SHAKA ZULU

by

Joshua Sinclair

(Limited Autographed Edition)

© Joshua Sinclair 1985/2001/2013

For Marie Louise
Without her support and dedication,
this book would never have seen the light of day

FORWARD
SUMMIT 1882

London. King's Cross Terminus. A sweltering late August morning. A South-Western Railways train idled by the platform, its locomotive disgorging a cloud of billowing smoke over a restless throng of Londoners held at bay by a cordon of police. The thick, muggy air, reeking of fetidness, sweat and coal, was shot through with the vibrant sting of expectation.

"There he is!" shrieked a young woman riding up on her toes, stretching her thin body and craning her neck to purchase a better view over the crowd. "Bless me! - He's o'er there!"

Alerted by the cry, the mob lunged forward, bodies jammed against the police line like cattle gone berserk, eyes wide and peeled to glimpse the focal point of their frenzied attention: - four men making their way down the platform, towards the train. Upon spotting the four men, the crowd became a whirling, eddying pool surging with roars of, "Crikey!", "'ere he is, o'er yonder!", "Bloody 'ell, look'at 'im - black as gloom!"

Violent, chafing, easily entranced by the curious and the terrifying, this madding congregation of Londoners was not too atypical of the Victorian Era during which uncultivated people in both the highest and lowest ranks of life would flock to "freak shows", as they were named, like the renowned Bartholomew Fair of Paddington, to view, agape and exhilarated, all the prodigies exhibited therein, pitiable, misshapen and deformed creatures endowed with less of the human than the beast.

This was the London that, in just a few brief years, would elevate to unabashed stardom a wretched, saintly creature named Joseph Carey Merrick, the "Elephant Man".

The show here at King's Cross proved to be just as satiating for the unscrupulousness of the maddened, as they strained to b6etter view the four men who were nearing the first class coaches. Indeed, with the exception of one Mr. Henrique Shepstone, a young, somewhat frail-looking man in his thirties, these men were black, amongst the first Africans to bless London with their unique colouring and phenotypical countenance.

Observing the dire crowd, Shepstone fervently wished himself elsewhere as he stole a tense glance at his companions. Though the three black men were dressed in elegant European suits, all three wore the traditional Zulu "isiCoco", a head-ring of polished wax into which the hair is woven to form a band around the top of the head, the Zulu equivalent to the "wedding ring".

Towering over the small group strode Cetshwayo KaMpande Zulu, a tall muscular man with finely chiselled black features, highlighted by a short, superbly sculpted beard. His pound or two of superfluous flesh was expertly concealed beneath a tailored double-breasted suit. Cetshwayo's air was regal as he cast a sidelong gaze, surveying the crowd, fascinated by its fascination.

The young woman who had first spied the extraordinary group, a Miss Penelope P. Smith, now found that she could see nothing at all, -- the crowd had packed too densely round her. With the rabid obstinacy of the obsessed curiosity-seeker, Penelope dropped to all fours and began, rather unwisely and unceremoniously, to thread her way through the forest of legs, shoving and prodding ruthlessly. Upon gaining the cordon, she darted under a policeman and reached Cetshwayo, flinging her arms around him.

The black man was too amazed to react. Shepstone, in shock, was temporarily just as useless as he stammered for assistance. The other two Blacks started tugging at the young woman, trying to pry her loose from her prey. At length, a handful of Bobbies arrived to the rescue. But before they could disengage her embrace, Penelope P. Smith had planted a kiss on the lips of Cetshwayo kaMpande and was thus bathed in limelight for the first and last time in her life.

"Crikey!, I bloody kissed 'im!" she trilled in triumph, as police dragged her away.

A couple of Bobbies quickly spirited Cetshwayo to the safety of a first class coach. Shepstone and the two black escorts hurried after him.

Eyeing the mob indignantly, a stationmaster moved down the train, slamming shut the doors. "Bleedin' glocky, if you ask me," he grumbled under his breath with an air of disapproval. "The scurvy soaks kill our boys 'n we treat 'em like bloody royalty, we do!" He then blew his whistle and cried, "All aboard!" as another whistle shrilled, further down the platform. The locomotive's engines began to chug, as the valve gears hissed, causing vaporous white steam to blanche the billowing smoke as the train gained speed and laboured out of the glass-panelled terminus.

As the South-Western Railways sped across the chalk North Downs of Surrey with their scattered Greenland rocks and jagged outcroppings, Henrique Shepstone shifted his weight in the comfort of his cushioned first class seat and settled down to the perusal of a recently acquired copy of "The Illustrated London News". A flashy lampoon caught his eye. It was headed:

ZULU KING TO VICTORIA - WILL WE WIN THE PEACE?-- The lampoon depicted the Queen on the back of an African elephant. Standing next to the elephant was Cetshwayo donning the traditional attire of a Zulu King (comprising leopard skins, oxtails, a cap of silver monkey skin and fully armed with shield, short stabbing assegai, and knobkerrie). The caption read: "Victoria to little Ben: "Ben, do you think we should give him a ride?"

Shepstone gazed vacantly at the page before him, his thoughts marshalling an interpretation of the lampoon's meaning. It came easily. "ZULU KING TO VICTORIA" referred to the meeting, a summit conference of sorts, which was to take place that very day at Osbourne. "WILL WE WIN THE PEACE?" was a speculation on the ultimate outcome of the recent, though already quite legendary, Anglo-Zulu Wars. The reference to "Ben," – Benjamin Disreali, of course, Her Majesty's Prime Minister - "do you think we should give him a ride" most likely alluded, Shepstone knew, to whether or not Victoria should allow Cetshwayo to join the British Empire.

The young Englishman lifted his gaze from the illustrated gazette and turned to glance at the proud countenance of the black man seated by the window of their luxurious coach. "Cetshwayo kaMpande Zulu" -- Shepstone turned the name over in his mind. A name that was almost unpronounceable to those uninitiated to the melodious orchestrations of the Zulu language with its canorous vowels spoken with honesty, as they are written, in the romantic tradition of Italian and other Latin vernaculars; with its three lingual "clicks" punctuating, like percussion instruments in a symphony, the consonants "c", "x" and "q"; with its elegant syntax, as refined as the phrasal architecture of Greek or Hebrew.

Cetshwayo kaMpande Zulu, a name as mysterious and exotic to the British as the noble monarch it distinguished, the proud successor to the quasi mythical King Shaka ka-Senzangakona Zulu.

Cetshwayo sat leaning against the mahogany sill of the window, his reddened, watery eyes locked on the passing scenery while Shepstone lit his pipe, and leaning back against the padded headrest, watched the blue smoke rings as they chased each other up to the ceiling. The man's thoughts gradually eased into resonance with the swaying of the train and the gentle clickety-clack of the metal wheels on the rails, evoking images of the past few months, the unforgettable period of his life linked to the Zulu monarch and the aftermath of the bloodiest war in the history of the British Empire:-- the Anglo-Zulu Wars of 1879...

***

It had begun in 1877, when Britain had annexed the vast Southern African Territory of the Transvaal, straddling the mighty Vaal River from the lofty peaks of the Drakensberg Mountains, eastward, to the fantastic expanses of sunburnt black rocks, rich orange sands and jagged-edged khors of the immense Kalahari Desert. Along with this territory, Great Britain had inherited the inflammatory borderlands dispute between Boer and Zulu. Sir Bartle Frere, British High Commissioner of Native Affairs for South Africa, had convinced himself that the sheer might and expansionist policies of the Zulu Kingdom were a menace to the peace and security of his domain. So, with a brazen self-assuredness so characteristic of Britannia's colonial ascendancy, Frere had served upon King Cetshwayo an ultimatum demanding the demobilization of the mighty Zulu Army and the subservience of the Zulu King to the British. With an unwavering impudence so characteristic of the Zulus' own imperial ascendancy, Cetshwayo, nettled, had rejected Frere's official request. The British had retaliated by taking to arms.

In January of 1879, Lt. General Frederic Augustus Thesiger, the second Baron Chelmsford, had launched an invasion in three columns aimed at the heart of the Zulu Kingdom: the town of Ulundi, Cetshwayo's royal homestead on the wide Mahlabatini plains. On January 20th, Chelmsford had camped on the plain, pitching a line of tents across a stony slope at the foot of a huge crouching sphinx of red rock called Isandhlwana -- Isandhlwana, a name that would forever be embossed in blood in the annals of British history.

Early on January 22nd, British scouts had returned to the camp reporting a large force of Zulus in the valley near the rocky promontory. Chelmsford, eager to fight, had lost no time. Pulling out of the camp with six companies, he had marched down the valley, white helmets shimmering in the mist of the African dawn. Several hours after the General had left, the 1,700 troops manning the camp had looked up to behold a sight that will not be seen again on this planet.

Along the entire five-mile length of the Nqutu plateau, 20,000 Zulus were spilling over the rim – a breaking sea of shields with a spindrift of spears; an army of highly disciplined warriors under the able leadership of Cetshwayo's prime minister, Mnyamana, converging at a dead run upon the British camp and its astounded defenders.

A murderous rifle fire had ensued, lashing out from the widely spaced units of Chelmsford's encampment at the slope of Isandhlwana. At first the

British guns had harvested unbelievable numbers from the packed Zulu ranks, but then Her Majesty's defence had faltered and faded for a reason that is as comically absurd as it is tragic. In fact, the rifles' ammunition of paper cartridges had been packed in boxes with screwed-down lids and - in the heat of the conflict - screwdrivers had been veritably impossible to locate. Frantic, men had torn at the wooden planks in an attempt to pry the boxes open while the tidal wave of spears had showered and swept towards them. A few fortunate soldiers had managed to fight their way out, but of those who had tried to hold the position, some 1,300 men; there had been no survivors.

Hopelessly out-maneuvered on his own front, Chelmsford had received a garbled message of the attack, but not until it had been too late had he learned what had happened -- one of the worst defeats that had ever been suffered by a modern army at the hands of so-called "savages".

As the Zulus had continued to charge down the Nqutu escarpment, others - Cetshwayo's Undi Regiment, several thousand strong - had veered to the rear of the rocky promontory to block the British escape route. Then, towards late afternoon, the Zulus had turned south to the Buffalo River, forded it, and, tingling with the sensation of imminent victory, trotted off towards another British outpost at Rorke's Drift.

At the time none of the British at the 'Drift' had known they would soon be part of an epic. There had been 141 men in all under the command of Lt. John Chard – 8 officers, 97 able-bodied non-commissioned officers and men, and 36 laid up in the mission station building that served as a hospital.

Alerted by the arrival of a survivor from Isandhlwana, Chard had hastily organised a wall of heavy sacks of cornmeal, large biscuit boxes, and some wagons around the hospital. The makeshift barrier had still been rising when lookouts had come tumbling down the hillside behind the mission station, one yelling, "Here they come, black as hell and thick as grass!"

The British soldiers had gaped out in awe as more than 4000 shouting Zulus had cascaded towards them. It had been 4:30 in the afternoon, and the steady fire from the single-shot breech-loading rifles had kicked a cloud of smoke towards leaden skies.

For hour after hour, rattling rifle fire and bayonets had blunted and stopped each Zulu charge. The ferocity of the combat had left mounds of dead before the boxes and bags, but eventually the Zulu wave had broken into the hospital building. As the roof had caught fire, the sick and wounded had been dragged from room to room by comrades who had turned to fight at every step. Most of them had miraculously made their way through the glare of the conflagration to the last outpost of defense, a circle of meal bags thrown up in front of the mission's storehouse. There the battle had closed to massive rushes of Zulu warriors, shields forming a solid wall, spears glittering in the firelight of dusk, met by thundering volleys from the densely packed survivors who were "pinned like rats in a hole".

The attack had raged for 12 hours. At about 4 a.m. it had slowed, then stopped. Men had fallen exhausted against one another, grasping for canteens to quench scorched throats. Seventeen British soldiers had been killed, and untold hundreds of Zulus.

If medals are a measure of valour and the fierceness of combat, that fight had few if any equals in the history of Western warfare. Eleven of the defenders of Rorke's Drift won the Victoria Cross, Great Britain's highest military decoration - one of the largest numbers ever awarded for a single engagement.

As for the rest of it, the Anglo-Zulu War of 1879 had been a grim colonial formality. Chelmsford had mounted a second invasion and pushed on to Ulundi, where he had decimated the remains of Cetshwayo's regiments and burned to the ground the king's homestead. For the first time in the life of their kingdom, the Zulus had become a subject people, and their king, Cetshwayo, the dethroned monarch of Africa's most valiant and most illustrious realm.

***

The approach to Osborne House by carriage led up Royal Avenue. The Avenue was a wide dirt road flanked on either side by a elegant double row of cedars and ilexes that shaded the margin of a deep-green lawn rolling gently to meet a gathering of willows 'weeping' round a pond of ducks and swans. Cetshwayo sniffed at the air and had a half smile as he recognised the sweet scent of roses. Moving forward in the carriage, the king rested his elbows on the back of the driver's perch and was soon lost in the compelling vision of Victoria's residence on the Isle of Wight, with its luxurious and lavish Italianate roof, domed ceilings and verandas.

The carriage stopped at the entrance to the mansion where two servants in livery scurried out to meet it. With Shepstone in the lead, Cetshwayo and his two black escorts were shown down a stone path toward a beach where a lolling cross-section of British nobility was enjoying the breath of salty summer under a bright sun and fleecy clouds in which seagulls whined playfully. The Princess of Wales and the Duchess of York, in appropriate swimming attire, were reclining beneath a striped canopy; Prince Edward of York, a youngster of six, played with the eight-year-old Earl of Athlone precociously building colonies of sand castles. The future Queen Mary, and George -- destined to become George V -- both still in their teens, splashed in the trolling waves that sprawled on to the shoreline.

At the edge of the beach, stockinged feet dipped in the sea, her diminutive size engulfed in a wicker chair crowned by a white canopy, sat Her Imperial Majesty, Victoria R.I. (Regina et Imperatrix, Queen and Empress), chatting with the Earl of Kimberley, her Colonial Secretary.

No one in the distinguished group seemed to take notice of the new arrivals.

Prompted by Cetshwayo's chin lifted in a gesture of mild disdain, Shepstone stepped forward and coughed respectfully, inciting reactions, which were as diverse as the personalities of those present on that shore. Prince Edward looked up from his sand castles. As he and the Earl of Athlone spotted the three Blacks, their eyes sprang large and their mouths dropped open in sheer wonder. The Princess of Wales and the Duchess of York tilted their heads in curiosity. Kimberley turned slightly, brow raised, monocle-fitted eye deigning the newcomers with a perusal of interest.

Since apparently no on else could trust themselves to speak, Shepstone, marshalling his courage and composure, stepped forward. "His highness, Cetshwayo kaMpande Zulu," he started, introducing the foreign dignitaries in his tow to the Queen, "and his chief indunas, Mkhosana of the Zungu and Ngobohzana of the Mpungose."

The three Black men nodded respectfully.

Exercising the whims of her imperial prerogative, Victoria did not nod back - not even curtly, as was her manner. Instead, in an act which appeared to be unjustifiably discourteous, Victoria turned away, offering the Zulu delegation her imperial back.

Shepstone glanced sheepishly at Cetshwayo, his spectacles magnifying the disconcertion in his tiny green eyes.

After an interminable moment in which bated breaths accompanied flittering glimpses, Victoria, with the aid of her ivory cane, rose to her feet. A lady-in-waiting scooped up the chair and rotated it 180 degrees. The Queen then executed a slow but determined about-face and, petulantly waving away Kimberley's offer of assistance, resumed her sitting position. Stroking a toy Pomeranian that had jumped onto her lap, Victoria regarded Cetshwayo, scanning the features of the "Barbarian of Isandhlwana".

The Zulu Wars of 1879 had left Victoria with a burning desire to meet the man that had so vigorously thrashed her valiant troops. "We must have these singularly brave warriors as friends," she had told William Gladstone, "not enemies! We must harness that nerve, that muscle, that energy!" When the meeting with Cetshwayo had been arranged, and the Zulu king was already sailing towards Plymouth, Victoria had urged Sir Bartle Frere to enlighten her upcoming visit by describing the king. Hard-pressed to explain away the difference between Cetshwayo as he appeared in reality - tall, imposing, dignified - and the mental picture of the monstrous, ruthless creature that Frere's own propaganda had done so much to create, the British High Commissioner had written to the Queen in response: "Long habit of uncontradicted command gives great dignity to his general manner, and takes in the casual observer with the belief that he is a very superior being; but you will look in vain for kingly attributes, as we understand them, apart from those associated with superior force and cunning."

Victoria R.I., who was far from what could be called a "casual observer", decided at once that she was faced with a "superior being", and she now waited for him to make the next move.

Cetshwayo was not surprised to find that he was instantly taken by the Queen's dignity, by her regal composure and the boundless resolution in her childlike features. He had expected that. He had conjured up the image of a white "Nandi", the mother of Shaka, who had been (and still was in the hearts of the People of the Heavens) the "Nkosikazi" of Africa.

Matching Victoria's dignity with his own, Cetshwayo shifted his weight, passing over the growing discomfort of his tight-fitting shoes, and addressed the British regent in Zulu.

"Sibonga umusa weNdlovukhazi yabamhlophe nendlela esemukelwe ngayo kulelizwe," he started, accentuating his even, steady voice with the rhythmic clicks of his native tongue, his full lips forming the words with the care of one who fervently believes that his own language, honed in the land of his birth, is the worthiest representative of his innermost feelings. "Sifisa ukwakha ubuhlobo okwonomphelo..."

The Pomeranian, reacting to the unfamiliar clicking, cocked its ears, screwed its neck and, bewildered, peered up at the black man.

Amused by the clicking, the children, Prince Edward and the Earl of Athlone, started to giggle. Like a benevolent father, Cetshwayo let his voice trail off and, feigning anger, cast a stern look in Edward's direction. Feeling the reprimand in those eyes, the boy froze. Yet the Earl, having failed to notice Cetshwayo's frown, continued to giggle till Edward silenced him with a swat of the hand. The shadow of a smile tugged at Cetshwayo's lips as he thought of his own children and how amused they would be by the oddities of the British world

Victoria was caught up in Cetshwayo's smile and her own eyes twinkled as she thought, with satisfaction, "Looks extraordinarily kind for a 'barbarian', doesn't he?"

Cetshwayo picked up where he had left off. When he finished, the King turned to Shepstone, who began to translate: "His Highness thanks Her Imperial Majesty for the kind way he has been received in Great Britain. He says that in speaking to Her Majesty, he is but a child before his mother".

Victoria lifted an imperious brow. "How charmingly ironic," she mused as the Pomeranian nibbled at her imperial ring. "It seems he said much more."

"The nature of the language, Ma'am," Shepstone proffered by way of explanation. "Poetic and idiomatic. I merely conveyed the essence."

Victoria swept the dog off her lap before it could pry the Seal of Britannia out of her ring and lifting a hand to her Colonial Secretary, prompting - "Lord Kimberley".

"Is His Highness aware of why Her Majesty agreed to see him?" asked Kimberley of Shepstone, taking a step forward, into the softer ground.

Cetshwayo waited for Shepstone to translate before responding in Zulu, and once again Shepstone conveyed the Zulu King's words, somewhat hesitantly. "His Highness says that he has travelled for many months over the waters, riding the 'Creature with the Great White Wings'. He says that during that long journey he prayed that the dream of his ancestor, King Shaka, could finally become a reality. He prayed, he says, that the sovereign of the Swallows and the sovereign of the Zulus could find lasting friendship in an air of mutual respect and harmony. He hopes, he says, he is here to seal that pact of friendship which will last forever."

Silence ensued and all were still - even Edward and the Earl. Only Victoria's hand moved, bringing a perfumed handkerchief to her jutting nose, her eyes still fixed on the Zulu - delving now, deep into his spirit.

A seagull glided across the sky, calling to the wind. Instinctively Cetshwayo looked up. Victoria followed his gaze. The seagull hung suspended, catching the air currents, hovering in the drift. Then, tucking back its wings, the bird dove through a cloud and levelled off, flapping back to a horizontal flight pattern and dipping, swooping out over the expanse of The Solent.

***

"The Colonial Office feels that any act of clemency towards Zululand would be a grave misreckoning of the Zulu threat."

In the audience room of Osborne House, Kimberley's voice was laced with urgency as he paced the parquet flooring, sharing his fears with the small gathering of nobility assembled in Victoria's seaside refuge, "Ma'am, gentlemen, we are at grips here with more than just a dispute over territorial borders and the revendications of a defeated king..."

Seated before an oak panelling, his indunas standing behind him like two towering, statuesque male caryatids, Cetshwayo looked anything but defeated as he graced Kimberley with his undivided attention, his soft-brown eyes following the Colonial Secretary as he paced back and forth. Seated to the king's left, Shepstone craned his neck towards the Zulu's ear, whispering a simultaneous translation.

"No! - We are called upon to defend Africa," the Colonial Secretary announced emphatically, stopping short, thrusting his closed fist into his open palm.

Shepstone looked up, intrigued by this last statement. Having rendered it in Zulu, he searched Cetshwayo's face for a reaction, wondering how the African would take the idea of Britain "defending" his continent.

The Zulu king remained indifferent to the remark.

"It is, I believe," continued Kimberley, starting to pace again, "our sovereign duty, Ma'am, to safeguard the well-being of our countrymen who have settled on those distant shores, as well as that of the Kaffir tribes who look to us to bring peace to a land that has, for the past 60 years, been devastated by one of the most formidable military empires ever created; the Empire of Shaka Zulu, here represented by Shaka's legitimate heir, King Cetshwayo."

As his interpreter dutifully transferred the English to Zulu, Cetshwayo searched Kimberley's face and found his eyes, holding the Colonial Secretary's stare evenly with his own. The Englishman had a fairly neutral look, Cetshwayo decided, certainly not virulent, or even faintly condemning, but it wasn't sympathetic either - and far from friendly. Cetshwayo's mind snagged on the word 'kaffir', which he knew came from Arabic 'kafir' and meant 'infidel' or, in the Arabic sense, anyone who was not Moslem. Not Moslem. The king's eyes roamed to those present in the room. "We're all kaffirs," he thought with a wry grin.

"Prof. Bramston...", prompted Kimberley, abruptly shifting his attention to the Oxford professor who sat in another section of the room together with the Colonial Under-Secretary Anthony Ashley, Sir Henry Bulwer, General Chelmsford, and H.R.H. Albert Edward, Prince of Wales.

Bramston, a stout, scholarly man with a somewhat bloated body, a long, pinched-in nose, and intense brown eyes magnified by thick lenses of glass, rose and, collecting his thoughts with a furrow of the brow, shuffled out to address the group. "1816 to '28," he began as he ventured out to take Kimberley's place in the centre of the room, "although some say '18 to '28. Finn says '16 and I tend to agree..."

Victoria peered at the aging scholar, running a restless eye over his crinkly three-piece suit, which had, for lack of interest on the part of its owner, seen better days. If Her Majesty wondered what the devil Bramston was talking about, it was not obvious in her averted gaze.

"...But then the history of Africa is bit of a muddle, isn't it?" Bramston inquired of no one in particular, finally answering his own question. "Yes. Of course it is. -- Take the origin of the Zulu people, for instance..." The professor let his voice trail off, disengaging his wire-rimmed spectacles from his diminutive ears and starting to clean them with such diligence that all present suddenly found themselves so engrossed in the fate of the optical instrument that when the man spoke again, the words seemed to be echoed from somewhere within the convex lenses. "Almost nothing is known of this tribe before the white man came! Like all the illiterate, they are people without a written Past. Why less than a century ago, and we find ourselves in their Prehistoric Age, with any of their earlier records almost as remote and undiscoverable as those of Mankind before its Birth! Do they descend from the Tekela Ngunis or the Ntungwa Ngunis?- Research in that area has..."

"The Zulu people as they were before the Whites came." Cetshwayo allowed the expression to echo in his mind dredging up memories of the 'colonies' that were better left dormant. "Before the Whites," a chauvinistic term that, like the Meridian of Greenwich, served as the mean with which the clocks of history were set.

"The Zulus are a people without a written Past," Bramston was repeating. The king cocked his eyes at a towering bookshelf laden with the tracings of culture. "Picture for a moment a European world possessed neither of written word nor archaeological remains," the professor continued, relentlessly, pacing the room, mindful never to turn his back on the Queen or the other nobles present. "Sumer and Egypt, Greece and Rome might then have never been; Plato might have taught and Shakespeare dreamed in vain; acquired knowledge might have never been preserved, nor been dispersed; all human thought, experience and worthy deed might have been lost in oblivion; Redemption remained unknown, and Revelation been forgotten or distorted."

Bramston's words lanced the heart of the Zulu sovereign. "Is the Redemption and Revelation of God limited to scribbling's on parchment?" Cetshwayo questioned himself in silence. "Can God not be 'read' by the heart alone? Could the Creator of the Eternal, Timeless Universe in which the Whites also believe have been petty enough to reveal Himself to a select few who have honed the pen at the expense of the spoken word?"

Bramston stopped in his tracks, his eyes meeting Victoria's deliberate stare, which silently urged the Oxford gentleman to get to the point. Nervously clearing his throat, the professor complied. "Shaka Zulu. Yes..." he started, "The founder of the Greater Zulu Nation and the Zulu Empire. Reigned from 1816 to 1828. Most definitely one of the greatest military geniuses in history. Certainly on the level of a Caesar or an Alexander the Great, though perhaps not as publicised."

The professor nervously cleared his throat and ambled to a linen map of Southern Africa. "Imagine, if you will, the prodigious feat accomplished by this XIX Century African Achilles, Shaka Zulu. In less than 12 years he transformed a handful of idyllic, relatively harmless herdsmen, who were, by nature, reluctant to engage in any form of warfare," the Professor paused for effect, his rounded eyes, magnified by the spectacles, scanning the noble assemblage, "... into a Spartan army of over 80,000 highly trained, ruthless warriors, extending his influence..." he plucked a cigar from his vest pocket and traced with it the area on the map, "...over most of South-East Africa. An empire comparable, in extension and might, to that of Napoleon! And - in treachery - to that of Genghis Kahn!

"Your Majesty, Gentlemen," Bramston's emphasis grew," - the war machine created by Shaka Zulu was so monolithic that it has survived his death by over half a century! True, the Crown has now defeated it, but that defeat is purely temporary."

Chelmsford, who had made the defeat possible, shifted uneasily in his chair, tugging at the edge of his military tunic as he raised a bushy brow in incense. The Professor plowed ahead, his conviction compelling. "It can and will rise again and again if we do not stop it once and for all!"

Swept away by his own theatrical impetus, Bramston let the thought hang in the air as he flipped over the map, revealing under it an 1820's drawing of King Shaka Zulu executed by one of the Whites who had passed through his magnificent court, British Naval Lieutenant James Saunders King. The drawing was that of a tall black man standing erect, proud, his beautiful cat-like features crowned by a quivering blue crane feather fastened to the forehead, his pastel-blue eyes swirling pools that compelled the observer to drown in the depths of their maelstrom, his full lips set in a obstinate smirk of superiority, his muscular nude body possessing the elongated, magnificent lineaments which evoked the artistic perfection of Greek sculptures such as Praxiteles. Though Shaka wore no drapings, skins, or adornments - save for the crane feather - the drawing was unmistakably that of a king, for indeed the fierceness of those eyes, the mesmerising beauty of that face, the incomparability of that physique could belong only to a king or a god.

Victoria was momentarily bewitched by the spell the drawing cast -- both evil and angelic, the spell of a Fallen Angel. She tore her gaze away from the drawing and caused it to rest on Cetshwayo.

The Zulu king's eyes had leapt to life at the sight of Shaka, the drawing being the first likeness he had ever seen of the legendary ancestor. Being introspective by nature, a student of life, Victoria caught that gaze and its glint of ecstasy.

"...Because King Shaka was no ordinary mortal!" Bramston went on as soon as he felt the impact of Shaka's image had had the desired effect. "For his people, he was more than a generalissimo,- he was a Messiah! A god-figure!" Bramston's closed fist lashed out at the drawing as he proclaimed, theatrically, "Like an African Mephistopheles, he gave the Zulus glory in return for their souls, wielding the forces of life and death on an endless battlefield of..."

Victoria raised a solicitous brow in the direction of Kimberley, who quickly interrupted Bramston's overly emphatic diatribe, dismissing him. "Thank you, Professor."

At Kimberley's beckoning, Bramston broke off abruptly, bowed to Victoria and shuffled back to his seat.

"The threat is real," said Kimberley, dryly, with a conviction he seemed to have borrowed from Bramston, "and the decision before us, clear. Therefore it is the suggestion of the Colonial Office, Ma'am, that we constitute in the Zulu Kingdom a progressive destruction and dislocation of the Zulu military and economic system..."

Ever vigilant, ever inquisitive, Victoria shifted her gaze to Cetshwayo. The king seemed impassive as he eyed Kimberley intently.

"...undermining the morale of the Zulu people," the Colonial Secretary pressed on, standing in front of Shaka's drawing, instinctively imitating the sketch's proud posture, "to a point where their capacity for armed aggression is fatally weakened. To accomplish this, Zululand would be divided into a number of independent territories, all under the watchful surveillance of the Crown. In so doing, we feel that the Zulus, deprived of central leadership, will revert to the state of innocuous bliss they enjoyed before the insane conditioning of Shaka."

Having finished, Kimberley cocked his eyes at Shepstone. "You may translate," he bid the youth.

After Shepstone's rapid, efficient translation, Cetshwayo offered his rebuttal in Zulu. His words were laced with calmness and dignity. "He says," translated Shepstone, "that the terms aggression and self-defence are often confused. Aggression means to attack without provocation. Self-defence is a divine right exercised by all peoples - irrespective of their colour - who feel threatened on their own soil."

Victoria's interest was aroused. "He has guts," she decided. "A man of principal and resolve. Most definitely the 'barbarian' of Isandhlwana!".

Victoria's eyes remained on Cetshwayo, who now regarded her calmly as Shepstone continued. "He says that things have changed in his country since King Shaka. Zulu power no longer issues from conquest, but from a bond of nationhood. He says the Crown might best profit by allowing that budding nation to govern itself".

* * *

"Self-determination?! Have we gone bloody bonkers, Ma'am?!"

Lt. Gen. Thesiger, 2nd Baron Chelmsford, now in his fifties, still as vital and as outraged as he had been at Isandhlwana, was somewhat overly intense in his objection to Zulu self-rule as he walked at Victoria's side, both leading the way into Osbourne's parlour where the Queen had bid her guests to join her for tea.

Victoria wrinkled her nose at the term "bloody" and cast Chelmsford a stricken look as she advanced with an ambling gait, slow yet determined, down her mansion's wood-panelled corridor.

"It's in their blood, warfare is," continued the General. "Killing's in their blasted souls," he thundered, adding, as an afterthought, "If they have any! We all saw that in '79 at Isandhlwana! Had the best damn regiment the British ever knew! The 24th! Armed to the hilt! Enough to win any damn war...!"

Shepstone stole a glance at Cetshwayo. "Thank heavens the Zulu doesn't understand," he thought.

"But no matter how many of those hyenas we shot down," Chelmsford went on, "a thousand more'd crop up out of the earth, vomited from Hell most likely! Screaming like bats possessed by the Devil himself!"

"Sounds rather heroic, Chelmsford," said Victoria, easing herself into her chair. "No wonder you were defeated. The vividness of your description betrays an apprehension close to panic on your part," she countered with a twinkle in her eye.

Chelmsford's gaze dropped, as he mumbled an apologetic, "Begging your pardon, Ma'am. Got carried away." And quickly added, "All the same, I tend to agree with Kimberley. If the Zulus won't bend, break 'em and be done with it, I say!"

"I rather think we'll be doing them a favour," interjected the Prince of Wales, dryly. "A return to the plough should prove to be most therapeutic for these savages! Might even bless them with a hint of civilization," he added, finding pride in his own arrogance.

"Am I meant to translate, M'Lords?,' inquired Shepstone of the group, straight-faced.

"That won't be necessary, sir," interrupted a deep, sonorous voice from the back of the room.

At first no one realized that it was Cetshwayo who had just spoken. His voice sounded quite different in English. Yet as the fact and its implications sank in, the room was gripped by complete silence.

Moving to the centre of the group, Cetshwayo continued, demonstrating his startling command of the English language and his total control of the anger that had been welling in his heart. "Savages?" Cetshwayo pondered the point so that all could hear, addressing his question especially to the flustered Prince of Wales and the shocked Lord Kimberley. "Yes. I suppose we are savages. Our customs. Our...," running an inspecting eye over the room's architecture and the frills that adorned it, "...ways and traditions are quite different from yours." Cetshwayo neared the Prince of Wales and held his gaze steadily with his own. "That is what you meant by 'savage', is it not, Your Royal Highness? 'Different'. To the point where the British would not feel…" searching for the word, "...'cosy'. I believe that is the right word, is it not, Shepstone?"

The entire company had been caught off guard, especially Shepstone, who, flushed to the hairline, found himself saying, somewhat agitatedly: "Yes. - That is the word."

"But then," Cetshwayo continued, pacing the room, hands clasped behind his back, with the scholarly command, effortless and unemotional, that appeared to mimic Bramston's own professorial inflections, "that is to be expected, isn't it, Lord Chelmsford? Our civilizations developed under quite different circumstances. In fact," the Zulu king allowed the irony to become manifest in his voice, "our meeting here is absurd. We have so little in common. Especially our concept of human respect". Turning to face Chelmsford, Cetshwayo chided, "I, for one, would never think of calling you or those present in this room 'savages' behind your backs, merely because you are different."

The mouth of the Prince of Wales fell open. It was not every day that such an exquisite group was called 'savage',- Her Imperial Majesty included. Accusing the insult, Kimberley's face contorted in anger. He stepped purposefully toward Cetshwayo, as if to challenge him to a duel. Chelmsford voiced that intent with a defiant and provocative: "Sir!" and rested a hand on his sword as if to draw its gleaming blade from the scabbard.

Victoria, her twinkling eyes on the Zulu, raised her hand to silence both men. "Thank you for your chivalry, Your Lordships; but we feel that anyone who shows such skill in mastering both our language and the situation deserves our undivided attention. Don't you agree? -- Lord Chelmsford?"

Chelmsford's face was coloured in anger, but what he said was, "Of course, Ma'am."

Victoria tapped her cane on the floor, her silver voice ringing, "'Undivided', Gentlemen.-- Thank you."

Having been clearly dismissed, Chelmsford, Kimberley, and the others filed out, casting Victoria worried glances that silently wondered if it was safe to leave the Queen alone with the -- 'savage'.

When the doors had slid shut leaving Victoria and Cetshwayo alone, the two studied each other whilst silence hung in the air. Then Victoria smiled. Cetshwayo followed her lead, offering the Queen and Empress a warm, gentle glimmer of his deep brown eyes.

"Your Majesty," the king said after a pause, "I don't believe we've been properly introduced. My name is Cetshwayo KaMpande. I am Zulu."

Victoria began to laugh, and Cetshwayo laughed with her - releasing their pent-up nervousness, ending the chapter, once and for all, on the Anglo-Zulu Wars.

* * *

Like the shrill laughter of spirited children, the cry of seagulls broke the stillness of The Solent as the grey and white birds swept elegantly over the channel, their carefree, airy flight cast against the carking, serried curtain of dark brume that had descended on the mainland. A foghorn bemoaned a tanker's trek across the murky haze that clung to the gathering storm clouds.

Victoria had further promoted the budding cordiality and good will she had struck with the Zulu regent by inviting him to the reserved confines of Osbourne's magnificent rose garden. In the midst of the petalled paradise, perfectly disposed red, white and pink roses formed the entwined initials so dear to the Queen: the initials "V" and "A" - "Victoria" and "Albert" ---

Albert of Saxe-Coburg had been the Queen's Prince Consort till his premature death in 1861. Victoria's love for this man, her husband, had been so great, her heart never completely recovered from the immense grief his demise had caused in her.

Cetshwayo sensed that greatness as he accompanied her down the seemingly endless rows of bushes, the tall black king diligently holding a basket and the diminutive monarch, now donning a quaint gardening outfit, snipping expertly, then gently depositing the flowers in the wicker container. Victoria looked up from her beloved roses and glanced pensively at the weather overhead, uttering under her breath: "Always from the sea, the Atlantic. The storm clouds, the winds of war – always from the sea."

Noticing the doleful glint in her eyes, Cetshwayo bent forward and relieved her of a rose stem, resting it in the basket. Catching his eye, Victoria chased away the chill of melancholy with a casual: "Have you gardens in your country, Your Highness?" she asked.

"Gardens?- No, I'm afraid even our roses grow wild," the king replied, his smile broadening.

Victoria broke out in a peal of laughter that echoed on the hovering clouds, causing them to murmur in a soft growl of thunder.

"But they are stunning," Cetshwayo added. "If you will permit me, Ma'am, I shall send you a variety of our best specimens."

Pausing to place another rose into the basket, Victoria screwed up her nose in an expression hinging on greed. The devout gardener, Victoria was lured by the thought of possessing a "variety" of tropical roses. Assuming regal distance, she answered, somewhat curtly: "You have our permission." Then, as an afterthought, she paused, raising her brow, "I don't suppose that would cause a political uproar, do you?"

Realising that Victoria's priorities were now evenly divided between her rose garden and Parliament, Cetshwayo confirmed reassuringly: "I wouldn't think so, Ma'am."

The Queen placed her shears in the basket, and rising with Cetshwayo's assistance, turned to face him with a gaze, direct and candid, that would leave little room for future speculation. "You strike me as a highly judicious man, King Cetshwayo. Tell me -- what does this Shaka Zulu, mean to you?"

Cetshwayo's answer also left no room for ambiguity. "He was everything that has been said today, Ma'am. A military genius. A born emperor. Perhaps a 'Messiah' of sorts. He was one of those rare men who had the courage to live his ideals, and the ability to instil his own dreams into the hearts of his countrymen."

"That is precisely why we cannot restore autonomy to your realm," Victoria held the man's gaze fixedly with her own. "Shaka Zulu is more alive today than ever. His military strength still prevails. You may be the king, but it is his spirit that rules your people. -- We are a practical woman, Your Highness," Victoria concluded, using the "pluralis majestatis", the royal plural. "We will not form an alliance with a legend."

The verdict had been pronounced. There could be no rebuttal. The two monarchs remained silent, facing each other. No anger, no tension - just the realization that the 'Osborne Meeting' had been brought to a close, the future of Zululand and its king sealed. Cetshwayo ka-Mpande would be the last independent king of an autonomous kwaZulu, the Kingdom of the People of the Heavens.

Or so it appeared in 1882.

The storm clouds had reached Osbourne. It started to drizzle. A flurry of servants appeared, shielding the two monarchs under the flared rotunda of a large umbrella. Yet neither budged. The servants waited, getting wet. At length, in the manner he had learned in Britain, Cetshwayo offered Victoria his arm. The gesture might have had a political significance, or more likely, it may have merely been one of courtesy. Yet the fact remained that Victoria took his arm, graciously, and allowed the king to escort her back to Osbourne House, out of the rain and into her refuge on the Isle of Wight.

Passing the bay window of the mansion's Audience Room, something caught Cetshwayo's eye. As the rain splashed and pattered against the glass pane blurring the darkened interior of the room, a flash of lightning cast a harsh ultraviolet glare on the drawing of the nude, imposing figure of Shaka Zulu, causing it to look all the more bewitching. Suddenly, with a devilish scream, a gust of wind threw open a window, catching the linen map of Southern Africa and flipping it back over the drawing. As if prompted by the hand of Time, another flash of lightning illuminated the map, casting a glow, which, as the bolt receded, shrank to a narrow beam of light pinpointing a spot near the centre of the vast empire,- the place where it had all begun...

CHAPTER I
"NANDI"(SWEETNESS)
MONTH OF UMNDULO: SEPTEMBER, 1786

In a period of Time Remote, the Courage and Curiosity of the nomadic Bantu ("The People") compelled them to follow the guideposts of Destiny. They pushed southward across the Boji Plain and past the Mighty Kilimanjaro, over the Pangani River and the Masai Steppes, past the Great Ruaha and down the African Rift to the Zambese. Then, fording the mighty river, they moved onward to the lands west of the Muchinga Slopes where some of The People settled, founding and fashioning one of the greatest and noblest centres of Civilisation this planet would ever know: Zimbabwe, - an African Civilisation comparable, in sophistication and grandeur, to the Rome of Augustus or the Greece of Pericles.

Remaining Restless, their Courage unabated, a fraction of The People, the "Nguni" Bantu, broke off and ventured even further South, crossing the Limpopo River and veering East, along the margin of the Drakensberg, skirting the foot of the range where a fraction of the fraction made their home on a patch of land no larger than the Isle of Wight, hugging the banks of the Umfolozi River fifty miles northwest of the Indian Ocean; a land free of mosquitoes, with a cool and invigorating atmosphere, and sweet grasslands teeming with game. When this small scion of The People discovered this land, they must have thought themselves as having passed through the Gates of Heaven - thus it was appropriate for them to name their first regent and themselves "Zulu".

Zulu means "The Heavens".

* * *

In the Month of Umndalo of 1786, the Heavens surged and ebbed over the territory of its tribe. Thunder rolled down the grassy orange, rock-strewn hills and lightning lit up the valleys with an anger so sustained that all the ferocity and cruelty of Africa seemed to be distilled into those dreadful blasts of sound and light.

The mauve storm clouds billowed, rippling in waves of lavender, hovering over the blackened landscape, stalking Nature like predators of the sky ready to lash out at creation. The advancing tempest was met with the stamping of hooves and the rustling of branches, as wildlife responded, fearing heaven's wrath. An antelope took flight and, bleating, shot straight up a cliff, leaping from ledge to unseen ledge with all the nimble- ness of a chamois. Newly born foals, with legs too long for their fleecy bodies, flitted, unsteadily, towards the safety of the open veld. A herd of ungainly blue wildebeest with scraggy manes galloped across the grass-lands, darting left and right with the quickness of minnows in a shallow stream.

A leopard stalked through the forest, the muscles along its elegant torso rippling as it moved. Suddenly the cat froze, the pupils of its eyes screwing out to large glimmering emerald discs, its body tense, on the alert. Raising its snout, it sniffed at the air. It was hard for the leopard to judge the distance of that offensive taint upon the shoulder of the wind, yet its origin was unmistakable: the acrid, pungent scent of man. Baring its fangs, the cat hissed.

Senzangakona's handsome features were also on the alert, his eyes fixed on his prey; his tall, muscular body naked, save for the scanty skins and oxtails that distinguished the prince of the Zulu Clan (a small tribe numbering approximately 2500 in this period of its history). Like the cat, he, too, stood frozen in place. Then, slowly raising his throwing assegai, he motioned to Igazi, another young Zulu who was also in his early twenties. Assenting to the silent command, Igazi nodded to his friend and padded to a position at the edge of the clearing, directly opposite a third youth, Lutuli.

The leopard shifted its gaze, reading the forest. A flash of lightning was reflect on its spotted face.

"Isaga!"

Senzangakona's cry pierced the thunder that followed. And suddenly the forest was alive with the screams of half a dozen men: "Isaga!, Isiho!" The men raced towards the animal, their assegais poised to strike. Startled by the attack, the leopard darted away from the youths, toward the clearing where, too late, it realized its mistake. The proud animal was trapped, surrounded by the hunters. Hissing, it bolted frantically first in one direction, then in the other. Tightening his grip on his assegai, Senzangakona kaJama Zulu moved in for the kill. "Kehli--, Kehli..." he teased.

The leopard turned to face its tormenter. Its eyes met and locked with those of the Zulu prince. For a captivating instant time stood still whilst the two stared at each other, the hunter and the hunted, deciding which would be which. Then the leopard bore its fangs again. Hissing, it gathered to spring. Covered by his friends, Senzangakona inched closer. The cat leapt into the air. Nimbly, Senzangakona dove to the ground, rolling under the beast. Then, rising, he spun round and hurled his assegai.

* * *

The rainy season had only just begun and the Mkumbane was still just a lazy stream of murky currents furrowing, like quicksilver on powdered iron, shallow tracks zigzagging through the red clay flecked with gravelly sediment. Returning from the hunt, the Zulu youths made their way along its banks. Carrying the leopard's carcass slung over his broad shoulders, Senzangakona strode with a gait, rapid and confident, of a man who was used to being in control. Igazi, Lutuli and the others followed, their joking and laughter mingling with the gurgling stream and the rumbling of the clouds overhead. The rain was imminent now.

Suddenly Senzangakona stopped, raising an open hand to silence his friends.

Igazi's eyes searched the woods near the stream as he readied his assegai. "What is it?" he whispered, his keen hearing sifting the sounds that were borne on the stirring wind, probing for the slightest indication of danger. Igazi's look of intense scrutiny relaxed to a glint of playfulness as a soft singing reached his ears, mingled with the chatter of female voices.

A mischievous smile tugged at Senzangakona's lips as he motioned to a gathering of young women of the Langeni Clan, neighbours of the Zulu, who were fetching water in shell and gourd-plant jugs. The girls also noticed the boisterous youths, yet in their coyness, they were doing their best not to show it.

Registering Senzangakona's playful grin, the Zulus exchanged knowing glances. "Haven't you had enough 'hunting' for one day?" Igazi asked the prince, teasingly.

A phosphorescent flash of lightning highlighted the remark followed, seconds later, by a deafening clap of thunder that shook the skies.

Senzangakona ran a restless eye over the blue-black clouds heavy with rain rumbling feverishly above him. "I suppose so..." he admitted reluctantly and, shifting the weight of the mighty leopard draped over his shoulders, started off, casting one last, lingering gaze at the appetising girls at the stream who were now hurriedly filling their water-jugs in the wake of another crash of thunder.

Abruptly and for no apparent reason, Senzangakona stopped short, his eyes narrowing inquisitively as he gazed with mounting engagement at one of the girls who was still kneeling at the edge of the water. Her lissom body, naked save for a short wrapping of hide round the lower waist, was bent over the vessel she was filling. Sensing the youth's caressing glance, the girl lifted her gaze in a manner, demurring and calculated, that would afford the young man the enchanting vision of her gorgeous, perfectly-sculpted features graced by high cheekbones, a light-brown complexion, and luminous, greenish-brown eyes that glowed with the entrancing allure of both serpent and feline.

Senzangakona's features ironed out, his blood chilled by the woman's spellbinding beauty, and, for the second time that day, the prince found himself trying to stare down a 'cat' - an exquisite cat.

As if to punctuate the sudden tempest that raged in the man's soul, the skies finally opened, unloading their deluge of tropical rain. Slowly, elegantly, effortlessly, the girl rose and placed the jug on her head. For a fleeting instant she paused to permit Senzangakona to review her tall, voluptuous body. Drops of rainwater glistened on her ebony skin accentuating her aura of sensuousness as they ran over her firm naked breasts, down her soft, flat stomach and belly enhanced by the velvety cleavage of tightened muscle, and onto her hide kilt, its uppermost fold spanning full hips and delimiting a wisp of pubic hair. As she stood, magnificent, the girl was well aware of the effect she was having on the man;- that, too, was part of the demure and the calculation.

Senzangakona graced the delicious female with one of his brazen, disarming smiles; but the girl remained straight-faced, distant - it took more than a smile to disarm her, even if that smile was addressed by a handsome youth wearing the skins and swathings of a prince.

"Nandi!" beckoned Mahlana, one of the girls in her company.
"Nandi..." echoed Senzangakona quietly, dropping his gaze, savouring the name that, in his native tongue, meant "sweetness".

When he looked up again, Nandi was gone - the apparition had vanished as unexpectedly as it had appeared.

***

Drenched to the bone, the mud and clay clinging to her feet, Nandi raced through the rain, towards the Village of the Langeni Clan and her father's homestead. Reaching the top of a hill overlooking her family's small cluster of huts and scant herd of cattle, she stopped to catch her breath, sucking the damp, refreshing air deep into her lungs.

As another spasm of thunder rattled the tortured skies, Nandi's hurried down to one of the huts, the largest, and entered.

Seated on mats on the right-hand side of the dwelling (the side reserved for males) was Bhebhe,- a man in his fifties, wearing the skins and furs of a Langeni 'paterfamilias', his features, parched by years of hard work and outdoor life, were blessed with a glint of compassion honed by a deep humanity. With him sat Gendeyana, a young man of the Qwabes Clan, not particularly muscular, nor especially handsome, yet possessed, nevertheless, with an expression, warm and genuine, that augured a heart that was patient and kind. Accompanying Gendeyana were his two brothers, both older.

Grimy, wet, the chill of the storm still clinging to her glowing skin, Nandi looked more sensuous than ever as, upon entering, she cast a sidelong glance at the Qwabe visitors and felt a vague foreboding. "Sakubona, Father..." Nandi greeted Bhebhe respectfully (with he familiar 'sakubona' or, literally, 'I see you') and sank down onto a mat on the left side of the hut next to her mother, Mfunda, who, though nearing fifty, was gifted with a beauty that still held its ground quite well, even when threatened with the nearness of her daughter's exceptional appearance.

Bending towards the warmth of the fire, Nandi began to dry her hair, her manner cat-like, graceful, and shamelessly seductive. As she did so, she glanced furtively at Gendeyana with a look of scrutiny, registering his expression of affection, recognising his love for her with the rising venom of contempt.

"Gendeyana has honoured our family," Bhebhe started, his words measured, his cadence hieratic, "by asking for your hand in marriage."

Still riveted on the Qwabe youth, Nandi's eyes narrowed, her gaze now piercing, accusing.

Bhebhe glossed over his daughter's look. He had anticipated her reaction. "We have agreed on a bride-price," her father went on, "of ten cattle, which I find most generous, considering the economic conditions of your suitor". Bhebhe wiped his damp forehead, passing his tongue over parched lips. 'Reading' this customary 'marriage contract' was difficult for him. He disliked treating his daughter as if she were an object. "Being that you will be his first wife, we have decided that, no matter how many others he should marry, you will remain his Principal Wife, with rights to your own private hut, private garden, granary, and stack for firewood..."

Gendeyana and his brothers smiled. They were proud of these conditions. They felt they were being most generous and, within the structure of their world, they were. What they failed to see was that Nandi wanted nothing to do with that structure and with their world where the condition of the woman was a notch above slavery. Where once wed and graciously installed in her husband's homestead, the woman became the property of the 'purchasing family'. Should she run away, Nandi knew she would be brought back. Should she refuse her husband access, she would be compelled by force. Where virtually everything she did - rising, working, eating, sleeping, cooking, bearing children - would be conditioned by the will of a husband who it was hoped would be broad-minded, tolerant, considerate, and -- easily satisfied! Yet, - and this being even harder for Nandi to accept,- most women revelled in the game and played along quite willingly, making this 'slavery' purely voluntary and, thus, fairly benevolent. Most women were quite content to relinquish their freedom in return for - security.

"But not me," Nandi mused. She felt that her security had to come from herself, from within. " In addition," Bhebhe's voice pressed on, "the first son you will bear him will be considered principal heir to his father's inheritance."

Again Gendeyana smiled, nodding with satisfaction. Simmering in the wrath caused by this mortification of womanhood, Nandi did not return that smile. Nor did her father. "We have decided," concluded the hieratic voice, "that upon your return from the wedding of your mother's family to the House of we will officially announce your betrothal to Gendeyana of the amaMbedweni sub-clan of the Qwabes."

Bhebhe fell silent. A silence, which hovered heavily in the small confines of the hut. Nandi lowered her gaze and her thoughts were soon lost in the burning fire, which crackled with tiny explosions that sent spurts of blue, pungent smoke into the air. Her brain was also searing, crackling with the pungent smoke of life's betrayals. Her eyes widened, engulfing the lapping flames, as she crossed her arms, the hands clasping her elbows, tightening the grip till the skin over the knuckles blanched with tension. Her mind was reeling. She felt that pride, reason, argument - all was gone, and there remained only the brutal humiliation of force. She suddenly felt like a flower whose life-giving stem had been broken by a gust of wind, whose petals were already withering. The condition of the wife, thus defined, was, for Nandi, a form of slow death. Stung into bitter protest, Nandi looked up and spoke, without first requesting permission - a behaviour which, normally considered rude in a woman, was unforgivable in the presence of her "betrothed".

"Ten cattle, Gendeyana?" she asked, her tone ironic, scornful, gathering volume. "That is most generous! And what do you expect from me in return for your 'payment'? - Moral virtues? Gentle submissiveness?"

"Nandi!" scolded her mother.

"Mother," she retorted, "if I am to be bought for a handful of milk cows, I have the right to know what is expected of me!" Her eyes shot back to Gendeyana who accused the impact of that spiteful glare. "Gentle submissiveness..." she repeated, the lustre of irony on her face fading swiftly into tight-lipped fury, her long, slender fingers clenching into fists. "Along with willing service and domestic diligence! Not to forget my generative organs! They must be healthy, mustn't they, Gendeyana? It would be criminal for you to waste all those good cows on a sterile bitch!"

Having spat out the last two words, Nandi hurled off her kaross and took her leave of the hut - forming a void of shocked stupor behind her.

Mfunda searched for her husband's eyes and found them oppressed by a sad sense of resigned wisdom, mingled with the profound pity of an old man helpless before a childish disaster. In his eyes was an understanding born of love, which shrouded a deeper feeling of outrage.

"My apologies to you and your brothers, Gendeyana," Bhebhe uttered with a deep sigh and a great weight on his heart as he clenched his own wrist, feeling his pulse-beat. "If, after this outburst, you feel that my daughter is no longer suitable, I ..."

"No need for that, Baba," Gendeyana quickly interjected, wanting to save Bhebhe any further embarrassment, adding with genuine conviction, "I want Nandi. I love her for what she is, you see."

* * *

It had almost stopped raining. The dark clouds were rolling back into the north and rays of sunlight were timidly pricking through.

Bhebhe found Nandi near the stockade of the cattle-fold. She was shivering, as if a cold fingertip had touched her heart, and her lips were pressed in fury. Bhebhe accosted her, gently placing one of his large, calloused hands on her shoulder. "It's as hard for me as it is for you, Nandi. You're the last person on earth I'd want to sell for a 'handful of milk cows'."

Nandi turned to gaze deeply into her father's eyes where she could see no trace of resentment, but rather a willingness to make her happy. Seeing his warmth, his gentle love, her anger dwindled, and she melted into the hollow of his embrace. "Oh, father, I'm sorry."

Bhebhe held his daughter as one clutches his most cherished possession in the throes of a hurricane. "So am I," he murmured, softly. "No man has the right to sire a wild-cat unless he has the wisdom to tame her."

Nandi smiled through her tears. Bhebhe lifted her chin with his fingertips and searched the deep pools of her gaze. "Nandi... what is it you really want?" He was serious now, his voice grave.

"I don't know, father. I suppose I want something...different. Something that's there for me -- only for me!"

"We all do at your age," her father noted, remembering his own 'roaming youth', the 'alluring vastness of the unexplored'. "What sort of 'different' did you have in mind?"

"Something..." she cast a longing glance at the clouds, searching the sky and her mind for words to describe an unreasoning quest. "...unreachable for all but me," she finally said. "Something nobody else can have."

"Then I hope you don't find it," Bhebhe replied, the simplicity of his tone enhanced by the complexity of human experience, "or you will be very much alone. I have always tried to make you happy, my daughter. But I am helpless now. No matter how much I love you, I have neither the strength nor the influence to change our traditions to please my rebel offspring. All I can suggest is that you try to break through that shell you have built round your heart and use your courage to face the situation for what it is. - Gendeyana is a good man. He has the patience to tolerate your temper because he truly loves you. For what more could you ask?"

Nandi's face hardened with resolve. "Much more, father. Much more."

***

A majestic rainbow framed the hills that rose between the Mkumbane and the Mpembeni rivers, its shimmering multi-coloured blade of light rising out of the orange grasslands, vaulting the skies, and burying itself in the brown currents of the Umfolozi which ran swiftly towards the distant ocean. Timidly at first, then with growing confidence, Nature's wildlife sniffed at the tangy dankness and read the heavens wondering if the wrath of Africa had been momentarily quelled.

The royal homestead of Senzangakona's father, the Zulu king, Jama kaNdaba, was blessed with the name "Nobamba" - meaning "The Place of Unity", an appellation which reflected Jama's reign - one of peace and unity. Far larger and more populated than Bhebhe's dwelling, with a smattering of helpers and maidservants (as befitted a king's 'palace'), the homestead was now, in the aftermath of the storm, alive with domestic activity. Young maidens were returning to the fields to resume the tedious process of planting the millet and sorghum seeds. Older women took up their splinters of sharpened bone and poised aged hands in the deftness of mat weaving. Young lads entered the sanctity of the stockade and bent to the task of milking cows, collecting the warm white nectar in clay vessels. Another youth inspected the frayed shoulder of his hut, gutted by the wind and storm and set to work repairing it before nightfall.

His stride secure, even despotic in gait, like the walk of a man who is accustomed to being completely exclusive, Senzangakona entered Nobamba carrying the august leopard on his mighty shoulders, both the impressive prize of the hunt and the lofty air of the noble hunter evoking the gaping admiration of his Zulu clans-men. Easing the beast off his shoulders, the Prince deposited the carcass next to a skin-dresser who was in the process of pegging and stretching the thick, rubbery hide of a buffalo. "I want it ready for the celebration," Senzangakona perfunctorily commanded, dismissing the skin-dresser, leaving him bent in a helpless bow of submission.

"Fine looking animal," said Mkabayi kaJama, casting the leopard a deliberate sidelong glance, her voice laced with chiding.

Senzangakona turned to face his sister's petulant sneer, which, along with her smugness, had become a permanent attribute of her once handsome features – now hardened and 'mothballed' by spinsterhood. Accustomed to her ironic and cantankerous nature, the Prince evenly matched her sarcasm with his own. "It's not every day a man marries," he smiled.

"Especially this man," she replied, simmering in her virulence.

* * *

Princess Mkabayi kaJama, sister of Senzangakona ka-Jama, daughter of King Jama kaNdaba Zulu was a misfit from birth, an exception to the rule.

In the tradition of the Nguni Bantu, whenever twins were born it was held to be an event of evil-portent heralding the flagellum of Apocalypse on the father and his immediate relatives. A cow or goat were at once slaughtered by the hapless family to the ancestral spirits in hopes that they would placate the forces of the Universe and dissuade them from their nefarious course. Then, after all this pious worship, one of the twins was also slaughtered: - the first-born.

Mkabayi was a twin. The first-born. Immediately after she and her mother, Mtaniya kaManyelela, had gone their separate ways, so to say, and whilst her twin sister, Mmama, was in the process of being plucked from the womb, Jama's councillors and "inyanga" (medicine men) descended upon the Zulu King appealing to him that it was vital that the first-born be returned, post-haste, to her ancestors lest the Heavens themselves should open, raining ruin upon the Zulu's homestead and clan. Belonging to a tough, wiry breed, active, sharp and bold, and being quite a misfit himself, Jama sharply refused: - he would not murder his own daughter! The Zulu Council of Elders met to apprise their regent that, though of fiery temperament and independent disposition, Jama was still subject to the superior laws of justice and reason. The king stubbornly rebutted that "justice" was one thing and superstition another, and that as long as the child was his, he would be subject to his own reason alone! Ergo, Mkabayi would live!

And live she did, though her childhood was marred by isolation being that most of the Zulus considered her a living curse and, as a consequence, kept their distance, as one would avoid a leper. Mkabayi reacted to the rejection of her clansmen and women by voluntarily assuming the role of the outcast. As she grew in age and bitterness, indeed as she honed her bitterness into over-whelming ambition, the twin learned to rebuff the Zulus more than they could ever shun her, becoming a product of her own loneliness, a hardened child first, then a jaundiced young maiden with no courter nor lover, and finally, a spinster void of femininity and simmering in virulence. Irascible and domineering by nature, only one balm could soothe the irritation of her heart: - power.

* * *

"Have you seen my bride-to-be?" Senzangakona asked as he strode casually at her side, a brazen smile twitching on his lips.

"I chose her, my dear brother. Or have you forgotten?" answered Mkabayi, her own lips wearing her usual smugness.

Momentarily breaking off the exchange, the Prince nonchalantly beckoned to a young maiden who was carrying a pot of beer. The maiden, Noliwa, very obediently scurried to his side and proffered the drink. Senzangakona grinned at the girl, his eyes dancing with pleasure over her shapeliness. Having drunk his fill, his moods like the winter sky, bright one moment and overcast the next, Senzangakona dismissed Noliwa with the same ease and abruptness with which he had dismissed the skin dresser.

"And what is she like - this bride of mine," he inquired with feigned interest, picking up the conversation where he had broken off as he wiped the beer's froth from his mouth with the back of his hand.

"The daughter of Sodubo of the Nzuza Clan, whom our father would like to entrap in an alliance, - that is what she's like," said Mkabayi, comfortably in control, falling into step with her brother as he moved round the perimeter of the fold.

"And I'm to be the bait?" he retorted, cocking his head with playful inquisitiveness.

"My brother - my one and only brother," said she, wryly, "need I remind you that you are the heir to the Zulu throne and not I because of what is between your legs. Would it be asking too much if you occasionally used it for the betterment of our kingdom?"

"I don't have much choice in the matter, do I?" Senzangakona answered, amused.

"No," Mkabayi was smiling, yet her eyes were serious. Then, in a harder voice, she added, "Remember that."

CHAPTER II
"KHEHLA"(WEDDING)

The deep blue-black of night was abruptly lightened to hues of mauve-violet, with the larger stars still glinting brightly on the sky's canvas. Behind the stars, the whitish glow of dawn crept higher and higher, deepening into a rose-pink, with the fan-like rays of the still invisible sun shooting and quivering across it.

The colours of daybreak were then pervaded by the distant booming of the umSenge drum, as if the sun's rays, like flittering fingers, were dancing over the musical instrument, 'milking' forth the booming sound from its reeds. The uluGibane (a stringed bow made of bent reed and ox-tendon), the umTshingo (a reed pipe), the iMpempe (a quill- whistle), and other instruments joined in the music's crescendo. When the sun finally burst forth, instantly dispelling the lingering moisture of night, the clapping of young men and women was added to the rhythm, soon punctuated by joyous singing and shrill ululating, as the orchestration swelled to a fever pitch.

The Zulu royal homestead was immersed in the merriment of a wedding celebration; the clan's entire populace having flocked to Nobamba to witness Prince Senzangakona's marriage to the House of Nzuza.

The three sacrificial beasts (the 'isiGodo') were being led across the auburn fields and up the rocky slopes towards Jama's cattle-fold. The animals were to be offered up to the bride's ancestral spirits as a prayer for healthy and plentiful offspring. One of these, a fierce-looking bull, did not appear as though he would easily be delivered to such sacrifice.

Behind the expiatory beasts was the bridal party, an impressive sight with the explosion of colours and designs belonging to the magnificent plumes, animal skins and tails characteristic of their specific clan. The party consisted of Sodubo, King of the Nzuza Clan with his numerous consorts and, next to the wives, his daughter, Mkabi, Senzangakona's bride-to-be, a somewhat common-looking, homely girl, distracted with fear and confusion as if she, too, were being led to some sort of sacrificial rite of which, like the isiGodo, she was to be the unwilling victim.

Dignitaries from two other clans related by blood to the bridal party completed the procession to Nobamba. They were Kondlo, King of the Qwabes, a powerful-looking man striding forcefully across the veld in the company of his ten year old son, Prince Pakatwayo, his wives, his servants, and his royal entourage of Elders.

The second clan, the Langeni, flanked the Qwabes and was represented by its king, Mbenghi, tall, lanky, of stately figure and carriage,

Mbenghi's two wives, the twelve-year-old Prince Makedama, and Gama, the most respected exponent of the Langeni council.

Completing the attendance of the two clans were the 'commoners' Bhebhe of the Langeni, with Mfunda and Nandi,- and the Qwabe Gendeyana and his brothers.

Her attire unpretentious, geared to enhance her shapely frame, Nandi advanced barefoot over the caked saffron marl, casting a lingering glance in the direction of the Zulu homestead. A lustful yearning stirred within her, as she allowed a playful smile to steal across her lips.

* * *

"Sodubo of the Nzuza, Kondlo of the Qwabes, Mbenghi of the Langeni..." Jama intoned, addressing his three regal guests, his open hands raised in peace and prayer, his voice riding the loftiness of pious inflection, "I welcome you and your families to the House of Zulu---"

Noting fatigue in his father's voice, Senzangakona ran a pensive hand over his newly acquired leopard-skin and turned to face the Zulu king with a critical gaze. Dressed in full regalia, seated on a draped tree-stump at the top of the cattle-fold and under a large shield held by a servant to shade the king from the midday rays of the sun, Jama possessed the awesome, lordly posture and countenance of a true king. "He's ill," the Prince thought with a chill of realisation, "and at one time or another, he must die, leaving the throne…to his son."

And with the throne, responsibility. Carefree and capricious by nature, the prince was staggered by the thought that he would ever be held accountable for his actions. He stole a glance at the royal females: his mother, Mtaniya, Mmama (insignificant; living, as she always had, in the shadow of her stalwart sister), and the haughty twin, Mkabayi. He was not surprised to find that Mkabayi was staring at him with a thin smile as if she were privy to his thoughts and fears. "She has always done that," he thought with rising resentment. "A part of her has always lived inside me, waiting, like a parasite, to feast at the banquet of my misgivings when I ascend the throne of Zulu."

"May the festivities of today bind our clans in peace," Jama concluded, his penetrating, feverish eyes fixed on the visiting sovereigns. "So I pray to our ancestors."

Senzangakona joined his father in that prayer. Peace would make life that much easier when he ascended the throne. "So I pray..."- trying to fashion for himself an air of regal piety, the Prince shifted his gaze to take in the neighbouring clans. Suddenly his eyes snagged on someone standing in the midst of the Langeni.

Some time had passed since their "meeting" at the Mkumbane Stream, yet the mere sight of Nandi caused the delicious encounter to resurface in his mind with all its original intensity. Yet Nandi did not return his glint of recognition, her face remaining void of emotion as she looked at him with blank eyes. The Prince frowned. "Has she forgotten me?" he wondered and quickly dismissed the thought as absurd, adding, "Of course not! She's just playing. Teasing me." His smile broadened at the prospect of really meeting her. -- "Later," he thought. "After my wedding."

* * *

"Ngitole, wena wakwaZulu," Mkabi beseeched as she knelt at Jama's feet, her head bowed, her face covered with a veil of leaves -- "Adopt me, O thou of the Zulu Clan".

Placing his hands over Mkabi's head, Jama responded to her plea by chanting, solemnly: "Mina ngiyaku-londo-lozwa nguWe. U-ngi-Pate kaHle, naNi ngi-yoku-pPata ka-Hle (It is I who shall be cared for by thee; treat me well, and I shall so treat thee)."

"How shall I treat her," Senzangakona pondered as he stared at his first wife, the future Nkosikazi of the Zulus, forcing himself to imagine her spongy flesh under his touch and her own hands groping for him. Feeling the revulsion rising within him, the newly wed looked away. His eyes, thirsty for the sight of something more attractive, soon quenched their desire on the alluring firmness and velvety softness of Nandi - the girl whose name meant 'sweetness'.

Mkabayi glanced at Senzangakona and was troubled upon noticing the shameless level of desire with which he was regarding the Langeni maiden. Turning her attention to Nandi, Mkabayi glossed over her remarkable beauty, - that, in itself, did not bother the Zulu princess who had, long ago, grown callous to beauty, beyond any degree of envy, accepting it as something which was simply beyond her reach and therefore something to be ignored. No, it wasn't envy that troubled Mkabayi as her gaze lingered on Nandi, it was something else: recognition. She recognised in Nandi's feline eyes a predacious glint of ambition which, when coupled with superior beauty, could reek havoc in the life of a man as weak as she knew her brother to be.

As if sensing her probing gaze, for the first time, Nandi shifted her attention to Mkabayi, allowing the two women to take stock of one other.

The animosity was immediate, mutual, and intense. They both knew that, in time, that initial feeling would grow to make them rivals.

* * *

With murder in his heart, the bull furiously dug into the turf with his front's hooves and, snorting, charged. His pointed horns swept past Igazi. The scrambled out of the animal's way, feeling the beast's hot breath flushing the skin on his back and smelling the sweet, musty odor of his sweaty hide. The bull lunged into the fencing of the cattle-fold, splintering the hefty branches of the palisade with an upward swoop of his left horn. He then turned and, head low, horns poised, ignoring several other of his tormenters, once again concentrated his attack on Igazi. Nearing the youth, the animal jerked his head up, and Igazi reached out, over the uplifted snout and grabbed hold of the horns, riding them. The youth struggled to pull the beast down, yet, lacking the body weight and strength to control the animal's forward thrust, the Zulu failed to purchase ground in the powdery turf and, with a violent jolt, was soon hurled painfully against the stockade.

Mkabayi smiled. She seemed to be on the bull's side. Captivated by the battle between man and beast, the members of the bridal party clung to the perimeter of the fold, cheering, applauding, shouting encouragement.

Nandi's large eyes, glistening with the brightness of fever, betrayed her excitement. Seeing her glean of arousal, Senzangakona responded to the opportunity of impressing her and rose from his place between Jama and the Zulu Elder Mudli (in his fifties; a gaunt, elegant figure, his face hard-set, as if chiselled in granite, with deep lines, the scars of many crises). The handsome Prince began to prepare for the 'combat'. Slowly, his manner deliberate, his eyes never leaving Nandi, Senzangakona slipped off his cumbersome leopard-skin and trinkets. Then, naked save for his loincloth, his tall, muscular body poised for combat, Senzangakona moved towards the corral, the adrenalin buzzing in his veins at the closeness of danger.

Nandi watched him; her face flushed with expectation.

Intrigued, Jama looked thoughtfully at his son and the Langeni girl. "Yes, a most lovely creature," the king admitted, evoking memories of his own tempestuous youth in which a woman like Nandi would have easily caused him to lose his head. Yet his son should know better than to punctuate his desires by making them the plaything of public opinion. For a king, for a future king, everything, even desire should be seen in the light of calm reflection. There is no room for passion on the throne - save for the passion of pride. With growing concern, Jama watched his son stride away, towards the corral and felt that his own honour was riding with his heir.

Reaching the turf of the stockade, his macho blood boiling, Senzangakona flashed a smile in Nandi's direction. And, for the first time, realising that she was now the centre of attention, Nandi smiled back. She then cast Mkabayi a sidelong glance laced with another smile – one of defiance.

Senzangakona strode into the cattle-fold, his eyes trained on the bull. Closing the distance between himself and the beast, the Prince motioned, with a brusque wave of the hand, to Lutuli, Igazi and the others to leave the enclosure. Igazi hesitated, apprehensive. In fact, alone and without weapons, even Senzangakona might have trouble taking on a bull as mighty and combative as this. Yet the Prince insisted and reluctantly Igazi and the others were forced to obey.

Sniffing the stimulating odour of adrenalin, the beast turned to face the man who was venturing this lone challenge. A hush fell on the gathering.

Senzangakona advanced, smiling, teasing the bull. "Kehli... Kehli...", he taunted, moving in on the animal so as to provoke a charge.

The beast shifted his massive weight, rocking forward, then back, gaining momentum, savouring the imminent attack. Suddenly he dug his rear hooves into the ground and propelled himself forward, pitching headlong towards Senzangakona. The Prince wait- ed and, in an instant, the bull was upon him, the animal's horns lowered, ready to stab. Before impact, the Zulu deftly moved to the side, as the beast snorted past him, his hide touching flesh, leaving a stain of muggy perspiration. Smiling with confidence, Senzangakona playfully slapped the bull's rump.

Laughter applauded the man's feat of daring.

The animal charged again and again, and the prince sidestepped, moving well clear of the arching, pointed horns. Nervous, exasperated, the bull stopped and shook his mighty head and sneezed, expelling a furious gust of rage. He turned and, snorting again, allowed his eyes to focus on the blurred contours of the Zulu. And it was then that Senzangakona's over-confidence betrayed him. Lowering his head, struggling against dizziness, the bull charged anew, quickly changed direction and, catching the prince off guard, tore across the side of his chest with his pointed horn leaving a bleeding gash.

The onlookers were in an uproar as they surged against the stockade, aghast. Mkabi closed her eyes, fully expecting to become a widow on her wedding day; as Jama seethed at the stupidity of his son's recklessness, mumbling, under his breath, "You fool!"

Only Nandi remained gelidly impassive, her feline eyes locked on the Prince in the aloofness of expectation.

With a strength born of fury, reviling himself for having been so careless, Senzangakona raced to the bull and grabbed hold of his horns. Though immensely strong, the animal's massive body rendered him slow to respond to the man's quick, agile attack and, almost before the bull could react, Senzangakona had wrestled him to the ground. Kicking wildly the bull sought to regain his footing, but as he raised his head, he gave the prince just the leverage he needed. Administering the animal's own strength against him, Senzangakona forced the horns downward as the bull thrust his weight in the opposite direction. With a dull wrenching sound the creature's spine snapped, tearing at nerve centers, driving a rib into his lung.

Senzangakona got to his feet leaving the wretched animal swaying on his flank, vomiting blood and pulmonary fluid, confused and terrified as the darkness of death descended upon his flittering eyes. Then, with a last, jerky kick of the legs, the bull quavered and slumped onto the turf, a lifeless heap.

Bathed in dust, blood and grime and in the praising stares of his clansmen, the victorious prince walked out of the stockade, his broad chest heaving with exertion, his teeth gleaming from lips parted in a self-satisfied grin. A royal valet, Ghubela, a thin, wiry, wisp of a man with frightened eyes, like those of a beaten dog, and a twitching hesitant manner, scurried to Senzangakona's side and draped the leopard-skin over the Prince's muscular shoulders which now glistening with perspiration. In sign of shared triumph and relief, one of the Zulus started to play the umSenge drum. The other instruments fell in with his rhythm, as voices began to sing the praises of their courageous prince.

Wallowing in the glory, Senzangakona accosted the Langeni maidens in charge of the sorghum beer. He stopped to review the females, his eyes lingering on each with a flirtatious glint as he systematically moved down the line towards Nandi. Pretending to have chosen her at random, he motioned to the beauty to come forward with her beer.

Nandi did not budge.

Senzangakona's brow furrowed, incredulously, his mind unable to accept her reluctance to comply with his wishes. Perhaps she hadn't seen his gesture, he thought by way of explanation, and motioned again.

And again Nandi didn't budge, her indifference to his command becoming more manifest to Senzangakona as well as to the entire bridal party.

Noliwa and the other maidens stared in wide-eyed amazement at Nandi's incredible defiance and in bated apprehension at Senzangakona, waiting for his anger to burst forth. Yet the Prince remained surprisingly calm, his penetrating gaze fixed on Nandi who returned his look with a hint of intransigence.

Perhaps she doesn't understand, he thought and turned to Ghubela, silently prompting the man's assistance. On cue, Ghubela announced to Nandi, his tone official, "Prince Senzangakona is thirsty."

Nandi favoured Ghubela with the blankest stare of disinterest and, once again -- did not stir from her place in line.

Feeling the mounting tension that shot through the air like an electric current, the musicians stopped playing, and an awkward silence suddenly gripped Nobamba.

Senzangakona shot Ghubela an intense look, a look which made the valet feel personally responsible for Nandi's outrageous behavior. "Prince Senzangakona has chosen you to give him your beer." Unruffled, her lovely features void of expression, Nandi lifted a brow and replied to the valet, "Ask your prince if I am to consider myself flattered."

Mkabayi had trouble stifling a smile, while Bhebhe, far from being amused, watched his daughter apprehensively, waiting, as were Jama, Mudli, Kondlo, and the others, for the Prince's reaction.

They did not have long to wait.

"Come here," Senzangakona ordered Nandi, his lips thinning as if all humor had been ironed from them.

Nandi's back straightened, as if she were about to take a step forward. All hearts missed a beat, anticipating that step. Perhaps it was the shadow of victory in Senzangakona's eyes that stopped her, or perhaps she had never intended to move. Whatever the reason, Nandi merely shifted her weight to her other foot…and did not obey.

Senzangakona knew he'd allowed the girl to go too far, placing him in an increasingly embarrassing position. But there was no turning back now, no forgetting the incident; his pride was at stake, he had to react. With a few rapid strides, he closed the gap between himself and Nandi. Grabbing her round the waist, Senzangakona forcibly lifted Nandi off the ground, carrying her thrashing body and the vessel of beer back to the place from whence he had beckoned her.

Insulted by the affront to his betrothed, Gendeyana moved to retaliate, but Bhebhe stopped him. "No!" the older man said. "That would only make matters worse."

As soon as Senzangakona set the struggling girl down on her feet, freeing her arms, Nandi's hand furiously lashed out like a whip and struck the Prince across the face, stunning him into a gaping, wide-eyed look of utter bewilderment. Nandi's slap resounded throughout the gathering and was echoed from the Heavens and on the faces of the Zulus.

As the initial amazement slowly subsided along with the throbbing on his cheek, Senzangakona deliberated his method of reprisal and decided that it would best serve his own purpose and that of his honour if, rather than strike back, he forced the female into submission. His eyes widening with anger, Senzangakona took Nandi's arm, holding her wrist in a vice-like grip. Her powerful physical attraction for him having been made all the more urgent by her teasing, the two now glared at each other with a mixture of passion and wrath - love and hatred. Emotions so intense, they seemed to have blocked out the rest of the world. They were 'making love' with their eyes, both aware of the desire flaring between them. The 'rest of the world' looked on in silence, shocked by the prince's reaction - puzzled by the smile that unexpectedly dawned on his face. When Nandi smiled back, provocatively, the prince, enraged, clenched her hand, forcing the fingers round the handle of the calabash. Guiding her hand in his powerful grasp, he forced her to bring the beer to his lips. His eyes locked on hers, he drank. Then, having had his fill, confident that he had made up for lost face by having forced her to comply with his wish, the prince released his grip on her and, turning his back in a deliberate gesture of dismissal, strode away.

As Nandi moved back to her place among the maidens, her eyes twinkled and a delicate, barely discernible smile of triumph played on her lips. Unlike Senzangakona, she knew she had cause to be confident.

With a look of intense annoyance, Jama registered her smile, making his son's indignation his own. Furiously, the king motioned to the musicians to quickly fill the uncomfortable void that followed the unusual confrontation. The notes of the umSenge were picked up where they had dwindled. Awkwardly at first, then with growing eagerness the other musicians followed suit. Some of the women started to dance, others sang. The gathering began to breathe again, the celebration gradually regaining life and lost gaity.

Senzangakona walked to the water jugs, where a few young boys cleansed his body of the grime and blood acquired in his fight with the bull. An inyanga medicated the wound inflicted by the horn with a paste of herbs and roots. While receiving this attention, Senzangakona mulled over his two conflicts of the day. The first, the one with the bull, though ostensibly more violent, would soon be dismissed from mind and body with the simple administration of some water and a few medicinal herbs. The other - Nandi's - would leave deeper traces, more difficult to 'wash away'. She had won the initial round, he reluctantly admitted to himself - but that was merely the first encounter. There would be others. He would see to that.

CHAPTER III
"UKUZIDLA"(PRIDE)

The Heavens over the Mkumbane were burnished with a deep blue gloss that shone, resplendent, like the cutting edge of daylight on the horny armour of the fruit beetle. The sun's rays were disseminated evenly throughout creation, inspiriting man, beast, and plant with the equalising passion of their glow. As the rays penetrated the moist vegetation that cleaved to the stream, the sun's glow was suddenly embodied into shafts of glistening mist - like a ghost appears at the behest of a medium assuming a glow that varies in intensity and shape with the density of the ethereal solution in which it travels.

As Senzangakona sat at the margin of the Mkumbane, his lean, athletic figure bathed in another radiant shaft of sunlight, he looked thoughtfully at the stream's currents as they frothed round a stone, its waters parting, demurringly, to suit the stubborn obstacle. "What am I doing here?" he sighed, his mind railing against the absurdity of the situation in which his heart had led him. "A man, a full grown man of suitable countenance," he estimated, then nodded adding, "- of more than suitable countenance, who can have and has had any girl on whom he's set his eyes and fancy,- sitting here waiting."

He looked down at himself and suddenly felt ridiculous as his thoughts pressed on with, "waiting with an itch in his loins like a boy fresh out of puberty and into the first Spring of his manhood. But this isn't Spring, it's Winter," he growled under his breath, hitching himself to his feet, "and I'm a fool! And I'd better leave before the branch breaks!"

Senzangakona had already reached the edge of the stream's embankment when the sound of rustling reached his ears, causing him to freeze in his steps, his assegai coiled at eye level. Without turning, the man allowed his sharpened senses, those of an accomplished hunter, to read his surroundings. He heard a voice, a lone voice, the muffled singing of a female, approaching, her bare feet padding on the rocky banks of the stream. He heard the female stop and kneel; then splashing, the stirring of water as a gourd was filled.

Senzangakona felt a smile tugging at the corners of his mouth, sweeping back his lips and throwing all caution to the winds. Like the finch, he, too, was destined to learn the hard way. Turning now, he retraced his steps to the bank of the Mkumbane and stopped, standing in the soft earth, shoulders back, head upright, arms akimbo, brow knit and eyes half-closed in annoyance as he peered at the maiden on the opposite bank of the waterway. Senzangakona was not quite sure how much of his original annoyance was genuine and how much feigned on Nandi's behalf, yet as he waited, and waited for the girl to acknowledge his imposing presence, the anger that surfaced in him was as real as the adrenalin that buzzed through his veins. The Prince cleared his throat, loud enough to be audible, modulated so as to convey the unnerved condition of its bearer.

Nandi lifted an eye and cast a gaze in the direction of the opposing bank, regarding Senzangakona with cool indifference, as one would gloss over a tree in a forest. When the girl's attention returned to her gourd, the prince, in his offence, made his first mistake by admitting, stonily: "You have kept me waiting."

"Have I?" Nandi remarked, and Senzangakona then made his second mistake by interpreting her indifference as remorse. "But it doesn't matter," he conceded, open-handedly, flashing a smile one would bestow upon a domestic animal before tossing a morsel of food. "You're here now."

That was the third mistake: taking for granted the ever-fickle disposition of the gentler sex. Rising, her manner remaining distant, Nandi turned and walked away. Senzangakona's lips parted with incredulity. His arms slumped to his side as if suddenly deprived of all use. "Where are you going?" he found himself saying in a voice that cracked and a tone that was meeker than planned.

"Home," Nandi replied, matter-of-factly, breaking her streak of obstinate silence with a monosyllable.

"Home?" Senzangakona has the misfortune of echoing, as he snagged on yet another mistake by letting his disconcertion shine through the cloud of incredulity.

"Home," the word was batted back, riding on the crest of sarcasm.

Struggling to regain control of events he'd never controlled, Senzangakona raised his voice in a pitch of groping rage. "Come here!" he uttered, repeating the command Nandi had disregarded at his wedding.

"You know better than that," Nandi curtly remarked as she set the pot of water on her head and sauntered gracefully up a hillside towards the auburn flatness of the open veld.

Somewhat belatedly, Senzangakona decided he had had enough. Infuriated, he ventured to ford the stream with long, purposeful strides which quickly closed the gap between himself and Nandi's aloofness. Yet, as a further confirmation of the finch's error and the necessity to be in step with Nature, Senzangakona lost his footing on the mucky surface of a stone slab and slipped backwards, falling into the shallow currents of the Mkumbane.

Hearing the splash and the muffled groan which came soon after, Nandi turned to look over her shoulder. Seeing the comedy of the situation, her coolness was suddenly warmed by a rising wave of mirth which burst into uncontrolled laughter.

At first, Senzangakona simmered in the fumes of his wrath and wounded pride, squinting at the girl with homicidal eyes. Then, realizing the absurdity of his situation, his rage gave way to the resilient, therapeutic self-criticism of youth, and he joined Nandi in her laughter.

"How good it feels," she considered, "that exhilarating laughter that sits on the threshold of freedom, of - love." She was afraid to think the word, let alone speak it. - Love. It left her suspicious. Laughter had to be enough for now.

And, in her laughter, Nandi was caught off guard by the instinct of the hunter. In a gesture that was more of a blurred flash than a motion, Senzangakona lunged forward, grabbing Nandi by the ankle, dragging her down, causing her pot of water to crash onto the rocky bank in an explosion of shards and chips. Then, pinning back her flailing arms, wresting her body flat against the rocky terrain, the prince slid his leg over her belly and rolled on top of her. Like a panic-stricken animal enmeshed in the constraining bonds of a snare, Nandi's body writhed wildly in his grasp, kicking, squirming, howling with rage as she violently fought to break free. Baring her teeth, the girl snapped at the man's face. "Let go of me! Let go!," she snarled furiously like a rabid mongrel, twisting her long fingers in an effort to claw into his flesh.

Nandi's fierce struggle coupled with the nearness, the fragrance of her body only served to heighten Senzangakona's desire, bringing it to a level of frenzy. He clamped his hand over her mouth and felt her teeth sink into the soft flesh of his palm, drawing blood and sending a bolt of pain racing down his arm. Yet somehow the pain translated as passion in his heart and, forcing her mouth shut, he pressed his lips against hers, staining them with his own blood.

Gradually, as her own passion overwhelmed her, Nandi closed her eyes, feeling Senzangakona's kisses moving down her neck, over her shoulders, to her breasts. Like one struggles against the abduction of inebriation, engaging one's mind to concentrate so as not to be claimed by the swirling darkness of torpor, Nandi struggled against her own passion. The focal point of her concentration became the reminder that this was not the way she had visualised it in the seclusion of her dreams. Loving was giving, she had decided - even as a young child, in the wake of her father's serene affection - and a gift cannot be stolen.

Senzangakona suddenly felt her body go limp under his touch. Troubled by what appeared to be a sudden submissiveness, the prince looked up and met her glare and was momentarily stunned by its steely glitter. In a voice that had the uncanny inflection of disembodiment, Nandi held his gaze steadily with her own and asked, "May I go now, or did you have rape in mind?"

That question thus voiced had the chilling effect of mollifying the prince's desire into shameful mortification. In a manner that was as awkward as the silence that accompanied it, Senzangakona relinquished his hold on the girl and pulled himself to his feet, standing in the midst of the shallow stream with a lost, confused look of childish remorse.

Nandi also rose, her body wet, caked with mud and clay. She ran an eye over the fragments of the shattered pot and had a wry smile. Something else had been shattered, she felt, something deep within her. Arching back her shoulders, restoring composure and dignity to her bearing, she strode away - away from the stream.

Senzangakona shifted his gaze to look at her with wondering eyes, the events of that afternoon searing in his brain, leaving him distracted with his burden of quandary. "Why did you come?" he finally asked, in a hollow voice.

The question had the effect of freezing Nandi in her tracks. Why had she come? The tinge of resolve was drained from her eyes, leaving the restless disorientation of a person who, having ventured too far, suddenly realises she's lost track of the way home. She didn't trust herself to answer because, indeed, she had no answer, no tangible purpose for coming, just the unreasoned stirring of desire.

The prince felt her hesitation and, intrigued by the vulnerability it betrayed, considered, out loud: "What a complexity of emotions you are, Nandi. Your heart is a labyrinth in which one could easily find himself right back where he started." His voice softened, beseeching: "I must see you again," and asked, his voice regaining in self-mastery, "Tomorrow?"

A silent pause ensued. Then: "I'll think about it," she answered, stiffly, non-committal, and started off again.

Senzangakona's gaze stayed with her until her figure vanished - its beauty claimed by the beauty of the landscape.

Jama kaNdaba Zulu knew that the wisdom of Life consists in putting out of sight all the reminders of our folly, of our weakness, of our mortality; all that bears witness to Man's inefficiency: - the vestiges of our failures, the hints of our lingering fears, the bodies of our beloved dead. Yet the king also knew that, in a greater sense, these reminders can serve to redeem Man, helping us to bear the burden of our ineptness as creatures. Thus, though buried and out of the way, our dead are ever-present in our prayers, ennobling the mortal soul; and our follies and weaknesses, with their fears and failures, are as much a source of embarrassment as a font of learning and growth. Indeed, far from putting his weaknesses out of sight, Man must face them in the light of day and strive to overcome them.

These were the thoughts that Jama was turning over in his mind as he sat on his throne of coiled grass (the 'inKata') within the confines of Nobamba's Royal Hut. He had asked to see his son, to speak with his heir in the presence of the Council of Elders, and he now dropped his gaze to Senzangakona's kneeling figure bowed before him.

"Sakubona, my son," Jama greeted him, gently.

"Baba," the prince uttered, looking up, searching for his father's eyes through the billowing fumes disgorged by the lapping flames in the hearth.

"Come closer."

Senzangakona rose from the warming glow of the smoldering fire, crossed the polished, mirror-like black floor of the hut, casting an inquisitive sidelong glance at Mudli and the other Council Elders who sat, stone-faced, their eyes rivetted on the youth making him feel ill-at-ease, outnumbered. His eyes returned to his father, as he sank to the floor, legs crossed, facing the king.

Jama remained silent, pensive. When he finally spoke, he asked: "Have you met with her?"

Senzangakona furrowed his brow in disbelief. That was the last thing he expected to be asked. Confused, seeking elucidation, he inquired, "'Her', Baba?"

"The Langeni woman."

The prince's heart stood still, stopped dead by utter amazement. How did his father know of his meeting with Nandi, he pondered.

As if reading his mind, Jama added, "Need I remind you, my son, that your spies are, above all, my spies."

A wry smile twitched on Senzangakona's lips. Ghubela, he told himself, the name echoing in his mind, summoning the anger born of betrayal.

"Well..?" Jama prodded, his expression becoming stern.

"Yes, father. I have," the prince admitted.

"And have you," Jama paused, seeking the most appropriate phrasing, finally deciding upon - "finally dismissed her from your mind?"

Senzangakona's bewildered eyes flittered from his father to the Council and back. "What an absurd line of questioning," he marvelled and asked out loud, his voice betraying his amused astonishment, "Have the esteemed members of the Council met to discuss a woman?"

Jama did not appreciated his son's irony. He insisted, the tone skirting anger: "Answer me!"

"It was meaningless, father," the youth retorted. "The encounter left me somewhat confused," he wanted to add, but didn't.

"Does that mean you intend to see her again?"

Senzangakona was irked by this line of questioning which he felt to be a full-scale invasion of his personal life. He voiced this with a defiant, "I feel that is my private concern, Father."

"A man who is to be king must learn that a king has no 'private concerns'!" Jama's anger became manifest in the harsh manner in which he stressed the word 'king'. His level of anger rose upon continuing, "Everything you do, everything you say, everything you think, even when you are alone, can be turned against you if your subjects chose to do so!- Now tell me..." he spat the words out, "do you intend to see her again?"

Jama's harsh tone made his son's defiance harder to subdue. "Haven't your spies told you, father?" he replied, his eyes locked on Jama's.

"I want to hear it from your own lips," the king shot back, unwaveringly, his tone remaining sharp.

Senzangakona felt that the floor of the hut was suddenly uncomfortably hard. He shifted his weight as if to find the most comfortable position in which to reply: "I'm not sure. - Perhaps."

Jama fell silent and sighed deeply, favouring Mudli with a look that betrayed his concern. "Yes," he reflected, "it is quite a task to grapple with another's intimate needs. It is even more of a task to make another aware of them - especially when one attempts to overcome the lack of objectivity inherent in Youth." Plucking some tobacco out of a snuffbox, Jama drew a pinch into each nostril, and felt the nicotine race into his blood, clearing the cobwebs from his head. Changing his line of questioning, the king returned his attention to his son, inquiring, matter-of-factly: "This Langeni girl -- how would you define her behavior at your wedding?"

Senzangakona found himself reacting to the emotional and the physical scrutiny of his father and the Elders by assuming a levity of spirit which hinged on reckless diversion. If he had suspected that Nandi had made a fool of him at the wedding, it was now confirmed to him beyond doubt. He could read it in their self-righteous expressions. His recklessness was heightened by a feeling that he had nothing to lose – except Nandi. And, as his eyes fell on Mudli, he suddenly saw, with irrefutable clarity, that that was what this meeting was all about: losing Nandi. "She was - provocative, I suppose," he finally answered, with a touch of hesitance.

"And your own?" Jama queried. "How would you define your own behavior?"

"Firm," said Senzangakona, half believing it.

"Do you think the others who were present at your wedding would agree with you?"

"With respect to what, father?" asked the prince, genuinely puzzled.

"Well, suppose you were King Kondlo of the Qwabes or Sodubo of the Nzuza. What opinion would you have had of her?"

Senzangakona grinned, his eyes sparkling as her obstinate image appeared before him. "I would think she was a beautiful, hard-headed, insolent shrew!"

"Disobedient?" suggested Jama, leaning slightly forward, his eyes fastening on his heir. "Rebellious?"

"Definitely," said Senzangakona, still smiling.

"Dangerous?"

The prince suddenly felt like leaving, running far away from this probing old man who was his father. "I'd be willing to wager that you'd want her yourself - if you were twenty years younger," he felt like telling him, and had the sudden suspicion that jealousy might be at the root of this relentless inquisition. "Dangerous? Yes, I suppose so," he retorted, with a hint of smugness. "If one didn't know how to handle her."

"I see," Jama said, curtly, leaning back now, crossing his arms in front of his chest, narrowing his gaze as he moved inexorably forward, following a course known only to himself.

"Would you have felt - being Kondlo or Sodubo - that she had somehow insulted you?"

Abruptly Senzangakona realised he was being cornered by a better hunter than he. "Yes. But father, I ..."

"Humiliated you?" Jama went on without mercy.

Senzangakona closed his hands into fists. His voice sounded strained upon acknowledging: "There was an attempt at that, yes."

"And wouldn't you find it fitting," his father suggested, "that a man treated in such an abominable way would have enough pride to never want to see the woman again?!"

"Perhaps I would, father. If I were Kondlo or Sodubo. But I am not."

"No!", Jama said with emphasis, having led his son to the designated mark. "You are not. You are much more! You are the heir to the throne of the 'People of the Heavens', the amaZulu! Soon you will be their leader. They will look to you for courage." There was now something akin to pleading in the king's voice. "They will respect you as long as you value your own pride and the pride of your people above everything else. - Pride, my son," the pleading was now real and rode on a wave of incense, "or have you forgotten what that is?"

Senzangakona's face ironed out. His eyes registering the blow of his father's grave reprimand. The prince glanced at the Elders and decided that he had been wrong - he had a lot more than Nandi to lose; the respect of the Council was at stake. Deprived of that respect, his own reign would be sheer aggravation, the agony of a man condemned to slow death at the death of his father. Senzangakona suddenly wished he had an older brother.

"Have you lost sight of what you were born to be?" Jama inquired, making his reprimand more poignant. "Has she blinded you?" The prince's gaze caught his father's and locked. "There is already talk of this woman...'Nandi'," Jama added, his voice lowered in confidence, "of how she has...bewitched you."

The prince was chilled by the thought. For a fleeting instant it somehow rang true, though Senzangakona was utterly unable to reason why. Rationalising the sensation of bewitchment is beyond human means, even when one is the product of a society where Superstition is the altar upon which the Unexplained and the Exceptional are sacrificed, like virgins of the Intellect, to a god that renders Man deaf, dumb and blind to the world's suffering; a society in which men and women are reared to look upon the Supernatural as a legitimate entity that exists, symbiotically, with the Natural and is called upon, when necessary, to fulfill the beneficial office of whispering to the soul that which the mind is not meant to overhear. In the depths of his soul, it rang true - yet he knew not why and therefore answered in a manner that would shroud his inner feelings in a thick veil of flippant disregard. "Oh, father! That's just the idle gossip of old women! We know better!"

"My son, you are at an age when a man is most prone to lose his head over a woman who constitutes a challenge. At an age when one needs guidance most - especially if he is to become the ruler of his people."

The indulgent tone was short-lived, as Jama resolved to administer the guidance with a firm hand. "You say you are not sure yet whether or not you will see her again. So I will make that decision for you."

Jama's features hardened as he hitched himself erect on his throne of rushes, his expression hieratic. Senzangakona, Mudli and the Elders knew that the king was no longer addressing his son, but rather a subject of his realm.

"By right that girl should have been punished for her effrontery to a prince of the amaZulu!" Jama decreed. "If she was not, it is only because she is related to the clan of Kondlo of the Qwabes, an ally whom I value. Yet if this obsession of yours persists, I may be forced to endanger that alliance with a brother clan in order to safeguard your honor and the trust of my House. – In consequence, you will erase that woman from your mind." The verdict rang out in the hut. "That is not a request. That is an order."

* * *

Nandi's heart was exultant when she reached the Mkumbane and tentatively stepped into its glimmering, gurgling waters and allowed the stream to swirl and eddy round her ankles, as if welcoming her return like a dear friend with whom one has shared a secret emotion. With coy anticipation, she snatched a glimpse of the place where she had met Senzangakona the day before, the spot where she now expected him to be.

But there was no one there.

Nandi curled up next to a rock to wait, her legs drawn up against her breast and clutched in a snug embrace. Resting her chin on her knees, a set smile of delightful anticipation on her lips, she allowed her mind to drift leisurely, tasting moments of total happiness. Her thoughts was borne afloat in the trance-like stupor of wakeful dreaming in which Fantasy and Reality are blended to suit the needs of the spirit, like the coloured paints of an Artist blend to suit the projections of his mind. In this state, she fancied that she saw the image of Senzangakona on the surface of the stream's rippling waters. The man appeared behind her and gently curled his strong arms round her waist, holding her body, pressing it to his own, softly kissing her neck. And, in the reflection, she abandoned herself to his touch.

Yet, as she stirred, opening her eyes, she was still alone, still cuddled up next to the rock, embraced only by the lingering warmth of her Fantasy. Instinctively she cast an urgent glance at her surroundings fully expecting to see the Zulu prince standing over her, flashing one of his confident smiles laced with his usual fierce self-confidence. But he was nit there.

"He'll come," she repeated, refusing to acknowledge any other likelihood.

The sun shown lower on the heavenly vault, its lustrous face partially obscured by swollen storm clouds. The wind was rising, bustling through the trees with a smell of rain.

Nandi sat in the long shadows of early evening, her figure unmoving, deprived of feeling, like a lifeless shell of a human form. Her vacant gaze was fixed upon her own reflection which was sharper now as the surface of the stream took on the opaque, silvery hues of the sky.

It started to rain, and the patter of drops on her face prompted a resurfacing of emotions and - with them - the ebbing of Fantasy and the Illusions it evokes. Her heart was seized by the chill of infinite loneliness which arose from the realisation that for the first time in her life she had allowed herself to be vulnerable and had been hurt. The humiliation and the pain it caused was deeper and more intense than any she had ever experienced.

Rising on unsteady legs, Nandi ran away from that pain and her own emotions, up the slope, through the driving rain. Upon reaching the edge of the vast expanse of open veld, Nandi stopped to catch her breath, and faltering, scowled against the rain as she fought back the urge to turn around; - an urge she could not overcome.

Nandi spun round and glared down at the contours of the Mkumbane, now blurred by a thick curtain of turbulence. Her blood froze as she narrowed her eyes, wiping the rain from them with the back of her hand, peering through the downpour. It took her a moment to focus properly, then, when she was certain, she smiled and her heart leapt with joy as the tension and bitterness were miraculously drained from her features leaving them radiant with the glow of deliverance. Quickly, she ran down the hill and was swept into his arms.

Their embrace burned with urgency and passion. Senzangakona was both surprised and delighted by the unexpected intensity of Nandi's show of affection. And he willingly returned it, her own desire prompting his. As they held each other, their caresses becoming more fervent, they spoke in a feverish whisper, their murmurs rising above the whistling of the rain.

"I didn't think you would come any more," she told him, her lips grazing the lobe of his ear, lightly, like the touch of a fingertip on the petal of a rose.

"It was difficult," Senzangakona admitted, combing back her drenched hair with a gentle touch.

Nandi tilted her head and gazed into his eyes with genuine wonder. "Why," she inquired.

"I had to be sure I wasn't followed," the prince answered with a wry smile. Nandi's frown prompted a further, "There are those who seem to think I should be wary of you," he explained.

"Of me?" Nandi echoed, searching his eyes, realizing for the first time that they were tinted a dark green.

"They tell me you have a rebellious spirit," he went on, his smile becoming mischievous. "And that you are dangerous." He kissed her. "Are you?"

"Yes," she teased, returning his kiss, adding, "Do you?"

"What?"

"Think I'm dangerous?"

"Definitely!"

They both laughed, impervious to the rain now pouring down in torrents. Their laughter faded, as their gazes met and they sank to the ground, their bodies entwined in the swift currents of the Mkumbane.

A flash of lightning pierced the unfathomable and pellucid depths of the raging Heavens bathing the top of a distant hill overlooking the stream where two figures stood in the rippling tapestries of wind and rain, their grisly silhouettes cast against the lavender clouds and billowing blue-black hues of the tempest. Another bolt of harsh light washed the silhouettes in a steely glitter that made their ghostly features look all the more horrid. The two figures, that of an old woman, and at her feet, the immobile shape of a hyena, seemed to be waiting, watching, probing - the animal's glistening fangs bared in an uncanny smile that was poised upon the gateway of ghoulish laughter.

By Birth, by Nature and by Appointment a wielder of powers that issue from Eternity to forge the course of Man in the remoteness of Time Immortal, the woman, Sitayi by name, was a 'sangoma', a diviner in the most Chaldean of traditions. A further bluish flash of lightning pierced the sky casting its sinister glow on her twisted body, defining the gruesome assortment of dried and inflated bladders that hung round her neck and over her shriveled breasts, fleetingly illuminating her skeletal countenance, ageless in definition, sharp and angular under parched flesh, bedaubed with white clay paint.

Possessed by the vehemence of the tempest, Sitayi looked up, her blind, vacant orbs of pastel-blue reaching beyond the human faculty of sight into the Infinite as she searched the storm for the Sign of Genesis.

It came. In the glaring blast that shown through the darkness with a brilliance of red, the crimson colour of blood.

It was heard. In a thundering blast that shook the earth with the March of War.

And after the Sign of Genesis had come, Sitayi knew all was well. She and the hyena turned away from the Mkumbane and shambled off, down the hill, as the rippling shroud of rain claimed them back onto the still, silent shores of Mystery.

CHAPTER IV
"THANDA"(LOVE)
MONTH OF UNTLOLANJA: DECEMBER, 1786

The marvellous stillness preceding the dawn pervaded the world, and the stars, together with the faint glimmer of their dying rays, seemed to shed upon the earth the assurance of security. The young moon, recurved and shining low in the west, was smooth and cool to the eye like a sliver of ice, its perfect gleaming circle of light clinging to the perfect curvature of the dark horizon as Senzangakona reached the vast, crouching plateau in the heart of The emaKosini, the 'Place of Kings', where he had built his new homestead, 'esiKlebe-ni', the 'Site of Eagles'.

Stopping at its gates, his arms akimbo, he looked thoughtfully at his residence which was now stirring to life at the advent of a new day. His gaze strayed from his own large hut, the Main Hut of the homestead's lord looming over a cluster of fig trees at the top of the cattle-fold, past the smaller storage huts which would soon be brimming with grain, to the thatched dwelling of Mkabi, his first and, for now, his only wife,- the meek creature who would sit as his side as the Nkosikasi, the Queen of Queens, when he ascends the throne of Zulu.

Senzangakona looked at his own homestead feeling little or no affinity with that cluster of huts strung round a corral and embraced by its outer palisade of thorn branches. And, as the word 'embrace' came to mind, the prince knew why esiKlebeni felt foreign to him. There was no love there.

Mkabi, his wife. He saw her now as she came out of her hut and humbly beckoned the attendance of handmaidens, and he winced inwardly at the sight of the drab woman he had married for reasons that had nothing to do with love, but were conditioned by the alliance his sister and father wished to secure with a neighboring tribe in the name of power. He looked at her eyes, ever startled in their candidness by life and its ways. He looked at her dolorously drooping features, so indicative of her dismal, subservient personality – ever patient, never complaining, never rebelling, subsisting on the border of the animal and the human. He imagined her sitting, cowering at his side in the tense moments that would follow their copulation, and he thought: "The Queen of Queens! The woman I married!"

Senzangakona snarled contemptuously, feeling the bitter taste of his own venom rising within him -- rising together with the soothing sweetness of a faint, melodious voice from the recent past whispering, "Marry me."

Senzangakona faltered, reaching out for the sturdy posts of the homestead's gates, resting on them as his mind grew fuzzy, blurred by the shifting and confused gusts of memory that evoked jumbled images and dashed his soul into a spell of deep uncertainty. Groping for a foothold in that void of swirling images, he longingly grasped the sweetness of that voice and drifted back to...

"Marry me," Nandi had breathed, lying on her back in the sea of grain, her lovely features washed by the fondling rays of the midday sun reflected on the saffron hues of the young millet. Senzangakona lay next to the girl, gently caressing her face with the tips of his fingers. When he had failed to respond to her behest, fearing that her words had been carried off by the gentle breeze that played through the swaying seedlings, Nandi had opened her eyes and repeated, staring steadfast at her prince, her tone taking on fervency, "Marry me, Senzangakona."

As the words had finally sank in, the prince grew tense and withdrew his hand from its caressing. Sitting up, he had allowed his gaze to wander pensively over the captivating landscape, snagging on a small family of white and amber vervet monkeys sunning themselves on the straight polished limb of a sisal tree. "I cannot," he had murmured after a pause. "Not now, at least."

Sensing an inflection of regret in his words, Nandi had risen and threaded her arm through his, resting her cheek on the wide sheaf of muscle on his shoulder. "Why not?" she had rebutted, her voice softening to sweetness. "For the past weeks - and months, you've told me repeatedly how much you love me; that you didn't know what love was until you met me."

The prince had been somehow irritated by the banality of his own words thus echoed - out of context, out of the mutual tenderness and passion in which they were originally spoken. Yet far from wanting to taint the afternoon's romantic encounter with his rising annoyance, the man had retained his good humor and a flippant air. "Have I?" he had answered, brushing by her remark with a thin smile, adding with sarcasm, "I should be more careful what I say."

Nandi, however, had grown in her earnestness. "Why can't our relationship, our love be out in the light of day, for all to see?!" she had pleaded, as the pent-up yearnings of her privations had suddenly flowed, unsuppressed, from her heart. "Why do you deny me, the woman you love, the right to be seen at your side, while you parade in public with that - that," Nandi had faltered, her chest heaving, the words bursting forth with an explosion of jealous rage, "silly little bitch you married!"

Senzangakona's disarming peal of laughter had only served to boost Nandi's level of anger and outrage. "I am tired of seeing you in secret!" she had confessed, her voice louder now and strained by her exasperated pleading. "Overrule the Council, overrule your father!" she had exhorted, her tone rising to a fever pitch.

"I told you. The choice of Mkabi was political. I agreed to it. Willingly. It was in the interests of my clan." Senzangakona had answered, concluding: "You wouldn't understand."

"Oh, yes I do." Nandi had pressed him tenaciously. "Perhaps I understand more than you do. - I see how much is at stake."

Senzangakona had run an inspecting glance over Nandi's body, over the shapely hips, the firm breasts, his gaze finally meeting and locking with hers.

"Your sister, Mkabayi!" Nandi had hissed. "She is afraid of me. Afraid of a strong woman at your side. One who loves you and could one day oppose her will."

Somewhat impervious to her words that had now struck senses he believed deadened to their sting, the Zulu had studied the girl through narrowed eyes, searching beneath her beauty - for the first time. No woman, except Mkabayi herself, had ever dared to speak to him in such a manner.

Intent on her own purpose, Nandi had failed to sense his shift in mood. "Your sister needs to have you all for herself," she had gone on, inexorably, "so that, through you, she can sit on the Zulu throne at the death of your father. She needs you to embody her own schemes and ambitions! And she will allow no one to get in the way of these schemes and ambitions. That is why she purposely wanted your Principal Wife to be a docile, insignificant creature. One who is hardly fit to share your body, let alone your mind, your hopes, your dreams..."

As Senzangakona had studied Nandi, he had felt that the blight of futility that so often lies in wait for the heart's pleadings had fallen upon her own appeal and had suddenly made it a thing of empty sounds. His mind had been spinning and all that he had felt was the loneliness he could presage for the future, a future without her; alone with his frustration and...

"...the Queen of Queens." The words reverberated in his mind as his gaze lingered on his wife, Mkabi, unnerved by the accuracy of Nandi's description of her, more convinced than ever that the true Queens of Queens was the woman he had lost in a manner that still roused pain in its recollection.

Wearily, the prince ambled through the gates of esiKlebeni, moving towards the Main Hut casting his wife Mkabi a sidelong glance, his eyes dropping to the bridal apron that covered her belly slightly swollen with child in the first quarter of pregnancy. The Child of the Heir to the House of Zulu.

The Child whose Day of Birth would mark the Birth of the First Born.

CHAPTER V
"JAMA"(THE AUSTERE)

Jama feared the Unknown as all men do, or rather less than most mortals inasmuch as his wisdom had served to alleviate his apprehension with a dose of the gambler's foolhardiness. Yet now his fear grew unabated at the approaching shadow of Death.

He sensed Life was slowly, relentlessly dropping out of his centre of influence, -- life with its colours, its designs, and its meaning, like a picture created by fancy on a canvas of stone, upon which, after long contemplation, the artist turns his back for the last time.

In preparation for the Great Umkosi, the King had donned his ceremonial attire: the skins of baboon, wildcat, and leopard, the tails of moss and lichens which dangled from his once powerful arms and legs now emaciated by age and disease. The royal valet and two sinister witchdoctors (their grisly skeletal shapes hideously clad in hides of crocodile with the blown entrails of bullock tied round their necks and chests and the bladders of birds and wild beasts decking, like fringes, their matted hair and horrid countenances) hovered round the King creaming curious concoctions and potions, vile-smelling roots and herbs, ashes and other grimy emollients onto his skin while Jama's Principal Wife Mtaniya looked on helplessly, her heart reaching out to the man whose life she'd shared for over forty years.

Jama shifted his gaze to Mudli who, upon entering the hut, knelt at the doorway in sign of reverence to his monarch. "It is time, Nkosi," the Elder spoke softly, as Jama motioned to him to come closer.

"I know," the King replied, his voice distant, different.

Hearing that voice, his gaze resting on his sovereign's ailing features, Mudli was gripped by anguish comparable to Mtaniya's. The Elder had served Jama, faithfully, untiringly, unselfishly, for as long as both men could remember, ever since the two, as boyhood friends and comrades, had decided to prepare, together, for the throne - one as King, the other as Councilor. And now, after all those years, like his king, Mudli also wondered what would be the measure of the immortality of 'their' reign and how he, Mudli, could safeguard the throne from the whims of Jama's reluctant heir.

"You are not well, Nkosi," Mudli said with genuine concern. "Should we not defer the celebration?"

"Defer?" Jama mused with a wry smile. There is so much in the life of a king that he would wish to defer but cannot. As he had told his son, a monarch's mind, his heart, and his soul belong to his people and from his people nothing can be withheld because, like children, they require attention at all times. - Especially today. The Umkosi was the official opening of the new season's food consumption with the king's blessing of the crops. Prior to this ceremony, nobody in the clan was permitted to partake even of his own 'first fruits' - on pain of death.

"You know better than that, Elder," Jama murmured to Mudli. "They need my blessing in order to partake of the new crops. If I fail to appear in today's celebration, they will interpret my illness as a curse - one which would reek havoc and starvation." Straightening up, calling upon all his resources of energy, Jama concluded, "Pray the Ancestors give me strength, for I am not only the Zulus' sovereign, but their bond with the Language of the Heavens."

Mtaniya closed her eyes in silent prayer.

The tumult was instantaneous, deafening as Jama appeared at the threshold of the Royal Hut and stood, alone, facing his subjects, some invisible force holding him erect, his expression, both solemn and grave, drawn taut in an effort to conceal a grimace of suffering, his hand clutching the Royal Assegai as if to squeeze from it the supernatural strength of his Ancestors.

As suddenly as the uproar had burst forth, silence descended on the populace. The Zulus then sank to their knees, bowing their heads reverently, as Mudli chanted, announcing his king: "Bayete Nkosi, wena OmNyama! Wena Silo! Wena Ngonyama yeZulu! Bayete! - Hail the King! Thou the Awe-Inspiring! thou the Wild Beast! thou the Lion of the Heavens! Hail!"

"Bayete, Nkosi! Bayete!" came the stentorian echo of the hundreds of Zulus solemnly greeted their king.

Flanked by the two witchdoctors, with a great effort of his superior will, Jama moved with a regal stride towards the cattle-fold where the clan women and children had collected symbolic samples of the first fruits in a small pile awaiting the monarch's benediction.

Mkabayi watched her father advance towards the fold and her breath caught upon noticing that, in the harsh revealing rays of the rising sun, Jama's face seemed a death mask. A sudden wave of unreasoning grief overcame her otherwise level, coldly pragmatic mind, as she was face with this irrefutable evidence of an imminent succession to the Zulu throne. Her gaze scanned the long line of Zulu warriors, grouped according to age, until it reached the imposing figure of her brother, regal and handsome.

Following Igazi's lead, Senzangakona thrust his spear high over his head and fell into the boisterous chorus that echoed throughout Nobamba. "Bayete, Nkosi! Bayete!" the words rang out. "Hail to the King!" As if suddenly disembodied, the spirit momentarily fled from Senzangakona, and hovering overhead, turned to view himself, the future Lord of the Heavens just as a disturbing voice reached out from the Past, - the voice of Nandi.

"Imagine yourself as king," the voice murmured causing the prince to focus once again on his father's gaunt figure as it neared the top of the cattlefold. "That's not something you just step into - like a robe! Being a king is a quality, a condition of excellence that must issue from within your very soul!" Nandi's voice bore her usual persistence.

"Bayete, Nkosi! Bayete!" the prince shouted again, with the others in the corral, trying to dispel the woman's hold on the most remote recesses of his mind.

"You will need someone strong at your side," the voice from the Past suggested, implacably, in an eerie whisper. "Someone strong in your moments of private weakness! One who loves you and with whom you can share your fears. That is why you need me! In my heart you will find the strength to reach for your own greatness and to become the king you were born to be!"

Igazi's prompting nudged Senzangakona out of his daze and back to the Present. Finding that the men had started chanting the iNgoma (the 'Chief's Song'), the Zulu prince fell in with the singing, his own voice instantly absorbed in the harmonious chorus.

Jama had now reached the pile of first fruits and was assisted by the witchdoctors in the smearing a dark, greasy medicinal paste on the tip of the Royal Assegai. Spearing one of the melons, Jama raised it in the air, pointing it at the luminous crimson globe of the rising sun, framing the fruit in the centre of the celestial ball.

"Wo, vuma, Nbaba! Hayi! Zi! Zi!" Jama's voice sang out weakly, in a murmur, hoarse, as if heard from a distance.

"Wo, wuma, Ndaba! Wo, ye, wo, ye! Wayi wuma indaba yemkhomto!" came the responsory chant from the men with a strength that was meant to compensate for the feeble tone of their king.

Jama's outstretched arm started to tremble. Clenching his teeth, feeling his muscles tightening painfully, the old king fought to keep the Royal Assegai raised as he chanted, tremulously: "Wo, vuma, Ndaba...ha-yi, zi--"

The Zulu King then faltered, the words failing on his lips, his proud spirit struggling to sustain the weight of a body that was now looking upon death as a high and rare favour, a supreme grace.

Abruptly, as if his skeleton had turned to straw, Jama slumped to the ground. The two witchdoctors let out a shrill cry, hooting and flailing their arms with a ghoulish display of dread and disconcertion, as the Zulu populace stood spellbound, aghast.

Igazi and Lutuli quickly ran to Jama's side, and lifting the King in their arms, hurriedly spirited him to the privacy of the Royal Hut. As Mudli scurried beside them, his eyes fixed on his sovereign's senseless body, he heard Jama's voice echoing, "...they will interpret my disease as a curse --".

Mudli paused, looking thoughtfully at the panic that had gripped his tribesmen and, setting aside his sorrow for his sovereign and friend, concentrated on the wellbeing of the Zulu kingdom. When Igazi reappeared from within the hut, the Elder clutched him by the arm, the firmness of his grip matching the intensity of resolve that blazed in his eyes. "Go to the head of each homestead, Igazi," Mudli ordered, "and inform him that the ceremony has been consummated as required by ritual. The first fruits are blessed and the clan is free to partake of them."

Igazi nodded. The Elder's words and the ardent manner in which they were conveyed served to dispel any doubt the youth might have had that the situation was grave.

"And, Igazi," Mudli added, the fire kindling in his reddened eyes, his grip on the youth's arm tightening for emphasis. "Tell them their king is merely,-" he hesitated before underlining the word: "...indisposed."

"Yes, Elder."

In the chaos that followed Jama's collapse, the confusion was such that no one took heed of Senzangakona's wife Mkabi as she, too, fell to the ground clutching her swollen belly. No one noticed her grimace of torment, her body writhing convulsively; nor did her painful whimpers reach the ears of her kinsmen as the excruciating pain tore at her womb and the greyish froth flecked with blood rose from her mouth, oozing through her clenched teeth.

In that chaos, Mkabi was alone as she swooned from consciousness, and she alone saw, or thought she saw in the whirling, eddying pool of darkness that swelled round her the vacant pastel-blue eyes of a sangoma named Sitayi and the muffled snarl of a hyena.

CHAPTER VI
"UBUFAZI"(WOMANHOOD)

By nightfall, Jama was delirious.

His body, motionless in the circle of light thrown by the glow of the fire, lay encased in wrappings of cowhide and inhumed in the stinging, acrid odour of the asphyxiating fumes disgorged by the herbs that hissed and crackled over the hearth.

The two witchdoctors were wafted round the King's limp frame like so many vultures, picking at him with their sinewy claws, chanting mysterious, fiendish incantations as they administered foul-smelling potions poured through mud-caked reeds into his nose, ears and mouth rendering the monarch's appearance all the more uncannily frightful.

Kneeling in a corner of the hut, her arms crossed over her breasts, her hands curled round the nape of her neck, Mtaniya rocked back and forth, the tempo of her swaying in cadence with the throbbing pulse-beat of her anguish. Jama had been her companion through every vital instant of her life - from the budding, rose-scented freshness of puberty to the stale, dusty smell of old age.

And now, as her gaze bore the burden of his dying image, she realised that every emotion of the past forty years, every feeling, every hope, every fear, every joy, had been a shared emotion with no life of its own beyond the life of the other. She no longer existed without Jama - his breath filled her lungs.

And, without Jama, she need not exist. That is why there were no tears to moisten her eyes: - though wakeful, she shared her husband's trance. Oblivious to all... Even the presence of her son who sat, silently, unmoving, his expression inscrutable, his eyes riveted on the grisly witchdoctors hovering round the human shell that was his father. Senzangakona's heart, still lodged in the freshness of youth, instinctively fled from that scene of death, which nettled his senses more than the rank fetor of the burning hearth. Yet, fleeing, his mind found itself on the threshold of another loss of life - not through death, but by way of a different departure...

"You are closer to me than you could ever be to your own people," Nandi had confided, her tone soft, her fingers touching the hair of his temple, running in a light caress down his cheek, gently tracing the margin of his strong, incisive jaw line, yet her eyes had been somehow hard, laced with a subtle scheming. "We have made love. Not mated, as you tell me you do with Mkabi!"

Stung by the remark, Senzangakona's eyes had narrowed as he had cast Nandi a deliberate glare, irritated by her habit of storing words uttered in confidence for a later, more spiteful, use.

"We love each other. We share secrets through emotions. And when you are the man I can help you become, I want to be with you, at your side...just the two of us, reflecting each other in love and strength."

Not having liked the idea of her 'helping him become' the man he thought he already was, Senzangakona's had suddenly felt defensive. "You shouldn't use your tongue like a spear. That's not becoming of a woman. Didn't your father, or rather your mother teach you that?"

Nandi's face had ironed out, as she had became conscious of the abrupt hardening in her heart, the deep hurt caused by the mocking bite in the man's tone. Lifting his head from her lap, the man had sat up, a set smile on his features. "Are you trying to turn me against the Council and my family? Is that what you want, my sweet?" he had queried with an eerie cutting edge to his voice. "You cannot, you know. Whatever they may appear to be in your eyes, for me - good or bad - they are still my people." With emphasis, he went on. "I would never go against my people. Not for anyone - and not for you. Remember that. If you really understood me the way you say you do, you would know."

"But,-" Nandi had sighed, trying to regain confidence in her own sentiment. "I love you. You will need my love."

The prince had regarded her with a wide, immense stare that seemed to embrace their entire relationship. "Could it be that what you call love is really a desire, a need to possess?" he had started, remaining calm, composed. "Could it be that you're afraid that if you don't possess me, you'll lose me and what you call your influence over me? You want to trade love for control over my life, Nandi. Well,- that's a trade I'm not prepared to make."

Nandi had been crestfallen. Never before had she experienced emotional pain of such intensity, rending her heart with a tangibly physical distress.

"And as far as my 'moments of private weakness' are concerned,-" the prince had gone on, his strength mounting in light of her uneasiness, his tone becoming all the more derisive as he got to his feet, stretching his body as if to limber the muscles after a long sleep. "Nandi, my beautiful little ambitious Langeni...my only 'private weakness', as you call it, is you. - But you see," he had taunted, lifting his brow jestingly, "I do not really need you. Not in the way you think I do." Pausing for effect, looking down at the beautiful girl at his feet whose sensuousness even now filled him with longing, he had pressed on, "I'm not going to marry you."

Nandi had faltered, the gleam of infinite bitterness surfacing in her eyes.

"I already have a queen, and she knows how to behave like one. The sangomas tell me she will soon bear me a son. So she is serving her purpose as a woman quite well."

Senzangakona had watched Nandi's eyes turn to ice, stung in her pride by Mkabi's pregnancy and by the crude implication of the 'purpose of the woman' thus defined. The realisation had struck her that Senzangakona was in truth like all the other chauvinistic men of her culture - and, in that moment, even worse.

He had felt her rage welling as she had risen, and looking at her steely expression; he had been surprised to feel a odd sense of pleasure, of satisfaction.

"Prince Senzangakona," she had said, ominously, finally finding the voice to react. "In the name of our Ancestors you will be punished for the way you used me. The day will come when you will beg me to come back to you, when you will want me...my way! I promise you that!"

Senzangakona could not help but laugh at so much arrogance, yet he had yearned to strike her down for what she had just said, all the more so as he had felt her words might probably reflect the truth.

Having felt the threat of violence in him, Nandi had recoiled from the prince shouting, "Get away from me!---"

"--get away from me!" her voice resounded in his mind, tingling with passionate anger, as his eyes remained trained on his father's suffered frame. Senzangakona suddenly felt a disquieting commiseration for Nandi, his father, himself, everybody he had ever known, and the earth, the sky, the very air he drew into his anguished chest; loathing that air because it made him live, loathing Nandi because she had made them both suffer.

As the feeling grew more unbearable, the prince had the chilling sensation that he was being watched by a wild predator and found that his gaze gravitated to one of the witchdoctors. A burst of clear flame suddenly lit up the man's broad, dark, pock-marked face - where the thin lips, stained a deep red and looking like the bleeding gash of a fresh wound, were drawn back in a spectral smile; where the firelight gleamed on a solitary eye lending it a fierce animation as it remained fixed on Senzangakona with a sinister look of contempt.

* * *

    The darkness of night had entered Nandi's heart, bringing with it the sense of immense sadness that comes with irreparable loss. Far from being Life's protagonist, a position she had always fought to retain, Nandi now assumed the more passive role of allowing her profound unhappiness to lead her through existence with a self-imposed indifference to all that had once filled her with hope, desire, joy. Even the defiance was gone, and with it, her reason for caring.

    She spoke little and confided in no one, not even in her father. And those who loved her, Bhebhe, Mfunda, Gendeyana - not knowing, with any certainty, the cause of her deep sadness - felt helpless and waited, with a patience born of respect, for the day when her silent suffering would reach out for solace and the need to be shared.

    That day came sooner than expected and in a manner no one as anticipated - especially Nandi.

    The woman was working in her father's garden, mechanically attending to her chores with a toil void of purpose, as had become her habit, when she suddenly felt a dizziness sweep over her. Struggling to regain her balance, Nandi rested her hand on a tree, fighting back a wave of nausea, breathing deeply to quell the convulsions in her stomach. The basket she was carrying slipped out of her grasp, its contents spilling, as a spasm of acute pain swept through her body. Again she was swept by vertigo and she gritted her teeth, her stubbornness resisting her malady.

    Then, with a gasping cry of pain that alarmed those nearby, she crumbled to the ground. In an instant, Gendeyana was at Nandi's side. Lifting her in his arms, under the distressed and solicitous eyes of Bhebhe and Mfunda, and the inquisitive frowns of some of her clansmen, the man carried her to the main hut.

* * *

As the sun had set that night on Senzangakona's esiKlebeni homestead, the prince had been annoyed by the disturbance of the handmaiden Noliwa who had urged him to hurry to his woman's side. "If she's ill, its a matter for the sangoma not me!" he had grunted, caring little for the empty formalities of observance that accompany the maladies of others.

    "The sangoma is already at her side, Ndabezitha," Noliwa had answered, her tone betraying her anxiety. "It is she who urges the prince to hurry."

Mkabi lay in her hut, her gaunt, wasted features glistening with perspiration in the reflected light of the dancing flames. When Senzangakona entered the abode, her pale, chapped lips parted in an enfeebled smile that caused a glint of relief to rise to her eyes. "He has come," she told herself. "That means he cares after all." Her heart leapt at the thought that under his brusque frigidness there could be even the remote semblance of affection; that the child she carried in her womb could find a place in its father's heart.

As the Zulu prince's gaze brushed over his wife's wasted countenance set in a smile of genuine love, a feeling akin to revulsion embittered his mouth screwing his features into a scowl. The man's attention shifted to the ghastly old woman squatting by the fire: the sangoma Majola - a wretched creature of undefinable years and distasteful appearance; her head partly shaven, with the remaining hair smeared with fat and charcoal; one eyelid painted black, the other red; her clothing hideous with its skins of warthog and vulture feathers swaying over dangling skulls of baboon and rat.

Without looking up, sensing the prince's searching gaze on her, as if reading his mind, she answered his unspoken inquisitive. "Your woman, Baba," Majola's screechy voice grated through the moldy dankness of the hut. ""The child is opposing its mother's fluids."

"Then do something!" Senzangakona said with annoyance. "That's why you're here, I presume!"

Casting an accusing eye at Mkabi, Majola's abrasive tone imputed: "She refuses to take the potions. You must speak to her, Ndabezitha. You are her master."

Angrily, Senzangakona scooped up the wooden bowl containing the revolting potion and pressed it to Mkabi's lips. "Drink!" he commanded.

"No! Please! I cannot!" she pleaded in terror.

"Drink!" repeatedly the prince. "It will do you good.

With trusting eyes riveted on her husband, Mkabi forced herself to take a couple of swallows of the murky liquid. Then, turning on her side, she retched convulsively, vomiting the potion onto the sweat-drenched straw of her mat.

Sickened by his wife, the man turned to the sangoma. "Have you worked the spell?" he asked, his whisper laced with insistence.

In the light of the crackling fire, the old woman looked all the more terrifying, as the shadows played over her wrinkled features. With a touch of evil conspiracy, she croaked in a hush: "Yes, Baba. I have. It will be a boy -- if it lives."

"He must live! You make sure he does, you old wench - or you'll regret it!"

Majola seemed amused by the Zulu's menacing reply. "It is difficult, difficult," she sibilated, her voice like a soft wind rustling through thorny branches. "The Life Force is too weak for both to survive." She started to rock on her haunches, from side to side, like the metronome on the Hour-Glass of Death. "When the time comes, Baba, we may have to choose."

Like a vile odour, these words rode a breath of air, as Senzangakona cast his wife a guarded sidelong glance. Glimpsing the foreboding purpose of that gaze, Mkabi protectively cupped her hands over her swollen belly.

He had departed shortly before dawn. The midday sun had found him racing across the vast plateaus near the Mpungose. By afternoon his cadenced footfalls had reached the waters of the umHlatuze.

And, by sunset, the Langeni messenger boy, a child of ten with the spirit of a fullgrown man, came racing down the slopes that shouldered the Zulu Village heading for Nobamba.

Igazi greeted him and watched, with a diverted grin, as the boy stood drinking his fill of water with a thirst that seemed unquenchable. When the child looked up from the bowl and noticed Mudli, he sank to his knees before the Zulu Elder.

"Sakubona, little one," Mudli greeted him with a gentle smile.

"Ngi-Bona wena, Baba, - And I see thee, my father," responded the child.

"What brings you to Nobamba," Mudli asked. "And in such a hurry," he added, noticing the boy's lanky body glowing with perspiration, his face flushed with the day's exertion.

"An urgent message, Baba. From Mbenghi, King of the Langeni."

"In what regard?" the Elder inquired, his brow knitting with interest.

The boy paused before answering and gulped a swallow of air as if to catch his breath or, better, as if to brace himself for the portentous news of which he was the humble carrier. "Nandi daughter of Bhebhe...is with child."

Igazi found Mudli's eyes, as an icy finger touched both their hearts - chilling them.

CHAPTER VII
"SANGOMA"(DIVINER)

He loved it all: the landscape of brown golds and brilliant emeralds under the dome of hot sapphire; the towering sugar cane whispering in the flaw with its plume-like tassels spilling their seeds onto the greedy red earth; the loquacious banana palms that rattled their leaves volubly in the salty night breeze. He loved the heavy, honeyed scents of the wattle blossoms and the euphorbia and the dank, tarty smell of the hippo and the nyala deer; the narrow and sombre creeks of the Hluhluwe, black, tortuous, smooth, that ran like byways of mystery through lands in which Man was a stranger. He loved the sorrow-faced baboons that profaned quiet waterways with their capricious capers and insane gestures of clownish madness.

He loved the land, and the immensity of it was the source of his pride.

He loved everything that was his home, inanimate and animate, and its immutable, eternal cycle of Genesis and Decay was, for him, a source of consolation.

But, above all, Jama loved his people and his family, and their wellbeing was, for him, a source of constant concern. Especially his son who would fuse his people with his family when he succeeded him as King of the Zulus, Lord and Champion of the Heavens.

As Jama lay reclined on his mat, his exhausted eyes searching the fire, he decided that if he was still alive it was only because the Ancestors had blessed him with an extra heartbeat or two in with which to put his house in order.

If what the Langeni messenger had announced was true - and Jama had no reason to doubt it - the situation was indeed grave and begged for all of the king's wisdom. He knew that, according to custom, an unmarried girl that was foolish or foolhardy enough to get herself pregnant was said to have received from her lover an 'umLanjwana'. The word, while implying the unlawful pregnancy, was used to signify the consequent feud or mutual enmity that was sure to arise between the two clans concerned. Such an occurrence (always considered the fault of the man) was regarded by the girl's people almost as seriously as the murder of one of their men, inasmuch as the girl would now have her prospects ruined for life, having become mere soiled or secondhand goods. As a rule, Jama knew, the man would be forced to marry her or his clan would risk the wrath of the other.

The decision was clearly put before him: either a feud with the Langeni, a neighboring tribe of which the Zulus had always been fond, or a forced union between his son and the dangerous shrew upon whom

Senzangakona had haplessly rested his lustful eye. Both prospects left Jama disconcerted; -- would he leave his clan with an intertribal feud or a domestic tragedy?

Neither!, he determined and resolved to discover the truth and then to seal it in the secrecy of denial and death. Extreme remedies to suit the exceptional purposes of a man whose soul was poised to take flight from the body. *

Resurfacing from his momentary abstraction, Jama rolled his head to meet Mudli's gaze through the lapping flames.

"Yes, you are right, Mudli, the plan is valid. And necessary," he breathed, weakly. "Though it grieves my heart to go to the Earth with the taint of murder."

"Then let the burden rest on my soul, Nkosi."

"My faithful friend," Jama smiled as a gleam of amusement blessed his gaunt features. "I wish I could. But that decision is neither yours nor mine. - Rather, the question is: will she go? Don't forget her pride, Mudli. It is one I have rarely encountered in any woman, especially in one so young."

"She will go, Baba," Mudli smiled, reassuringly. "She will want to know what your son has to say to her that is so secret and...urgent. Hope will make her go, my sovereign. The hope that he will once again disobey his father's word."

The king was silent, musing. Mudli sat unmoving, his eyes on his monarch and friend, respectfully waiting for the dying man to break the muted stillness that seemed to belong to him.

"Mudli," he finally uttered after a long pause.

"Yes, Nkosi."

"Watch over him." Mudli knew he was referring to Senzangakona, and he drew closer to listen. "Protect him," the king went on. "From those around him. Protect him from himself. He will need you." Jama's fleshless, cadaverous hand snaked out from under the cowhide blanket, sought the Elder's touch, closing round Mudli's arm with a grip that betrayed the urgency of imminent departure. "Just as I have needed you."

Mudli placed his own hand over his sovereign's, stroking it with a gesture akin to a caress, his eyes trained on Jama's spindly features with a glint that evinced more than affection,- love.

"I shall, Jama kaNdaba Zulu. I swear I shall."

"Then have my son come to me now. I am ready."

Senzangakona neared his father and knelt beside him. Jama's gaze penetrated the prince's soul, flooding it, leaving no room for fear or bitterness in that brimming sea of love.

"So you have disobeyed my orders?" came the remark together with a gaze that was at once judging and merciful.

"No, father. I have not."

"My son, you send me to our Ancestors with a lie?"

The prince sensed that Jama's words were more of a statement than a query. He felt his father's searching gaze and dropped his eyes, answering, "You told me to forget that woman, father - to erase her from my mind. I have...now." With melancholy, Senzangakona pronounced the verdict that he, himself, had reached in his passionate relationship: "The Son of Jama truly remembers no one by the name of Nandi, daughter of Bhebhe."

Jama was somehow appeased by the reply, though he knew it was partially founded on a lie. Solemnly, his eyes riveted on his son, the king addressed his Elder. "Mudli, see that the messenger has food and send him back. He shall announce to his king that the Son of Jama remembers no one by the name of Nandi, daughter of Bhebhe. If the woman says she is pregnant, it is either the work of another man or the 'I-Shaka', the disease of the beetle."

Mudli knew Jama meant the disease also referred to as the 'iKambi' - an intestinal germ ('beetle') often held responsible for the suppression of menstruation.

"He shall also tell Mbenghi of the Langeni," Jama went on, his features hardening, his voice raised in indignation, "to spare the Royal House of Zulu any other such defamation...or it will mean war!"

As Mudli bowed and left the hut to carry out the command (which he feared would be his king's last official directive), Jama reached out and took his son's hand in his own. "There was so much left unfinished," the old man told himself. "So much yet to be said."

*

The night was very dark and the Nkandla Forest crouched unseen by the stars under a veil of motionless clouds that, driven before the salty breath of the sea, had drifted slowly inland from the eastward.

In the darkness of that night, as the clouds hung overhead, silent, menacing over the tree-tops, withholding their blessing of rain, nursing the wrath of their thunder, Nandi made her way through the heart of the tenebrous forest. Senzangakona had sent word that he wished to meet with her, and as Nandi ventured to the site of their rendezvous, her satisfaction had the taste of triumph: if Senzangakona still wanted her, he would have to accept her conditions this time.

Suddenly a rustling reached her ear. She froze, her hands instinctively clasping her belly. Widening her feline eyes, she scanned the shadows round her, probing the darkness for the cause of the sound. When silence fell upon her scrutiny, Nandi reassured herself that the sound could have been the fruit of imagination and tried to shrug off her fear. Yet, after a moment, the rustling returned. Closer this time. Nandi stopped again, listening, her veins charged with adrenalin. Unmoving, becoming one with the forest, she peered up at the shadows and sinister branches that hovered over head, as her mind raced to appease itself with a logical explanation for the stirring that had frightened her. Breathing deeply, Nandi was on the verge of resuming her trek, when - in a terrifying instant - a shadow sprang from the tenebrous void, imprisoning her in a vice-like grasp. The terror-stricken woman opened her mouth to scream, but before her cry could take shape, a hand closed forcibly over her lips, silencing them as she felt the cold blade of an assegai press against her throat.

Nandi thrashed in that grip, her legs kicking ferociously, her arms wildly pummeling the air, her teeth finding the softness of flesh, biting into it, drawing blood. With a strength born of desperation, she succeeded in tearing herself loose from that clutch and, breaking away, running from her mysterious assailant. But the shadow was on her again, with a suffocating, grappling hold. Nandi sank her nails into the shadow's hand, plying back the parched, leathery fingers that clutched the spear. Yet her attacker's strength prevailed and, tightening its hold on the assegai, the shadow raised the weapon, wrenching the blade so that its razor-sharp point was trained on Nandi's jugular. As the blade drew nearer, ready to strike,- a bloodcurdling peal of laughter pierced the darkness, reverberating round them. The hand froze in mid-air and the shadow, startled by the laughter, involuntarily loosened its hold on Nandi.

Snatching at the advantage, the woman darted away, seeking the cover of thick vegetation, only to find herself faced with the chilling sight of terrifying luminous eyes that peered at her out of the darkness. Another evil laugh shook the night, joined by an eerie chorus of devilish cackling.

A hyena loped into view; one of a pack. Her courage the fruit of despair, Nandi picked up a branch and prepared to defend her own life and that of the child she was carrying. Yet the pack of hideous beasts moved silently past the woman, and, as Nandi watched them wide-eyed and appalled, she had the bewitching impression that one of the hyenas regarded her with a gaze laced with a mesmerising glint that was almost human.

Before her soul could react to the full portent of that look, the pack had reached the shadow of her assailer and were suddenly upon it - with bared, gleaming fangs tearing into pulpy flesh, with muffled screams laced with the dread of death and mingled with the greedy snarling sounds of the butchery.

Then all was silence; - all save for the shrill laughter of the hyenas as they formed a semicircle round Nandi, the beasts' eyes on her, luring her into a dimension that transcended the natural into a level of spectral terror. Nandi gaped at the animals in horror, spellbound, waiting to die. But the hyenas did not move from their circular formation, remaining straight, motionless, like the soldiers of some ghastly regiment sent to protect her and the child yet to be born.

Instinctively Nandi dropped her gaze to the blood-stained shadow that had been her attacker. The man looked at her. Almost imperceptibly at first, his lips started to move. Intrigued, momentarily ignoring the pack, Nandi inched closer to his mangled frame and, as his features became discernible in the night, realisation struck her with the force of a mighty blow, fraying her nerves beyond endurance. "Ghubela!"

Her scream resounded in the darkness, as she recognised in that blood-caked face the semblance of Senzangakona's valet. As her tearful eyes remained on the Zulu, Ghubela's lips pulled back and a homicidal and loathsome smile bared his yellowed teeth, forming two deep folds down his shallow, calloused cheeks. And as the smile was born, so was it imprisoned in death.

Nandi sank to the ground, weeping hysterically, the sobs coming in uncontrollable spasms. When suddenly the forest was illuminated by a magical, enchanting light, which wiped away all memory of the horror and despair that had gripped her.

Like a whisper on the lips of Timelessness, softly, urgently, a bewitching voice called out to her: "Nandi, daughter of Bhebhe."

An old woman moved out of the darkness, into the throbbing glow of the entrancing light, through the statuesque, immovable ranks of the beastly regiment, her blind, vacant pastel-blue orbs fixed on the young woman as she neared her, floating more than walking on the illuminated shaft that clung to the moist earth.

Nandi caught her breath at the vision of the sangoma, Sitayi, as the old woman's whisper beckoned to her from a dimension beyond the Now and

Here. "Come, Nandi. It is time for you and the son you shall bear to learn of your destiny."

Sitayi turned and, leading the way, moved back into the darkness; the hyenas filed silently after her like faithful, guarding angels of the Unknown.

In a trance, Nandi found herself following.

The sun, whose concentrated glare dwarfs the earth into a restless mote of dust, had risen behind the vault of the horizon, and the diffused light from an opal sky seemed to cast upon the world the shadows and the brilliance that gave the illusion of a calm and pensive greatness.

In the footsteps of her inscrutable guide Sitayi, Nandi had ventured through the blackness of night, down paths and byways arcane and unfathomable by mere mortals, skirting streams and currents that rushed unseen in the tenebrous mists;- then, rising, ascending, higher and higher it seemed, as Sitayi's shadowy figure untiringly lead the way over arching ramps of stone and sloping paths of granite, higher and higher, up courses of gravelly sand and along passages of ice - till it had seemed to Nandi that she and her exceptional escort had reached the roof of the world.

When the darkness gradually ebbed before the advancing paleness of day, Nandi had found herself near the summit of a tall mountain, indeed the roof of the world, its tundral landscape barren save for a tattered lean-to propped against a jagged boulder, its calfhide walls flapping in the wind that howled and whistled through rocky crevasses and glacial chasms.

And now, as the sun shone forth dwarfing the earth, Nandi followed Sitayi to the foot of a towering spiral of ice that rose straight up from the summit of the mountain like a finger pointed at the sky, its tip vanishing in the dizzying heights. Steps, steep and perfectly levigated, were cut into the natural curve of the spiral forming a staircase that wound upwards like the cochleariform swirl of an immense crystal shell.

As if responding to an unspoken command, the regiment of hyenas, which had flanked them on their trek, froze in place at the foot of the seemingly endless stairway, standing like statues at the threshold of some pagan temple.

Sitayi raised a sinewy finger and, her sightless eyes gleaming with an bewitching sparkle, motioned Nandi to follow. The two women started up the glimmering steps, towards the top of the stairway and the 'Isiqongo kwaNkosi', the Pinnacle of Kings'.

Hours later, when the sun was already weary from its long journey across the sky and was yearning for the bed of Dusk, Sitayi reached the

Platform of the Pinnacle and padded out to a polished railing of ice that circumvented its margins. Nandi followed and, resting a hand on the railing, allowed her gaze to drift out.

She gasped, catching her breath, as an immense panorama sprang into view, clutching her heart in a vice of ecstasy and consternation. At her feet, over five thousand meters below, stretched a landscape so immeasurably vast that her eyes ached in the attempt to encompass it; a great expanse of woodlands, somber and green, undulating as far as the violet and purple range of mountains, and the canvas of the veld, saffron and amber, rolling like a sea, with glints of winding rivers that flowed into the opaque blueness of the Indian Ocean.

Raising a gracile arm, Sitayi made a sweeping gesture over the landscape, her vacant orbs reflecting its immensity as her voice rose to meet the sibilating wind that seemed to diffuse her words throughout creation.

Nandi stood transfixed as Sitayi announced to her the secrets of the Prophecy of the Child---

"From your womb shall come the Language of the Heavens emblazed in the heart of him who shall be great. His Condition shall be that of the First Born - the Child of the Prophecy, Nkosi yama Kosi...the King of Kings. His fame and that of his House shall radiate into the sun, giving birth to a mighty nation of red spears and thundering shields of light. His shadow and the Glory of the amaZulu shall spread throughout this earth, ruling over Nations and their Kings as far as the eye can see."

Sitayi punctuated the words with a mysterious authority that seemed derived from the Heavens themselves---

"All things shall obey him. All shall kneel at his feet. For he shall be their only King: - the Sacred Sovereign of whom the Ancestors spoke when they sang to the Wind."

When the sangoma finished, and her voice faded into the wind, Nandi's eyes met the sun as it quit the earth, leaving the long shadows of night.

CHAPTER VIII
"UKUSHONA"(DEATH)

The reflection of death was in the Zulus who regarded their monarch's body as if it were the shadow of infinite wisdom buried in a distant grave to which they no longer had access.

With a vague, barely discernible shudder, Senzangakona felt a great emptiness enter his heart. It seemed to him that there was within his chest a great space without any definite borders where his thoughts wandered forlornly, unable to escape, unable to rest, unable to relieve him from the fearful oppression of their existence. And of these thoughts, the most oppressing was the conviction that a period of his life was irreversibly undone and that the Past was beyond recall. As he gaped at that mummy with a stare that seemed to probe the heart of some awful vision, he induced himself to remember that Life remained, that even though his father was dead, gone, forever perhaps, he, Senzangakona, was still young, alive, and that he and all that lived would survive this day of death!

The prince had a sudden, urgent craving for sensations; for touching, feeling, seeing, hearing, caressing - for the fresh, the green, the budding. In the background of his senses, he heard that the wailing had stopped giving way to the chanting of the Zulu men, a melodious dirge that was reminiscent of a lullaby. Looking up, his eyes caught his sister's, and Mkabayi nodded to him, deliberately, bestowing upon him her first silent directive to his own upcoming reign.

Senzangakona found himself smiling, as he complied with her muted prompting and resumed his officiating of the royal funeral. Accompanied by Igazi and Lutuli, Senzangakona neared his father's body, raised a flap of black hide and secured it over Jama's face making the Darkness complete. The three men then gently lifted the corpse in its sitting position and carried it, ceremoniously, towards the gaping burial site.

As the dirge rose in volume and reverence, Jama's royal valet was led into the grave, up to the polished niche of smooth stone upon which the king's body would be seated. The countenance of the faithful valet was devoid of expression save for a flittering glint of anxiety that danced across his wide, unblinking eyes as he knelt between two Zulu men, bowing his head. After a moment of silent meditation, perhaps prayer, the valet looked up at them, a fresh dose of courage on the placid smile he now wore, the sign that he was ready. Before that smile could distort to terror, in an instant, the two men had twisted the valet's head, snapping the spine, inducing a relatively painless, quick death. His lifeless frame was then toted across the grave and propped up on the niche where it would serve as the king's 'cushion' if his 'brooding' should turn to 'slumber'.

After Senzangakona, Igazi, and Lutuli had placed the remains of Jama kaNdaba on the site that was his final throne, the prince was left in solitary contemplation of the corpse, feeling the breath of his father's spirit still hovering round it, delaying final departure, like the intangible form of a wistful breeze. Standing in the pit he now shared with the kneeling figure bound in black hide, Senzangakona realised, with an odd sensation, that this was the first time he could remember when he'd been alone with his father. The life of a king has no private moments, Jama had told him. Well, Senzangakona would soon know how true that was.

Impervious now to the others who were present at the funeral, Senzangakona started to enjoy this somewhat odd private moment with his father. He did not want it to end, yet, after a while, a great while, he told himself it must end - forever.

'Tucking him in the niche', as was the custom, he placed a stone on his father's knees and one under each foot. Then, scooping up a handful of dirt, he sprinkled it over the protrusion that was Jama's head, uttering, "Bayete, Nkosi," and adding, with a warm familiarity that had always been lacking in their conversations when his father had been alive, "Hamba kahle, Baba - Go well, my father. I loved you more than you knew. More than I was ever allowed to tell you. Thank you for giving me life. Thank you for now showing me that it is short, so terribly short. - Help me." As Nandi's words came oppressively to mind, the prince's voice faltered, quivering slightly with the plea: "Help me to be the king I was born to be."

Then the wistful breeze that was the breath of Jama's spirit finally departed, leaving his son with a sensation of peace.

In Death.

"Umkonto wenKosi o-y-isiMakade," Mudli chanted, the Royal Assegai raised in his closed fist, its polished blade reflecting the sunlight and the spellbound faces of the entire Zulu population which was spread out in the valley surrounding esiKlebeni; men, women, and children on their knees, bowing to their new king.

"Nantso-ke inKosi yeNu, Bakiti, namhla-nje! – Behold him, ye of our clan who is your king this day!" the Elder concluded, the timber of his voice reaching the hieratic as he turned to face Senzangakona who was seated on the inKata, the Royal Throne of pressed grass, wearing the fastuous clothes of a Zulu king at Coronation - the resplendence of leopard skins and glistening ivory trinkets dangling from neck, arms and ankles.

Senzangakona turned to the Elder and received from him the spear that was the symbol of his hereditary reign and power. "It seems heavier, today," he mused with a thin smile, clutching the assegai in his strong hand, thrusting it over his head as he shifted his gaze to meet those of his people.

"Bayete, Nkosi!" The valley was alive with the cry. "Bayete, Nkosi!" the mountains echoed, awaking the silent streams and the distant woodlands with the sonorous greeting of the Heaven's new Lord.

Mkabayi watched her brother, critically, as a glow akin to triumph graced her eyes. She, too, smiled, sharing in his praise, her ambition tingling from head to foot. In the somber resolve of her expression, that smile was like the first ray of light on a stormy day- break, darting evanescent and pale through gloomy clouds; the ray that is the forerunner of sunrise and of thunder.

Seven weeks later, on the seventh day of the seventh month of the Eve of Untulikasi, in the Year 1787, a crescent dart of fire shot through the night, tearing in two the distant, barely discernible contours of the horizon, lighting up the gloom of the earth with a dazzling and ghastly flame which was followed, at a heartbeat, by a clap of thunder that resounded from the depths of the Heavens, reverberating throughout the earth with a rushing noise, like the frightened gasp of a startled Creation. Then the heavy air that welled over the soil of Africa was pierced by a sharp gust of wind, bringing with it the chill of falling rain; and all the innumerable tree-tops of the Kingdom of the Heavens swayed down under the forceful squall, springing back again in a tumultuous convulsion of shuddering branches and clashing leaves which seemed to whip across the face of the storm, heightening its fury, causing wildlife to flee in the wake of its mindless force.

In that tempest, impenetrable, cool, flooded with darkness, the night,- the blind night that saw nothing, heard a scream, unexpected, piercing - a scream beginning at once in the highest pitch of a woman's voice and then cut short, so short that it suggested the swift work of death. But, an instant later, the woman's voice returned in a painful whimper followed, almost immediately, by the cry of a newborn babe.

Then the woman, Nandi, laughed. Her laughter – which was heard over the cries of the child and the rumbling of the skies - had the bizarre, indefinable stigma of a burst of deliverance, which, like the child, seemed to have been torn from her against her will, brought violently to the surface from under her bitterness, from the secreted recesses of a Love that was aborted before the full gestation of Emotion.

Before her lips shed the tingle of her laughter, Nandi, daughter of Bhebhe gave the child, a boy, the name I-Shaka kaSenzangakona Zulu.

<blockquote>
Shaka Zulu.
The First Born of his House.
The Child that was the Language.
Nkosi yama Kosi - the King of Kings...
</blockquote>

...and from her Pulpit high atop of the Pinnacle of Kings, Sitayi read the night, and her heart conceived that all was good and well, and wielding the Force of the Heavens to Hone the Child, the sangoma swept up the Wind bringing Darkness to the Birth of the Heir Apparent...

The tempest raged unabated over esiKlebeni. Senzangakona struggled against the howling wind and the slashing rain as he made his way through the unrelenting shadows of night punctuated by blinding bolts of incandescent light.

Noliwa had brought him the message. Just a few moments before. A child had been born, she had told the king. A boy! Thrilled by the news, Senzangakona had swept excitedly past the maiden, out of his hut and into the darkness. His delight had driven him away before Noliwa could tell him more. Before she could tell him...

Upon reaching the hazy, darkened outline of the hut he knew to be Mkabi's, Senzangakona was startled by a violent flash that lanced the sky bathing the grisly figure of the sangoma Majola in a ghoulish wash of phosphorescence. In that instant of light, the king saw that the old woman stood facing him, her hunched frame holding a tiny object cradled in her fleshless arms. He guessed almost immediately that the miniature bundle in her grasp must be his son, and his face took on the fierceness of the storm as he strode towards the woman, ready to lash out at her for exposing the gracile creature to the violence of the elements. Yet when he neared the sangoma, he saw that her face was twisted round so that her keen eyes were trained on him with a look that abruptly dashed his soul into a maelstrom of anguish, rendering him momentarily speechless. In that void in which Time and Space ceased to exist, her croaking voice reached him like a knife slicing through the tumult of the tortured skies. "The Life Force was too weak for both to survive, Baba," Majola's words cudgelled his spirit. "It chose in favour of the woman."

On the Pinnacle of Kings, Sitayi raised her vacant pastel-blue orbs and felt the soothing caress of Timelessness and stretching out her hand, with a sweeping gesture, she caused the rains to cease, the clouds to roll back, and the stars to twinkle on the mauve vault of The Heavens.

CHAPTER IX
"I-SHAKA"(THE BEETLE)
MONTH OF UNCWABA (AUGUST, 1787)

"They have tried to kill you once, Nandi. They may try again."

Two weeks had passed, and Nandi now found herself in the Royal Homestead of the Langeni Village, under the shady cupola of a spreading euphorbia tree, in the presence of her King Mbenghi and his esteemed councillor, the Elder Gama.

"Are you sure you wish to return to the Zulu Kingdom?" Mbenghi continued, his inquiring glance, grave and severe, bent on the kneeling figure of Nandi. "Do you feel it is safe for you, and for the child."

Her face set with resolve, Nandi nodded, pressing to her breast Shaka's fragile body swaddled in soft hides. "Nkosi," she remarked, her voice charged with a determination that rode the wave of pleading, "He must claim his rightful place at his father's side."

"And does your family agree with this decision?"

Thinking of her loving father Bhebhe and her mother Mfunda, Nandi's face was hardened by the conviction that her family had truly been wronged and that the justice she sought was more than warranted. "Yes, Baba. They share in my pain and indignation."

"Very well," said Mbenghi with a deep sigh, raising his brow as if to underline his reluctance to acquiesce. "If that is your decision. But remember, Nandi - the pain and indignation are also our own. If you feel you have made a mistake, do not hesitate to return. We are your people and the well-being of you and your family is most important to us all."

Nandi was moved by Mbenghi's words, sensing his devotion and respect for her family, feeling how he and the Langeni villagers held her father in the highest regard.

"You will accompany them, Gama," Mbenghi ordered, turning to his Elder. "With a party of armed men."

"And if they should decline to acknowledge the mother and child?" Gama considered out loud.

"It would mean war," the Langeni king answered, flatly.

Senzangakona furiously paced the polished black floor of his large Royal Hut as Mkabayi silently looked on, taking pleasure in her brother's uneasiness.

"They will be here tomorrow, Nkosi," Mudli told the son of Jama, his departed friend, striving to conduct himself with the same respect and dignity of bearing that had characterised the Elder's manner during the previous reign. "The messengers tell me it is an important party. King Mbenghi's senior advisor is accompanying them." Lowering his voice to a timber of severity, he punctuated, "Much will be at stake when they arrive. Important decisions will need to be reached."

"And what do you advise, Elder?" the king queried, running a nervous hand over his dry lips.

"When the infant is laid before us," said Mudli, simply, "we should assume our due responsibility. You must accept the child as your own, Nkosi."

"So we are to be dictated to by this unpredictable girl and her clan?" Senzangakona cried out, in frustration. "We are to endure this humiliation?"

"'Unpredictable'?" Mudli considered, his voice laced with a touch of reprimand. "Need I remind you, Nkosi, that you were once warned of such a possibility. – In your father's wisdom and that of the Council, this woman and the threat she represented were most predictable from the very start."

Mkabayi was clearly enjoying the situation. The set smile she had been sporting throughout the latter part of the exchange suddenly broadened, causing her brother to inquire, stiffly, "Does my sister wish to address the king, or is she here merely to punctuate his misgivings?"

"The way I see it, my brother, the king's hands are tied," she started, instantly making him wish he hadn't prompted her response. "He has but two alternatives: accept the child and face a little ridicule, but no actual conflict, or...reject it and face outright war with the Langeni." Then, her manner presenting a curious combination of feigned reticence and audacity, the woman proffered, "I suggest you choose the path Mudli advised. I feel it is the best for your people and...your image. Jama's reign was one of peace. What would be said of his successor if he were to usher a period of war before the earth grew cold on our father's grave?"

Senzangakona's and Mkabayi's gazes remained locked in a brief battle of wills, the king's own sullen glare inflamed by his reluctance to be told what to do so soon in a reign that already presages an unrelenting frustration of purpose. Finally, tearing his eyes away from his sister, fashioning for himself an air of regal ascendancy, the king turned his back on the two and uttered a curt and somewhat flowery, "In the name of my beloved father, Jama kaNdaba, I shall do what I can to preserve and cherish the peace he maintained in this land."

Casting Mkabayi a deliberate sidelong glance, Mudli nodded with a smile, "A wise decision, Nkosi. I see you share in your father's clarity of purpose."

Senzangakona's eyes darted to the Elder in search of a trace of sarcasm. There was none.

The new Royal Homestead at esiKlebeni was vaster than Nobamba, but even so it could hardly contain the numerous Zulu villagers who had flocked to witness the second meeting between Senzangakona and Nandi. If it was to be anything like the first memorable encounter at the wedding celebration, they knew it would definitely be an event they would not want to miss.

From the top of the homestead's sloping palisades, Mudli witnessed the arrival of the Langeni party that included Nandi and baby Shaka, Bhebhe, Mfunda, Gama and a detachment of Langeni warriors.

"Inform the king that they have arrived," the Elder instructed.

Igazi struck off towards Senzangakona's hut as Mudli's gaze settled on Mkabi who, with the help of Noliwa, was shuffling on unsteady legs toward the homestead's gates to greet her paternal aunt, Nandi's mother Mfunda. As his eyes lingered on the Queen of Queens, her usual cheerless manner made all the more doleful by the recent trauma of her child, born dead, the Elder felt a pang of compassion.

"Greetings, Aunt Mfunda," Mkabi addressed the woman. "And, Nandi," she said, smiling at her timidly. "Welcome."

At first Nandi stiffly accepted the embrace of the woman for whom she had felt so much hatred, but upon noticing Mkabi's haggard, drawn features, Nandi's anger subsided before a feeling of pity and she found herself somehow warming to the woman.

"You don't look well," Mfunda remarked.

Mkabi dropped her gaze, sheepishly avoiding Mfunda's questioning look, somewhat absorbed, as though she was watching at the bottom of a gloomy abyss the mournful procession of her thoughts. "My child. It was stillborn." Her eyes flickered to Nandi as she added, almost inaudibly: "It was a little boy."

A chill ran down Nandi's spine. The pieces of Sitayi's revelation were starting to fall into place, Nandi reflected with mounting fascination for the role she and her child were playing in the inscrutable design of the Prophecy. The Magical had seen to it that her child was not only the first born, but, indeed, the only living Son of Zulu. Stirring from her musing, she now saw the Zulu king standing before her, his imposing frame looming over the group.

Nandi held Senzangakona's gaze steadily with her own as the two assessed each other, unflinchingly, like opponents before a mortal struggle. "They tell me there is a child," the Zulu king broke the silence. "I wish to see it."

Extending her arms, Nandi proffered the child, not as a gift, she was beyond giving, but as a trophy of sorts.

Senzangakona cradled it in his powerful arms and, bracing himself, gently uncovered the baby's face. Ever suspicious, the king exposed the rest of the tiny body, checking the genitals. At the confirmation that it was indeed a boy, he could barely suppress a feeling of exhilaration. Then, when Shaka offered his father a beaming, toothless grin, the joy surfaced on the king's lips in a faint smile, which he quickly curbed, along with a surge of feelings that threatened to burst through the ramparts of his control.

"You realise there will be no wedding feast," he said dryly to Gama, feigning annoyance,

"That will still not deny the child his right to you as his father," Bhebhe commented gravely.

Senzangakona knit his brow as if Bhebhe's reply left room for reflection. Feeling all eyes on him, the king started to enjoy being the center of attention, the focal point of suspense - it somehow made up for the gnawing dissatisfaction that still dwelled in him as a consequence of his recent meeting with Mudli and Mkabayi. Looking at Bhebhe with a twinkle in his eye, Senzangakona announced: "Ten cattle," breaking the tension and thus admitting Nandi of the Langeni to the Clan of the amaZulu.

The king's eyes roamed past Mudli, to Gama, Nandi, and back to Bhebhe, knowing full well that they could not accept his offer without accepting offense. "Fifteen," the king grudgingly raised his own offer, as if giving way to reckless generosity.

"Fifty-five," countered Nandi, flatly.

Mudli compressed his lips with a show of indignation coupled with rising anger. "Your insolence, woman, is becoming unbearable. Be it clear that your presence in this kingdom is due only to the age-old respect we nurture for the Langeni king and his people. Were it not for that mutual respect, we would not feel obliged to suffer you and that child of deceit."

Nandi's face ironed out with rage as she faced the Elder, her own indignation matching his. "No, Elder," she spat out as a wave of astonishment rippled through the Zulus. No woman had ever dared to offer rebuttal to an esteemed dignitary such as Mudli. "Respect, has nothing to do with it. You know as well as I that if your king refuses to acknowledge my child as his own it would mean war."

Spinning round to face his king, flushed with rage, Mudli uttered through clenched teeth, "Baba! How much longer shall we be addressed in such manner by this woman?"

Senzangakona's eyes remain trained on Nandi, feeling strangely aroused by her inimitable strength of character. "Why do you waste your strength in anger, Elder? - We should all be amused by this woman's insolent behaviour," the king replied, adding with a wry smile as his glance shifted to Mudli with a playful gleam: "we had 'predicted' it, had we not?" Then, his manner becoming suave, Senzangakona returned his attention to Nandi, his voice composed, riding the edge of scorn, "Fifty-five cattle? What makes you think you're worth that much?"

"The memory of words once spoken by the father of this child," Nandi retorted, evenly, "assuring me that I was the only woman he wanted at his side. The only one worthy of his love. And now the only one who has given him a child." As she spoke, she felt an odd feeling akin to triumph welling up within her, dispelling all restraints of compassion and all remorse. She willed herself not to glance at Mkabi as she added, "And how much is all that worth?" In the blindness of that triumph, she sensed more than saw the disconsolate pain she had inflicted on Mkabi, she sensed more than saw the sharp reproach in Bhebhe's eyes, she sensed more than saw Gama's disquieting stare silently urging her to put an end to the spiteful duel which was now claiming innocent victims, yet she felt Senzangakona's grasp tightening on her arm, wrenching her round to face him - and then she saw the glint in his eyes which she knew too well to be the spark that would light his flaming rage.

But instead of giving vent to that rage, the king allowed an eerie smile to steal across his lips as he placed the child back into Nandi's arms and, turning on his heels, strode away causing the blood to drain from her face. Nandi faltered, gripped by the sensation that she might have gambled too much this time and lost it all.

A rigid and absolute silence reigned in esiKlebeni, and all eyes were on Senzangakona as he strode away from the Langeni party, his mind racing to find a way out of the dilemma in which he had cast himself. Suddenly he stopped dead, his instinct, that of the hunter, awakened with the solution to his dilemma: he would sacrifice Mkabi's pride to save his own. Turning, he glanced back at Nandi and her father. "So be it. Fifty-five cattle." Then, directing an unmerciful stare at Mkabi, he repeated: "Fifty-five cattle...for a son!"

Her head high, holding Shaka as her banner, looking like a queen and conducting herself every inch as such, Nandi strode into esiKlebeni while the Zulus parted before the daughter of Bhebhe and her son. Though remaining illegitimate, the 'I-Shaka' was now permitted to bear the designation 'kaSenzangakona Zulu'.

Shaka Zulu.

CHAPTER X
"UMTHONGA"(MASTER)
MONTH OF UMANDULO(SEPTEMBER, 1793)

After her highly unorthodox and unceremonious instalment as the second wife of Senzangakona kaJama Zulu, Nandi soon realised, in a matter of days in fact – as soon as the stupor caused by her enlivened encounter with Senzangakona and Mudli had worn off - that her father Bhebhe had been right about something else: few have the influence to change traditions to suit their rebel hearts.

Like David at the portals of Goliath's camp, Nandi had stood at the gates of esiKlebeni and, in one tempestuous hour, defied the giant that was the social system of her people. She had broken all the rules:- she, a woman, regarded as having been created to serve her men, cook food, and till the fields, had scorned Sovereign, Elders, and Council, and far from being the 'Nkosikasi', the Queen, Nandi was considered an outcast, her presence at esiKlebeni suffered by all as a temporary evil which would, she felt, be eliminated as soon as the right opportunity arose. Especially Mudli, who had grown to hate the woman and her child who had caused the generous heart of Jama to worry so throughout his last troubled days on earth, waited for the chance to purge the Zulu Village of those who were the living reminder to all of his king's weaknesses.

And Nandi looked upon the Elder with due circumspection. Ever since Igazi had confided to her that it was Mudli, and not Senzangakona, who had plotted with Jama to assassinate her, Nandi guarded herself and Shaka from the fleeting glances of the Elder whom, whilst confiding in her offspring in the reserved privacy of their small hut, she compared to a fox stealing from its burrow at night - the very image of craft and of plotting.

On the other hand, Senzangakona drew closer to the Elder, willingly responding to his suggestion that the king try to forget the arrogant Langeni. Complying, in his need to forget or out of spite for the phantom of his memory, the Son of Zulu wed, in the brief space of those few years, Bibi, Fudukazi, Langazana, Mzondwase, Mpikase, Magulana, Kishwase, and Mjanisi - eight in all. Yet, far from forgetting Nandi, Senzangakona floundered in this sea of matrons whom he found as dismal and unappealing as his first wife and yearned more than ever for that one woman who still held his heart and ensnared his mind, the beautiful maiden who, though now within reach, was forever tacitly forbidden to him in the name of the pride he had promised his father to value above all else.

Nandi's life was, indeed, that of a proscribed being. She rarely communed with anyone, and when she did it was only with Shaka or with the three persons who had somehow grown close to her: Igazi who, having witnessed Senzangakona's affair with the Langeni from its outset, knew that both parties had been guilty of wronging and hurting the other and, in light of that understanding, had become Nandi's only true friend and confidant without, however, relinquishing any of his affection for the king; Mkabi, the only genuinely innocent victim of the lovers' struggle, the would-be rival who, though bitterly humiliated, found solace in the thought that she and the lovely Langeni could have something in common:- the king's rejection; and, oddly enough, Mkabayi, the twin whose life was spared making her an outcast in her own right, felt an affinity with Nandi and Shaka and often came to visit the boy, spending long hours in the child's company during which Nandi had the distinct impression that her son was being subjected to the scrutiny of a wise and experienced connoisseur in matters of leadership. In Shaka's perfectly proportioned, chiselled features, graced with high cheekbones, a tawny complexion, and luminous greenish-brown eyes, catlike, reminiscent of her mother's, Mkabayi glimpsed the proud allure of the vague and the unknown, of the unforeseen and the sudden, of all that is dangerous, strong, alive, human, and wild, unfettered. In a way Shaka was for both Nandi and Mkabayi not only the product of his father's seed, but the seed of what his father could have been. For both women, Shaka was the promise of the power that had been denied them in the man they loved.

And there was something else. The Prophecy. They shared it -- with Mudli. They saw it unravelled before them: no matter how many wives the king had, Nandi's child remained - stubbornly - the only born!

Before Nomcoba, his sister..

He had come to her, in the night, in the darkness of a shrouded moon, wearing the stinging odour of sorghum, yet inebriated not with beer but with the solitude of his body, with the loneliness of his soul in the presence of her seemingly lofty indifference.

He had come to kill her - or so he had whispered, hissing but inches from her face with a violence that aroused sensations she thought extinct. Yet at the warm touch of the woman whom he called the cause of all his misfortunes, the anger had peeled almost instantly off his scorching mind leaving only an extreme need of consolation. Perhaps - he had told her, letting the spear fall limp in his open hand - perhaps if he must resign himself to his fate, she might help him to forget. For a moment.

As Nandi had looked at his kneeling figure, sad, absorbed, spear in hand, the very picture of the vanquished warrior, she had heard an inward voice, one speaking of unavailing regret. Forget! Her own heart suddenly welled with the same desire, the dire need to find an island of peace in that ocean of profound despair - even if that island was a mirage. For a moment forgetfulness in his arms had seemed possible, and she had closed her eyes giving herself up to that need.

Then - when the passion was spent, Shaka had been there, standing before them, his eyes, still those of a child, astounded into perfect stillness - delving deep into the mystery of a violence beyond the grasp of his years.

"Get out!" Senzangakona had growled, twisting his neck round to glare at his son as he had rolled off his mother's body.

"Get out! Now!" his father had yelled angrily, allowing passion and wrath to mix in Shaka's heart, clouding love and hatred into one immense, obscure emotion that, for Shaka, translated only as pain in the tears he had seen spilling from Nandi's eyes. *

Nomcoba, Shaka's sister. Conceived together with Shaka's fear of the Unknown.

She had ceased to count the years. Yet they had passed. Six altogether. As Shaka the boy started to observe his acquired habitat, the Life of which he was a part, the Nature of which he felt he was a dispensable element, his heart reached out, all-encompassing in its insatiable desire to grasp the unfathomable design of survival. The fear and fascination, the inspiration and the wonder of the kill - of death near, unavoidable, often unseen, filled his soul with unrest and stirred the most indistinct and intimate of thoughts. Death -- that unquiet and confounding demon of inextinguishable desires and fears - became his companion, his inseparable friend.

In was in this engagement of mind that in his sixth year Shaka sat high atop of a rocky promontory near the Zulu homestead were he was apt to spend the hours between his chores in silent, enthralled contemplation of Nature, his heart open to impressions, his mind ready to learn.

His attention was snagged on a comical, shabby troop of long-nosed monkeys that crowded the bough of a giant wild fig tree which loomed over the muddy waters of the Empembeni River. Shaka smiled as the primates chattered in a flurry of mad, disordinate gesticulations communicating with hands and drawn up, twisted lips in what appeared to be a farsical parody of Mankind.

Then suddenly the boy froze, the smile vanishing from his own lips as his blood charged with a buzz of adrenalin. Ever so slowly Shaka shifted his eyes searching the banks of the river. His glance ran over a small clearing on the edge of the water and rested fondly on the sleek, honey-coloured contours of a baby kudu, its budding gracile horns barely visible under the tufts of fur between its large, oval ears. The deer was alone, far from its mother and its herd. Unmoving, Shaka followed the kudu's agile prancing as it leapt down the banks and, bending its slender legs, lowered its head to drink.

Then, shifting his gaze, the boy scanned the river for what he had sensed was there and his eyes fell on a full-grown lioness standing stock-still, its slanting gaze riveted on the kudu, its body poised, ready to advance for the kill.

Sensing the danger, the kudu jerked its head up, sniffing the air. Shaka watched with bated breath, his charmed eyes darting from hunter to hunted, his soul transported by a nervous tingling of boundless curiosity, as the lioness stalked towards its prey, every muscle in her sinewy body drawn tight, ready. Then, fangs bared, the cat made her move darting after the kudu which had now bolted off, running for its life, the lioness close behind. Closing the gap with a mighty bound, the hunter clipped her victim's legs with a sweep of her paw, bringing the lighter animal sprawling to the ground. In an instant, the big cat had sunk her fangs into the deer's throat, tearing from the depth's of the kudu's being an excruciating cry of pain and of terror. As the blood gushed freely from the torn flesh, the lioness dragged her still trashing victim off toward a nearby formation of rocks where her lazy mate and young cubs awaited their 'breakfast'.

With the images of this recent 'kill' still lingering in his inquisitive mind, Shaka joined his mother who was crossing the velvety, rolling hills, returning to esiKlebeni with her afternoon's ration of fresh water. As the boy fell into step with the tall, beautiful woman who, through suffering, now looked somewhat older than her 24 years of age, Shaka shared with Nandi his fascination for Life's seemingly implacable violence. The woman listened silently, intently to her son's restless inquiry into the more vivid colours and the more passionate sensations of existence and, far from being surprised by a depth of reasoning which would belie his tender years, Nandi primed herself to give adequate kindling to the raging flames of her child's probing mind, the mind of the one she knew would soon speak with the Language of the Heavens.

"Aggression," she started when her son had finished, her voice even, firm, resolute, her words derived from experience and tapped from the font of the magical. "Everything that lives, Shaka. - Lions, impalas, kudu, leopards, the elephant. Everything is aggressive. It is in the nature of life. We are either the Masters of that instinct, or its Victims. We either learn how to die or how to kill. There is no middle way."

"When did the antelope learn how to die, mother?" the youth asked pensively.

"When it was born, Shaka," she replied. "It is a Victim...by nature. It was created to thrash in the dust, covered in its own blood, trying to hold on to its dignity in death."

"And what am I?" Shaka mused out loud after having momentarily pondered over his mother's words.

"A Master," she told him, with a proud smile, her arm curling round his broad shoulder. "A Master – from birth!"

"Am I the Lion?"

Her smile broadened as she confirmed, "You are the Lion."

Another pause ensued as the two magnificent creatures strode side by side over the veld. Shaka wrinkled his brow in consideration, finally asking: "And my father. What is he?"

At the mention of Senzangakona, Nandi's countenance lost the twinkle of pride it had enjoyed whilst she reflected upon her son, and took on an expression of helpless anger tinged with deep sadness. Retrieving her arm from her son's shoulders, she crossed it with the other, over her chest, in a gesture that was vaguely defensive. "Your father, Shaka?" she considered, her tone almost hushed. "He, too, is a Lion from birth. - Yet he chooses the way of the Victim because, for the Master, learning how to die is often simpler than - living."

The King of the Zulus, the 'Reluctant Master', had taken to drinking - heavily. The large quantities of beer serving to dull the senses and to help him draw a temporary blank on the utter wreck of his affections, indeed on all his feelings, in a chaotic disorder of thoughts and memories conjured out of context, bereft of purpose.

Edging towards thirty now, the Zulu king found himself doing something which, in his budding youth, would have appeared to be an act of outrageous cowardice, - namely: looking over his shoulder; in the physical sense as well as the spiritual. It was then that he knew, with frustrating pangs of conscience, that Nandi was not the cause of his weakness, but merely one of its consequences. It was then that he fathomed that by some fickle blunder of Fate, Senzangakona kaJama Zulu was in reality a mediocre soul residing in the stalwart body of a magnificent warrior. And he feared that over the years the body would inevitably degenerate to match the soul thus laying open his great secret through the loss of his pretence of appearance.

And the thought led him round full circle and back to drinking until, over the years, a general air of squalid neglect pervaded his being.

It was therefore not surprising for Nandi and Shaka to find, upon their return from the Empembeni, that the Lord of the Zulus was indecorously slouched by the flickering glow of a hearty fire, his lips stained with the fat of beef, the foam of sorghum and the moronic smirk that distinguished the sinister cheerfulness of a mind sodden with alcohol. In the king's company were his wives (sans Mkabi, who shied away from these boisterous gatherings in which she knew she would ultimately become the brunt of her husband's mocking) and a groveling congregation of clansmen who thoroughly enjoyed their king finding him far more accessible than his haughty father had been.

Nandi's expression came straight from a tormented heart as she inched closer to the fire, her fingers playing with the fringes of her kilt in an absent-minded caress as she stood absorbed in thought. Glancing down at Senzangakona's sprawled form, the woman was surprised to feel, through her indifference, a great pitying tenderness for that man she once had considered the master of her life. A sense of absolute loneliness came home to her heart with a force that made her shudder.

At her side, his magnificent features the mirror image of his mother's; Shaka intuited Nandi's deep sorrow and used her suffering to foment the fever of his own rising anger. As a wave of heat passed through him, the boy's small hands closed in fists trembling in the suppression of his feelings, his lips pressed tightly together, his eyes glaring at the inebriated mist of revulsion that clung to the man who had sired him, doing little to conceal his distaste. Shaka's thoughts leapt back to that summer night in which, secreted in the shadows of his mother's hut, he had witnessed Nandi's nude body, wet with perspiration, strained against the straps tied to her ankles and wrists as Noliwa, Mkabi, and two old women held her in place. As the cords grew taut with Nandi's writhing, the sangoma Majola positioned herself between the woman's legs. After a terrifying series of short, tortured gasps, a shrill cry coming from the bottom of Nandi's heart was expelled through her parted lips as the sangoma drew from her the slimy, blood-drenched form of a tiny, wretched-looking creature. In his memory, Shaka now saw that slippery being that vaguely resembled the human and the exhausted features of his mother as the ghastly, vein-streaked placenta was torn from her womb. As then, he now heard Noliwa speak excitedly, joyously of a child, Nomcoba, the king's daughter.

Opening his eyes, stirring from his nightmarish abstraction, Shaka saw that his father had reached out for Nandi, closing his powerful hand round the back of her neck. The woman's expression remained coldly distant as he yanked her face closer to his own and hissed, his nostrils flaring and his eyes flashing with the storm that raged within him, "Hail, Nandi! Queen of the Zulus! The whore who trapped the mighty leopard with a bastard cub!" He burst into a short, joyless laugh, then added with severe gravity, "Hail, Nkosikasi! Ndlovukazi! Hail, Queen of Whores!"

His words were applauded by the delighted tittering of his wives and the boisterous laughter of the intoxicated men. In that general merriment, Nandi and her son were like two islands of trapped stillness in a hurricane. The woman's eyes fell on Shaka and in that gaze, the boy read the reflection of his father's aggression. And he responded to what he interpreted as a silent command. Racing to their side, Shaka fastened his tiny hands round his father's, trying to release Nandi from his grip. Finding that this strategy was soon frustrated by the king's superior strength, in a courageous act of unparalleled effrontery, Shaka took hold of the Royal Assegai resting at his father's side and, with a resolve and strength far beyond his years, forced its polished blade against the king's neck, drawing blood. "Don't you ever hurt my mother again," Shaka threatened his father, his voice razor-sharp and steady.

Horrified the Zulus remained riveted in place, speechless as Nandi's eyes shone with a feeling of immense gratification and pride for her young man, her valiant warrior.

Shaka's act had an instant sobering effect on Senzangakona, the stupor of alcohol giving way to one of incredulity. He peered at his son as if seeing him for the first time and, for a fleeting instant, Nandi had the impression that she saw pride in the king's eyes, admiration for his son's unbounded courage. Yet, as her gaze met Senzangakona's, even that hope was shattered, for all she could read in those sunken eyes that shown strangely in the red half-light of the fire was indignant fury.

Grasping his son's wrist, Senzangakona twisted it round, pointing the blade at the boy's chest. As the air was suddenly charged with terror, Shaka looked deeply into his father's eyes without a trace of fear, indeed the boy wore a glint that challenged the king to strike. Seeing that eerie look in his own flesh and blood, the king's anger was suddenly dead within him and, his eyes flitting to his subjects with growing unease, Senzangakona snatched the Royal Assegai from Shaka's grasp and rose, glaring down at the boy, mocking him: "My little cub has the arrogance of his mother! We shall have to tame him as well!" Cocking back his arm, the king hurled the spear at his son, causing the blade to sink deep into the earth, a thread's distance from Shaka's side.

"And if we cannot tame him," Senzangakona roared, angrily, his gaze locked on Nandi's. "We shall be forced to pluck him from our midst, like a thorn from one's flesh. - Now remove your beetle from my sight, woman - before I forget I'm its father!"

Shaka sat on the river's banks, a solitary figure, immovable in the night, gazing vacantly at the various degrees of unshaped blackness which marked the places of trees, of riverside bushes, of hills and jutting rocks against the backdrop of a starred sky. Stirring, his anger still brooding within him, the boy hurled a stone into the limpid waters of the river and watched the ripples move out in ever expanding, concentric circles, framing the reflection of the full moon on the surface of the Empembeni.

Intrigued by this play of gentle motion, Shaka tossed another stone at the moon's reflection and smiled to himself as the ripples were renewed. Riding up on his haunches, the boy leaned forward and sank his hand into the water in an attempt to scoop up the reflection of the heavenly globe. Finding this impossible, he frowned and, reaching out, craned his neck as if to get closer to the moon's reflection, when suddenly he saw his own features mirrored on the dimly lit surface of the river.

And he was instantly spellbound by that image of his own face which, as he continued to stare in fascination, gradually took on, in his mind, the lineaments of Nandi, her features hardened by that look of suffering to which the boy had inadvertently been made privy in her moments of great passion and unbearable pain.

In a need to free himself from that recurring image of his mother's suffering which was now, on the river's surface, vividly superposed upon his own reflection, the two faces becoming one in the immensity of their communal spirits, Shaka furiously punched the water with his small fist, shattering the reflection into shards of glimmering, rippling vengeance.

In the darkness of night, Senzangakona was deep in slumber, his body propped up against the outer thatching of the Royal Hut, one arm thrown over his face as if to ward of the enemies of his dreams. At his side lay the remnants of his bout with alcohol,- the crockery of a broken pot and an overturned gourd from which dripped a steady spill of beer onto a smoldering fire, the liquid hissing as it extinguished the heat of the embers:- the residues befitting the Master who chose to live like a Victim.

Returning from the river, Shaka stopped to gaze at his father's sleeping frame strongly outlined in the chairoscuro of the full moon. His face steeled against any form of sentiment, the boy strode nearer and closed his hand round the Royal Assegai, yanking it out of the soft turf. Then, as the boy's eyes leapt to life with an eerie glitter, he took a step closer to the man who had sired him and raised the spear, its blade gleaming in the moonlight, mirroring the gleam in Shaka's eyes. The boy drew back his arm as if to sink the assegai into his father's chest, but finally relented, sinking the assegai into the ground just a breath away from his father's throat. Then the boy moved off, into the darkness…

…and in that darkness, Mkabayi watched him move off. She spent the night awake. Wondering how best to minister to a valour as inscrutable as that of the Child.

***

CHAPTER XI
"ISILO"(VICTIM)

"It is as your father, the great Jama, suspected," Mudli said, coldly unemotional. "He is the Child of the Prophecy."

The blood drained from Senzangakona's features. "Do you realise what you're saying, Elder?" he responded, knitting his brow in disbelief.

Sitting in the shadows of the large hut, Mkabayi kept her own counsel, silently listening, observing the two men as they spoke about the small boy whose future she now held in the circle of her emotions and influence.

"During the harvest before his death," Mudli started in a consequential way, "King Jama was visited by Sopane of the Mountain."

At the mention of the legendary and formidable diviner of the Nzuza Clan whose powers were said to be unrivalled throughout the land, Senzangakona leaned forward on his throne of rushes, his face moving into the wash of the fire's lapping flames that seemed to punctuate the sudden attentiveness in his glaring eyes. The king knew that Sopane's visits to the land of mortals were rare and all too often the harbingers of portentous events. If this human vulture had swooped down from his nest in the mountains to meet with his father, Senzangakona wanted to know why - especially when it concerned his own flesh and blood.

"Go on, Elder."

"The sangoma told your father that a Child had been conceived in the Land of the Heavens, the Child of the Cycle of Blood predicted by Those Who Inhabit The Mountains. Sopane urged your father to prevent the full gestation of the Infant lest his Birth herald the upheaval of life as we know it and the birth of an era in which the name 'amaZulu' would signify death and terror." Mudli paused, for emphasis perhaps, before adding, "That is why King Jama planned that the Langeni woman should not live to bear her son."

Mkabayi stole a keen glance at Mudli, her astonished expression betraying her shock at the revelation.

A wave of heat passed through Senzangakona, flushing his face and causing him to break out in cold perspiration. The man was stunned and aggrieved, profoundly, bitterly, with the immense and blank desolation of one confronted with a truth both bizarre and terrifying. So his father had taken more resolute precautions and gone further than just admonishing his son, Senzangakona mused, the rancid taste of delusion causing him to grimace. With a wry smile, Senzangakona's mind drifted back to that last talk he had had with his father: one of shared emotions, one of mutual respect, mutual trust, one of love. So he had never really trusted me, the Zulu considered, his lips compressed with a show of affliction. "In what way?" the king asked with repressed emotion.

"It was the final act of his reign, and of his life; one which unfortunately was not blessed with success," Mudli retorted, going on to relate the facts behind the sham rendezvous in Nkandla Forest, the plot to assassinate Nandi at the hands of Ghubela, the discovery of the valet's mangled body after days of exposure to the elements and to predators, and finally the news by way of the young Langeni messenger that Nandi was well and with child - the proof that the plan had unavailingly failed.

Senzangakona listened, aghast, disconcerted. He was seeing an aspect of his father which was completely new to him; a ruthlessness, which belied the gentle warmth that had been his touch, the deep pools of compassion that had been his eyes. "He did this?" The king's voice was hollow.

"For the good of..."

"I know, Elder," Senzangakona interrupted, his tone suddenly strident with anger, riding a wave of biting sarcasm. "For the good of the kingdom. - But why?" He was almost shouting now. "Why, Mudli?!"

"Fear, Nkosi," Mudli answered gravely. "Of what that child would do to our clan - to our people."

"The great Jama - resorting to the murder of a helpless, pregnant woman -- at the mere urging of a wretched sangoma?! - Don't you find that beneath his dignity, Elder?!"

Defending the memory of his beloved friend and king, Mudli rebuked Senzangakona's accusing manner with a tone of righteous indignation as he solemnly announced with irrepressible conviction: "King Jama's suspicions were based on more than Sopane's admonitions, Nkosi. Your father came to his resolve upon verifying that the signs of the Child's life correspond with uncanny precision to those predicted by the Prophets: He was born in Untulikazi, the Month of the Prophecy; he is illegitimate, the Condition of the Prophecy; he was conceived during the Moon of Pleiades, the Constellation of the Prophecy; you are the seventh successor of Zulu kaMalandela Zulu, the Reign of the Prophecy; his moment of birth coincided with the death of your principal wife's son, - that is the curse of the Prophecy!"

The chill of Mudli's words and the spectral images they conjured in Senzangakona's mind caused the king to freeze, immobile. Managing to push aside his unreasoning apprehension, the king forced a superior, careless smile scoffing the Elder's ominous words. "I am surprised, Mudli. You are a wise man. Rational. Yet you lend your king's ear to the supernatural by suggesting he give credence to this -- folklore? - The Child of the Prophecy, indeed!" Senzangakona shot a glance at his sister expecting her hard-boiled realism to find diversion in this old wives' tale! Yet, to the king's surprise and bewilderment, far from being amused, Mkabayi's face wore an odd, indefinable look of intent that left him all the more baffled by the entire affair.

"A king's power to rule over the lives of others is in itself magical, Nkosi," Mudli responded, straight-faced, unwaveringly. "If he should ever lose contact with the supernatural from whence his power is derived, he would relinquish his right to rule. When he starts to doubt the validity of...'folklore', he is lost."

Intrigued by the answer, Mkabayi stole a glance at her brother, reading the impact Mudli's words have had on the man's soul, waiting for his reaction. "And if what you say is true...?" the king finally spoke.

"He must die." The other man replied with a tone and expression conveying no regret, no spiritual discomfort - no emotion at all, in fact, save for the respectful urging that the task be dealt with in short order.

Senzangakona's entire being suddenly railed against the thought of sacrificing his own son. Once again, he cocked his blazing eye at Mkabayi as if to solicit a response from her. "Shaka was her blood as well, after all," he told himself. "She cannot remain indifferent to that blood being shed in the name of the irrational!" But avoiding her brother's stare, the woman dropped her gaze contemplatively, the keen glimmer in her eyes being the only sign of any inner turmoil. "Has everyone gone mad?!" Senzangakona asked himself, then muttered out loud to Mudli in an eerie whisper laced with the pure abstract terror of such a deed: "Kill?! My only son?!"

"That, too," Mudli pressed on relentlessly, "is part of the curse, Nkosi. Since you met that woman, you have had but two children - both hers. All your other wives are barren." Raising an emphatic brow, he stressed: "Miraculously so."

Senzangakona felt as though he was being made the victim of some paradoxical conspiracy. His stomach churned queasily with the memory of Nandi's adamant warnings that his sister and the Council would inevitably try to isolate him, to bid for control over his life by severing him from all that he loved. Is that why Mudli wanted Shaka's death?, he wondered. Was it a plot to which Mkabayi was a silent party? Senzangakona suddenly felt exposed. All the more so when Mkabayi finally spoke, her question reflecting his innermost thoughts.

"You hesitate, my brother?" she asked, flatly. "Is it out of love?"

"Is your concern more for these strangers than for the future of your own kingdom?" Mudli chimed in.

"He is no stranger!" Senzangakona roared angrily, feeling very much like a caged animal. "He is my blood!"

"Yes, Nkosi. Your blood," echoed the Elder, his tone foreboding. "It was your blood he shed to protect his mother! That did not go unnoticed, - and cannot go unpunished!" Sensing the king's helpless confusion, Mudli exchanged a quick glance with Mkabayi and approached his monarch. "I fear these are matters beyond the light of our mortal comprehension and competence, Baba." The Elder's voice was persuasive, almost caressing as he went on in a confidential manner. "We shall call upon Sopane of the Nzuza. His powers over these mysteries far exceed our own. He will read the secrets of the Child and provide the proof you need. Then, Nkosi," the Elder concluded, an awesome light appearing in his eye, subtly spinning his web, "you shall deliberate as you feel best - for the welfare of all."

Senzangakona looked up and, with a bitter smile, stared blankly ahead, his thoughts lost in the eddying; sinister fog in which all Hope is lost in Magic's gigantic deception.

It was an odious face - crafty, vicious, malignant, and shifty; a large face, seared with a thousand wrinkles and marked with every evil passion, every imponderable intent of darkness, while the sunken, bile-shot eyes and the high, thin, fleshless nose conveyed the impression of decrepitude and cragginess proper of some fierce, malefic bird of prey.

The body, hunchbacked, misshapen, twisted in tubercles of callous flesh, was tinted a pinkish white, the pale, colourless hue of the albino, and crooked in a low, stooping demeanour, perpetually frozen in the attitude of the beggar and the knave, with shoulders thrust forward in protrusions of bone and gristle. It was a monstrous figure with a suggestion of hunger and rapacity. And the soul was not like the clear water of a river, but muddy with turmoil, clogged with slabs of bark, the residue of sin and iniquity, messy with whole chunks of ground that had been gouged out of the shores of the diabolical.

Such was the inner and outer semblance of the famed Sopane of the Mountain, wretched son of the Nzuza Clan, diviner of the unfathomable and the mysterious.

The villagers were spellbound, petrified with revulsion and fear, as the miserable creature hobbled and shuffled grotesquely across the cattlefold, eyes shut tightly, his oversized bald head glistening like an infected pustule, the skulls of bats and mice dangling from his neck, colliding with an eerie clanging sound against the tarnished bronze pendants and bells which were fastened to his ears and to the porcupine quills draped round his shoulders. Sopane's entranced, ghoulish chanting, interfused with shrill ululating and hissing, was accompanied by the crazed yelping of his insidious subordinates, Mgidi and Mqalane, both younger than their master, their grisly figures also marred by the effects of rickets and other osteopathic deformities, as the fiendish procession danced towards the homestead's main hut, the three men leaping and vaulting in the air with freakish pirouettes and a wing-like flapping of the arms making them look like so many vultures caught in the throes of a slow, tortured death.

Nandi stood before her hut, bewitched, gaping from a distance at the macabre cortege as the merciless, stark, implacable talons of premonition clawed at her soul, tearing at the fiber of her being. Perceiving the tempest that raged within the woman, Sopane suddenly froze in a attitude of attentiveness, his eyes springing open, the jaundiced orbs darting to Nandi as his lips set in a malicious and abominable smile, a smile that laid bare her innermost sentiments and fears, exposing them to the icy breath of witchcraft. And on the firmament of her soul thus revealed to him, Sopane saw the confirmation of the Child and knew.

Nandi and Shaka were sent for and brought under escort to the Royal Hut. Nandi's blood ran cold as she approached the foul smelling sangoma, his ghastly features regarding her with an oddly possessive expression of expectation. Sensing that the danger she had intuited was now imminent; Nandi instinctively hugged her son, cradling him against her breast defensively. Yet the boy was snatched from her and delivered into the hands of the Nzuza diviner and his helpers. In desperation the woman fought to free Shaka from the clutches of these fiends, kicking at the Zulu guards who held her at bay, her arms thrashing out at their faces, her nails raking their skins, biting down hard with her teeth, nearly severing one of the guard's fingers before she was hauled away hut.   Left alone, with only his own courage and wits to rely upon, Shaka was pinned in place by the sinewy skeletal arms of Mqalane and Mgidi, as Sopane knelt down at the boys feet, bringing the blade of a sacrificial spear to the boy's ankle. Shaka stood unflinching as the blade lanced his tender flesh, the gash instantly flooding with a glistening surge of dark crimson, as the blood disgorged freely and was collected, by Sopane, in- to a small bowl of baked clay. As the bowl filled, Sopane shut his eyes, the nearness of the blood of the Child causing his senses to swoon in resonance with the Melody of the Ages.

The fire was burning brightly, cracking ominously as it sent spurts of blue, pungent smoke into the stifling interior of the Main Hut. Squatting before the hearth, Sopane leaned forward and, chanting in a deathly whisper - like the hushed litany of an infernal dirge,- touched the bowl to his mouth, spat into it, then gently rested it on the burning embers, as Mgidi and Mqalane sprinkled a peppering of the ashes of cremated human organs and the powder of ground herbs over the blood.

While the others - Senzangakona, Mkabayi and Mudli - looked on, spellbound, their eyes widened in disbelief as the bowl began to glow with a magical light of its own, a greenish phosphorescence of throbbing radiance that grew in brilliance with each pulse-beat, emitting a bewitching whimper - like the wail of boundless despair imprisoned in the shackles of Hell. The supernatural whimper mingled with Sopane's chanting, both voices gaining force, their pitch rising higher and higher like an evil chorus swelling in the praises of the Impondera- ble. Then, as the pitch became deafening, Sopane's grue- some features tightened, quivering uncontrollably, a patina of sweat forming on his colourless skin causing it to take on the greenish glow emanating from the bowl; a glow which had now waxed stronger, overpowering the light of the fire, pervading the entire hut like a spiralling, pulsating phantom.

Outside the dwelling, a bolt of lightning suddenly crashed through a clear blue sky, and out of the still- ness, the wind howled, bending all life before its brut- al and mindless fury. Summoned by the elements, the thunder spoke in one prolonged roll disclosing the turmoil of agony that suddenly afflicted all Creation; - and when the rain came, driving, hissing, it was as if the Heavens had burst forth with the tears of Eternal Sorrow.

Back in his hut, Shaka was in a trance, his body racked by the violent throes of a seizure as intense as the one that gripped the celestial vault. As Nandi held him tightly in her embrace, baffled and terrified by her son's sudden, unexplainable fit of convulsions, Shaka's feverish soul responded to the soothing, silky textures of a distant call, the call of Sitayi: "The Grandson of Jama," came the old woman's hushed whisper, "must prepare to hear the words of his forefathers. Seven nights hence, alone, he must rest beside the Pond of Mageba and Ndaba, East of the Great Mountain. There shall his destiny be sealed."

And, in Shaka's soul, as Reality and Illusion fused to form Destiny, he saw the huge globe of the sun a mere degree or two above the horizon, and, from the heated surface of the moist ground, he saw a mist begin to rise; a mist thin, invisible to the eye of Man yet dense enough to change the face of the sun into a glowing red disc, vertical and hot, rising above an expanse of saffron veld. Cast against the glowing red globe, striding away from the horizon, Shaka's soul saw the tall, magnificent figure of Nandi and, next to her, himself. The two walked over the immensity of the landscape, hour after hour, mile after mile, side by side, untiring in their resolve and purpose.

Then, as the edges of the sun touched the circular expanse of the sea, casting a track of light, straight and shining, resplendent in gold and scarlet, - he saw a path that seemed to lead from the earth directly into Heaven - Nandi stopped in their journey and faced Shaka, telling him tenderly: "You must go on alone now, my son. Follow the route as I explained it. And do not be afraid, for I shall be with you - always."

And Shaka's soul saw himself embrace his mother, his eyes welling with tears. Then, upon Nandi's gentle urging, he turned away from her and struck off towards a majestic, mystical mountain - its cliffs imbued with hues of deep red and shimmering silver, its summit jeweled with crystals and ornamented with pinnacles of white limestone and filigrees of ice sparkling with the radiating threads of light emitted by the dying sun.

Night found the boy by the banks of a mist-enshrouded pond - the Pond of Mageba and Ndaba. Heedless of a pair of buck drinking from the calm waters and of the crocodiles half-submerged by the murky banks, Shaka climbed through the thick undergrowth of decaying branches and fallen logs until he came to the edge of the pool and stood bathed in the hazy, unreal light of the full moon which shot through the fog, lending the setting a quality of enchantment. As Shaka surveyed his surroundings, waiting anxiously, attentively, the mist hovering over the pond slowly began to swirl and to lift, revealing four animals crouched near the opposing shore - a lion, a leopard, a hyena, and a jackal; all with their gleaming eyes trained on the boy.

Instinctively, Shaka prepared to defend himself from he beasts, snatching a large branch from the ground, weighing it in his hands, clasping it like a weapon. But, as he glared at the four animals placidly resting on a bed of vegetation like statues on a cloth a green velvet, Shaka slowly realised that they meant him no harm and, his curiosity returning at the departure of fear, the boy shifted his attention back to the magic pond and found, to his amazement, that its murky waters were churning and bubbling. He stood dumbfounded, eyes gaping, mouth opened in wonder, as, with a loud splash, a huge Cobra lifted itself out of the water, its hood fully distended, its luminous, perfectly round, rubineous eyes peering at the spellbound child. Swaying back and forth, the Cobra rose to a height where it towered over Shaka. Then, in a deep resonant voice it half- spoke, half-chanted: "Bayete, wena wa sendhlu nKulu! Hail thou who art as great as the dreams of his Nation."

"Who are you?" Shaka asked, surprised by the steadiness of his voice.

"In me is the Spirit of the People of the Heavens," the Cobra thundered. "I speak with the voice of Malandela, Zulu, Ntombela, Punga, Mageba, and Ndaba. This day thou art my Son and I thy Father. Ask and I shall give thee the nations for thy heritage, the ends of the earth for thy domain. He who acknowledges thy name shall grow in thy glory; he who does not, shall meet everlasting ruin. The Bond of this our Covenant shall last so long as thou shalt retain the condition of a Son before his Father. - Seek no more, lest the Father turn against the Son with the blood of his blood."

The resonant voice was suddenly still, leaving silence - save for the soft whistling of the swirling mist and the strained breathing of the Child who stood perfectly unmoving, marmoreal.

"Step forward, Shaka Zulu," the voice returned with the soothing summons, "and prepare to be consecrated."

Mesmerised, the boy found himself moving forward, into the shallow pond. As he did so, the waters began to stir round him, spinning faster and faster, rising in a column that engulfed the boy in a shaft of shimmering crystal which was slowly tinged the colour of blood. The hushed whistling of the waters grew into the boisterous cry of thousands of voices intoning the salute to the king: - "Bayete, Nkosi! wena wa sendhlu nKulu!"

And when the cry was suddenly abated, Sitayi's voice murmured in an uncanny whisper: "You are Zulu. You possess the Heavens. Your power, your glory, and your kingdom are the gift of your Heritage. Do not betray that heritage, or your death will be the death of your people..."

...and Shaka's soul withdrew from the Dimension of Destiny to return to the measure of Reality, as another wave of convulsions racked his feverish, tortured body. Nandi pressed him to her breast, sobbing helplessly as the storm continued to rage outside, the forceful wind hissing through the hut's thatching.

Then, as suddenly and mysteriously as it had begun, the storm subsided and the tempest was dead in the night -- a dome of deep blue sprinkled with shining dots of luminescence returning to crown esiKlebeni in peace.

The bowl containing the Child's life fluid stopped glowing and was, with a prodigious suddenness, transformed into a semi-circular chunk of deep-black coal, crumbling to ashes in the sangoma's wiry fingers. The maddened chanting seemed to stick in Sopane's throat, causing him to choke, to gasp for air with a raspy grating that was born deep in his lungs, his mouth wide in a grotesque, twisted yawn, similar to that of a fish deprived of his natural environment. Then, with a hollow gurgling, the evil bird of prey slumped forward, unconscious.

The electrifying stillness that followed was finally broken by the Zulu king. His chest heaving with a deep sigh, Senzangakona rose gravely to his feet uttering: "Give them whatever payment they require, Mudli." Pausing at the hut's doorframe, the king added, wearily: "Tomorrow the curse will be broken."

Before leaving, Senzangakona cast a deliberate glance in the direction of his sister. In that look, which lasted for a mere fleeting instant, Mkabayi detected a muted, despairing supplication - like that of a beast glaring out through the constraining bars of a cage. Feeling the impact of that entreaty, Mkabayi pensively dropped her gaze to the crackling flames.

CHAPTER XII
"IGAZI"(BLOOD)

"Shaka!" came Nandi's gentle voice.

The boy stirred on his mat, shaking the cobwebs from his mind with a painful sluggishness. His eyes fluttered, blinking repeatedly and were gradually forced open, turning to peer at his mother through the tingling haze that lingered from his fever.

"Come, Shaka. We must leave at once."

"Where are we going, mother?" he asked in confusion.

"Home," she said with finality.

With Nomcoba strapped to her back in a cowhide pouch and holding Shaka by the hand, Nandi made her way through the night, following the shadow of a man that furtively led them away from the ill-defined circular contours of the esiKlebeni homestead toward the sloping hills cast against the harsh moonshine.

Upon reaching the summit of the furthest of these hills, Nandi stopped to glance back at the impalpable images of the Zulu village enshrouded in the stillness of night. Pushing aside the last six years of her life, an existence which she now saw had been made up of sad remorse and frightened hope, Nandi looked toward the future and turned to the kind features of the man who had delivered them from of the claws of Magic's decree.

"We owe you our lives, Igazi," she said with a thin, weary smile.

"No, Nandi," he smiled back. "Though I cherish your lives, the idea of your escape was not mine."

For an instant Nandi entertained the hope that the architect of their salvation might be the man who had been the cause of her nemesis. In light of that hope, she felt fully willing and oddly capable of forgetting and forgiving all and she asked, the glint of expectation dancing across her eyes: "Then whose was it?"

"You will know in time." Igazi answered evasively. "But now you must hurry. At daybreak he will be looking for you, and you must reach the Langeni Village before then."

The full impact of her anguish swept back into her heart, strangling the half-born hope that had dared to intrude upon her suffering. " 'He' will be looking for us," she echoed, her shoulders drooping slightly forward as the burden returned. "For a moment I thought..."

Her voice trailed off, and Igazi tried to coax away her incurable despair. "You better than anyone should know that Life is capricious. It never ceases to surprise us. But go now, Nkosikasi, and may the Ancestors be with you."

"Nkosikasi?" Nandi echoed the word pensively. "That is the title of the Principal Wife of Zulu, Igazi. Not an outcast."

Unflinchingly, the man replied, his gaze steadily holding Nandi's. "You are the Principal Wife of Zulu, Nandi. You are the Queen! - I knew that six years ago, when you strode into esiKlebeni as if you owned the place!"

A thin smile of recollection tugged at the corners of Nandi's lips, and she laughed, momentarily dispelling the grief. Igazi laughed with her, enjoying this fleeting, joyful moment with the woman he had always loved from a distance. "Some day you will return to claim your rightful place," Igazi was serious now, in earnest. "And he," the man indicated Shaka, "will be your shield."

Embracing Igazi, Nandi took Shaka's hand and, shifting Nomcoba's weight on her back, started off, towards her future.

Moving towards his hut through the shadows and the silence, Igazi sensed the presence of another wakeful being near the smouldering embers of a campfire. The man stopped in his tracks, stiffening slightly.

"That was foolish, Igazi," a voice told him in a tone of regretful irritation riding the inflection of immense fatigue. "Very foolish,- very...foolish," the man repeated as if reading in the fire the refrain of some satanic litany belonging to the ritual of death. "Why?" he asked, lifting a wondering gaze, searching Igazi's face through the mantle of heat rising from the embers, somehow hoping that warmth would dispel the icy veil that now clothed their friendship.

Igazi found he was unable to speak - there was too much, or perhaps too little with which to form a coherent phrase. He merely ambled towards his king and gazed down at him.

"It's not too late," Senzangakona considered, his eyes returning to the fire. "I could still send out some men to intercept them before they reach their village. It shouldn't be too hard to catch up to a woman on foot with a child and a baby."

The last few words were strained through the vice of unbounded affliction, his eyes moistening with tears as the thought struck him like a forceful blow: - that woman and those children were his, and in the immeasurable facets of their being they reflected, like the polished surfaces of a prism, every colour, every hue, every timbre of sound, every pattern of light that was his own being. What more could a man cherish than the woman he loves and the gift that is their progeny. What more is there in life?

Nothing, save for - friendship, and his eyes returned to Igazi who now spoke softly. "No. It shouldn't be hard at all, Nkosi."

Senzangakona sat unmoving. His eyes locked on those of his friend. "You know what this means." The king's was a statement more than a question, "-- an act in defiance of your king."

Though he was the one that must die, Igazi felt his soul flinching in empathy with his king at the realisation that his own death would leave an insurmountable void in his friend's life.

"Of course no one knows, - no one besides you and I," Senzangakona conceded, his words a veiled suggestion that a conspiracy amongst friends would be more than acceptable to the king. The spear was flashing in his hand as he underlined the entreaty. "No one need really know."

"Perhaps, Nkosi," was Igazi's level reply. "Yet we have hunted together too long to not recognise survival when we stare it in the eye." The man's gaze darted to the assegai in the king's hand. "For your own dignity as well as mine, you must grant me the punishment due."

"I can change the punishment. I am the king, after all. I give the orders!" His mounting despair and the inner conflict it produced transpired in the king's voice.

A thin smile was born on Igazi's generous lips. "And can you order my heart and your own to forget betrayal?"

"It may be possible," Senzangakona replied, his fear of complete loneliness overriding the call of duty in an effort to rewrite the unwritten laws of Mankind.

"Yes. It may be," Igazi seemed to agree. "It may also be possible to order the brook not to run to the river, and the river not to rush to the sea. If you speak loudly. If you speak angrily. Maybe they will obey. - Yet, I believe that the brook will not listen and the river will rush all the faster to the sea in which it is lost forever." Gently lifting the blade of the king's spear so that the point is over his own heart, Igazi whispered, withdrawing into his courage: "Strike, my friend. Strike swiftly."

Senzangakona sensed that his arm had thrust forward, plunging the spear's blade deep into Igazi's heart. Aghast, the king looked down at the blood gushing out of his friend's chest and shivered, feeling that the warmth of life was abandoning him as well. When Igazi slumped forward, Senzangakona caught him in his arms, staining them a deep crimson, and lowered his friend's body to the ground, yanking the assegai from his side.

"Why?" the king's question came again, laced with insurmountable desolation, bitter, profound.

Coughing through a punctured lung, fighting back the pain and darkness, Igazi murmured, "They had you trapped again. You needed a way out. It was either your son's life or...this."

"I could have overruled Mudli and the Council," Senzangakona proffered.

"You were never very good at that," Igazi reminded his king, his smile burnished with the gloss of humour.

"No. I never was," Senzangakona confessed with a wry grin.

"Bayete, Nkosi," breathed Igazi, clutching his friend's arm.

And then he was dead.

"Hamba kahle, my friend. - Go well," was the hushed reply.

Senzangakona kaJama Zulu lifted his gaze from the body of his closest friend and glanced at the huge globe of the sun, which had risen to shed warmth on the king's disconsolate grief.

Can the beginning of another day bring hope to a man who has lost everything he cherished?, he wondered, the outline of the sun blurred by his tears. Can even a king command the brook not to rush to the river?

The dawn found three exhausted figures struggling up the rocky incline bordering the Langeni Village: - Nandi with Nomcoba and Shaka now leading the way.

Though Nandi's legs were scratched and bleeding, though her physical and spiritual strength had been sapped to a point beyond caring, beyond feeling, - though Nandi had no reason whatsoever to smile, she was smiling - joyously - as she and her children made their way towards Bhebhe's homestead, the point in Time and Space which she now looked upon as a haven in a storm.

Approaching the dwelling of her childhood, Nandi noticed, crowding the top of her homestead, a small gathering of people, some faces still familiar, others changed beyond recognition by the advance of Time. She saw her mother Mfunda, and King Mbenghi, his son Prince Makedama - now a young man, the Elder Gama, other esteemed members of the Langeni Council and the old women of the village who, smacking their breasts, were immersed in a woeful, disparaging lament.

As Nandi looked closer, she wondered why there was no sign of Bhebhe. Then she knew, and the blood drained from her face, the tingling of sheer horror pervading her soul. Nandi caught her breath, her eyes falling on the clearing at the top of the cattlefold where she saw...a pit, four feet deep, six long, and three wide - as was the custom with commoners. In the pit, sitting upright, only his head and shoulders visible above the edge of his grave, was Bhebhe, his features congealed in an expression that, even in death, promised soothing compassion and understanding.

Feeling that her legs had suddenly gone limp, Nandi reached out for Shaka's hand, squeezing it for comfort as the boy stared, wide-eyed and unblinking at the frightening semblance of his grandfather. "The inimitable power of Death," he thought, looking at his mother's grief. "Death: the Lord of Grief, the Lord of Pain, the Lord of Suffering. The Lord of...The Kill.

One is either its Master or its Victim, he resolved in his young mind. There is no middle way.

"The way has been clearly laid before us, Nkosi," came Mudli's eloquence as the Elder paced the soft turf near the euphorbia tree where the Council had met to deliberate on the event of the previous day. "And I would suggest that we do not close our eyes to the solution Fate has offered."

"And what might that be, Elder?"

Mkabayi, Lutuli, and the other members of the Council (a dozen men in all of varying ages, each representing one or more Zulu homesteads) shifted their attention to the king, keenly aware of the uncommon aura of antagonism that now enveloped his spirit. The man seemed stronger somehow, more resolute: - the facade of a man who can barely conceal the profound grief at the loss of a person with whom he had shared his heart.

"They have been 'coaxed' into exile," Mudli went on, unruffled, "by the treachery of your induna. - We could not have planned it better, Nkosi. Now you must take the next obvious step and ask that they be returned to you."

"The Langeni are proud, Elder," mused the king, his voice laced with a touch of weariness as if everything in life, especially living, had become too much for him. "They may refuse -- and that would mean war."

"Exactly," Mudli continued, moving down a somewhat sinister path of intention, pausing for an instant as if to give greater effect to: "And in that war there will be casualties...one of which will be the boy. -- The threat of the Prophecy will be nipped in the bud, so to say, without you personally having to soil your hands with the blood of the child." As Senzangakona shot the Elder an intense look, Mudli completely the sketch of his plan with a disturbingly dapper: "Thus allowing both your honour and...your conscience to remain intact."

Senzangakona smiled sarcastically. "It pleases me immensely," said Senzangakona to all present, "that my sister and my councillors show such undying concern for my honour." The smile became sardonic upon adding, "I am also delighted that in so doing they have acknowledged its existence -- my honour's, that is." The king rose from his throne and, hands clasped behind his back, paced the red earth under the shade of the euphorbia. "Yet need I remind them that I have already soiled my hands - and my conscience - with the blood of my friend!? Need I remind them that it was due to their advice that I accepted the 'I-Shaka' in the first place - in order to avoid outright conflict with the Langeni. Am I to understand that you now advise me to have this war after all? For the sake of this boy? - What will the amaZulu people say of their king? That he is a fool, a--"

"That," interrupted Mudli with due firmness, "is my foremost preoccupation, Nkosi: your people and what they will say." The Elder twisted round to face the Council, adding with vibrant outrage: "A king cannot tolerate being abandoned by a woman!"

"So tell the people that it was my own doing. I, the king, chased her away because I was tired of her arrogance."

"Very well, Nkosi," Mudli readily agreed; too readily, Senzangakona mused. "And how shall I explain the sudden violent death of Igazi?"

"Elder," the king said with irritation, trying to banish from his mind the image of his dying friend. "You are trying my patience."

"That is my calling, Nkosi."

"Then let me make your calling less burdensome for both of us," said Senzangakona, parrying Mudli's conniving with a firm hand. "They are gone! And, however their departure might be interpreted, the fact remains that she is a woman, alone, with two children and no one to care for them." Lowering his voice, the king went on: "She and her children are disgraced, Elder. - And if I - a king - now risk war to get them back, it would be virtually like proclaiming that I love them, that I need them!"

Senzangakona's voice snagged on the word 'need'. In her attentiveness, Mkabayi caught the inflection and responded with a thin smile.

"But if I forget them," the tone became an eerie hush. "Well...for her son, that punishment will be worse than death. The unwanted child of an exiled mother. Not a Zulu. No longer a Langeni. A boy destined to grow up without a clan. Far worse than death, Mudli. - You tell my subjects that. Tell them that I remember no one by the name of Nandi daughter of Bhebhe."

"Forget," the word echoed in his mind. And, in that instant, with chilling insight, Senzangakona perceived that that might now have become the purpose of his life: -- forgetting Nandi and her children. How long would it take?, he asked himself. Would the longed-for oblivion come before sunset, would it come before the next moon, would it come only with death?

He suddenly yearned to be alone.

But he was not. Unwavering in his intent, Mudli was retorting, "Indeed, Nkosi. And I trust that explanation will satisfy your subjects. In a way, the people have always believed that witchcraft was at the source of the Langeni woman's extraordinary temperament, and Sopane's presence here has served to confirm that suspicion. - Yes, they should be quite content with the banishment of the 'witch' and her son. - But we who know of the Prophecy are aware that the true implications of mere banishment are much more serious." At the mention of the Prophecy, Mudli's grave discourse had taken on a rising level of urgency. "If the Child is allowed to live, he will bring death and terror! The upheaval of life as we know it! That is what the Ancestors meant when they spoke of this boy! That is their warning! All that we believe in, all that we stand for - all that we are - will be lost! Forever. In an empire that is destined to become an unbridled monolith of destruction!" Having vehemently delivered the last few phrases in one strained breath, the Elder paused to fill his lungs. Then, with measured eloquence, Mudli lowered his tone, becoming suddenly confidential. "Baba, I sympathize with the fact that you are reluctant to bring about the death of your own son. But of one thing you must be convinced..." He emphasized passionately. "He is not your son!"

As gasp of astonishment was torn from the Council and the king's eyes flared with incense, Mudli hastened to add: "The son of your loins, yes! But his conception and birth were guided by the hands of evil!"

At the termination of this further display of Mudli's rhetoric, and whilst a wave of comments rippled through the Council, Senzangakona studied the Elder, long and hard, the steadfast gaze of his thoughtful eyes seeking the truth within the heart of the man who had loved and faithfully served his father. He then broke his silence as his command rang out: "Erase them from your mind, Elder! That is an order! The same order I received from my father over seven years ago!"

Realising with a pang of helplessness that the king's order left no room for further rebuttal, flustered by this abrupt dismissal, Mudli pursed his lips to conceal his annoyance and, bowing, strode away from the site of the meeting. Lutuli and the other members of the Council followed his lead, leaving Senzangakona alone with his sister.

After sitting for a few moments in silent thought, the king asked without looking at her: "Did it have to be Igazi? Couldn't you have used someone else?"

Taken somewhat unawares by the question, Mkabayi hesitated. "Answer me," her brother urged with increasing impatience.

"He was the only one I could trust," she finally admitted, flatly. "He loved you both."

Silence set in once more as Senzangakona listened to the breeze playing with the leaves of the euphorbia, his thoughts returning to the friend who had loved him enough to sacrifice his own life to save that of his son.

His son. Senzangakona turned a wondering eye to his sister. "This...Prophecy. What do you make of it?

"Mudli is right," she answered, absorbed, as if heeding the dictates of an inner voice. "A new order will come, and the Spear of the Prophecy will clear the way. Mudli foresees the destruction of all we believe in and calls this - 'evil'. But is it evil to destroy a homestead to make room for one which is larger and better? Our father, Mudli and those of his generation are the straw to be cut and bound together so that the New House of the amaZulu can be formed."

Senzangakona turned to face Mkabayi and their eyes locked as she continued, "The House ordained since the beginning of Time. The Prophecy tells us that when the straw shall be ripe, it shall be cut with the Spear and that the Spear shall be wielded by the Child."

Senzangakona lowered his gaze, Mkabayi's words swirling round him in a vortex that seemed to fashion itself into the quiescent crater of a volcano, its abyss glowing brightly, enchantingly, in a trapped stillness, - as on the eve of its eruption.

"The New Order, the Rebirth that Shaka heralds is not evil, my brother." Mkabayi's voice dropped to an eerie whisper. "It is our destiny.

CHAPTER XIII
"UKUQALWA"(AGGRESSION)
SEASON OF UNYAKA (SUMMER, 1802)

Nzobo kaMpepha had come in the heart of the night with a group of ruffians. Holding their torches high, they had furtively intruded upon the stillness of the homestead where Mfunda, Nandi, Shaka and little Nomcoba had found well-earned slumber after a long day of toiling in the nearby field where a small crop of grain marked all that the tiny family had to depend upon in the face of the famine's onslaught.

The group had silently spread out and, upon Nzobo's wave of the hand, they had touched the torches to the dry thatching of the huts, to the straw palisades of the cattlefold and, finally, to the tender grain rippling in the night.

As the flames had swept through their homestead, Shaka had clutched his spear and gently rebutted Mfunda's restraining hand with a calm yet resolute, "They think we are victims, Grandmother. It is time they learned that we know how to kill." And he had strode off, through the flames, to execute - in the way of Nature - the verdict of Justice. Justice only! Nothing was further from his thoughts than such a fruitless thing as revenge. Justice. It was his duty, he felt, that it should be done - and by his own hand, the hand of the family's only male.

"Nzobo kaMpepha!" he had cried out in the night as if the name personified all the hatred the Langeni Villagers harboured for the outcasts.

Nzobo kaMpepha: Shaka was now ready to claim his first human kill.

"Nzobo kaMpepha!"

The belligerent call roused the members of Mpepha's homestead who stirred, the sleep still buzzing in their hazed minds, and scurried from their huts to the sloping summit of the cattlefold where they stopped to peer, startled and bemused, at the imposing figure framed in the gates of the residence, arms akimbo, his majestic body washed blue and glistening in the light of the moon.

"Nzobo kaMpepha," Shaka repeated, lowering his powerful voice. He was smiling now, yet the steely glitter in his feline eyes conveyed no pleasure. "My body is soiled with the charred ruins of my home," Shaka commented, evenly, gazing down at his muscular chest streaked and smudged with the black of coal and ashes. "I have come to wash it in your blood."

Tightening his grasp on his assegai, Shaka strode into the Langeni homestead, shoulders back, his figure tall, with an appearance and bearing both masterful and arresting, his beautiful features graced with an ascetic austerity and a fixity of purpose suggesting a grown man,- not a boy of barely fourteen.

Nzobo, close to seventeen years of age considerably bigger than Shaka, parried the challenge with a smile of his own, thin, sardonic, self-assured, his eyes blunted with stolid unconcern. By way of an answer, Nzobo neared a cluster of spears propped against the fold's palisade. Reaching down, the Langeni youth snatched up one of the weapons and weighed it in his hand as, eyes locked on Shaka, he moved to close the gap between himself and his younger opponent.

"Stop them, Mpepha," Nzobo's mother urged her husband with an anxious plea.

"No," was Mpepha's reply as he, too, reached for an assegai and shifted his threatening gaze to the arrogant intruder. "It's time we were rid of that whore's bastard."

The mordant resolve of Mpepha's statement reflected a bitterness that was prevalent in all the members of his homestead as they gathered round the two youths cheering excited in favour of Nzobo as he and Shaka circled each other, spears flashing in the moonlight, eyes locked, muscles coiled and ready to strike.

Nzobo lunged. Anticipating the move, Shaka parried easily, their spears crossing, the hafts crashing in the thick sound of wood against wood. Taking advantage of his greater bulk and size, Nzobo abruptly thrust forward, catching Shaka off-balance, propelling him back against a pile of earthen pots which shattered beneath the boy's weight as he fell to the ground causing the sharp, jagged shards to cut painfully into his flesh.

Laughing at Shaka's prone figure sprawled in the midst of the crockery, the Langeni spectators - which seemed to be growing in number as nearby homesteads were awakened and their sleepy, bewildered inhabitants gravitated to the site of the combat - renewed their boisterous goading, encouraging Nzobo to dispense with the unwanted "whore's bastard" in due haste. One of the on-lookers punctuated his verbal rallying by handing Nzobo a shield which the boy readily grasped against his sturdy left forearm.

Impervious to the current of public opinion which was plainly flowing against him - indeed, quite accustomed to it, it would seem - Shaka was alive only to the concentration and keen-witted assessment so vital to one who takes the battle to heart and he hitched himself to his feet, his eyes wide, trained on the Langeni, his commitment to victory heightened by the loud jeering that flooded round the cattle enclosure in which he was pitted against a rival almost twice his size. Once again the two boy's circled, Nzobo fully armed now and quite confident of his ability to secure a quick and lasting subjugation of his opponent thus winning the hearts of his clansmen and popularity.

Shaka jabbed with his spear, yet his attack somehow lacked conviction, and Nzobo had no trouble swatting his adversary's weapon aside with a sweep of his shield. Then doubling back with his sweeping gesture, he caught Shaka on the side of the body, driving the lighter boy backwards, through the twisted fig branches of the stockade and onto the grimy turf saturated with mud and dung.

Again the small crowd hugging the fold laughed in amusement, thoroughly enjoying Shaka's humiliation. Even Mpepha was smiling now, the spear limp in his hand at the certainty that his son was well in control of the fight.

And, while those around him were engrossed in their laughter, Shaka took advantage of their distraction and allowed his thoughts to race freely, analyzing the combat and his own failings in an attempt to rectify his seemingly inferior position. As usual, his mind probed his experience, and his inner analytical scrutiny snagged on the effectiveness of close combat in the animal kingdom, especially when a smaller, yet more aggressive creature is matched in mortal duel with a larger beast, and the boy started the rough mental sketch of a battle strategy...

Close combat. Rule One: Avoid fighting at an arm's reach, especially when your own arms are shorter than your opponents.

Knitting his brow, Shaka's eyes bent upon the spear in his hands. Something was wrong with the haft, he considered. It was long, too long. Longer than his own arm, and, what's worse, longer than his opponent's arm.

Close combat. Rule two: The blade is what an assegai is all about, Shaka reminded himself. Not the haft!

Close combat means keep close to the blade! If the haft gets in the way, then....

Gripping the spear's wooden handle in both hands, Shaka broke it over his knee and smiled at the confortable feel of the shorter weapon, his hand a mere inch or two from the cold metal shoulder of the blade.

Misunderstanding, surprised by Shaka's gestures, Nzobo teased. "What? Giving up so soon? - I was just starting to enjoy myself!"

As Nzobo's words unleashed another burst of amusement, Shaka rose to his feet and advanced on his opponent, his shortened weapon held in his hand like a dagger of sorts, blade thrust forward as if to stab.

Nzobo's eyes narrowed in suspicion as he peered at the odd weapon in his opponent's hand, as Shaka moved deftly towards the Langeni, his confidence mounting, his own tone laced with amusement and jeering as he beckoned him like a hunter would his prey. "Kehli...Kehli...," Shaka taunted. "Tubu. Tubuuu..."

Irked by Shaka's awesome grin and the disturbing glint in his catlike eyes, Nzobo furiously launched in to the other boy. But Shaka was quicker, agilely darting to the side, easily parrying the other's attack. Then, finding a gap between Nzobo's spear and shield, Shaka lashed out with his weapon, its blade finding flesh and cutting a gash on Nzobo's flank.

Pleased with the experiment, Shaka nodded to himself, musing -- close combat; rule three: move in close, inside your opponent's grasp, within his barrier of defense, exposing his bare chest to the thrust of your blade.

Feeling the sharp pain on his side, Nzobo gave a startled cry and stared at his wound in disbelief - as if it had appeared miraculously, his eyes widening in anger and astonishment as they darted back to Shaka, overwhelmed by the speed and perfect execution of the younger boy's bloody assault. Mpepha tightened his grip on his assegai, ready to come to his son's aid, yet still holding back out of respect for the boy's pride.

Furious now, Nzobo lunged at Shaka, repeatedly, blindly, yet his long, unwieldy spear failed to purchase ground in the constraint of close combat. As a feeling of enjoyment tingled throughout his athletic frame, Shaka dueled with his partner, easily in control now, waiting for the moment to strike. It came when Nzobo thrust forward with his spear, missing his target, sweeping past Shaka who instinctively bent over and clipped the taller boy's legs, sending him toppling to the ground.

Close combat. Rule four: Balance and Leverage are everything. Master them and you become the Master of The Kill -- no matter how formidable the odds.

In an instant Shaka was on top of Nzobo, his knee over the Langeni's neck, choking him, pinning him to the ground. Mpepha cried out in anguish, not daring to hurl his assegai for fear of killing his own son. As he and his clansmen looked on helplessly, Shaka brought the blade of his assegai to Nzobo's chest, the point hovering over the heart, ready to silence forever its cadenced beating, ready to taste, for the first time, The Kill in a human...

"Shaka, no!"

Mfunda's voice rang out! A sudden stillness pervaded Mpepha's homestead as Mfunda's cry was echoed upon the electrified faces of all present, dispelling with its urgency the taint of death that hung ominously in the air.

Chilled by his grandmother's command, Shaka's gaze leapt from the frightened countenance of the figure he held pinned to the turf to the old woman who moved purposefully into the homestead and strode past the searching stares of the onlookers towards her daughter's son. "Let him go!" She commanded in a tone that demanded obedience.

Mfunda's then glimpsed the assegai in Mpehpa's grip. "I'm just in the nick of time, I see." She voiced her contempt for the man.

"The honor of my homestead has been challenged," Mpepha retorted. "It is in the tradition of our family that my son respond to that challenge."

"Is it also in the tradition of your family that your son destroy the hard work of a couple of helpless women?" And seeing that the man had no idea what she was referring to, Mfunda quickly added: "Some one burned our crops tonight, Mpepha. The fruit of a year's work. All the food we had to get us through the seasons to come. And we have every good reason to believe that some one was was your son, Nzobo."

Mpepha's astounded gaze darted to a distance hillock where a curtain of billowing smoke shrouded the bluish glare of the moon. Momentarily petrified by the sight and its implications, the man passed a hand cautiously over his dark hair, as if he were not quite familiar with it, before casting a piercing sidelong glance at the figure of his son.

"Is that true, Nzobo?" he demanded in a gruff voice.

By way of an answer, Nzobo bowed his head, pressing his bloodstained hand against the gaping wound on his flank.

"Is it true?!" Mpepha roared, punctuating his anger by sinking his spear deep into the red earth at his feet.

"Yes, Father," was the murmured reply.

Mpepha's head jerked to the side, a reflex born of a spasm of choler. "Shaka," he deliberated in a hollow voice, barely hesitating to think, "take six of my best cattle and lead them back to your homestead." Then, raising his head as if taking the starry night to witness: "I apologize, Mfunda...For my son."

Nzobo sensed the agony, the wrath in his father's apology, and the boy's lips pursed into a narrow line, his eyes shifting to Shaka, the fixity of his fierce gaze raging with an avenging tempest that had in it the germ of unreasoning violence.

Perched on the low, drooping branch of the mopani tree, Nomcoba watched the elephant herd with entrancement and the tingle of delight. At almost nine years of age now, the girl had finally overcome her original trepidation caused by the monstrous size of the beasts and had grown to become aware of the endearing bond that seemed to unite all the members of the herd. To her they began to seem almost human - especially since Nomcoba's relationship with the animal kingdom had been in the most part affected by Shaka's own endearing bond with Creation - a biased outlook in which, as a rule, animals were preferred to Man.

Seated next to his sister, his arm, etched with a fine definition of sinewy sheaths of muscle, curled affectionately round her shoulders, Shaka reflected upon the massive bulk of the patriarch bull elephant. Ever crotchety with the gnawing pain of his arthritic joints, the bull drank noisily from the waters of the nearby pond, shallowed by the drought's poverty of rainfall, trumpeting with pleasure as he arched back his trunk, squirting the muddy water down his throat and slapping the oozing grime on to his dusty grey head. As a further sign of the civilty and instinctive mutual regard that distinguishes the animal kingdom, Shaka pointed out to his sister that the herd treated the revered patriarch with due respect, leaving one side of the pool for him alone. The respect due to the Wise Man and the King, the King of Kings, he told Nomcoba, the Great Bull Elephant, the Respected Lord of All Animals who lives on the side of life reserved for him alone.

"Alone," Shaka repeated, his gaze drifting to the opposite side of the pool where the cows drank and bathed, and the young calves, looking like fattened, wriggling pigs, cavorted round their mothers' legs and under their bellies, trunks entwined in a loving embrace.

"Alone," Shaka murmured once more, his arm tightening round Nomcoba's shoulders.

"When will mother be a queen?" she asked, somewhat incongruously.

"She already is a queen, Nomcoba," Shaka retorted, a thin smile gracing his lips, his eyes twinkling with love and devotion. "The Queen of Queens. The Great Female Elephant. And soon - as soon as I'm old enough - she'll have her own throne, and people will flock from miles around to bow at her feet and bring her gifts."

Nomcoba smiled at the image presented to her mind as she rested her head on her brother's broad shoulder, - when suddenly she felt his muscles tense under her touch.

"What is it, Shaka?" she inquired, her gaze following his to the herd, which was now shuffling nervously, trunks raised, ears distended forward to catch the wind and the sounds of which it was a messenger.

"They sense something. - Danger." The boy noted as his eyes turned to scan the surroundings.

When he saw them, he felt his blood charging with adrenalin, the heat of it spreading down his limbs, his mouth drying. "Run, Nomcoba," he hissed with urgency. "Run!"

Alarmed, the girl's wide, unblinking gaze fell on Nzobo and a dozen or more older boys. The group was advancing towards them, the smiles they wore, the sparkle in their eyes, the hefty sticks clutched in their fists evincing the hatred that welled in their hearts.

"Run!!" Shaka shouted, and Nomcoba leapt down from the branch and tried to flee, only to find herself imprisoned in Nzobo's vicelike grip.

"No," scowled the son of Mpepha with mock ferocity, savouring the moment. "I want her to see this."

Slowly, like a cat slinking down from its lofty perch, Shaka eased off the branch and lowered himself onto the soft, grimy soil that delimited the pond.

Sensing the brooding violence of the upcoming conflict, the patriarch bull elephant heaved himself upright and, glistening with mud, his trunk swinging before him with the reliable cadence of a century-old metronome, strode away into the woodlands, his bloated, water-filled belly rumbling in a silent command. Obediently the rest of the herd trooped off after its Lord.

Eyes locked on his opponents, Shaka moved towards the group of Langeni boys and watched them spread out, surrounding him. Nzobo transferred Nomcoba's writhing body into the clutches of a companion and, weighing the stick in his hands, readied himself.

Snatching at the advantage of surprise, Shaka suddenly charged, ducking under Nzobo's stick, hitting the Langeni in the ribs with his shoulder as he came up off his bent knees. Nzobo expelled a gust of air and struggled to regain the breath that had been driven out of him, as Shaka whipped his arm around the back of his neck. Instead of resisting, Nzobo put all his weight into the direction of Shaka's pull. The two boys cart-wheeled onto the ground, their arms locked, chest to chest, their breathing hissing into each other's faces as they tumbled onto the oozing mud and into the murky waters of the pond. They rolled and Nzobo came up on top, straddling Shaka, his hands cupped over the younger boy's face, holding it under the pool's surface with the full weight of his body. His lungs screaming for air, Shaka's arms flailed in the water, his hands struggling to purchase a hold on the slime and muck in which he floundered, trapped under Nzobo's bulky frame.

Suddenly Nzobo felt Shaka's body fall limp, lifeless. Grinning at his comrades with satisfaction, the Langeni loosened his grip, ever so slightly - yet just enough for Shaka to break free, rising out of the water like a fish sprung from Hell, rearing back on his shoulders and bucking forward, butting the top of his head against Nzobo's mouth.

A tortured groan was wrenched from the Langeni's throat as one of his incisors was snapped off at the gum, his mouth glutting with a flow of deep crimson. Nzobo drooped over backwards, onto the muddy bank, and lay stunned, as Shaka quickly fell on top of him and reached for his unprotected throat with both hands. Finding the ligatures of muscle girding the pointed hard lump of the thyroid cartilage, Shaka drove his thumbs into the base of the muscle, yanking back with such force that Nzobo uttered a rumbling, tortured moan as the mucus and saliva gurgled spasmodically in his trachea. Shaka continued to pull back the muscular casing round the larynx, stretching the ligatures to the point of snapping...

...when the blow, hard and stinging, glanced off his ear, numbing one side of his face, deadening it with a dull, flashing pain that raced down his neck to his shoulder. Shaka staggered slightly, his fingers still curled round Nzobo's carotid. The next blow caught him across the bridge of the nose, the jagged bark of the stick crunching against his cheekbone, splitting the flesh. Feeling his hands grow weak, as if they had abruptly been drained of all strength, the boy slumped onto his side, his fingers instinctively moving to the throbbing wound on his face, touching the warm, sticky coating of blood that oozed down his cheek.

The rest of the blows came in a continuous barrage that assailed his body without respite - striking him on the chest, the legs, the arms, the stomach, the groin. He felt vomit rise and scald the back of his throat, yet, resisting with a courage that was embedded deep within his spirit, on the level of the subliminal, Shaka swallowed back the vomit and clung to consciousness with all his remaining strength, struggling to not slip over the edge into the black void of oblivion. Focusing his mind on the distant, muted sound of Nomcoba's hysterical sobbing, in an attempt to hold on to wakefulness, Shaka's soul reached out for his sister's voice and he tried to open his eyes, now swollen and caked with blood, in an effort to see her.

Yet the force of another stinging impact exploded below Shaka's eye; a heavy blow that jarred his chin causing his teeth to clash together and to bite through his own tongue. The last sensation of which he was aware was of the blood filling his mouth - as darkness mercifully took him in its embrace.

Later, as Nandi and Nomcoba looked on with helpless apprehension, and as Mfunda toiled in the half-gutted, scorched shell that was the remnant of her hut doctoring Shaka's wounds with herbs and poultices, the boy felt himself resurfacing to wakefulness, a flash of pain sweeping through him as full consciousness returned.

    Discerning the dancing flicker of the hearth's fire through the narrow slits of his tumescent eyelids, groping, Shaka reached out and found his mother's hand. Squeezing it, his bruised lips, caked with dark crusts of blood, trembled and moved, his voice choking and spasmodic as the pulpy flesh of his swollen tongue formed the words: "Mercy is the trait of Victims, mother. - Never again---!" His squeezing was suddenly laced with urgency. "Never again will I leave an enemy behind!"

CHAPTER XIV
"HAMBA KAHLE"(GO WELL)

"Next time, - if you allow there to be a next time, they will kill him, Nandi."

Makedama's face was taut and his eyes heavy, like those of a man weighed down with some great anxiety. Having barely turned twenty-eight, the son of Mbenghi of the Langeni had recently inherited, at the death of his father, a throne made cumbersome by a Famine named Madlatule and a female named Nandi - both quite out of control.

As Makedama gazed at her alert greenish-brown eyes, ever wise and shrewd, missing nothing, at her features somewhat lined and scored by the years of suffering, yet ever magnificent in a beauty, the Langeni king found it difficult to add: "They see you and your family as the enemy. They think you have bewitched their land."

Nandi laughed lightly, and in the gloom of Makedama's words, this flash of joyous sound was incongruous and somewhat chilling. The treachery of Man and of the intricate web of Man's social structures, narrow-minded, reclusive, discriminating, had long ceased to surprise the woman;-- very little, in fact, surprised her anymore, and, with her very characteristic brand of cynicism, she had come to expect the worst from people. Indeed, in Nandi's heart the initial shock and the pain of Senzangakona's betrayal had been swiftly replaced by a simmering anger of gelid ferocity; and, during the long, extraordinarily hard period of the last nine years (a period in which she was forced to provide for a family of four - almost single-handedly, fulfilling the role of both mother and father for two growing children), that anger had been honed into her own (and subsequently Shaka's) avenging need to survive - a need that went beyond sentiment and emotion into the realm of vaunting ambition. As Nandi had constantly reminded her son throughout his formative years, everything they owned would have to be hard won, the fruit of a life rooted in single-mindedness of design, gruelling work and relentless sacrifice.

It was that fixity of purpose that her mouth settled into its familiar resolute lines and she finally retorted to her king, the corners of her smile still lingering on her lips: "I have been held responsible for quite a few things in my life, Nkosi, but never anything as eventful as a famine!"

Makedama found himself smiling at the remark as Nandi's own expression grew serious, etched with bitterness and scorn. "But I suppose it was to be expected, Nkosi," she mused out loud, sharing her bitter thoughts with her king. "What else could their superstitious minds tell them? Their envy blinds them; they are made deaf and dumb by their mediocrity. Ever since we returned here, my family and I have been seen as the cause of all their woes, but -- after all..." her lips contorted with contempt, "who is better suited than a...'witch' to be their scapegoat?"

Makedama sat silently, looking at the woman he had known and looked upon with great affection since childhood.

"But we have survived, Nkosi, in spite of their hatred and ridicule," Nandi continued, rendering the tide of Makedama's pity all the more painful to bear. "We have survived, and that makes them feel very uncomfortable. They have to be rid of us - we are the reflection of their weakness."

'Weakness', Makedama mused. How foreign that word sounded on her lips.

"As soon as possible," the king sighed gravely. "For your own good," his voice dwindled to whispering sadness. "There's no telling what people might do when the hunger really starts to madden their minds."

Their eyes met again in silence, interlocutory.

"It is not a decision I make lightly, Nandi. Remember that. I have always admired you. Always. If you didn't like the way things were, you tried to change them. An enviable quality, yet one that - in a woman – is not only unique, but preposterous!" His lips wore a gentle smile that vanished in the wake of his confession: "But no matter what I personally may think, I am king now and I have become the tool of my subjects, and though my heart might rail against a decision that may well be the fruit of their - 'mediocrity', I am bound by the pathos of my position."

"Then let me make your position easier, Nkosi. We shall leave as soon as possible."

Makedama was conscious of the relief he felt at Nandi's decision. He was also aware of a pang of guilt, which caused him to suggest: "Your mother may stay here, if she'd like. In my homestead. - She may be too old to travel."

Nandi was deeply moved by Makedama's generosity, a most unusual commodity in a world that, for her, seemed to harbour only hostility. Yet the idea of Mfunda remaining behind, far from her grandson's side, was hard to conceive, especially in the light of the recent past. "Thank you, Baba," she murmured by way of answer to Makedama's generous offer, her glance resting fondly on her king. "But I think my mother wants to stay near Shaka. As a salutary influence. I think she's afraid that without her proper guidance, he'll turn out to be like me:-- a misfit."

They both laughed at the remark, a peal of tense laughter born quickly to veil their mutual embarrassment and soon stifled by the suffocating uneasiness of a forced farewell.

"Sala kahle, Baba," Nandi bowed to her king.

"Hamba kahle, Nandi," Makedama sadly replied. "Go well. Go in peace..."

It was in response to a need for Peace, her soul's demand for a settling of accounts, Nandi returned to the site of her encounters with Senzangakona on the banks of the Mkumbane, where her gaze reached out for the river's churning waters, caressing them, and her eyes sought and found the place where she had gone to fetch water, so long - so very long ago.

Softly padding to the bank, she bent down as she had then, scooping up the crystal clear water in a fond embrace. With a quizzical smile she realised that her hands were trembling with excitement, as she found herself lifting her gaze and beholding his image as it emerged from the Past on the spot where she had first seen him, a strapping young man with a disarming smile, his body wet with rain, a leopard slung over his power- ful shoulders.

Closing her eyes, forcing the lids shut tightly, Nandi splashed water on her face in an effort to dispel the image, and with it the drowning maelstrom of impressions it evoked. Yet when her eyes opened once more, her attention was gravitated to her own reflection on the water's surface and, appearing behind it, she saw the reflection of Senzangakona - exactly as she had seen it so many years before. The man gently curled his brawny arms round her waist, pressing her body against his own, softly kissing her neck.

And Nandi allowed herself to flow with the tide of those sensations, until, with a chilling certainty, she realised that the reflection and the touch were real, that the vision from the Past was present. Gasping, the woman struggled in his arms, breaking free from his embrace, turning to face him.

They stared at each other in profound stillness, with astounded, searching eyes, with eyes maddened by the memories of things far off, lost in the currents of Time. His gaze, dulled by age and sorrow, by concern, looked closely into hers, and she met the deepened expression of his solitude with a look so steady it caused him to catch his breath in a pang of profound disconcertion. In an instant, she saw the night of his soul, and its workings, simple and violent, were laid bare before her with a disturbing charm that aroused her desire.

He reached out again and took her in his embrace, his whispered words choked with emotion: "I was told you were leaving and I came here, day after day, hoping - knowing I would see you. - You are still as beautiful as ever. No--. More beautiful!"

She shivered under his burning touch and tried to suppress the flash of heat that gripped her craving body - her flesh which had so long been denied sensual fulfilment. She was ripe, over-ripe for love, and her loneliness was a hunger so intense that it seemed it could never be assuaged. As his passion ignited her own, she gave way to her hunger with a lustful moan and melted into his arms. And though her eyes remained open, there was no sun in the sky and no gleam on the water; there was no horizon, no outline, no shape for the eye to rest upon, nothing for the hand to grasp - an obscurity without limit in Space and Time that seemed to submerge the Universe like an overwhelming deluge.

Later - when the hunger was spent and reason returned - they laid side by side, on the banks of the Mkum- bane, silently gazing into its waters, their senses emptied, dulled, silenced, shied in the wake of Desire's abatement. Breaking the spell of their craving for one another - a tingling which still lingered on their raw flesh, Senzangakona sat up and cast a stone into the water, his attention captured by the concentrical ripples splayed by its fall.

"Tell me about him, Nandi," he finally said, after a long pause.

Watching the ripples fretting over the water's surface, dispelling the stone's mark on the river, Nandi answered him, speaking softly, in an uncanny whisper, well aware that her words, like the ripples, would dispel the magic of the moment they had just enjoyed together. "He's not like you," she started, her vengeance mounting. "I've searched his heart for some fragment of the man I once loved - but there is none, not anymore."

Not anymore.

The ripples were gone now, and the surface of the beloved Mkumbane had ironed out to match the sombre expression of the Zulu king as he listened -- barely breathing.

"He is still a boy," Nandi went on, "yet his pride is greater than that of any grown man. He has dedication, the courage of a lion, and a strong nature, wild and free, unfettered by tradition. And he is loyal - as loyal as any mother could wish."

And as he listened - barely breathing - his heart torn asunder, Senzangakona saw it all,--he saw it in himself: the past, the future, all of it, shifting and indistinct like the shapes the eye sees when the spirit takes leave of itself.

"And his mind is sharp, as sharp as the blade of his assegai. He is swift in making decisions and fearless in carrying out his resolutions. His body is of iron and his beauty that of a leopard. And his love - like mine - is as great as his hatred."

Senzangakona turned to find that her eyes were on him, her gaze distant - her soul once again...beyond his reach.

She rose and started off, away from the banks of the Mkumbane, away from him, and as she strode off it seemed to the King of the Zulus that he was saying good-bye to all the world, that he was taking a last leave of his own self, and the sudden and violent impact of her departure clutched at his entire being scarring it with deep agony, - a pain both physical and spiritual which left him throbbing in the pit of his being.

Reaching the top of the hill, Nandi turned and looked back. Her eyes met his and he realised that he had never seen her before. There had always been too many things, to many thoughts, to many people. - Never. He had never seen her. But now the world was dead, and all was gone, and she was there for him to see.

Fleeing from her gelid look like from the cold white glare of lightning, Senzangakona turned away from Nandi in a bid to regain possession of himself, his old self which had things to do, words to speak as well as to hear - the self which must live on. Yet he felt only an immensity of contradictions, of delight, of dread, exultation and despair, of a life that could not be faced and yet was not to be avoided:- of a life without her.

When he looked back, she was gone.

"Nandi!" the cry came from the bottom of his heart and flew out into the world through lips parted in agony

Beyond the hill, Nandi heard her name rend the Heavens, causing the sky above her to colour the deep crimson of blood. She sank to her knees and remained still, very still, her hands clasping her ankles, her head resting on her knees. And her mind was thinking of him, of the days of their youth, of the moments of their joy, of their life and of their passion; and she thought of all that had been their love and she wept for what could have been.

And wept.

The tears of those who mourn over the dead next to the grave they have dug for themselves.

CHAPTER XV
"MADLATULE" ("LET ONE EAT WHAT ONE CAN AND SAY NAUGHT")

The land lay silent, still, and golden under the deluge of scorching rays that seemed flung down from the serenity of the Heavens like the assegais of a crazed hunter - rays that dulled all sound and all motion, that buried all shadows, that choked every breath.

No voice was heard in the stillness of day, save for the faint murmur of the wind that swirled and eddied in the loose, powdery soil. No motion was set against the blazing sky, save for the lone figures of four outcasts wandering across the arid countryside like the indistinct procession of thoughts that grip the soul upon awakening from a nightmare.

Like a mirage projected on curtains of rising heat, the outlines of the four figures quivered against the vault of the horizon where the saffron textures of arid land were one with the whiteness of the sky. The outcasts moved silently, each coping in his or her own way with the hardships of the journey: Shaka, his athletic, perfectly-trained physique easily contending with the hazards of the trek and the weight of the pack of meagre belongings which he carried strapped to his broad back along with a bundle of gleaming assegais; Nandi, stoic, her crusted lips pursed with unflinching resolve, her exhaustion kindling the fire of her undying vigour and drive; Nomcoba, weary, holding Shaka's hand, needing his strength to carry on; Mfunda, drained, pushing her body beyond the natural limits set by her age.

Well knowing that to all intents and purposes he was the 'man' now, that the safety of his small family unit depended largely upon his own strength and resourceful- ness, Shaka was greatly stimulated by this burden of responsibility, his soul basking in the exhilaration of leadership. As he peered through narrowed eyes at the sun's blinding glare reflected on the barren landscape and as his gaze took in the great expanses seared by the heat, the arid bushes and trees, shriveled, desiccated, as he felt the hot winds howling across the land carrying misery in their wake, Shaka sensed deep within his spirit that the challenge of survival was made sweeter by the nearness of Death, and that the closer Death came, the less he feared it.

And its nearness was irrefutable. As was their despair.

The hours and days of wandering transpired with no known course, no definite goal, no hope save for the delusions conjured by the mind's unremitting resilience.

They journeyed in solitude, over vast stretches of wilting grasslands framed in the immensity of a cloud- less sky, across rocky promontories and jagged ravines that cut into the bare flesh of their feet and hands, under the scourge of the sun at its zenith that greedily sucked precious moisture from their bodies, over forsaken terrains that wore the disturbing taint of graveyards.

It seemed to them that the whole world was deserted as they alone walked on and on, their paths untraversed by the paths of others; and the men they did meet passed by them in silent search of food and survival, - walking slow, unsmiling, with downcast eyes, as if the melancholy of an overburdened earth had weighted their feet, bowed their shoulders, borne down their glances.

And the animals they met had the burnt odour of the stale, dying earth: lions, sick and starving, their ribs racked out under scraggy hide; winged creatures soaring across the phosphorescent globe of the sun fleeing East towards the ocean in search of rain; zebra and giraffe, elephant and wildebeest, in forlorn herds that, oblivious of man, roamed the land for water like ghosts haunting the realm of the living in quest of eternal peace. Yet there was no sign of the symbol of Zulu, the mighty leopard, almost as if, in its monumental pride, the august feline had favoured withdrawing from the world to suffer under cover, in the seclusion noble beasts seek when Death stalks them.

And Death was stalking everywhere.

And when the late evening shadows turned the plains a soft mauve giving definition to the land so that the low hillocks emerged from the glare of the day and the glassy curtains of heat magnified and distorted the globe of the sun as it melted into the horizon, -- when the heat withdrew to night, the noble wanderers reached the gates of a lone homestead, one of many they had visited in the course of their nomadic wayfaring. As elsewhere, here, too, their request for food and shelter was greeted by the merciless litany of the famine: - there was nothing to eat, they were told by the wispy old man who peered at them from hollowed orbs; nothing at all, he told them, his hushed whisper barely rising above the chilling notes of a distant dirge, nothing to find except hunger, disease and death.

Yet, as Time and Space and white sunlight mingled and became one, the four pushed on, their nerve and endurance riding the crest of a Destiny that would want them to survive. They ate tubers and the thorny iMfino herb which pricked their tongues already swollen and parched with desiccation, they ground umCaba maize and fed themselves on the bitter leaves of the iNtshungu plant, they skinned lizards and snakes and chewed their sticky, revolting flesh being careful not to vomit lest they should lose precious body fluids; and they sucked the sparse juice of the acacia gum and the isiGwamba plant, the ama-hluke lily and the uboqo root -- and they survived.

Miraculously. And like the birds of the air, the outcasts were drawn eastward, along the tortuous, thirsty river-bed of the once mighty Mfolozi, past the territories of the Ntombela tribe and the Zungu, over the uPate Plains, past the lands of the Sibiya, the Mpanza, the Dludla and the Cambini, scaling the majestic eNtsangoyana Mountains into the flatlands of the Mkawanazi clan, the Nzimeleni and the Nxele, through the iDukuduku Forest and the ter- ritories of the Ntolozi and the Sokulu, on towards the Indian Ocean. But no clan would give them refuge; no tribe had a place in its womb for the Son of Zulu, for the Child and his family...

...and the Child, the "Sacred Sovereign of whom the Ancestors spoke when they sang to the Wind" would pre- serve the memory of this impudence and avidity of his fellow Nguni Bantu; he would preserve it forever! Not out of a need for revenge. Merely Justice.

Then, on the last eve of the seventh month, when the sun had mercifully sunk behind the hills, and the shades of the evening had deepened over the land, the tortured body of Mfunda could take no more, and the old woman collapsed into Shaka's arms; and as the boy hugged her close, he felt her ribs grating at his chest, and the feeble pulsing of her heart beneath the flaccid folds of her breast augured the advent of the imponderable - the Child's companion, Death.

Under the apprehensive gazes of Nandi and Nomcoba, Shaka carried the limp, emaciated frame of the proud matron to the shadows of a twisted thorn tree and rested her on the dusty ground. Holding a tuber to her parched, cracked lips he squeezed from it a film of acrid moisture which stung the scabs on Mfunda's tongue as it oozed down her scalding throat. Closing her eyes, the old woman slumped into a lifeless state, distinguishable from death only by the presence of laboured, raspy breathing.

"She can't take much more of this," Nandi whispered as she gazed at her mother, her own exhaustion manifest on features drawn taut by inhuman exertion. ""We must find a place to stay. At least for a while."

Shaka's mind was racing as he started to gather kindling wood and dry grass, igniting the campfire with a spark of flint struck against hard stone. Fanning the spark to life, he considered out loud: "That's almost impossible, mother. You know that as well as I. Sooner or later we're going to have to face that the famine is everywhere and we'll never outdistance it. There are no crops, no grazing ground, no game worth hunting, and no village that will make the sacrifice of taking on four extra mouths to feed. You've seen what's happened, mother. Even if we offer to work for our keep, our labour means nothing if the land is sterile. - We must find another way." Nandi's steady gaze met her son's and locked.

"I've been thinking, mother," Shaka went on. "Our chances might be better if we separated."

Nomcoba was stunned by the remark, the thought of being separated from her mother and Shaka leaving her momentarily stunned.

"The induna I spoke with at the last homestead would be willing to take grandmother," the boy said in a con- sequential way, as if the decision had already been made. "And we could leave Nomcoba at one of the next villages, and you and I could continue south. Then, when the famine is over, and the rains return..."

"No!" came Mfunda's eerie rebuttal riding the sharp edge of urgency. "We are a family! A...family!" When her tortured lungs filled again, the uncanny voice returned with: "No matter what happens, we must stay united! We have fought too hard and too long for our identity to loose it now!"

"Family," Shaka silently mouthed the word, sensing how odd, how unfamiliar it felt on his lips. Looking away from his grandmother, Shaka's face turned to gaze pensively beyond a smattering of sandy hillocks to the Indian Ocean, the measureless expanse of smooth water that lay sparkling before him like a floor of jewels, brilliant, vast, and as empty as the slate-grey sky - as empty as the word "family".

In that very instant, not far away, in the land of the Mtetwas, south of the eNtseleni River and east of eNkwenkwe Hill, another face - wrinkled, thin, aged - was also contemplating the vastness of the Indian Ocean and the validity of man's allegiance to those he calls his "family". King Jobe, tall, powerful, his piercing eyes alive with a glint of youthfulness that belied his advanced years, turned away from the sea's salty breeze and faced his son's critical eye. "Who?" he questioned, incredulous.

"Tana and Godongwana," answered Prince Mawewe, a small, dapper man, with a sharp, abrupt manner and an incisive manner of speech.

Jobe knit his brow in disbelief. "I find that hard to believe, Mawewe. They have always been loyal sons. Why would they now conspire to kill me?"

"Because they have always been loyal sons, Baba," Mawewe retorted, his eloquence swelling as he carefully spun his web. "Remember what you taught us - 'loyalty to the king means wanting what is best for his people'. Un- fortunately that maxim leaves a great deal of room for interpretation and can be easily distorted in the hearts of the ambitious. Tana and Godongwana feel that you are too old to rule in these times of hardship. They feel that the people would best profit if one of them were on your throne in your stead."

Jobe narrowed his eyes. "And what of the people themselves? What have they to say?"

"They are hungry, Baba. It is easy to sway their minds."

The king caught something strange in his son's voice. He was not sure what it was exactly, but it vexed him, anyway. "And you, Mawewe," he inquired of his son testily. "What do you think?"

"As long as the Ancestors give you life, father, our kingdom could have no better ruler," was the pat answer. "What my brothers condemn as senility, I value as wisdom."

"Of course." Jobe agreed, still bothered by the tone of his son's voice. "And what would you suggest I do about this...conspiracy?"

"Nip it in the bud, baba."

"Kill my own flesh?"

"Before it turns against you, my father."

After a pause, a thin smile dawned on Jobe's lips as he regarded his son. "Could it be, Mawewe," the Mtetwa king suggested, "that you, too, have been swayed by - 'hunger'? With your brothers gone, nothing would stand in the way of your taking my place on the throne."

Unwavering, Mawewe met the accusation with a composed, smiling countenance. "Baba, if I truly wanted to be king at the expense of fratricide, I would not betray the conspiracy, I would be its leader."

Their eyes locked. Both smiles faded. Then, rising from his mat near the ocean's salty breath, Jobe turned to look up at the multitude of stars that were appearing against the mantle of night. "Ask Tana and Godongwana to come to me," he ordered his son. "So that I might question them."

"And if they should refuse, father?" was Mawewe's subtle suggestion.

Jobe spun round to face the other man. "It would be proof of their guilt," he shot back, his haggard features clouding over with anger.

Confident that his father's suspicions had been sufficiently aroused against his two brothers, Mawewe hurried off to execute the rest of his ambitious plot. At the prince's bidding, Mtetwa warriors were dispatched to the homesteads of Tana and Godongwana. Officially the guards were ordered to bring the two men before the king - for questioning, they were told. Yet this 'official' version was greatly divorced from the more covert directives Mawewe had earlier imparted upon his own faithful warriors: the secret command that, far from the eyes of witnesses, his brothers, Tana and Godongwana, should attempt to escape from the king's guards (or so it was to appear) and should, as a result, be executed for this apparently treasonous behaviour.

Yet, unbeknownst to Mawewe and men of his stature, Destiny, the irrefutable Mistress of Life's often sinuous Courses, far from ever bending to suit Man's schemes, enfetters Man most in the instant in which Man feels he has outwitted Fate.

Consequently, the prince's plot was unravelled as planned - as planned by Destiny, that is: Tana was killed "attempting to escape"; yet his brother Godongwana, sensing the true conspiracy of the moment, made pretense real by eluding the assassins Mawewe had dispatched and fleeing for his life through the thatched palisades of his homestead into the cover of a moonless night with a barbed assegai sunk deep into his bleeding back.

Accordingly, at the lowly hands of an ambitious knave, Destiny had thus fomented the lustrous Cycle of the Child heralding the Language of the House and Its Glory. The Exile of the Child would coincide with the Wandering of the betrayed Mtetwa, Godongwana, who would be known as "uMafavuke njenge" (he who died and rose again).

Mtetwa: the First Nation of the House, the Furnace at which the Blade would be forged.

The Child was ready for the Encounter sanctioned by Sitayi at the Pinnacle of Kings.

As ordained, the Child followed the call of the Nation "emthabatha lapha liphuma khona (beckoning him from whence the sun rises), emsingisa lapha lishona khona (and leading him to where it sets)".

Life from life, Death to Death -- such is the Way of Masters.

Feeling the smooth haft of his throwing assegai securely clutched in his fist, Shaka's eyes remained riveted on the eland as he padded along the edge of the clearing, moving closer for the kill. Suddenly the boy froze, every muscle, every nerve in his prodigious body pulled taut, perfectly still, only his eyes shifting slowly to gaze at a patch of umbrage spread thinly under the distended limbs of a fig tree.

Unmoving, the leopard faced Shaka at a distance of less then forty paces. She, too, was a big animal, and though she was quite young and lacking in experience, the leopard looked quick and strong, her hide, still clean and unscarred by claw or thorn, glowing in hues of white with buttery-yellow spots sketched onto blotches of black and deep tan.

The two predators, man and leopard, peered at each other, feline eyes locked with a gleam of hunger's rapacity. Ever so slightly, the leopard started swaying her tail from side to side, flicking its white tuft as if swatting at imaginary flies. She then extended her neck and humped her shoulders, lowering her head and opening her jaws so that her long ivory fangs sparkled in the sun's reflected light - and, her emerald eyes still locked on Shaka, the leopard hissed at the boy, a warning to stay clear of her prey.

The eland sensed the antagonism of the two hunters and stood stock-still, its adrenalin buzzing through its slender legs as they bent slightly, poised for flight.

Shaka's adrenalin was also racing as his gaze moved from the cat to the large antelope and back. Then, a thin smile caressing his lips, the boy seemed to withdraw his hunter's bid as he retreated behind a cluster of bushes.

Satisfied that she had won the silent battle with Man, the leopard turned her attention to the eland and crouched low against the earth, the great muscles on her chest and thighs swelling, rigid with tension, her ears cocked. Then, after a seemingly interminable pause, the cat sprang forward, streaking through the air.

The eland threw up its head and erupted into a snorting stampede, a veil of fine dust clinging behind it like a mist.

Yet the leopard was in fast pursuit, soon closing the gap that separated her from her prey. With elegant, even strides, she drew up alongside the eland and hooked expertly at one of its galloping forelegs, clipping it, her yellowed claws sinking deep into the eland's flesh, striking bone.

The antelope dropped in a tumbling heap, somersaulting forward, its legs splayed in the dust, and, like a flash, the leopard swept under its powerful horns and bit hard into the base of the eland's skull, driving her fangs into the spine, crunching the vertebrae and severing the flow of life.

Then the leopard's ravenous snarling was stilled as the cat's startled eyes met Shaka's. The boy aimed carefully, hurling his spear, pegging her proud heart, which burst through her ivory fangs in a splash of scarlet.

That evening, after the tormenting sun had sunk to rest behind the horizon, and as the eland's carcass still roasted over a hearty fire, the family was enjoying the unexpected freshness of returned hope. Having finally eaten their fill, Shaka, Nandi and Nomcoba sat huddled round the open hearth, chatting leisurely, their smiles and the levity of their conversation momentarily dispersing from their spirits the long shadows of past sufferings. Even Mfunda seemed somehow revived as she listened to her daughter and grandchildren, their cheerful mood smoothing away the lines of care and exhaustion that had marred the old woman's features, giving them the semblance of a death mask.

As is the way with hunters, Shaka was soon bragging good-naturedly about his exceptional feat: bagging both an eland and a leopard "with one fling of the spear"- as he put it. "You should've seen the glint in her eye when she realised I had outwitted her," Shaka boasted, running a caressing hand over the leopard's glossy hide as he stretched it taut, scraping the remaining shards of flesh from the underside of its thick skin. "She thought I had given up because that's what I led her to think. And that was her downfall! - She allowed her enemy to do her thinking for her."

All of a sudden an ominous snarl reached them from the unseen recesses of the night, causing the blood to run cold in their veins. Stiffening, Shaka instinctively reached for his assegai as he peered into the darkness and caught the gleam of a single eye glaring back at him. "Move closer to the fire," the boy whispered as his hand closed round the spear. "Slowly. Nothing abrupt."

"What is it, Shaka?" Nomcoba breathed as her heart raced inside her.

"News travels fast," was her brother's ice-cold rejoinder.

As they all looked on, petrified, the gleaming eye moved closer to the flickering light of the fire, becoming a pair of eyes, then - the odious, gnarling muzzle of a wild dog, its teeth bared and glistening with saliva, the smell of the roasting meat and hissing blood driving its hideous soul frantic with the devilry of lingering starvation. As the animal advanced upon the campsite, the silhouettes of other wild dogs were cast against the slate of night as they, too, advanced, their avid growling rending the night's stillness like the fiendish laughter of demons about to feast on the flesh of angels.

Completely unnerved by her sheer blank fright, her pure abstract terror, Nomcoba hunched next to the fire, behind her brother's broad back. Judging the danger in its right proportion, with his usual keen, sanguine temperament, ever-lucid in intent, uncoloured by emotion in purpose and purview, Shaka's eyes strained after the shapes of the beasts, counting them as they circled closer and closer to their quest. One, two, three --- twelve in all. A formidable enemy, he mused.

"Give them what they want, Shaka!" Mfunda hissed, her tone laced with pleading.

"I don't mind sharing, grandmother," Shaka commented with a suggestion of irony in his steady voice. "But first they must earn their prize. As I have."

As the dogs' circles became narrower, Nandi scooped up an assegai and flanked her son, her eyes meeting his and settling in an expression of resolve.

Abruptly, the lead dog made a fearsome snapping sound and rushed forward, flinging itself into the air and onto Shaka's back, missing its hold as the boy swung round, but badly raking him with deep claw marks. Grit- ting his teeth with a fury born of pain, Shaka seized hold of the animal and smashed its head to the ground, quickly dispatching it with a thrust of his blade.

Yet as he turned, two more dogs were upon him. Dodging, Shaka was able to spear one of the beasts, thus freeing both hands to contend with the other. Grabbing the animal by the throat to avoid its slashing teeth, he lifted it off the ground with one hand and, taking hold of its head over the ears, he twisted it round till the spine snapped.

Another of the dogs had launched itself on Nandi. The woman, being no stranger to the use of an assegai, readied to check the beast's assault. Holding the spear in both hands, the projecting blade before her, Nandi lashed out as the dog reached mid-air, ripping open its belly like an over-ripe melon, bringing the screaming animal slamming to the ground in a spray of sticky blood and entrails.

Normally the loss of four of their number would be enough to turn a pack of dogs, yet these hunger-crazed animals were relentless as they contested their right to the succulent carcasses of the eland and the leopard. Side by side, Nandi and Shaka matched the dogs' inexorable attacks with their own seemingly unyielding resources. Three more of the animals were slaughtered, yet the other six persisted in giving battle, snarling and clawing, wild figures in the night, delirious, their abrasive hides staining Shaka's and Nandi's skin, the animals' froth and slime commingling with human sweat and blood. The sanguinary conflict went on with an unnerving crescendo, till -- "No more! No more!" screamed Mfunda hysterically, tearing off a chunk of the eland's roasted meat and hurling it out to the dogs who instantly collected round it, suddenly concentrating their maddened foray on the morsels of tender flesh.

"Enough!" the old woman cried, falling to her knees, panting with exertion as her breathing wheezed in her grief-stricken breast. "Throw it all to them. - Let the beasts have it all and be gone!"

Reluctantly, Shaka shifted his gaze to the remnants of the eland's carcass and, lifting it by the sharpened pole on which it was skewered, the boy flung it out into the night, into the midst of the gnarling pack. Then, as if to make their defeat all the more poignant, Shaka took the skinned body of the leopard by the hind legs and swung it out, away from the campfire, in the direction of their ravenous visitors. The four outcasts sat with bated breaths, listening to the heinous sound of the dogs' feast, the rapacious crunching of bones, the tearing of flesh, the fierce growls that punctuated the beasts' contention of their prize.

Suddenly Nandi started to weep, violent, unconstrained sobs that racked her body in spasms of indistinct mumbling that gradually took shape, becoming an echo of Mfunda's plea: "Enough, Shaka!", Nandi whimpered. "Enough - enough...enough..." she repeated the refrain of gloom, falling forward as if her body were slowly deflating, sinking her head into the hollow of her joined legs.

Shaka curled a strong, consoling arm round his mother, rocking her body close to his own, murmuring words of comfort and hope.

As Mfunda looked at her grandson, her moist eyes saw a boy of barely fifteen giving solace when he himself would need it, taking the place of the father he was never allowed to have; as she now looked at him she tried to think of his childhood, and, as her eyes closed driving the tears down her sunken cheeks, she suddenly realised that he had never had one.

Nomcoba twitched and moaned in her sleep, her delicate spirit troubled by the visions of her nightmares:- those terrifying processions of thought that accompany fear incarnate. Next to her, Mfunda was huddled near the burning embers in a restless state of vigilant repose.

Though the threat of the wild dogs had passed, Shaka remained wide awake, staring out at the night, his mind turning over thoughts, intentions, resolves. Sensing another wakeful presence next to him, Shaka addressed his mother without turning to her, sensing more than seeing her reaction to his words. "Mother," he started in a hushed tone, levelly, "you once spoke to me of a man named Gendeyana of the Ama-Mbedweni - in the land of the Qwabes."

Feeling a sudden tightening at her back, Nandi squared her shoulders and rode forward on her haunches, her body tingling with the sting of remembrance. The mention of Gendeyana, the meek suitor of her past who, in the words of her father, Bhebhe, had had "truly loved her", brought a rush of memories; and with them came sorrow riding on the crest of a lover's regret.

"You said he loved you," Shaka went on, coldly analytical, as if, for him, the whims of love could be made to serve a rational purpose. "You said he wanted to marry you before you met..." reluctant to mention his father, Shaka interrupted the thought, ending with a curt: "Is that true?"

"That...that was a long time ago, Shaka," Nandi found the voice to answer.

"A long time?" Shaka repeated, finally turning to face her, adding with a furrow of his brow. "Do you think he would remember?"

Nandi stared at her son - long and hard, a searching look. It was obvious now that the boy had taken over the reigns of the family. Though she couldn't quite pinpoint when and how it had happened, there was no escaping that the realisation of the fact occasioned some of the sad- ness to peel off the woman's mind, leaving an odd contentment - and a sense of security.

"Perhaps," she considered almost in a whisper. "I think perhaps he might remember."

"Good. Then that's where we'll go." The boy seemed fearless of the future as he spoke, and his plans displayed a sagacity that was only limited by his ignorance of the emotions his mother had secreted from him. Rising, he dismissed the entire affair as concluded by announcing: "I'll get some more firewood."

"Shaka,"

The urgency in Nandi's voice caused the boy to stop and look down at her.

"I said that was a long time ago."

At the sight of his mother's beautiful features made all the more breath taking by the warming reddish glow of the embers, the boy had a gentle smile. "I know, mother. But we must try him. We've no other choice."

When the moon had sunk lower in the sky, its slanting rays found Shaka padding through the dark with the burden of firewood strapped to his back, his senses ever alert, scanning the night for prey or predator.

An indefinable presence suddenly snagged the boy's attention, arresting him in his steps. Shaka probed his surroundings in an attempt to give a form, a shape, to give body to the vague sensation, subliminal in circumspection, which had compelled him to stop. Fleetingly, the shape was made visible to him, but only barely. It looked like a phantom of soft light, its glow barely distinguishable from that of the moon, save for the fact that it was moving, quickly -- a phantom that assumed the shape of the ageless, blind sangoma named Sitayi.

Intrigued, Shaka found himself following that shape to a barren river-bed, where the phantom vanished, its fading radiance briefly lingering over the unconscious body of a man.

Nearing the slumped figure, Shaka could make out the projecting shadow of an assegai sunk into the man's back; the almost imperceptible motion of the weapon's haft indicating that the man, Godongwana, Prince of the Mtetwa, was still breathing, faintly.

Lifting the man into his arms, Shaka strode back towards his camp.

Thus the Encounter - as ordained.

Mfunda's own breathing was faint, raspy, laboured, as Nandi bent over her mother, gingerly running a caressing finger over her death mask, her heart gripped by a helplessness that struggled against resignation.

"Nandi," came the voice, as old and as tired as the body from which it fled.

"Sleep, mother."

"When you were a small child, you never wanted to sleep because it meant closing your eyes - and you were afraid of the dark. And I always used to say to you, 'Don't worry, Nandi. Tomorrow the light will return. I promise you - tomorrow it will return'."

Mfunda paused thinking of Shaka, then—"Now it is my turn to be afraid. If I close my eye, I know that no one can make me the same promise. If I now close my eyes, the light may never return and the darkness that has been at my side since the death of your father will say to me, 'You've had your share of life, old woman, make room for some one else to breath.'"

Reaching out, Mfunda took her daughter's hand and squeezed it, and as Nandi felt the hard, bony surface of Mfunda's fingers, she suddenly sensed the intangible and vague atmosphere of peril that would guide her life at her mother's death.

"Nandi, give him room to breath. He is still so young! All of life; all of love; all of happiness is still ahead of him. Yet to be explored. Yet to be enjoyed. His body is young - straight, tall! His head is high, his eyes challenging the sun! If you truly love him, don't cripple him! Don't make him old before his time! Don't stoop his broad shoulders with the weight of your hatred and revenge! Give him the youth Youth needs! - If you truly love him--" the old woman's voice rose with the need for light one feels at the approach of a tunnel. "Give him hope! Even when no hope can be found!

Free his soul from darkness! - Let him believe that tomorrow the light will return!"

Then her lips were still, and Nandi's eyes became moist, and crying in choked bitterness, she retorted: "And what about me, mother?! What happened to my life?! To my love?! To my happiness?! To my Youth?! Where is it, mother?!" she was shouting now, rousing Nomcoba's sleepy incredulousness.'

"Where is it?!" Nandi screamed in anguish.

"In him." Mfunda answered before taking her leave of the Earth with its marvels and pettiness, with its clamourous, cruel battles of hunger and thought, with its mercy and retribution, to enter the realm of brilliance reserved for those who believe that tomorrow the light will return.

Nestled in the shadows of night, Godongwana's limp frame cradled in his strong arms, Shaka stood gazing at his mother's figure weeping over the figure of his mother's mother, and her tears appealed to those qualities of his being that belonged to survival, and the boy conceived how scarcely equipped for the task of exis- tence is this species of animal called Man.

Whilst the darkness rolled back into the south and the stars began to pale before the threat of dawn, Shaka, Nomcoba and Nandi stood in silence at the foot of Mfunda's grave, beneath the tangled branches of the thorn tree.

Lifting a large slab of stone, Shaka placed it at the head of the grave. Then, scooping up some loose dirt, he sprinkled it over the old matron's final rest- ing place.

"I will be back, grandmother," he solemnly promised. "To claim this land in your name."

For weeks to follow the Mtetwa Godongwana lay in a deep coma, shivering, delirious, whilst the family fought to reclaim the life of this stranger from the near mortal injury left by the barbed assegai of his brother's assassins.

Daily, Nandi lanced the man's festering wound, making tiny incisions over and round the injured flesh, al- lowing the suppuration of the infected lesion to flow out. Then, with a metal blade heated red-hot at the campfire, Shaka cauterized the deep laceration, searing together tissue and skin, causing the living meat to hiss and smoke as the mucus evaporated and dried.

With hands grown calloused and sore, day after day, under the relentless rays of a cloudless sky, Nandi dug the sterile earth for roots and tubers, whilst Nomcoba picked the amber leaves of the ubuHlungwana plant, steeping them in the film of their own moisture, obtaining a medicinal extract which was diligently rubbed into Godongwana's wound.

At length, the long weeks of nursing and the endless nights of silent vigil were rewarded. Godongwana opened his eyes and for the first time looked up at the family with a faint smile of deliverance.

Then - as more days passed at the campsite by the thorn tree - the flow of Life became stronger in Gondogwana's veins and his appreciation turned into genuine affection as he, Shaka, Nandi, and Nomcoba sat round the campfire exchanging stories - of survival in the wake of betrayal.

At long last, when he was able to travel, the out-casts - four again - departed from the salty breath of the sea and set out across the territory of the Mbonam-bini clan, westward, over the barren bed of the once fertile eNtseleni River, into the lands of the Tembu, the Dube and the Ngadini, over the parched tracings of the iMfule River, across the emTonjaneni Heights, past the drought-stricken farms of the Cube tribe, the Wos-slyana, the Ndlela, and the Cunu.

For months they travelled, heading west towards the lands of the Qwabes in hopes of finding Gendeyana alive and his spirit, once kind and generous, untarnished by the drought's tribulations.

Though it had never been openly voiced, there seemed to be a tacit agreement that the Mtetwa, now very much a part of the family (an older brother, perhaps - being that Godongwana was nearly thirty), would remain with Shaka, Nandi and Nomcoba when they reached their destination. Yet, upon crossing the eNqutu Hills, when the rays of dawn were first cast upon the distant, majestic peaks of the towering "umThangala" - the legendary "Wall" of unexplored mountain range that constituted the end of the Nguni Bantu's 'Known World', - Godongwana turned to his companions and voiced his desire to carry on 'wandering' alone. "This is where I must leave you, my friends" he told them with a pang of deep regret, explaining that their paths must now part for the call of his own Destiny was different from theirs.

"Where will you go?" Shaka inquired of the man.

"West. Over the umThangala."

Shaka lifted his gaze to the distant mountains and peered longingly at their lofty, snow-capped peaks rising, it seemed, to the very roof of the sky. "But no one's ever been over the umThangala. - No one except the Ancestors."

"Then the Ancestors shall guide me, Shaka," Godon-gwana answered with a smile. "Just as they guided me to you. - Hamba kahle, my friends, I pray that we meet again and that I may be given the means to repay you for the life you have returned to me."

"Sala kahle, - 'Dingiswayo', stay well, 'Wanderer'," Shaka answered with a grin.

Godongwana smiled at the nickname 'Dingiswayo - Wanderer', a term, which could well, have suited any one of them. Then, before starting off, up the natural path that led towards the foot of the range, he slipped off the leopard-skin that was draped over his shoulders and returned it to Shaka.

"Keep it," the boy urged. "You deserve it far more than I. Your fight with death was more heroic than my tangle with that leopard. Besides," he added, gazing back at the mountains, "you'll need it. It looks cold up there."

The Mtetwa stood staring for a long moment at Shaka, Nandi, and Nomcoba - his 'family' -, committing their weathered features to memory...for life. Then, with an embrace and a last farewell, he turned and strode off to follow the Call of Destiny on the footsteps of the Ancestors.

As the huge orange globe of the sun set on yet another rainless day, Shaka, Nandi, and Nomcoba entered the land of the Qwabes and were, at last, on the edge of the vast plateau overlooking the tiny village of the ama-Mbedweni nestled on the banks of the parched ama-Tikulu River.

Turning from his labour, one of Gendeyana's brothers spotted three exhausted travellers standing at the gates of his small homestead. "Gendeyana," he called with tense eagerness.

Gendeyana glanced up from his work. He, too, bore the scars of the Famine, looking frighteningly thin, his fleshless features a far cry from those of the rather prosperous young man who had once asked for Nandi's hand in marriage. Yet his eyes had retained the same glow of kindness and patience. Squinting against the sun, Gende-yana peered down at the gates of his homestead and, when his eyes had focused properly and his mind had registered what he saw -- the man gasped. "Nandi," he mouthed in an incredulous whisper.

Nandi gazed back and nodded - simply.

Gendeyana's smile was one of infinite pleasure as he neared the woman and embraced her. "And you must be...Shaka," Gendeyana said, turning to the tall young man with the steady, searching gaze.

"You have heard of me?"

"Yes," Gendeyana laughed good-naturedly thinking back to the surprise pregnancy of the girl who had been his betrothed, - an otherwise tormenting recollection which, in the present context, seemed so terribly comical to him. "Yes. I have heard of you."

The subtle irony of the situation was not lost on Nandi and she joined him in his laughter - finally al- lowing the months of stress to drain from her spirit in this joyous outburst.

Shaka and Nomcoba exchanged a quizzical glance, both wondering what the 'adults' found so funny.

That same afternoon billowing blue-black clouds began to form in the South and, rolling northwards, they veiled the mighty sun, taming its rays with the rumbling impatience of their swollen fleece. Lightning bolted, thunder crashed, and then -- after almost a year of drought - the skies opened drenching the earth with life-giving rain, causing the surrounding villages to share their uncontrollable joy with the newcomers Shaka, Nandi, and Nomcoba, jumping and dancing with frenzied gaiety, yelling, screaming, singing and cheering, laughing and crying, their faces to the sky as the celestial torrent washed away the tension, the fear, and the pain.

For the time being.

It was later said that many in the land of the Qwabes - especially Gendeyana and his brothers - bestowed upon the three outcasts the credit for such good fortune, seeing their arrival as the harbinger of food and plenty.

This fact should stand as yet another landmark of Fate's whims. Indeed, that an exiled 'witch' and her bastard son and daughter should be considered by some as the cause of a Famine is, in itself, whimsical, - yet that the same 'witch' and her children should then be looked upon by others as the precursors of 'food and plenty' is the sort of capricious behaviour that leaves Man to consider, despondent, whether his own ephemeral role in the Universe is some sort of spoof.

CHAPTER XVI
"UMTHANGALA"(THE WALL)
MONTH OF SEKUYISIKATI SOKUVUNA (APRIL, 1806)

"He's in the land of Kondlo of the Qwabes," the Zulu messenger told his king. "Living with his mother and sister in the homestead of a man named Gendeyana."

As Senzangakona waved the messenger away, a wry smile tugged at the corners of his full lips causing the sacks of loose flesh on his jowls and chin line to rise in rubbery folds of skin. At forty-three, the son of Jama looked old, much older than his years, and profoundly fatigued in both body and soul. It was as if the sorghum and sorrow to which he had become addicted made the coming of each day an event to be endured with stoic sufferance.

"Ah, yes - Gendeyana," the king nodded to himself, his gaze fixed on a point in space where he seemed to see the procession of images from his past, dredging up memories that were better left dormant. It had been four years since he'd last seen Nandi, four long years, yet the sound of his own voice crying out her name on the banks of the Mkumbane still echoed in his soul.

"I should've suspected she'd go back to him - as a last resort. Though I'm sure it must have been very humiliating for her. - She was never one to...go back."

Mkabayi caught an odd inflection in the way her brother spoke the words 'go back', and she twisted round to peer at him critically, realising with a twinge of jealousy how little she really knew about his true relationship with Nandi, what it had been - what it was today. She'd need to know more, she decided, much more! The emotional stability of her brother and, more important, the political future of the kingdom was at stake - the future the Ancestors had entrusted to the Child.

And it was Mkabayi's conviction that the Ancestors needed her to prepare the way for the Child. The others round her were either incompetent or, as in the case of Mudli, a threat to Shaka and the New Order he would bring. No!, it was up to her, she knew. Accordingly, she must stay strong where her brother was weak, she must see clearly where his vision was blurred by the lingering image of the Langeni woman, an image his mind was powerless to dispel.

Her probing eyes trained on Senzangakona, she added, almost parenthetically: "She has another son now. His name is Ngwadi."

The Zulu King could barely hide his displeasure. Another son. His lips pursed in a scowl as the vision of Nandi and Gendeyana embraced in love making obtruded itself upon his mind. "How humiliating." He murmured.

Glimpsing her brother's suffering, Mkabayi prided herself in never having fallen in love: that unreasoning emotion that obscures and changes even the innermost facts of life. Yes, she reconfirmed to herself, she must guide the way; a man in love cannot be expected to see clearly the path before him, especially if it leads away from the object of his affections. With this in mind, she prompted:- "But far more humiliating for us, my brother."

Senzangakona turned to look at her.

"Twelve years ago," she said, as if repeating some- thing learned by heart. "I helped your son escape because I believed that that solution was for the good of our people. At the time, you said that his exile would be, for him, a punishment worse than death. I now believe that his exile may well become our own punishment.

"King Kondlo of the Qwabes," she went on, "has given him a home in his lands. Makedama of the Langeni has asked for his return to his mother's people. Whether it be out of true friendship or fear - they all want that young man on their side because they all sense his future greatness. Yet we who know of the Prophecy and its implications remain silent. Stubbornly antagonistic. And that, baba," Mkabayi neared her king with an inflection of vehemence, "is suicide! I think the time has come for Shaka to take his place as a legitimate member of the royal house of Zulu together with the other sons your wives have finally borne you: Dingane, Magwaza, Sigiyana..." Her voice trailed off for she had no need to mention the others: Mpande, Nzibe, Bakuza, Kolekile, Gowujana, Sigwebana, Gqugqu, Mfihlo, Nxojana - twelve in all. None of which could hold up to inspection when faced with the first born -- the Child.

Knowing this, Senzangakona had a bitter smile as he considered: "His place in the royal house? At my side? That's ludicrous, my sister. Have you forgotten the events that led to his exile? Why his mother must feel only antagonism towards my house and me. Even if I selected him as my sole heir to the throne, she would--"

"Exactly," interrupted Mkabayi with fiery rancour. "That woman! How much longer will you allow her to influence your son? To turn him against his own father, his own people?!"

The king shot her a sidelong glance marred by a sardonic grin. "I had the impression you rather liked her when she was here. So much of your time was spent in her company."

"Not hers! The boy's!" Mkabayi quickly rebutted. "My interest was only in him and his future! Even Igazi and the escape. I did that for him, not for her! Just as now it is he we must think of - not her!"

Senzangakona remained silent, his eyes wandering to a rippling field of millet, as his sister pressed on. "He was only six when he left here. Too young to understand what you felt for her, yet old enough to store impressions that could easily be honed into hatred. Mkabayi lowered her voice to a disturbing undertone. "Baba, your son, the Child of the Prophecy, will soon be a man. And when he is, he will come to claim his right as leader of the amaZulu. - With or without your blessing."

As Senzangakona hesitated, his sister added ominous- ly: "Win him back, my brother. Win him back from that woman before I regret having saved his life!"

King Kondlo of the Qwabes was seated on his throne of rushes at the top of his large cattlefold flanked by his lavish court, the most richly splendid in the land (or so it was said), comprised of his son Pakatwayo and his servants, the king's six wives and their handmaidens, the king's private servants, the Qwabe Council of Elders and their servants, the king's guards - and, of course, the ever-haranguing jester with his commemorative chanting embroidered with metaphor, satire and rhyming verse.

The eyes of the multitude of Qwabe clansmen and women - who had flocked to the royal homestead to be part of the king's ceremony - gravitated to the gates of the vast residence as soon as Shaka and his family made their appearance.

Nineteen years of age now, standing over a meter ninety in height, with a statuesque, robust, magnificently-proportioned physique, all muscle and sinew, Shaka strode into the homestead, his air commanding, august and impressive, the fire and perspicacity in his eye completing the image he projected of the exceptional leader, the man born to bear the wings and the shackles of Glory.

At Shaka's side, dwarfed by his regal stature, were Nandi and Gendeyana. Together the three marched to the top of the cattlefold and, stopping in front of the king, knelt in unison giving the traditional greeting of respect.

"Bayete, Nkosi," they said with a single voice.

"Sakubona, my friends," responded Kondlo in a friendly tone.

As they rose to their feet, Shaka's gaze shifted to Pakatwayo and, for a fleeting moment, he read in the prince's expression the ill-will, the resentment and the brooding violence of intention proper to soul's given to grudging others their success, merited or otherwise. And as Shaka saw that sinister look, he stored it in his heart, as a warning - in case their paths should cross again under different circumstances.

"Lutuli..." Kondlo called out.

At the mention of the Zulu, Nandi froze into perfect stillness, only her eyes moving to glimpse the figure of Senzangakona's boyhood confederate. Expecting to find the slim, somewhat attractive athlete who, together with Igazi, had shared the acquaintance of her youth, Nandi was shocked to see a middle-aged man, over-weight and mellowed by time beyond the spring and bounce needed to resist Time's mellowing.

"Prince Shaka," Lutuli addressed the young man caus- ing a complete hush to fall on the gathering.

And causing Nandi to catch her breath. "Prince"? - impossible!...

Prince Shaka! - As her heart leapt within her, Nandi cast her son a deliberate sidelong glance. Their eyes met, briefly, and in them was the sparkle of triumph. This was the first time Shaka had officially been addressed with the title 'prince'. Had Senzangakona, like Lutuli, also mellowed beyond the spring and bounce of pride.

"Prince Shaka," Lutuli announced, "I bring you a missive from your father, King Senzangakona kaJama. He is grieved that his son has chosen to wander in distant lands..."

Shaka was used to the injustices of the world and, like his mother, he had even grown to expect them. That is why he merely smiled - a wry smile - upon hearing that he had 'chosen to wander', leaving his father 'grieved'.

"King Senzangakona," Lutuli continued, "asks for his son's return to the home of his forefathers so that he can publically, and before his own people, he proclaimed a legitimate heir to the throne of the House of Zulu."

Yes, Gendeyana mused sorrowfully, the day had come.

Yes, Nandi nodded to herself, one need only rely on patience and Age.

"Is that the extent of the message, Lutuli?" Kondlo asked when the Zulu had stopped speaking.

"No, Nkosi," Lutuli retorted, his tone laced with the reluctance of a man faced with an unpleasant chore. Looking back at Shaka, trying to avoid Nandi's gaze, the Zulu remarked: "My king requests the return of his son. Only his son."

Nandi flushed, her hands tightening into fists, the knuckles blanching with rage. He had humiliated her again, publically. Her eyes shot back to her son and she saw that he was strangely calm, composed, unemotional. Is his own quest for power so great that...- With a rising sense of uncertainty that teetered on the precipice of disappointment, Nandi broke off the thought in mid- sentence, not daring to even consider the possibility that her son might want to walk his path alone.

"What have you to say, Prince Shaka?" Kondlo asked.

A heavy atmosphere of oppressive quietude pervaded the homestead. All eyes were on the Zulu prince, waiting.

"A legitimate heir, you say, Lutuli," Shaka finally inquired, enunciating each word distinctly, with soft precision, the deep rolling tones of his voice filling the air round him without effort.

"Yes, Ndabezitha," Lutuli answered.

"The son of an illegitimate wife?" asked Shaka, stonefaced, each pronounced word taking on a visible shape.

Lutuli said nothing. Nandi remained still, her heart racing in her breast.

"I am confused, Lutuli," the Zulu Prince confessed, his brow furrowed with theatrical inflection. "How can an heir be legitimate if his mother has never been officially wed?"

The Qwabe court froze at the remark. All gazes now shifted to Lutuli who faltered somewhat and said: "If the king so wills it, so shall it be."

"I see," Shaka raised his brow, nodding. "That must be it," he added with growing sarcasm, causing a muffled ripple of laughter to stir through the onlookers, effecting King Kondlo who smiled, his eyes riveted on Shaka. "Your king must be powerful indeed to alter our traditions to such an extent," Shaka said with slow, ironic emphasis evoking another ripple of laughter and a din of heated comments. It was slowly becoming clear to all that Shaka was indeed, as Kondlo had put it, "extraordinarily unpredictable".

When Shaka spoke again the irony was gone from his voice and his eyes were bent with gelid resolve. "Go back and tell your king, Lutuli, that Shaka Zulu remembers no one by the name of Senzangakona, son of Jama."

The din of comments burst forth in unleashed surprise. Nandi's eyes returned to her son, twinkling with infinite affection. Her triumph was now complete: - Senzangakona's insulting phrase had come round full circle.

"I have no wish to be part of this man's royal house for I do not recognise his authority, nor do I acknowledge the sovereignty of his family," Shaka's bellowing voice was now modulated over the crowd's uproar. "I, Shaka Zulu, am already by birth a prince of the People of the Heavens, and shall, by Destiny, be their king! Nothing and no one can change that! Not even the hypocrisy of a father who has brought only hardship and disgrace to the true descendant of Zulu kaMalandela."

Kondlo glanced at his son. When their eyes met, Pakatwayo quickly dropped his gaze.

"Tell the Zulus to prepare themselves, Lutuli," Shaka went on, relentlessly, his voice ringing with the crystal clarity of a waterfall bathed in sunshine. "Tell them that sooner than they dare think, I will return. But not alone!" Shaka curled his brawny arm round his mother, squeezing her. "My mother will be at my side. As Nkosikazi indlovukazi, the Queen of Queens! The Great Female Elephant of the People of the Heavens!

A hush fell on the gathering. Suddenly Kondlo became the center of attention as all waited for the Qwabe monarch to react to Shaka's unheard-of loyalty - and intransigence.

The king's eyes remained locked on Shaka, delving deep into the Zulu's imponderable soul, sensing how his own spirit was bewitched by that soul and the flash of its energy, its commanding sadness, and its ambition, immense and towering, like a crested wave running over the troubled shallows of the sands. "It is not within my competence, Prince Shaka, to judge you for the stand you have taken against your father," he finally responded. "I am sure that, in your heart, it is justified - and I respect that, just as I have learned to respect you for the time you have been my guest. As you can well understand, your attitude places me in a very delicate position. Circumstances would force me to request that you and your family leave my domains."

Gendeyana braced himself for the decree of banishment that he was certain was now forthcoming. Indeed, he thought, Kondlo's hands were tied. He could not allow Shaka's offensive defilement to go unpunished. If he were to, he would become an accomplice in the insult propagated against King Senzangakona. Yet instead of wearing the sombre expression which should accompany banishment's proclamation, to the surprise of all - especially Pakatwayo's, Kondlo's lips curled in a warm smile as he remarked to Shaka: "Circumstances would force me to, if I were one to be forced by circumstances." The king's smile broadened. "Fortunately I am not." Squaring his shoulders, Kondlo solemnly declared: "I, Kondlo son of Mncini, true descendant of Qwabe will bring no further hardship and disgrace to the true descendant of Zulu. You and your family may remain in my kingdom for as long as you see fit."

Another current of startled comments bolted through the homestead. In his remark, Kondlo had not only sided with Shaka against his father, he had officially acknowledged Shaka's legitimacy as future king of the Zulus. A bold step indeed. Yet one taken not without proper consideration. In fact, Kondlo had decided long ago, shortly after Nandi's arrival in his domains, that if it should ever come to choosing between Senzangakona and his son, he would stand with the Zulu that most resembled his valiant friend Jama. And, as Shaka grew to manhood, the choice became academic.

Nandi's face was aglow at this remarkable turn of events, and even Gendeyana ventured back to the thres- hold of hope; though he had always felt in his heart that Nandi would never be his for the keeping, he now yearned that those he had grown to love, to need, those who were now his life would stay with him after all.

But Shaka soon dashed that hope in the simplicity of his noble manner. "Thank you, Nkosi," he nodded to the king, "your words do honour to the Sons of Qwabe. Though it would be my great privilege to stay on as your guest, I will not repay your generosity and loyalty by jeopard- ising you and your kingdom."

Again general surprise rocked the court.

"I believe, Baba, that it is best for us to leave," the Zulu prince concluded with intimacy, causing another wave of astonishment to ripple through the crowd. "I and my family have been blamed enough in the past. I will not allow us to be the cause of a useless war. The time is not ripe for conflict...Not yet." Bowing low, Shaka bid Kondlo, "Bayete, Nkosi. Wena wa sendhlu nKulu - Hail thou of the Royal House. May the Ancestors give you health, prosperity and long life as a reward for your nobleness of heart, the courage of your judgment and convictions, and the benevolence of your proud nature. I pray that one day I may bestow upon you and your people the good will you have bestowed upon me and my family."

"Sala kahle, Shaka Zulu," Kondlo returned the salute with a note of sadness. "Wena wa sendhlu nKulu. - thou, truly, of the royal house."

When Shaka, Nandi and Gendeyana had taken their leave, Pakatwayo commented to his father: "That Zulu, father! Have you ever seen such arrogance. Surely the man is mad!"

"Or enlightened. Only time will tell. But one thing is sure, Pakatwayo," Kondlo's voice had become grave as he found his son's eyes, "if he should be true to his word and become king of the Zulus - he won't stop there!"

At the gates of his homestead, Gendeyana embraced Nandi for what he was certain would be the last time; - Fate, he knew, could never be so generous as to allow their paths to cross again. Nandi returned the embrace, genuinely sad to leave this kind man of whom she had, in her own way, grown fond, feeling for him a love of sorts -- not the wild senseless passion that was the conflagration of her life, a passion that was still only partially, extinct -- but a gentle sort of love, a quiet acceptance, the relaxing warmth that causes lizards to sit for hours, immovable on a patch of sunshine.

There was no mention of the possibility that, even for a short period of time, she, Nomcoba and Ngwadi might stay on alone, without Shaka. The very thought of the woman being separated from her son was so inconceivable to those who knew her, that those who loved her, like Gendeyana, knew better than to confront the sombre intensity of her emerald-green eyes with so outrageous a prospect.

No, Gendeyana knew better. Nandi and Shaka were one, just as, in its flight, the seagull is one with the sky.

After taking his sorrowful leave of Nomcoba (fourteen now, looking more and more the reflection of her father's handsomeness) and his own son, Ngwadi (almost three), with the promise that he would join them soon, for a visit, Gendeyana lifted his gaze to meet Shaka's steady feline eyes.

"We still want you to come with us, Baba," Shaka told the man who had been his foster father. "If you should reconsider, we will be on the banks of the iMfongosi, by the Cliffs of uGangeni. We will wait for three days. Then - if you do not come - we will move on."

"I cannot come, Shaka," Gendeyana confessed, his voice choked with emotion. "She doesn't belong to me. She was never meant to belong to me."

Shaka considered the point in his usual manner, de- tached, objective, coldly unemotional, and then nodded in agreement. Yes, she was never meant to belong - just as he himself could was never meant to belong. Their stay in his homestead was merely an act of convenience. Resting his mighty hands on the man's shoulders, the Zulu Prince saluted him with affection. "I will never forget you, Baba," he said. "One day I will give you the glory you deserve."

"Not all of us can cope with glory, Shaka," answered the other man with a sad smile.

And as the outcasts - four again - Shaka, Nandi, Nomcoba and Ngwadi walked away across the amber fields, Gendeyana's eyes moistened. Cocking his head, his gaze fled from the sight of the departing 'family' as the tears welled in his soul spilling down his cheeks. Suddenly he was assailed by an irresistible longing to look again at that woman that was his life and, in this moment of final parting, his heart clung to her as one clutched a priceless and disputed possession.

Yet they were gone.

Turning, slowly, Gendeyana's gaze drifted to the huts where the family had lived, to the fields where he had played with the children, to the brook next to which his son had been conceived. He looked at the homestead he had built for them and, taking a torch, he lit it and set fire to his heart.

Those who knew Gendeyana of the amaMbedweni subclan of the Qwabes towards the end of his life, before his premature death, of a broken heart, it was said -- those who knew him those last few years of his earthly per- manence swore that he never mentioned her, as if her image had utterly gone from his mind - dismissed, no longer before his eyes to nuture his imagination into love and longing. They all swore that she had vanished from his memory.

Yet Gendeyana was a simple man. To liberate his soul was for him too great an undertaking, - a matter of desperate effort, of doubtful success.

And when he died, of a broken heart, they say that despair was imprisoned in his soul for eternity.

Age, -- Patience, they are often not enough.

"It's insurrection!"

Mudli's vehemence was addressed to Senzangakona, Mkabayi, and the esteemed members of the Zulu Council of Elders who had met to discuss Shaka's intransigence.

"Not only has he transgressed the most sacrosanct rules of reverence and submission that bind a son to his father," the Elder continued, his oratory laced with supreme indignation, "he has also publicly discredited you, Nkosi, and your Royal House by challenging your supremacy as ruler of the Zulus."

Expressionless, Mkabayi's eyes ran over Mudli's slender frame, rendered somehow more spindly by the March of Time. "Frankly, Elder," Mkabayi started, as if in response to her brother's silent bidding, "his reaction should not come as such a surprise to us. After so many years of forced exile, we should have anticipated his hostility."

Mudli nodded to Mkabayi. "Perhaps, Udadewethu. But we would be fools to condone it! Especially since his hostility surpasses the limits of treason!"

"Treason, Mudli?" the king asked with a knitted brow.

"Yes, Nkosi!" Mudli left no room for doubt. "His offense is not only against the State, it is in defilement of all our values - all we believe in, all that we stand for! His statement before Kondlo was nothing short of a declaration of war on his own people! And the fact that Kondlo has seemingly remained indifferent to the affront makes the matter all the more dangerous for us!"

"I presume you are about to tell me that my pride is at stake," Senzangakona interrupted with a hint of sarcasm.

"Our pride, Baba! The pride of your entire kingdom! And its future!" The Elder's voice took on a tone, eerie and ominous, that presaged disaster. "We must safeguard the future of the amaZulu from the Evil that he and the Prophecy stand for." After pausing an instant to allow the thought to sink in, Mudli declared with a snarl of contempt: "He must be brought back, Baba, charged with high treason and executed according to the laws of the land!"

Murmurs of agreement shook the Council.

Once again, Senzangakona was burdened by the weight of immeasurable sadness, one that left him breathing with difficulty. Having recently buried his mother Mtaniya, the king was loathe to even consider another death, especially the execution of his respected son. Yes, respected! In spite of himself, Senzangakona felt respect for Shaka and the stand he had taken. In his heart of hearts, he was even proud. Turning to his sister the king spoke confidingly, as if they were alone. "It seems we've come round full circle, haven't we, Mkabayi? A vicious circle. Exile to avoid death - and now the death penalty as a consequence of his exile. It would seem that there are many destinies in this Prophecy. Mine is to kill my first-born son. Or perhaps my resourceful sister can think of another way of saving him?"

Mkabayi held her brother's gaze steadily with her own. There was no doubt now. He was asking for help. "My purpose, Nkosi," Mkabayi remarked, her eyes directed on Mudli and the Council, "is not and never was to 'save him' personally. I only wish what is best for our people and, in this specific case, to prevent a miscarriage of justice. The Elder is right. We are faced with an act of high treason. But who, ultimately, is to blame for that crime? - The boy or his mother?"

Mudli's brow furrowed with suspicion, Senzangakona's with incredulity.

"Can we truthfully say that Shaka's actions and words are the fruit of his own disloyalty," she pressed on, her voice gaining in conviction and volume, "or are they instead a projection of the defiance we have had cause to observe in his mother."

Senzangakona gelidly regarded his sister. Is she really going to sacrifice Nandi to save Shaka? he wondered and listened intently, waving back Mudli's attempt at a rebuttal.

"Our society is founded on the precept that a father's word is law, his will supreme, his person sacred," Mkabayi strode closer to the Council. "It is a mother's privilege and duty to raise her children according to that precept. If she fails to do so, or, indeed, if she turns the child against his father, the fault of his insubordination lies with her. She is responsible, not the son!"

An impressive defense, Senzangakona thought as his eyes remained glued to his sister, captivated by her diatribe.

Mkabayi took a deep breath and continued: "The Elder insists that Shaka represents evil. I humbly submit that what he calls evil is merely the fruit of his mother's conditioning. I submit that what the boy represents is not evil - but power! We have seen that in all Shaka's actions! Why destroy that power when we can harness it for the good of our people?! - He's still young! He can still be moulded by us -- if and only if we finally put an end to his mother's influence! She, not Shaka, must be tried for treason and - if found guilty - executed according to the laws of the land!"

The Council exploded with contrasting comments - most of which applauded the woman's oratory and logic.

Senzangakona remained stunned, his eyes catching Mkabayi's and locking. I won't feed Nandi to the Coun- cil, those eyes told his sister. I won't offer her up as an oblation to the future of the amaZulu. Not Nandi. Not even for Shaka! If a choice must be made, I shall cling to the Past, not the Future!

"I must congratulate you, Udadewethu," Mudli was saying with cordial praise. "Your mind is as nimble as that of the fox."

Mkabayi pursed her lips to iron back the smile.

"Yet," the Elder went on, "if what you say is true, no one would 'ultimately' be responsible for his or her actions because we are all products of our upbringing and environment. If what you say is true, our laws become meaningless. - Yet I must agree with you on one point, Udadewethu. Shaka does represent power. Unharnessed power! At the age of six - before his mother's influence became determining - he had already manifested the seed of his treachery by threatening to kill his father!"

As Mkabayi dropped her gaze, another murmur of agreement shook the Council.

"And now," Mudli remarked emphatically, "at the age of nineteen, he has publically threatened him again! Yet you continue to justify him, Udadewethu...Has this Child blinded you? Has he bewitched you?!"

Struck by the magnitude of the accusation, Mkabayi's fiery gaze shot back to the Elder.

"What will it take to open your eyes? The death of our king?!"

"Enough!" Senzangakona shouted over the verbal roar that burst from the Council. "Enough," the king's voice became suddenly weary. "We have hesitated too long. - Bring him back, Mudli. It is time this intrigue was settled once and for all!"

CHAPTER XVII
"IMVUMELANO"(COVENANT)

"Is he dead yet, mother?" Ngwadi asked with a distinct catch in his breath, his voice sounding low and timid.

Death. The Lord of Grief, the Lord of Pain, the Lord of The Kill. - One is either its Master or its Victim, there is no middle way.

At nineteen, Shaka had the invincible conviction - one which would accompany him throughout his life - that those who attempt to use the strain of Superstition as an explanation of the more tenuous and incomprehensible events of which Man is protagonist, and especially those who use it as a justification for untimely Death and as a palliative for the fear of the unknown that accompanies dying, fail deplorably to see Man's true relationship with Life and the living. Shaka believed that whatever fell under the dominion of our senses was in Nature and, however inexplicable, could not differ in its essence from all the other effects of the visible and tangible world of which we are a self-conscious part. What is in Nature can be explained by Nature - one need not go further than the senses.

In was in this frame of mind that Shaka turned to his brother upon hearing his remark and, intrigued, strode down from his vantage point on the towering Cliffs of uGangeni, and neared the makeshift stone hearth where Nandi and Nomcoba were boiling maize to soften it for the making of iziNkobe bread.

Nandi shifted her loving gaze to her toddler son who was flat against the earth, peering inquisitively at the immobile features of a reed buck that Shaka had recently procured for dinner. "Yes, Ngwadi," Nandi replied. "He's dead."

"How can you tell? Is it because he's stopped moving?" Ngwadi asked with the insistence proper to children his age.

"It's in the eyes," Shaka broke in knowledgeably.

Ngwadi knitted his brow and peered deep into the buck's eyes. "I don't see anything," the boy finally remarked, disappointed.

Shaka and Nandi exchanged an amused grin. "Look closely, Ngwadi," Shaka prompted. "Can you notice something's gone. In the eyes."

His manner increasingly watchful, Ngwadi stretched closer to the buck, his eyes becoming one with the animal's. As the boy's gaze penetrated the innermost truth of the buck's stillness, a smile of realisation slowly dawned on his young features.

"See it now?" Shaka asked.

"Yes," said Ngwadi with mounting excitement. "I see it!" Yet the frown suddenly returned, as the toddler looked up at his brother. "But where has it gone?"

Shaka's attentive gaze quickly scanned his surroundings, falling upon the crackling campfire. "Into the fire," he finally told his brother.

Ngwadi studied the fire and nodded in silent agreement. Indeed, the lapping tongues of flame did look alive and, in their greedy swells of crackling crimson and blue, they looked as if they might well have stolen that life from another being. "And what happens to it when the fire dies?"

Ngwadi inquired with a show of keenness that belied his years and touched Nandi's proud heart.

"It becomes smoke," Shaka quickly retorted, his eyes trained on the surging smoke that, rising from the fire, thinned and vanished into the afternoon sky. "And the smoke becomes air."

Ngwadi gaped at his brother, wide-eyed. "So the life of the dead is all around us," the boy concluded, in a hushed, religious tone, feeling the swirl of sensations that suddenly swelled within him.

The life of the dead is all around us.

Ngwadi's words had a more urgent meaning for Shaka as he sat on his solitary lookout high atop of the Cliffs of uGangeni, assegai in hand, his ever-vigilant eyes probing the shadows of the night which was washed a harsh blue by the moon's phosphorescence. Shaka knew that Death was indeed all around them, waiting, stalk- ing.

In fact, ever since the outcasts had left Gendeyana's homestead and pushed off in search of another village, another future laced with the unpredictables of Fate, Shaka had kept close watch in the certainty that sooner or later the Zulus would be after him. It was to be expected, he knew. After his hostile remarks at Kondlo's residence, made all the more caustic by the fact that they were uttered in the guise of a public denigration of Senzangakona and his house, the Zulu king's reputation was at stake and, though irresolute of character, he would be forced by others - Mudli perhaps, or even Mkabayi - to react with due severity.

Yes, he knew, the Zulus would come and soon their spears would be within reach. And just as the reminder of that threat struck him, Shaka suddenly stiffened, easing forward on his rocky perch, inspecting the shadows that hugged the cliffs' smooth flanks, listening, sensing that the moment of confrontation was already upon him. His roving eye sought the lurking enemy and was arrested by the fleeting shine of the moon's reflection on a blade, by the geometric shape of a shield cast against the slate of night's darkness, by a filament of shadow that matched the narrow outline of a spear. His hearing screened the sounds of Nature and was checked by the snapping of a branch underfoot, the rustling of leaves, the soft steps of approaching warriors.

Silently slinking down from the cliffs' summit, Shaka padded over the spongy earth near the banks of the iMfongosi and reached the campsite where his mother, Nomcoba and Ngwadi were fast asleep by the warming glow of a smoldering fire. "Mother!" Shaka whispered, rousing Nandi from her shallow slumber. "They're here!"

Nandi knew full well who 'they' were and she now searched her son's eyes for a plan of action.

"Go to grandmother's grave," he ordered her. "I'll join you there. By the new moon."

When Nandi opened her mouth to speak, Shaka gently touched a restraining finger to her lips and, with a reassuring smile answered her silent inquisitive by repeating with slow emphasis: "I will join you there. By the new moon."

Nandi reluctantly nodded in agreement and embraced her son.

"And, mother," he adjoined with a contemptuous certitude born of angry resolve, "this is the last time we're running! - The very last time!" And kissing her, Shaka stole away, claimed by the darkness and the daunting intrigues of the man who had sired him.

Sprinting through the misty-enshrouded murkiness that clung to the waters of the iMfongosi, Shaka raced halfway across the shallow river before sighting, on the opposite bank, over a dozen Zulu warriors advancing towards him. Stopping short in his tracks, Shaka spun round only to find that the other bank was now also lined with warriors, their menacing figures silhouetted against the glow of the moon. They, too, were moving in on their human prey.

Realising that his only means of escape was the river itself, Shaka began to run along its slippery bed, following its course, the warriors close behind. Yet even this bid to elude his would-be captors was short-lived for, all too soon, the bed of the tortuous iMfon- gosi rose slightly and leveled off to a slanting incline where the river's waters sped headlong towards a lofty waterfall.

Reaching the fall, Shaka stopped at its margins and peered at the breath-taking drop - over fifty meters of perpendicular rock mantled in the gleaming sparkle of rushing water that hurtled downwards forming, at the fall's base, swirling, foam-streaked eddies and whirl- pools that, unraveling at mid-stream, plunged onwards, running deep and strong over jagged boulders and scattered debris.

Trapped on the edge of this mammoth precipice, Shaka's mind raced as he turned to look back at his tormentors and found that they were closing in, both banks of the river alive with their spears and feathered head-dresses. As the instants passed, it became increasingly more obvious that the young man's only route of escape was the headlong drop at his feet. Yet Shaka still hesitated, his spirit railing against this apparently suicidal leap into the misty void.

The decision was soon forced upon him as one of the warriors, Dilikana by name, a husky, thick-set brute with a bulldog neck and features to match, cocked his arm and hurled his weapon through the air. The missile sank into the brawny muscle on Shaka's thigh, barely above the knee, striking the man with an impact that drove the spear deep into his flesh, spinning him round, causing him to lose hold of his own assegai and his footing as he plunged over and down.

It seemed to Shaka that he was falling forever - through the void of darkness. Then suddenly he struck the surface of the river with a force that verily drove the air from his lungs, as the frosty, tumultuous torrents of racing water clasped him in their whirling embrace and pulled him away with the current.

Clinging to his last shreds of consciousness, Shaka fought for breath, fought to keep his head above the surface, as he groped for the spear in an attempt to yank it out of his throbbing thigh, yet the elements impeded his task, pummeling at his arms, sweeping him downstream with a force so overwhelming it made all voluntary movement impossible. As he slid along the racing spill of foaming rapids, he felt the skin stripped from his hip and shoulder as he bounced and scraped against the roughness of the riverbed. The spear's haft was struck by a swirl of debris and the blade was thrust even deeper into his flesh, tearing at the mouth of the wound, sending a jolt of pain shooting to his head. The young man's mouth opened in a silent, tortured gasp as icy currents gushed down his straining throat, burning it, making him choke and retch for each breath.

Again the spear scraped against the river's bed, yet this time the haft was abruptly snagged by a tangle of strong roots and jammed solid between two large boulders. When the spear caught, Shaka's forward progress was stopped with a pain so intense it flashed in his mind with the brightness of lightning.

Struggling to overcome the agony, the youth closed a powerful hand round one of the roots and, with the other hand, snapped the spear's haft in two and finally succeeded in yanking the blade out of his leg. Then, as the blood gushed from the gaping lesion disgorging into the frothing currents, Shaka handed his way along the root's sticky shaft in an effort to reach the rocks that lay imbedded on the river's muddy shore.

By now, Dilikana and several of the Zulus had reached the top of the waterfall where they stood gaping down at the swirling torrent in search of their human quarry. Upon realising that there was no sign of Shaka, Dilikana cast a worried look at his comrades. In fact, the Zulu king's instructions had been all too explicit: the 'prince' was to be brought back alive. If Shaka were to die in the process of abduction, the entire party would be held responsible for his murder. Being the one to have hurled the spear, Dilikana's worry turned to apprehension when one of his comrades cried out an excited "Over there!"

The man was pointing to the shadowy contours that clung to a portion of the iMfongosi's muddy banks. In the shadows, the silhouette of a human figure seemed to detach itself from the river's grinding currents and, pulling itself up onto the bank, the figure appeared to remain slumped on the grimy shore, drained of all energy.

Suddenly boosted in both spirit and purpose, Dilikana barked out a command to capture the silhouetted apparition whom he knew to be Shaka, and, within seconds, the detachment of Zulus was clambering down the rocky slopes that flanked the waterfall in renewed pursuit of their prey. His strength greatly depleted by his injuries and exhaustion, his body battered and strained beyond the natural limits of most mortals, Shaka, not being like most mortals, viewed the approaching Zulu contingency with stoic self-command, firm in the persuasion that he would survive to fulfill his Covenant with the Spirit of the Heavens as it had been announced to him as a young boy at the Pond of Mageba and Ndaba; "This day thou art my son and I thy Father. Ask and I shall give you the Nations for thy Heritage, the ends of the earth for thy domain."

Confident of his mission as a Master, Shaka rose on unsteady legs and, gritting his teeth, fled from his pursuers in his own pursuit - of Destiny.

All night he ran, without respite for himself and his tortured body, losing blood from his throbbing wound, yet miraculously gaining ground on those who gave him chase, his own speed, though greatly diminished by his injury, remaining well above that of his trackers.

And when the long, cold, weary night was over, and the deep blue-black sky had lightened to a wonderful mauve-violet, with the larger stars still glinting brightly out of it, Shaka found that the character of the scenery around him had changed and that the river's thick vegetation had given way to a more barren terrain strewn with jagged black khors opening out onto hard rolling plains covered thickly with snaggy outcroppings and gullies.

In his desperate flight, the youth had soon realised that as long as he kept moving, the pain in his leg was almost bearable,- yet when he slowed or stopped to catch his breath, the agony became debilitating. The youth knew that he was fast nearing the limits of even his own endurance and that his escape was becoming a battle of mind and will over a failing body. Yet he pressed on, unrelenting, as the Zulus, who were also beginning to feel the weight of fatigue, started gradually to close the gap that separated them from their formidable prize.

By the end of the third day, the pain in Shaka's wound had somewhat subsided, deadening to a dull throbbing sensation that seemed distant, detached from his own body almost as if the injury were slowly taking leave of his flesh. Yet the initial relief procured by this turn of events was soon mitigated to apprehension upon the discovery that numbness was slowly setting in and that the area round the crusted scab on his thigh was deepening in colour to the telltale red and blue of gangrene.

When night closed on the forth day, Shaka noticed the blades of the Zulus' assegais reflecting the glow of the moon like so many tiny, flickering torches and the first pangs of despair clutched at his heart. In fact, those reflected spears were but a few hundred meters behind him. As the youth stopped to rest, he pressed his hand against his thigh, and a chilling terror accompanied the awareness that the skin under his touch had the sinister texture of something foreign, a limb dismembered, the cold smoothness of a corpse. Instinctively, Shaka slapped his leg over the wound and was heartened to feel a slight stinging. But, as the sensation died away, a sinister notion took root in his mind: - the leg muscles would soon no longer respond to the dictates of the nerve centers and, when that happened, running, indeed even walking would become virtually impossible.

Shaka closed his eyes, momentarily resting the back of his head against the cold hardness of a rocky sarsen, marshalling his thoughts round the burden of his hopeless plight - one seemingly without solution. Yet, when his eyes reopened, the answer was suddenly before him, its huge, gently sloping outline looming against the greying hues of dawn: - a mountain, prodigious, majestic, its base stretching from horizon to horizon, its summit verily touching the Heavens.

There was no need to run, Shaka told himself with a faint smile. No need even to walk. Though his leg was nearly useless, his hands, his arms were still strong and perfectly reliable.

No need to run. He would climb!

Within an hour, Shaka had reached the base of the mountain and started his ascent. As Dilikana and his companions gaped in awe at the climbing figure that was slowly but powerfully moving up the face of a rocky cliff, the leader of the Zulu detachment wondered what manner of man was this I-Shaka, who, having miraculously survived the thrust of a spear and a fall that would have claimed the life of even the most fortunate of men, was now, after four days without food, water, or rest attempting to scale one of the highest peeks in the land. Were the rumours true? he marvelled. Did this 'beetle' really possess powers unknown to other mortals?

With a muffled curse and a deep sigh, Dilikana urged his men onward in pursuit of a man who was proving to be as stubbornly elusive as the end of a rainbow.

The birth of the sixth day found Shaka suspended on the face of the cliff at an altitude of over a thousand meters, with sheer rock above him, and below - the void. He was practically climbing with only his arms now using his good leg as a pivot point and as one of support, while his injured limb was merely dragged behind, a useless burden of flesh and bone without feeling, without purpose save for the hope that it would one day regain its flow of life.

Shaka had stopped worrying about the leg and its frightening deep purple colouring. He had even ceased to worry about the Zulus who were awkwardly plodding up the mountain behind him, losing ground with the passing of time. No, the youth was too overcome by his hunger and thirst to think of anything but the mitigation of these cravings which overrode even the blazing heat of the fever that seemed to consume his brain in its fire.

The immensity of his need for food and water, made desperate by his great loss of blood, thrilled every fiber of his body with a commanding urgency that obliterated all else. And, in the shadow of this need, Shaka was climbing on instinct alone, his powerful fingers mechanically purchasing their hold on the cliff's narrow ridges and cracks, pulling the body higher and higher without consciously reasoning where the next point of support would be found. It seemed that his hands were climbing with a will of their own.

When his eyes, their vision blurred, weakened by the turmoil of his senses, saw, or thought they saw what looked like a large nest, that of an eagle. And in the nest his eyes saw, or imagined they saw an egg, tinted white with spots of grey and brown, polished and gleaming in the sun's rays - an egg, succulent and appetising.

Slowly Shaka began to inch his way towards that savoury meal. Then, nearing it, averring that the vision was real and recognising it as the home of the mighty Lammergeyer, the Lord of Africa's Eagles, Shaka's heart leapt with expectancy, as he eased himself up onto the ledge on which the nest was perched and searched the skies for signs of the mother.

There were none. Not for the time being at least. With baited breath, his gaze still locked on the blue skies above and below him, Shaka reached for the large egg and, breaking it open, hungrily began to devour its creamy contents, his head reeling with delight at the taste of the morsels of chunky flesh.

Then he froze.

A grey-blue Lammergeyer swept across the sky with a slanting and ponderous flight, its boundless wings drenched in clear sunshine, its white crown brilliant against the deep blue of the celestial vault. Then, soaring higher, the eagle became a dark and motionless speck before it buckled its head forward and swooped down, diving -- towards Shaka.

In an instant the youth was ready for the mighty bird's attack. Inspecting the cliff at his shoulders, Shaka selected a sharpened sliver of granite that jutted out of the stone wall and, breaking off the chunk, he held the shard in his hand, the point projecting outward like the blade of an assegai.

As the eagle approached, it broke its forward thrust by opening and displaying its outstretched wings - with their full prodigious span of well over four meters. Then, curling the burnished tips of its feathered coverts, back-flapping, the eagle propelled its legs forward, its deadly talons reaching out for its unwelcome guest.

Feeling the overpowering displacement of air caused by the flapping of the gigantic hovering bird, the immense blast of wind almost drawing Shaka off his perch and into the void, the man pressed himself back against the face of the cliff, his one hand tightening its grip on the ledge as the other lashed forward with the granite shard, the stone's cutting edge slicing across the Lammergeyer's belly, drawing blood.

The mammoth bird let out a bloodcurdling shriek of pain and outrage before tucking back its wings and shooting down and away from the face of the cliff. Then, after a moment's respite, it soared back up, circling. drifting with the wind, studying the man with its keen ebony eyes, preparing its next attack.

Shaka, too, was preparing his defense. Gulping down the last few swallows of his pulpy meal, the youth clasped the stone sliver like a dagger, pressing himself against the cliff, his eyes locked on the eagle as it continued to circle, hovering overhead.

Then, suddenly, with a speed Shaka would not have believed possible, the bird was on him, the weight of its body oppressive, its claws scratching at his face and shoulders, its enormous wings fluttering over him, obscuring the light of day in the long shadows of its relentless assault, its pointed beak picking at his arms and shoulders, goring his flesh.

Nearly overwhelmed by the huge eagle's flagrant onslaught, Shaka goaded and thrust with his granite shard, his arms flailing in his valiant struggle to ward off the attack of the deadly talons that poked and slashed at him, lacerating his chest, bathing it in his own blood as well as that of his assailant, while the flashing redness of the sharp angular beak stabbed at his face in an attempt to gouge the eyes.

Unable to adequately parry the enraged Lammergeyer's foray, Shaka found that he could only take punishment and deal it out in return in hopes that the eagle's resistance would give out before his did. Yet, as the struggle dragged on inexorably, it appeared increasingly clear that the two opponents were evenly matched, both possessing unremitting endurance and undying prowess:- a deadlock that begs for the intervention of Fortune.

And Fortune appeared in the flash of sunlight that was reflected from the cliff's shiny surface onto the eagle's ebony orbs. For an instant, when that light caught the bird's eye, the mighty Lammergeyer was distracted and looked away.

Just a fleeting instant, but long enough for Shaka to sway the course of the conflict in his favour. Like a blurred flash of movement, the youth's hand snaked between the talons and his shard sank deep into solid flesh. The eagle cried out in anger, furiously stabbing at the man with its beak; yet its attack was losing force, as Shaka, with mounting rage, the fever in his brain igniting the passion of his wrath, slashed at the animal's body, slicing open its belly in a flow of slimey blood and viscera, piercing the mighty chest with thrust after thrust until the Lammergeyer's heart and its uncanny shrieking were silenced forever, and its mammoth body fell limp into Shaka's embrace.

His eyes flaming with triumph, the Zulu prince slit open the eagle's throat and brought his lips to the gash, drinking the warm blood that flowed forth to quench his raging thirst. Then, tossing the carcass aside, Shaka rose on his good leg and, squinting against the sun, peered up at the mountain's summit that loomed a good five hundred meters above him. Calling upon his final reserves of will power, the youth reached up for a handhold and resumed his climb.

The next afternoon, when Dilikana and his Zulu comrades reached the Lammergeyer's nest, they fully expected to find the mangled remains of their illustrious fugitive. In fact, having observed the previous day's conflict - from a ledge well below the two contenders - the Zulus, gaping witnesses to the eagle's enraged shrieking and to the crushing flutter of its monstrous wings, had little or no doubt as to the outcome of a battle in which the opponents appeared so disparate. Indeed, Dilikana had commented sarcastically that the 'prince' had already found his executioner and that there would be no need for a trail - just a burial.

But now, upon their arrival on the site of the butchery, the warriors stood in dumbfounded disbelief as they gazed at the blood-caked remains of the colossal Lammergeyer. Dilikana lifted his eyes to the cliff's towering peak and moved his lips in a silent murmur. To this day no one can swear whether that hushed remark was uttered in prayer or in cursing.

The impervious landscape on the mountain's summit was carpeted with a thick layer of snow and ice. The wind howled over the crest of the majestic glacial plateau, chilling the pinnacles and spines that rose out of the wintry blanket of eternal frost. It was into this extraordinary, inhospitable world that Shaka pulled himself at last, clawing his way over the edge of the rise.

Tittering on the verge of delirium, his body shivering with cold, his head scorched with heat, the youth might well have believed, as he first gaped at the summit's surreal contours, that this forbiding landscape was the fruit of his feverish imagination, for never before in his life had he seen anything like it - never before had his spirit viewed the magical candor of snow. Yet the reality of what he saw became clear as soon as his curiosity took over and, pulling his body forward, he dragged himself into the bed of snow, touching it, tasting it, intrigued and captivated by its colour, its nipping chill, and its granular consistency that turned to liquid upon inspection.

Looking up in amazement, Shaka gaped, awe-struck, at his niveous surroundings. When his gaze wandered over the blanket of shintillating whiteness, it sought out and found the opposing side of the peak. Rising onto his knee, Shaka made his way to the other end of the summit and, as his eyes beheld what lay beyond, his breath caught in his throat causing his heart to race within his chest and his astonishment to become disbelief.

Stretching out below him, washed in the crystal clear orange light of a dying sun, was the sweep of a landscape that seemed interminably, immeasureably huge to Shaka's mortal eyes with velvety hills stretching to meet the sky, plains unrolling towards the horizon, rivers angled silver in the sunlight, the emerald canvas of the great expanding woodlands, and, far beyond it all, the sparkling opaque blueness of the ocean.

Shaka's gaze was suddenly gravitated towards another mountain, distant and magical, its sloping summit far higher than the one Shaka had just scaled. As the youth bore the mysterious image of that distant peak with its pinnacles shining bright in the rays of the setting sun, he suddenly saw an apparition, miraculous, mystifying, unreal -- the image of an immense cloud that, before Shaka's eyes, slowly took on the shape of a narrow splinter of stone, over a thousand meters in length, that rose straight up from the mountain's peak, like a finger pointed at the sky, its tip vanishing into the reeling heights of the celestial dome. On the splinter, Shaka could barely make out a flight of stairs, steep as a ladder, cut into the stone's surface.

Staggered by the dizzying vision of the Pinnacle of Kings, the site where his mother had first learned of The Prophecy, believing that vision to be an hallucination, Shaka sank back, resting in the snow, the ebony colouring of his magnificent body contrasting with the frosty whiteness of his surroundings, both colours blending in the tenuous light of the dying day.

After the snow's initial cold impact, Shaka was delighted to feel a warming glow pervade his frozen frame. In the temporary invigoration procured by that warmth, the youth scooped up some of the snow and began to cleanse away the blood from his face, his chest and shoulders, his arms and, finally, his legs. The gelid frosty substance felt good on his bruised and battered flesh, and, gradually, as a smile caressed his lips, Shaka felt the fatigue overpower him as the cold deadened the remnants of pain.

Nodding off, the prince entered a dreamlike state where his mind entertained a dance of thoughts, a whirl of remembrance that rode on the crest of a lingering cosiness, the soft touch of his mother, his cheek on her breasts, his own voice - at the age of seven - asking, with insistence...

"Tell me, mother."
"It was all so unreal, Shaka. So...magical."
The fire danced merrily at the center of their hut in Mfunda's homestead, and, as Shaka gazed into the flames, watching them crackle with tiny explosions of white and blue, his voice took on the strain of urgency.
"Please tell me."
"It was on top of a mountain," Nandi started, hugging her son close to her, her eyes wandering to the flames as they took on the distant glint of one transported into the Past and its Mysteries. "On top of a high mountain. With a stairway of stone that lead to the clouds. I followed her up and up---"

"Who?"

"Sitayi," Nandi answered, pronouncing the name in a religious whisper, as one utters that which ears daren't hear. "The sangoma. - We went up and up and up. And it was cold," the woman winced, her smile returning as she added, "and magnificent. I could see--"

"What?"

"Everything! The river. The hills. The valley. The ocean. I felt like I could reach out and grasp the universe."

"And tell me again, mother. What did she say?"

Nandi lapsed into a gentle hush. There was a suggestion of fabulousness in her dreamy voice.

"From your womb shall come the Language of the Heavens emblazed in the heart of him who shall be great. All things shall obey him. All shall kneel at his feet. For he shall be their only king - the Sacred Sovereign of whom the Ancestors spoke when they sang to the wind."

"Who are they, mother?" the boy of seven asked, snuggling up closer to his mother, his smile of enchantment reflecting her own. "The Ancestors?"

Those who came before us and from whom all things descend," Nandi answered, patiently.

"Where do they live?"

"In us."

"In us?"

"In our hearts. In our thoughts. In our deeds. -- In us and through us."

When the twelfth sun had set on his flight from his father's warriors, after five more days and nights of arduous scaling down the steep cliffs that constituted the mountain's opposing flank, Shaka finally reached the foot of the immense stone escarpment and eased his tortured body onto the relative softness of a grassy slope. Looking out at the flatlands below him, barely discernible in the tenuous light of a crescent moon, Shaka knew that in his condition he would never be able to cross them. In fact, the plague of gangrene that had taken possession of his leg was already infecting the rest of his body, and the fever that raged in his veins along with the merciless demands of hunger's tyranny would soon draw his mind to the threshold of madness.

He would never be able to cross the flatlands. Yet he had no choice. He must keep running. Lifting his febrile gaze, Shaka scanned the cliffs above him for signs of his pursuers and spotted the moon's reflection on the shiny blades of their assegais. Half a day's distance, he calculated. Perhaps less. By the greying of dawn they should reach his present position.

Half a day. How wonderful it would be to rest just half a day. Yet, Shaka's finely-honed logic, ever vigilant, ever circumspect, easily deduced that in his present physical state the only chance he had to make good his escape was to stay well ahead of the Zulus.

"A Zulu, you say?" inquired Dingiswayo lifting a brow to General Buza who was respectfully kneeling at before him.

"Yes, Nkosi," answered the rugged troop commander of the valiant iziCwe Regiment, his heavily lined, dusky face drawn in an expression that seemed perpetually enslaved by a grimace of disapproval.

"Far from home, isn't he?" the king commented.

"Through no choice of his own, it would seem," General Buza replied in a gruff voice.

"And what is his name, General?"

"They call him...'Shaka', Nkosi."

At the mention of the name, the king's keen eyes were suddenly aglow with the glint of remembrance. Lapsing into a momentary abstraction, Dingiswayo rose from his throne and crossed to the edge of the clearing at the top of his vast cattlefold where he stood silently gazing, with vague interest, at his mulling throng of portly cattle - the sign of his recently acquired and hard won wealth and prosperity.

Shaka. - How long had it been?, the king mused, his hand instinctively curling under his arm to finger the smooth knot of scar tissue that had formed on his back.

How long? - Over four years since his brother's betrayal, four long years since the unselfish devotion of 'the outcasts'.

Shaka. - How often Dingiswayo had wondered what had become of that valiant young man. And now ---.

Ngomane, the king's chief induna and commander of the newly formed Mtetwa armies, a tall, distinguished-looking man in his mid-thirties, observed his monarch's silent reverie with interest and intrigue. Since Dingiswayo's return to the Mtetwa kingdom (after the news of his father Jobe's death had reached him beyond the "Wall" of the umThangala Mountains) and since his installment as king of his tribe (after Mawewe had fled north for fear of his brother's reprisal), Ngomane had become the monarch's only true confidant, sharing Dingiswayo's thoughts, his dreams and his hopes, as well as his concrete plans for the restructuring of his kingdom. The chief induna had also heard of how his sovereign's life had once been saved, and, as he now gazed at him, he found his thoughts returning to that remarkable tale.

"I wish to see him as soon as he is well," Dingiswayo finally told Buza, breaking the silence that he himself had imposed.

"So will that detachment of Zulus," Buza remarked with a sombre attitude. "They've been quite adamant about taking him prisoner, Baba. They say he's wanted by his king for treason."

"When a dozen armed soldiers fail to capture one dying man, they've little to be adamant about," the king bluntly replied, adding with a twinkle of amusement in his eye: "If my kingdom had armies like that, I'd be proud to bear the brunt of treason."

Ngomane turned to Buza with a diverted smile, yet, as was his manner, the general remained stiffly formal.

"Thank you, Buza. That will be all," the king told his soldier, dismissing him with a wave of the hand.

As Buza strode off to join his regiment (which had been instructed to 'play host' to the Zulus during their stay in the lands of the Mtetwa), Dingiswayo shifted his gaze to the magnificent leopardskin that hung at the threshold of the Royal Hut - the handsome hunting prize that had been given by one fugitive to another, the gift that a man named Godongwana had received together with his life and the name 'Dingiswayo', the 'Wanderer'.

"Is he the one of whom you spoke?" Ngomane asked.

"Yes, Ngomane. He is," the king confessed in a voice made heavy with the burden of despair. "When I was dying, Fate willed that we should meet, and he saved me. And now that he is dying, we meet again - as if Fate had willed that the time was ripe for me to settle an old account."

"I hear that his condition is desperate, Baba," Ngomane told his king, sharing the weight of his frustration.

"He must live, Ngomane!" Dingiswayo rejoined with a note of pleading. "He must. - If he were to die, the spectre of my unpaid debt would haunt me forever."

On the Pinnacle of Kings, two lone figures, Sitayi and Majola, stood above the clouds, their bodies suspended on the sea of ivory fleece.

Over the howling of the wind, Majola asked: "And what of the Nation?"

"It shall rise from his first grave," Sitayi uttered in a phantasmal whisper. "In ten-and-two, last for ten- and-two, and be buried with the second son of his father's son."

"Who will cast the Earth?"

"Those with the skins of sorghum," the sangoma hissed with a grimace of revulsion. "They will darken the Heavens and stand as the Elect, governing those who were foolish and judging that which their pale hearts cannot grasp."

"And the Appeaser?" Majola inquired. "When will he come?"

"On the Day of Fear. To judge the Elect and to bring Light back to the Heavens."

"And what of the Nation?"

"It is His," the blind sangoma smiled, the blueness of her orbs one with the sky. "It will always be His. Such is the Covenant of Loyalty."

Situated on the vast ridges and plains between Tzangonyana and Dondota, extending from the Heights of enTseleni to the Umfolosi River -- Dingiswayo's Mtetwa kingdom was saddened by the suffering of the beautiful, brave stranger who had "yehla ngogoma ebelwehle amaphiva namashongololo" ("descended the steep ridges which were walked upon only by water buck and millipedes"), and the many inhabitants of the kingdom feared for his life.

Pampata, the lovely young peasant girl, orphaned granddaughter of the wise Mbiya, had discovered his seemingly lifeless figure slumped on the pebble-strewn banks of the Guluzana, the stream where she was accustomed to fetch water at the dawning of each day.

She had grinned at first, coyishly, and blushed upon taking timid stock of his exceptional body - the imposing physique of a great athlete and warrior. Then, on closer inspection, Pampata had been shocked to see his gangrenous leg, his bruises, and the multitude of infected wounds that riddled his tortured flesh. Having feared that he was already dead - indeed his breathing was so shallow as to go almost unnoticed by an eye not trained to such scrutiny - the girl had pressed her hand to his cheek and felt the raging fever.

Upon turning to rush for help, Pampata had found herself faced with Dilikana and his contingency of Zulus. The men - whom she had instinctively distrusted on first sight - had told Pampata that they would tend to the fallen warrior who was - or so Dilikana had told her - a fugitive from justice and the armies of his king.

Yet, as Pampata had gazed back at Shaka's delicate, regal features, she had found it hard to believe that such a magnificent creature would ever willingly wrong anyone - especially his own people - and, consequently, she had insisted on seeking the advice and assistance of her grandfather, Mbiya, who - she had told Dilikana - was far more versed than she in matters of such intertribal subtlety.

Being the sort whose patience is easily and quickly tried, Dilikana had soon tired of this exchange with Pampata - which he had angrily defined as a waste of time - and, brushing the girl aside, he had ordered his men to heft Shaka's body onto their shoulders and be off with him.

The Zulus had been in the process of doing just that when Mbiya himself had appeared on the scene and surveyed the warriors with the level, perceptive eye and the righteousness of intent that had, over the years, won him the respect of his clansmen and women. Then the stalwart old man had listened to his granddaughter's simple words rebuked by the unmannerly invectives of the Zulu commander and had not been hard put to deduce that something was amiss.

Calling upon the aid of the iziCwe Regiment that had been patrolling in the vicinity Mbiya had wisely entrusted the entire matter to General Buza's authority and, through Buza, delivered the stranger into the hands of his king, Dingiswayo.

And now Pampata, who had found him by the stream, was at his side. As was Mbiya, intent on the administering of herbs and medicinal drugs which the old man expertly applied to the suppurating gashes he had lanced on Shaka's decaying limb in an effort to save both it and the body it had served.

Lifting his gaze to peer briefly through the fumes and smoke disgorged by the hut's generous fire, Mbiya cast a loving eye in the direction of his granddaughter and was immensely touched by her prone figure bent over the unmoving contours of the Zulu prince and by the tears that ran down her soft cheeks; he was moved by her youth, her innocence, her pretty beauty, which had the simple charm and the delicate vigour of a wild-flower. Mbiya looked at the young woman, almost sixteen now, the child he loved more than his own life, and he swore that he would do all he could to save 'her' prince.

Yet, as the fire's fumes filtered through the hut into the breeze of day and into the stillness of night, as Mbiya laboured on his patient, and as women scurried in and out with more herbs and fresh water - a tense urgency transpiring in their manner, it became more and more apparent to all that Shaka's life dangled from a fine thread.

That, indeed, he would die -- without a miracle of some kind.

Although Shaka would not have wanted others to resort to giving credence to Superstition - even at a time when his own life was riding the crest of thin air - he would also not have been contrary to their believing in the Supernatural as the Caretaker of Masters. Indeed, had the youth not been in a coma, he would most likely have done so himself.

Or perhaps he did. Anyway - that belief was averred.

In fact, though it was a fine, clear day and the sun was shining bright and undisturbed from horizon to horizon - an immense cloud suddenly formed and came up running over the Heavens and hovered overhead, arrested by the restraining hand of Magic. Presently, to the South there appeared a livid trembling gleam, faint and sad, like the vanishing memory of dying moonlight. And, to the North, another cloud appeared, blacker than the first, growing at a tremendous rate, consuming the lighter textures of the sky like a spot of ink expands over the leaf of the indigo. With the cloud came the Wind, screaming in great gusts that sent even the mightiest of trees bending in reverence; and the Rain, slashing at Nature, as Thunder raised its stentorian roar over Lightning's incandescent fingers.

And out of the tempest came Majola - the skins, skulls, and ghastly trinkets that adorned her withered body dashed and tossed by the wind, her wretched eyes narrowed against the rain, her grisly features bathed in the revealing harsh light of the heavenly bolts of fire.

Through Nature's flagellum she strode, under the eyes of the spellbound Mtetwas, past the astounded gazes of Dilikana and his Zulus...across the fields, through the gates of Mbiya's homestead and towards the hut where Shaka lay on the threshold of death.

Majola entered that hut without question, without opposition, for no one, not even Mbiya, dared confront the Supernatural with the artless guises of mortal Man.

For three days and two nights, the ageless sangoma remained with Shaka, alone, unaided, unseen in her task and toil, while the population of the Mtetwa Kingdom assembled round the homestead -- a vast throng of men, women, and children - carpeting the valleys and hills near the site of the dying prince like a silent, vigilant, immovable sea of brooding compassion.

On the eve of the third day, the clouds dispersed, and tranquillity returned in the wake of a splendid rainbow. Majola appeared at the threshold of the hut and, without uttering a word, without casting a gaze at any of those present, without acknowledging - even in her inscrutable thoughts - the eyes that glared at her in mystification, she vanished as magically as she had appeared, on the distant horizon, her wistful spirit claimed by the setting globe of the sun.

Later, when Shaka opened his eyes, he found the gentle presence of Mbiya and Pampata at his side. When Pampata saw his enthralling eyes fixed upon her with an uncontrolled expression of affection and gratitude, she experienced a hitherto unknown feeling of shyness, mixed with alarm and desire. Confused and dazzled by these unusual sensations, she instinctively fled from his gaze to the glow of the hearth, finding the brilliance of the embers less blinding than the eyes of that splendid prince.

"Who are you?" Shaka breathed in a feeble tone of deliverance.

"I am Mbiya. And this is my granddaughter Pampata."

Reaching out, Shaka took both their hands in his own and smiled.

"Thank you, Mbiya. Thank you, Pampata...For saving my life."

"No, my son," Mbiya answered, pensively shaking his head from side to side. "Miracles are not within our reach."

Shaka tightened his hold on their hands and his smile broadened infecting his eyes with its ardour.

"Aren't they?"

Mbiya frowned, puzzled by the remark.

"Your kindness, Mbiya," Shaka said in a tender hush. "That is miracle enough for a man who has lived as I have."

The next day Shaka was escorted to Dingiswayo's lodgings by an impressive contingency of guards. The prince was flanked on one side by Buza and a detachment of iziCwe warriors and, on the other, by the Zulus and their leader Dilikana - who stubbornly continued to regard Shaka as his prisoner and was greatly irked by the Mtetwas' interference (as he called it) into the internal affairs of a foreign tribe.

Upon reaching the recently built Mtetwa Royal Homestead, O-Yengweni, as it was called ('The Place of the Trickster' - in bitter commemoration of Mawewe's defilement of his father Jobe's trust), Shaka was amazed to find a huge residence, unrivalled in both size and splendour by anything the youth had seen in his long years of roaming.

The exterior palisade that circumvented the entire abode was well over three hundred meters in diameter, and Shaka could count at least fifty huts within the embracing arms of the high thorn bushes, but, as he extended his purview, the Zulu prince realised that the real number of huts must be well over two hundred. - Two hundred! Incredible, the youth considered - a residence five times larger than Kondlo's already enormous court at emTamdeni! What sort of man could have built such a home?! What ambition! What greatness!

And the cattle! Over a thousand head Shaka guessed, casting an astonished eye at the fold brimming with a sea of flesh and hide under a forest of glistening horns.

Amazing, he told himself shaking his head in disbelief. This new king of the Mtetwas must be truly without peers and his power greater than any he had thought possible. Hopefully he will also be compassionate and look kindly upon him and his family, the Zulu prayed as his eye fell upon Dilikana's threatening features. Hopefully, he, Shaka, will be spared the humiliation of Senzangakona's requital.

With these thoughts droning in his mind, flanked by Dilikana and Buza, Shaka approached the large clearing by the Royal Hut and, committing his fate to the care of Justice, the youth strode purposefully towards yet another kismet and knelt before the monarch's seated figure.

"Bayete, Nkosi," Shaka saluted the potentate.

"Rise, my friend," Dingiswayo answered. "It is my fortune that you have recovered."

Shaka knitted a stunned brow, struck by that voice which sounded so remotely familiar, yet one he had trouble placing. Looking up, the youth's eyes fell on the leopardskin draped symbolically over the Royal Hut and his gaze was gravitated to the smiling semblance of the man he had last seen striking off, over the "Wall", for the Unknown World.

"It would appear that out destinies are interlocked, Shaka," the king commented, his eyes dancing with pleasure.

"Dingiswayo," Shaka exclaimed, truly delighted to see him, and rose to better greet the long lost member of his 'family'.

The two men fell into each other's arms, embracing as brothers.

Dilikana chanced a perplexed look at Buza, but the latter was as puzzled as the Zulu by his king's unfamiliar familiarity.

"What is this talk of treason?" the king finally demanded from Shaka, his full lips still riding the intimacy of a benevolent smile.

"I'm not completely sure," the prince shrugged good-naturedly. "But I have the feeling my father has decided that a dead son is less of an inconvenience than a live one."

"Yes," nodded Dingiswayo, raising a knowing brow. "Such is the way of monarchs. They all desperately want sons who take after them until their sons decided to take after them."

Shaka grinned at the remark, feeling the last vestiges of his recent struggle with death peeling from his spirit before the Mtetwa's overwhelming cordiality. Dingiswayo's attention flitted across Dilikana's features as he asked Shaka, somewhat playfully: "What do you want me to do with him?"

"Whatever you feel you must, Baba," smiled the prince, his eyes twinkling mischievously.

Nodding, his face ironing out with severity, Dingiswayo turned to face the Zulu commander, who suddenly found himself wishing he were somewhere else.

"I want you and your men out of my kingdom by sunset," the Mtetwa ordered and then looked away, as if the man were no longer there.

"But..." Dilikana stammered. "But what will I tell my king, Nkosi?"

"That his son is my guest," the king rejoined tersely.

Summoning up his courage, the Zulu commander levelled his shoulders and offered, as proud rebuttal: "I feel it is my duty to inform you, Nkosi, that your attitude could lead to war."

Dingiswayo shot Dilikana an enduring glance. "War?" the king echoed, arching a brow. "Buza, what tribes have thus far been incorporated in the Mtetwa Paramountcy?"

The word 'paramountcy' was not lost upon Shaka. He knew it signified one kingdom, one power ruling supreme over others in a confederacy of tribes under the supervision and control of one 'paramount king', - a king who could, if he so wished, wield absolute powers that were dictatorial in all but name.

A Kingdom of Kingdoms. One Nation. Shaka listened intently, his curiosity notably roused.

Realising the nature of his king's question, Buza answered nonchalantly, his statement geared to impress the Zulu visitor. "The emaTenjini, the emaNgadini, the Moonabi, the Sokanas, the Dube, the Sokulu, the emaDlazini, the Nxele, the Nzimeleni, and the Ncube, Baba - along with several other smaller coastal tribes," the general listed, adding somewhat conceitedly: "Thus far!."

Dilikana's mouth was opened in amazement.

"And what do our standing armies number, Buza?" the king asked, his eyes still locked on the Zulu commander.

"Including my iziCwe, the uYengondlovu, and the iNyelezi -- Five regiments, Nkosi. Each composed of approximately 200 warriors - all highly trained and fitted for battle...day and night."

Thrilled by what he heard, Shaka felt the blood racing in his veins, charging his thoughts with excitement. A nation with a standing army of over a thousand warriors trained in discipline and ready for action both day and night! The concept seemed to bring Shaka's own ambitions into focus. Suddenly, for the first time in his life and for reasons that were still not completely clear to the youth, he felt close, very close to the illusive dream that haunts the sleep of Masters.

"And what is the size of the Zulu army, Buza?" the king went on, driving home his point.

The commander of the iziCwe answered, in the same matter-of-fact tone, that, like all the other Nguni Bantu tribes, the Zulus had no standing army - in fact no army at all to speak of. In the event of conflict, the Zulus would be obliged to militarize virtually overnight, forcing shepherds to abandon their staffs and farmers their plows for the weaponry of war, - a war in which only the most experienced hunters would be of any actual military value.

"We calculate, Baba," Buza concluded, "that the Zulus might be able to rely on an army of a hundred to a hundred and fifty men. No more."

"Does that substantiate my 'attitude', Zulu?" the king inquired of the hapless Dilikana.

The Zulu nodded in silence.

"As I said - you have until sunset."

The falling sun seemed to be arrested for a moment in its descent, and it sat on the far edge of the unbroken expanse of amber veld, whilst from its brilliant globe shot out on the darkening surface of the earth a track of light, straight and shining, resplendent and direct - a path of gold and crimson that led from the horizon to the makeshift hut Nandi had built near the thorn tree that marked her mother's gravesite.

Nomcoba was already fast asleep near the smouldering campfire, and Nandi sat next to her, cradling Ngwadi's slumbering figure in her arms, rocking back and forth as if to give the mediocre son of Gendeyana the solace she had never been able to convey upon the magnificent offspring of the Love of her life.

Yes, mediocre. Nandi knew - as only a mother can - that the soul of the child she now held, the blood of her blood, was a blood diluted by complacency, by the false contentment of life's vanquished, by the serenity that justifies the defeated, by the poise that masks the commonplace.

As Nandi now held Ngwadi - she thought of Shaka. What if he were dead?

Notwithstanding the sense of insecurity that gripped her, she had no image of his death before her. She felt him intensely alive - and, consequently, she, too, felt alive in a flush of strength, with an impression of novelty as though his life and her own had been the gift of that very moment.

She even found herself smiling. And yet the doubt lingered. What if he were--?

Looking up, Nandi noticed a cloud of dust on the horizon, near the setting son - a cloud moving towards her. As it approached, she could make out the figures of men, soldiers - an army.

Resting Ngwadi on the ground, the woman reached for her assegai and prepared to defend her family - when, all of a sudden, her fierce, narrowed eyes were overspread by a strange look of beatitude as she beheld, in the distance, his figure marching towards her, aloof, mysterious, his erect and careless attitude suggesting - as always - assurance and power.

When Shaka reached the gravesite, he took his mother in his arms and, as she wept over her own fortune in having such a son, he caressed her face and whispered: "Come, mother. I'm taking you home."

"Peace," said Dingiswayo, as he and Shaka strolled through the gorgeous countryside that flourished near his imposing homestead. "It may sound incongruous, nevertheless that is the ultimate purpose of my standing armies. - To bring peace, unity and a common identity to all the Nguni Bantu peoples - to all of Africa! I firmly believe that that is our only chance if we want our civilisation to survive."

As Shaka walked at the king's side, the youth was in awe of Dingiswayo's words and he listened in silence, without interruption, without any other thoughts save for thoughts of what he was hearing. Though the Mtetwa's ideas were new in concept, visionary in scope, and revolutionary in spirit, they seemed to reflect perceptions and convictions that were already very much a part of Shaka's own prospective, and the other man's ideas danced in his own brain to very much the same music.

"After I left you and your family," Dingiswayo went on, "and crossed the umThangala, I 'wandered', as you so accurately described it; and in my journeys across the unknown lands that lie West of here, I was brought into contact with other peoples and other ideas which broadened my outlook on life---"

The king told Shaka of the remarkable civilisation that he had run in to in his travels: the White Man - or the "Swallows", as Dingiswayo called them (due to the fact that, like the swallow, the Whites built their 'nest's' with mud and wattle). This unusual breed of people, he said, with skins the colour of sorghum, had come from far away riding over the seas on immense animals with great white wings and had established their advanced outposts many moons' to the South. He also told Shaka that he had learned that beyond the seas the Swallows were far more numerous than all the Ngunis combined, and that their armies there were uncountable and equipped with death-dealing staffs which vomited thunder, smoke and death, and still bigger staffs, like logs, which were the most fearsome of all. Dingiswayo stressed that these beings were strong not only because of these death-dealing instruments, but because they possessed an orderly system of government in which all lesser chiefs and kings acknowledged one supreme lord as head over all, a unifying system which did away with petty fighting and ensured lasting power and peace;-- indeed, Dingiswayo emphasised, due to their weapons and orderly system, the Whites were powerful enough to constitute a threat to the Nguni and to all of Africa if their greed ever became as uncontrollable as that of the locust.

Consequently the Nguni must adopt a similar system of orderly government, the king propounded with vehemence, - and find a unity of their own, if they are to offer proper resistance to the relentless advance of these...locusts.

"We Nguni are a multitude of hundreds of separate kindred clans," Dingiswayo went on to stress, "all speaking the same language, or dialects of the same language, all leading the same mode of life, all with the same basic type of social organisation, and yet, we have nothing in common - no common purpose, no common ambition, no common aspiration. We are like so many beautiful flowers growing from the same earth and on the same plot who lack the courage to call themselves a garden. We are a garden, Shaka! Africa is a garden! Lets protect it from the locusts!"

Both men fell silent, gazing out at the rich fields alive with grain, at a lazy herd of elephant basking in the mud of a river bank, at the graceful flight of the guineafowl.

Africa, the garden in the shape of a heart.

"Things must change," Dingiswayo suddenly filled the silence with the appeal of his words. "This land and its people must be shaken out of their complacent stupor. By force, if need be! We must impose unity by incorporating all these wayward tribes under a common leadership - the Mtetwa Paramountcy, first, then..." the king's eyes verily sparkled as he added, "the Nguni Paramountcy and the Bantu Nation! One vast, united empire encompassing all the surrounding lands, as far as the eye can see!"

Shaka froze, chilled by Dingiswayo's vision thus phrased. His mind reeling, once again the youth heard the voice of the Pond with its sonorous consecration: 'Seek and I shall give thee the nations for thy heritage, the end of the earth for thy domain -- as far as the eye can see!"

Yes, Shaka told himself, it was true - his own destiny and Dingiswayo's were interlocked.

"And I will need you to help build that Nation," the king went on. "Your courage, your valour, your strength. To start with, I want you to be the general of one of my regiments. Any regiment,- you pick it!"

Shaka was greatly moved by Dingiswayo's generosity and his heart yearned to grasp the opportunity offered him - the opportunity literally of a lifetime! Yet his intrinsic sense of justice refuted any special treatment - even by the man whose life he'd saved."

"Thank you, Baba," Shaka said. "But I cannot accept. Though my courage, my valour and my strength are at your service, I cannot be a general. I am not worthy of that honor. Not yet, that is. You and I have suffered enough to know that a man must always earn his way through life!"

Dingiswayo smiled.

"Though I truly wish to lead one of your regiments, Nkosi, I will do so only through merit and merit alone! - I ask that you give me the chance to prove my talents as a common soldier. - To start with." The Mtetwa king looked deeply into the young man's eyes and, as if reading something there, uttered, softly: "Dignity. A quality rarely found nowadays. - Very well, Shaka, you will join the iziCwe regiment. With the other warriors of your age group -- as a 'common soldier'." Dingiswayo had a broad smile as he placed a hand on Shaka's shoulder. "Though I doubt you will remain that for long. You were born to be a leader, Shaka. Be it through merit or by destiny - nothing and no one can stand in your way."

What had his mother told him when he was a child of seven? He would recognise his destiny when the time was right for him to see it.

He saw it. Clearly. Now he saw it.

"My son is his guest?" repeated Senzangakona, aghast. "Is that all he had to say?"

Mudli and the other members of the Council shifted their stupefied gazes to Dilikana who was looking steadfastly at the ground at his feet. The utter failure of his mission was a heavy burden to carry, especially in the presence of his king and the Council.

"More or less, Nkosi," was Dilikana's evasive response.

"More - or less?" Senzangakona growled in a low rumble.

Dilikana's eyes had nowhere to search for support, so they continued to stare at the polished black floor of the Zulu Royal Hut.

"I had the impression, Baba," the beaten warrior remarked with difficulty, "that they already knew each other. Shaka and the Mtetwa king, that is. Like --- old acquaintances."

The Zulu king's brow furrowed as he glanced with bloodshot eyes at his sister to see if she could shed any light on this miraculous turn of events. But Mkabayi merely rewarded her brother's perturbed, drunken glare with a knowing nod; - hadn't she warned Senzangakona that he must win his son back, before it was too late, before others, like Dingiswayo, won him over first? Hadn't she been against the entire idea of sending armed guards to bring him back? Hadn't she further told him that having one's son stand trial for the mistakes made in his upbringing was certainly not the most appropriate way of winning his affection.

"Old acquaintances?" Senzangakona echoed in a hollow voice as his eyes fled from his sister's merciless smirk. "How much longer am I to endure this?" he queried of no one in particular, slumping down onto his mat and into a monotonous reverie of self pity. "Since the day he was conceived, this 'I-Shaka' has brought me only disrepute and outrage."

Mkabayi could not resist restating her past admonitions. "It is as I said, my brother. They see his greatness and fear him as a potential enemy."

"Perhaps, Mkbayai." The king shifted his gaze back to the woman. He looked weary and bitter. "Yet there is something I fear more, much more - becoming Shaka's puppet!"

Mudli and the members of the Council exchanged tense glances as the king continued his confession, mumbling sulkily.

"The boy is already on my throne, making decisions for me, forcing my hand, indirectly wielding the future of my realm. Although I am king of the Zulus, he is ultimately manipulating the fate of my House through his powerful 'acquaintances'. If this is allowed to continue, we will be virtually isolated! The time has come for me to force the issue." Senzangakona gazed dejectedly into space and spluttered recklessly, in a tone of drunken bereavement, as if he now realised that his son was indeed lost forever: "The time has come for war."

Jarred by the thought of a war with the Mtetwas, Mudli was shocked, as were Lutuli and the other members of the Council. When the Elder finally regained his composure, he beseeched his king to abandon the idea, stressing that a war with Dingiswayo would be suicidal! The Mtetwas greatly outnumbered the Zulus. And when Dilikana remarked upon the size of the Paramountcy, its standing armies, its trained regiments - each two hundred strong, the Council was nearly bubbling with animation, commenting heatedly on the dreadful fate that would await their kingdom if they were to take up arms against such a formidable foe.

"Perhaps through diplomatic channels," Mudli suggested to his king. "Dingiswayo appears to be a man of honour. If he were made to understand your outrage, your---"

"No more messengers!" Senzangakona roared. "No more discussions! We're outnumbered, I know, but Dingiswayo's expansionistic policy has won him many enemies who would be only too pleased to form an alliance against the Mtetwas. King Pungashe of the Butelezi Clan, for instance. I'm sure that when we speak of Dingiswayo, he and I will find that we have a great deal in common."

The Zulu king lifted his gaze to the polished royal assegai hanging on the wall of his hut and repeated his decision with mounting resolve and a voice slurred by his inebriation. "War! - there is no other way. Our dignity is at stake. And perhaps my throne!"

CHAPTER XVIII
"IMPI" (REGIMENT)

For the most part, the Task of Warfare, like that of the Artist, is sought out primarily by the Discontented -- those nomadic travellers of the human condition who need the presence of a strong passion to justify their own restless anger, the penetrating power of their souls which, acting like a corrosive fluid, eats away at the generally inexpugnable strength of common sense. Indeed, for these "Travellers" nothing is more repulsive, more foreign than a sense which is common, and they flee from it in search of an appeal which is not dependent on any fixed manner of action, but finds fulfillment in the extravagance of Delight and Wonder, in Pity, Pain, Beauty and the Horrid, in Death and in the other mysteries that surround our lives. The Discontented, like the Artist, have a dire need to be honest, not as a moral consideration - there is little or no place in such souls for doctrines and codes of conduct which are effected by the norms of healthy human behaviour inasmuch as they find any human behaviour that is conditioned by collective norms as unhealthy and a manner of conduct which betrays the purpose of the Individual Soul, - no, their need for honesty is one of pure survival. And thus they both, the Discontented and the Artist, in their own way, approach the remorseless rush of Time in a single-minded effort to attain a clearness of sincerity in their toil, in their joy, in their hope, in their fears, in their love and hatred, and in the uncertain fate which binds men to each other and all Mankind to the visible world. Yet, whereas for the Artist this attainment of sincerity is often a diversion, a task approached in tenderness and faith, as if dealing with mere dream-stuff, for the Discontented that same quest - whether for Good or for Evil - has the overtones of an obsession, a desire wrought to its highest pitch. When, as often occurs, the Discontented are also Artists, the tenderness and faith of their approach to dream-stuff has a need for honesty in survival that is as urgent as the next heartbeat. Shaka Zulu was a Discontented Artist. Over the years that spanned his military career - guiding him from common soldier to emperor, warfare became more and more the outlet for the undying restlessness of his anger, for the penetrating power of his mind, and for the corrosive need for honesty that, for him, became the very essence of survival. Yet that was later -- but now, at the inception of this tempestuous career, as Shaka followed the brisk pace of General Buza who was leading him through the iziCwe Regimental Homestead at emaNgweni in the Kingdom of the Mtetwa - on this his very first day as a common soldier, the Zulu prince had no clear way of knowing in which direction his nomadic travels through life would take him. He only felt, as he walked through the military residence carrying the uniform he'd been issued - consisting of white oxtail anklets and wristbands, a kilt of fur strips, a black plumed skin cap and oxhide sandals, together with his weapons: three long throwing assegais and a small oval shield, - he felt, as he followed Buza to the hut he'd been assigned, an odd expectation, an anxious impatience that rushed through his veins giving him an intensity of existence that he experienced only when hunting in the open veld. But this anxious expectation, this foretaste of experience was not even remotely akin to Romance. Shaka knew - from the most tender of ages - that journeying in search of Romance was like trying to catch the horizon which always lies a little distance before us and yet has the elusiveness of something we have already passed. He knew that to live in search of Romance was to seek an imaginative lie that extinguishes, in a whirl of emotions, a true understanding of Life. No, in his need for honesty, for sincerity, in his ardent belief in discipline, Shaka would never have sought the deception of Romance. What he felt, instead, was the kindling of a fire that would consume his life.

Notwithstanding this feeling of controlled exhilaration, something bothered Shaka as he crossed the regimental homestead, something that caused his stomach to churn queasily.

It wasn't the belligerent, domineering manner of General Buza that annoyed him, nor was it the authoritative way in which the iziCwe commander swung his knobkerrie against the palm of his hand, looking all too ready to inflict punishment with his heavy club at the slightest provocation. No, having lived amongst suffering and adversity, Shaka was hardened to violence and to the temperament of violent men. In fact, in such military surroundings, where discipline is often mistaken for submission, the youth expected to find varying forms of brutality, and Buza's brusque conduct - the fruit of ignorance, Shaka deduced - was a calculated waste of energy. Nor was it the diffidence and aggression that transpired in the reserved stares of the soldiers who eyed Shaka as he passed them, showering looks of suspicion and envy upon the stranger who, though an old friend of the king, preferred to start in the ranks of common soldiers: an act of suspect munificence and one which had the taint of a spy's intrigue. No, this did not annoy Shaka. In fact, as he allowed his gaze to linger on the hostile eyes of the iziCwe warriors - who snapped to attention as Buza passed them with his lethal knobkerrie - the Zulu youth had a wry inward smile thinking of all the times in his life when he was made to feel unwelcome. He was used to that hostility, he reminded himself. Besides, he thought, - quite objectively speaking, his peers had every good reason to be envious of him - many reasons, in fact. In addition to his fraternal relationship with Dingiswayo which, at first sight, Shaka had to admit did look rather suspect especially to a hardliner like Buza who could very well consider Shaka's friendship with the king as a threat to his own career if the Zulu ever decided to take the king up on his offer and ask to be general of the iziCwe, - in addition to this, Shaka realised that the soldiers' envy and almost immediate dislike for him could have been sparked by the fame that had preceded him to the land of the Mtetwas: - the strong stand he had taken with his father, the respect and loyalty shown him by the powerful Kondlo who had officially recognised his status as a true prince of the House of Zulu, his miraculous escape from Dilikana and his men, and, to top off these celebrated feats, his recent victory over Death at the hand of the Supernatural in the guise of the sangoma Majola. Yes, Shaka nodded to himself, more than enough reason to be envious, particularly if one were to append to the list his physical and intellectual attributes: his exceptional height and physique, his superior intelligence, his extraordinarily refined experience (far greater than that of most men his age), his aura and charismatic comportment that would obviously make lesser men cringe with umbrage and, of course!, - his arrogance, he added with a smile as he caught himself thus singing his own praises. No, that was not what bothered him, for he knew that sooner or later Masters must become accustomed to the resentment of Victims. What bothered Shaka was the gnawing premonition that he might soon fall prey to an emotion he had not yet experienced: - loneliness. Though the youth had trained himself to go for long periods without the so-called necessities of life:- food, water, sleep, warmth, shelter from the sun and rain, relief from pain, and without the basics of living:- the friendship of his peers, their companionship, a home, a father, a true family, an identity, security, hope, solace, -- though the youth had been schooled in the suppression of Life's 'confining elements', he had never - in his almost twenty tragic years of earthly permanence - been deprived of Nandi for a long period of time. And now, at emaNgweni, he would have to live away from his mother for over a year, relying on only a few occasional visits to bridge the loneliness. Nandi - ever Nandi. - Like his father before him, he would have to learn to live without her. And, like his father before him, he now felt the premonition of that great sacrifice. At the far side of the homestead, bordering on a ravine flanked by a high, rocky promontory, Shaka was shown the hut he would share with four other men and, as he and Buza ducked through the threshold of the thatched abode, the Zulu prince found himself suddenly enveloped in an oppressive human stench and in the company of an unlikely assortment of housemates who, upon first inspection, seemed to substantiate the hostility that Shaka had felt in the other soldiers. Near the door was a wiry young man that went by the name of Joko - or so Shaka was told by Buza who took the gruff liberty of introducing the disparate group. Somewhat seedy in character, with a thick hanging lip and a strong jutting chin, Joko looked up from the cowhide shield he was mending and inspected the newcomer with eyes narrowed challengingly over sunken, pockmarked cheeks. Behind him, Mtonga, short, with chunky legs and arms, and a protruding belly, spat a chunk of chewing tobacco into the hearth and grunted a greeting that was echoed, as a surly rumble, by Dlaba, another youth who was slumped on the ground indecorously scratching his testicles as he cast the newcomer a dispassionate sidelong glance. Nodding back curtly, Shaka turned his clear eyes to gaze through the seething smoke at a quick face, precocious, sagacious in lineaments, with deep downward lines on each side of a thin, wide mouth. Those lines, belonging to the features of a recruit named Nqoboka, curled back and up in a smile of genuine pleasure. Then, surprisingly, Nqoboka uttered a warm greeting, which came like a patch of blue sky in a thunderstorm to shed a ray of sunshine upon the chilling animosity that had gripped the hut since Shaka's arrival. Finding Nqoboka's smile contagious, Shaka grinned back, taking an instant liking to this man who represented the first sign of camaraderie in a military establishment in which fellowship, especially towards new recruits like Shaka, should be the order of the day. Fellowship - and discipline. As Shaka spent the remainder of his first afternoon at emaNgweni exploring his new surroundings, "acclimatizing" as Buza had curtly put it, the Zulu prince soon realised that something was fundamentally wrong with the regiment's discipline. In fact, though the soldiers readily responded to Buza's authoritative presence, by snapping to order as soon as the commander's knobkerrie smacked against the palm of his hand, this was not discipline, but rather an acquired reflex action based on fear. And, though Shaka knew full well from his investigation of Nature - that a basis of fear was necessary in all communities because animals (especially humans) were generally more inclined to submitting to the leader who made himself dreaded, than to one who merely strove to be beloved - the young man had also intuited that lasting discipline, the only sort a leader can truly rely upon in battle, was an active effort of the entire being, a training, a conditioning of the heart, the mind, and the soul to produce a pattern of behaviour which would lead to a moral, physical and mental improvement of the Individual, not a passive condition where punishment was received in an effort to break the will - not unlike the whippings received by a dog or by any domestic animal. In fact, far from attempting to break the Will, - discipline should aspire to fortify it, creating an enlightenment of character in which the mind's coordination of the body and the heart becomes as vital as that of the legs in walking. A discipline that comes from within, not from without. A principle from which purpose is derived - not punishment.   As he went about his afternoon's "acclimatisation", Shaka realised that the uniform he had been issued also appealed to his critical sense. - Anklets, caps, fur strips, kilts, and the like, and especially the sandals! What use did a soldier have for all this paraphernalia? Men should fight like the leopard - wearing little more than the uniform they were issued by Creation! And the spears - something was wrong with them as well, though Shaka could not yet put his finger on exactly what it was. They were too long, of course. That was obvious at first glance. But the problem was greater, he knew, and made a mental note to investigate the matter further, and was, in fact, about to bring it up with Buza at the campsite dinner when he was suddenly put off by the general's visible reluctance to commune with the newcomer.

Yes, Shaka confirmed to himself with a burdened sigh as he ate alone, segregated from the others - it was quite understandable that his peers and Buza should express their envy through hostility that they should find it hard to cope with his arrogance. Yet, having developed as a natural mechanism of self-defence in a world full of enemies, Shaka's arrogance was now an integral part of his being as necessary to a smooth interaction of the psychic components needed for security and confidence, as his keen eyesight was to the physical coordination necessary for hunting.

If his 'military comrades' couldn't accept him for what he was, he determined to continue to live as he always had - as a recluse.

Alone. Without Nandi - the only person to whose soul he could confide his innermost thoughts.

That night he was sleepless and sat alone with his thoughts, perched high atop of the promontory overlooking the homestead. His eyes on the night, Shaka felt an peculiar sense of solitude flow through his being as if his blood had turned to a rushing current of ice; a unshakable feeling that momentarily cast the shadow of doubt on his fixity of purpose. The youth felt himself faltering, losing his psychological balance, his head spinning as he lowered his gaze to the blackness of the void at his feet.

When a voice was heard at his shoulders - a voice soft, soothing, with a tone of polite affection.

"I know how you feel," the voice told him.

Far from being frightened by that tempering sound, Shaka swivelled his head round and stared up at a young man of medium height and sturdy build, with a round, full face, placidly noble in its expression and cherubic in the twinkle of its eyes, a face that betrayed simple faith in others and compelled respect for itself. The face of a man who quietly introduced himself as Mgoboziovela-entabeni ("Mgobozi-who-came-over-the-rise") and asked if he could sit down next to Shaka, proceeding to do so without waiting for an answer.

"I didn't like it here either at first," Mgobozi went on, his eyes wandering to the stars. "But then that was my fault. I had my hopes set too high."

Shaka narrowed his eyes as if to take better stock of this appealing stranger.

"I came here thinking I was going to become ..." Mgobozi raised a brow and emphasized, "- a soldier. Of course I had no idea what that really meant - being a soldier, I mean - but somehow in my ingenuousness I fancied it had something to do with 'heroism'! But, as I say, it was my fault. I was looking for a purpose, a good reason to be alive, and maybe even something worth dying for."

Shaka was attracted by the word 'purpose' inasmuch as it reflected his own existential search, and he gazed at Mgobozi, intrigued, captivated.

"But you know what I found?" the young man asked, again rhetorically. "I found that a soldier's life is like any other life - just dirtier."

Shaka smiled.

The other's expression became sombre.

"There are almost two hundred men down there," Mgobozi reflected, his gaze wandering over the flickering campfires that dotted the obscurity of the military homestead. "Two hundred men. All with the same problem. All coping with it in their own way, all looking for some one to come along and give them a good reason for being a soldier. - But no one's done that yet. That's why you can say we're two hundred men in a regiment, - not a regiment of two hundred men. And, like you, we all feel terribly lonely. Perhaps even terribly cheated."

Shaka's smile faded - his eyes rivetted on Mgobozi.

"I just thought you should know that," he added, rising to take his leave. "When you're lonely, it's nice to know you're not alone. - Good night. Thanks for the talk. - By the way, roll call's at the crack of dawn, but no one ever lines up till mid-morning, when Buza makes his rounds. - So sleep late if you want to."

Shaka's smile returned as he watched the youth amble off into the night - a warm smile of genuine affection.

"Good night, Mgobozi," the Zulu replied to the darkness and spent the rest of the night awake - one Discontented Artist pondering over the strife of another. *

As the radiant globe of the next morning's sun lifted above the pinnacles overlooking emaNgweni, the homestead's soldiers were still cosily nestled in their slumber; - it seemed that sleeping late was the norm.

Yet Shaka was up and in the process of shaking Mgobozi out of his dreams.

"Wake up," the Zulu urged.

Opening one eye, Mgobozi tried to focus on his new acquaintance. When he had, he uttered a curt "mornin'" and, rolling over, went back to sleep.

"Mgobozi," Shaka urged anew. "You said you were looking for a purpose. Maybe we can find one together."

"Tomorrow," Mgobozi answered without budging.

"Mgobozi," the Zulu repeated the name, slowly now, with punctuated emphasis. "If roll-call's at the crack of dawn...roll-call's at the crack of dawn."

With a big, long sigh, Mgobozi turned to look back at Shaka. This time both eyes were open and he was grinning. "Me and my big mouth."

Quietly, so as not to rouse the others, the two men donned their uniforms. Shaka found he had trouble determining how one went about placing sandals on feet.

"Don't tell me you've never worn them!" Mgobozi remarked in wonder.

"I've never had to," Shaka replied in helpless apology, his expression reflecting a grief befitting a far greater crime.

"Well, you'll have to here!" was the stern answer. "Buza's very strict about uniform."

"Wake up, you lazy bastards!" shouted Buza an hour or so later! "Wake up you pack of old women! - Off your asses!"

The commander of the iziCwe was shouting his very characteristic reveille, as he made his morning rounds accompanied by his direct subordinate, Kuta, an officer of mild manners and dapper disposition who seemed greatly perturbed as he followed in Buza's tow, wincing at the crassness of his superior.

And Buza was truly in the foulest of moods as he ventured from hut to hut, nudging the warriors out of their slumber with a liberal use of his mouth and his knobkerrie, provoking a chorus of grumbles, groans, coughs, and curses.

Upon reaching Shaka's hut, Buza stopped, a sardonic smile dancing across his boorish features. Clenching his blunt weapon, the commander ducked into the abode and, cocking back his arm, readied the knobkerrie for its infliction of pain, and roared: "On your feet, you---!"

The words stuck in his throat as he noticed, to his utter dismay, that Shaka's sleeping mat was neatly folded in his corner of the hut and that the Zulu himself was nowhere to be seen. Feeling cheated, enraged, Buza retaliated by clubbing Dlaba out of his troubled repose, before stomping deliberately out of the hut.

"Where's that new recruit?!" Buza barked to Kuta.

"Up there, sir," the officer replied, evenly, nodding in the direction of the slope where roll-call was held, the place where Shaka and Mgobozi were now standing at attention, fully dressed and ready to be counted.

"I knew that upstart was trouble! - " the general grunted, leaving Kuta to frown at the remark.

"Trouble, sir? - I would think it's about time the soldiers obey orders of their own free will. Without... 'coaxing'," Kuta's eyes rested on the knobkerrie. "The Zulu's a good example for the men. You should be happy."

"I know his kind! He's just doing it to aggravate me, Kuta!" was Buza's mindless rejoinder. "But, maybe you're right," the commander added, his lips pulling back over a remarkably perfect set of white teeth that seemed more than ready to bite. "Maybe he can be an example for the men."

"Look at this man! He's been here less than a day and already he's understood more about military life than any of you miscreants!" Buza was addressing the men lined up for training. Reference, of course, was being made to Shaka with a tone that presaged only malice of intent.

"This morning," the general now allowed sarcasm to creep into his rising voice," at the crack of dawn -- at the crack of dawn, mind you! - he was fully dressed and ready for action in the company of his confederate here!"

Buza jabbed his knobkerrie in the direction of Mgobozi who wondered, with a knitted brow, what the commander intended by 'confederate'. It sounded almost as if the two men had taken part in some sort of conspiracy! "I find that highly commendable - highly commendable -," Buza's sarcasm was becoming farcical. "And I want each and every one of you to follow his example. Tomorrow morning, when the sun peeks over those mountains," he continued, lowering the extended knobkerrie till it was level with the mountains, "I want to see each and every one of you out here, fully dressed and ready for action, like this man. Is that understood?! - There will be no more slackers in my regiment!"

Kuta sighed, closing his eyes at this transparent ploy. By making Shaka an example, Buza was bringing into focus the hostility nurtured against the Zulu, a hostility that up to that point had remained only a vague feeling, one with no precise definition or directive. Yet, in light of this 'example', the men now knew why they disliked Shaka: he was going to cost them precious sleep.

One by one Joko, Dlaba, Mtonga, and the other men turned to peer at the newcomer out of the corners of their spiteful eyes. Only Mgobozi and Nqoboka stared straight ahead, cursing Buza under their breaths.

Shaka was also staring straight ahead, his expression void of emotion. Though he presaged that the situation had become explosive, he remained unruffled.

This was certainly not the first time he'd been unpopular.

And that unpopularity grew.

Later that same morning, Kuta took the men out for their daily run. In a compact group, with Joko, Mgobozi and Nqoboka in the lead, their feet protected from the sharp rocks by the ox hide soles of their sandals, the warriors moved along at a good pace. All, that is, except one - Shaka. Gone was the man's leopard-like speed, as he slipped and slid in the unusual footgear until he had soon fallen to the rear of the formation and well behind the regiment.

Joko, Dlaba and a few of the others began to grin at the newcomer's awkwardness, and before long the entire group - save for Mgobozi and Nqoboka - was enjoying a good laugh at Shaka's expense. Then, when the Zulu suddenly stumbled on the rocky terrain and fell flat on his face, the laughter burst forth in a tidal wave of mirth. Even Mgobozi had to grin - in spite of his sorrow for the other's humiliation.

Furious, Shaka came up spitting dirt. Clenching his teeth in subdued rage, he tore off the offending sandals and, getting to his feet, began to run, at a great speed now, easily catching up to the others, racing past them and disappearing into the distance, - leaving the iziCwe to gape in wonder.

Some were impressed, others more envious than ever. At least one, Mgobozi, was bursting with pleasure. Yet, whatever the emotion they felt, nobody was laughing anymore.

When Buza heard of this he stomped off to brood in seclusion, pondering over the future of his relationship with the Zulu and wondering when the first true confrontation would come about. He felt, no, he knew it was impending. It was just a matter of time!

The General of the iziCwe did not have long to wait.

Not long at all...

When Shaka first joined the iziCwe and thus became part of his very first regiment, the Bantu attitude towards warfare was easy-going to say the least. Indeed when opposing armies met on the field of battle, there was never any deep-felt malice, no hateful intent to kill their neighbours with whom but yesterday they had joined in merry beer-drink or love dance, there was no longing to burn down their neighbours' homes or destroy their herds - there was merely a naively enthusiastic patriotic duty to safeguard their kingdom's interest and a deep-rooted ambition to excel in Sport and Contest.

In the 'war' itself, the armies spent more time and laid greater store on the ceremonial than on actual combat, and the warriors would often stand before their rivals in full battle array, complete with spears, - yet, instead of resorting to their Arms, they would provoke the enemy to action by pungent taunts and insults. Then, finally, when spirits raged high, the warriors would let the javelins fly (from safe distances), each soldier politely returning the darts of his rival, till at length those who tired first of this javelin hurling contest would take to their heels and flee, whereupon a rush would be made by the 'victors' for male and female prisoners and enemy cattle, the former to be ransomed for payment, the latter to be permanently retained by the victorious clan. If there were any slain (only those who had accidentally stood in the way of a spear would be slain), heart-felt condolences were exchanged.

The actual threat of warfare was economic and rarely, if ever, one of bloodshed.

In fact, even when Mudli warned Senzangakona that conflict with the Mtetwa Paramountcy would be "suicidal", the Elder was referring to a great loss of cattle, land, and ransomed subjects - not a loss of life!

Indeed, that is why Mudli dreaded the advent of the Child inasmuch as it was portended that he would bring "the upheaval of life as we know it" (Mudli's words) and "the birth of an era in which the name amaZulu would signify death and terror" (also the Elder's words).

For Mudli and others of the Zulu Council, the upheaval of life as they knew it meant that the Child would usher in a era of death and terror by changing the method of waging battle, by turning warfare from a mere 'sport' into Total War and...carnage.

And the Child of the Prophecy did just that...

But not yet - not in 1807, at the beginning of his military career. - Not on the day of the first of his many confrontations with General Buza.

On the vast clearing skirting the perimeter of emaNgweni's outer palisade, the iziCwe was employed in combat training. The regiment was evenly divided into two lines of warriors standing shoulder-to-shoulder. As was the current Nguni Bantu custom, the two lines, or fronts, faced each other at a distance of approximately fifty meters. In turn, as was the regulation of combat, the men on each front hurled their assegais at the opposing line where their comrades would diligently snatch up the 'discarded' darts and hurl them back.

Back and forth. Back and forth. In the exercise known as war.

Though Shaka was definitely the best man on the field, launching his spears with exceptional strength and aim, causing the warriors on the opposing front to take special heed of his pitches, moving well back and away from the landing site of his dangerous projectiles, -- though he was, as usual, the best, the Zulu was far from pleased. To him it was frustratingly obvious that the distances between the fronts were too great and that the spears - being long, heavy and unwieldy - lost most of their forward thrust upon sailing through the air and became virtually innocuous by the time they'd travelled a parabola arching over the full fifty meters.

Being of the conviction that the instruction of combat, like all other disciplines, was a growing process of the mind and the spirit, enhanced and enriched by new ideas and by the interaction of observations, perceptions and experience, Shaka took leave of his post and struck off in the direction of General Buza and Kuta who were watching the training from the comfortable shade of an euphorbia tree.

"Excuse me, sir," the Zulu youth addressed his commander in a terse, formal manner. "Aren't the fronts too far apart?"

Ever so slowly, Buza's churlish countenance screwed into an expression of restrained amazement. Certain that he had heard incorrectly, the general grunted: "What?"

"The fronts, sir. They are too far apart?"

His interest stirred, Kuta cast the young man an inquiring glance, as Buza still struggled for comprehension. The Zulu's remark appeared, at first hearing, to be part of a procedure called 'thinking'. Soldiers - thinking?! The idea seemed quite foreign to the general as he echoed, his expression becoming one of blank astonishment: "Too far apart?"

"Yes, General," Shaka replied, eyes level with his commander, unblinking. "By the time our spears reach the enemy line, they have no thrust left."

Buza peered at Shaka hard and long. Upon realising that the Zulu's words had been uttered as a criticism of warfare's tactics - tactics which Buza had grown to consider, with undying respect, as among Life's immutables - the General of the iziCwe allowed a smile to twitch on his lips as he thought: "The upstart just got here and already he's trying to change everything! Typical!" Out loud he replied, his manner depreciatory: "I see. And what do you suggest we do about that?"

Shaka was not intimidated by the edge of sarcasm he sensed in the other man's voice. Remaining calmly adamant in his reasoning, the youth suggested: "Rush the other line, sir. Get in closer. So we can throw our spears with more precision. And more effectiveness."

Though Buza remained obnoxiously narrow-minded, Kuta's eye were unable to conceal the intense engagement of his interest - what Shaka was saying made sense to him.

"The regulation distance is fifty paces. Now get back to your line," the general barked, in dismissal of both the subject and Shaka, and allowed his gaze to stare vacantly ahead.

"I know, General," Shaka would not be put off. "But I don't think it's effective."

Buza's eyes were clouding over with an impatience that bred anger. "Wars have been fought like that for as long as wars have been fought, and now you come along and say it's not effective," he snapped back sharply.

"Yes, sir," Shaka admitted with a simplicity and nonchalance that brought a thin smile to Kuta's lips.

"Who do you think you are?!" Buza was shouting now, attracting the attention of Joko, Mgobozi, and the handful of men nearest the site of the verbal conflict.

"A soldier, General," was the sanguine reply. "Trying to do his job as best he can."

Those words had a sudden appeal for Mgobozi who moved closer, listening intently, Nqoboka at his side.

"Has it occurred to you, 'soldier'," Buza chided, growing in his hatred of the new recruit, "that if we start rushing them, they might start rushing us? That if they have more casualties, so will we?"

"I've thought of that, sir," Shaka was quick to retort. "I think it would be advisable to make our shields bigger. Large enough to cover the whole body. That way we can get as close as we need to and still be protected."

A small knot of interest was forming round Mgobozi, Joko, and Nqoboka. The critical eyes shifted from Shaka back to Buza.

Though tingling with anger, the commander of the iziCwe veiled his wrath in contemptuous irony, putting on a show for the watchful men. "Why don't we just go into battle wearing our huts?!" he jeered.

A bit of laughter and a snicker or two rewarded the general's attempt at humour. Impervious to the mocking, Shaka answered the question, his tone remaining formal.

"Too cumbersome, General," he said deadpan, causing the laughter to mount and even Joko to smile, in spite of himself.

Buza was enraged.

"Regulation distance is fifty paces! Regulation shields are five palms by three! You will abide by regulation! Is that clear, 'soldier'?!"

"Yes, sir," Shaka said in a hollow voice, feeling the deep disappointment welling within him, surging, threatening to crash through the shackles of his self-control. Then, realising that all remonstrance was futile with a creature of habit like Buza, the Zulu struck off, past the lingering gazes of his peers, to return to the ludicrous regulations of a game called war.

As Shaka marched off, Kuta followed him with his gaze. Dingiswayo was right, he mused. The young man is indeed exceptional. In his report to the king, Kuta made a mental note to include Shaka's extraordinary self-control to his other attributes. Even he, Kuta, who knew Buza to be, in the transparent clarity of his character, one of those men who seemed to live, feel, and suffer in a sort of mental twilight, would have had trouble remaining so composed in the face of the general's bovine intellectual dexterity. "I wonder how far the Zulu can be bent before he snaps?" Kuta wondered and smiled considering that he might have had the answer to his question if Buza had noticed his feet. Shaka wasn't wearing his sandals. *

Despite the fact that many of the men of the iziCwe secretly agreed with Shaka's viewpoint and started to respect him for opening to question and dispute the rigid standards that Buza seemed to defend with unreasoning obtusity, and although many wished that they could openly take sides with the newcomer, no one did at first, - no one save for Nqoboka and Mgobozi.

This was primarily due to the fact that individuals - especially in explosive, brash environs like those of a military camp - are not usually apt to have the moral fortitude and intrepidness necessary to stand up and be counted for their own personal convictions and would rather, for the sake of safety in numbers, be incorporated into the cuddly womb of the "mob", assimilating and sharing the opinions, the judgments and the modes of action dictated by this amorphous body of unlimited resources, unbounded prejudices, and of a spawning intent that leads irrevocably to murder.

Persons disposed to this sort of cowardly "marriage of convenience" with their Fellow Man (and unfortunately most individuals might well fall into this category) care little if the mob is right or wrong, as long as they can feel they belong. This cosy feeling of passive association with crowds is characteristic of the Way of Victims.

And though Joko himself was not wholly a Victim - indeed, as Time would prove, he had a great many of the Master's qualities -, he found himself, all the same, catapulted into a position of "mobbish prominence" where full-fledged Victims flocked round him, like crows round an ear of corn, expecting to be fed in their aggressiveness with a proper line of action.

Not being a strategist, Joko deliberated that the best release for their pent-up violence was assault.

And so it was that one evening, in a segregated corner of the homestead's campsite, whilst Shaka, Mgobozi and Nqoboka were having supper alone - as was their custom, the Zulu suddenly looked up from his meal and sensed the presence of his tormentors.

Dark silhouettes detached themselves from the nebulous shades of approaching darkness and spread out, surrounding the outcast and his two comrades. As the silhouettes neared the flickering glow of the fire, knobkerries casts their long, narrow shadows on the craggy, pockmarked features of Joko and, next to him, on the grinning faces of Mtonga, Dlaba, and the faces of the menacing throng from the iziCwe - over twenty in all.

"You stay out of this," Shaka told Mgobozi and Nqoboka as he rose to give battle. "It's my fight. I'm used to it."

"Are you kidding?" Mgobozi answered with a broad smile, as his hand closed round a sturdy branch and he hefted it in his grip. "I wouldn't miss this for the world! It's finally starting to get exciting around here!"

Shaka smiled back as Nqoboka flanked him, and the three men prepared for the onslaught.

"Where are your sandals?"

It was the "crack of dawn" and Buza was moving down the roll-call line, inspecting, with a clefted frown, the battered features of Joko, Mtonga, and the others who, with their assortment of swollen lips, black eyes, scabbed chins, gashed cheekbones and other divers injuries of the flesh, looked rather worse for wear. Reaching Shaka - who, like Mgobozi and Nqoboka, was far less battered, with a mere bruise or two, a split lip and few scratches as souvenirs of the previous night's fisticuffs and clubbings - Buza echoed his roaring interrogatory.

"I said, where are your sandals?!"

The fact that Buza's question regarding the footgear was so divorced from a more logical comment on the appearance of this remarkable assemblage of thrashed humans, led both Shaka and Kuta to suspect that the general might well have had a hand in his troops' 'after dinner recreation'.

"I haven't been wearing them, sir. I've found that I don't need them. They slow me down."

As usual, the apathy of Shaka's response incited the anger of his superior.

"Are you trying to tell me that your feet are tougher than ox hide soles?!"

"Yes, General."

Buza fell into a silent reverie, pondering over Shaka's curt answer as he paced back and forth in front of his soldiers. The vexation that corrugated his face ironed out and was transformed into a malicious grin when his eyes fell upon the lapping flames of the morning's campfire. Plucking a burning branch out of the open hearth, gingerly, so as not to singe his fingers, the general swung it forward and let it fall to the ground in front of Shaka.

"Put it out," he ordered. "With your foot."

Joko allowed his swollen lips to pull back in a contemptuous grin, his eye catching Buza's in terms of scornful intimacy, as Kuta stiffened at this intolerable display of brutality.

But, unfaltering, Shaka stepped forward and placed his foot on the burning branch. As all looked on with bated breaths, dumbfounded, the Zulu ground his heel into the flaming bark, splintering the wood and crushing the flames into the sandy earth. Throughout this singular exploit, as the branch hissed beneath his foot, searing his flesh, the youth bore no signs of pain - save, perhaps, for a vein standing out on his forehead, a hand clenched in restrained emotion, a slight quiver of the nostril.

Then, when the fire was spent - along with Joko's scornful smile (which had drooped to gaping amazement) - Shaka returned to his place in line repeating: "As I said, General, they slow me down."

Furious at being made to look the fool, Buza shouted: "I don't care if you can put out a volcano with those feet. Soldiers wear sandals, you are a soldier, you will wear sandals! - Put them back on!"

"Buza's so efficient, he's become counter-productive," Shaka told Mgobozi and Nqoboka as they consumed their afternoon meal in the privacy of their niche at the foot of the homestead's cliffs. "He lacks imagination, resourcefulness. His mind is as nimble as a slab of stone."

"But isn't that the way it should be?" Mgobozi inquired plucking an uTiti, a boiled sweet potato, out of the communal bowl from which they were eating. "Shouldn't soldiers simply obey orders without thinking?"

"Yes, Mgobozi, soldiers should," Shaka retorted swallowing a mouthful of roasted sesame seeds, "but not generals. - As the architects of warfare, generals must be innovative! Not opposed to change, but in favour of it! Yet the way armies are now conceived, warfare is not a vital process, it's stagnant, a game for children and fools, with no pride, no valour, and no purpose!" Shaka scowled in frustration, his voice lowered scornfully as he concluded: "But of course war can never have a purpose or a creative process without killing!"

Mgobozi frowned looking up from the juicy sweat antelope meat in his hand.

"What can be creative about killing?"

A twinkle came to lighten Shaka's eye as he answered, almost in a whisper: "Dying is the supreme act of creativity, my friend. Even more so than birth. And the general, the true General as I see him, should be called upon to wield Life and Death on the battlefield, and, in that capacity, he must be creative! If not -- well, then he's simply a murderer!"

"How can you tell the difference?" was Nqoboka's amazed query.

"You can, Nqoboka," Shaka smiled confidently. "You can feel it!" Suddenly the lustre of the Zulu's twinkle faded into a vacant glassiness that left both Nqoboka and Mgobozi gaping at their friend's eerie abstraction with a touch of foreboding.
"You can feel the difference," Shaka repeated under his breath. "In your soul."

* * *

Nandi stiffened in apprehension of the odious, crafty, ageless features of Sopane of the Mountain, wretched son of the Nzuza Clan, and the woman narrowed her eyes at the diviner, peering hatefully at his haggard face branded with a thousand wrinkles and marred with the gloom of eternal darkness and at the bile-shot orbs that, sensing her presence, scanned the crowd at Dingiswayo's Royal Homestead with the inspecting scrutiny of the iniquitous and the malefic.

When those diabolical orbs came to rest on Nandi, they sprang to light with the frightening glint of recognition, and Sopane remembered that woman and her child, the boy whose blood had evoked the Image of the Ages, the Fire of the Bond, "Llanga eliphahl'elinye Ngemisebe" (The Fire of the Heavenly Globe that eclipses the sky in its glow), he remembered the Magical Storm that had raged over King Senzangakona's Zulu homestead at esiKlebeni, he remembered the Glowing Bowl - and seeing Nandi he knew the Child was near, and his hideous gaze squinted through the lapping flames of his torch as he searched for him along the line of iziCwe warriors...

As was the custom in the era when warfare was still "traditional" and lacking, as Shaka put it, in the vitality of the creative process, armies on the point of engaging in the Contest of War were 'doctored' by medicine men who, like Sopane and his execrable companions, Mgidi and Mqalane, were renowned for their gift of bestowing victory upon the armies they treated.

The treatment itself was rather showy and would be performed at the Royal Homestead of the clan, before the king, his Elders, his Council, the assembled nobility and the most illustrious of his realm. With the warriors to be treated drawn up in single file in the centre of the cattle fold, the medicine man lit his famous grass war-torch (the isiHlanti seMpi) that blazed fiercely in his hand (the blaze being kept at full force by the diviner's assistants who would, from time to time, squirt a mouthful of fat onto the torch, instantly reviving the flame in a burst of crackling blue and hissing black).

Thus equipped with this undying brand, the medicine man made his way up the line of warriors, holding the torch but inches from each man's face. Bidding him to gaze intently into the blazing flame, the doctor would ask: "U-m-Bonile yiNi?", "Do you see it?" - meaning, "Do you see your victory in the fire?" To which each warrior would answer, "Yebo, Baba!", "Yes, father!"

So much for Superstition: the Assuager of Victims.

So unlike the Supernatural: the Guide of Masters, the spiritual power Shaka would later bestow upon his own standing army -- one that would grow to be over 80,000 strong. But, then, in Shaka's Empire this sort of Superstition would be unnecessary. There would be no need to glimpse victory in a torch's fire when the blaze of that Victory would rage across Africa.

...and, when Sopane's gaze found Shaka in the line of iziCwe warriors, the hunchbacked witchdoctor crouched low and fingered the tubercles of callous flesh on his chin, eyeing the Child with a long, bewitching stare that silenced, in the sheer weight of its rapacious intent, the frenetic beating of the drums and the shrill drone of the stringed bows.

An awe-stricken hush descended upon the homestead, all eyes fixed on Sopane and Shaka whose souls were now joined by an imperceptible current that flowed between them, emanating, throughout the assemblage, the galvanizing energy of its bewitching spell.

Caught in that incantation, Dingiswayo glared at his friend and perceived a feeling of dread, something akin to terror. The king suddenly felt as if his spirit had been enslaved by a dizzying whirl of darkness, a vortex of disconcerting emptiness like that of a mind enchanted by a glimpse of Hell -- a spellbinding sensation that left him wondering if he'd momentarily lost touch with his own sanity.

This sense of utter consternation must have transpired quite visibly on Dingiswayo's countenance for his chief induna Ngomane, who was seated beside him, thought the king had been taken ill and inquired after his Child. - When it is time."

"Where is he? - The Nameless One?" Shaka queried.

"Amongst Those Who Inhabit the Forest. He is "Luhlezi Ludlongophele" - The One Who Lives in Great Rage. -- He is War. It is his task."

Sopane's bilious gaze met Shaka's and locked.

"When it is time," the wretched hunchback repeated, his putrid breath spiralling through the torch's flames. "Go to him as the Bearer of the Weapon. He will forge it onto Death. - As was ordained."

* * *

The sloping terrains of the emaYimane Neck that separated the Mtetwa Kingdom from the territory of the Dlamini Clan were alive with an atmosphere of festivity. There was none of the flashing verve that is bred in the hero's quest for blood, none of the reckless passion evoked by unrequited violence, no hatred, no fierce contempt, no intense egoism inflamed to conquest, - and no sign of Death, that smiling, jeering, inviting, lurking, grand, insipid, and savage Spirit, always mute and with an air of whispering. - No, there was no measure of War - merely the frolicking festivity proper to the farce called "traditional warfare".

The two armies that were the day's contenders, the Mtetwa's iziCwe and the Dlamini's iGunqumwza - dressed in the distinctive, colourful uniforms proper to their clan affiliation, were lined up on the narrow strip of land delimiting the battlefield, facing each other at the standard distance of fifty paces.

On the south side of the field, idly lounging on the grassy slopes that stretched upwards over the face of a hillock, were the Dlamini royal family, its Council and the large gathering of the clan's gleeful spectators who had turned out on this sunny afternoon to cheer their warriors on to victory; these spectators - men, women and children comfortably sprawled and scattered over the scented meadows that faced the site of the Contest - were engaged in eating, chatting, shouting, playing, singing, waving to each other and to their "champions on the field", carousing amongst their goats and cattle, guzzling large quantities of beer and generally having a good time in the manner of a leisurely afternoon of diversion.

The Mtetwa public, occupying the northern slopes bordering the battlefield, were equally distracted in their convivial, holiday attitude. Dingiswayo sat on top of the rocky hillock, looking quite distinguished next to Ngomane and the Council, with Mbiya, Nandi, Nomcoba, Ngwadi and Pampata installed on the grass nearby.

They all looked thrilled in the anticipation of the upcoming dispute: Dingiswayo, very much the proud patron of his "home team"; Ngomane, reflecting his monarch's preened glory; Pampata, sharing a vein of sororal joviality with her now inseparable friend Nomcoba, both girls veritably tingling with impatience as they awaited the display of valour which they knew would be forthcoming from their hero, Shaka.

Indeed, most of the Mtetwas were geared to keep a keen eye on the notable newcomer who was prefigured to be the best man on the field. Yet the crowd's interest was not the fruit of an affinity it felt for Shaka. Far from being their champion, the young man was still very much a outsider for the Mtetwa public, a figure of prominence to whose aloofness no one could properly relate, an illustrious loner who, it was known, fraternized with few and belonged to none - save perhaps to his mother and family. No, the Mtetwas' interest in Shaka was prompted by the aura of mystery that, from the start, had been so much a part of his image - an arresting charisma that could only be enhanced by his awesome association with priests and witches like Sopane and Majola; and now, on the field of Contest, Dingiswayo's subjects were anxious to see this mysterious loner in action.

But only Nandi could guess how Shaka would react to playing the buffoon in the travesty that was about to be staged for the entertainment of fools.

On the "stage", the proud Zulu himself was aghast. This battle, his first such experience, hadn't even begun yet and it was already proving to be far worse than he had ever dreaded, and even his capacity for tolerating the stupidity of his fellow men - a capacity made quite generous by his disenchantment with life - was being taxed to its fullest. As his mother had anticipated, Shaka felt very much the buffoon, the court jester dressed in the plumes and fineries of mock warfare on the verge of engaging his exceptional prowess in the spoofery of conquest. The Zulu's eyes wandered past the idle, loafing throng that sat ready to be entertained and fell upon the proud figure of Dingiswayo - and Shaka's heart screamed out to the monarch: "Is this your new order? Is this farce the manner in which you intend to shake our people out of their complacent stupor? Are we to thus pave the way for the mighty empire to which you aspire?"

But Dingiswayo could not see his valiant warrior's distress. The king's eyes were on the Dlamini line where one of the enemy soldiers had initiated the day's "conflict" by indecorously shouting insults at the opposing front.

"Ya-Ntsiniza, ya-Ti sina!," the Dlamini was yelling, "You dogs who merely show your gums and snarl, but are afraid to bite!" How appropriate, Shaka thought with a bitter grimace of repulsion, as Joko stepped forward and hollered back, "Ya-nTsini zaNja, nje-ya! nje-ya! nje-ya! - You, too, are merely dogs that bare their teeth and run. All of you!"

After another round of ludicrous insults, an assegai was finally hurled through the air by one of the Dlamini soldiers. As his clansmen and women cheered the gallantry of his brazen act, the spear hobbled across the sky and finally landed, innocuously, at the feet of the iziCwe. Joko strode out and retrieved the dart, then, returning to his regulation distance of fifty paces, the lanky warrior waved to his public (who shouted back all its encouragement) and hurled the weapon which the enemy eventually parried - with great ease.

Back and forth. Back and forth. In the game known as warfare.

Shaka's critical gaze lingered on Joko, Dlaba and the other members of his regiment as they took part in this farce, and he reflected upon their absurd behaviour - so unlike the explosive belligerence he had experienced in the fisticuffs at emaNgweni. If these men could be trained to openly manifest on the fields of battle the pent-up aggression that is so much a part of their private life, Shaka knew that war could become the vital process he envisaged. If only they could be trained to transfer their anger, their hatred, their vengeance - all those emotions which breed violence - if they could learn to harness that brute force and hone it into a controlled, rational war machine, then Mgobozi might truly find the purpose in soldiery that he sought. If only---

Shaka was jarred from his train of thought by the sound of his own name echoing all around him. Looking up, he realised that the crowds - both Dlamini and Mtetwa - were calling out to him, "Shaka!", "Shaka!", goading him to take part in the Contest. As his features hardened with resolve, the Zulu prince determined to please his "fans". He would take part in the event, but not as the buffoon.

Breaking away from his formation, Shaka strode off in the direction of the Dlamini front, moving closer and closer - leaving the regulation distance of fifty paces far behind him.

"Where does he think he's going?" roared Buza at Kuta. "He can't do that! It's against regulations!"

"He doesn't strike me as the type who knows the meaning of the word 'can't', General," Kuta replied, a beguiled smile gracing his lips.

"Come back here, Zulu!" Buza bellowed, as Dingiswayo and Ngomane followed Shaka with engrossed attentiveness and a pinch of wonder, and as the crowds looked on, dumbfounded and confused by this deliberate transgression of the rules.

Stopping at about ten meters from the Dlamini army, Shaka directed his piercing stare at the enemy - in sign of defiance. One of the Dlamini warriors accepted the challenge and stepped forward, facing his unorthodox, taunting rival. Gripping his assegai with decisiveness, Shaka raced towards the other man and rammed his shield against that of his opponent. The Dlamini, caught unawares by this unexpected and unheard-of military tactic, toppled backwards. In an impromptu assault, his actions following the dictates of instinct, with no proper strategy save for the impulse of the moment, Shaka fell on top of the other warrior, and, as an astonished hush fell on those present at emaYimane, the two men rolled on the ground, shield locked against shield.

The Zulu struggled to enhance his "madness" with a method of execution, yet his movements were awkward and slowed by the sandals and by his lack of a precise, concentrated line of attack. Both men were relying on strength alone, and Muscle without a Mind to guide it is apt to frustrate even the most worthy of endeavours.

After a brief and rather bizarre romp in the dust, Shaka made a bid to end the duel by swinging round his assegai in an effort to stab the enemy. But the spear's haft was too long, too unwieldy, and, to Shaka's further frustration, the blade broke off leaving the man clutching a useless, blunt weapon. Nonetheless, Shaka raised the haft as if to sink its splintered end into the other man's chest. But before inflicting the blow, the Zulu desisted. This was not the way - not the way to kill with dignity.

Tossing away the broken assegai, disgusted with himself, Shaka ripped off his sandals and hurled them at the Dlamini warrior, stomping back across the inglorious battlefield with the signs of bitter defeat marring his beautiful features.

The weighty silence that followed was suddenly broken by a peal of laughter. Followed by another. And yet another. Until the sloping hillocks were flooded with mirth, as both clans found unbridled merriment in Shaka's fledging attempts at breaking from the norms of traditional combat. Indeed, the young man's maladroit efforts had proven to be more of a farce than the war itself.

Joko, Dlaba, Mtonga, and especially Buza were verily racked in the throes of hilarity, as Dingiswayo remained of sombre expression, his mind probing into the recondite forces that lay buried within the Zulu's enigmatic soul.

Mgobozi lowered his gaze in sympathy, while Pampata looked at her prince, wide-eyed and unblinking, broken- hearted.

And Nandi's face was a piece of ice as she watched her son stride off alone - in search of the creative process called War in which True Generals are not murderers.

* * *

The bitter taste of humiliation was not new to Shaka. He had had to savour it often throughout his life and it now left him indifferent. Indeed, having learned from his mother to expect the worst from people, he came to look upon mocking and derision as requisites of living and, should he chance to bear the brunt of infamy, he remained surprisingly calm, appeased, without rancour, without uneasiness, as if his mortification atoned for his own and his mother's bitterness, purifying them both.

Nor were anger and frustration new to the youth. - Shaka realised that anyone who experiments with Life and Creation, anyone who seeks growth through trial and error must bargain with the anger of frustration, seeing it as an integral part of any growing process.

But defeat - defeat was unacceptable in a life where success was the measure of survival. On the field of emaYimane, his attempt at innovation had been met with defeat. He must now discover why that happened, what he had done wrong, and what he must do to rectify his mistakes. He must make up for defeat, - make amends for the unacceptable!

That is why Shaka spent the next few weeks alone - roaming over the ridges, the plateaus, the plains and the grasslands surrounding the Mtetwa Kingdom; alone -- thinking, developing, fashioning dreams into reality.

The first thing that came to mind was a chapter from his youth - but not in the form of vague, abstract reminiscing that is so proper to Romanticism - no, a very specific moment of his childhood was evoked; to wit, the turbulent night when his crops had been burned, - the night he had engaged Nzobo in a struggle that most likely would have led to the Langeni's death had it not been for Mfunda's timely intercession.

On that occasion, four rules of close combat had taken shape in Shaka's mind and he now dug into his past to re-evoke those principles.

Rule One: get in close, avoid fighting at an arm's reach.

Rule Two: the blade is essential, not the haft! If the length of the spear prevents one from properly wielding the blade - shorten it!

As he had done almost five years before, Shaka now took the wooden haft of his spear in both hands and broke it over his knee to one-third its length, weighing the shortened weapon in his grip, pleased with its newly acquired manageability.

Close Combat, Rule Three: move within your opponent's barrier of defense, exposing his bare chest to the thrust of your blade.

Rule Four: Balance and Leverage are everything, master them and you become the Master of The Kill - no matter how formidable the odds.

With this lesson from his youth in mind, determined to make up for the defeat of emaYimane by developing a viable new combat technique, Shaka trained day and night, practicing with his new spear against the invisible enemies his imagination summoned for the occasion, - drilling himself hour after hour, taking stances, doing sudden turns and kicks in the air, thrusting with the blade, jabbing - over and over - attacking in perfected methods of close combat, thrusting again, parrying retreating, falling to the ground, rolling out of the way of the enemy's spear.

Day and night.

With barely no sleep. His body exhausted and dripping with perspiration. Thrust. Lead. Roll. Kick. Parry. Practicing until the movements flowed into one another with a perfection of style, with a totality of rhythmn, with an excellence of balance.

Attack. Retreat. Thrust forward. Jab. Thrust back. Parry. - Developing the faultless steps to the Ballet of War.

Faster and faster.

Spinning. Thrusting. Diving to the ground. Rolling. Spinning once again. Kicking. Over and over. His confidence mounting with each sleepless night. His method enhanced and refined with the passing of each day.

Day after day. Incorporating the ramming motion that had been so disastrous against the Dlamini. Adding a hooking movement to the forward thrust of the shield. Gripping the shortened haft near the blade. Jabbing it repeatedly into the invisible enemy. Adjusting the upright stance, feet firmly on the ground, knees bent slightly for greater dynamic equilibrium.

Then, at the end of the fifth week, his features drawn tight with exhaustion, his veins throbbing with the animation of discovery, Shaka knew that defeat had left him and he lay down to rest on the rocky summit of the emaNdawe Plateau.

For four days and four nights he slept. And in his dreams, he had the vision of a Gleaming Assegai of polished silver, its blade longer, broader, heavier than any he had ever seen, its haft shorter and thicker than any he could conceive. It was a wondrous weapon that had the contours of a sword and the lightness of a dagger, the sharpness of a lancet and as solid as an axe. The Spear of the Child. "Ilemb'eleq'amany'amalembe ngokukhalipha". "The Spear that is mightier than all others". The Child had become the Bearer of the Weapon.

CHAPTER XIX
"IXWA: - THE SOUND OF DEATH"

"'War', they call it! It's amazing, mother," Shaka was saying as he and Nandi walked high atop of the emaNdwade Plateau where the youth had recently terminated his forced training, - Shaka's majestic figure towering over his mother's lithesome, elegant frame. "They've been fighting in that same ludicrous way for as long as anyone can remember, yet they still don't see what a farce it is. Why hasn't some one tried to change things before?!"

"For the same reason that nothing else has changed 'for as long as anyone can remember'," Nandi retorted with a touch of resentment. "Our people instinctively reject new ideas, Shaka. They're like turtles, building hard shells round themselves to protect their hearts from the outside world and the evolution of Life."

Shaka was reminded of Dingiswayo's insight that was so similar to Nandi's own caustic critique of her people. Indeed, Nandi's analogy with the turtles was reminiscent of the Mtetwa king's comment on "the darkness of our culture's complacency".

"They need some one like you to break through those shells," the woman was telling her son. "Some one to show them that without the courage to change, there is no future. - They need you, Shaka! And your valour," Nandi had stopped now and was facing him, the reflection of his own immovable Fate in her eyes. "The time is fast approaching for you to take your place as the leader you were born to be. So you must be careful. Very careful. You cannot afford to jeopardise, in public, your own pride and the legitimacy of your mission."

Sensing the gentle reprimand in Nandi's words, Shaka dropped his gaze, his features taking on an uncharacteristic look of boyish contrition, the compunctious mien of a child faced with a scolding. When he looked up again and their eyes met and locked, both mother and son became aware of the fact that the umbilical cord that had bound them at Shaka's birth had never been properly severed, and that a great deal of Shaka's courage was still dependent on the unobstructed flow of that lifeline.

"Yes. I felt like a fool," Shaka said as if that confession was a logical corollary to what she had just said.

"I can imagine," was her somewhat insensitive reply as she started off again, Shaka at her side, the sharpness of her remark attenuated by: "Most innovators make fools of themselves at first. The important thing is to prove that you're right in the long run." Nandi gave her son a deliberate sidelong glance. "Can you--?" Her eyes fell on the shortened assegai in his hand. "Prove that you're right?"

"Yes, mother. I can," came the resolute answer.

"Then you've made a mistake," she said stiffly, looking away. "You should have waited till you were ready. Completely ready. You can't experiment with new techniques in the moment when their effectiveness is most important. That's too late. You can risk falling flat on your face. Which is exactly what happened."

They both smiled now. The first lighter texture in the dark shades that were colouring their conversation.

"But don't let it worry you," her smiled broadened. "I would've done the same and often have. In fact, I don't think I've ever been completely ready for anything in my life."

"How are things with Mbiya?" Shaka found himself asking, the question spurred by Nandi's admission.

"He's a good man," there was no feeling, no emotion in her response. She had been installed in the Mbiya's homestead and felt quite comfortable there. It was as good a place to live as any, and one that provided the necessary requirements for Nomcoba and Ngwadi: food, shelter, clothing, human warmth, an air of friendliness which was quite heartening at times. It was a superficial life, Nandi knew, one quite suitable for a woman who no longer dared to probe under the surface of anything.

"And he loves me," Nandi added, as if to give evidence of Mbiya's 'goodness'. "That's never counted for much in the past - except with your father..."

She shot her son a deliberate glance, suddenly sorry she had mentioned Senzangakona and their relationship, and was pleased to see that the statement had apparently glanced off Shaka's awareness. The boy was still looking straight ahead, his expression unmoved.

Yet, though his face did not reveal it, Nandi's words had been driven deep into Shaka's soul, and the discovery of the truth they avowed suddenly came home to him with all its revealing power. So she had loved him, he told himself. And, to all intents and purposes, she still did. She probably always will. As he now thought of that fact, he found it impossible to remain indifferent. Had Shaka been a little older, he would have felt the comforting assurance that the situation between his mother and Senzangakona was well beyond his grasp; but he now suffered because he was too young to see it whole and in a manner detached from himself.

"But the fact that Mbiya loves me," Nandi's voice was echoing in Shaka's brain, "is assuring. I suppose as I grow older, being loved will always be more important than actually loving." A distant smile graced her lips as she continued, under her breath. "It's like everything else in life. Give and take. The activity of Youth reflects the passiveness of Age. The love you give when you're young, you receive when you're old. And there's no cheating there." The smile vanished as she added: "Unfortunately it is also the same for hatred."

When her eyes wandered back to Shaka, she found that he was staring directly at her, his feline eyes wearing the glint of sorrow. Disturbed by that look, Nandi quickly added, on a lighter note: "Will you be coming to stay with us for a while. Nomcoba and your brother miss you terribly. It's important you know, for a boy Ngwadi's age to have some one to look up to."

Shaka said nothing, yet his eyes retorted: - Yes, mother, I know. Painful as it may be for the two of us to remember, I was once that age too.

As if reading his thoughts, Nandi added, softly: "Your visit would make us all very happy."

"I can't come, mother. Not now. I've been away from the regiment long enough. I wouldn't want Dingiswayo to think I'm a quitter. - But this time, mother, when I go back to emaNgweni...," he raised the assegai in his hand, "I'll be ready. Completely ready!"

"Good," she replied in a choked voice.

As Shaka strode away, Nandi watched him, and a tear came to her eye as she remembered his childhood and the words Mfunda had uttered before her death, "Give him hope! Even when no hope can be found! Free his soul from darkness!"

Darkness. - As Nandi had said, it is the same for hatred. Those who hate in their Youth must be fortunate enough to die young.

As Fate would have it in its Mercy, the Child found favour with the Infinite and was blessed with that fortune.

**

In the semidarkness of the evening, "UmZizima", the Venerable Realm of Those Who Inhabit the Forest, looked dismally foreboding. Columns of misty light filtered down through the trees and thick vegetation, bestowing an unreal, uncanny quality upon the wooded kingdom and, nearby, under the sinister splendour of that moonlit sky, the sea, blue and profound, remained still, without a stir, without a ripple - viscous, stagnant, dead.

His back to the body of water, Shaka stood staring at the hazy glow of a flickering fire, now bright, now faint, that glimmered out of the black shadows, - the fire of a campsite nestled deep within the ominous forest. From his vantage point on the edge of the thick vegetation, Shaka could see a collection of odd, upright huts with flat sloping roofs upon which were perched congregations of vultures that sat picking on the blood-caked carrions of wolf and rodent. Save for the glow of the campfire, the inhospitable village appeared deserted, the doors of the thatched abodes gaping like wide, toothless mouths frozen in screams of disconcertion.

A row of tall, twisted poles crowned with human skulls seemed to form a path leading from Shaka's position to the cluster of huts, and it was along this path that the Zulu now made his way towards the sinister homestead. Reaching its portals, framed in towering thorn trees, the youth squared his broad shoulders and entered.

As he strode in the direction of the campfire, it seemed to Shaka that baleful shadows lurked in the secreted recesses of the forest and that grotesque, monstrous faces peered at him out of the darkness, glimpsing his every move as he neared the entrails of the kingdom. Approaching the open hearth's glimmering flames that cast their dancing show of light on to the campsite, Shaka could make out a group of crouched figures that were huddled round the crackling blaze, - figures lying in strange, fantastic poses, bowed shoulders, bent knees, heads thrown back and chins pointed upwards in utter despair, with here and there a dark, lack-lustre eye turned upon the newcomer.

As the Zulu reached the gruesome gathering, some of the huddled figures turned to look at him, revealing, in the harsh light of the fire, their hideous, deformed faces - the heinous semblances of the Freaks. Then, as Shaka drew closer, the Freaks uttered indistinct, ghastly sounds, screeching and cawing like bats and ravens, and quickly scrambled off into the shadows, leaving only one of their number sitting alone, his face turned down upon the glow of the fire.

The imposing, solitary figure - that of the Magician Mabodla, son of Ntlabati of the Mbanambi People - clad in lion's skins with the head and mane of a lion draped over his own head and shoulders, seemed to ignore the visitor, his eyes remaining trained on the spitting flames.

"Sakubona, Baba," Shaka greeted the man in a solemn tone.

Without looking up, Mabodla acknowledged the greeting with: "Ngibona wena, Son of Zulu."

"You know me?" Shaka had trouble hiding the inflection of amazement in his tone.

"Those who Inhabit the Mountains have told us of your birth," said the Magician of UmZizima in a voice that caressed the spirit of the other man. "They said you would come to us. We have been waiting."

Mabodla now lifted his gaze showing his features to be strikingly handsome, ageless in their rugged beauty, incongruous in these hideous surroundings. Like those of Sitayi, Mabodla's eyes were also a light, pastel-blue. Yet, unlike the sangoma, the man could see. "How may we serve you?" he asked, his voice changing, becoming more severe.

"I need your craft, Baba. Your Magic."

"To what purpose?" The voice changed again, as if two different souls were flitting in and out of his body.

"The forging of a weapon."

The Magician nodded to himself, pensively. He then signalled Shaka to sit next to him by the fire. When the Zulu had done so, Mabodla urged: "Describe it - this weapon."

Plucking a stick out of the fire, Shaka smoothed the ground near the hearth's outer rim and, with quick, deliberate strokes, began to sketch, in the wash of the flames' light, the design of the Assegai that had appeared to him in his dreams. As he did so, the Freaks, intrigued and curious, began to re-emerge from the darkness, forming a circle round Shaka and the Magician, peering with quick, keen eyes at the progressive phases in the drawing of the formidable instrument of War.

When Shaka had finished, Mabodla studied the design and considered out loud: "It will take time. We must begin at the beginning. A new furnace. New bellows. New iron tempered with the best fats." He looked up and his eyes locked with Shaka's.

"Only then will it be invincible."

Under the Magician's supervision, the Freaks - True Artisans of the Weapon - began at the beginning. From a flock of prize goats, Mabodla selected a choice ram that was slaughtered and skinned. The goat hide was then dried, tanned, pounded, and initiated to its regal purpose with fantastic rituals from time immemorial.

Shaka watched with enthralled fascination - an innocent, captivated witness to an age old craft - as some of the Freaks cut and shaped the goat hide into bellows, while others began to fashion a new furnace, cylindrical in shape, that was placed in the remotest and most tenebrous recesses of the enchanted forest, - a furnace thirteen meters high and seven wide, made from the magic clay found only on the Pinnacle of Kings.

When the initial work was complete, Mabodla strode to the mouth of the furnace and, lifting his arms to the Heavens, uttered a soft melodious litany of incantations that engaged the mind and inveigled the soul in the gracious timber of their harmony. Looking up, his gaze transpiercing the night, the Magician of UmZizima cried out to the Elements, invoking their ingratiating benediction upon the work of Man and the restless toil of Man's heart.

Suddenly a flash of lightning arched across the blackened sky, bathing the forest's mist in a harsh light that verily throbbed with a bluish glow. The lightning struck the furnace, igniting its charge of iron-ore and charcoal in a burst of pulsating crimson. Shaka stood spellbound, as the Freaks howled with beguiling, hysterical laughter incited by their master's power over the forces of Nature.

His enraptured features dancing in the light of the flames, the Son of Ntlabati whispered: "It can begin."

The Freaks worked the bellows and shovelled the fuel, while Mabodla, manning the mouth of the furnace, his body glistening with sweat, smelted a clean bar of iron-ore and silver. Shaka watched, mesmerised, as the bar glowed in phosphorescence, shedding its impurities, turning from deep red to incandescent white.

Then gradually, as if with a mind of its own, the fiery, incandescent bar of pure iron and silver began to assume the shape of a blade - Shaka's Blade; and, as it did so, the Magician withdrew it from the furnace and rested it on an anvil of granite, beating it with a huge martel, defining its magnificence with each smiting of the weighty bludgeon. When he was satisfied with the labour of his hand, Mabodla placed the blade near the open shaft of the furnace and turned to scan the forest, as if searching.

"What is it, Baba?" Shaka inquired, feeling the mounting tension that shot, electric, through the air.

"Our work is done. Now we must wait."

"For what?" the Zulu questioned, stealing an eager glance at the forest's darkness.

"For the Nameless One," Mabodla said in a chilling whisper. "Only he can give the blade a life of its own. Only he can provide the ingredients of Human Death."

As Mabodla spoke these words, his gaze rested on Shaka, the Child, Hero, Conqueror, unwitting instrument of forces beyond the clear discernment of even the wisest of mortals, - Shaka, the One of Whom They Sang to the Wind, "UShaka ngiyesab'ukuthi nguShaka, UMahlom'ehlathini" - "Shaka, I fear to say he is Shaka, He who was armed in the Forest", - as the Magician now looked upon the Child and saw his beauty and his tender apprehension he realised that this young man was also: I-Shaka, the unwitting victim of his own Mastery.

Then, before these troubling thoughts could be dispelled from Mabodla's mind, footsteps were heard in the darkened entrails of the forest - followed by -- sniffing.

"He comes," said the Son of Ntlabati, as the Freaks fearfully covered their heads with their goatskin hoods.

A rustling was heard - that of a creature, a man perhaps, or a beast. The rustling seemed to be approaching and, as Shaka's keen senses scanned the darkness, the night air was torn by a diabolical shriek followed by cackling laughter.

Then - all was silent. Shaka stood frozen in place, barely breathing. Shortly, the silence was broken once again by the ghastly sound of crunching and rending, as if some great carnivore were devouring bones and flesh.

Suddenly a hyena strode out of the shadows, followed by a tall, robust man wearing a fur cape of pelts about his shoulders, with strips of fur round his waist and hanging down his huge thighs, and tails draped over his face, partially concealing the fiendish sparkle of his crazed eyes. The mammoth being carried a heavy spear in his right hand and, in the left, a soiled goatskin bag.

"Is he the Child of whom they spoke?" the Nameless One asked Mabodla.

"He is."

The Nameless One stepped towards Shaka and gazed at him - a long, inspecting gaze. Then, without giving any apparent sign of the fruit of his scrutiny, the creature spoke, with throaty enunciation, "I wish to see it."

Mabodla lifted the Blade and held it out to the Nameless One who peered at the extraordinary weapon, the fire in his eyes matching the throbbing glow of the Spear. Extending his parched, scabrous hands, the man cupped them round the incandescent metal, barely touching it with the tips of his scaly fingers. Turning to Shaka, he uttered with saturnine solemnity, his voice hollow - like a carrion gutted by vermin: "As you possess this blade, it will possess you. With each mortal blow it inflicts, you will lose a fragment of yourself. - Life from Life. Death to Death. - Son of Zulu, do you choose the Way of the Blade?"

"I do, Baba," Shaka replied, coldly unemotional.

"Is your yearning so great for the kinship for which you were born?"

"It is, Baba."

"So be it."

The Nameless One turned from Shaka and withdrew to a remote section of the clearing where he was joined by Mabodla. In a low voice the two conversed. The Nameless One opened his cloth bag and produced a handful of human viscera still dripping with blood.

Returning to the furnace, the Magician held the glistening fat and the deep red flesh of human entrails over the glowing blade and, bowing slightly, in reverence, he lay the viscera on top of the heated metal. As the fat sizzled noisily, a smile of achievement was born on Shaka's lips.

"The Spirit of the Blade speaks," the Zulu said.

"The Spirit of Shaka speaks," Mabodla suggested in a melancholy tone.

Over the sizzling flesh, the voice of the Nameless One came ominous and uncanny.

"Son of Zulu - let the first rays of tomorrow's sun seal within your Weapon the destiny of your People. For, like the sun, you shall cast your Spirit to the ends of the earth."

Life from Life. Death to Death. -- Such is the Curse of Masters.

*

As the night flowed inexorably towards day, Shaka was led - by Sitayi, Majola and Mabodla - to the foot of a towering spiral of ice that slanted upwards from the summit of the Great Mountain, - the spiral's tip vanishing in the dizzying heights of the firmament.

At the Magician's bidding, the Son of Zulu started up the gleaming steps of the seemingly endless staircase that wound upwards - into the starlight.

Alone, Shaka reached the summit of the mountain and strode to the polished railing of the Platform perched atop of the Pinnacle of Kings.

And when the advent of Day brought the flashing rays of the sun, Shaka held his Weapon against the vault of the horizon and allowed the glistening metal to drink of the golden dawn until the Spear's own light burst forth against the Heavens with the radiance and magnitude of brilliance proper only to the birth of a star, and in that radiance came -- the Second Birth of the Child.

* * *

Slowly inching his way round the corner, Shaka stopped to gaze at the hazy light of the campfire burning within the recesses of the huge cave.

Then, with mounting assuredness and with a malicious twinkle of anticipation, the young warrior tightened his grip on his new weapon and stealthily padded into the stench of the grotto's interior.

The cave was just as Shaka had remembered it from his first encounter almost six months before: the cluster of bearded vultures perched on their convoluting branches, the dried skins and the strips of meat hanging in the billowing smoke, the remains of grisly meals and, of course, the cave's lord himself - Inkomo, the Mad Giant of Sondude.

The Titan sat near the fire, his asthmatic breathing punctuating the crunching sounds he made as his massive yellowed teeth ground into the thigh-bone of an ox followed by a loud guzzling which accompanied the ingestion of the bone's marrow.

Suddenly one of the bearded vultures sensed the Zulu's presence and looked up from its meal of rodents, jerking its head to the side, its glossy eyes peering through the smoke. Noticing his "pet's" suspicious behaviour, the Mad Giant knitted a prominent brow and swivelled his immense head round to gaze in the direction indicated by his winged predator.

When he saw Shaka smiling at him, disarmingly, the Titan was not disarmed, indeed, he grunted and, slowly, as recognition crept over his garbled features, he grunted again, with more feeling, his jaundiced eyes widening with fury as he lifted his mutilated hand and narrowed his eyes at the thin air that had once been occupied by his thumb.

Emitting a hollow growl, his breathing becoming more laboured as his anger choked his windpipe, Inkomo heaved the ox's carcass against the wall of the cave and, reaching for his mighty axe, rose heavily to his feet. Then, quickly closing the distance between his own monumental figure and that of his unwelcomed guest, the giant brought the axe down. Yet Shaka nimbly rolled to the right of the club that struck the floor of the cave with a tremendous blow, sending rocks and boulders hurtling in all directions.

Blinded by his own fury, the Titan awkwardly chased the Zulu through the interior of his abode, repeatedly clubbing the ground in an attempt to slay the intruder, but Shaka avoided the deadly blows, agilely rolling out of the axe's way, smiling all the while at his colossal pursuer.

When Shaka's smile finally faded, he was ready to strike. Gripping his phenomenal Assegai, the Zulu swept past Inkomo, gashing the giant's chest with the gleaming blade. Growling with anger and pain, the sight of his own blood causing his venom to run over, his wrath to mount, the Mad Giant - who now truly deserved the name - howled with despair and, tossing away his club, advanced on the other man, barehanded, as if to strangle him.

Shaka positioned himself facing Inkomo and, as the Titan came towards him, the Zulu ducked under his sweeping grasp and, with a quick, precise thrust of his weapon, sank the blade into the giant's flesh, driving it deep into the flank, piercing the mammoth heart.

Inkomo's eyes sprang wide with incredulity as he emitted a pitiful, bloodcurdling cry and sank to his knees. Feeling the flow of life deserting him, in one last, desperate attempt to kill Shaka, the giant lashed out and closed his huge hands round the other's throat. Shaka gasped for air and struggled to loosen Inkomo's grip, yet his adversary's strength, even on Death's threshold, was too formidable. As the Zulu started to swoon, the world blackening and spinning round him - the giant's arms suddenly fell limp, his eyes rolled back and his body came crashing to the ground in a lifeless mountain of muscle.

Fully regaining his senses, Shaka stood over the body of the Titan of Sondude and yanked his Spear out of the giant's carcass. The sucking sound made by the blade as it was withdrawn from the deep wound gave the Zulu the onomatopoeic name for his new weapon.

"Ix-wa" - he called it, repeating the sound it made.

Ixwa -- the Sound of Death.

* * *

"Well, what a pleasant surprise! Welcome back, Shaka! We've missed you!"

On the slope over emaNgweni, Shaka was standing in the roll-call line-up, shoulders back, his tall figure erect, proud, his steady gaze void of expression, level with Buza's mounting sarcasm.

A few of the men snickered at the general's remark. Joko laughed out loud (an act of insubordination which Buza would normally have frowned upon, especially when the men were at attention, yet one the commander chose to disregard on this particular morning - considering the special occasion of the Zulu's return to the iziCwe after an absence of almost two months). Mgobozi was smiling as well - not at Buza's words (as usual he found little or no diversion in the general's moronic comments), but because he and Nqoboka were happy that their friend appeared to have overcome the blemish to his pride procured in the Dlamini War and was back in his ranks again.

Though there were some pronounced abnormalities about Shaka's military attire. His shield, for instance, which was well above the regulation dimensions, measuring, from base to spire, over fifteen palms or a little under two meters; and the sandals, inasmuch as he was wearing none; and, of course, the mighty Ixwa (which Shaka held concealed behind his huge shield). There was also something else peculiar about the Zulu's gear: a large ox hide bag resting at his feet, a bag that seemed, judging from its contours, to contain something circular in shape, a melon, a ball perhaps, or a ---

Yet, for the moment, Buza found reason to disregard Shaka's uniform and its obvious deviation from the norm as he pursued his initial irony.

"Do you have a valid reason for being absent without leave?" the commander inquired.

"Yes, sir. I had some thinking to do."

"Ah! - So we have a 'thinker' in our ranks, do we?" Buza teased, raising his brow in feigned admiration, encouraging another roar of laughter from Joko's apparently insatiable mirth. "And what exactly were you 'thinking' about--?" The general's smile suddenly turned to a scowl of anger. "Your act of insubordination in the Dlamini War," he was roaring now, "or your attempt to make fools of me and my regiment?" "Yes, sir," Shaka replied, unflinching.

"Yes, sir, what?" Buza insisted on knowing.

"Yes, sir, that is what I was thinking about."

"Ah!" the general tilted his head back. "And what conclusions might you have reached?"

"I was foolish."

A slight frown clouded Mgobozi's features. This sort of admission seemed so foreign to Shaka's character. Buza, on the other hand, was infinitely pleased with this "confession" (or so he deemed it). Perhaps something could be done with this Zulu after all, the commander considered and beamed: "Good! Very good! I admire a man who admits he's wrong."

"I didn't say I was wrong, sir. Just foolish." Shaka said, continuing to offer the general a cool and upright gaze.

Mgobozi shot Nqoboka a diverted smile, as Buza deigned the Zulu with a look of savage spite.

"Where are your sandals?" he asked, quickly adding: "Ah, yes. I almost forgot. You 'misplaced' them on the battlefield, didn't you?" More snickers down the line rewarded the general's sharp witticism as he pressed on with his bantering, trying to regain control of the situation. "We can provide you with other, you know. Or do they still - 'slow you down'?"

"Yes, sir. They do."

"I see. And what might this be?" Buza was indicating the large shield with his knobkerrie.

"A shield, sir?"

"A trifle large, isn't it?"

"I don't think so, General. Just the right size, I'd say."

"For what?! Fording a river?!"

Joko's laughter burst forth and flooded through the regiment. "No, sir. It's for fighting a battle," Shaka said with grave tranquillity.

"Yes, of course. You're the expert on that, aren't you?"

More laughter. Uncontrolled now - a high, ringing outcry that left Mgobozi and Nqoboka feeling like two islands of compassion in a ocean of ridicule. Yet Shaka remained surprisingly serene as he stood straight, proud, staring directly ahead, unshaken by the chaffing.

"And where are your spears? Or have you been 'thinking' that we ought to fight without weapons?"

Another wave of mirth surged over the slope, - a rolling crest of jocundity that was abruptly and categorically suppressed, like the climbing swell of white capped breakers crashing against cliffs of granite; indeed the laughter was curbed so sharply that many of the men found themselves literally gagging, breathless, as they gaped, crestfallen, petrified, at the Ixwa which Shaka had produced by way of answer to Buza's jeering remark and was now gripping in his outstretched hand, its gleaming Blade mirroring the rays of the sun in a blinding fan-like display of colours.

In silence, the iziCwe favoured the Zulu and his Spear with opened mouths and the blankest stares of astonishment Shaka had ever seen on a human countenance. The Ixwa truly seemed to possess a magical quality, a compelling aura and spirit of its own - that indefinable something which forces it upon the mind and the heart of Man.

Buza's lips had lost their colour. Catching hold of his balance, a glitter of moisture on his bullish brow, the general stammered, rather awkwardly: "It's not regulation."

"I know it isn't, commander." Shaka rejoined, feeling vaguely sorry for the crushed officer. When Buza found the steadiness of voice to offer trifling objections to a favourable adoption of the Spear as a "regulation" weapon - arguments such as the fact that it was too short to throw, that its blade was too heavy to manage, and so on, - Shaka courteously suggested that an indication of the new weapon's effectiveness might well be given by the exceptional contents of his cowhide bag. And, with no further ado, the Zulu flipped over the large pouch and caused a huge, furry ball, caked with blood and fleshy pulp, to bounce on the soft turf and roll across the clearing, coming to a halt at Buza's feet.

Not being totally familiar with the physiognomy of legendary creatures, it took the general a moment or two to realise that the furry ball at his feet was the head of Inkomo, Titan of Sondude. When he had, he gasped, dumbfounded: "You killed Inkomo?"

"We had an old score to settle," said Shaka, nonchalantly. "Our last encounter gave me a chance to test my 'Ixwa' - as I've called it. That's the sound it makes at the Kill. -- ix-wa."

The iziCwe general uttered a request for Shaka to demonstrate how it worked - this 'Ixwa' of his (the actual name of the Spear being murmured by the commander in a hushed tone which betrayed an emotion akin to frightened regard). Complying with Buza's entreaty, as the men looked on with mystified, inquiring glances, Shaka broke from his ranks and, moving out to the clearing facing the regiment, asked for three volunteers to fight against him.

There was hesitation, naturally. Most feared Shaka in a one-to-one situation, and a three-to-one was little better; and then there was the new Spear of course, and the sheer terror its bewitching gleam evoked. Indeed, even the most brazen of men find cause to dally in the face of the fabulous. Shaka egged on a few of them, especially Joko, Mtonga and Dlaba, reminding his foes that they had once so craved to fight him, they had stopped at nothing - not even the laws of a fair fight. And yet they now held back? Did they find an ambush more manly than the open combat he was now offering, he taunted.

Faced with this reproach, feeling his pride very much at stake, Joko clutched his shield and assegais and ventured out to join the Zulu in the centre of the clearing. Mtonga was soon at his side.

"I said three volunteers," Shaka restated. "Would you mind joining them, General?"

Buza peered suspiciously at the Zulu before deciding to acquiesce so as not to lose face with his men. Snatching a shield and throwing assegais from Mgobozi, the commander took his place next to Joko and Mtonga, facing Shaka at a distance of about twenty meters.

"All right, now," the Zulu said calmly when his opponents were properly lined up. "Kill me."

Mgobozi's blood was suddenly charged with adrenalin. The commander of the iziCwe was just the type to take advantage of this opportunity to rid himself of the pestiferous Zulu, offering as an excuse to Dingiswayo that it had been the other man's idea, that, in fact, he had urged him to do so!

Instead, Buza grunted: "I have no time for games!"

"I assure you, General," Shaka told him. "This is no game." And he added, with a touch of his own jeering now: "Come on. I'm waiting. Don't stand there like a pack of old women. Kill me!"

"You arrogant bastard," Buza cried and fired his assegai that Shaka parried with ease, swatting it away with a sideward sweep of his shield.

"That's what the larger shield is for," he commented to the troops, his eyes still fixed on his opponents. "Better deflection. Once you get accustomed to its weight, you can parry a shower of enemy spears, making them practically innocuous. - Come on, Joko, Mtonga," Shaka urged them, "- the least you could do is offer your commander some support."

Stung, Joko and Mtonga readily joined Buza in his attack. As Shaka continued to easily deflect the darts they hurled, harmlessly tossing them back from time to time so that his assailants would not be left unarmed, he spoke to the iziCwe, calmly, casually - like an instructor giving a lesson to a class.

"From the very beginning," he told the captivated men, "I had a feeling that something was wrong. But I couldn't quite put my finger on what it was. Of course the spears were wrong - and the shields, the sandals, all those things we call 'regulation'. But there was something else, something at the core of it all that bothered me. Then, as I took time to consider the mistakes I had made during actual combat, I discovered, in a greater sense, what was wrong with the entire concept of traditional warfare. - Energy! - Precious energy is wasted!"

Buza was hurling spears with all his might now in an attempt to silence the Zulu. Yet Shaka went on, his voice unaltered by the barrage that rained upon him.

"Never having been a soldier, in my investigation I had to relate warfare to something I know well, something we all know well: hunting. The two have a great deal in common. When you hunt, you must save your energy for the Kill, because the Kill is what hunting is all about. Yet in conventional warfare, we do the exact opposite. We waste all our energy shouting, singing, cheering, waving to friends and hurling insults - and spears that are as harmless as the insults. And when it comes time for the Kill, we have no energy left, no real desire to do any harm. So we all run home and call it a day!"

Mgobozi grinned.

"In fact," Shaka added, "we don't fight like men at all. If anything, we resemble a bunch of ranting baboons!"

Some of the other men grinned as well. Though they were loath to admit it, Shaka's words made sense.

"I believe there are two ways to solve this problem," the Zulu went on with a positive note. "New weapons and a new method of combat. A frontal attack, moving in closer. Man to man." Shaka also smiled now. "My first attempt at this was a disaster."

Mgobozi, Nqoboka, and even Dlaba laughed at the disarming admission.

"But now," Shaka's gaze shifted to Inkomo's gruesome features frozen in a gaping expression of terror, " I believe we can say it works. -- Watch."

Abruptly Shaka raced towards his three adversaries, his body cramped behind his shield to ward off the oncoming spears. With agile, perfectly measured, swift motions, the athletic Zulu leapt through the air, feet forward, and disarmed Joko and Mtonga, sending both men flying to the ground. He then spun round and charged Buza - who had become somewhat apprehensive now - verbally describing his movements as he executed them on the commander: "Contact. Hook the enemy's shield with your own. Pull back and away, exposing his bare flank. Then - aim for the heart."

Indeed, as his words indicated, Shaka made contact with Buza, hooked the commander's shield with his own, pulled his opponents shield back and away exposing Buza's left flank, and thrust the gleaming blade of his Ixwa towards the general's chest, right over the heart -- stopping a hair's-breath from the man's skin.

The blood drained from Buza's glaring features as his entire military life flashed before his eyes - the good, the bad, the progressive (what little there was) and the obtuse. Indeed, the commander of the iziCwe was so overwhelmed by Shaka's speed of execution, he lay on the ground, astounded into perfect stillness, wondering whether he was still alive.

"As you see, it's quick and clean," Shaka remarked as he relinquished his stunned prey. "Very little energy is lost. And it's highly effective. - Here, Mgobozi. Try it."

Mgobozi reached for the Ixwa that Shaka held out to him, and as soon as he felt it firmly in his grip, a charmed smile dawned on his face. He gazed at the magical Weapon in his hand, in awe of its potential power.

Facing Joko - who had just gotten to his feet - Mgobozi repeated the lesson learned, executing the movements as he voiced: "Contact. Lock shields. Pull back and away. Aim for the heart," and stopped his thrust as the tip of the Spear barely touched Joko's chest.

Mgobozi passed the prestigious Assegai on to Nqoboka who also tried "The Method" (as it would later be called).

Then, one by one, the other members of the iziCwe took turns practicing on each other -- Contact. Lock shields. Pull back and away. Aim for the heart.

All the men - even Joko.

Contact. Lock shields. Pull back and away. Aim for the heart.

"What is this charade?" Buza finally screamed, beside himself with rage, incensed by this display of regimental anarchy.

"For lack of a better word, General," Shaka retorted with an even tone. "I would call it -- War."

CHAPTER XX
"UKULWA"(WAR)

Kings and so-called men of government must appear to be proud of their firmness of character, of their steadfastness of purpose, of their directness of aim. They must go straight towards their pre-set goals, to the accomplishment of virtue, sometimes of crime, in an uplifting persuasion that what they do is the best for their people. They must never falter on their journey down the path of government and must never miss a step in the stride of their leadership, walking with their heads up and their eyes set on their haughty aspirations, careful not to stumble over the bodies of the wise and the unburied remains of their predecessors. Kings and governors must never lose their way. They must always know where they are going and what they want.

Or so it would appear.

Yet Senzangakona kaJama, King of the Zulus, had faltered greatly on the day following his heated meeting with the Council. Though he had been - in principle - relatively content with the stand he had taken, finding it had been firm, steadfast, blessed with directness of aim and other "kingly attributes", he had been troubled all the same by the fact that the driving force behind his decisiveness had not been a clear plan of action born of vigilance, but, instead, the hazy stratagems born of emotion that the mind elicits in the fumes of inebriation.

The day following the meeting, Senzangakona had sat alone in the recesses of his royal hut nursing the mala- dies procured by too much sorghum, his bloodshot eyes lost in the fire's lapping flames, his throbbing brain racing to fit together the puzzle of words uttered and heard in the course of the Council's discussion.

The debate's conclusive remarks had easily resurfaced in the king's mind, causing him to wince in recollection. - "The time has come for war!", he had remembered saying - adamantly, too adamantly. "No more messengers! No more discussions! War! Our dignity is at stake - and perhaps my throne!"

War! - A word of few letters, monosyllable, easily uttered. Yet a word of great consequence with implications that would merit far more than two consonants and a vowel.

And, as he had gazed into the fire, Senzangakona had pondered over the word's implications for him. There was, of course, no going back on this decision. In his drunken state he had overruled Mudli, Mkabayi and the other Elders! No more discussions!, he had said. Well, there could be no more. In that, his pride was really at stake.

So war it was and war it would be. The Zulus, a small clan without a standing army, against the Mtetwas, a huge paramountcy with over one thousand troops.

What had Mudli called it? - Suicidal?

Apparently, it was! - Yet, Senzangakona had had a plan. Vague. Indefinite. Reckless, perhaps. But a plan all the same in which he had contemplated enlisting the alliance of King Pungashe of the strong Butelezi tribe in order to form a confederacy of three or four clans that would face Dingiswayo as a united front. Four against one - the only chance of a "fair" fight against such superior odds.

But would Pungashe agree to such an alliance? The Zulu King had hoped he would, and had spent the next few weeks in concentrated thought, without the disturbance of Man or alcohol, devising a workable, convincing strategy to present to the Butelezi monarch. Senzangakona had known that without such a strategy, a seasoned ruler like Pungashe would never have agreed to stand at the Zulu's side against five regiments of highly trained men, and without Pungashe's patronage no other clan in the area would enlist its support in this united front.

So Senzangakona stayed sober and prepared for the meeting where he had hoped to show his peer that he possessed the firmness of character, the steadfastness of purpose, and the directness of aim proper to kings and so-called men of government. Yet, in a more personal sense, he prepared for the meeting in which he hoped to find an ally to help him make good his bid to avoid "becoming Shaka's puppet" (as he had put it in the Council meeting).

Indeed, Senzangakona needed Pungashe to finally rid himself of his first-born son.

The summit was held shortly after the harvest of 1808, a few days after Shaka first introduced his revolutionary "Method" of combat to his comrades in the iziCwe.

The site of the meeting was the foot of a hillock that jutted majestically out of a hard, rolling plain covered thickly with sage-green tufts of grass, - a plain over which Pungashe's sonorous voice rang loud and fiercely.

"We'd be fools to declare war!" the Butelezi king was saying, "It would be like begging for defeat!"

"I don't think so, Pungashe," Senzangakona replied, his gaze turning to the tall monarch who, though well over sixty, was still youthful, with ferret-like eyes, a cynical mouth and a face that looked ruddy and verily glowing with health.

"In fact, I think declaring war is our only hope of avoiding defeat," the Zulu went on, making a conscious effort to keep his voice steady, his tone confident. "We have every reason to believe that Dingiswayo will continue his march West. He's just conquered the Dlamini - only five miles from out borders. We're next, and if we don't make our move first, he'll declare war and catch us off guard."

Pungashe furrowed his brow and turned to his brother Mevana and his overweight, slovenly son, Msicwa, and seemed to look through both men as he asked, rhetorically: "Have you any idea how large his armies are?"

"Yes, Pungashe," Senzangakona answered. "But I know we can do it."

"Defeat over a thousand men?" The Butelezi asked with a rising level of suspicion. "How?"

The Zulu king cast Mudli a fleeting glance before proffering the suggestion: "By constructing a unified offensive. A confederacy of four tribes."

A sly smile danced across Mevana's lips. "We're the stronger tribe, Senzangakona. A confederacy would obviously be to your advantage more than ours."

"Stronger or not, if you Butelezi face Dingiswayo alone, you'll lose." Senzangakona held Mevana's eyes steadily with his own. "If we face him together, we have a good chance of winning. I would say that that sort of collaboration is of mutual advantage!"

Mudli could not conceal a look of admiration for his monarch. He had rarely - if ever - seen the son of Jama in such "regal" form. Perhaps it was the absence of Mkabayi, the Elder considered with a touch of malice.

"Four tribes, you say," Pungashe remarked as if warming to the idea. "Which did you have in mind?"

"Logically those which now feel most threatened by Mtetwa expansionism: my Zulus, your Butelezi, the Mbateni, and the Kumalo."

"Have you already spoken to the other kings?" The question was Mevana's.

"Yes," Senzangakona nodded feeling a modicum of relief as his idea seemed to take root. "Kali of the Mbateni agrees it is the best and only way."

"And the Kumalos?" Pungashe queried.

"King Donda has already offered his support."

"If we give ours, I take it," Msicwa intimated with a scurrilous smirk.

But Senzangakona was keenly on his guard against the Butelezi's imperious comment. Indeed, he had bargained for a far more venomous remark.

"As we said, Msicwa," the Zulu was offering the fat man a charming smile, "- your backing the confederacy would be to all our advantage."

Mudli found himself smiling. His king's rebuttal was poised and direct, one truly worthy of the Elder himself.

"But that would still provide us with only six hundred men. Against over twice that number."

The observation was Mevana's, and Senzangakona was ready for it.

"I'm aware of that, Mevana."

"Perhaps it would be more propitious to seek a larger union. Five tribes, perhaps. Or six."

"That would make matters more complicated, Mevana. I trust, we'll have enough trouble with four kings. Five or six monarchs would create a unruly dispersal of allegiance amongst the troops and defeat the whole concept of a united front. - Besides, I believe I've devised another solution to our problem." As the other men looked on, the Zulu monarch knelt down and started to scratch a rudimentary map on the powdery red surface of the hard, rocky terrain. "This," he explained, referring to the map, "is the Umfolozi River with its tributaries, the eMpenbeni and the iNzololo. Here is the Kingdom of the Butelezi," he scratched a circle round a large area south of the uMfolozi and indicated next to it: "and here are the Zulus, the Kumalo, the Mbateni - and here, the Mtetwa. If we made the mistake of meeting Dingiswayo's armies north of the Umfolozi, then, as Pungashe put it, we'd be begging for defeat. The land there is flat, exposed on all sides - and we'd be most vulnerable because of our inferior number. But," Senzangakona looked up, scanning the men's eyes, "if we lure the Mtetwas south of the Umfolozi, the landscape would work to our advantage. We could mass our army here," he referred to the map again, "on the slopes between the eMpenbeni River and the summit of nNtuzuma Hill. From that commanding position our 600 men will seem like 6000."

Though Pungashe knew the plan was valid, he steeled himself against its hasty approval and asked guardedly: "What makes you think we can lure the Mtetwas south of the Umfolosi? Dingiswayo's no fool. He'll sense it's a trap."

"Perhaps you're right, Pungashe," the Zulu remarked. "But I don't think so. Dingiswayo has never been beaten, which means he might very well be blinded by victory and by confidence in his armies' superior strength.

That will make him reckless, I would guess. Especially if he thinks he's marching only against the Butelezi."

"What?" Pungashe frowned.

Senzangakona glanced at Mudli, his eyes twinkling with boyish mischief.

"Dingiswayo won't know there are four tribes, Pungashe. You alone will declare war and when he faces you - he'll find us waiting at your side." The Zulu wore a broad smile as he concluded, "The Mtetwas might have a larger army, but we'll have a commanding field position and - the element of surprise!"

Mevana and Msicwa seemed verily transported by the seductive strategy. Pungashe remained marginally uncomfortable.

"You said 'confederacy'. Could it be that there is something more behind this unique plan of yours?" the old monarch voiced his concern. "A paramountcy of your own, for instance?"

Senzangakona's features hardened, as he rose to face the other king's accusation.

"I have no such ambition, Pungashe. - What I want when we win is very, very personal."

*

"I'm impressed, Baba," Mudli told his monarch as they strode over the open veld, on their way home from the summit. "Your scheme is truly worthy of a great king."

Senzangakona laughed out loud, and, as he laughed, Mudli fancied that he saw in him the carefree youth he had once been, the valiant prince who might have really become a great king had it not been for "her".

"You mean you didn't think I had it in me, don't you?" Senzangakona asked, his tone remaining jovial.

By way of an answer, Mudli pursed his lips and gazed vacantly out at the countryside, his eyes resting on a stray herd of giraffe galloping across the plain, a thin mist of dust clinging to their playful prancing.

"We're alone now, Elder," Senzangakona would not be put off. "No Council to convince. No inconvenient royal sister in the way. Just the two of us. - Answer me."

"I have, Nkosi," Mudli told his king, curtly. "My words had no subtle meaning. I merely wished to praise our Ancestors for the amazing way in which they en- lighten our regents."

Again the Zulu king laughed out loud - a hearty peal that carried across the veld, causing the giraffe to take notice and pivot their long necks in alert, questioning glances. "Diplomacy!" the Zulu king roared. "If anything, you should praise the Ancestors for the amazing way in which you've just answered my question!"

A smile twitched on Mudli's lips.

"Elder, you've been my chief induna and Councillor for over twenty long years, and my father's before me--."

The Elder's head bobbed up and down, his thoughts drifting back to all those years, - to the shades and textures that had coloured his life, and to the great Jama and to how, through Jama, he, Mudli, had become humanised and initiated to the tender, complex, elusive subtleties of Life, how he had learned to understand the repulsions, the fear, the shrinkings, the evasions, the delusions and the decadence of Man, and how Jama had taught him to believe in his People.

Belief. Yes, that was at the root diplomacy. Belief and love.

"Don't you ever tire of diplomacy?" Senzangakona was asking him. "Don't you ever want to say what you really feel?"

"Oh, but I usually do, Nkosi," Mudli answered. "With diplomacy."

After many hours of journeying, when the men had almost reached the Zulu village, Senzangakona glimpsed, in the distance, the gutted ruins of Nobamba, the royal homestead that had once been his father's, the place where he had met Nandi, and his mind drifted ruthlessly back to his youth.

"Do you think he'll be in one of the Mtetwa regiments?" the king asked, his expression burdened with thoughts of Shaka.

"Who, Baba?"

"You know whom I mean, Mudli."

"With his talents, I would be surprised if he weren't," the Elder's eyes flashed with bitterness.

"Funny, isn't it? This is the first time in my life I've done something truly 'regal', and he is at the core of it. His shadow always seems to be looming over me."

Mudli's features darkened.

"It is the way of Evil, Baba."

"And my sister maintains it is Good. Quite frankly I don't care anymore which one of you is right. I just want him to die, Mudli!"

Both men stopped and faced each other. The king repeated, his voice choked with sorrow: "I just pray that he dies in that war!"

* * *

"He just isn't made for military life, Nkosi. He's too headstrong. Too independent! Bad for morale!"

After Kuta had made his enthusiastic report to the Mtetwa king concerning Shaka's new combat technique, his "Method", Dingiswayo had expressed great interest in learning more about his friend's military brainchild and had arranged for an audience to be held with those most closely related to the Zulu and his life at emaNgweni: to wit, Kuta, Buza, and Ngomane (the Commander-in-Chief of all the Mtetwa regiments).

Though ostensibly the subject to be discussed would be the Method itself and its validity in combat, Dingiswayo was secretly looking for the slightest opportunity to advance Shaka from the lowly state of common soldier without transgressing the youth's self-appointed goal of promotion through "merit and merit alone". Consequently, Dingiswayo had resolved - long before the meeting - that if this new technique had value - any value at all - he would jump at the chance to credit it as the basis for Shaka's immediate graduation in ranks.

That is why the king was now troubled by Buza's negative report, as he knit his brow at the general, his eyes darting to the knobkerrie that the other man kept slapping disturbingly against the palm of his hand.

"In what way is he not made for military life, Gene- real?" Dingiswayo inquired.

"No discipline, Baba!' the boorish man answered. "I've done what I could, but he just doesn't know the meaning of the word."

The king's gaze sifted to Ngomane and both men had a thin knowing smile. Obviously the man was either lying or too narrow-minded to see the truth. Kuta's reports on Shaka had depicted a very disciplined, very dedicated warrior who had all the qualities of a great military leader, and Dingiswayo had every reason to find these reports trustworthy inasmuch as they reflected the personality of the Zulu as the king himself knew it to be.

"No discipline?" Dingiswayo echoed.

"You saw it yourself, Baba," Buza insisted. "In the war with the Dlamini! His conduct was irresponsible!"

"Really?" Ngomane wondered. "I found it intriguing."

Buza faltered at the remark. Though crude in his military insight, the general was soldier enough to sense when he was outnumbered and surrounded. He felt that now and decided to hold his ground in silence.

"Does this method of his work?" Ngomane got down to the subject at hand.

"It's hard to tell, Ndabezitha," Kuta answered with his usual frankness. "It's still in an experimental stage. Yet I assure you that from what I've seen, it's most fascinating. The Zulu slaughtered Inkomo single-handedly, if that can be any indication." "So I've heard. A remarkable feat!" Ngomane commented, raising a brow.

"It's remarkable, all right!" Buza voiced, not being able to hold it back. "If you want to turn my men into killers, it's damn remarkable!"

"There's always been a fine distinction between soldiering and killing, General," Ngomane observed. "Many would say that soldiers are potential killers inasmuch as they are all armed with deadly weapons. - Weapons that could and have killed."

"Yes, but only when killing was in the best inter- sets of victory, Ndabezitha," rebuked the General of the iziCwe, his brow furrowed with stubborn concern. Ngomane's reply had a touch of the philosophical speculation to it and Buza was far from one to engage in such natty pursuits of the mind. He was a practical man and, as such, continued: "And so far we've been victorious in all our wars with virtually no bloodshed! I don't see why we should change a winning strategy for one that is still, as Kuta put it, in an experimental stage!"

"Point well taken, General," Dingiswayo said, believing it. Indeed Buza's stand was valid and anyone who did not admit it was as insensitive as the general him- self was known to be.

"Nkosi," Buza bowed to his king, accepting the compliment with a pleased grin.

"Yet," Dingiswayo instantly interjected, "there may be times when new techniques are useful. As you say, we've been victorious so far, but that is still no reason to press our luck."

"I don't think I understand, Baba." Buza relapsed into a more defensive pose.

Calmly, Dingiswayo guided the general down the path of his own logic, leading him to the desired conclusion.

"Then let me see if I can make it clear, General. - You've been in the military for quite some time, haven't you?"

"Yes, Nkosi," Buza arched his back with self-esteem. "I had the pleasure of serving your father in the Bush- men Regiment. It wasn't a standing army like yours, but I can say we were almost always fit and ready for action - with very little drinking going on!"

As Ngomane observed the general's artless poses of pride and prejudice, he had a sudden pang of tenderness for the other man's somewhat primitive ways.

"And what was conventional warfare like in those days?" Dingiswayo asked.

"Same as today, Baba! We went by the tried and tested. It's the only way to fight."

"Yes," the Mtetwa king regarded the general pensively. "But what if, for the sake of argument, you were to go into battle and find that the enemy was fighting differently - not according to regulation?"

"That couldn't happen, Nkosi. Our honour code prohibits it. The enemy can't just start fighting any way it wants to! That would be ludicrous! - What would become of war?!"

"But what if it did happen, General?"

Buza was completely thrown by the question and stared blankly ahead, muttering: "Well, we'd...be caught off guard, I suppose."

"And might that change the course of the battle?"

"Most likely."

"In other words," Dingiswayo moved in to close the dialectic circle round Buza, "fighting differently might possibly help win a war."

"Without a doubt, Baba," Kuta jumped in to complete the deduction.

Ngomane could now easily surmise the potential in Dingiswayo's line of reasoning, and, enthralled by the intriguing possibilities at hand, the Mtetwa Commander-in-Chief broke in, as if thinking out loud: "A special brigade trained in Shaka's new Method. To be held in reserve. On the sidelines of the battlefield, as it were. Just in case the tried and true should not be enough and the 'best interests of victory' would necessitate something 'different'..."

"Exactly," Dingiswayo assented, an adventurous smile gracing his lips.

Buza's eyes leapt from Ngomane to Dingiswayo and back. Somewhere in the course of that round trip, the general realised that he may be losing touch with the situation in its fullness. Kuta's question came to bolster that fear.

"When, Baba?"

"I sincerely hope we won't need it, Kuta. But I wouldn't mind having this unit on reserve against the Butelezi. - They've declared war, it seems."

"The Butelezi? -But they're no threat to us," Kuta interjected.

"We know that and they know that," Dingiswayo considered musingly, his gaze falling on his numerous head of cattle packed shoulder-to-shoulder in the vast stockade, an immense herd he's secured by being clever and careful, the king reminded himself, uttering under his breath:

"They should want to avoid, and yet they declare it? Now why would an old fox like Pungashe do that?"

"I can't imagine," Ngomane admitted in a serious tone. "But whatever it is, I'm sure it's intended to be a surprise."

"Yes," Dingiswayo agreed. "So we'd better have a surprise of our own ready."

"How many men would you want in the brigade, Nkosi," Kuta inquired.

"Fifty, I'd say. To start with. All volunteers, of course - they usually make the best soldiers. Do you think Shaka can raise that much support?"

"I'm sure he can, Baba. He and this new weapon of his have a great deal of charisma."

"Good. Will you see to it, Kuta? And make sure Shaka has all the freedom of action he needs. In fact," Dingiswayo's gaze shifted to Buza, his order leaving no doubt in the general's mind that Shaka had, indeed, been promoted, "from now on, I think it would be best if he and his brigade answered only to me."

Buza dropped his gaze, his bushy brow clouding over as he tightened his grip on his knobkerrie. He had been right all along, he reflected, brewing in his anger. The Zulu was trouble. He had cost him to lose face with Dingiswayo and Ngomane, to lose a portion of his authority to Kuta, and probably to lose face with some of his men. Yes, he was trouble and good riddance to him!

The next day at emaNgweni, when Kuta announced the formation of the new brigade that would be equipped with the Method and the Ixwa and asked for volunteers, Shaka almost also cost Buza to lose his entire regiment. In fact, the overture of being part of a Reserve Unit, a Special Brigade of exceptionally trained soldiers who answered only to the king himself and who were called upon to engage in battle when all else failed, had such dazzling, heroic, epical possibilities - all too alluring for men in the prime of their Youth's quest for Romance - that few if any could resist this once-in-a-lifetime bid for Glory! As Mgobozi had told Shaka at their first encounter, "there are over two hundred men here all looking for some one to come along and give them a good reason for being a soldier." -- What better reason could any man seek than to be in a special brigade with a remarkable method as yet untested: a unit of hand-picked men, volunteers, the "King's Own", the "Brigade of The Last Resort", and - above all - a detachment armed with the enchanting Ixwa! Indeed the overture rode on the notes of a hero's dream!

And all two hundred men stepped forward to volunteer. Not all at once, of course. There was even a touch of reticence at first. A quite understandable reaction considering that Buza was standing nearby with his belligerent knobkerrie and remembering that most of the men instinctively still feared the general. Mgobozi was the first to break from his ranks and be counted in the brigade. Nqoboka was next. Then came Joko (Shaka was not overly surprised, he had always known that his aggression, like that of many of the other men, would respond to the appropriate lure), and Dlaba, Mtonga, and - one by one - all the rest (as further proof that, even in glory, Man needs to share in the moral fortitude of the mob's cuddy womb).

But, as decided, only fifty took part in the new team that was instantly known as "Shaka's Fifty", or "Shaka's Brigade", "Shaka Own", and, by those who later saw it in action, "Isankahlu kaShaka" - "Shaka's Fury".

So the preparation of the Brigade began: the cutting and shaping of the men's new shields which, like Shaka's own, would be large enough to cover most of the body, yet light enough to be held in one hand and wielded with ease; the forging of the ixwas (under Shaka's direction, a new furnace was built and each man smelt his own iron, tempering and modelling it into the shape of the glorious blade - the men's new spears identical to Shaka's in all but the "Ingredients of Human Death" proper to "The Nameless One" which would remain the supremacy of the Child); besides the ixwas and the improved shields, the Brigade had nothing else by way of uniform, indeed the men went into battle nude (save for a small umuTsha, or loincloth);

And the training: -- running (fifty kilometres a day, day in and day out, in all weather, over the most hazardous terrains, with feet bloodied and bruised, the men's endurance and will-power driven beyond the limits of what was considered humanly possible; day in and day out, trotting in tight formation, snaking their way across the veld, carrying their outsized shields tightly together to form an impenetrable barrier around the sides of the formation, in silence or singing and stomping their feet in a rhythmic, heroic cadence, - running until soles toughened to the hardness of leather, until legs became as strong as tree-trunks, until lungs became as elastic and powerful as the surging waves of the sea, until the mind became the body's tyrant, driving it without respite and towards goals once thought fantastic, unreachable); practicing the Ballet of War that Shaka had perfected on the emaNwade Plateau (the stances, the kicks and turns, thrusting, jabbing, alternative stances and jabs of close combat, parrying, attacking, retreating, rolling clear of an enemy charge, then again, thrust, lead, roll, kick, parry, jab --- perfecting the style, the totality of rhythm, the excellence of balance and leverage); training in The Method (the classic sequence of The Kill:

Body to body contact. The shield hooked under the opponent's and yanked back exposing the enemy's flank. The thrust of the ixwa into the heart. - Contact. Lock shields. Pull back and away. Aim for the heart. - Over and over. Drilling in the Method until it became second nature, executed at lightning speed without flaw, without hesitation, without thinking, without remorse).

Throughout the training - that spanned the next several months - Shaka imparted to his men the concepts of warfare as he saw them, as they were developing in his mind.

This Philosophy of War, if it can so be termed, was first expressed as a reaction to standard warfare and as a justification of his new technique...

"Lions, leopards, cheetahs, the lynx, the mamba -- all the Masters of Nature have three things in common when they fight: Strategy, Speed, and Physical Contact. When the leopard hunts the impala, he first stalks his prey, approaching under cover, waiting for the best moment to strike. That's Strategy. - Next, he uses his Speed to outrun his victim. - And, finally, Physical Contact, when he sinks his fangs into the impala's throat. That is the way of Masters! --

"Yet we Humans, the Warrior Species - who should be the Masters of the Animal Kingdom - fight like Victims. First of all, our Strategy is ludicrous. Instead of silently stalking our prey, like the leopard, we go out of our way to make our presence known by shouting, screaming and ranting like men possessed! - Then, our armies have no Speed because their feet are dependent on sandals! And, finally, our present form of warfare has no Physical Contact - no close combat! In fact, we toss away our weapons hoping that the enemy will be courteous enough to return them to us. Can you imagine a lion hurling his fangs at an antelope. Or a cheetah shouting out to its prey, 'Watch out! I'm coming to kill you!'? - Of course not! If they did, they'd starve to death. Or can you imagine a lynx with leather strapped to his paws?!"

Later Shaka's Philosophy started to reflect more existential considerations. Indeed, as the months of training went on and the men started to become truly proud of the physical aspect of their bodies, of their new-found stamina, of their exceptional endurance, of their will-power, - as the 'Fifty' began to develop a full awareness of themselves and as they grew closer to Shaka and started to feel genuine affection for their 'mentor', the Son of Zulu began to appeal to their hearts and souls...

"I never said this would be easy. But then, we're grown men, not children! By now we should know that whatever comes easy in life is short-lived. I believe that has something to do with purpose. We either have it or we don't. We either decide to go through life as winners, or as losers. The choice is ultimately ours and ours alone. We are the architects of our own success and, if we fail, we have no one to blame but ourselves. Our daily victories are lasting only if they are the result of superior will-power, of an active participation in the course of our destinies - of Commitment!

"And in War, where the losers may pay for their failures with their own lives, that commitment to winning must be total! Again - we return to the word purpose., There is nothing more dangerous than a soldier who has no idea what he's doing on the battle! He can cause not only his own death, but that of his comrades.

"So let me make it clear once and for all, - our purpose in War is to kill or be killed. That's what we're doing on the battlefield. There's no use veiling it in petty idealism! What we're talking about is blood - ours or theirs!"

Indeed, Shaka's innate honesty together with his natural martial genius made it easier for his men to grant him the absolute obedience he demanded of them. In fact, the 'Fifty' went further than that - they trusted him with their lives. And Shaka never betrayed that trust because he knew how painful betrayal was...

"In our training, I will; drive you to the limits of human endurance! You will test your will powers over and over again until you've developed them into finely- honed weapons -- as effective as the Ixwa. In return for your dedication, I promise you Glory. - If anyone here feels that bruised feet are too high a price to pay for Glory, let him say so now. I'd rather have ten good men than fifty complaining little boys. Besides, I can tell you from experience - the first five months of running are the hardest. From then on you'll forget you ever had feet."

Honesty, friendship...and a genial technique of oratory...

"Like the vertebrae of a snake, we are the separate links that join together to make up the backbone of one single animal! - In combat we must be one person - one mind! One will which is the sum total of all our commitments - the Will to win at all costs.

"I don't want to see any individual acts of heroism on the battlefield. If any one of you needs to prove that he's better than the rest of us, do it in training, not in War! We are a team and I expect victory through teamwork - nothing more, nothing less! When we win, we will all be heroes. Your pride is the pride of the brigade. Your honour is loyalty to your fellow soldiers!"

And a genial technique of waging war...

Shaka's most important brainchild in this particular period of his military career was the so-called "cattle- horn formation" of attack. In this revolutionary technique (that the Zulu devised one day whilst gazing idly at Dingiswayo's great populace of bulls and cows), his brigade was divided into three main divisions: - the "iKandha" or central "head" of the formation (which was made up of the heaviest and strongest of his warriors) and, on both sides of the head, the "izimPondo" or lateral "horns" (consisting of his lightest warriors, the fastest runners). In actual combat, the three divisions were to remain together at first, the horns tucked behind the head in a compact group. Then, after the initial assault (in which the entire brigade would advance upon the enemy at a fast trot, engaging it in close combat and literally battering it into a forced withdrawal), the horns themselves would be deployed, breaking off from this group and suddenly sweeping out at top speed, encircling the enemy in their "open arms". This circle would them cut back and close in on the enemy as the arms tightened against the advancing head.

Shaka himself first explained as...

"Like the human body, we will have several components, all working together in harmony. The eyes. The ears. The chest, The legs. - Yet the most vital will be the head and the horns - for when we fight, we will be as aggressive as the bull.

"Twenty men in the centre displayed in four rows of five. They will make up the 'head' of the formation. And, on both sides of the head, two divisions of fifteen men each - our fastest runners - will be the horns.

"The head will advance first, with the horns hidden behind it -- that's Phase One!

"Then, when I give the word, the horns will sweep out on both sides -- that's Phase Two!

"And, Phase Three -- like encircling arms, the horns will surround the enemy and close in!" "And after each Kill," he directed his men on the last day of training before the war against the Butelezi at eNtuzuma Hill, "- after each Kill, when you yank your blade out of the enemy's heart you will shout - loud enough for the Heavens to hear it - 'Ngadla'!"

"Ngadla!" - The war cry of the Child's insatiable hunger for the Way of the Blade.

"Ngadla!" -- "I have eaten!"

CHAPTER XXI
"THABAS NKOSI"(THE HILL OF THE KING)
THE BATTLE OF ENTUZUMA HILL

The Nguni Bantu have a Folk Tale about how all the birds of the world got together one day to decide which of them should be king. After much deliberation, they agreed to hold a contest and the one that could fly the highest was to be appointed. As the time for the competition drew near, the smallest of the birds, the uCilo (a tiny lark), crept underneath the wings of the Eagle. Soon the race began and the Eagle soared up high above the rest. Yet just as he began to think that he was king, the uCilo came out of his hiding place and easily flew up still higher than the Eagle.

The other birds, and the Eagle in particular, were very angry at the way they had been tricked and decided to punish the tiny Lark for his cunning. But before they could catch him however, the uCilo flew into a hole in the ground, the mouth of which was too narrow for the other birds to follow.

Determined to keep a watch on the Lark and capture him when he came out to eat, the birds chose the Owl to guard the hole. But after a while the Owl grew sleepy and thought to himself that there would be no harm in closing one eye while keeping watch with the other. So he guarded the hole, first with one eye, then with the other, till finally, to his dismay, when he shut his left eye he forgot to open the right. The uCilo, who had been quietly awaiting his chance, took advantage of the sleeping Owl and escaped.

When the birds found out what had happened, they were very angry with the Owl, and from that day the Owl has been in such disgrace that he hides away during the day and only comes out at night, when he will not be seen by anyone.

It might have been this punishment that made the Owl wise. Indeed, unlike the blustery fools of the world who insist on "rushing in where Angels fear to tread", the Owl, accustomed to living at night, in the darkness, became perforce more cautious.

Yet it was broad daylight at eNtuzuma Hill in the dry, wintry season of ubuSika, in the Month of April, 1809, and King Dingiswayo of the Mtetwas had brought his entire army to engage in battle at the urging of King Pungashe of the Butelezi.

Dingiswayo gazed round him at the festive atmosphere that gripped his subjects - the Mtetwa public, the excited "fans" who had accompanied his armies on the long march south of the Umfolozi and were now lounging and loafing idly on the grassy banks of the eMpenbeni River, under the high, wooded slopes of eNtuzuma, waiting to see the "home team" engaged in the classic Contest of warfare.

As the king's roaming eye distractedly took in the Mtetwa men, women, and children singing, laughing, running, playing, chatting, joking, and joyously indulging in the behaviour that was an accessory of this traditional "sport", Dingiswayo's thoughts clung to Pungashe, whom he had known since his childhood days when the Butelezi had often visited his father Jobe, and he decided that if Pungashe were a bird, he, too, would be an owl, or, more properly, a cross between the Owl and the Lark - both wise and clever.

Too wise, too clever. And the gnawing question came back to mind: why had he declared war well knowing that his own forces were so inferior to the Mtetwa? As he pondered over this query, Dingiswayo's gaze detached itself from the festive antics of his subjects and swung out to the clearing under eNtuzuma were his five regiments (now numbering over 1200 troops with the new Dlamini recruits) were assembled in their ornate, imposing attire of plumes, furs and coloured shields, a spangled spectacle that flooded the narrow valley between the eMpenbeni and the Hill with rippling waves of ornate flourish: - the two hundred men of the Uyengondlovu Regiment with their black and white shields and red plumes; the two hundred men of the iNyakeni with red and black shields and white plumes; the iNyelezi Regiment and its three hundred men gripping solid black shields and wearing flashy yellow plumes; the three hundred of the iziPikili, red and orange with black; and, finally, the iziCwe, shields solid red, plumes a jet black.

Yet, though splendid, the sight of his numerous troops, usually the cause of great pride and elation, could today bring little solace to Dingiswayo as his mind lingered on the surprise Pungashe might have in store for him. Indeed, the king's face registered an expression akin to relief only when his gaze shifted further to take in the new brigade, "Shaka's Fifty", positioned slightly to the side of the other troops, ten serried lines of five men abreast, all standing at attention, all in stony silence - eyes staring straight ahead, unflinching, ixwas gleaming in the afternoon sun. As Dingiswayo surveyed his brigade, he fervently hoped that in the unpretentious, Spartan simplicity of these men, devoid of fatuous plumes, feathers, furs and the like, "adorned" only with single-minded volition and courage, that in their hearts would be the answer to any threat Pungashe might pose. He hoped that, once again, if need be, Shaka would be in a position to save his life, the life of his kingdom.

In light of this hope, Dingiswayo turned around and looked up at eNtuzuma Hill where he saw the Butelezi forces grouped on the wooded slopes.

"How many would you say there are, Baba?" Ngomane was at his side, his eyes also trained on the Hill.

"Three hundred," Dingiswayo murmured, narrowing his eyes. "Three-fifty maybe. Not more."

"Then I see your point, Nkosi," Ngomane remarked, with a rising level of incredulity in his voice. "It doesn't make sense. Even if his position is better than ours, we still outnumber them four to one. Has Pungashe gone mad?"

"Perhaps, Ngomane," Dingiswayo answered with a thin smile. "That's one explanation that hadn't occurred to me. Let's test his sanity, shall we? - Dispatch a herald to the Butelezi, Ngomane. Inform their king that, in view of our overwhelming superiority, I wish to save him needless injury and humiliation. I am therefore willing to call off the conflict and offer an amnesty if he will acknowledge my over lordship and join the Mtetwa paramountcy."

"I don't think that will be necessary, Baba," Ngomane's words were delivered in a low, thoughtful manner, suddenly solicitous. "Look."

Amazement crept over Dingiswayo's features as he stole a glance in the direction his induna indicated and saw a second army appear on the Butelezi's left flank, the Mbateni warriors of King Kali. Then, an instant later, before the Mtetwa monarch could further react, two other armies came into view, the Kumalos of King Donda and Senzangakona's Zulus - both manning the Butelezi's right flank, all four armies literally carpeting the summit of the hill.

A flurry of heated comments rippled through the Mtetwa spectators as the idle conversation, the laughing and the joking were abruptly shot through with keen tension and gaping astonishment.

Buza was thoroughly afflicted at the sight of the Butelezi's surprise tactic. For the commander this unexpected forgathering of troops smacked of a deep lack of fairness on the part of Pungashe (indeed the enemy king had gone against conventional warfare's honour code by deliberately misleading his prospective opponent - by not playing by the rules, so to say). The general was on the point of sharing his outrage with Kuta, when his eyes fell on Shaka's Brigade and the painful thought struck him that on this particular day no one was really 'playing by the rules'. Would eNtuzuma mark the end of tradition? he wondered, feeling suddenly very lost, very cheated.

Nandi, who was on the grassy slopes in the midst of the onlookers, was also spellbound by the unexpected presence of the Zulu army and its king in the enemy lines, and shuddered profoundly, feeling a thread pull at the fabric of her mind.

Like Nandi's, Dingiswayo's eyes had travelled to Senzangakona and he was filled with distress as he mused out loud, his thoughts on Shaka: "Can I ask a son to fight against his own father?"

"We need him, Baba," Ngomane stressed grimly, in a veiled blank voice as he reviewed the enemy's commanding position. "As you so accurately suspected, without a surprise of our own, our chance of victory is now greatly reduced."

Their eyes locked as the decision weighed suspended between them.

"Then I shall allow the choice to be his," Dingiswayo resolved and strode down the lines of Mtetwa regiments and, under the intense watchful gazes of his troops, stopped next to the "Fifty".

When Dingiswayo had put the question to him, exhibiting that the final decision rested completely upon his friend's judgment, Shaka shifted his gaze to look up at the Zulus. Though he hadn't seen the man in well over sixteen years, since the early days of his troubled childhood, the years at esiKlebeni, and though the Zulu sovereign had changed considerably, his once proud, athletic frame having degenerated to the less flattering figure of a debauched alcoholic, - though Senzangakona looked strikingly different, Shaka recognised the man at once, and when their eyes met in the force of an incur- table perception and the father identified the son as mysteriously as the son had known the father, the great distances that separated them at eNtuzuma seemed to vanish - and they both felt, father and son, that they could suddenly reach and touch one another; and in that spellbinding instant in which this magical proximity of the two men seemed to rest on the fragile vane of a feather, Shaka spun round, turning his back on Senzangakona, dismissing the one who sired him.

"My men have worked too hard and trained for too long, Baba," Shaka formally announced to his king, remaining as coldly unemotional as was his manner. "I will let nothing stand in the way of their glory." Shooting a sidelong glance back at his father's position, Shaka added, stiffly: "Nothing!"

"My compliments, Senzangakona," Pungashe approached the Zulu king with a humourless smile. "You were right. They look very vulnerable indeed."

As the Butelezi King cocked his head to peer down at the Mtetwa troops which, though numerous, looked quite assailable indeed in their open position at the foot of the hill, Senzangakona nodded in response.

Yes, the Zulu king thought, they look very vulnerable. Yet his eyes were not on the armies of his enemy, they were on that woman, the Love of his Youth and of his Life who was seated on the grassy slopes near the eMpenbeni, and his eyes were on her children, his children he had to remind himself, Shaka and Nomcoba, almost adults now, who had been the innocent human offerings of that Love. Before coming to the site of the battle, Senzangakona had wondered, with anxious trepidation, whether Shaka would be there - on the field of war - and if so, whether he, his father, would be able to signal him out in the packed regimental files. Yet, those fears were superfluous for recognition came almost instantaneously, though Senzangakona himself could not discern why. Perhaps it was something imperceptible in the lines of Shaka's attitude that made him stand out. Or his exceptional beauty - the mirror image of his mother's - which seemed to soften the suggestion of ruthless pride that enveloped him like a fortress of granite. Perhaps it was his statuesque physique, or his---

Senzangakona's thoughts were abruptly cleaved as he shifted his gaze from Shaka back to Nandi and found that the woman's eyes were trained on his. And still sensitive like a bond slave to the mesmerising appeal of those eyes, he was moved to a twitching smile by the subtle relenting of her grace. And Nandi smiled back, though the smile was not for him, he knew, but the reflection of some deep and impenetrable thought - as if she were already savouring the sweet taste of victory, her son's imminent triumph over this man who had rejected and humiliated her, as if, for Nandi, the Battle of eNtuzuma Hill had taken on the textures of a "family feud" since the appearance of Senzangakona in the enemy ranks, a "lover's quarrel" in which her "champion", Shaka, was about to engage in combat for the sake of her honour. Faced with that smile Senzangakona suddenly felt drained of the strength and determination he had enjoyed whilst plotting and planning for the conflict, - he felt like forfeiting the battle, indeed forfeiting his existence and abandoning himself forever to this feeling of immense deception, of extreme fatigue.

Beside him, seeing his eyes on that woman and the expression they wore, Mudli became increasingly aware of his king's turmoil and, for the first time perhaps, realised the extent of his pain. The Elder was about to rouse the Zulu from his reverie, when Donda stepped in to perform the task instead.

"How do you suggest we deploy our armies?" the Kumalo king inquired of Senzangakona.

When the Zulu stirred and answered, he wondered at his own self-control and at the steadiness of his voice.

"Pungashe has the greatest manpower, so it seems to me that his regiment should go down and engage the enemy first. You," he nodded to Donda, his tone growing in authority, "Kali and I will stay on the hill and cover his position."

"That would mean splitting our forces," Kali objected. "I was under the impression that a united, concentrated front was at the root of your original idea."

"Yes, Kali. And we will remain united inasmuch as our attack will be coordinated. Remember, we have the commanding position, and we must use it to our best advantage. By dividing our troops," he was now addressing all three kings, "we'll be able to fight on two different levels - one up here, on the hill's summit and another below, at its foot. An attack like that is very hard to parry because the enemy's eyes cannot be on both levels at the same time. Sooner or later, our spears will hit home. And, even if they don't, our barrage will make throwing their own spears most awkward."

The monarchs exchanged glances of agreement. The Zulu's reply to their objections made sense.

Mudli felt an ever-deepening respect for his king and his seemingly natural ability as a general, an unknown facet of his character. Perhaps he had been wrong, the Elder mused. The war with the Langeni that had loomed over the Zulus more than two decades ago should have been fought. Its victory would have spared Senzangakona the tragedy that his life had become.

"The concentrated attack will come later," the Zulu was continuing. "Once our spears start to become a nuisance, we'll sweep down the hill and join the Butelezi forces for the final rush - driving the Mtetwas back across the eMpenbeni. - Are we in agreement?"

There was little more to say. Nodding their assent, Donda and Kali returned to their troops. Pungashe stayed behind just long enough to add: "Again, my compliments, Senzangakona. I never thought you had your father's acumen."

As if he had read Mudli's mind, Senzangakona replied: "I've been waiting over twenty years for this war, Pungashe. I don't intend to let anything go wrong."

The Butelezi eyed the Zulu with a sombre expression, a dozen explanations for the man's cryptic response flashing through his mind.

Pungashe was on the verge of seeking more elucidation, when he thought better of it and, spinning round, strode off to his troops.

"'My father's acumen'! No, I'll never have that!" Senzangakona echoed with self-abasement. "But I should have taken heed of Jama's acumen! If I had, I wouldn't be here today trying to win back my life from the son who should never have been born."

The "son" in question was standing next to Mgobozi and Joko, the three men's eyes on the Hill.

"Two fronts. One above. One below. Two separate points of attack," Shaka stated, analysing their opponent's strategy. "A very clever way of approaching conventional warfare. Whoever's behind this idea is an exceptional strategist."

"Maybe he's been reading your mind?" Mgobozi suggested with a smile.

"No," Shaka said. "If he'd been reading my mind, he would know that splitting his troops though a valid strategy in principle is the last thing he should do here. In fact he's just relinquished the only chance he ever had of winning."

Moments later, as agreed, Pungashe's forces reached the bottom of the Hill and fanned out in combat formation, defining a straight line of warriors that skirted the edge of the valley. Nkalakata, the Butelezi commander and the undisputed champion of his armed forces, - a tall, brawny man with the facial lineaments of a pugnacious, weathered fighter, stepped to the centre of his ranks and glared at the enemy with spiteful eyes narrowed in a silent challenge.

Ngomane gave the sign and the five regular Mtetwa regiments moved forward, advancing to a distance of 50 paces from the Butelezi formation.

Sensing the tingling vibrations that accompanied the beginning of their favourite "game", feeling the "lust of battle" upon them, the Mtetwa public began to cheer, shouting words of encouragement to their "team"; and the "players" shouted back, waving to their families, smiling with the artless confidence of those who walk in the mists of mediocrity's contentment.

Only Shaka and his men remained silent, immovable, patient.

His eyes flaming with primitive unharnessed aggression, Nkalakata raised his voice in a piercing cry that gave way to a warrior's chant. The Butelezi forces echoed that chant, their voices resounding from the hills of eNtuzuma where the Zulus, the Mbateni, and the Kumalo regiments waited to join the conflict.

When the Mtetwa troops answered the war cry, adding to it a rhythmic, heroic dance, frenzied and disordinate, the Butelezis started to dance as well, working their hearts into the rage of combat. Presently, as was the custom, Nkalakata began to intersperse his chanting with insults, to which the Mtetwas responded in kind.

Now the "game" had begun in earnest.

Suddenly intrigued by the odd detachment of men who stood silent, stoic, immobile, Nkalakata cast a suspicious gaze in the direction of Shaka's Fifty and, laughing at their silence - which he interpreted as a sign of cowardice, the Butelezi commander tried to provoke the men into remonstrance with his clownish, mocking words and gestures. Yet "Shaka's Own" would not be bullyragged, no matter how bantering the abuse.

Upset by his inability to instigate the brigade, Nkalakata seemed to suddenly forget the thousand, as he concentrated his efforts on the Fifty and hurled his spear, which sailed mightily through the air and was easily deflected by Shaka's shield. Yet, when the Butelezi commander - and indeed when all present at eNtuzuma waited for Shaka to pick up the assegai and toss it back (as was the norm), they found that their expectation was soon frustrated by the Zulu's complete disregard for the weapon at his feet. Indeed, Shaka remained in place, calm, offering Nkalakata his cool, upright gaze.

Furious, the proud Butelezi hurled another spear. Which Shaka again deflected, and left forgotten at his feet.

The Mtetwa Public - who had heard so much of this exceptional brigade and had expected it to be the afternoon's special attraction - now felt extremely cheated by this "unmanly" show of military indifference. Indeed, they would have asked for their money back (if that had also been the norm of custom), but, having paid nothing for the show but their token of faith, they retracted this confidence by showering the Fifty with expressions of disapprobation.

Though Shaka and the Fifty had well anticipated this reaction, and though Nandi stiffly ignored it, Pampata was shattered by this affront to her hero and gaped at the booing crowd, her eyes moistening with tears as she thought of "her prince" with the unselfish concern and dedication of a loving maiden who has inadvertently rested the whole meaning and joy of her world on the delicate thread of a hero's safety.

Buza was also deeply disturbed by this turn of events. Yet the commander of the iziCwe was moved to anger not tears and, mentally consolidating his hatred of Shaka, Buza motioned to his men to come to the rescue and return the fire. Obligingly, the iziCwe obeyed, and spears were launched at the Butelezi line. Parried and retrieved by Pungashe's troops, the spears were tossed back.

Back and forth. Back and forth. The public seemed somewhat appeased as the game resumed. When---

Senzangakona sensed that the time was right to move to the next stage of his plan: - the concentrated effort of all fronts. Catching the glances of both Kali and Donda, the Zulu sovereign raised his hand to give the order, yet as he was about to do so, he suddenly sensed that a pair of eyes were on him, a penetrating stare that caused the king to shift his gaze which was instantly ensnared by Shaka's. Once again the two men, father and son, looked at each other over the distances of the battlefield. Having noticed that both Kali and Donda awaited Senzangakona's signal to act, Shaka realised that the "clever strategist behind the Butelezi's idea" was none other than his own father and, for an instant, a fleeting instant, the way a fisherman spies the moving shadow of a large fish in the purple depths of the ocean's bottom, Shaka now spied a fragment of the man his mother once loved. As he did so, the young man smiled. And his father smiled back. And in this instant, this fleeting fraction of a second that was abruptly gone, never to come again, to be remembered only as a flash of light in the infinite vastness of consummate darkness, - in this twinkling of Time, Shaka felt respect for the other man and a sentiment as close to love as pitted hatred can conceive.

And then it was gone, and Senzangakona clenched his teeth with suppressed emotion and, as his heart cried out "too late! Too late!", he lowered his arm, giving the sign to attack as if each new dart was to be directed at Shaka and Shaka alone!

A shower of spears rained from the hill, clouding the sun. A moment later, another barrage of Butelezi spears was hurled head-on at the Mtetwas. The timing of the attack was perfect, and both barrages caught Dingiswayo's forces simultaneously. Shaka's men remained unhurt as the missiles merely bounced off the protective shell of their large shields, but many of the men in the regular regiments were wounded or killed as they tried vainly to parry assegais which seemed to be coming at them from all directions.

Buza and the other commanders shouted out to their troops, urging them to return the fire, but as the confused warriors tried to obey yet another barrage of darts blackened the sky, catching the Mtetwa forces completely open and off-guard. Dozens of soldiers fell to the ground.

Snorting in pain, spitting up blood and pulmonary fluid, Buza sank to his knees, struggling to pull the assegai out of his punctured aorta. Yet he soon realised that his effort was futile - as vain as had been his attempt to dislodge the Method from the Pulse of History. Slumping forward with an angry groan, the general gave up his life, the inglorious spectator of someone else's war.

When yet another shower of spears was hurled by the enemy's concentrated attack, Dingiswayo and Ngomane turned to glare anxiously at the tight formation of warriors that was prophetically becoming their last resort.

"What is he waiting for!?" Ngomane snarled angrily, his eyes on Shaka's brigade. "Why doesn't he do something?!"

As if sensing the induna's irate plea, Shaka uttered to his men, in a tone that had the impersonal ring of a voice without a master: "Stand by."

With calculated movements the Fifty lined up in ten rows of five men each, as Shaka, alone, his large shield and Ixwa poised for combat, advanced on the Butelezi line.

Nandi watched her son's actions in a seemingly detached manner, with clinical scrutiny while, next to the woman, Nomcoba's and Pampata's eyes grew wide with apprehension as they saw their hero racing towards the forest of spears in this completely unorthodox manner.

The Butelezi, the Kumalo, the Mbateni, and the Zulus were also taken aback by the unprecedented sight of Shaka rushing their lines and, as he quickly closed the distance between himself and Nkalakata, the troops stopped their attack to gape in wonder at the nude man racing towards them with his gigantic shield and extraordinary spear. In fact, as he drew closer, his appearance struck some as so comical that they began to laugh.

Even Nkalakata, who was accustomed to taking hissoldiering
seriously, found himself amused by the approaching warrior. But the man's laughter was short-lived. Within seconds, Shaka had closed with him, hooked his shield behind the Butelezi's, pulled back and away exposing the man's flank and thrusting his Ixwa deep into his chest - with such force that the Blade pierced Nkalakata's heart and lung and came tearing out through the back of his rib cage. Yet the truly terrifying part of the Kill - as far as the onlookers were concerned - was not the powerful thrust, nor the gushing blood, nor Nkalakata's ghastly cry of sheer anguish as if his soul had been virtually wrenched from his body, - no, what was truly terrifying was the Speed of execution:- it had taken Shaka but a few seconds - a few bloodcurdling seconds - to dispatch the Butelezi to his Ancestors.

Pungashe jumped to his feet as his troop commander fell. Senzangakona and Mudli turned to ice, their faces frozen in masks of surprise and horror. Dingiswayo and Ngomane stood spellbound; - never, in their wildest imagination, had they thus conceived "The Method" in action!.

No one at eNtuzuma moved, as all gaped, speechless, breathless. It was as if the Spectre of Death Itself had come to visit the assembled populace of the five clans. Indeed, all five clans suddenly seemed to form one single front, with but one enemy - Shaka, his Method, his Brigade.

As Nkalakata crumbled to the ground, Shaka disengaged his weapon and broke the spell of silence that hung over the battlefield by shouting a bewitching "Ngadla!" that resounded from the Heavens like a clap of thunder. As the cry was echoed from the summit of eNtuzuma, the Master of the Brigade roared: "Phase One!"

In compact formation, the Fifty broke into a dead run, speeding towards the Butelezi line, their bare feet pounding the earth with a vengeance. Shaka preceded his men, continuing his assault on the stunned, defenceless Butelezi warriors. -- Contact. Lock shields. Pull back and away. Aim for the heart. -- "Ngadla!"

In an instant the Fifty were at Shaka's side and the formation literally rammed the enemy with its large shields like the head of a charging bull.

"Phase two!" Shaka shouted.

On cue, as the first four rows of the Brigade continued to push back the enemy line, engaging it in close combat, the last six rows branched out in to two thinly-spaced "horns" of fifteen men each which swept out and down both sides of the startled Butelezi line, joining Shaka and their comrades in the carnage.

Contact. Lock shields. Pull back and away. Aim for the heart. - "Ngadla!"

Joko as part of the chest, Mtonga and Nqoboka with the left horn, and Dlaba with the right, put to death one Butelezi after another with a speed and precision that sent their victims gaping incredulously into the jaws of death. Yet, next to Shaka, Mgobozi was the hero of the day as he burned his way through the enemy formation, grinning with mounting confidence, his bare chest bathed in spurted blood.

Contact. Lock shields. Pull back and away. Aim for the heart. - The men danced through the Ballet of War for their enthralled, captivated audience.

As the enemy scrambled to retreat, wounded men slipping and sliding over the oozing entrails of their gutted comrades, Shaka bellowed: "Phase Three!"

The two horns of the Brigade launched into action, circling behind the Butelezi, trapping them in their deadly embrace, as the head continued to pound its way into the enemy.

Breaking away from the Brigade, Shaka, Mgobozi, Nqoboka, Joko and a handful of the Fifty, stormed the hill, rushing towards the forces of the three remaining kings. Though the Zulus, the Kumalos and the Mbateni -

stirred into action by the urgings of both Pungashe and Senzangakona - far outnumbered Shaka's small detachment, their long throwing assegais were virtually worthless at short range and the Fifty's massacre continued claiming, among others, the tortured souls of Dilikana and his comrades (who had once had the misfortune of giving chase to the Child).

His eyes on the bloodbath, Mudli uttered under his breathe, with an ominous inflection of doom: "'He will usher in a new Era in which the name amaZulu will signify death and terror'. Such is the Prophecy. And today we have seen it in action." The Elder's eyes met Senzangakona's and locked. "The Seed of Evil has been planted and will grow nourished by the Blood of eNtuzuma Hill. It is too late. By changing the course of war, he has changed the course of our history."

"What a war machine!" Ngomane commented on the opposite side of the field, his excited words ascribing a measure of validity to the Method. "Fifty men fighting like one thousand! In one afternoon, Shaka has made centuries of conventional warfare look like child's play!"

"Yes, Ngomane," Dingiswayo's voice was hollow, suddenly tired, sounding so very weary that Ngomane turned to look at his king with genuine concern. "But I fear he's done the same to centuries of conventional peace. Made it child's play. After today, there's no turning back." His intimation seemed to reflect Mudli's own fears. "The war machine has been initiated and will grow of its own momentum. From now on, one factor will be paramount in all our dealings with other clans: - fear. And fear is known to breed hatred!"

*

"SI-GI-DI!" shouted Mgobozi raising his ixwa in Shaka's acclaim.

"SI-GI-DI" echoed the "Fifty", their spears thrust towards the Heavens, their feet pounding the ground in a single quake of thunderous tribute as they extolled the leader of their brigade with the mighty praise name "Sigidi" - 'One who fights like a thousand'.

"One who fights like a thousand," Dingiswayo repeated the praise, as he strode at Shaka's side. The two men were walking on their own, not far from the long lines of Mtetwa soldiers who were marching back from eNtuzuma, on their way home.

Shaka had a wry smile as he listened to the exalted chanting of those who had become his clansmen and, far from basking in the elusive warmth of that acclaim, he commented offhandedly: "Our people are so accustomed to mediocrity, they jump at the chance of taking some one seriously. They are so starved for a collective pride, they'll turn anyone with a purpose into a hero. - My men and I didn't fight like 'one thousand', we fought like fifty who knew what they were doing."

"What exactly were you doing, Shaka?"

Shaka frowned at the puzzling question and retorted, levelly: "Turning defeat into victory, Baba."

"Is that all?"

With a quick sidelong glance, Shaka perceived that Dingiswayo was eyeing him somewhat critically. Annoyed by that look and by the subtle reproach that transpired in his king's curt inquisitive, a somewhat accusatory tone that seemed totally uncalled-for after Shaka's glorious rout of the enemy, the Zulu left the question unanswered as he shifted his gaze to the multitude of stars that were starting to peek through the darkening vault of the sky.

"There was something I glimpsed in your eyes, Shaka," Dingiswayo pressed on. "A glint that betrayed an inner motivation surpassing that of a soldier in the line of duty. You were finding an emotional outlet in war - and that can prove dangerous in some one as sensitive as you."

Shaka allowed a little impatience to pierce under his casual manner.

"How can a man fight without emotion, Baba? How can you achieve victory without totally pledging your heart to the spirit of combat?"

"Even at the risk of losing that heart?"

The Zulu stiffened, lowering his head in aspect of profound meditation.

"War must always remain a means, Shaka, a last resort - never an end in itself!"

"And what is the end?" the Zulu asked stiffly.

"Peace."

Shaka's rejoinder came in the murmur of a voice, which flowed, with a trace of resigned sadness in its depth.

"War and peace are both an end and a means, almost interchangeable in their intents. There can be no peace without war - and we need war to impose peace."

"Do you need war, Shaka - to find peace?"

The young man was stung by the question. He had given up the habit of relating to his inner needs for so long that the sudden mention of deep-seated motivations irked him exceedingly. Shaka was piqued by his king's line of questioning not so much because it was what could be called 'personal' (the term 'personal' meant little to a man whose emotions had become deeply effected by his logic), but because the Zulu sincerely believed it to be a waste of time and an unnecessary commingling of terms - war was war and sentiment was something else.

Dingiswayo sensed his friend's irritation and realised that it was to be expected. Youth that is fresh enough to believe in innocence, in guilt, and in itself will never search for faults in its Glory. Yet, the king knew that for Shaka's own good, he must strive to make his point clear.

"We've both suffered, Shaka. Far more than men should if they wish to keep an objectivity about life. Our dreams are haunted by hatred, by the ghosts of those who have made us suffer. I suppose we're allowed to kill them in our dreams, there's very little we can do to prevent that. But once that urge to kill spills into our waking life, we become misfits. Extraordinary misfits -- Heroes!" The boisterous refrain of 'SI-GI-DI!' echoed over the king's words. "Once we allow our personal defeats to be projected onto the battlefield, war becomes a very convenient means of release. An end in itself! And when that happens, our victories turn into massacre. - Like today's."

Their eyes locked.

"You'd won the battle, Shaka! You'd won it long before you drenched eNtuzuma in blood."

Stung into protest, Shaka jerked his head to the side and rebutted defensively: "Your words surprise me, Baba! I thought you would be pleased by the performance of the brigade."

"I am, Shaka. I have to be. Success seems to be the criterion of wisdom. In fact, we need you and your brigade more than ever now. You're the only one who can harness this monster you created. 'Regulation tactics' are no tactics at all anymore. Word gets out and from now on I suspect we'll find our enemies more prepared and full of surprises. That's why Ngomane and I have discussed your promotion. As you know, Buza fell in combat and we feel you should take his place."   Dingiswayo could not help but grin at the excitement he read in Shaka's eyes.

"Commander of the iziCwe?"

"'Through merit and merit alone', as you put it. And there was a great deal of that going on today."

Shaka was more confused than ever now.

"I don't understand, Baba. You speak of merit, of promotion - yet I sense that your voice is laced only with sorrow and reproach."

The Mtetwa king looked at Shaka intensely, at the youth's chiselled features framed in the yellow glow of the ascending moon, such soft features, he mused, too soft, too gentle to house the seed of such deliberate violence; and Dingiswayo's sentient heart felt a pang of penetrating sadness, and, queerly enough, his thoughts returned to the Folk Tale of the Owl and he considered how, like the Owl, Hatred also often hides from Light and is revealed only in Darkness, when its Terror blazes like a tongue of flame that touches and withdraws before it turns the heart to ashes. I must bring him back to Light, the King decided - slowly back to Light.

Barely raising his voice above a whisper, Dingiswayo answered: "Your merit and your promotion are public, Shaka. My words were only for you, as a friend. You saved my life. Now I must try to keep you from ruining your own."

CHAPTER XXII
"UMPHATI"(COMMANDER)

Like so many other aspects of the Child's life, the evolution and development of The Method was also destined to follow the fatidic course dictated by the Prophets and the Wise of the Land. In fact, as was put forth in the premonitory words of King Dingiswayo, Shaka's "war machine had been initiated and would grow of its own momentum".

And so it was to be.

The War Machine grew and spread throughout the land, as did Shaka's Fame. Indeed, like all exceptional men, Shaka's greatness could soon be measured by his fame - and his fame was the greatest thing around for many a day's journey.

And, for many a day's journey - the War machine grew and thundered across the countryside, the long serried formation of warriors gripping their huge shields and pounding the earth like a colossal maddened serpent with cowhide scales.

After the iziCwe had been thoroughly trained in the Method and prepared - both physically and spiritually - to engage in combat as effectively as had the original Fifty, the Son of Zulu, as the new commander of the Mtetwa regiment, deemed that his king had been correct -- word of the new close combat strategy would indeed get out and surprises would definitely be forthcoming. Therefore, Shaka determined that it would be best if he and his regiment indulged in "precautionary campaigns" in which his troops would "visit" neighbouring tribes and "coax" them into the Mtetwa Paramountcy before these tribes had a chance to devise any "surprises" of their own or any ingenuous measures with which to safeguard themselves from the Method.

The first series of such campaigns was to last only one dry season (i.e. from April to September, the months in which warfare took place) - or so Dingiswayo and Ngomane had deliberated in their meetings with Shaka. And there was not to be any violence unless tribes actually refused to enter the Paramountcy and then such violence was to be limited to only the bare essential.

Yet as often happens in such explosive intertribal situations where "absorption" into another kingdom can be seen as a form of "vanquishment" and where a "reluctance to be absorbed can easily be confused with an outright "refusal", and where the term "bare essential" is inevitably destined to be read as merely "essential", then "necessary", and then "customary" - indeed as often happens in armed campaigns that have the flavour of imperialism, "coaxing the allegiance of reluctant tribes with barely essential violence" is likely to degenerate into a policy of progressive conquest in which waging war becomes not the exception but the rule.

Especially when the commander is as extraordinary a person as the Child and his warriors are trained to be as dedicated as Mgobozi, Nqoboka, Joko, Mtonga, Dlaba and the rest - all of them, men who now began to see in soldiering not only a purpose, a way of life that gave them glory, a feeling of fulfilment and the thrill of gratification, but, indeed, their sole purpose for living! The men of the iziCwe and then, progressively, as Shaka was given command of the other regiments, all the Mtetwa warriors became "professional soldiers in a standing army" - a concept totally new to the Nguni Bantu and to Africa - the totally new concept of Total War!

And so it was that Shaka and the iziCwe set out in the dry season of 1810 to indulge in a precautionary campaign that was meant to last but a few months. Yet this prophetic April of 1810 was instead to mark the beginning of a plague of ceaseless warfare that spanned over eighteen years.

The first five of those years marked the turning point for Southern Africa, - and the Log of the Pinnacle thus relates those years of Initiation to Fear, Blood, and Death as the Diary of the Child had written it on the Wind:

- Battle of eNtsangoyana Ridge, April 1810. Shaka Zulu commander of the iziCWe. The Cambini Clan: defeated, three hundred and twelve of their population slaughtered. Six of their homesteads burnt to the ground and razed. All cattle confiscated as the prize of victory. -- Survivors incorporated into the Mtetwa Paramountcy. Mtetwa losses: none.

- Battle of iHluhluwe River, May, 1810. Shaka Zulu commander of the iziCwe. The Nxele Clan: defeated. Two hundred and fifty of their populace slaughtered. All homestead burned and razed. All cattle confiscated. Survivors incorporated into the Mtetwa Paramountcy. Mtetwa losses: none.

- Battle of Hlopekulu Hill, June, 1810. Shaka Zulu commander of the iziCwe and iNyelezi Regiments. The Zungu Clan: defeated. Four hundred and sixteen of the population slaughtered. All homesteads razed. All cattle confiscated. No survivors. Mtetwa losses: two.

- Battle of Umona Creek, July, 1810. Shaka Zulu commander of the iziCwe and iNyelezi Regiments. The Dludla Clan: defeated. Two hundred and seven slaughtered. Seven homesteads burned and razed. All cattle confiscated. Survivors incorporated in the Mtetwa Paramountcy. Mtetwa losses: seven.

- Battle of eShowe, August, 1810. Shaka Zulu commander of the iziCwe, iNyelezi, and Uyengondlovo Regiments. The eMbo Clan: defeated.

one hundred and ten slaughtered. Six villages burned and razed. Cattle also slaughtered due to infected waters of eNadi River. Survivors of battle died of isiHudo (known today as dysentery). Mtetwa losses: twenty-two (due to disease).

- Battle of iBuse Bank, April, 1811. Shaka Zulu commander of the iziCwe, iNyelezi, and Uyengondlovo Regiments. The Ximba Clan: defeated. 311 slaughtered. 6 homesteads burned and razed. All cattle confiscated. Survivors incorporated in the Mtetwa paramountcy. Mtetwa losses: 2.

- Battle of umLalazi River, Battle of eHlobane Mountain, Battle of uSutu River, Battle of eNkwenkwe Hill, Battle of isiHlalo Ridge, Battle of iNcandu River, Battle of emaJuba Hill, Battle of umZinyati River, Battle of iNgagane Ridge, Battle of uBivane Plateau, Battle of iBululwane Plains, Battle of iNgula River, Battle of oKdini Plains, Battle of iXopo Neck, Battle of iVuna River. May, 1811 to June, 1815. Shaka Zulu commander of the iziCwe, iNyelezi, Uyengondlovo, iziPikili, and iNyakeni Regiments. Nibele, Msane, Kosa, ezeBisini, emaQungebeni, emaHlutshini, Mazibuko, mKwanazi, emDletsini, emaNcubeni, Mabaso, Sibiya, Mnqomakazi, and emaNtshalini clans: defeated. 229 homesteads burned and razed. 2824 slaughtered. All cattle (equalling 3500 head) confiscated. Survivors incorporated in the Mtetwa Paramountcy. Mtetwa losses: 63.

*

- Battle of Mkumbane Stream. September, 1815. At this auspicious stream, so eventful in the lives of both Shaka and Nandi, the small forces of King Makedama's Langeni Clan were defeated in what would be known - for centuries to come - as one of the most brutal massacres in the history of a Southern Africa. It was said that the blood flowed for an entire day and an entire night, colouring a deep crimson the sloping banks where Prince Senzangakona had first seen that magnificent young maiden who was to be the tragedy of his life, colouring a radiant pink the gurgling currents from which Nandi had fetched water, colouring the eddies, the tiny whirlpools and the deeper courses of the stream where the Child had been conceived, tainting the colour of blood the place of that last encounter over which hung suspended, imprisoned in Timelessness, the disconcerting cry that was torn from the depths of a man's agony, the resounding name of that woman: - "Nandi!"

After the bloodbath, Shaka Zulu returned to the site of Bhebhe's Homestead where he had lived and suffered as a child. His eyes ran over the gutted remains of the hut where he and his mother had lived, the tiny family plot (now gone to seed), the outer fencing (half hidden by the tall grass, still marred by the cinders of the fire that had consumed it so long ago). As Shaka looked at the remains of what had once been his home, in stillness, in silence, as one would look upon the Grave of one's Youth, the commander of the Mtetwa forces had the odd impression of the nearness of the Shaka he had once been, Shaka the boy of barely fourteen. And in that stillness, he heard the blood beating in his ears with a confused rushing noise in which there seemed to be a voice, the voice of that boy, uttering the words: "They think we are victims, grandmother. It is time they learned that we know how to kill."

The Commander shuddered - for the delusions of the sense of hearing are the most vivid of all, and because of their nature have a compelling character, especially if the voice heard is from one's own past. A thin smile tugged on Shaka's lips as he repeated "learned how to kill?", yes, I have learned.   And the voice came again - with yet another lesson: "Mercy is the trait of victims, mother. Never again will I leave an enemy behind."

Never again.

That, too, was a lesson learned.

"You were kind to my mother and me when we needed it most, Makedama," Shaka was telling the Langeni King as they ate in each other's company after the massacre. "I won't forget that. I will spare your village."

Makedama had a bitter smile. It would take him the rest of his life, he knew - no, all of eternity - to forget the sight of so much blood! His response was uttered slowly, with a sinister sarcasm.

"I am glad to see that you have grown in the ways of Justice, Shaka."

Yet Shaka's own sarcasm could be far more sinister.

"You disapprove of me, Makedama?"

"I disapprove of the legendary 'Sigidi', the one who fights like a thousand, and I wonder how many see him for what he really is -- a killer!"

Shaka shot the other man a piercing look, as if to silence him, his eyes sparkling with rage, hurt and indignation. Yet Makedama would not be silent; why should he? he had nothing more to lose.

"A killer who's contaminated his armies with his own coldblooded thirst for revenge! That's your real motivation, isn't it? Revenge! - King Dingiswayo has little or nothing to do with your campaigns - he, too, is a victim of your thirst! And building the Mtetwa Confederacy? - you don't really care about that! It's just pretence! The wars you wage are, in fact, very private. -- Each of your battle's is a trial in which the enemy is condemned to death for having caused yours and your mother's hardships!"

Shaka's expression remained glacial, his eyes fixed on the Langeni King, the hearth's lapping flames reflected on that gaze, igniting it with the fire of wrath. Yet the wise king calmly continued his courageous appeal.

"Each village you burn to the ground is the home you were denied! Each man whose chest you burst open you make responsible for Nandi's suffering. Each child you leave crying on the heaped carcasses of his family is paying for that one child who was denied a real family so long ago!" Makedama raised his voice to a feverish cry. "Stop it, Shaka! Stop it! Your thirst for revenge has already been quenched a thousand times over - Sigidi!"

Jumping to his feet, Shaka snatched up his Ixwa and trained the Blade on Makedama, its point over the heart, the mortal blow ready to be inflicted. As the commander gazed at the king, a storm raged within his heart, and Makedama watched Shaka, composed, ready to die if need be, praying that his words - spoken out of true affection for Nandi's son - would burn through Shaka's hatred like sunshine through the morning mist.

Yet Shaka was well beyond that sort of warming influence. His own fire - the blazing furnace that was his heart - eclipsed the sun. Overcoming his initial rage, Shaka let the Ixwa fall limp in his hand and uttered in an uncanny whisper: "As I said, you were kind to my mother and me."

Sitting back down on the mat, resuming his meal, the commander inquired, an eerie smile tugging at his lips: "There once lived a man in your village named Mpepha. He had a son, I believe...Nzobo---"

The tangled thorn tree still marked the place where Mfunda was laid to rest. Though the gravesite, covered in snarled shrubbery and wild grass, looked forsaken - it was not, it had never been.

Not by Shaka.

As his troops stood serried in their ranks and at attention, looking on in the severity of complete silence, Shaka tossed a handful of dirt onto the stone slab that covered his grandmother's resting place.

"I have returned, grandmother," Shaka spoke thickly, addressing the grave. "To fulfil my promise. To claim this land in your name."

After a contemplative pause, the shadow of tenderness that had graced Shaka's features was hardened to a look of bitter resolve as he turned to face Nzobo, now a man of almost thirty, and his father Mpepha. The two men - held firmly in the restraining grips of Joko and Mgobozi - were overwhelmed with fear, a confounding terror which had literally unhinged their reason and left them gaping in mumbled pleading like babbling idiots. The horror grew as Shaka addressed them.

"Do you remember the woman who is buried here?" he asked, in an unearthly murmur. "Her name was...Mfunda. You must remember her, Nzobo. She once saved your life!"

Nzobo stammered a response that sounded somewhat like an affirmative and Shaka smiled - his irony mounting with a spooky inflection. And even his troops - hardened men, devoted to him and inured to death - were chilled by the degree of hatred that his words and his manner emanated.

"There, you see, you do remember. She was the mother of my mother. I loved her very much. - You know how she died? Starvation. A slow, painful way to die - especially for an old woman. - But her death could have been avoided, you know. If some one hadn't burned our crops. If some one hadn't broken her heart by forcing her to pass the last few years of her life as an outcast. -- Now what would you do, Nzobo, if she had been your grandmother?"

Nzobo found his breath and modulated it into a quavering: "Shaka!"

"Don't worry, Nzobo," Shaka said gelidly. "Your death won't be like hers. It will be quick."

Shaka shot Mgobozi a stern glance and nodded, ordering him to proceed with the execution. Yet the warrior hesitated.

"What is it, my friend?" Shaka asked.

"They are unarmed."

A thin smile played with the commander's lips.

"Moral scruples, Mgobozi," he queried. "How many men did you kill today? Twenty? Thirty? More? - Yet these two dogs arouse your pity? -- Very well," Shaka took a couple of ixwas and pressed them in Nzobo's and Mpepha's hand, "now they are armed. - Obey the order."

Mgobozi held Shaka's gaze steadily with his own. After a long, tense pause, the soldier jerked his blade back at an angle, plunging it into Nzobo's neck, slicing through the throat, almost severing the head from the body. An instant later, Joko sank his own ixwa into Mpepha's windpipe, silencing forever his gurgled cry of utter anguish.

As the blood spurted from the severed jugulars, it rained in heavy purple gobs onto the stone slab of Mfunda's grave --- "claiming the land in her name."

- Battle of Mkumbane Stream. September, 1815. Shaka Zulu commander of the iziCwe, iNyelezi, Uyengondlovo, iziPikili, and iNyakeni Regiments. Langeni Clan: defeated. All homesteads - save for that of King Makedama and his family burnt and razed. All cattle - save for that of King Makedama and his family - confiscated. 934 slaughtered. 2 executed for armed treason. No survivors - save for King Makedama and his family who were incorporated into the Mtetwa Paramountcy. Mtetwa losses: none.

*

April, 1810 to September, 1815. Over thirty clans defeated in five short years. The Nation, the Empire was becoming a reality - slowly but surely.

And he was tired. Ever so tired, as he sat alone on the banks of Empenbeni, near the huge campsite where his numerous troops had stopped between battles to bivouac for the night.

Leaning forward, Shaka craned his neck searching for his own reflection on the surface of the river. Though twenty-eight now, the commander was pleased to see that Time and years of war had done little to alter his original youthful beauty. He looked the same as when he had started his career, he thought, looking at that silvery reflection on the river. Or, almost the same, at least. His expression had changed somewhat, around the mouth and on the jawline, - it was harder, harsher. His eyes, too, betrayed a change. They had become sadder and now reflected a deep fatigue of the soul.

Tiring of his own image, Shaka's attention moved to the reflection of the full moon. Picking up a stone, he tossed it into the river, onto the moon, and watched as the ripples moved out from the central glowing disc in ever-expanding circles, unrepeatable once set in motion.

His mind drifted back to the little boy of six who had sat by this same river and tried to scoop up in his hands the reflection of this heavenly globe, and he had a faint smile as he remembered that boy and he wondered - deep in his heart - what had happened to him. Was he still trying to grasp the moon, or had he given up? Was he still chasing reflections of the sky, or had all his illusions drowned under those rippling waves?

"Sigidi," Mgobozi's voice roused Shaka from this gentle stroll through his own heart.

"What is it, Mgobozi?"

Tired. He's so very tired, Mgobozi thought upon hearing his friend's voice.

"A messenger has come. King Dingiswayo wants you and the regiments to return to base."

Shaka stiffened slightly and shifted his weight, turning to face his friend and soldier.

"What reason did Dingiswayo give?"

"A king need not give a reason, remember. You told me that."
Both man smiled.

"It's just as well, I suppose. The men need a rest. Some time with their," he had trouble with the term, "-- loved ones."

"So do you, Shaka. You haven't been home in over three years."

The commander pondered over the remark and replied - not with self-pity, but as a mere ascertainment of the fact in itself: "The only home I know today is right here with my troops."

Mgobozi was visibly saddened by the confession. His friend's weariness seemed chronic inasmuch as he had no place to go where he could rest.

"Tell the messenger we'll leave at dawn, Mgobozi. And break the good news to the men. They're relieved from active duty until after the harvest."

"Yes, Sigidi."

"But if anyone puts on any extra weight, they'll have me to answer to!"

Grinning, Mgobozi turned to leave with, "Good night, Sigidi."
"Good night, general."

Mgobozi froze in his footsteps and, eyes springing wide, gaped at his commander who laughed out loud.

"That's about the way I looked when Dingiswayo gave me the iziCwe."

"The iziCwe," Mgobozi echoed in a half-trance.

"Yes. And Nqoboka will command the iziPikili. Joko, the uYengonglovu. Mtonga, the iNyakeni, and Dlaba, the iNyelezi. The promotions will be official as soon as I receive the king's blessing."

Mgobozi's gaping incredulity was transformed to delight.

"Thank you, Shaka. For the confidence."

"Save your thanks, Mgobozi," the commander answered, his smile fading. "I'm not sure I did you a favour."

* * *

-

In his lasting conviction that "Superstition was a palliative of the soul, the fabrication of minds insensitive to the intimate intricacies of our relation to the dead and to the living, a desecration of our most tender memories, an outrage to our dignity", - in his realistic relationship with Nature, Shaka, throughout his reign as Emperor Supreme of Southern Africa, did away with almost all, if not all of man's spiritual palliatives - those irrational delusions that give birth to existential fallacies in which the Mind is sacrificed on the altar of Fanatic Obsession.

One such palliative was "ukuSula iZembe". Originating in the remotest recesses of Bantu tradition, this practice, also known (rather guilelessly) as the "Wiping of the Spear", dictated that, having killed in battle, a warrior must "wipe his spear" or, more explicitly, have intercourse with a woman. Until he had done so, he was to be considered unclean, and could not enter the social life of the tribe. Thus, a woman, if unmarried, accosted by any warrior for this "ceremony" was morally bound to agree with it, and, conversely, it was the soldier's duty to take the first suitable woman who came his way.

And so it was that towards the end of 1815, hearing that her prince was on his way back from his notorious campaigns, Pampata decided to set the stage for this fascinating ritual.

This was, of course, not the first time Pampata had entertained the idea of making love to Shaka. Yet, since he made no advances of his own - in fact it seemed that he remembered rarely, if ever, that she even existed - the girl had soon realised that she might have to employ the more recherché aspects of her macho culture to get the job done. Thus, in her great tumult of passion, like a flash of lightning she stumbled upon the idea of the "wiping of the spear" (giggling inwardly as she did so).

She had thought of availing herself of the ukusula izembe after the war with the Butelezi and had even been so bold as to share her plan with Nomcoba. Yet Shaka's sister had been instrumental in putting her off. Her brother wasn't much for those primitive rituals, Nomcoba had told her (leaving Pampata, a virgin, to eagerly fantasize over what could be so "primitive" about lovemaking); - "Besides," she had added with a flippant smile, "my brother thinks sandals slow him down. Can you imagine what he must think about women!"

Yet Pampata had not given up. Indeed, the thought of being thus united with the man who had become the idol of her Youth, the object of her overriding infatuation, of her obsession, of her desire, the man who was the ever-valiant protagonist of all her dreams, in slumber as in waking, -- the thought of making love to Shaka became the epitome of her reason for living and the very thought of it, no, even the thought of the thought of it caused her to blush like a ripe beet bathed in the October sun.

She must have him, she resolved with the tenacity of a woman in love and set out, at the end of 1815, to make sure she was the first "available female" he saw on his journey back from war.

Shaka's gait was sure, powerful, quick, belying the fatigue of years of warfare, as he strode down the banks of the Umfolozi River, on his way towards Dingiswayo's Royal Homestead in the Mtetwa Kingdom. The commander's mind was turning over his imminent meeting with the King, his imagination staging the encounter in countless different ways, each leaving him uneasy and restless, when, suddenly, he heard rustling in the bushes near the water's edge and, gripping his Ixwa, spun round, ready to strike. Only just in time did he recognise Pampata, wide-eyed and petrified as she gaped at the Blade.

Shaka gazed at the lovely young woman as a smile tried to force its way to his lips.

"You almost got yourself killed," he told her, feigning reprimand.

A broad smile verily glowed on Pampata's features as she looked up at her hero, her eyes twinkling.

"I'm glad you're back, Shaka."

The Son of Zulu peered down at the girl and grinned. She was one of those creatures, he mused, whose mere existence was enough to awaken an unselfish delight. Yet a soldier had little time for such musing, he reminded himself and turning, he strode off, answering over his shoulder, by was of dismissal: "Thank you, Pampata. It is good to be back."

Yet Pampata would not be dismissed, and she raced after the man, slipping and splashing along the riverbank. When finally she reached his side, she did her utmost to nonchalantly stay in step with him - an arduous task considering his exceptional height and the vibrant buoyancy of his pace. Shaka cast a deliberate sidelong glance at the girl struggling at his side, making a mental note - in his usual unemotional way - of how rather lovely she'd become over the years.

Recognising the appreciative glint in his eye, Pampata screwed up her courage and made the first advance by commenting, with added emphasis: "I came to the river to look for you, Shaka."

As soon as the words had escaped her lips, the girl shot him an expectant glance, well anticipating his pleased reaction to her amorous confession. She read nothing on his gaze except what looked like an ever-increasing desire to be left alone.

"...on purpose, Shaka," she stressed coyly, with a forced little laugh that betrayed her utter inexperience in such intricate matters of the heart (an ineptitude second only to Shaka's own). "I purposely wanted to be the first woman you set eyes on. The one to welcome you home."

Still no reaction as the man continued to look straight ahead, his pace quickening slightly.

Pampata's mind was racing as she literally chased after the Zulu. Perhaps he didn't know about the custom, she considered. Or perhaps he just didn't want her. But why? she queried in her heart. Any other man would be gladdened and honoured by her offer. Any other man. But, then, Shaka was not like any other man, she had to remind herself.

Maybe she should give up the whole idea - save herself the embarrassment! - No, she determined. This was the moment she'd been waiting for since she first set eyes on him. Waiting with a longing and desire that yearned to find fulfilment. And now that she was beside him, she wanted to reach out and touch him, to feel his hands on her body, to hear him softly whisper her name - she wanted to kiss him and make love to him with an urgency that cramped her stomach with pain.

"Shaka," she called out to him, gently. "According to the custom, you should - we should---"

"Old wives' tales!" the Zulu grunted, cutting her short.

Suddenly she felt alone, and shamed, and she reacted with anger.

"Don't you find me suitable enough to make love to?!" she snapped, causing him to finally stop. Turning around, Shaka looked at her as if he was seeing the woman for the first time. A smile came to his beautiful features and grew to laughter.

"I appointed five troop commanders this week. You should be the sixth. Though somewhat awkward, your strategy is most laudable."

"Is that all you can talk about?" She was furious now, hurt, and decided not to quell that emotion. "Commanders! Troops! Strategy!"

"That's all that matters to me."

"Is it?" she asked, lowering her voice to a gentle murmur as she ran her light touch over his skin.

"Make love to me, Shaka," she whispered.

As he faltered, her eyes travelled the length of his magnificent body, drinking in the muscles that rippled beneath the ebony skin, the trim leanness that exuded such pure, savage masculinity. As her fingertips brushed over his brawny chest, trailing down his stomach and lingering on his belly, Shaka experienced a sensation that was totally new to him, one that left his mind reeling, groping for a secure hold in the realm of past experience. Yet there was none.

The decision to momentarily relinquish his mind's prevailing control over his body was, for Shaka, not a conscious act of the Will. Later he would tell himself that it was a reflex judgment, born of weariness, perhaps, or a profound need for affection, and compounded by his innate curiosity, one that rarely left anything to the imagination that could actually be perceived with the senses. Anyway - whatever the cause - Shaka now let himself go, as her caresses grew bolder.

Acting as his guide, Pampata curled his mighty arms round her waist and felt a sweet, wild throb in her belly at the nearness of his warmth. And as he felt her body against his tingling flesh, his desire took over, and Shaka tightened his embrace, clinging to her, eager to feel more of her touch. Then, closing his eyes, his head swimming, his legs giving way, Shaka sank to his knees, onto the muddy banks of the Umfolozi.

Caught in his embrace, feeling his fear, his anger, his love, his arrogance, his strength, the plethora of emotions whirling tempestuously in the maelstrom that was his heart, Pampata's eyes moistened, loving, pitying, desiring the man of her life.

Tenderly, awkwardly, innocently the two caressed, leading each other closer and closer to the consummation of their desire. But that moment never came.

When Pampata reached expectantly for his manhood, Shaka's eyes clouded, in confusion at first, then in shame at this humiliating betrayal of his own body - the body that had always responded to whatever the mind told it to do. Yet, as the anguish welled within him, Shaka realised that this was not a matter of logic, nor one of the mind. It was emotion. Pure, unfettered emotion. Something that was beyond his control, something he had buried so long ago.

Furious with himself for having been thus trapped, caught off-guard, defeated by a woman, Shaka got angrily to his feet and raced off -- escaping. To forget this mortification. And to find himself again through forgetfulness!

"Shaka!," Pampata yelled after him, tears streaming down her cheeks, sobbing, fearing she had lost him forever.

"Shaka!" the name fled from her lips, speeding down the currents of the Umfolozi. "I love you, Shaka!"

* * *

"Your request is absurd, Baba. The success of my campaigns is partially derived from the momentum of my war machine," Shaka was resolute, his voice rising with the strength of his own persuasion. "To now break that impelling thrust would be pure folly!"

Dingiswayo, Ngomane, Kuta, and the other esteemed members of the Mtetwa Council of Elders were following Shaka's authoritative figure with their concerned gazes as the commander paced back and forth on the rocky clearing in front of the Royal Hut.

"By the next moon, my troops must be on the march again!"

"If I and the Council so decide," Dingiswayo affirmed, avowing himself of cold, regal strictness.

Shaka's reply was immediate and forceful.

"How can you put me in command of your regiments, and yet deny me a free hand in military decisions!"

"You have had a free hand, Shaka," the King rebuked, fired by the other's anger into a berating rejoinder. "And judging from the reports I've received, you've used that freedom to the fullest. The 'Fear of Shaka', as they call it, is spreading throughout the land."

"So is your empire, Baba," Shaka snapped back. "In the wake of that fear!"

Accustomed to being addressed deferentially, Dingiswayo accused the blow of his commander's sharp revindications. Yet, instead of warming in his indignation, the king found that his anger was suddenly dead within him. There can be no adequate rebuttal to the Truth, irate or otherwise, and the truth was as Shaka spoke it - the Method was building an empire, the Mtetwa Empire. Sitting back on his throne of rushes, Dingiswayo composed himself to silence, his eyes locked on those of his friend, his heart realising that a rift had widened between them since Shaka had taken command of the armies, a rift which he fervently hoped would not prove to be insurmountable.

Nearing his king, sensing the other man's undying friendship, Shaka placated his tone, making it more conciliatory as he appealed to the more practical aspects of the situation as it presented itself.

"Five years ago, Baba, you spoke to me of the Nguni Bantu Nation. Then it was a mere dream, a fantastic quest. Yet today only two powers threaten your position as supreme overlord of our people: the Qwabes of Pakatwayo and the Ndwandwe Confederacy of King Zwide! Mighty kingdoms, both of them - but not inexpugnable!" Shaka's voice rose in vehemence as he broadened the direct influence of his appeal to include Ngomane and the Council. "We must continue the campaigns while this "Fear of Shaka" remains effective! While my armies have the impetus of uninterrupted Victory. We must strike now - and, if we do, I am confident that soon we will see our dream become reality."

"When I spoke of that Nation, I wanted the name Mtetwa to stand for peace!" Dingiswayo's heart was on fire again. "Not Total War! I wanted my armies to bring, subjugation - not destruction!"

"To subdue another tribe, you must strike it once and for all," the commander's voice was fierce and eager, with the desire to be understood.

"That is the only conquest that is truly lasting! - Total war! Total obedience to the Paramount King! Total destruction to anyone who raises even a whisper against him! - A man in your position, Nkosi, wields an incredible amount of power. Only one thing can back up that power, make it credible: - adequate military strength! The ability to destroy. There is no other way!"

"Yes, Shaka! There is! - Faith!" Uttered by such a man as Dingiswayo, these simple words were bereft of shallow sentimentalism, of the nectared fancies of vagaries; the word Faith was tendered not as some bizarre solution to a commonplace dilemma, but as an objectively viable means to a definite end, as a vehicle of comportment that was quite down-to-earth and very much within one's reach. Yet Shaka refuted it with a scowl.

"Faith?!" the commander spat out the word. "In what?!"

"The human Being," was the reply. "In Reason! In each man's desire to believe in himself and in his fellow man."

Shaka stood suddenly frozen in place, gazing at his king with a grimace of repulsion - not for Dingiswayo himself, of course, but for the words he had just delivered in a manner that left the commander staggered. "Man's desire to believe in his fellow man"! The Zulu felt like laughing out loud! And, as the searching fixity of his gaze remained on the Mtetwa monarch, Shaka asked himself how such a "believer in Man" could ever hope to rule an empire of men and men's falsehoods -- the falsehoods that inevitably triumph through stupidity, through doubt, through pity, through sentiment, through compassion! "How can a man believe in himself without the assurance of strength?" Shaka continued the thought, out loud. "How can this world of peace you envisage exist without standing armies? Do you really believe, Baba that an empire like yours can be run on Faith alone, on Reason? Do you really think the time will come when you can disband your armies without losing your realm! - The Human Being is violent, Baba, and, whether we wish to acknowledge it or not, usually the only Reason that makes sense to him is this!" Shaka raised his Ixwa, allowing its gleaming Blade to cast the sun's reflection onto the intent expressions of the Council's Elders.

The pain of conscious defeat crept over Dingiswayo's features as he heard his friend's words and was left saddened by his inability to touch the other's heart. How divergent are the lessons one learns from suffering, he considered. Odd that two men can look upon the same truth, and that one can find it a lie.

"Zwide of the Ndwandwes is preparing an attack," Shaka's tone had become suddenly formal. "His army is as large if not larger than ours. He has heard of our battle tactics and has devised others that I fear may be just as effective. And, in his Reason, he has only one wish, Baba," Shaka's expression wore a humourless smile, "to crush your Paramountcy into oblivion. And, believe me, he won't do it with Faith. - But, as you say, the final decision of what action to take is yours and the Council's." The Zulu took a slight, theatrical pause before concluding, with a brisk tone: "And so it shall remain. - I ask you to accept my resignation as commander of your regiments."

The Council was crestfallen.

Nodding, Shaka took his leave with, "Bayete, Nkosi" and strode away - leaving a gaping void of apprehension behind him. It was instantly obvious to all - especially Dingiswayo and Ngomane - that accepting Shaka's resignation was completely out of the question. Though vast and powerful (due mostly to Shaka's own efforts), the Paramountcy was practically defenceless without the Zulu - the core of the realm's survival being lodged in the Method and its execution.

"Ngomane," the Mtetwa King prompted with a hollow voice.

The induna's eyes met those of his king and, reading Dingiswayo's apprehension, Ngomane nodded in silent consent and struck off, in pursuit of the Son of Zulu.

"You played your hand well," Ngomane told Shaka when he had fallen into step with him. "What do you want?"

"Complete control of the Armed Forces. Without any more interference from the King and Council."

Ngomane was frozen in his tracks, shocked by the request, his voice strained with incredulity as he muttered: "That would virtually give you control of the State."

Shaka spun round to face him.

"If Zwide defeats us, Ngomane. There will be no State! Winning the Campaign against the Ndwandwe Confederacy is a matter of life and death! For me. For you. For the Council. And for Dingiswayo and his dream! If I am to bear that responsibility as a commander, I will have no time to waste with idealism and speculations on the redeeming qualities of Mankind! - Ngomane," Shaka bent his flaming eyes on the other man, "Zwide wants our blood, not our Humanity!"

The Council's deliberation lasted all night. Not that there was any real doubt in anyone's mind that ultimately the Zulu's request would find a favourable vote of confidence. It was just that the decision to bestow Power upon another is often subject to the imponderables of Fear - especially when the Power to be transmitted is so immense. And Fear has a habit of retarding the mind's ability to pronounce judgment.

By dawn, Shaka had the answer to his request.

Ngomane found him sitting high atop of a promontory, gazing out at the immensity of the Mtetwa Kingdom, his eyes resting fondly on all that he saw as if each hill, each tree, each flower, each blade of grass were a personal, cherished possession. Sensing the induna at his side, he turned to face him and spoke slowly, absently, as if his thoughts were still lost in the vagueness of his sensations.

"Do I have it?" Shaka asked.

"Yes," Ngomane answered, softly, his eyes also reaching out to the landscape. "You have it. Complete control. Without interference."

The induna cast Shaka a deliberate sidelong glance, searching the young man's features for a sign of relief, triumph, joy perhaps - or contentment. Yet the Zulu's face proffered no emotion.

"Five years," Ngomane considered in a soft murmur. "You've come a long way from being just the leader of a small brigade. - This decision makes you second to the king and - in many ways - just as powerful."

"The strength of a king lies in the power of his generals, Ngomane. And, in the Perfect State, the King is the General."

"Is that what you want, Shaka? - To be both?"

The Zulu cocked his head to peer at the induna. He wore a thin smile as he remarked: "I want only what is mine by destiny."

On the Platform of the Pinnacle, above the clouds, above the kingdoms of the world and their men, above the greed and glory, above the artless poses of the proud, above all those fated to share in Man's tragic and grotesque miseries, - Sitayi turned her blind orbs to the Wind's Song: "Bayete, wena wa sendhlu nKulu! Hail thou who art as great as the dreams of his Nation. Ask and I shall give thee the ends of the earth for thy domain. He who acknowledges thy name shall grow in thy Glory; he who does not, shall meet everlasting ruin."

The Earth of ten-and-two was Cast.

The Child was soon to become the Inheritor of the Bond. The Chosen Son of his father's House.

Death to Birth. - Such was the Way of Loyalty.

CHAPTER XXIII
"SENZANGAKONA"(THE RIGHTFUL-DOER)
MONTH OF UMBASA: FEBRUARY, 1816

Stillness reigned over the Royal Homestead of esiKlebeni - it was a great peace, all-encompassing, as if the Earth had been one grave, as if all Hope were buried in some remote place, out of the knowledge of Mankind.

Sitting in the reserved company of his own thoughts, motionless, Mudli watched with unseeing eyes the horizon against the thin light of the false dawn as it passed through all the stages of daybreak until the deep purple of its outlined vault shown gloriously with the gold of the rising sun; he listened, with unhearing ears, to the vague, distant sounds of waking that filtered through the relentless dirge of despair and sorrow.

And as he sat, alone, the Zulu Elder watched the sunrise, heard the voices and thought of Jama and of his son and of how, nearing sixty now, Senzangakona should have started to be more tolerant of Life, less hard on himself and should have begun to take a more charitable view of living and existence.

Peculiar, the Elder considered, that a man who, in his Youth, had been looked upon as weak and superficial, as somewhat shallow and exclusively interested in his own pursuit of activities like hunting and womanising, disdainful of life's preoccupations and of the call of duty, -- odd, Mudli mused, that a young lad who had been so "carefree" had become - overnight almost - so burdened with care, so troubled and so wary of Life.

All because of her.

Yes, he should have had a more romantic outlook on Life now that he's nearing sixty. More tolerance at the approach of death.

Or would there be time enough? Mudli wondered, and his mind finally came to rest on the distant dirge, the wailing of the old Zulu women that enshrouded, like a thick black mantle, the Royal Hut in which the king lay dying.

A damp chill touched the marrow of Mudli's old bones and caused the man to shudder and stir from his musings. Rising heavily on his feet, feeling the stiffness in his legs, the Elder ambled round the cattle fold, past the sombre expressions of the royal family - Mkabi and the other wives: twelve in all, the sons and daughters: seventeen in all - and moved with a laboured gait towards the king's hut through which gusts of dense, billowing smoke were disgorged, veiling the orange globe of the sun.

"Mudli? -- Is that you?" came the raspy, suffered voice.

Yes, Nkosi. It is I." - It had always been Mudli when Mudli was needed. For so many years. For the reigns of two kings, Mudli mused, - Would he now have the pain of also burying Jama's son?

The air within the hut was suffocating. Clouds of greyish smoke, spewed by the blazing fire, interwoven with long filaments of ferret-like vapours and fumes rising from the bowls of medicinal herbs. Barely visible through the concentrated effluvium, Senzangakona kaJama Zulu lay on his mat, breathing with difficulty, his greatly emaciated frame racked by intermittent fits of convulsions. Moving to his sovereign's side, Mudli knelt next to Mkabayi, concealing with difficulty the grief that tore at his heart at the sight of Senzangakona's skeletal features, the facial skin clinging, shrunken and wrinkled, to the protuberances of bone that were his nose, his cheeks and the orbits of his eyes.

"Mudli?" the king repeated, reaching out for the Elder with a gnarled hand that swung jerkingly on a knotty wrist.

"I am here, Baba," Mudli reassured his monarch, his anguish concealed under a soothing voice, as he took the bony hand in his and pressed it to his heart.

"Mkabayi?" the Zulu sovereign breathed with a pinch of urgency.

"I am still here, my brother. At your side."

As she reached out and took the man's other hand, her eyes met Mudli's and locked, just for an instant, before her grief-stricken gaze fled his in something that resembled embarrassment.

"Are we alone?" Senzangakona asked, and though his eyes were open, wide open, he had no way of knowing. The whole world looked hazy to him, as if he were looking at it through a veil of tears.

A disease known as chronic uremia - a condition that results from "uValo", alcoholism.

Yet Senzangakona had no way of knowing from what he suffered, he just suffered. Indeed, that is the way his life had been since his dependency on the panacea called sorghum - he never knew why he suffered, he just did. And his vision, well that had been hazy for quite some time - ever since he'd met her, life had worn the impalpable distinctness of a dream.

"Yes, Baba," Mudli answered. "We are alone."

"I'm terrified!" the king confessed, tightening his hold on the other's arm.

"A normal reaction, Baba," the Elder fought to keep his voice steady. "We are all afraid to depart from the surroundings to which we are accustomed. I suppose we will all feel terrified when the time comes.

Unexpectedly, Senzangakona laughed out loud - a catarrhal peal of laughter. "In the middle of a thunderstorm you would rationalise the detrimental qualities of sunshine! - You have always had an answer for everything, Mudli. And now even death! - You should've been king, not me! You would have safeguarded those 'surroundings to which we are accustomed' far better than I did!"

Mudli pursed his lips at the thought, as Senzangakona took a long breath, filling his tortured lungs with air.

"No, it's not death that terrifies me," the king went on. "It's my father. That look of disapproval he always had on his face. What do I tell him when we meet again? You were right, father. I was incompetent. But it wasn't my fault I was your only son - the only heir to the throne! I never asked to be king. I just wanted to be---" the man's voice suddenly trailed off as he knit his brow, his tired mind racing as he added, with true disconcertion, "What is it I wanted to be? I can't seem to remember. It must've been something! Every man wants to be something! - Why can't I remember?" a thin smile tugged at his parched lips, "Perhaps because I was never meant to be anything. Perhaps I just wanted to be nothing...to remain - a son, to remain - without care, without being the possession of my people. Perhaps I just wanted to have me all to myself!"

"Baba!" there was gentle reproach in Mudli's tone.

"No, Mudli. Don't be disapproving. Accept me - accept me at least now for what I am. For what I never was. - Let me talk! Death and confession go hand in hand, don't they? Besides, no one's listening. Just the two of you, my 'Royal Faultfinders'. It's only right that you should be here to prepare me for Jama - he'll be my judge for eternity."

A tear fell onto Senzangakona's hand. Feeling it, the king reached up and ran his trembling fingertips over his sister's cheek.

"Tears? How lovely, my sister." Lowering his voice to a hush, he repeated, "How lovely. There were so many times when I would've needed you to cry. So many times when I would've wanted you to wipe my tears. So many of them."

The man's face suddenly clouded over as if remembering a last, burdensome duty to which he must attend.

"My sons, Mudli. I need an official heir don't I? And Shaka will most likely kill whomever I pick. So who shall it be. - That is a hard decision to make, and you must help me one last time. " Sensing his Elder's reluctance to make the choice, the Zulu monarch murmured: "Very well. Let it be Bibi's son, Sigiyana. - The night Nandi fled, the night I killed Igazi, the night that was the beginning of my end -- he was conceived. Let Sigiyana rule for as long as Shaka allows him to. For as long as Shaka..."

And thus, with the name of the Child on his lips, Senzangakona kaJama Zulu, King of the People of the Heavens, grandson of the Mighty Ndaba, great grandson of Mageba, Seventh Descendant of the Legendary Zulu kaMalandela, went to the Earth - in anguish and in sorrow for his wasted life, - oppressed by the Injustice of the world and surprised to perceive how long he had lived under the burden of that Injustice without truly realising his unfortunate state, annoyed by the uneasy suspicion of his undiscerning stupidity;--

And thus he died - not happy, not peaceful and not at peace with himself, not hoping, not accomplished, not satisfied, not believing, not successful, not powerful...

Not.

Not seeing the world except through the haziness of tears, yet seeing clearly that all he had ever wanted was not to be a king, not to be something, but to remain a happy, carefree, great -- nothing!

The great man he could've been just being a Nothing.

So much wasted greatness! Why hadn't she allowed him to be the man he was really born to be?!

Why, Nandi, my love?

Why?!

Nandi ever Nandi...

CHAPTER XXIV
"HAYIDESI"(UNDERWORLD)

Ten days' journey North of the iHluhluwe River, four days West of the Bay of Ntlozi, three weeks trek from the land of the Mtetwas, the adventurous and intrepid traveller might have found - in those bygone days before the Second Advent of the Child - the mighty and magical eTshaneni Mountains dominating the rolling valleys of the umSunduze.

Though The eTshaneni Range might well have appeared magnificent at first sight, in the broad light of day, when the fiery rays of the sun played with the profiles of the rocky crests and ridges bestowing them with a gilded aura of radiance that suggested the divine and the blessed, this view of breathtaking beauty was quite divorced from the true spirit of the lost, nefarious world that was concealed within these mountains. In fact, to accurately perceive the menacing character of eTshaneni, the traveller ought to first have approached the range at night, when the blackness of its contours blotted out the stars with its vague mass, like a low thundercloud brooding over the earth and ready to burst into flames and crashes. Indeed, notwithstanding the semblances of beauty and exaltation eTshaneni affords when the earth is washed in sunlight, the range is in truth a remote and dangerous place, filled with fog shrouded gorges, beast-infested lairs, and fathomless canyons and crags that find their bowels deep within the Dark Earth.

And in the most forsaken recesses of this ghastly range of mountains arose a series of man-made towers that projected upwards out of the cold rock and damp masonry like mutilated fingers pointing blasphemously at the Heavens. These towers engirded, like the battlements of a medieval European stronghold, the accursed African Citadel of Dlovunga, the sinister Realm of Those Who Inhabit the Underworld.

Dlovunga was a mountain fortress of granite and limestone, surrounded by a deep moat of dark, stagnant water over which was suspended a long, narrow bridge that threaded into the citadel's only point of access: the imposing Gates of Jade guarded by over a dozen famished lions; - Dlovunga was an immense acropolis where walls of black adamant jutted courageously out of silvery quartz and slimy porous rock, where steeples of copper and bronze commingled with pavilions of glimmering mica; - Dlovunga was a stronghold of bastions whose grisly inhabitants haunted dwellings made of thatching, of wood, of stone, or lived in the infinite network of caves and labyrinths that were gouged into the rock and plunged into the most alien recesses of the Underworld; and, above all, Dlovunga was the impregnable Kingdom of the Omnipotent King Zwide, Lord of the Ndwandwes.

Ntombazi, the ageless mother of King Zwide, clutched the leather straps bound to the iron collars of her pet jackals, holding the vicious, snarling animals at bay with her strong, brawny arms as she led them through a narrow tunnel towards the wrought iron cage where a troop of vervet monkeys were chattering nervously. The woman's horrendous face wore a look of sadistic anticipation as she neared the terrified apes and lit a torch casting its harsh light onto her ghastly face with its web of wrinkles traced round eyes grotesque in their decrepitude, round a toothless mouth with pulpy, bleeding gums, and over hanging, yellow cheeks, that rippled with her cackling.

Reaching out her bony appendage, the Witch, Mistress of Dlovunga, threw back a rusty bolt and eased open the cage's trap door. Then, her gleeful cackling heightened by her ghoulish thrill, the woman freed the jackals that eagerly leapt into the cage, onto the frantic monkeys, silencing their hysterical chatter and replacing it with the hideous sounds that accompany the tearing of skin, the rending of flesh, and the crunching of bones. As Ntombazi looked at the carnage, laughing all the while, her fierce crow-footed eyes reflected how many forms of evil are akin to madness, darkening the soul of the living and dashing the dead into the putrid bowels of eternal perdition.

Suddenly the Witch heard the shrill sound of a trumpet echoing from one of Dlovunga's bastions. Spinning round, the wicked woman hobbled out into the light of day and screwed her eyes up to the tower where a sentinel was blowing a long reed horn, the signal announcing the return of the immense Ndwandwe Army from one of its conquering campaigns.

Her smile broadening, Ntombazi hurriedly scampered across the citadel's jagged cliffs and scrambled up a wooden ladder towards one of the fortress's lofty lookout towers. Upon reaching the top of the ladder, the woman clawed her way across the granite to the edge of the lookout and craned her neck to gaze down at the mammoth cloud of dust that moved slowly towards Dlovunga - the cloud shrouding the returning troops of her son's ponderous Confederacy, thousands of warriors marching in a huge formation behind General Soshangane kaZikode Gaza, the Commander-in-Chief of the Ndwandwe forces - a tall, majestic-looking warrior, a mere twenty-five years of age. At Soshangane's side, next to the other victorious generals, strode the defeated kings: - Mashobane kaMosesa of the Northern Kumalo Clan; Mashobane's son Mzilikazi, twenty-three years of age, of finely-sculpted, powerful features, over a meter-ninety in height, a youth comparable only to Shaka himself in both beauty and commanding musculature; and, the second vanquished regent, King Mlota kaLatali, Overlord of the large Mabaso and Ngwane Clans.

Ntombazi's toothless mouth contorted in silent laughter as her jaundiced eyes darted to the two men standing high atop of a thatched turret constructed at the summit of a quartz pinnacle.

"Soshangane returns victorious," grinned one of the two men, King Zwide of the Ndwandwes, aged 50, with ruddy, weathered features and quick eyes betraying a shrewd, determined spirit - one without scruples.

The man beside him, also tall, also without the burden of scruples, stood silently gazing at the armies as a feeling of power welled within his soul. This man, King Pakatwayo kaKondlo, now forty years of age and, of late, King of the Qwabes, swivelled his head and forced himself to look at his host.

"The northern tribes are now firmly consolidated in my Confederacy," Zwide boasted. "We now stand alone, Pakatwayo. You and I against Dingiswayo."

*

The Ndwandwe generals, led by Soshangane and followed by the defeated kings and Prince Mzilikazi, made their way across the narrow bridge, through the Gates of Jade - where the vicious lions were jerked back to allow entry - and down a network of tunnels dug into the core of the earth.

After a seemingly interminable trek, the men entered an enormous vaulted cavern - the Grand Hall of the Council - a fantastic grotto, sparkling, intricate, a palace of jewels, with glittering roof and walls ornamented with filigrees of white limestone, - with bizarre and colourful sculptures of countless dripstone configurations, - and illuminated by a series of torches that cast their flickering glow on the vitreous formations causing them to come alive with the brilliance of incandescent prisms.

When the members of the Council had taken their places in the Grand Hall and were seated upon their crystalline thrones next to Queen Ntombazi, General Soshangane, Prince Nomahlanjana and his four brothers, and the honoured guest King Pakatwayo, - and when the distinguished prisoners, Mashobane, Mzilikazi, and Mlota had been securely locked within the confines of the large Crystal Cage, - King Zwide - his huge headdress spilling a shower of glistening black plumes over his strapping shoulders and down his broad back - strode to the centre of the floor and directed his words at the Qwabe monarch, his voice echoing throughout the mammoth cavern of light.

"All the land stretching from the Pongola River to the Tugela. That's what is at stake, Pakatwayo," the Lord of Dlovunga emphasized, pacing the center of the hall, his eyes aflame. "The largest Empire this land has ever known! And it can be ours! If we have the wisdom centre where Dingiswayo has sown."

Pakatwayo eyed Zwide with a raised brow.

"Indeed, with his naive plea for 'unity' and a 'common Nguni identity', Dingiswayo has done most of the hard work for us! Almost half that territory is already in the Mtetwa Paramountcy. - You and I, Pakatwayo, control the other half." The Ndwandwe's lips pulled back over large gleaming teeth. "Now all we have to do is step in and take it all."

A faint smile altered for an instant the clear, firm design of Pakatwayo's lips.

"You make it sound easy, Zwide," said the son of Kondlo.

"It can be. If we work together!"

"They say that under Shaka's leadership, Dingiswayo's armies are nearly invincible," the Qwabes commented, remaining extremely guarded in his deliberation.

"Of course they seem invincible!" Zwide rebutted, without relaxing for a moment his vehement conviction. "In the face of incompetent opponents, any army would! Just ask yourself, Pakatwayo - whom have they fought so far? Pungashe? Senzangakona? Kali? Donda? Makedama?! - How can those meagre tribes compare with our combined military might?!" The king spun round to address his Commander-in-Chief. "After our latest victory, Soshangane, how many troops do we have at our disposal?"

"Approximately 25,000, Nkosi," the commander retorted with crisp officiality and added as he cast a deliberate glance at the Crystal Cage, "counting our newly acquired 'allies'."

Mzilikazi caught his breath, shocked by the huge number, far greater than he had ever imagined it to be, as Zwide's voice rose emphatically.

"Which means thirty thousand, Pakatwayo," he roared, nearing the other monarch. "If we include your own armies!"

"And the Mtetwas? What do they number?" The question was posed by the Qwabe.

"Reports put it at seven thousand," Soshangane was quick to supply the answer. "Though I believe that figure is overly generous. Say six thousand at the most."

"Six thousand against thirty!" The Lord of Dlovunga was roaring now. "Do you find those odds invincible?!"

"Not at all," Pakatwayo said calmly, trimming all emotion from his voice. "In fact, I'm fascinated! You seem to have more than enough troops to win this war alone - to secure this empire for yourself. Why do you need me?" Zwide and his mother, the Ndwandwe Queen, exchanged a meaningful glance before the man acknowledged with a forced grin: "Honest question. Deserves an honest answer."

In the Crystal Cage, Mzilikazi had to stifle a grimace of amusement at the thought of this mendacious man bringing up the notion of honesty.

"Yes," Zwide's head was bobbing up and down with a nod of agreement as he took a seat on his monumental throne of jade and porphyry and rested his chin on his joined fingertips. "We could probably win alone. But the risk factor would be greater, and I'm the sort of man who avoids risking whenever possible." The Ndwandwe looked up and his eyes met the Qwabe's. "Were you not with us, Pakatwayo, you might be tempted to join them. I consider that a big risk. - Besides that, I need you and the strategic position of your kingdom. - In order to make my plan work, I must rely on both fronts: the Qwabes to the South of the Mtetwas, and the Ndwandwes to the North - both attacking at the same time, forcing the enemy to fight in two different directions and disperse their manpower to the point where..." the king had a pitiful scowl, "- well, even their six thousand will seem like only a handful."

"Again, you make it sound very easy, Zwide," Pakatwayo objected. "Don't you think Dingiswayo's spies have told him I'm here. Don't you think he'll guess what we're planning and act in consequence?"

"Not if you lead him to think that you have refused our offer of alliance. That after our meeting today you have decided that you want nothing to do with the Ndwandwes. For 'personal reasons' - I'm sure you'll think of some...It shouldn't be hard."

Pakatwayo glanced at Ntombazi's grotesque features creased in a devilish grin. No, the Qwabe told himself, it shouldn't be hard at all. To Zwide he murmured: "Go on."

"You will tell the Mtetwas that you prefer to fight on their side." Zwide's expression had become severe and his words were steeped with the harshness of a command. "You will be convincing. Dingiswayo must be led to believe that you are his ally. Right up to the moment the battle begins. Then - you will suddenly change fronts. Catching the good king completely off guard."

Prince Mzilikazi's keen eyes shot from Zwide to Pakatwayo, studying both men, awaiting the Qwabe's response. It came with a wry smile.

"The 'good king' might fall for that. But do you really think a military genius like Shaka will?"

For the first time, Queen Ntombazi chilled the interior of the Grand Hall with the sordid, wolfish rumble that was her voice, causing those who were not accustomed to its sound to have a sudden start, jolted by an icy shiver of dread.

"He will," the Witch said, in an eerie monotone. "If you are persuasive enough. Your father Kondlo was Shaka's friend, was he not? Appeal to that, if you must. Use any argument you wish, but," Pakatwayo felt the woman's fiendish eyes ravishing his soul as her wrinkled lips formed the words, "win Shaka's trust. It is imperative!"

Fleeing from the woman's yellow-tinged eyes, from the savageness of her speech, the Qwabe king's attention came to rest on the Crystal Cage where Mzilikazi was peering at him, the prince's expression etched with reproach. A sardonic smile suddenly danced across Pakatwayo's features as he indicated the cage and remarked to Zwide: "I thought you shunned risks. What about them? They have heard everything."

Ntombazi rolled her deep-sunken orbs in a look of ghoulish diversion.

"You needn't worry about them," the Queen noted as she rose from her throne and moved, haltingly, with a shambling gait, to a section of the Grand Hall next to the Cage where the recesses of a large alcove lay mantled in an oppressive darkness. As she ambled towards the niche, she explained: "We have ways of securing complete fidelity from our conquered chieftains. A way which I find quite -- full proof!"

Nodding to a royal guard, the Mistress of Dlovunga ordered that the torches in the interior of the alcove to be lit. When they were, their lapping flames cast a grisly light onto an assortment of thirty or more mummified human heads fastened to a long transverse post spanning the niche's entire width. The woman's soul numbing smile grew even more grotesque as she reached out her arthritic hand to caress the heads and to identify a few of them in turn, the choicest of the lot.

"Zayi, King of the Ngudlubela," she announced to those present in the Grand Hall, causing her son and the Esteemed Members of the Council to nod assentingly in expressions of immense pride and satisfaction, and causing Pakatwayo, Mzilikazi and the 'allied' kings to gape in abhorrence at the terrifying collection of desiccated skulls.

"Lange, of the Nxumalos," she went on, her fingers lingering on the head's plaited hair. "Mangete, King of the Nwenis. Tshana of the Manqueles.

Zihlandlo, ruler of the Timba Clan and..." Ntombazi hesitated as she turned to glare spectrally at the Cage and hissed: "Mlota, King of the Ntshalini."

A creeping paralysis of terror gripped Mlota as a pair of Ndwandwe guards threw back the Cage's bolts and swung open the iron door. The ruler of the Ntshalini Clan struggled only briefly, barely formulating the semblance of a plea for clemency before the axe sliced through his neck and his severed head plummeted to the ground, rolling to a halt at Ntombazi's feet. Cackling merrily, the Witch scooped up the head and held it high for the inspection of all, the blood gushing down her arms. Then, content with the new addition to her abominable collection, the woman fastened the newly acquired head to the post and, laughing wildly, turned to focus her maniacal gaze on Mzilikazi's father, Mashobane.

"Mashobane, King of the Northern Kumalos," she sibilated, causing Mzilikazi she leap out of the Crystal Cage in defence of his father and, with a bloodcurdling cry of fury, to fasten his mighty hands round Ntombazi's throat. Glaring at the man, the Witch swelled her sinewy neck muscles against his powerful grip, her lips staining with the blood-specked froth of rabid fury. But before Mzilikazi could strangle her gurgling yelp of savagery, Zwide bludgeoned the prince's skull with his knobkerrie, sending him slumping to the ground, unconscious.

Unshaken by the man's attack, Ntombazi focused once again on her victim and repeated: "Mashobane, King of the Northern Kumalos."

Again the axe came down, drenching the quartzite pavement of the Grand Hall with a sticky film of deep purple blood.

"Who's next?" the Qwabe king asked gravely. "Pakatwayo, King of the Qwabes?"

"Oh, no!" Zwide was quick to reassure him. "As I said. We need you!"

"No, Zwide," Pakatwayo shot back with a sizeable amount of courage - considering the bloodbath he's just witnessed. "We need each other. Or Shaka will have both out heads!"

* * *

"Has he named a successor," Shaka asked Dingiswayo.

"Sigiyana," the Mtetwa king answered.

"The least likely candidate amongst his legitimate sons! He must've been influenced. - Even in death he has shown his weakness!"

The three most important men in the Mtetwa Kingdom - Shaka, Dingiswayo, and Ngomane - strode alone, across the magnificence of their realm.

Dingiswayo gazed at Shaka out of the corner of his eye, deeply disturbed by the cold indifference with which the youth was reacting to Senzangakona's death. No grief. No regret. No feeling whatsoever, it seemed. The Zulu was treating the demise of his father as a mere matter of state business.

"Shaka," the king dropped his voice to a reverential murmur. "I'm sorry."

"Sorry, Baba?" Shaka was genuinely surprised by the comment. "Why should you be sorry? The man's death works to my advantage."

Ngomane joined his hands behind his back as he allowed his eyes to roam out to the landscape in front of him, wondering in disbelief how two men like Shaka and Dingiswayo, two close friends who owed each other their lives, two brothers in all but blood - how could they be so very disparate in matters of the heart? On opposite poles in matters of sentiment. This disparity became all the more obvious to Ngomane when he heard the exchange:--

"But he was your father!"

"As Jobe was yours. He, too, tried to kill his son. Did you shed a tear when he died?"

"Yes. I did," Dingiswayo's voice was saddened at the recollection.

"Bloodlines!" Shaka said with a droll smirk. "They are always demanding our allegiance. Yet most of the time it's unwarranted. Just because a man gives you life doesn't mean you have to love him. Cry at his funeral! Carry the burden of his memories! - My conception was a moment of pleasure for him,- the beginning of a lifetime of suffering for me! -- If I have tears, I will shed them for myself, not for the man who sired me!"

Yes, Ngomane nodded to himself. On opposite poles!

"How many regiments will you take to esiKlebeni?" The Mtetwa king finally asked, after a brief pause for reflection, his question taking both Shaka and Ngomane unawares.

"You astonish me, Baba," Shaka said. "Are you implying that I march in and take the Zulu throne? Interfere in the internal affairs of a subjugated tribe. - That doesn't sound like your policy."

"Isn't that what you've wanted all your life? Isn't that what your military career is all about? Taking the Zulu throne? And I am certainly not one to keep a man from his destiny. Besides," a slight smile tugged on the king's lips, "you have control over the Armed Forces, Shaka. You may do it regardless of what my 'policy' might be. So I thought it would be more dignified for both of us if the idea appeared to be my own."

Shaka afforded his king a long searching gaze that radiated benevolence.

"The iziCwe should be enough," he answered, softly. "I won't disturb the other troops. They're in intensive training for the Zwide campaign. In fact, I may just march into esiKlebeni with the original 'Fifty' - for old time's sake." Shaka shifted his attention to Ngomane. "I'll need someone to officiate at my coronation. I obviously can't use Mudli. He'd just as soon stab me with the Zulu Royal Assegai. - Would you do me the honour, Ngomane?"

"It would be my pleasure, Shaka," the induna smiled, gratified by the privilege bestowed upon.

Taking the leopard skin from round his shoulders, the one given him at the outset of his "wandering", Dingiswayo handed it back to Shaka.

"I think it is rightfully yours now, Shaka. It has come round full circle: - wanderer to wanderer, king to king."

The Zulu took the leopard skin, gently fondling it in his grasp, and when he spoke again, his voice conveyed his pleasure, and his great affection for the other man.

"You will always be my overlord, Baba."

"Shaka Zulu is destined to have no overlords. We both know that. I only pray that we remain friends."

* * *

The infamous Pit of Dlovunga was a dungeon, an abyss of torture, a gaping crater of misery, a chasm of excruciating death.

Carved into a natural vein of pure calcite, the Pit's rectangular floor (measuring five square meters) was as hard as a diamond and its four walls (each four meters high) as perfectly levigated as polished glass - walls which afforded no footholds, no means of scaling, no manner of escape.

Prince Mzilikazi was slumped in a corner of the Pit, his massive frame resting limply against a cold, crystal wall. Slowly he stirred to wakefulness and instinctively grimaced as a wave of sharp pain jolted through his brain. Bringing his hand to the throbbing gash above his forehead, he gingerly touched the wound inflicted by Zwide's knobkerrie and, as he did so, a wave of recollection swept through his mind, bringing with it the sorrowful realisation that his father had most assuredly already fallen victim to the hideous Mistress of the Citadel.

As the thought of his father's death and of the horrid manner in which it was dealt blazed through the prince's spirit, setting it aflame with a desire for vengeance, the man opened his eyes and was suddenly faced with a spectral sight that verily caused his blood to run cold. At his side, a hair's-breadth from his face, was a human skull blanched by the sun, its wide, vacant orbs and grinning mouth frozen in an expression of heinous amusement. Too petrified to move, Mzilikazi shifted his unblinking gaze to a cluster of human bones collected round a gutted rib cage, shreds of purulent flesh still clinging to a few of the ribs and reddened by devouring throngs of hungry ants.

Overcoming the initial abhorrence that had chilled him, the Kumalo prince hitched himself up, inspecting the grisly interior of his horrifying confinement, finding it cluttered with the macabre remains of its past guests: the carrions of jackals in various stages of decay, the animals' twisted frames interlocked with human skeletons as if the ghastly struggle in which man and beast had been engaged was perpetrated for Eternity. Then, lifting his gaze, Mzilikazi's eyes took in the mouth of the Pit yawning onto the delicate play of rose pink and gold that heralded the dawning of a new day.

Somewhat heartened by that daybreak, rising on heavy legs, Mzilikazi marshalled his brooding disconcertion and terror into the lucidness of reasoning necessary for survival, and concentrated his scrutiny on the Pit's walls, finding, to his utter dismay, that they were indeed devoid of any means of scaling. As his mind raced to formulate an alternative plan, he heard it: - a muffled growl that seemed to come from the portals of Hell, and he froze in place as he looked up and spotted the odious features of Ntombazi peering down at him from the mouth of the chasm, the gaping wound that was her mouth curled in a gleeful smile. Next to the Witch appeared a pair of ferocious jackals, their fangs, drenched with saliva, gleaming in the first rays of daylight. Ntombazi cocked back her brawny arm and hurled an assegai into the Pit. The spear sailed through the crisp morning air and fell harmlessly at Mzilikazi's feet.

"The spears are to make it more interesting," the Witch said, her smile turning to delighted cackling as, at the wave of her hand, one after the other the two beasts leapt down onto their victim.

The Kumalo successfully fought back the jackals' initial onslaught, spinning free of the beasts and lashing out with the back of his fist, clipping one of the animals directly below the muzzle, snapping its windpipe. Then, snatching up the assegai, gripping it in his hand, the man stood poised, his eyes trained on the other snarling beast, ready for its attack.

He did not have long to wait. The jackal sprang upwards, landing on Mzilikazi's chest, going for the man's head, slashing open the skin on the cheekbone just below the eye in a clean sabre-stroke of white teeth. The prince turned at the instant of impact and, using his shoulder and his massive strength, he punched the animal back and spun free of its razor-sharp claws. But, in an instant, the beast was upon him again, his teeth going for a hold on the man's throat, catching only his ear, splitting it open so that the blood gushed out to commingle with the crimson blotches on the prince's cheek.

The force of the jackal's second charge threw Mzilikazi to the ground, and man and beast rolled on the floor of the Pit, bodies interlocked, twisting and wrenching amidst the gruesome cadavers and skeletons that cluttered the ground beneath them. The Kumalo purchased leverage under the big animal's chest, literally lifting it into the air with one hand whilst the other brought the spear's blade to its belly and plunged it into the bare, shiny dark skin below the ribs.

The jackal screamed and relinquished its hold on the man, spinning violently to the side so that the blade of the assegai tore out of the belly, ripping a flap of stomach lining through which grimy, purple entrails bulged immediately.

Yet the beast was not yet beaten. Again it charged, making solid contact with Mzilikazi's chest as the blood disgorged from its wound, bathing the Kumalo in its sticky, warm flow. And again the man sank the blade of his weapon into the jackal's side, tearing through the flesh until the rubbery pink tubes of the animal's guts were pulled out of the stomach cavity and hung free, becoming tangled with Mzilikazi's flailing legs. Then - with one last vicious growl - the jackal finally fell limp. Breathing heavily, his body bruised and lacerated, the prince fell back against the wall of the Pit, his chest heaving with exertion.

Suddenly the sound of clapping was heard. The Kumalo's gaze shot up to the mouth of the cave where Ntombazi was applauding his prowess with a satisfied twinkle in her jaundiced eyes.

"Good. Very good," she screeched. "But then I could see that you were a man of superior qualities. Not like the others!" Her gaze flitted to the skeletons that were scattered near the prince. "They all perished with the first two beasts. How long will take before you succumb? Four? Six. Ten? - We shall see."

As his heart raced within his chest, once again the prince heard growling.

A fresh pair of jackals came into view at the mouth of the Pit, their gnarling jaws set against the blood- red radiance of dawn.

* * *

"Your father's people are like jackals, Shaka," Nandi told her son as she looked up at the serene purity of the night that enveloped them in its tepid breath. "They bare their fangs, but, like the jackal, their threats are those of cowards. - You should have no trouble winning from them what has been legitimately yours since the day you were conceived."

Nandi's tone was museful, laced with a note of deep introspection. It seemed to Shaka that her words were part of a shared inner reverie. Indeed, when she fell silent, her mind reached out to the coming dawn when she and her son would enter the Zulu village and take possession of the Destiny to which she had been a helpless and hapless protagonist since she first heard of the Prophecy on the Platform of the Pinnacle. She now felt an overwhelming sense of immensity at the realisation that that Dream would become reality and, as that sense of greatness gave way to the malaise of uneasiness, her father's words resurfaced in her mind - "If you reach that unreachable, you may well be very much alone". Alone. No, she told herself, not alone. She has Shaka! She will always have Shaka!

Shaka glanced at his mother, at her beautiful features, still radiant and youthful in the mellow wash of the moonlight, and he saw her distant, pensive gaze and pondered over the state of her heart. If Senzangakona's death had affected her, it was not visible on her stately, determined expression. Tenderly he probed.

"Has it saddened you? His death, I mean?"

Nandi dropped her gaze, staring directly into the amorphous forms of the night's shadows, listening to the inner voices of her soul speaking in hushed tones of the man that was her Love, voices that spoke in fierce contempt, in angry tenderness, and in mingled accents of pity and regret. There was no mistaking her love - it was there, it would always be there; it had come and stayed under circumstances that left no room for doubt in the matter. And now that she was alone with her love, she listened to the voices of her solitude, not in agitation but, on the contrary, oppressed by the sensation that something had happened to her that could not be undone: - she had lost him, forever.

Had his death saddened her? She couldn't tell really. The part of her that could have been saddened died with him, so there was no pain, no feeling, just the numbness of an empty world steeped in an infinity of silence. But what could she tell her son? How could she answer his legitimate query.

She couldn't. So she sat silently and listened - to her own heartbeat counting the seconds that passed until Shaka said: "It's a shame, isn't it? That the man you loved never deserved your love."

Stunned by the remark, she turned to her son and saw that he was looking at her, directly at her, waiting for her reply. And this time she knew she could not remain silent. She wanted to tell him that you love not because of what is in the other, you love because of something that is in you - something alive - something in yourself. Yet instead she replied: "The heart is very capricious, Shaka. Often impossible to control."

"No, mother. Like the mind, the heart can be trained to function predictably."

She searched his eyes and when she realised he meant it, she had a faint knowing smile.

"You say that because you're still young. You've not been in love yet. Wait and---"

"I love you, mother," he said in earnest, interrupting her. "I've always loved you."

The woman was warmed by his affection and, taking his powerful arm, she rested her head on his shoulder.

"I know, Shaka," she said with a gentle smile. "And I love you. - But the love I mean is different."

She felt him stiffen under her touch and wondered why,- yet she had no way of knowing that his thoughts had suddenly been wrenched back to his humiliating session with Pampata, to his aborted sexual performance, to the betrayal of his body.

"We have no need for that love, mother," he uttered in a disturbingly hollow voice.

"Every man needs that love, Shaka," she told him, not stubbornly, but with kind persuasion.

"Did he?" Was his curt rejoinder.

When their eyes locked, Nandi's moistened with tears and Shaka took her in his arms, gently rocking her as he whispered: "You have taught me to survive, mother. To become the king he was meant to be. And I have survived! And I will be that king! - But if you now ask me to share his faults, you might as well bury me with him."

She started to cry, the tears raining onto Shaka's chest. Cradling her face in his large hand, the Zulu lifted it so that their eyes met again."

"The man is dead, mother," he told her. "Do not cry for him - for yourself. Do not cry for what was, for what could have been - Forget the Past! Think of us, mother! We are the future!"

* * *

As once again the sky over the Pit was shot through with the reddish filaments of a new day - his second - Mzilikazi finished the execution of yet another beast, and fell back, against the cold crystal of the grave like abyss that was his prison, and, as his gashed, bleeding chest heaved with the exhaustion of his superhuman struggle, his gaze reached out to the floor of the cave where the six carcasses of his would-be executioners lay in a heap of torn flesh and tangled fur matted with blood.

"How many will it take?" the Witch had asked. Six? Ten? - And the prince sighed knowing that soon, before he could rest sufficiently, two more beasts would appear to torment his existence. And then, if his strength were to persist, two more - and two more, until death finally came to liberate him from the wretchedness of Dlovunga and its macabre Queen.

Suddenly the man froze, his brow knitting with an idea. Reaching out, he ran his hand over one of the jackals' furry hides as his eyes darted up to the jagged cliffs looming over the mouth of the cave.

"It's a chance, a mere chance," he thought, "- but it just might work! No, it must work," he determined. There was no other choice.

His blood racing with adrenalin, the prince set to work, skinning the jackals with his spear and cutting their sturdy hide into strips.

Less than an hour had elapsed before Mzilikazi tugged on his makeshift rope of joined and braided strips of fur, testing its strength, and smiled. Satisfied that it would hold the weight of his body, the prince fastened a heavy thighbone to one end of the long cord and, with a mighty thrust, pitched it up, out of the Pit and around a sliver of rock that protruded from the side of an over-hanging cliff. He then tugged on the rope, tightening its hold on the rocky sliver, before beginning his ascent.

Reaching the mouth of the Pit, Mzilikazi eased himself over the edge and searched his surroundings for signs of the gruesome human plague that was Ntombazi. He spied her in the distance, her hobbling figure cast against the rising sun as she eagerly moved towards the site of her grim diversion in the company of yet another pair of voracious jackals.

Moving quickly, Mzilikazi retrieved his makeshift rope and scrambled off across the rocky terrain towards the Citadel's lofty cliffs.

CHAPTER XXV
"BAYETE ZULU ELIPEZULU"
("HAIL THOU OF THE HIGH HEAVENS")

In the Journey of Life some are left behind because they are naturally feeble and irresolute; some because they miss the way; and many because they leave the Path by choice, and, instead of pressing onward with a steady pace, they delight themselves with momentary deviations, turning aside to pluck every flower and repose in every shade.

The Son of Zulu - who was not much for plucking flowers and reposing in the shade - went down the Path of his Journey through Life with a swift, determined pace and with a "method of attack" that very much resembled his fabled cattle horn formation: - his "head" ramming stubbornly against Life's Weakness, Life's Insecurity, Life's Fears, and Life's Doubts, while the "horns" swept out, embracing all that could be Life's Glory.

The Method.

Make contact with your Destiny. Lock shields with your Purpose. Pull back and away exposing the Truth. Aim for your Goal, thrust into Its Heart and shout "Ngadla!" - "I have eaten!"

Such was the Child's predestined Journey: to move down the Path of Life, unswerving, steadfast, to repose only in the shade of Early Death and to pluck only one Flower, the Lily of Success that lay not on the side of the road, - but at its End.

That was the Method of his Life.

The Path that led to the Sovereignty of the Heavens.

As the Prophets had sung to the Wind.

What had Dingiswayo told him? "Isn't that what you've always wanted? Isn't that what your military career is all about? Taking the Zulu Throne?"

On that brisk morning on the Month of uLutudlana in the Year 1816, as the lavender sky above the Umfolozi River was streaked with the first warming rays of sunlight, Shaka's answer to Dingiswayo's queries was "Yes! Definitely! That is what it was all about!"

And on that morning, at its dawning, according to Ritual of Annointment proscribed by the Prophets and the Wise, Shaka stood naked, ankle deep in the speeding currents of the river, under the grave, watchful gazes of Nandi, Nomcoba (now 24), Ngwadi (a tall thirteen), Ngomane, Mgobozi, Nqoboka, Joko, Mtonga, Dlaba and the other members of the original "Fifty", as Pampata officiated at the service, preparing and dressing the Child's body for the Coronation.

His magnificent, statuesque frame was rinsed and soaped clean with a paste of fat and ground millet. Then, when it was dry, the skin was smeared with an emulsion of red ochre, which left a ruddy, silky gloss on his smooth flesh that shone brilliant over his rippling muscles and upon the severe handsomeness of his features.

Fringes made from the tails of spotted genets and the fluffy fur of blue-grey monkeys were draped over Shaka's massive shoulders, while Pampata fitted splendid copper ringlets with hanging ivory tassels - that jingled enchantingly in the gentle breeze - round the Zulu's legs, just above each sinewy calf.

Then Pampata placed upon his head a fabulous crown adorned with the hides of the Cheetah, the Lynx, and the Lion, the quills of the Bateleur and the Lammergeyer Eagles, the colourful plumes of the Kingfisher and the Marabou, and fitted with a long, quivering Blue Crane feather. And lastly, the now legendary leopard skin was cloaked upon his back and the Ixwa came to rest in his powerful grasp as he thrust it up, towards the sky.   "SI-GI-DI," Mgobozi roared, breaking the religious silence that had prevailed throughout the anointment.

"SI-GI-DI," echoed the Fifty.

"Are you ready, Shaka?" Ngomane asked as he prepared to strike off on the long trek to esiKlebeni.

"I am ready," said the Child.

And he was.

* * *

"Umkonto wenkosi o-y-isiMakade," spoke Mudli, holding high the Zulu Royal Assegai as he presided over the Coronation of the new Zulu monarch whom Senzangakona had designated before his death. "Nantso-ke inKosi yeNu, naKiti, namhla-nje! -- Behold him, ye of our Clan, who is your king today!"

Solemnly Mudli handed Sigiyana the Assegai, the symbol of Zulu Power, the symbol of the youth's new office as king, and the legitimate heir to the throne clutched the spear in his hand, firmly, as if fearful that he might drop it or that it might inadvertently be snatched away.

Indeed, as Sigiyana lifted his gaze to take in the sight of the Zulu population spread out in the valley at the foot of EsiKlebeni, on its knees, bowing low in homage, the young man's eyes caught sight of a group of distant, approaching figures that glimmered against the radiance of the sky with the hazy distinctness of a mirage. And as Mudli also narrowed his eyes on the horizon, making out the tall, mighty frame of Shaka and, behind him, the gleaming ixwas of his Fifty, the Elder truly wished that what he was seeing was a mirage instead of the image of imminent ruin.

A sudden wave of fear washed through the Zulu population as, one by one, gazes were lifted to view the party that was advancing towards them and eyes were transformed from attitudes of submission to the wide, gaping semblance of terror upon seeing the celebrated, marvellous I-Shaka - donning his magnificent, awe-inspiring attire of plumes, tails, furs and ivory - as he strode up the slopes towards the Royal Homestead in the company of his family and his valiant troops.

And, with immense trepidation, the sea of Zulus verily parted before Shaka and his procession, cowering before his regal stride, quickly scampering out of his way like beaten dogs glimpsing their master's switch.

Up through the gates of the outer palisade Shaka strode, round the cattle fold and towards the site of the coronation.

Besides Sigiyana - who was in a state of trance-like hysteria, the Royal Assegai literally trembling in his hand - Senzangakona's other sons were also spellbound by the advent of their illustrious half-brother. Especially one of them, Dingane by name, the son of wife Mpikase, a short, husky youth in his early twenties, with a body, flabby and amorphous, that lacked discipline and a face, puffy and insipid, that lacked any clear definition of character, a commonly face, the sort one looks at but never sees, the sort that is easily lost in a crowd, - especially Dingane glared at his half-brother and wished in breathless earnest that he could, indeed, be now lost in a crowd.

Only two of the official Royal Entourage seemed to react with rational: Mkabayi who hardly concealed a propensity to absolutely glow at the sight of the Child of the Prophecy, and Mudli, proud defender of the status quo, seasoned diplomat, and loyal servant of his kings, who ordered, sharply, in a voice that rose with vibrancy: "In the name of all that is sacred - leave this homestead. Now!"

"You sound terrified, Elder," Shaka responded, moving towards the man and stopping a few paces from the Zulu throne. "Does my presence frighten you? Or is it your guilt that makes you quake?"

Mudli's face contorted with loathing. Drawing up the venom in his spittle, the Elder spat on Shaka's face causing a hot flash of terror to bolt through the gathering as all present awaited the scourge of Shaka's wrath.

Yet the Zulu's face did not darken with rage. Instead, it lit up with a buoyant lift of sarcasm. "An esteemed member of the Royal Council spitting on the face of his king? That is an act of High Treason, Elder."

"You're not my king," Mudli hissed, years of hatred bursting forth from his soul. "Even your blood-thirsty warriors cannot win my allegiance, my respect! Senzangakona kaJama Zulu - the true descendant of Zulu kaMalandela - has dictated his choice and I will defend that decision with my life! I will not allow you to defile the divine rituals of our tribe." His voice rose, fired with indignation. "Leave these sacred grounds!"

Shaka's tone became glacial.

"As I said - treason." His eyes shot to Senzangakona's heir. "Sigiyana, would you please execute the sentence."

The new Zulu monarch - who was already counting the cursory seconds to the end of his tragic reign - was dumbstruck by the command and sat petrified on his throne, open-mouthed and gasping as if his half-brother's words had knocked the wind of him. Ravished by Shaka's flashing eyes that remained fixed on him with rising impatience, Sigiyana started to tremble, his teeth chattering, his arms quivering with a fearful attack that symptomatically hedged on epilepsy, as the Royal Assegai swayed incontrollable in his hand, on the verge of slip ping to the ground. Leaning over, his eyes still locked on the terrified youth, Shaka whispered: "Did you not hear me? - I said execute the sentence."

Sigiyana caught his breath, his eyes darting to Mudli with a pleading glance, silently begging the Elder to take pity upon him, to have understanding, forgiveness perhaps, as he clasped the Royal Assegai in both hands, steadying it, and thrust out his arms, sinking the Symbol of Zulu Power into the belly of the man who had, for over fifty years, personified that Symbol.

Incredulous, the Elder clutched at the spear in his stomach and sank to his knees, as the entire Zulu population looked on in glacial silence, passively awaiting the next act in the tragedy of their kingdom.

Mkabayi closed her eyes, shuddering slightly at the blow dealt to Mudli, her courageous rival, gallant to the end, and in her heart she felt grief for his imminent death and for the manner in which it was inflicted, one so beneath the dignity and pride that had otherwise characterised his existence. When she opened her eyes, her gaze met Nandi's and both women were transported back to their first meeting, at the time of Senzangakona's wedding - almost thirty years before - when the young Langeni shrew had denied the handsome prince's request for beer. At that time Mkabayi had wondered whether Nandi would threaten her rightful place at the side of her flesh and blood, her brother Senzangakona. And now, as Nandi met Mkabayi's domineering glare, she wondered whether the Zulu spinsters would contend for a place at the side of her own flesh and blood, her son - the Child of the Prophecy.

His lips stained with the deep-red flow that pulsated freely from his mouth, Mudli saw the approach of Death and addressed it.

"Now there is darkness," he said in a faint voice, one that so resembled a distant cry of distress. "I pray it is not...not too late. I pray...that the Ancestors will preserve our People...our Kingdom. Safeguard our Past. As it...as it was..."

When Mudli was still, Shaka allowed his fierce eyes to linger on the old man's lifeless frame and the Zulu offered a response to the Elder's dying words.

"No, Mudli," he whispered with a bitter scorn for the Past. "Nothing will be as it was. - Ever again!" To drive home the bleak significance of his words, Shaka yanked the Royal Assegai out of the man's body and broke the weapon over his knee.

Thus, with this sacrilegious act that left the Zulus crestfallen, the Child severed the People of the Heavens from their past and catapulted them into a fathomless void of obscurity and fear, an unknown future that left the populace scared, - not as one is scared whilst his judgment and his reason still try to resist, but completely, boundlessly, and, as it were, innocently scared - like little children lost in the all-enveloping blackness of night.

The same fear that shone in the eyes of Sigiyana when Shaka turned to address his faint-hearted relative.

"Do you acknowledge me as king of the Zulus, my brother?" he asked the shaken man. "As the legitimate heir to the throne in your stead?"

Falling to his knees, embracing Shaka's legs, the whimpering, blubbering dastard babbled: "Yes...yes, Shaka! You are my lord! My master! - Bayete! Bayete, Nkosi!'

"And you," Shaka hissed, sickened by Sigiyana's revolting cravenness, "are a snivelling fool."

With a gurgling sound, Senzangakona's legitimate heir slumped to the ground, as the Ixwa was driven through his chest, bursting his heart. Then, extracting his weapon from his half-brother's body, Shaka brusquely wiped the Blade on Sigiyana's headdress and, pushing him aside with a sweep of the foot, he took his place on the Zulu throne, his proud countenance facing his horrified subjects.

If Ngomane had been shaken by the bloodbath, it was not clearly discernible on his grave features as he strode to Shaka's side.

"Is there anyone here who contests the righteousness of this decision?" The Mtetwa induna inquired, raising his voice to be heard by all present. "If so, let him speak now, or hereafter be silent."

Ngomane's eyes searched the crowd, eyeing significantly Senzangakona's others sons and the members of the Zulu Royal Family before concluding: "No one speaks? - Very well. Then salute your king!"

Dingane was the first to sink to his knees and, offering another example of the cowardice that seemed a predominant streak in the post-Shakan stock of his father's house, the grandson of Jama fearfully exclaimed: "Bayete, Nkosi. Bayete Zulu Elipezulu!"

"Bayete Nkosi!" came the responsorial cry from the entire populace, an ovation offered in a tremulous distraction that was soon interwoven with the heroic roar of the Fifty as they proclaimed with one voice, pounding the earth with their feet, "Bayete, Sigidi! Bayete, Nkosi! Wena wa sendhlu nKulu!"

His face aglow with power and the inordinate gratification of complete fulfilment, Shaka raised his hand and beckoned to Nandi. The woman hesitated for only a heartbeat, then strode majestically, magnificently towards the Zulu throne, her movements measured and with a rhythmic undulation of her noble figure, slow, deliberate, as if she were restraining herself.

And, for the second time in the life of their clan, the Zulus parted before the daughter of Bhebhe as she crossed to the top of esiKlebeni; yet, unlike the first time, when she had been the whore with a bastard son who had cost the clan fifty-five cattle, - she was now the Nkosikazi, the revered Queen of Queens of the people who had once despised her, the Great Female Elephant of Zulu whose bastard son would cost the clan not a handful of cows, but its Past, its Present, and its Future - and the most precious commodity it had: its Identity!

Mkabayi was also thinking of the Future and the Identity of the amaZulu as she watched Nandi take her place at her son's side and she considered, with a wry smile, how today, just like so many years before, the Langeni shrew owed her presence in the Zulu homestead to her son - only to her son. "I wonder if she knows," Mkabayi mused, "I wonder if she realises that he belongs to the Nation now! Or has she built her life round him without ever really facing the possibility that he may one day no longer need her, no longer have room for her in his life?"

When Nandi was seated beside her son on the throne, he queried, gelidly: "Aside from this man, mother," Shaka's glance brushed scornfully over Mudli's body, "is there anyone else here who has offended you?"

Nandi's face hardened, her feline eyes moving past Mkabi, and the terrified faces of Fudukazi, Langazana, Bibi, and Senzangakona's other wives, to come to a rest on Mkabayi. The late king's sister held her stare with cold indifference, her expression betraying no fear, though she knew full well that Nandi now had power over her life.

"No," Nandi said, looking away, remembering that Mkabayi had once saved her son from his father's spear. "No one."

"So be it," said the Son of Zulu and, taking his mother's hand, gently rested it over his own, both hands clutching the Ixwa - the new Symbol of Zulu Sovereignty.

"Bayete, Nkosi!" came the extolment of the new king, the salute repeated in a crescendo that dwarfed the valley in its impetus.

"Bayete Nkosi!" was the greeting on everyone's lips, installing the Child as the Language of the Heavens, initiating the New Era in which the Fame of the House of the amaZulu will radiate into the sun.

Of those present, only Pampata remained silent, her eyes moist with tears as she pondered over the inscrutable soul of the man she loved and wondered, heart-broken, of the cruel, selfish design that Fate held in store for him. Of those present, and because of her love, only Pampata spied the truth as had Mabodla, the Magician of UmZizima. Only she saw, with terrifying clarity that the Great I-Shaka was no only King, Hero, and Conqueror, but also the unwitting instrument of forces wielded beyond his Heart's comprehension, the unwitting victim of his own Destiny.

*

That evening, as planned, feasting followed the coronation. Yet the feeling that pervaded the festivities was definitely not as planned. In fact, the Zulus had the distinct sensation that, in the wake of this forced transition of power, their lives would never again be "as planned". So, as the oxen roasted over a campfire and the beer ran freely, the Zulus ate, drank and danced in a frenzy of fear that Shaka himself defined most appropriately.

"Controlled panic," the new Zulu sovereign noted, observing his subjects with detached, caustic interest as he and Ngomane sat eating together at the threshold of the Royal Hut. "They're all drunk! I've never seen such forced merriment in all my life! They're floundering in a state of pure shock!" Taking a hearty bite of veal with an appetite made voracious by his recent triumph, Shaka added, almost in passing: "A state of shock from which I trust they shall never recover!"

"What do you mean 'never recover'?" Ngomane asked, puzzled by the heartless remark. "They're your people now, Shaka."

"That's why I hope they'll never recover," the Zulu rejoined, smiling, and continued, shedding light on his companion's growing bewilderment, "Haven't you realised what's happened, Ngomane? In it's entirety, I mean. -- When I marched into esiKlebeni and took the throne, the one factor that made my act successful was fear! I have, to all intents and purposes, instituted a reign if fear. And now the only way I have of truly preserving my power and the undying fidelity of my subjects," a hint of irony transpired in Shaka's tone, "is to keep that fear very much alive!"

"How?" Ngomane had lost interest in his food.

"By cutting them off from their past. From their roots! And projecting them into an unknown future in which there will be but one directive - my own! And even in that there will be doubt! I'll keep them guessing: - What is Shaka? Where is he going? What will he do? What does he want?"

"What does he want?"

Shaka's sudden graveness of expression contrasted enigmatically with the mischievous twinkle in his eye.

"Change, Ngomane. Shaka wants change! - I will effect a complete upheaval of all their emotional anchors: - their traditions, their customs, their family bonds, their beliefs and superstitions! All that Man thinks he needs will be abolished! From this day forward all rules, all laws, all state ordinances will be provisional and subject to change at a moment's notice!" The twinkle in Shaka's eye contaminated the rest of his features and he smiled. "I'll keep their heads spinning until they're all dizzy! That's the only way to keep my throne, Ngomane. Power through Fear of the Unknown."

"That can be dangerous, Shaka," the Mtetwa induna replied, voicing his moral reflection, calmly, as if Shaka's chilling scenario for the future were only a passing storm cloud on an otherwise splendid day. "Traditions are hard to die. The human heart is very resilient. If you push them too far, I'm afraid that sooner or later they'll assassinate you."

"I was meant to die at the age of six, Ngomane. Since then, every year has been a year of grace. But I have taken my precautions," his tone became confident. "Two to be exact. First, I have formed a special security force for my protection made up of the youngest and most alert warriors of my regiments who will veritably 'cling' to me like mist. In fact, that's what I've called this special force - the 'Ufasimba', the Mist! -- Then, second, every available assassin in my kingdom will be kept busy venting his aggression in warfare. Those who refuse will be eliminated."

"And when there are no wars?" Was Ngomane's query as it became increasingly clearer to the man that Shaka was in earnest.

"I'll create them," came the smug answer. "Even after Zwide, there's still a great deal of land to conquer. In fact, from what Dingiswayo has told me, I suppose that one day soon we'll have to give a thought to the Swallows." Shaka rested a confident hand on Ngomane's shoulder. "No, Ngomane, there should be no difficulty keeping our soldiers happy! - Indeed, I wouldn't be surprised if War became the natural state of things."

A knowing grin tugged on Ngomane's features as his eyes locked with Shaka's.

" 'Total war. Total obedience to the Paramount King. Total destruction of anyone who raises even a whisper against him.' That's what you said to Dingiswayo. But you were really thinking about your own future, weren't you?"

"Those ideas are mine," the Zulu King was coldly ironic now. "I can hardly divorce them from myself - even if they are suggested to another."

Abruptly a hush gripped the festivities, as Shaka's and Ngomane's attention was gravitated towards a man being led by Mgobozi and Joko into the king's presence. The man, Mzilikazi, his powerful body stained with blood and marred by the wounds he had sustained in his struggle with Ntombazi's "pets", was thrust unceremoniously to the ground at Shaka's feet.

When Mzilikazi looked up, his proud eyes met Shaka's and the two men had the sudden, strange feeling that they were glimpsing in the other reflections of themselves. Without having yet uttered a word, both men knew that a fellowship had asserted itself, stronger than any either man had ever known.

*

"25,000 troops?!" exclaimed Shaka, incredulous, his piercing gaze darting to Mzilikazi who sat near the fire of the Zulu Royal Hut, the brilliant light of the hearth bathing his muscular body in its uniform glow as Pampata gently administered compresses of herbs and poultices on his infected lacerations.

"I never dreamed they were that strong!" The Zulu's eyes roamed restlessly over the sparkling flames, as if reading the answer to some silent interrogative on their glowing surfaces. "The Qwabes switching fronts in the heat of battle!" His eyes flitted to Ngomane. " A juvenile tactic! Zwide must be mad to think Dingiswayo and I would have fallen into that trap."

"That's exactly what Pakatwayo said," Mzilikazi responded, wincing slightly as Pampata spread a burning paste on his shoulder.

"A spark of light in the darkness of his treachery," Ngomane commented grimly.

Shaka's gaze returned to rest suspiciously on his exceptional visitor.

"How do I know you're not part of this plan?" he asked Mzilikazi.

"You don't," the other man grinned disarmingly. "But I'm sure you have your own full proof ways of verifying that."

Shaka's eyes remained on the Kumalo, glinting, as his mind raced, judging the other man, when Mgobozi was suddenly at the threshold of the hut.

"Sigidi," he saluted upon entering. "A runner has come from the Qwabes. Pakatwayo wishes to meet with you. To discuss an alliance against the Ndwandwes."

A diverted smile twitching on his lips, the Zulu King's gaze brushed past Ngomane's and Mzilikazi's.

"Mgobozi, tell the messenger that we will meet with Pakatwayo tomorrow, to discuss this 'alliance' of his. - Tell him we come in peace." As Mgobozi bowed to leave, Shaka added, "And, Mgobozi - alert the regiments. All five. We march on the Qwabe capital at dawn."

Mgobozi was greatly puzzled by the two seemingly contradictory orders of "meeting in peace with all your regiments at hand". Yet Shaka was a man one obeyed with- out question and the commander of the iziCwe nodded and took his leave.

"You," the Zulu said to Mzilikazi, "will come with us, of course. As a...full proof 'verification'."

* * *

The meeting between Shaka and Pakatwayo began well enough as the two kings strolled through the large Royal Homestead at emaTandeni discussing the political situation as it was evolving in their kingdoms. And the Qwabe, being a good twelve years older than the Zulu, seemed very relaxed, very much in control.

"Congratulations, Shaka," Pakatwayo said casually. "But then we always knew the Zulu throne was yours for the taking.

"We?"

"My father and I. He thought very highly of you, Shaka. He trusted you, and, through him, I've learned to do the same."

Shaka's thoughts wandered back to that somewhat reposed, somewhat happy period of his life in the land of the Qwabes, under the affectionate wing of the good Gendeyana. He recalled Kondlo's courageous stand on behalf of himself and he recalled his own prophetic words which had recently come true: "Tell the Zulus to prepare themselves, Lutuli," he had said at the age of nineteen, "tell them that sooner than they dare think, I will return. But not alone. My mother will be at my side, as the Nkosikazi indlovukazi, the Queen of Queens!"

Nineteen! An interesting age, he thought. One in which a man is easily reckless and easily apt to dream: the power of reflection being weak and the power of imagination strong.

"Yes," Shaka finally replied with a tender smile. "Kondlo was a great man. The last of the enlightened rulers of your tribe." Pakatwayo's eyes darted to Shaka, cushioning the Zulu's veiled insult with a broad smile.

"May he rest in peace," said the new Qwabe king.

"Your message sounded most...intriguing, Pakatwayo," Shaka remarked, getting down to the question at hand. "And somewhat incredible. Especially in light of your visit with Zwide."

The Qwabe was not phased by the remark. As he had mentioned to Zwide himself, he had expected the Mtetwas to know of his presence in Dlovunga.

"I don't deny that the thought of an alliance with the Ndwandwes was tantalising. Very tantalising! Their armies are quite numerous and---"

"25,000," Shaka inserted, curtly.

"Ye-es," the Qwabe faltered, just for an instant. He hadn't anticipated that Shaka would be privy to that particular piece of information. Yet, quickly recovering from the sting, he added, "Exactly. 25,000. With an army that size, security is the name of the game!"

"That depends on the game you're playing, Pakatwayo."

The Qwabe avoided meeting Shaka's eyes as he went on.

"And what dissuaded you from forming that 'tantalising' alliance?" Shaka wanted to know.

"Loyalty!" was the answer, riding an emphatic wave. "As I said, my father thought highly of you, and, out of loyalty to his memory, I now feel our clans must stand together!"

"I agree whole-heartedly, Pakatwayo," Shaka was starting to enjoy himself. "In fact, I would take it a step further. Why don't we join the clans under one name: Zulu. Under one king: Shaka!"

Pakatwayo spun round to face the other man, his eyes alight with rage at Shaka's intransigence. Yet, before the Qwabe could voice this wrath, Shaka called out: "Mzilikazi!"

Mzilikazi kaMashone Kumalo strode grinning into emaTandeni causing the blood to drain from Pakatwayo's features and the man to stand riveted in place, stammering: "The--the Kumalo!"

"The Kumalo," Shaka agreed.

"But," Pakatwayo said, forcing a spurt of laughter though his hair was verily stirring at the roots. "But you wouldn't take his word against mine! The word of a complete stranger against that of an old friend!"

"An old friend"? Shaka said to himself with a wry smile, thinking of the prince who so long ago wanted to turn his father against the "arrogant Zulu". "I no longer need to take his word for it, Pakatwayo," the Zulu said out loud. "The expression on your face when you saw him was all the truth I needed to know."

As Shaka and Mzilikazi exchanged meaningful glances, the Zulu raised his arm and, on cue, the thundering war cry "SI-GI-DI!" was heard echoing in the vicinity of the Qwabe homestead, engiring it in its heroic embrace.

In muted amazement, Pakatwayo cast a wild, terrified glance at the surrounding hillsides and was dumbstruck to see the thousands who now made up Shaka's armies. Knowing there was no time, no opportunity for retaliation, the Qwabe King spat: "You tricked me, Shaka! You said you would come in peace!"

"But I have, Pakatwayo." Shaka retorted gelidly. - "The same peace you offered me."

* * *

By the nightfall of the fifth day, the Qwabe runner had reached Dlovunga and been admitted through the Gates of Jade.

An hour later, Zwide was at his mother's side, his nervous inward impatience growing intolerable as he spoke: "Pakatwayo has fallen."

"The Kumalo?" Ntombazi asked, without flinching.

"Yes."

"Unfortunate he got away," she groaned, and the incipient grimness vanished out of her hideous aspect when a toothless smile appeared on her parched lips as she formulated the words: "Then he must die. Tonight! - His death must come to reek havoc! And, in the wake of that chaos, you will build your empire!"

"But what of their Prophets, Mother?" Zwide inquired, tensely. "They spoke of another sovereign."

"The fatuous dreams of Those Who Inhabit the Mountains," the Witch hissed, her thin lips wrenching in a scowl of contempt. "Our power is greater! We possess the Spirit of the Underworld!"

The eyes of the Mistress of Dlovunga were suddenly set alight with violent and causeless excitement, the glimmer of a malicious and abominable thought, and when she spoke, her jaundiced orbs seemed to spy the vacant orbs of Sitayi, as Ntombazi expelled with a putrid breath: "She knows that! She cannot stand in our way!"

CHAPTER XXVI
"DINGISWAYO"(THE WANDERER)

Through the jagged aperture in the dome of clouds, the light of a few stars fell upon the disconcerting black sea of brooding Evil that was Dlovunga, - as its Mistress, Ntombazi, the Mother of Horror, hobbled through the Citadel carrying a flaming torch and a soiled cowhide bag clutched in her arthritic hand. The creature made her way past the grim inhabitants of the rocky fortress who were going about the chores that preceded their retirement for the day, past the goats, sheep and poultry that were being led back to their thatched pens and coops, past the idle herds of cattle that ambled lazily up the inclines towards their stalls, and along the narrow roads which skirted the slanting cliffs of the immense acropolis.

Reaching the outskirts of a more uninhabited area of the kingdom, Ntombazi quickened her shambling gait, moving with mounting anticipation towards the gaping entrance to Dlovunga's vast labyrinth of caves manned day and night by armed Ndwandwe warriors who now saluted their Queen as her foul features tottered past the men and were immediately engulfed in the darkness of a descending passage leading into the earth's viscera, the light of her torch retreating and vanishing in the darkness like the last dying star on a firmament of hopelessness.

With a steady, determined step, the old woman made her way deeper and deeper into the bowels of the Underworld, the light of her torch flickering past countless dripstone formations and the huge fossils of colossal reptiles and monsters that once roamed the Earth in the Mezozoic, - deeper and deeper until at length Ntombazi came to the edge of a subterranean stream which entered the course of a small waterfall - both the stream and the fall magically shining with a light of their own, casting a scintillating brilliance of bioluminescence (such as that of phytoplankton) onto the walls and high ceilings of the underground chamber.

Stopping a few paces from the silvery watercourse, the Witch knelt by the stream and her leathery fingers curled round a large quartzite stone. Lifting the stone with relative ease, she rolled it aside and her features took on a ghastly expression of pure delight as she set her glittering yellow-orbed eyes on the hollow left by the quartzite stone where a nest of white scorpions lay exposed in a wash of phosphorescent light.

Frightened by the sudden exposure to the light, the terrifying white insects snapped at the air with their claw like pincers, their venomous tails curled forward, ready to strike. This outer ring of combative arthropods seemed to be guarding the large female scorpion that was nestled in the centre of the nest, the eggs of its young still clinging to its back.

Leaning her torch against a stone, Ntombazi clutched the end of the cowhide bag so that it stood open and reached out, her bare hand hovering over the nest. Then, with a swift, precise movement, the Witch snatched up the female and flung it into the bag. As she did so, one of the other creatures succeeded in stinging her, yet, unflinching, the woman brought the offended hand to her thin lips and sucked out the venom, spitting it back onto the writhing occupants of the nest.

Then, before hobbling off, the old woman brought the sharp blade of a spear to a calcite formation and chipped away at the rock, exposing the petrified skeleton of a bat. Easing the fragile, prehistoric bones out of their stone encasement, Ntombazi gingerly slipped them into the bag together with the scorpion. Rising with a satisfied smile, the wretched female struck back in the direction from when she had come.

A short while later, in the confines of the vaulting cavern that was her dwelling, Ntombazi began to unfold the Evil to which she had forfeited her soul. Squatting near a healthy fire, the woman boiled a dark liquid in a small vat. Into this concoction, she dropped the scorpion and watched, cackling merrily, as the insect tensed upon contact with the scalding liquid, its outer shell sizzling loudly, the eggs bursting open in tiny slimy explosions.

Ntombazi then stirred the potion, sprinkling over it the whitish powder derived from the crushed bat skeletons. Finally, she transferred a few spoonfuls of the steaming broth to a small bowl and -- drank.

* * *

As the stars shone over the peaceful realm of the good King Dingiswayo of the Mtetwas, the cheerful inhabitants of the Royal Homestead were also preparing to retire for the night as campfires filtered through the thatched huts and women prepared the evening repast.

As was customary for such a powerful king as Dingiswayo, a platoon of armed guards positioned itself at the gates of his homestead and around the perimeter of the palisades to watch over and protect their sovereign's slumber.

A young maiden carrying bowls of food and sorghum for the king's dinner made her way past the residence's entrance, past the soldiers on duty - who smiled at her in recognition - and to the large hut reserved as Dingiswayo's sleeping quarters. Upon slipping her shapely frame inside the hut's small doorframe, the maiden bowed her head and waited to be admitted further.

The king was alone. He looked more tired on this particular night, more pensive than usual, older than his years as he looked up and smiled at the lovely maiden.

"Sakubona, iNgane - come closer, my child," Dingiswayo beckoned her.

"Ngiyabonga, Baba," the girl answered, rising, nearing the king and humbly proferring the evening meal.

The king glanced at the food and nodded his acceptance, prompting the maiden to rest the bowls on the mat before him and proceed to wash his hand, pouring over them a thin rivulet of clear water.

Suddenly Dingiswayo's eyes shot open in a disbelief that turned to horror. The blood verily froze in his veins as he witnessed, gaping, that the girl's hands holding the bowl began to undergo a transformation, changing from the smooth, pale freshness of youth to the parched, calloused cragginess of advanced senility. Then, ever so slowly, the Mtetwa monarch shifted his terrified, incredulous gaze to meet the horrendous face of his supernatural visitor.

At dawn, another maiden knelt at the threshold, her head bowed, waiting to be admitted with the king's breakfast.

After a long pause, the girl frowned wondering why her monarch had not yet spoken. Perhaps he still slept, she mused, and raised her head to see and, when she had, a bloodcurdling scream issued from her lips, an anguished cry that swept across the homestead with the numbing gelidness of sheer abhorrence.

Simultaneously, as the sun warmed the Ndwandwe Citadel, Ntombazi lifted her odious face to smile at the blood-drenched head of Dingiswayo as she fastened it to the gruesome post in the Grand Hall of the Council in a privileged position, - the head - still frozen in a look of pure consternation - being placed high above the heads of the other, lesser kings.

"What will your people do now, Dingiswayo?" she screeched, addressing the appalling skull. "How will their minds explain that which the Mind cannot grasp?"

Ntombazi shot a look at her son who was leering beside her.

"Send a messenger to the Mtetwas," she ordered. "We march against them on the next full moon!"

* * *

"The Ndwandwe," Mzilikazi said dryly, bitterly, thinking of the death of his own father. "Queen Ntombazi."

The Kumalo was in the Mtetwa Royal Hut, together with Shaka and Ngomane, all three men glaring at the decapitated body of Dingiswayo wrapped in a cowhide blanket, - the traditional sitting position in which the corpse had been placed making the deceased sovereign look all the more macabre.

Shaka's heart had been fulgurated by the death of his mentor, his friend, his king, and he found himself voiceless as he neared the body and gently placed the leopard skin over the headless chest as if to bestow peace upon the gaping hole in his torso that seemed to thrust directly into the man's soul, exposing it.

The famous leopard skin: - Shaka's mind raced with the thought. Wanderer to Wanderer, King to King, Death to... The Zulu forced himself to repeat, in his heart, the eerie words pronounced by the Nameless One. "Life from Life, Death to Death. Such is the Way of the Blade."

Shaka's eyes shot to the Ixwa in his hand and, for an instant, for a fleeting instant, the Zulu had the disturbing sensation that he himself, with his own Blade, had dealt his friend the fatal blow. Yet, what had Mzilikazi just said the real cause was? The Ndwandwes? Queen Ntombazi. Yes, it was an explanation, Shaka considered. A logical one perhaps. Yet this rational explanation of the fantastic made it only more mysterious and weird. There was something devilish about it. Dingiswayo's death, and the manner in which it was executed was one of those experiences that throw a man out of conformity with the established order of his kind and make him a being of obscure suggestiexperiences thatulu was far from being a creature of obscure suggestion!

"How?!" he roared, his eyes flashing to Mzilikazi and Ngomane.

"A mystery, Shaka," Ngomane replied. "As usual guards were posted at the gates of the homestead, around its perimeter, and at the entrance to the king's hut. I have personally questioned the men and they swear that no one was anywhere near the king last night - no one except his private maid servant, and I don't think a woman could have the strength to inflict such an injury."

"The guards are lying," Shaka snapped back. "To cover up for their incompetence!"

"I seriously doubt that, Shaka," the induna's voice remained surprisingly steady. "They're your men. You trained them. No one could have slipped past them unnoticed."

"What are you saying, Ngomane?" Shaka's rage was laced with sarcasm. "That it didn't happen?!"

"I'm merely suggesting that the way it happened may have had nothing to do with human error."

The Zulu King had absolutely no intention of even entertaining the idea that it might have been witchcraft. That sort of Superstition was as foreign to him as begging for mercy.

"Nonsense!" he told Ngomane, as they left the hut and strode across the funereal atmosphere that had invaded the homestead's inhabitants.

"What we think is of little importance, Shaka," Ngomane remarked, gazing at the populace. "All that matters now is what they think?"

Shaka also cast a deliberate sidelong glance at the Mtetwas, his lips remaining pursed with rage.

"Especially our troops," the induna emphasized.

"And what has their reaction been?" Shaka asked through clenched teeth.

"They feel that whoever had the power to kill Dingiswayo right under the noses of our best guards, has the power to put a curse on all our armies."

"Ignorance!" Shaka hissed.

"Or - Fear of the Unknown."

The two men's eyes locked.

"Isn't that what you called it, Shaka? Well, fear is a powerful weapon. Often double-edged. It can undoubtedly be turned against you. Like in this case."

Oddly enough, a cunning smile suddenly came to grace Shaka's features.

"Then we shall have to temporarily cure that fear, won't we, Ngomane. With the best antidote of all: - Man's faith in himself!"

*

"Most of you know what 'Sigidi' stands for: - One who fights like a thousand." Shaka was standing high atop of a hillock addressing his entire army assembled in the immense valley near the Umfolozi River (the army now consisting of the five original regiments with over 1000 men each and the newly acquired Qwabe troops). Dressed in his royal vestments and fatuous regalia, his ivory tassels gently jingling in the wind, the Son of Zulu was a most impressive sight as he roared to the men, his commanding voice easily carrying to all ears.

"I have acquired that praise name, yet I must admit I don't deserve it."

Mgobozi and Nqoboka exchanged a puzzled frown.

"Not alone, that is," Shaka was quick to adjoin. "By right that title belongs to each of the members of a very special brigade formed almost eight years ago. "Shaka's Fifty", it was called."

Joko caught Mtonga's eye and winked proudly.

"When that brigade was first created," the Zulu filled the valley with his voice, "people laughed at us because we were doing things differently, using methods contrary to the so-called tradition of warfare. They laughed at us because we were going against the flow of accepted norms."

Kuta and Ngomane listened intently, well remembering their meeting with Buza and Dingiswayo.

"Yet those fifty men became the most formidable fighting unit ever known! Today heroes like Joko, Nqoboka, Dlaba, Mtonga -- and especially Mgobozi have become legends in the songs and tales of distant tribes."

Mgobozi looked down, blushing slightly as Nqoboka gave him a friendly swat on the back.

"Today these men are the pillars of what has become the strongest army in this land. And why? - Because they had the courage to be different! They discovered eight years ago that a man who thinks for himself and who believes in himself has the power to change the course of history. To mould History to his own Purpose!"

Ngomane's eyes wandered out to the troops and he scanned their captivated expressions, acknowledging with a wry smile that perhaps Shaka's greatest weapon was not his Blade, but his Mouth.

"I ask each and every one of you to make that same discovery in your own heart. Have the courage to be different and you will own the world! Be a 'Sigidi' - not only on the battlefield, but in every instant of your life! Challenge the 'thousands' of antiquated customs, ideals, and Superstitions that threaten your freedom of thought! In other word," his voice was bellowing now, "stand for something or you will fall for anything!"

"SI-GI--DI!" Joko shouted at the top of his voice.

"SI-GI--DI!" The valley echoed to the Heavens.

"King Dingiswayo was more than our overlord," Shaka went on when the men had returned to silence, "he was a father to us all. His death has left us with a sense of deep sadness and helpless rage. - Many of us now feel confused, adrift without clear directives! That is to be expected when a Nation like ours is suddenly deprived of a man of his greatness. Yet, in the name of that man, we must stay united as a fighting force! In fact, I say that out purpose, our directives are clearer than ever!" Shaka paused for an instant before pronouncing with deliberate vehemence, "We must avenge his death! Wipe the Ndwandwes from the face of the earth!"

Again, the roar "SI-GI-DI" overwhelmed the banks of the Umfolozi with the thunderous stomping of thousands of feet.

"Zwide would like us to believe that witchcraft was involved in Dingiswayo's assassination," the Zulu king commented when stillness had returned. "Again, an example of how some would want us shackled to accepted norms, willing to fall for anything! Yet the truth lies elsewhere!" Shaka started down the cliff, continuing to address his men as he drew nearer to them. "Our beloved paramount king met his death through treachery, not witchcraft!"

Ngomane's gaze narrowed with intrigue. "His royal guards and maid servant have confessed to their betrayal, and for that crime, the greatest of all crimes, they will suffer the most grave punishment we can inflict - impalement!"

Ngomane's face hardened. So Shaka had found the scapegoats, the induna reflected. He had found some one to exorcise the "curse" with human blood.

Indeed, a detachment of Ufasimba warriors soon appeared and led the "criminals' (the lovely maid servant and the two guards who had been posted outside the king's hut) to three sharpened posts projecting upright out of the ground. And, as the troops looked on, spellbound and horror-struck, the Ufasimba lifted the guards and the pitifully whimpering young girl over the sharpened posts and thrust downwards, pulling forcibly on the arms until the victims' anguished cries faded to silence, as their blood and entrails showered upon the grass, staining it a deep purple.

Complete silence ensued. The glorious smile momentarily faded from Mgobozi's full lips as the man lowered his gaze, paling with revulsion.

"Their bodies," Shaka concluded, "or what the buzzards will have left of them, will hang there even after death as a testimony to all of what awaits those who betray the nation." His voice suddenly became stern. "Now return to your training and let there be no more talk of witchcraft!"

"You never cease to amaze me, Shaka," Ngomane told the Zulu as he later stood at his side, both men watching the troops exercising in the Method. "I often wonder how much of what you say is born of genuine conviction."

"I'm a soldier, Ngomane," an almost imperceptible smile was tugging on Shaka's lips, " not a statesman. What I say is always influenced by a soldier's will to win."

"I'm sure that after today no one doubts who the next leader of the Mtetwa Paramountcy will be."

"I never asked for that." The Zulu's response came stiffly.

"You never have to ask, Shaka. Things just seem to fall naturally into place for you. Zulus, Qwabes, Mtetwas, and soon the Ndwandwes. - One vast empire. One mighty sovereign. In your own way, you're making Dingiswayo's dream come true! - The Nguni Bantu Nation!"

"No, Ngomane. The Zulu Nation!" The glowing intensity in Shaka's eyes underlined the fervour that blazed in his heart. "Zulu! - That will be the common identity! - My people will forget they were ever anything else!"

Zulu!

Thundering, the Language of the Heavens had spoken.

CHAPTER XXVII
"SAKUBONA"(I SEE YOU)
THE BATTLE OF QOKLI HILL

"We must lead them to believe what we want them to believe! Overwhelm them with the unexpected! That's the only way to make a bid for victory."

The morning air was still crisp, and the sun was rising behind the woodlands causing the contours of the tree-tops to be outlined by a thread of gold that gradually took on textures of light blue and green as the globe of heavenly light detached itself from the horizon and became one with the sky.

As was his custom when he wished to share secret designs and plans with his closest associates and most trusted generals and regimental commanders, Shaka had summoned Mgobozi, Nqoboka, Joko, Dlaba, Mtonga, Kuta and Ngomane (who had recently become Shaka's Chief Induna - his Prime Minister, so to say) to the high, flat stretches of amber and saffron that distinguished the impressive emTonjaneni Heights where, strolling in the brisk freshness of Nature, the Zulu felt free to divulge his stratagems confident that no foreign ears could hear his words, save for those of the Prophets and the Ancestors. On this particular morning, the one in which he had promised to disclose the strategy of the imminent and quite momentous conflict with the Ndwandwes of Zwide, Shaka had also requested the presence of Mzilikazi - a man whom he had instinctively grown to trust in the short period in which he had known him. There was great anticipation in the hearts of those present as they listened intently to the words of their commander (and, now, king) as he discussed the war they knew was to be Shaka's most significant. Indeed, as Ngomane had stated, winning against the Ndwandwes would be the fulfilment of Dingiswayo's dream - the great dream the Zulu himself had espoused. "Like at eNtuzuma," Shaka was saying as he strode across the plateau, "we now need the 'unexpected' to achieve victory - especially since our army is so outnumbered. In fact, even with our new Qwabe recruits, we still have only 9000 troops. That's nine against twenty-five!"

"We've won against greater odds," Mgobozi commented with his usual, somewhat reckless confidence.

"Yes, Mgobozi," Shaka smiled, resting an amicable hand on his general's shoulder, "but in those days my Method was still new and the enemy could easily be caught off guard. In this war, the Ndwandwes will be anticipating our past tactics, so we'll have to give them something new. Something they won't be expecting!" Shaka had a playful twinkle in his eye as he added, almost in passing: "That's why I've decided that Zwide's forces will face only half our troops."

The men stopped dead in their tracks, shocked by the Zulu's amazing revelation, and they all peered at Shaka inquisitively, hoping that he hadn't inadvertently lost his mind, praying that his words were uttered in jest.

"That's unexpected, all right," Mtonga remarked phlegmatically.

"With all due respect, Shaka," Ngomane proffered, "you cannot be serious!"

"I've never been more serious, Ngomane," was the reply.

"Then you'd better explain," suggested Kuta with mounting leeriness.

"It's all a matter of making Reality appear to suit the needs of your enemy's Fantasy," Shaka expounded with a general skittish air of innocent frolic that dashed his officers into an even greater state of sheer bewilderment. Taking note of their perplexity, the Zulu chose to clarify: "Think of what's happened so far and try to see it from the Ndwandwes' point of view. Zwide obviously thought that Dingiswayo's extraordinary death would cause our troops to panic, and, indeed, it almost did! So now we must lead him to think that his plan was successful!"

Shaka's captivated audience was still shrouded in a numbing mantle of befuddlement. Kuta shot quick glances at his companions to see if their understanding was any greater than his own, then, confident that the incomprehension was collective, he inquired of the Zulu: "How?"

"A messenger has arrived from Dlovunga with a declaration of war," Shaka said in slow, clear tones, "Zwide is meant to march against us on the next full moon. Before that messenger leaves our kingdom, he will be made privy to information which he will think is highly confidential."

"What sort of information?" Ngomane asked, starting to see some light in the obscure affair.

"The messenger will be led to think that our situation is desperate!" Shaka was starting to forcefully drive home his point. "He will hear that after the unexplained murder of our king, fearing the supernatural powers of Ntombazi and the Ndwandwes, over 4000 of our warriors fled - in panic - leaving us with a little more than half our armies in active service."

As understanding started to creep over Mzilikazi's features, his eyes grew suspicious.

"What makes you think Zwide will believe that, Shaka?" the Kumalo prince questioned.

"Because he wants to! - That's where the Reality and Fantasy come in," Shaka smiled. "The easiest thing in the world is to convince some one that he's right. It was Zwide's own plan, Mzilikazi, he wanted Dingiswayo's death to bring panic to our ranks and now I'm sure he wants to believe his plan worked. It's human nature!" "But where will the 4000 men really be?" Mgobozi was groping for clarity.

"With us, of course," Shaka replied somewhat carelessly. "But the Ndwandwes won't see them until it's too late!"

"Four thousand invisible men," Joko murmured raising a brow. "Talk about 'supernatural'!"

"Not invisible, Joko," Shaka was quick to correct. "Just hidden!"

"Where are you going to hide 4000 men?" Kuta queried, more confused than ever now.

"On the top of Qokli Hill."

Qokli Hill was a most peculiar geographical formation located approximately three kilometres from the wide banks of the Umfolozi River, part way between the Mtetwa Paramountcy and the Ndwandwe Confederacy. The hill was almost completely circular at its base, rising to an altitude of about 400 meters. What made Qokli ideal for Shaka's purposes, however, was that its top was shaped like a hollowed out cone (much like the summit of an extinct volcano) that formed a large concave basin surrounded by thick vegetation and high rock formations.

As the following afternoon the Zulu King led his commanders for an inspection of the hill's exceptional terrain, especially its crater-like summit, he shed more light on his "hidden troops" strategy.

"Our full fighting force will form two concentrical circles," he told the men as he strode round the edge of Qokli's basin. "An inner circle comprised of the troops which have supposedly abandoned us in a state of frightful panic - the troops which Zwide will not know about at the beginning of the conflict. In fact, this massive reserve unit of 4000 men will remain out of sight until we need them, silently hidden in the concave basin at the Hill's summit along with a generous supply of water, food and medication. As I've said, this inner circle will be virtually 'invisible' to the Ndwandwe Armies in the valley below who, I'm sure, are not even aware that Qokli has such a convenient crater.

"And the second circle?" Kuta asked.

"That will be the outer belt," Shaka continued the disclosure of his unique plan. "The circle of our remaining 5000 men who will be positioned on the hill itself, quite visible to all as our official fighting force."

Mzilikazi's stony uncertainty did not break down before Shaka's confident air.

"What about the third circle," the Kumalo mentioned sceptically. "The circle of Zwide's troops in the valley. We'll be surrounded, Shaka. It's suicidal!"

At Mzilikazi's remark, the other men had a moment of slight hesitation, of startled pause as their eyes shifted expectantly to Shaka. Once again, the Zulu's cool, mildly sportive manner elicited a few worried frowns.

"Yes, Mzilikazi. Suicidal!," he tone was almost triumphant. "That's exactly what I want the Ndwandwes to think...that our strategy is suicidal. In fact, most of what we do in this war will appear to be a mistake!" He grinned. "Their generals will think Shaka has lost his mind."

Kuta, who had had the same lurking suspicion since the outset of the strategy meetings, grumbled in a low voice: "If I didn't know you better, Shaka, I would be inclined to share that opinion.'

As further confirmation of the Zulu's excellent, exhilarated mood, he threw his head back and laughed very heartily, a high, ringing peal of laughter that left the commanders of his troops gaping in wonder.

*

Amongst the dozens upon dozens of innovations and ameliorations that Shaka bequeathed to the People of the Heavens, one of the most significant - from an educational point of view - was to create the institution of the "uDibi Boys".

According to this new practice, arrived at the age of 14 6, the former herd boy blossomed into an uDibi (a carrier-boy), that is to say he was now deemed big and strong enough to carry the baggage of his father, his friends and, above all, the baggage of the Zulu armies when they travelled on their endless campaigns. The peculiar privilege of this new status was the delight of seeing a bigger world, the world of warfare, and the great honour of accompanying Shaka's valiant soldiers on their distant journeying and perhaps the remarkable opportunity of being able to glimpse the Great Sigidi himself in the midst of combat.

The baggage carried by the boys was, of course, the soldiers' bare necessities (they never travelled with more): their karosses (which the boys carried upon their heads), the soldier's wooden pillow and sleeping mat (all rolled up together in a cylindrical bundle), their food-stuffs, sundry personal belongings, and the soldier's water supply. Though this might appear to have been a considerable load for such young lads, one must remember that the actual fighting of wars was a very strenuous task and the soldiers themselves (in Shakan times) were under strict orders to save all their energy for the actual battle. Thus, the men themselves were ordered to tote only their own weapons and shields, leaving the uDibi to build muscle and character by struggling under the greater weight of the other supplies.

Nor did the lads ever complain. Indeed, elevation to this high rank was an epic-making event in a boy's life inasmuch as it meant final withdrawal from the herd-boys and the first conscious realisation of budding manhood, the commencement of a public career, so to say. - It was the first big step towards a boy's dream: his installation in a regimental homestead and the beginning of his military life.

And it was over the next few hectic days following Shaka's unique strategic meetings that the uDibi Boys were kept quite busy trekking back and forth to Qokli with huge gourds and clay vats filled with food and copious calabashes spilling with water drawn from the currents of the nearby Umfolozi, along with medication and other supplies until the hill's crater-like basin was virtually crammed with enough "hidden" provisions to keep an army going for days on end.

For the next week, the boys worked diligently and quickly, day and night, to make absolutely sure all was in readiness well before the next full moon: - the deadline announced by Zwide, -- while the Zulu generals, under Shaka's ever-present directive, canvassed the hill, committing to memory its terrain, its vantage points, its covers, its densely packed vegetation, its staggered clearings and the like, grooming and preparing both their men and the hill itself for the upcoming conflict.

On one such day, Shaka was perched high atop of Qokli's only rocky ledge, the Zulu's eyes scanning the wide valley that stretched from the distant Umfolozi to the hill itself, the valley that would soon be swarming with Ndwandwe troops.

"Surrounded". Mzilikazi's comment burned in Shaka's mind with the deep preoccupation he had hidden from his commanders under a disarmingly playful air of confidence. Yet, deep in his heart, Shaka knew that, though his strategy was valid (no, - more than valid, it was genial), nothing in life was entirely infallible, especially when the human factor was predominant. Nothing except ---

Looking up, Shaka's eyes were lost in the deep blue immensity of the sky, the greatness, the imponderable greatness of the Heavens, and he wondered, deep in his soul, if the seed of infallibility was present in prophecy and if what the Ancestors had ordained would come to be - no matter what mortal Man might do to impede or promote its effectuation. And the mere chance that it might be so gave even a staunch pragmatist like

Shaka a sort of comfort, as though his soul had become suddenly reconciled to an eternity of blind Victory and Triumph.

"In me is the Spirit of the People of the Heavens," the Cobra had told Shaka the young boy. "I speak with the voices of Malandela, Zulu, Punga, Mageba, and Ndaba. This day thou art my Son and I thy Father. Ask and I shall give thee the nations for thy heritage, the end of the earth for thy domain..." - "Was that infallible?" Shaka now asked his heart and wondered whether the ultimate outcome of the Battle of Qokli Hill was already predestined.

And the words spoken to his mother so long ago came relentlessly back to mind: -- "When, mother? When will it happen?!"

Was it meant to happen now?

One Nation! Now? --

And Shaka remembered that dawn - that magical dawn after the Forging of the Spear at UmZizima, when he had been transported to the Pinnacle of Kings for the Consecration of the Blade.

What had Sitayi told him? - "Those Who Inhabit the Underworld! Defeat them, my Child and the Cycle shall be closed round its Emperor. Defeat them - destroy them and the Age of Fear will be accomplished."

Defeat them at Qokli!

Abandoning himself to the influence of words pronounced to him so long ago, Shaka now searched the blueness of the Sky, his gaze straining after a sign of his destiny, and he spotted, above the orderly work of his troops and the uDibi, a restless myriad of birds rolling and unrolling like dark ribbons across the firmament, then gathering in clouds, soaring and stooping in an ordinate play of shadows.

In the flight of those birds, Shaka read the fluctuating reality that is Life, now swooping, now soaring, and, with a sudden sense of weariness, he conceived that even if Victory should favour him at Qokli, the battle in his heart would rage on and on - until Victory itself would become his greatest defeat.

And he listened to the Wind for the sounds of war and the voices of combat and tried to hear his own voice shouting "Ngadla!" - when another sound, gentle, youthful, pleasant was heard at his shoulders.

"Are you trying to imagine it?" Ngwadi asked, padding closer to his brother.

Shaka turned to look at the illustrious uDibi Boy (indeed being Shaka's brother would make even the most unpretentious uDibi illustrious), and the Zulu gazed at him marvelling whether the young boy had read his mind.

"The 25,000 troops," Ngwadi explained, handing Shaka a bowl of water from which the man drank thirstily. "Are you trying to imagine what they'll look like?"

The Zulu King smiled, casting his gaze back out to the expanse of valley that unfurled at Qokli's foot.

"No, Ngwadi. It would be useless. I don't think I can conceive what 25,000 of anything looks like."

"Is Zwide coming?" the youth asked, his eyes lighting up at the prospect of seeing the infamous villain of Dlovunga.

"No. My scouts tell me that only Soshangane and Zwide's son Nomahlanjana are marching with his armies."

"But shouldn't a good king always be with his troops?" Ngwadi knitted his brow.

"Yes," Shaka answered, barely realising that he, himself was always with his men. "A good king should."

"I know why he's not coming," the boy grinned.

"Why?" Shaka asked, playing along.

"Because he's afraid to die."

The Zulu king rested a hand on his brother's shoulder and nodded, his expression becoming more serious.

"We're not afraid to die, are we, Shaka?" The uDibi asked with an innocence that left his brother somewhat shaken.

"No, Ngwadi," he replied, his voice slightly choked with emotion as his thoughts wandered back to the time, after their departure from Gendeyana, when his brother had asked him where the breath of Life goes after it leaves the dying.

"No, my brother," he repeated. "We're not afraid to die."

*

The Ndwandwe Army arrived within sight of Qokli by the first full moon and proceeded to ford the low waters of the Umfolozi on their march towards the hill.

And Shaka was ready for the enemy: the basin was fully stocked with supplies of food, water and medication (under the supervision of the carrier-boys who would also act as "waiters" and nurses if need be); the 4000 "secret" reserve units were silently huddled in the crater, well out of sight, their ixwas clutched in expectant hands, their hearts ready to engage in battle as soon as word was given; and the official troops (5000 in all) manning the rounded shoulders of the hill itself, all squatted in silent formation, weapons ready for Shaka's call to war.

The generals were gathered round their commander and king for a final briefing before the next day's combat. In due course, Shaka announced that Joko, Dlaba, Mtonga, and Nqoboka would be in charge of the 5000 regular troops, whilst Kuta and Mgobozi would command the hidden reserves.

Mgobozi was greatly disturbed by this decision inasmuch as he would be forced to remain "squatting in anticipation" throughout perhaps most of the combat - a prospect that left the brave warrior distressed to no end. And even Shaka's reminder that his friend's was indeed a command of great responsibility (the reserve units being the key to the entire conflict), did little to console the stocky general as he trudged into the basin to join his men.

At Shaka's bidding, Mzilikazi was the last to leave the rocky ledge where the generals had met. When the two men were alone, the Kumalo's gaze remained fixed on the approaching Ndwandwe troops.

"Do you think they'll try to reach the hill before dark?" he asked Shaka.

"No. They'll probably camp on this side of the Umfolozi and make their move at daybreak." Shaka turned to face the man. "More or less when you'll make your move."

The Kumalo cast Shaka an inquisitive frown.

"I'm putting you in command of 2000 of my frontline troops," the king explained, his expression betraying no emotion.

"A command?!" Mzilikazi was stunned by the offer. "You hardly know me!"

"I know all I need to know, Mzilikazi."

"Thank you for your trust, Shaka - but," the man was still shaken, "I'd like to know what you expect of me before I accept."

"You mean you might refuse this honour?" The king asked, smiling.

"Does that surprise you?" Mzilikazi smiled back.

"No. It merely confirms that my judgment is correct. You're prudent. That's a very important attribute in a commander." His face ironed out as he started to expound: "At daybreak I want you to lead your troops away from the hill, across the eTonjaneni Heights, then cut back and rejoin the rest of the army by sunset."

Mzilikazi's surprise was more than evident.

"What?! - You're outnumbered as it is, Shaka! Tomorrow you'll need every available man! What could you possible gain by sending two thousand precious men on a wild goose chase."

"You've just answered your own question," was Shaka's response, filling the Kumalo with mute wonder. "It will be a wild goose chase - for the Ndwandwe detachment that is sent to follow you. I want you to lead that detachment around in circles. Keep it away from Qokli until the sun sets!"

The Kumalo's searching gaze was on Shaka: "Is this one of those 'Shaka's-lost-his-mind' mistakes you were talking about?"

"Yes."

"Very well," Mzilikazi nodded, not nearly convinced. "I trust you know what you're doing. - I can only hope that this mistake of yours doesn't prove to be real."

*

Prince Nomahlanjana kaZwide Ndwandwe, the representative of his father on the field of battle, was hysterical by nature, sickly, thin, short, and with wrists like a boy of ten. Yet from that debile body (barely twenty years old), there issued a bullying voice with a resonance that belied his build.

"What is your report?!" Nomahlanjana's voice inquired of one of the Ndwandwe scouts who had just returned from a closer inspection of Qokli.

"It is as you anticipated, Ndabezitha. The hill is thinly held. Five regiments - four to five thousand men.

It was the crack of dawn and Nomahlanjana's yellowed teeth sparkled with the redness of the sun as he smiled at the distant form of Qokli.

"Food and water?" the prince asked the scout.

"Very little. It'll be a miracle, in fact, if they last the heat of one day's combat.

Zwide's son cast a glance at the heavenly globe and his smile broadened. Its throbbing golden rays did, indeed, herald the advent of scorching heat.

"So that is the strategy of the Great Shaka?" the Ndwandwe hissed with careless disregard. "A handful of men perched on a hill, fenced in like so many goats!" With a scowl, he added: "It'll be like slaughtering cattle in a stockade!"

"I don't understand it," Soshangane commented as he neared the prince, his eyes also trained on the hill. "This is not Shaka's way."

"There's nothing to understand, commander," Nomahlanjana's temerity swelled. "The facts speak for themselves! It's obvious that deprived of Dingiswayo's guidance, Shaka has gone astray. - And tomorrow his head will join those of worthier kings! - We march when the sun is there!" the tiny man roared, indicating with his knobkerrie a point in the sky a few degrees above the horizon.

The prince then spun round on his heels and marched off to join his pudgy brothers in the shade of a mimosa. He was disgusted! He'd expected a real battle, a real threat - not this!

An hour later, Nomahlanjana's anger grew to baffled incredulity as he stood, gaping, while Mzilikazi led two thousand men away from the hill, trotting off at a steady pace in the direction of the eTonjaneni Heights.

"Idiotic! - I've never seen such military incompetence! This man is highly, highly overrated! Why the last thing a commander in his inferior position should do is divide his troops! He's leaving the hill practically defenceless!"

An uneasy premonition of disaster oppressed Soshangane as he viewed Mzilikazi's odd manoeuvre.

"I wonder," the commander said under his breath. "Those two regiments could be a decoy. By dividing his troops, he's encouraging us to split ours as well - creating two fronts." Soshangane's face suddenly clouded over with resolve as he turned to inform his prince: "It is a trap, Ndabezitha!"

"A trap?!" Nomahlanjana's small head twisted round on his threadlike neck and his beady eyes rested on his commander with brows raised in astonishment. "Nonsense!" Then his tone grew coldly formal. "Follow them, Soshangane. Take a third of our troops with you!"

"Do you think that's wise, Ndabezitha?" the commander inquired of the man, trying to remain calm though all his military instinct railed against the prince's decision. "Shouldn't we rather take the hill first and then follow the other troops?"

Nomahlanjana was annoyed and his pursed lips showed as much.

"There are only three thousand men left on that hill, commander. Employing all 25,000 of our troops to defeat them would be an insult to our military pride!" His tone became scoffing. "I trust that 16,000 against three should suffice." The harshness returned. "Now do as I say!"

Soshangane did. - And it marked the End, and Shaka knew it as he watched in contemptuous amusement as Soshangane's detachment of over 8000 men separated from the rest of the Ndwandwe Forces and headed off, chasing Mzilikazi's decoy.

Within half an hour, the remaining Ndwandwe troops had surrounded Qokli Hill and stood milling about, chatting, joking, and waiting with impatience and overconfidence for the battle to begin, -- whilst on the hill itself, round its rim, Shaka's disciplined front liners (as well as the secreted reserves) sat on their haunches, ixwas ready, in attitudes of full alert, and in perfect stillness and silence.

Nomahlanjana was scowling as he rested against the bark of the mimosa tree, casually sipping beer whilst, with great smugness, he shared his thoughts with his brothers and his generals.

"Since they have little water and food, time is on our side. We can afford to draw out the conflict. They cannot. And since we outnumber them five to one, we can afford to have casualties. They cannot. -- In fact most aspects of this battle work to our favour."

Getting to his feet, the Ndwandwe wiped the froth of white sorghum from his mouth in a gesture of finality.

"We will send up three groups of 5000 men each," he ordered. "One now. One at noon - when the sun is the hottest - and one at sunset." As a smile danced across his lips, he added: "I trust sending the last group won't be necessary."

As ordered, the first 5000 Ndwandwe warriors marched half-way up the hill and, stopping, began to hurl abuses at Shaka's soldiers (as was still very much the norm in Ndwandwe warfare), inciting them to engage in conflict. Of course the Zulu's brave troops remained silent, immobile, unmoving in their places on the rim of the hill. Their confidence strengthened by this lack of response on the part of their "cowardly" opponents, the Ndwandwes moved up closer to the enemy, shouting louder now, as their generals gave the order to hurl the first spears.

When the shower of darts rained onto Shaka's front line troops, unwaveringly and in silence the men raised their large shields and easily parried the barrage. Seconds later, groups of uDibi boys scampered out of the protective basin and quickly gathered up the 'discarded' assegais, collecting them in piles round the hill's summit.

Somewhat astonished by this odd tactic, the Ndwandwe commanders ordered another barrage of spears and, again, Shaka's men unflinchingly lifted their shields, creating a solid buffer with which the assegais were easily deflected and, once again, the carrier-boys hurriedly scooped up the darts and hustled them back to the basin.

Exasperated by the enemy's reluctance to engage in combat, the Ndwandwes moved even closer to Shaka's men and prepared to hurl their last remaining spear (regulation, in fact, was three). In that instant, Shaka's voice roared from the hill's rocky ledge and was heard as far as the Umfolozi.

"Ayi!! Hlome!!" yelled the Son of Zulu. "Attack!" came his bloodcurdling cry to arms.

As a response to the command, with an incredible precision of movement, Shaka's 3000 warriors stood up as one man and, with perfect timing, split into four concentrical lines (with five paces between each row). Then, once again in perfect symmetry and in unison, the men executed their war salute: - the stamping of 3000 feet, followed by the deafening crash of ixwa against shield!

Overwhelmed by this thundering proclamation of war, unnerved by the disciplined precision of this ominous enemy, the Ndwandwes faltered, -- as Shaka's army began to roll forward and down the hill like an avalanche, closing with the enemy. The Ndwandwes were by no means weaklings and cowards, yet their strength and valour was no match for the superhuman determination of Qokli's defenders as they blazed through the Method - decimating their opponents.

Contact! Lock shields! Pull back and away! Aim for the heart! -- "Ngadla!"

In exquisite frustration, the reserve units under Mgobozi and Kuta sat in their crater feeling cheated as they listened to the battle raging nearby, -- whilst Shaka himself strode wildly back and forth, checking the progress of the conflict from all vantage points, satisfied with what he saw.

Contact! Lock shields. Pull back and----

Inadvertently, Mtonga pulled back slightly too late and found an enemy dart waiting for him. The Ndwandwe warrior - whose name and family of origin remain unknown to this day (though Shaka himself later went to great lengths to sift the blood-drenched hill for the body of a man clutching a spear without blade) - rammed his spear into Mtonga's side with such force that the haft broke in two, leaving the assegai's blade lodged in the man's chest, a touch to the left of the trachea, causing the proud member of the original Fifty to slump to the ground, as the bodies heaped round him.

On and on the battle raged, littering the slopes of Qokli with the dead and dying, as Shaka's warriors cut down the enemy that soon found itself without weapons - on and on went the Zulu rampage, without respite for the Ndwandwes, until a frustrated Nomahlanjana was forced to give the order to withdraw.

"Casualties?!" the Ndwandwe prince impatiently snapped to his commanders, adding: "Well?!", when the generals hesitated to respond to the pressing interrogative.

"Most of the first group, Ndabezitha, is still on that hill," was General Sixoloba's sombre reply.

"And what went wrong?!" Nomahlanjana barked.

"Nothing, Ndabezitha," another general said simply. "They're just better, that's all."

Sixoloba and Zwide's other surviving generals exchanged a meaningful glance. Though they had all been thoroughly briefed on Shaka's "Method", none of them had for an instant imagined that it could be so effective in practice, so inexorably accurate, so overbearing! Yes, they were not only better, this Method of theirs seemed inexpugnable!

"Things will be different at noon!" Nomahlanjana's sinister gaze moved to the hill. "They're still fresh now. Lets see how they fight after a few hours of thirst and hunger?"

"How did we do?" Mtonga asked feebly, straining to make out Mgobozi's features through the darkening veil of approaching death.

"As expected," Mgobozi kidded.

Mtonga's smile broadened in spite of a painful convulsion. Ngwadi rested the dying warrior's head on a soft cushion of leaves and brought a bowl of water to his bloodstained lips.

"No, Ngwadi," Mtonga waved away the water. "Save it for the battle." Then, narrowing his eyes, he asked: "Where is Shaka?"

"I am here, Mtonga," came the Zulu's sonorous voice.

Mtonga groped for Shaka's arm through the fog that seemed to envelope him, and, finding it, he gripped the firm muscle and asked, with urgency: "Is it true, Shaka?"

"Is what true, my friend?" Shaka responded, softly.

"That we are all Sigidi! Each of us! - Did you mean what you said?!"

"Yes, Mtonga. I meant it."

The dying warrior leaned back as if a great load had suddenly been eased from his heart and he murmured, almost to himself, smiling seraphically: "Good."

Mgobozi's lips quivered slightly and he bit them, forcing back a wave of emotion, while he watched Mtonga's hand feeling its way down Shaka's arm until it came to rest on the cold Blade of the Ixwa.

"Would you do me the honour, Shaka?" he asked his king, tilting the Blade till its point was over his own chest.

The Son of Zulu hesitated before his eyes locked with those of Mtonga for a fraction of a second. "Death to Death..." came the echo of The Nameless One.

Aim for the heart.

The Heart. Mtonga's burst open with one thrust of the Blade.

"Things will be different at noon," Nomahlanjana had told his generals. Well, regardless of what the prince might have thought, at noon -

as the vultures and buzzards pecked at the decaying flesh that was strewn over Qokli and the nearby valley, and as the sun blazed directly overhead - things on the hill were not much different.

Indeed, if anything, Shaka's troops - having had quite a bit to eat and drink - were fresher than ever and awaited, silently, stoically - ixwas cleaned and gleaming again - for combat to be resumed.

When it was, and the second batch of 5000 Ndwandwe troops marched on Qokli, the turbulent onslaught of the morning was quickly and chillingly repeated.

"SI-GI-DI!" came the boisterous battle cry, accompanied by the human quake of pounding feet and the thunder of ixwas crashed against shields, as Shaka's troops again stormed down on the oncoming Ndwandwes, engaging them in close combat, literally extinguishing row after row of warriors in a systematic massacre, a butchery without precedent, indescribable even by the evanescent Songs of Prowess and Victory that the Prophets sang to the Wind.

Two hours later, after another call to withdraw from the hill, Nomahlanjana's lips were twitching in reaction to the somewhat tragic complexion the battle was assuming. The nervous prince paced back and forth, plying the dusty turf in front of the mimosa, his beady eyes fixed on Qokli with a glint of rage and dismay.

"What keeps them going?!" he asked no one in particular. "They've had hardly any food since yesterday and water -- water! - Well, look at that sun!"

Nomahlanjana's frail arm swished through the arid air until his knobkerrie was pointing directly at the glowing heavenly orb as, his eyes also on fire, he repeated, shouting, "Look at that sun!"

Obediently, the Ndwandwe generals did, though they found little solace in this astronomical perusal - sun or no sun, they were losing the war! "How many men have we left?!" the prince suddenly wanted to know.

"8000, Ndabezitha," Sixoloba replied, adding a grave: "Battleworthy, that is."

"More than enough!" said Zwide's son in a show of laudable optimism. "More than enough to take the hill," he said once again, his voice strained as he wondered whether "more than enough" might be too little.

"A little over 6000, Shaka," Mgobozi told his friend and king. "Counting my reserve units."

"We're almost even!" the Zulu noted, his handsome features beaming with joy.

"Does that mean you're finally going to give me a chance to fight?" Mgobozi asked, his tone venting a portion of his pent-up frustration.

"Yes, Mgobozi," was the reply. "In the next attack, we'll be fighting side by side. - Tell your units to stand by."

As the sun fell low in the sky, and as the time was fast approaching for the third and final prearranged assault of the Ndwandwe Forces, the diminutive Prince of Dlovunga on whose gracile shoulders had been inattentively placed the future of his realm was briefing his generals for what would be the last time - the very last time.

"In this attack I don't want the men to hurl their spears! That's not been effective so far. In fact, it's proven to be a waste of time. Instead, they should use them as stabbing weapons, like that blasted Zulu does! Like this!"

By way of explanation, Nomahlanjana's isthmian fingers closed round a spear, near the metal blade, and he stabbed the air around him wildly.

"And no more shouting insults!" the prince added at the conclusion of his "stabbing" demonstration. "Shaka's men seem to have no ears - or no pride!"

The men "without ears and without pride" were squatting round the summit of Qokli, immobile, waiting, their hearing attuned to the sound of Destiny, their hearts swollen with the pride of imminent Glory.

Upon noticing that the Ndwandwes were moving up the hill without the customary barrage of insults and clutching their spears like daggers, Shaka whispered to Mgobozi, with a touch of sarcasm: "They're learning. A bit late, but they're learning..."

In fact, it was very late to learn.

When the Ndwandwes had advanced to less than eighty paces from Qokli's summit, Shaka nodded to Mgobozi who turned and signalled to Nqoboka who relayed the command to Kuta. Then with a earth-shaking "SI-GI-DI!"- the 4000 reserve troops disgorged from the hidden basin like devils vomited from Hell.

At the sight of the spellbinding apparition of this "supernatural" army that seemed to have been conjured up from thin air, erupting from the crater like molten lava from the bowels of a volcano, the Ndwandwe troops froze in place, jolted into a helpless stupor as the human "lava" surged and gushed down towards them. Those who found the courage and the coordination to resist the advance were drowned in their own blood; those who panicked and, dropping their spears, turned to flee, were soon caught and embraced in the pincers of the "cattle horn" as Shaka's voice resounded throughout the countryside with the staccato ordinances: "Phase One, Phase Two, Phase Three!"

By the time the sun had set leaving the blood-red glow of its rays to mingle with the crimson of Death that mantled the slopes and valleys of Qokli, all the Ndwandwes had fallen - all the soldiers, all the generals, all the commanders, all the sons of Zwide.

And even Nomahlanjana kaZwide Ndwandwe had been devoured by Shaka's troops, the look of utter consternation imprinted on his beady eyes for Eternity.

By the time the sun had set Mzilikazi was obediently returning with his 2000 troops - with which, as instructed, he had literally run the Ndwandwes round in circles, from the Heights of eTonjaneni to the Plains of the umHlatuze, and from the waters of the Umfolozi back to Qokli Hill.

Upon seeing the hundreds of buzzards and vultures circling, swooping, and greedily swarming round the site of the conflict, the Kumalo's heart stood still with the sheer dread that Shaka's plans had, indeed, been the fruit of madness and that his comrades-in-arms had been slaughtered by Zwide's Armies. Then, when the massacre came into view with all its full, horrendous impact, Mzilikazi grimaced in revulsion. Thousands of bodies were spewed on the hill and adjoining grasslands in attitudes of terror and despair, literally floating in a murky quagmire of blood, wallow and human waste.

Yet Mzilikazi's greatest surprise (which was more than shared by his 2000 troops) came upon seeing Shaka and his men flanking the sea of bodies, standing in serried ranks that looked like a restraining dike of human flesh erected against a purulent morass of refuse expelled from the viscera of Hades.

"How far behind are the Ndwandwes?" Shaka asked the Kumalo, yet Mzilikazi did not, could not hear for his pulse was throbbing loudly in his ears as he gaped, mesmerised at the carnage that a mere 6000 men had inflicted on almost three times their number. "Mzilikazi," Shaka spoke the name in an effort to get the attention of its bearer.

"Yes," the Kumalo's staggered gaze found Shaka.

"The Ndwandwes, Mzilikazi. Where are they?"

"Two...three miles back," Mzilikazi answered, trying to regain his composure.

"Give the order to retreat," the Zulu said to his generals, causing Mzilikazi's bafflement to heighten.

Retreat.

Though the order was in truth quite baffling for Mzilikazi, Mgobozi, Nqoboka, Kuta and the other men who had taken proud part in Shaka's victory at Qokli (for in fact the word itself, "retreat", had the flavour of vanquishment), all obeyed without uttering a single request for elucidation. No one any longer doubted that the Son of Zulu knew exactly what he was doing. He'd just proven it in a manner that was so irrefutable, the Universe itself stood in silent mystification.

Retreat. - Part of another Shakan innovation, a military strategy that had never before been practiced in Africa. The strategy of the "scorched earth" (as it is called today) by which a countryside is devastated before an army's evacuation so as to be useless to an advancing enemy or, in the sense of Qokli, a military policy of devastating all land and buildings in the course of a retreat so as to leave nothing of use to the enemy.

So Shaka and his men "retreated" from Qokli across the Umfolozi, over the oNdini Plains and the emaYimane Neck, past the imBekamuzi and the iNyalazi -- for eight days and eight nights, as Soshangane marched in anguishing pursuit. Yet, true to the scorched earth policy, in their retreat the Shakan Armies devastated everything in their path, levelling homesteads and villages, each man eating his fill and then burning all the remaining flour and wheat, burying all gourds and melons that could provide nourishment for the enemy, causing all food-stuffs to virtually vanish in the troops' wake -leaving the Ndwandwe pursuers with nothing but "scorched earth" and billowing clouds of smoke that formed a winding path across the landscape like a burning fuse of gunpowder racing towards the stock of explosives.

And the explosion came. On the morning of the ninth day. In the narrow ravine running through the iMfule Ridge. Soshangane and his men, famished and on the verge of complete exhaustion, entered the ravine to drink at the clear sparkling waters of its brooklets and found themselves surrounded by Shaka's men.

The battle - properly named that of iMfule - lasted barely one morning. The Morning of Blood, as it was later called. Almost all 8000 of the Ndwandwe troops met their death. The survivors, including General Soshangane himself, fled North.

Shaka's Victory was complete - or nearly so.

*

High atop of one of Dlovunga's steeples of copper and bronze, a sentinel blew his reed trumpet to signal the sighting of a distant cloud that rumbled across the earth - the cloud, or so he assumed, of the victorious Ndwandwe Forces returning with the spoils of war.

Grinning through pulpy, toothless gums, Ntombazi, the Citadel's hideous Witch, scrambled up a wooden ladder to one of the bastion's lookouts where, cackling with anticipation, she strained her jaundiced orbs to make out the hazy silhouettes of the approaching soldiers, well expecting to see the brazen features of her generals next to the proud countenances of Nomahlanjana and her other grandsons.

Yet, as she gazed out expectantly, a sudden chill gripped her body and a woeful gasp of sheer terror was torn from her wicked heart.

Below her, Shaka and his troops marched unopposed to the granite base of the fortress's outer wall, up the winding paths of mica and quartz, across the wooden bridge and through the Gates of Jade where the famished lions were set free to feed upon the living flesh of their screaming custodians.

As the conquering troops streamed into the fortress, panic broke loose amongst the citadel's sordid inhabitants. They swarmed the streets like crazed rats, some scurrying to the relative safety of Dlovunga's caves, others hurling themselves from its lofty cliffs into the void preferring suicide to what they feared awaited them at the hands of Shaka's men.

And that fear of unremitting reprisal was justified for, indeed, Sitayi's words rang loudly in Shaka's mind as he stormed into Dlovunga. "Those who Inhabit the Underworld," the blind sangoma had told the Child. "Defeat them! Destroy them! And the Cycle shall close round its Emperor!" And the Zulu took heed of the old woman's admonition.

"Kill every man, every women, and every child!" Shaka ordered to his troops. "Wipe these wretched beasts from the face of the earth! - And, find Zwide! I want him alive!"

"I think I might know where he is," Mzilikazi said in an eerie whisper as he shifted his gaze to the gaping mouth of jagged stone that yawned from the Underworld.

Holding their torches high, Zwide and Ntombazi quickly made their way down the fantastic labyrinth of rocky passages and crystal galleries that formed the immense network of the subterranean "Inner Sanctum" of Those Who Inhabit the Underworld. The Ndwandwe monarch was whimpering with fear as he trudged after his mother's frame, clutching the flaccid skin that hung from her back as if it were his lifeline with salvation.

The gruesome pair hobbled down another passage, and yet another until Ntombazi stopped before a solid wall of red, phosphorescent sandstone that framed a wavy curtain of transparent, vitreous stalactites. With an iniquitous leer, the old Witch raised her bony hand and gently caressed the wall which, shimmering magically, vanished, miraculously forming a translucent gateway into a huge chamber bathed in a soft blue, throbbing glow.

"Hurry," Ntombazi urged her son, motioning to the enchanted chamber.

"Aren't you coming with me, mother?" Zwide asked with trepidation.

"No, my son. For you there is a future in the world beyond ours. A future in which you must wait and plan revenge. For me..." an unholy smile tugged at the corners of her mouth. Yet the phrase was left unfinished, as the old woman's eyes lit up with an loathsome fury and she urged him, once again: "Go now! Hurry!"

And when he had, the wall of sandstone returned to seal his escape.

Shaka and Mzilikazi found the Mistress, Queen of Dlovunga sitting on her throne, in the Grand Hall of the Council. She seemed to be waiting for them, and she smiled and nodded a sinister greeting - or was it a farewell? - as she raised her hand, bringing the writhing body of a large female scorpion to her neck, the creature's pincer claws snapping at a hair's-breadth from her wrinkled skin.

"No," Mzilikazi roared, racing to the side of the woman who had procured him such agony and swatting the scorpion out of her clutches with one sharp strike of his assegai. "You killed my father. The manner of your death shall be my decision alone."

Sturdy ropes tied round her wrists and ankles, suspended and hanging like some blasphemous puppet in the Theatre of the Damned, Ntombazi, Queen of the Underworld was lowered into the Pit of Dlovunga. Screaming hysterically, her mouth frothing, her sallow eyes wide with devilish rage, her arms thrashing and flailing savagely she sank lower, until the ropes brought her within range of the hot breath of the fierce pack of snarling jackals. Over her own screeching - she could hear the beasts growling in anticipation of their grisly meal. Then - as her inhuman yelping and squalling echoed throughout the burning devastated Citadel - the first pair of fangs purchased the rubbery folds of her skin, tearing it from the muscle, exposing the oozing tissues round the bone. The next pair of fangs sank deeper, shredding the muscle and splintering into the marrow of the rib under it. And the next was even deeper...

"How long will it take?" Mzilikazi mused with a crooked smile as he watched the Witch being eaten alive. "How many times will they tear at your flesh before you succumb. Ten? Twenty? - We shall see."

The Witch lasted that day and the next full night before the putrid stench that was her soul left the feculence that was her body and fled into the Underworld - never to be glimpsed again by Man or by Beast.

Dlovunga itself lasted a few days longer than its Mistress before there came a mighty Wind and a great tumult of the Earth, and the Heavens reeled and the cliffs and ridges slid, and a colossal chasm opened beneath the Fortress swallowing it down into the Under- world with all its steeples of copper and bronze, with its fantastic grottos and palaces of jewels, with its towers, and with its evil Children and their scelerous designs.

They all vanished forever -- all save for Zwide and Soshangane who would later return with their plans for revenge and profane the Child in his trust of the Strangers.

Later. Yet now...

...by the end of the year 1822, Shaka Zulu, the Language of the Heavens, had extended his rule and influence over a territory larger than that of the continent of Europe, forming a colossal empire far greater than that of his contemporary Napoleon Bonaparte. More than 120 clans, kingships, realms and confederacies had been consolidated into a single political and military unit - the Zulu Nation - that paid homage to Shaka as supreme overlord and absolute sovereign. As integral part of this consolidation into a single vast empire, One Nation, all vanquished clans were forced to lose their own original identity and become - to all intents and purposes - Zulu, part of the Greater Zulu Family. All those who refused to do so were either exterminated on the spot or dispersed to points outside the empire where they faced a life of "wandering" as "homeless outcasts" (like, perhaps, that child who, time ago, was doomed to the same fate).

But, though immense at the end of 1822, the Empire of the Son of Zulu had yet to grow, reaching the most distant horizons of his world, -- horizons which bordered on the Empire of the Swallows.

CHAPTER XXVIII
"IZINKONJANE"(THE SWALLOWS)
MONTH OF UNTLOLANJA: DECEMBER, 1822

Thousands - men, women, and children - stood huddled, cowering in muted temerity on the edge of the dusty clearing near the Anglican mission station, their eyes, widened in scrutiny of the large Cross perched high atop of the Church, built of mud and wattle -- like the nest of the swallow.

Thousands stared at the Swallows' Cross and they knew it was a symbol, of something in which the Whites believed no doubt. A petition for rain, perhaps, a talisman, a Bearer of Fertility, a Token of the First Fruits, a sign of the Dead; and as they peered at the Symbol and as the pain throbbed in their bellies, they wondered whether It could bring them 0 morsel of food, shelter from the rain, Hope.

And their hearts begged, yet the Swallows' Cross remained silent on its wooden steeple, high enough for all to see, its clean symmetry looming unemotional over the imploring sadness of their appeal - as the hushed murmur of their laboured sighing seemed to fill the tepid African air with the undertones of the word "fingo".

"Fingo" - "Feed me".

And their terrified eyes flitted from the Cross to scan the Christian outpost from the edge of the clearing, and though their hearts longed to move closer, they stood still - like lepers afraid to cross over onto the soils of civilisation for fear of the punishment that comes from contaminating Complacency with the germ of their anguish.

Vukani, a young boy of the Xhosa Tribe, was the first to spot them, and when he stopped to gaze at the sea of pleading eyes filling the surrounding bush country, the boy was frozen in gaping astonishment.
"Teacher!" Vukani finally shouted upon finding his voice. "Teacher!" he called out, racing off, across the clearing, past the church and the wooden huts of the mission station, past the makeshift school where other Xhosa and Pondo children dressed in European attire turned to glare at the frantic boy. "Teacher!" he yelled out of breath as he rounded the cattle fold and shot up the hillock towards a tiny cottage and the knitted brow of Reverend Josiah Bellow, Anglican clergyman, esteemed pioneer of the B.B.C.A.M. (the British Board of Commissioners for African Missions).

"Simmer down, Vukani. - Simmer down, now," the reverend gently urged, curling a long, lanky arm round the boy. "Catch your breath."

"Fingoes!" the word exploded from Vukani's lips rousing the attention of a commanding figure standing at the threshold of Bellow's front door. The man - a Xhosa school teacher whose tall, lean physique was clothed in a dusty three-piece suit of English origin - turned to look down at the boy with the well-opened eyes of one accustomed to honest directness.

"Fingoes?" The teacher asked.

"Yebo, Baba!" Vukani replied in his native tongue, echoing the answer in his adopted language. "Yes, Teacher!"

"Where, Vukani? - Where?!"

"By the Church," the boy answered, pointing.

"Who in Heaven's name are they, Daniel?" Bellow asked a few minutes later as he stood gazing in bewilderment at the pitiful, somehow threatening sight of this silent, fearful, hungry throng of humanity that carpeted the countryside bordering the mission station.

"Displaced tribes," said the Xhosa who, after his conversion, had assumed the Christian name Daniel. "People who have lost everything," he added in a softer tone as he looked deep into the sorrowful, listless eyes of these people, his People, Bantu, - and realised that though his name was now "Daniel" and he spoke the Swallows' language with painstaking precision, and though he knew the Strangers from the Sea well enough to teach the children of his people to speak like them, to dress like them, and to find interest in the often squalid intrigues and petty revindications that made up the history of "Western Civilisation", - he realised that though he understood the Whites, it would be virtually impossible to explain to Rev. Bellow the African tragedy of the last decade---

---the tragedy of the "Mfecane", as it was called, meaning, literally, "the crushing" or the "hammering". The cataclysmic event, or so Daniel might have seen it, that was directly linked to the forced migration of more than two million people who fled like helots from the ferocious impact of Shaka's expansionism, spilling inevitably into the laps of the White settlers in British Kaffraria and, directly to its South, into the Colony of the Cape of Good Hope - known more simply as the Cape Colony---

--- Daniel realised that, even if he tried to explain his people's suffering, even if he went to the trouble of "translating" that suffering into the White man's English, Bellow would not understand because, quite simply, men like Bellow did not care. He and most missionaries like him had come to Africa as "a favour" to the africans, to save the souls of these "savages" who, without their generous intercession, were destined to rot in Hell for Eternity (or so they thought), and above all they had come to win for themselves Eternal Peace dedicating their lives to the work of God "among the heathens"; - indeed, their "mission" was a very selfish venture and those who recognised this - men like Daniel - had converted out of a true belief in Christ, not in His representatives, and in spite of the mission- aries' patronising ways.!

Daniel knew in his heart that men like Bellow had come to convert the "kaffirs", not to get involved in their problems!

And the Fingoes were a problem. As was Shaka.

"They have lost everything, the Fingoes," Daniel repeated, almost to himself. "Their land, their birthright, their homes, their families, their identity as Africans! And now they roam like scavengers and marauders begging for each day's respite."

"But who did this to them?" Bellow inquired, in a religious whisper.

"Shaka," Daniel responded grimly, causing a terrified groan to issue forth from the sea of humanity.

"Shaka?" the Anglican reverend was incredulous. "But his kingdom is over 400 miles North of here!"

"No, Reverend," Daniel's eyes met the Englishman's. "They say his regiments have reached the umZimkulu River and are moving South - towards our outposts in British Kaffraria and, ultimately, towards the Cape."

Bellow's features, already pale by nature, blanched at the thought.

"The Cape?! - We must alert the Governor!"

CHAPTER XXIX
"INDABA KASHAKA"(THE SHAKAN AFFAIR)

The skies over Berkshire, England were veiled in the usual curtain of light drizzle that God is kind enough to sprinkle generously upon His Majesty's homeland, keeping the threat of drought well away from Britain's shores.

And, on this particular day, as the galloping hoofs of his stately sorrels spun the wheels of his lacquered carriage in a brisk clip down the gravel path towards Windsor Castle, Henry Bathurst, the extremely distinguished and somewhat portly 3rd Earl of Bathurst, who had for over a decade worn the signation of His Majesty's Colonial Secretary for War and the Colonies, chanced to look out the tiny window of his carriage at the dreary sky above him and thought to himself that, though it was June (of 1823, in fact), it could be any month judging from those clouds, - April, perhaps, or September, May, or even August.

Dropping his gaze to the towering ilexes that flanked Windsor's approach, the Earl ran a pensive hand through his groomed salt and pepper whiskers and wondered what the weather was like at the Southernmost tip of Africa, its Cape, and, as he considered the Cape, he had a smile, one that betrayed fond possession. It belonged to him, in a way - the Cape did. It had since he'd given up his post as Master of the Mint to become Secretary in the Foreign Office.

"For War and the Colonies". Strange title, that! - Odd combination of responsibilities under one Royal Roof.

"War and the ---" His thoughts were abruptly gravitated back to the lengthy and quite troubling missive resting on his lap; the letter the Court Courier had brought round the previous morning - addressed to his office and dispatched, under urgent cover, from Sir Charles Somerset the British Governor at the Cape. From the sound of the governor's missive, it seemed possible that those two concepts, "War" and "Colonies", might make a match after all.

Threading a pair of reading glasses over his ears, he settled down to reread Somerset's letter, for the fifth time.

It went: "To Sir Henry Bathurst, His Majesty's....." Bathurst brushed over the rest of the address and got quickly to the greeting. "My Lord, - In consequence of Your Lordship's wish that I maintain close touch with Your Office concerning matters of Colonial bearing, I--"

"'Close touch', indeed," Bathurst said out loud into the empty carriage, his aristocratic features pulling back in a wry smile. "Over six thousand miles of ocean lie between you and me," he told Somerset's distant spirit, "and even though I am His Majesty's Official representative, no contrivance can prevent the effect of this distance in weakening government! Seas roll, and months pass between the order and the execution, and the want of a speedy explanation of a single point in a document or manuscript is enough to defeat a whole system! What had Edmund Burke said?" Bathurst pondered, "'Because of Nature's distance the Turk cannot govern Egypt and Arabia, and Curdistan, as he governs Thrace; nor has he the same dominion in Crimea and Algiers, which he has in Brusa and Smyrna! Despotism itself is obliged to truck and huckster, and the Sultan gets such obedience as he can'!"

And, Bathurst mused, I, too, get such obedience in the Colonies as I can. Especially in such a disordinate brew of humanity as the Cape: a slave-owning community with a White population numbering no more than 20,000 against some 28,000 slaves and perhaps 17,000 Hottentots and other so-called 'free blacks', where an autocratic governor like Somerset can take advantage of "Nature's distance" to rule by proclamation and practically by his own authority, without reference to London and using every opportunity for the obstruction of London's orders by adopting a perpetual policy of evasion.

"Close touch, indeed," the Earl grumbled, adjusting his reading glasses which had inadvertently steamed over (due to the rain, he surmised). "The only time Somerset remembers we even exist is when his is a call for help. As is this missive!" And, having made that point perfectly clear to the disinterested interior of the empty carriage, Bathurst went on to read:---

"I herewith wish to communicate in writing my deep concern for the future of the Crown's Colony at the Cape of Africa, and I beg leave to submit the following evidence regarding the menace of the Zulu Tribe under its king, Shaka Zulu.

"Since he ascended the throne of the Zulus (my reports put it at less than eight years ago), Shaka has forged one of the mightiest empires the African continent has ever known. In this brief period of years, his small insignificant clan has risen from obscurity and given its name to an all-powerful nation organised into a fearsome military machine. Reports of Shaka from---"

"Who goes there?" came the curt request from the Yeoman of the Guard at Windsor's gates.

"The Earl of Bathurst to see His Majesty," retorted the Earl's coachman.

As customary the Yeoman neared the carriage and quickly looked inside - just long enough to glimpse Bathurst peering back at him over his spectacles and through his bushy brows.

"Carry on, m'lord," the young guard barked officially as he snapped to attention, his rifle swinging up to his chest, the slender bayonet gleaming near his ear. As the Earl's eyes lingered on the young guard, his lips pulled back in a pensive smile. "It's men like him that make the colonies," the Colonial Secretary considered. The brazen young stock of the British Isles who are weaned on salt water, windlasses, flying jibs and brass blunderbusses and who take to the seas when they're barely old enough to swim, some to return only as changed men, others not to return at all -- their bones left bleaching on distant shores, so that wealth might flow to the living at home.

The living at home. - As the carriage rumbled over the pebble path that wound up to the castle, the Earl's eyes returned to Somerset's missive.

"Reports of this Shaka spread by Kaffir traders make him appear to be an horrendous fiend whose activities go far beyond the most primitive code. The Zulu is shown as a mass murderer, a depraved ogre whose thirst for conquest knows no limits. He has deluged his country with innocent blood, forgetting the most sacred ties of affection, turning father against son, son against mother in a bloodbath that defies description. Indeed, the recital of this monster's deeds would only throw Your Lordship into disarray at a moment when I most need your complete sanguineness.

"In fact, I regret to inform Your Lordship that it has reached my attention from sources I can define only as of the utmost trustworthiness, that the threat of Shaka Zulu may soon be directed against the White Settlers residing in the Crown's territories. If that were to happen, the Cape would find itself virtually defenceless and at the mercy of this ruthless barbarian.

"I respectfully remit this pressing matter to Your Lordship's judgment and that of His Majesty. - Signed: Sir Charles Somerset, Governor of the Cape Colony, Colonial Africa. Cape Town, January 7, 1823."

His description is strikingly vivid, Bathurst mused. So unlike Sir Charles to exaggerate. It can only mean that either the man has gone mad or -- God forbid, it was true!

* ** *

The state - both physical and spiritual - of His Majesty King George IV in the Year of Our Lord 1823 can be best conceived when one is confronted with the repellent creature depicted in Gillray's cartoon "A

Voluptuary under the Horrors of Digestion". This cartoon shows George slouched indecorously on an easy chair recovering from an enormous meal at Carlton House (the London home of the Prince of Wales), his huge belly bursting from his breeches and his florid face on the verge of apoplexy. In the drawing, the King is surrounded by empty wine bottles, unpaid bills and various patent medicines (including the famous cures for venereal disease, Veno's Vegetable Syrup and Leeke's Pills).

To better clarify the King's state, one might adjoin to this depiction the comments made by Leigh Hunt (the famous XIX Century poet and journalist, renowned for his biography on Lord Byron): "The King is a libertine over head and ears in debt and disgrace, a despiser of domestic ties, the champion of demi-reps, a man who is over sixty years of age and has not a single claim on the gratitude of his country or the respect of posterity."

"Good morning, Your Majesty," Bathurst nodded, bowing respectfully to the king.

"Is it, Sir Henry?" the king asked, with the biting petulence of those who are no longer enamoured of Life and its tortuous ways.

"Sir?" Bathurst queried, puzzled by the odd inquisitive that was adjoined to his otherwise innocuous greeting.

"Your face, Sir Henry. It bodes anything but a good morning."

Yet Sir Henry could do little to hide the slight disapproval that tinged his expression as he stepped into the spacious interior of the king's bedroom (which was quite tastefully furnished, as a tribute to George's patronage of the Fine Arts) and looked upon the rotund, "florid" frame of the monarch reclining in a sea of pillows and under a flurry of satin sheets and loose-fitting satin and lace garments. The king's royal person was still half asleep (though it was well past noon) and in the process of feeding itself a luscious breakfast made up of oysters and white Claret wine whilst a fussy hairdresser was precariously perched on the royal bed's headboard tugging at and backcoming the king's curly locks.

"Terribly sorry, Your Majesty," Bathurst uttered, apologizing for the expression on his own face.

"Don't apologise. Alter it!" was the pressing request.

Not being much of an actor, and not at all a liar, Bathurst did a very poor job of forcing a smile and the king scowled at the Earl's reflection in the gilded mirror he held in his pudgy hand. Disgusted, the monarch threw back his bedclothes and swung his fleshy pale legs clear of the mattress. Having achieved a standing position, George extended his arms like those of a scarecrow and, on cue, two servants hurriedly threaded his chunky arms into a crimson houserobe. Padding barefooted to a settee by a convoluting bay window, George once again deposited his obese frame onto another pile of cushions - panting heavily at the fatigue procured by such a protracted excursion without repose. The hairdresser, who had scurried after him, swung quickly round to the king's rear and resumed his attack on the regal ringlets.

Throughout this delicate royal manoeuvre, Bathurst stood waiting patiently. Being a religious man - or so he considered himself, an Evangelical in fact, with warm links with the Clapham Sect and the other institutions that were, like Sir Henry, fervently in favour of abolishing slavery, - the Colonial Secretary did not mind waiting. It gave him time to pray for his less fortunate brothers, as, in this case, for His Royal Majesty the King of England.

After a seemingly interminable pause, George returned his bored countenance to face the Earl.

"I am all attention, Sir Henry. Spit out what you must."

"It's the Colonies, Your Majesty," Bathurst started after clearing the meditation from his throat. "We seem to be faced with a slight problem."

"Your office always seems to be having 'slight problems' with the colonies."

"Well, sir, it is the Colonial Office and anyone who deals with melting pots is apt to be scorched once in a while."

The Earl's attempt at levity was rewarded by a tittering peal of laughter on the part of the hairdresser who, upon meeting the king's gelidly reproachful gaze, instantly quelled his merriment into a polite cough.

"Who is it this time," George stiffly inquired. "The Canadians?"

"No, Your Majesty," Bathurst responded with the tracings of a smile still lingering on his usually 'stiff upper lip'. "I'm pleased to report that the remainder of North America is still securely - 'under our thumb', shall we say."

George eyed the Colonial Secretary, critically. The Earl's indiscriminate use of the word "remainder" brought a slight rumble of disturbance to that great chamber of flesh that was the monarch's belly. And with the rumble came the reminder of his father.

George III, dignified father of George IV, had had the unforgivable misfortune of committing, in the late 1770s, the mistake that would subsequently be referred to (in private British circles) as the "Blunder of the XVIII Century": to wit, losing the thirteen North American colonies. This loss of America was such a terrible blow to all, that even Catherine the Great of Russia was said to have remarked: "Rather than have granted America her Independence (the word "granted" is here used rather loosely), as my brother monarch, King George has done, I would instead have fired a pistol at my head!"

The king's eldest son, the Prince of Wales (later to become George IV), almost took Catherine up on her suggestion, but desisted before the emotional plights of patricide, deciding that it would be far easier and not as messy to simply have his father declared insane (indeed their was a touch of madness to the whole affair) and take his place as Prince Regent.

And that is exactly what he did. In fact, at the time of this meeting with Bathurst, George IV had officially been king for only three years, though, 'de facto', he had been ruling the country for well over eleven.

"It's Africa, I'm afraid," Sir Henry was quick to detach the king's train of thought from the ungrateful Americas. "I've received this alarming missive from Lord Somerset at the Cape."

The Colonial Secretary produced the manuscript from his leather folder and proferred it for the king's inspection.

"You don't expect me to read it, do you?!" George growled indignantly, peering down his nose at the letter.

"It concerns the Zulus, Sir," Bathurst spoke, his upper lip stiffening as he replaced the 'unwelcomed' missive in its leather folder.

"The Zulus?!" George echoed, his pinguid face taking on an interesting combination of shock and hilarity. "Are you implying, Sir Henry, that the Colonial Office of the British Empire considers a tribe of savages running about in their birthday suits a problem? - What ineffable twaddle!"

Yes, "Nature's distance" plays many tricks on the Colonies, Bathurst inwardly considered, as his king burst into an uproarious discharge of laughter. One of its most dangerous tricks is the racism that produced slavery, the prejudice of men wearing satin against those distant, indistinct human shapes in "birthday suits."

"Unfortunately it is more than just a tribe, Your Majesty," Bathurst broke in, through the king's merriment, his voice calm and reserved. "We feel we are at grips here with a proper empire of over a million such birthday suits."

"They do multiply like bunnies, don't they," the British sovereign forced through his laughter, causing his eyes to water with the strain of his derision.

It would appear that both the deceased Mudli and the distinguished Earl had been reared at the same school of diplomacy - within their own specific contexts, of course, the kingdom of the one being far more civilised than that of the other - for Bathurst remained perfectly calm in the face of his king's pathetic display of joviality. "Your Majesty, the Zulus may be planning an attack on the Cape," Bathurst noted, levelly. "If that were to happen, we'd be faced with many such 'bunnies' under a March Hare named Shaka."

The announcement had an instant sobering effect on George who snapped back: "Well send down some reinforcements!"

"We had thought of that, Sir," Sir Henry retorted in defense of his Office's foresight. "But, you see, the Cape's awfully far. 6000 miles and four months by sea, to be precise. And, judging from the Governor's missive, I fear that by the time fresh troops are shipped in loco and trained in that form of native warfare, it may be too late."

"Then transfer some of our Bengali troops from India!"

Bathurst felt the urge to remind his king that though Britain had won the war against Napoleon, it had been, so to say, a Phyrric victory, one gained at the expense of thousands upon thousands of men and millions of gold sovereigns. And, today, quite frankly, Britain just did not dispose of as many troops as the ever-expanding Empire would need. Indeed, to be quite cautious, the Colonial Office should suggest that no further exploration be allowed to take place until the ranks of Britain's armed forces can be refurbished; - no more colonies until the armies are strong again.

"Secretary of War and the Colonies" -- yes, the title did make sense after all, Bathurst mused as he gazed at his king and decided to respond to George's suggestion as simply as possible.

"We cannot transfer the Bengali troops, Sir. - We'd lose India."

George frowned at the Colonial Secretary, irked that the man was ruining his day with problems that he should be competent enough to solve on his own.

"Then use mercenaries," the king suggested recklessly.

"'Not to be trusted'," Bathurst shot back. "To quote your own words, Your Majesty."

The king had had enough. Casting Bathurst a stern sidelong glance, George shrugged off his hairdresser and, rising heavily on his lardacous legs, he strode round to the bay window at his shoulders and peered up at the sky.

"Look out there, Sir Henry. What do you see -- falling?"

"Rain, Your Majesty," Bathurst pursed his lips with the taint of annoyance.

"And is that a frequent occurrence in England. Rain falling, I mean?"

"All too frequent, Sir," the Earl commented, remembering his own earlier considerations regarding the rain on his drive up to the Castle.

"And what do the Colonies represent for us, Sir Henry?"

Though Bathurst found George's overweening manner somewhat insulting, he politely replied, after reflecting slightly upon the question: "Sunshine, Sir?"

"Precisely," the king's podgy wet lips sagged in a smile. "And it is your privilege to safeguard that sunshine for England." The smile vanished as effortlessly as it had appeared. "Thomas Jefferson drove my father out of his wits. I trust you shall keep such fate from me. - Tend to these Zulus of yours, Bathurst, or it shall be our sad task to find someone who can."

* * *

Ever since the Summer of the Year of Our Lord 996, when the lovely Princess Gunnor of Denmark gave her husband, King Richard the Fearless, a model Viking sailboat for his 33rd birthday, the Sons of England have had their sights set on the Colonies.

And, almost 825 years later, when England began to extend her dominions beyond the seas and her foreign relations grew more complicated, it became quite natural for state employees to pass from the Offices of the Secretary of State for Foreign Affairs on one side of the doorway at Downing Street to the offices of the Secretary of State for War and the Colonies on the other.

Sir Henry Bathurst, as the head of half of Downing's doorway, was assisted by his parliamentary and permanent undersecretaries, and by a staff of subordinate officials. Besides these, the Earl had four permanent assistant undersecretaries: one for questions of law and in charge of the "remainder of North America", Australasia and Cook's discoveries in the Pacific; one for Africa; a third for the East and West Indies, emigration, prisons and hospitals; and a fourth for "other possessions".

In this grouping, Africa per se was under the jurisdiction of Assistant UnderSecretary David Worthing and his assistant, the young and spunky Tim Wilkins (who had, before joining the Office, made quite a name for himself in journalism as the cub reporter who had helped the Authorities trace Jacob Hornby - the infamous Essex Strangler to his lair in East London).

With a department thus specialised and manned by first-rate employees, the Earl could have easily and safely delegated Somerset's problem to Worthing and Wilkins without giving it another thought. Yet the threatening tone of King George's "Tend to the Zulus, Bathurst", drove Sir Henry to give the Shakan Affair, as it was called, top priority.

In fact, throughout the month of July, most of the employees in the Earl's section of Downing Street (and even some from across hall) were engaged in finding a solution to the problem of the crazed African March Hare. But the matter looked bleak inasmuch as the most obvious solution, that of sending down troops was quite out of the question - indeed, it was beyond the capabi- lities of Bathurst's office to conjure up soldiers that just did not exist.

But towards the beginning of August, when many in the department had given up hope, the handful who remained on the Shakan Affair were cheered by the performance of Tim Wilkins who, being a sport and true to form, came up with a grand idea.

It was a few minutes past two in the morning, and, being unable to sleep, Worthing, Wilkins, and Bathurst himself were haunting the Earl's private study at Downing Street with the oppressive weight of a predicament called Shaka Zulu.

"What's the good of owning one third of the world, George, if it keeps you up at night?" Bathurst said addressing Sir Thomas Lawrence's portrait of the king hanging dutifully over the fireplace.

"Oh, I suspect His Majesty is sleeping rather soundly by now," Worthing said in his usual rumbling, low, very British voice, the sort of voice that leaves the listener with the disturbing sensation that its owner should swallow more often. "Why shouldn't he? He has us to worry for him, doesn't he? Of course he does!"

"How tall would you say he is?" young Wilkins inquired without looking up from his sketchpad.

"Who, George?" Worthing retorted, frowning at the seemingly unrelated question as his eyes came to rest on the pencil in Tim's hand that was frantically dancing across the page. "Five-seven, five-eight, I'd say."

"Without his plimsoll slippers," Bathurst added wryly.

"No, I mean this Shaka chap," Wilkins insisted.

"Oh, I dunno..." Bathurst started and then suddenly frowned. "What the devil has this barbarian's height to do with our imbroglio?"

"How's this for a likeness?" Tim grinned as he flipped over the pad and showed his associates an extravagant Englishman's interpretation of what a "birthday suited" (to use George's words) savage king might look like.

"Well," Worthing's scrutiny was critical. "You've captured the spirit, m'lad. But as far as likeness goes, I dare say your guess is as wanting as any."

"You mean to say no White man had ever seen him?" the youth's question was laced with the seed of excitement.

"Not to our knowledge." The reply was Bathurst's.

"Which means that the reverse is also true..." Wilkins considered under his breath suddenly looking up, his freckles meeting in a broad smile. "What blind beetles we've been! Here we are trying to devise a way to confront Shaka with a regiment, when all we need is a suitable Caucasian!"

"What are you talking about?" the UnderSecretary queried as he watched Wilkins rise and start to nervously ply the study's parquet floor as if he were literally chasing his own ideas across the room.

"Worthing," Tim spoke as if thinking out loud. "For the sake of discourse, pretend you're this King Shaka. Or you, Sir Henry, pretend you're that ruthless cutthroat described in Somerset's missive."

"I say, Wilkins...!" Worthing snapped, finding the speculation to be an outrage against Bathurst's and his own decency. "Come now, Henry," the Earl broke in, calming his colleague. "Let the boy continue."

"Thank you, Sir Henry," Wilkins went on, causing Worthing to purse his lips in restrained chagrin. "Let's say you're toying with the idea of attacking the Whites, creatures you've never set eyes on. - You'd be wary, wouldn't you? Of course! - It's all very well to fight against known odds, but Lunarians! Well that's another kettle of fish, isn't it?!" Tim continued pacing as he ran a hand through his red hair and felt his thoughts taking shape. "And what if one of these Lunarians appeared at your court, like a diplomat of sorts - from the other world. And what if he said, 'Hold on now, Shaka, we know what you're up to. But hadn't you better hear me out before you go tipping the scales of war! We have spears that spit fire, you know. Here, look at one. Bang, bang, and a lion's dead at 600 paces! We have magic powder that produces lightning and hollowed trees that make thunder...!"

"You mean scare him?!" Worthing seemed shocked.

"In a way, yes, Worthing."

"He doesn't strike me as the type who would scare easily," Bathurst commented, pouring himself a tumbler of Brandy.

"No, Sir Henry, he is exactly the type! All primitives scare easily when confronted with what they think is the Supernatural!"

"But surely his spies have told him about our gunpowder and cannons!" The objection was Worthing's.

"Perhaps, Worthing, but those aren't our only superior weapons! We have another - one we call 'civilisation': 7000 years of tried and tested double-talk! If we cannot 'soothe' the savage beast, we can certainly try to confuse him long enough to mount a suitable military defensive."

When Wilkins had finished, he returned to his chair and sat silently looking at the two other men with a set smile. He seemed confident that they would come round to his idea and decided to wait it out.

Bathurst rose and took the youth's place pacing the floor as he nursed his Brandy casting occasional glances at Tim's sketch on the table. Finally he stopped and looked out the window at the odd hansom clamouring through the night.

"You realise this scheme of yours isn't very British - fair play and all that." Bathurst noted.

"Isn't it, Sir Henry?" Wilkins's tone was mildly ironic. "I would've thought that schemes like this were what the Colonial Office is all about."

Bathurst spun round and cast the youth a sharp look that quickly dissolved before Tim's twinkling eyes.

"And where do you suggest we locate such a 'Luna- rian' disposed to carry out this novel and rather questionable mission?" the Earl pursued the idea.

"I know just the man, Sir Henry," Wilkins riposted with the excitement of the imminent chase. "Had the pleasure of serving under him in His Majesty's Royal Navy. - Lt. Francis George Farewell's the name. A master of land, sea, and -- crazy enough to do it!"

CHAPTER XXX
"ULWANDLE"(SEA)
FRANCIS GEORGE FAREWELL, R.N.

The grassy clearing by the shores of the English Channel near Brighton, England was crowded with a festive group of men, women, and children dressed in their Sunday Georgian best, sporting umbrellas against the light drizzle and capes against the early morning chill. Pedlars both young and old, wearing ragged clothes that smacked of a Dickensian flavour, wove their way through the throng flogging their wares: Union Jacks, buttons, fish and chips, luke-warm soup, tea, and the like.

Taking advantage of the distraction afforded by an approaching carriage, a light-fingered young lad stealthily relieved an expensively dressed gentleman of his wallet and waistcoat watch. The carriage jostled over the damp meadow and grounded to a splashing halt. Wilkins and Worthing alighted from the coach and, turning up their collars against the rain, they stood with eyes narrowed on the furore round them.

"Are you sure this is the place?" Worthing was definitely put out by the meteorological precipitation and the commotion.

"Quite sure, Worthing," Tim replied, his eyes falling on a large white banner suspended above the crowd on which were painted the words BRIGHTON TO CALAIS BY LIGHTER THAN AIR. "Come along," the young man bid his superior as he struck off across the clearing, heading for the spot where the majority of the crowd was collecting. Remaining somewhat baffled and quite ruffled, Worthing trudged along in pursuit of Tim, peering quizzically at something bobbing above the heads of the throng.

The two men threaded and shoved their way through the crowd and, upon reaching the beach, stopped to gaze in wonderment at a large Montgolfier-type balloon anchored to the rocky strand, its silk gas-bag colourfully adorned with an immense Union Jack. In the balloon's car stood the solitary figure of a handsome man in his early thirties wearing a charming smile and the spiffy uniform of a lieutenant in the Royal Navy.

"Is that...?" Worthing asked, gaping at the huge apparatus for lighter than air travel.

"Lt. Farewell? Yes." Tim grinned and, waving at the man in the car, called out: "Lieutenant!". Ducking under the cordons that were girded round the vehicle, the young man neared Farewell as the lieutenant, not having heard Tim's beckoning, went on with his last minute check of the ship's instruments: spyglass, barometer, thermometer, compass, valves, and the like, as well as the gas burner situated at the mouth of the huge inverted bag.

"Lieutenant," Tim repeated causing Farewell to look up from his tinkering and gaze at Wilkins. A faint glimmer of recognition gnawed at the man's memory as he took in the lad's features, trying to place them. Suddenly the recollection came and the lieutenant smiled, snapping his fingers.

"'HMS Bacchante'," he told the red-haired youth. "Adriatic reconnaissance. - Wilkins! Tim Wilkins."

"Yes, sir," Tim beamed.

"Best first mate I ever had," Farewell remarked, ducking back into his car.

"Thank you, sir," Wilkins's smile broadened.

Worthing, having witnessed the brief "veteran's reunion" with growing impatience, cleared his throat repeatedly as a hint that Tim should get down to the reason for their unsettling trek through the mud and rain.

"Sir," Wilkins addressed the car in the recesses of which Farewell was still quite concealed, "I'd like to have you meet Mr. David Worthing, Assistant UnderSecretary for the Colony of Africa."

Instinctively, Worthing extended an open hand, well expecting to shake the lieutenant's, yet when Farewell reappeared from the depths of his vehicle, he was holding a heavy ballast which he heaved over the side of the car (barely missing Worthing's extended appendage) and commented, distractedly: "Ah, Africa! Interesting! Good of you to come!" Then, waving to the crowd (that had started to cheer), the lieutenant cut the ropes that bound him to the beach and started his ascent.

"But, sir..." Wilkins uttered helplessly as he and Worthing watched the balloon float upwards and, catching the breeze, carry their man out towards the turbulent waters of the English Channel.

"Of all the cheeky...!" Worthing grumbled, his eyes on the retreating Montgolfier.

"The sloops," Tim announced, his mind racing as his eyes fell on a few sloops bobbing near the shore ready to sail off in pursuit of the eccentric lieutenant with the more adventurous of the spectators and a generous gathering of newsmen.

"The what?!" Worthing echoed, aghast, suddenly reminded that he was one of the few proud members of the Colonial Office whose stomach was so opposed to sailing it became qualmish at the mere thought that "Britannia rules the Seas"! "I have no intention, Wilkins," he yelled out with resolve as he saw his younger colleague racing down to secure places in one of the shallow boats - "No intention whatsoever of chasing that blasted balloon across the Channel! - I say, there - Wilkins! Do you hear?!"

*

"Upon the whole, gentlemen, I see two major problems in your plan."

As a tribute to the stubbornness of Youth, Worthing had indeed "chased that blasted balloon" and its master and was now sitting in a luxurious suite in one of Calais' swankiest hotels. Worthing's complexion was somewhat yellowed (the trip had taken five hours and the waves were quite choppy), his suit frightfully dishevelled (the sloop was small and the reporters many), and the barometer of his disposition was definitely leaning towards the stormy.

Yet - though crimped and crinkled - they were finally sitting opposite Farewell, both men looking on as the eccentric lieutenant reclined in a tub placed in the center of the suite's livingroom - taking a bath.

"First--," the lieutenant started, and, without apparent warning, slid into the tub, disappearing under the suds, leaving his captive audience to gape in wonder.

Worthing pursed his lips. Even if the man had been a hero during the war, one of Admiral Hoste's and Nelson's most trusted young officers, even if he had distinguished himself in the Battles of Lissa and Cattaro, at Gibraltar and Trafalgar, Worthing resolved that he would take little more of this abuse as he leaned back on the couch and sat waiting patiently for the officer to reappear from beneath the suds.

"---making Shaka's acquaintance." Farewell continued the flow of his thought upon resurfacing. "That in itself should prove to be a major obstacle. -- Entrez," the lieutenant said in response to a knock at the door.

A porter entered the suite carrying Lt. Farewell's freshly pressed uniform, an evening newspaper, and a rolled piece of parchment.

"Mettez-le la bas," Farewell instructed the frenchman and watched him execute his orders, bidding him, as a pleasant dismissal, "Merci, c'est tout pour maintenant."

"Excellent French, sir. Impressive," Tim grinned with genuine admiration.

"I picked up a smattering during the war. You know what they say, Tim - 'Know thine enemy'." The lieutenant's faced suddenly became serious as he pressed on with: "Which brings us back to Shaka."

Rising from the tub, Farewell took the towel proffered by Wilkins and wrapping it round his waist, he padded to the desk and picked up the parchment scroll. Unrolling the scroll - which proved to be a recent and extremely accurate Royal Admiralty map of Southern Africa - the lieutenant hung it over a mantlepiece and referred to it, drying himself by the fire's hearty flames.

"To start with," he started, "let us - to use a nautical term - take the bearings of our problem. "This is the Cape Colony, with Port Elizabeth and Cape Town as its two principal harbours. And here - extending from the Great Kei River northwards to the Pongola River - is the unexplored area that the local colonists refer to as Natal, the territory believed to be the site of Shaka Zulu's empire."

Wilkins and Worthing were all ears, the older man being clearly impressed by Farewell's familiarity with Southern Africa. Indeed the UnderSecretary was slowly warming to this unconventional officer of H.M.'s Britannic Navy.

"Now, returning to my original query," Farewell went on as he started to dress, splashing cologne and talcum onto his lean, well proportioned physique. "How are we to make Shaka's acquaintance in order to carry out Tim's ingenious scheme?"

Wilkins smiled at Worthing who nodded back his approval.

"From reports I was privileged to acquire last winter during my trip to Portuguese Delagoa, it would appear that the new capital Shaka has built - a place the native's call 'Bulawayo', should be somewhere in this vicinity." He indicated a spot on the map that was buried in the northeastern corner of Natal. "Now, there are two ways of reaching it: overland from the Cape..." Farewell indicated the long trek, well over 1400 miles of rough and unexplored terrain. "Though I would exclude this option a priori considering that the only White man to attempt the journey - a Dr. Cowan, by name - was never heard of again."

Wilkins and Worthing exchanged an apprehensive wince as the lieutenant ploughed on unflinchingly with nonchalance and charm.

"Which leaves us with the only other option, - an approach by sea. Landing somewhere along this coast - the so-called 'Wild Coast' of Natal. From a survey made two years ago by the Protuguese Navy, the two most likely places for such a landing would seem to be St. Lucia Bay, here, or Rio de Natal, here..." Again the naval officer indicated the two sites on the map situated on the southeastern coast of Africa, the shores washed by the Indian Ocean.

"But that option could also prove to be a problem, I'm afraid," Farewell confessed as he slipped into the immaculately pressed tunic of his uniform.

"In what way, Lieutenant?" Worthing inquired.

"Well you see, gentlemen, no one's ever landed on that coast - and lived to brag about it, that is.

*

"It seems we're faced with a cul-de-sac, sir," Wilkins's preoccupation clearly transpired, as the three men made their way through the posh interior of the Calais Concert Hall, threading past the reporters that clung to Farewell with questions and interviews as if he were indeed some great celebrity, and took their places on a small lodge reserved for the lieutenant near the yawning stage where the orchestra was seated and ready to begin.

"Not exactly, Tim," Farewell said in response to Wilkins's remark, his voice lowered in a hush as the conductor raised his baton and the musicians fixed their eyes upon him with expectation. "The mere fact that no one else had conquered that coast doesn't mean that I won't. - God knows I've been faced with greater obstacles in my sailing days."

"Does that mean you're with us, sir?!" Tim virtually glowed with joy, his outcry eliciting a few indignant shushings from the Hall's parquet.

"Most definitely, Tim! I would never miss a chance to serve my king..." the lieutenant announced in a whisper, bringing a pleased smile and a bit of colour to Worthing's features, - both of which vanished when Farewell added, matter-of-factly,"...and collect the ivory."

"The what, sir?" Wilkins's furrowed brow was fixed on Farewell with a trace of perplexity.

"Later, gentleman," was Farewell's evasive reply as the orchestra intoned Beethoven's "Battle Symphony". "Let's hear how this Prussian has celebrated the feats of our beloved Wellington."

*

"Did you say ivory, Lieutenant," the UnderSecretary for Africa requested of Farewell as the trio made its way down the outer steps of the Concert Hall, Beethoven's notes still resounding in their ears. "Yes, I did, Worthing," Farewell smiled. "Natal is said to be a paradise for ivory hunters."

"But surely the financial side of it is---," Worthing rebutted, changing course with, "I mean, it's all very well but, well, as you said, serving the King and all, 'tisn't the sort of..."

"My dear Worthing," Farewell interrupted the man's disconcerted babble. "Hasn't it occurred to you that I shall need good, adventurous men to join me on this mission? Men who are able and, above all, willing to face the hazards of that coast and Shaka Zulu. Experience has taught me that men of that caliber are prone to be swayed by the prospect of riches--. What would you have me say to entice them to come with me? 'You're doing it for your king! For the glory of Britannia!'?"

Seeing the lieutenant's point, the UnderSecretary compressed his lips and nodded demurringly.

"I need their courage, Worthing," Farewell pointed out. "Not their patriotism! And there is always a price on courage. In this case it shall be paid in ivory. 'The Farewell Trading Company'," the naval man grinned, "I rather like the sound of that, don't you?"

Worthing cast Farewell a sidelong glance, wondering, as he observed the man's broad smile, whether the lieutenant himself - being a man of courage - was also in need of a bit of "enticement".

The Farewell Trading Company? "Why not?" Worthing mused, "It wouldn't be the first time explorers and colonial 'diplomats' paid themselves from the spoils of the land. Look at James Cook, Sir Francis Drake, - even Christopher Columbus. In fact," the Assistant Under- Secretary considered with a twitching smile, "without a pinch of greed there would be no Colonies at all!"

*

The large falcon sailed across the sky, its imposing wings spread, catching the air currents, soaring with the wind above the trees, circling the triangular gables on top of Holbrook House, near Severn Bay, Glouchester, England - the splendid manor house that had been the Farewell residence for generations. Suddenly the proud bird tucked back its wings and dove towards one of the mansion's lofty terraces landing on the gloved hand that Farewell held out to it. The lieutenant cast a glance at the noble bird, feeling the animal's courage, its power flowing into his own heart, and the two creatures, man and beast, exchanged a silent, fleeting look of mutual respect and understanding.

"Is that another of your hobbies, lieutenant? Falconry?" Worthing asked, trying to keep his tone casual, though he was in fact terrified by the nearness of the bird.

"If anything I am his hobby!" responded Farewell good-naturedly.

"Back in France, sir" Wilkins started by way of recapitulation. "You said there were two major problems to my plan..." The men had been in Holbrook House for almost two days now, and, though the idea of staying in the mansion as Farewell's guests had derived from a desire to better discuss and organise the mission to Natal and Shaka, what with all of the lieutenant's impressive interests and "hobbies" (horse breeding, billiards, archery, hunting, polo, an immense library with an entire section dedicated to anthropology and the sciences, a collection of model ships, a complete chemistry laboratory where Farewell toyed with alchemy, and the like) little or no real work had been done. Wilkins remark came as a sort of gentle reminder that they mustn't forget his "ingenious scheme".

"If I understood correctly, sir," the red-haired youth went on, "the first problem is reaching Shaka. What is the other?"

"Why the most obvious, Tim," Farewell replied transferring the falcon to a wooden perch. "The problem of convincing the king of a primitive empire that our civilisation is to be feared when, in fact, we're no match at all for him out there.

Once again the two men from the Colonial Office were confused as the lieutenant explained.

"Centuries of so-called 'enlightenment' do not necessarily make a country or its people militarily stronger. Indeed, as Attila the Hun proved, domestication is usually a weakening factor. You see, as our weapons become more and more sophisticated, our hearts forget how to kill."

"But surely that is one of the more commendable aspects of our society," Worthing noted.

"Oh, I quite agree," Farewell was quick to adjoin. "I'm all in favour of the 'perfect weapon' inasmuch as, by definition, it cannot be fired. But I'm afraid Shaka will see things quite differently."

The falcon tore at a piece of raw meat the lieutenant proferred, as the man continued, "The Zulu is probably very much like this falcon here. He won't fail to see that our polished ways have made us as vulnerable as fowl in a poultry yard. No, gentlemen. Fear is not the answer. I'm sure that Shaka is more of a specialist in that than we could ever be! When we tap those '7000 years of tried and tested double-talk', we'll have to find another emotion to work with. Jealousy, perhaps. Or pride, hatred, greed ---"

"Vanity, Francis," came a female voice from over his shoulder. "That's the greatest weakness of all males - be they falcons, Huns, Englishmen or Zulus!"

"Elizabeth!" Farewell exclaimed with a beaming smile as he spun round to face a strikingly beautiful woman who was advancing across the terrace towards the three men.

Wilkins and Worthing gaped at the woman who appeared to them luminous in the unfailing brilliance of her femininity. As she strode towards them, the sun suddenly peeked through the clouds and was reflected on a window pane causing the magnified light to fall across her path, igniting the mass of her tumbling long hair, making it appear incandescent, chiselled and fluid like the burnished helmet of Minerva.

Noticing, with pride, the reaction his wife was creating, Farewell verily preened as he introduced: "Elizabeth, meet Mr. Worthing and Tim Wilkins - they're with the Colonial office. - Gentlemen, my wife."

With those three words, "Gentlemen, my wife", Farewell seemed to take possession of the beautiful creature, suddenly thrusting her well out of anyone else's reach. Tim and his companion found it hard to link the adventurer Farewell to the constraining words "my wife" and, somewhat taken aback, the two men stood momentarily dazed.

"Terribly sorry, madam," Worthing stuttered upon stirring himself from his abstraction. "I---"

"There's no need for that, Mr. Worthing," Elizabeth smiled. "Most people find it hard to believe that Francis shares his life with anything but his dreams."

"Yet without the benefit of my wife's practical mind, my dreams would go hopelessly adrift," Francis added, addressing his guests though his gaze remained lost in the deep blue pools of Elizabeth's eyes. The two lovers exchanged a few words relative to the woman's brief holiday at the Farewell summer cottage in Swansea (from which Elizabeth had just returned), before the lieutenant mentioned, with a grin that anticipated his wife's joy: "I've grand news for you, darling. We shall soon be visiting your mother at the Cape!"

"Oh, Francis," she threw her arms round him. "Thank you!"

CHAPTER XXXI
"INTO EMOSAYO"(WHITE ELEPHANT)

The day over the Kingdom of the Heavens broke on dark lavender clouds heavy with rain. A flash of blue lightning pierced the skies, followed by a crash of deafening thunder, as the heavens opened, unloading their burden in a torrential storm that, in its hissing fury, strove to drown out the stentorian uproar of thousands of Shakan warriors shouting shrilly and beating their sticks against the earth in a quaking proclamation of the most dangerous of African sports - the Hunt of the Great Indlovu - the Mighty Elephant, the Potentate of Creation.

True to this Sport of Regiments, which Shaka looked upon as an activity as noble as that of Warfare, a long tightly serried line of warriors recruited from the proud Zulu ranks was stretched between two parallel tributaries of the Umfolozi River. The line advanced towards the point where the waterways met, snaking and undulating its way over the rough uneven terrain - rendered muddy by the deluging shower that poured down from the skies. As they advanced the warriors raised their quaking voices to the Heavens and beat the ground ahead of them with long swishing sticks - making as much noise as humanly possible in their systematic sweep over the countryside.

In the distance, the noise had the desired effect on a large herd of elephants. Hearing the approaching cacophony, the huge beasts cocked their enormous ears in alarm and raised their trunks over glistening tusks as the fear buzzed through their mammoth bodies. Their leader, a large bull, started to run, darting frantically away from the source of his apprehension, the equally terrified herd trotting close behind. The elephants began to stampede through the bush, the beasts' frantic trumpeting and the pounding of their massive legs upon the earth barely audible over the clamour of the Heavens and the outcry of its warriors.

The herd zigzagged wildly from tributary to tributary, their leader uncertain which direction to take, virtually boxed in by the two parallel waterways and the advancing line of intimidating Zulus from which the elephants fled.

Less than half a mile in front of the herd, Shaka, Mgobozi, Nqoboka, Joko, Mzilikazi, and a group of select soldiers were waiting on the steep slopes of a hill, each man holding a small axe (shaped slightly like a tomahawk) and his ixwa. Excitement shone on the men's eyes as they squinted through the rain at the herd that was being driven towards them.

Upon reaching the hill, the beasts slowed as they laboured up its acclivity, moving ever nearer to the waiting hunters. And, as the elephant lumbered past almost within touching distance, Shaka and the others watched from their hiding places, waiting to act. Then, as the last elephant of the herd, a medium-sized bull, reached their position, Mgobozi and Nqoboka attacked it from either side, closing with the bull, their axes inflicting deep gashes at the elephant's knees and at the great tendon at the hock of the hind leg (this being the only method of elephant hunting approved by Shaka: the noble "close combat" technique of the severed hamstring).

The wounded bull trumpeted with rage and turned, lurching to get at its assailants, its trunk lashing at the men. But Mgobozi and Nqoboka made sure they kept well behind the beast as they continued to inflict gash after gash over the hamstring until at last the poor beast could no longer stand and came crashing to the ground were it was speedily executed with a jab of the ixwa through the thinner skin of its throat and into the jugular. The same process was repeated by Joko and Mzilikazi as the two men set upon another bull, deftly crippling it with their axes before moving in for the kill.

Shaka was the last to enter the hunt, his axe and Ixwa poised for combat as he raced out of the bushes, his eyes alive with the exultation felt when the chase was upon him. Yet, as he peered through the driving rain to focus on his prey, the Zulu king froze, wide-eyed and spellbound, gaping at a gigantic bull that towered over the rest of the herd at a height of at least five meters, its immense tusks well over three meters in length and its flapping ears like the wings of the Lammergeyer. Yet, though staggering in its proportions, it was not the size of the bull that startled Shaka - it was its colour: the powdery albino cast of the legendary "iNto eMoSayo", the White Elephant.

Shaka stood in awe of the animal, incapable of moving, his eyes fixed on the gigantic creature. The White Bull tilted its mighty ears at right angles, lifting its trunk and trumpeting loudly as it swayed forward and charged. Yet the Great Sigidi, the Slayer of iNkomo the Mad Giant, remained strangely entranced, anchored to the ground at his feet, gaping at the beast as its gleaming, deathly tusks drew nearer and nearer.

"Shaka!" screamed Mgobozi over the storm, rousing his friend from his stupour a mere instant before the animal's tremendous sweeping tusks could sink into his chest.

At Mgobozi's call, the Zulu king quickly spun to the side as the smooth ivory scraped against his flank. Then, gritting his teeth, shouting a bloodcurdling "Ayi! Hlome!", Shaka finally responded and bound towards the white bull, his body dwarfed by its enormity. Deftly and expertly rolling under the animal, Shaka swung his axe, inflicting a terrific blow over the hamstring. The bull trumpeted loudly, squealing with rage and in pain, its colossal ears flapping through the deluging downpour as it spun around, its mighty trunk threshing through the storm in an attempt to cut down its assailant. Yet the Zulu nimbly darted behind the beast and inflicted another blow, severing the tendon.

As the pain flashed through its body, the bull roared with fury and closed its trunk round a tree, uprooting it and hurling it at Shaka. An instant before the crushing impact, the Zulu rolled again, moving out of the tree's trajectory and closed with the monstrous White bull, chopping at the back of the leg until the mountain of flesh, unable to stand any longer, came thundering to the ground in an earthquaking crash. Relentlessly, panting heavily, his eyes wide and flaming like those of a man possessed, Shaka scrambled up onto the elephant's side, slipping and sliding on its thick hide, ducking under its flailing trunk, until he reached the mammoth head and sank his Ixwa into the bull's neck, repeatedly, wildly, staining its albino hide in the deep-red flow of its blood, again and again he thrust the Ixwa, until the bull's desperate death cry pierced the thunder that wrenched the skies overhead. Again and again, Shaka inflicted his blows, long after the mountain of flesh found stillness in death - again and again, his chest heaving with uncontrollable wrath, until he finally looked up - his feverish eyes meeting those of Mgobozi, Mzilikazi, Joko, Nqoboka and the others.

And the men were suddenly conscious of something in Shaka's expression, something they had never seen before, - a chilling, unquenchable emotion that had entered the Zulu's soul like a pestilential disease and now glowed in Shaka's eyes with the intensity of its fever.

An emotion known as Fear.

*

"There is a saying among Those Who Inhabit the Mountains," Sitayi spoke in an eerie whisper as she peered over the crystal railing of the Platform of the Pinnacle at the immensity of the landscape that stretched from horizon to horizon, her vacant orbs reaching out "as far as the eye can see", to the great land "of nations and kings" over which the Language of the Heavens now ruled.

"It is said," Sitayi went on, her hushed words directed at the "Child" who was standing beside her, the long blue crane feather of his headdress flickering in the breeze, his ivory tassels jingling softly. "That when iNto eMosayo, the White Elephant, is seen, it is an omen - a warning of danger."

"What sort of danger?" Shaka uttered in a low voice - one that sounded disembodied.

"To that which you value most. Your power."

"No human would dare challenge my supremacy now," the Child boasted to the howling wind.

"So it is, Baba," Sitayi agreed. "Yet I speak not of humans. I speak of beings who have emerged from the Sea riding animals with great white wings - as white as the hide of the iNto eMosayo. Creatures that have skins the colour of sorghum, eyes as transparent as the waters of a flowing stream, and hair like a lion's tail."

"The Swallows?" the rebuttal was Majola's. "We have nothing to fear from them! They are Creatures of Greed and they will destroy each other with their lust before they become a threat to us!"

"So it is with the locust," Sitayi replied, her words rustling gently round the Child, caressing him, soothing his fear with the prudence born of wisdom. "A harmless solitary creature whose greed is usually directed only against its own. But when it feels crowded, its instincts tell it to migrate. And it does! In hungry swarms that devour everything in their paths! - Such is the plague of the locust. And when that plague begins, it is almost impossible to control."

"And the Swallows?" Shaka asked, stiffly.

"At the Dawn of Time, Nkosi, when your forefather Zulu kaMalandela bore the seed of the People of the Heavens, these beings were unheard-of. Now they are to the North, to the South, to the West. As close to you as a man can run in half a moon. - The Plague has begun and the Child must deal with it."

"How?" Shaka's voice rang out, demanding the knowledge he sought.

"By preserving the Identity you have given your Nation. Let the words of your Covenant with the Land and the People be your guide against the Plague."

As Shaka turned to gaze down at the immensity of his Kingdom, at Africa, he heard Sitayi's voice fly out to the Wind.

"Remember your Covenant," she repeated. "You are Zulu, you possess the Heavens, your Kingdom, your Power and your Glory are the Gift of your Heritage. Be true to that Heritage or your death will be the Death of your People."

CHAPTER XXXII
"INKUMBI"(LOCUST)
MONTH OF UMFUMFU: OCTOBER, 1823

The sleek bow of the "Elizabeth Catherine" ran completely under the glistening foam of the chilly waters of the Atlantic Ocean. The ship - a fine-looking, full-rigged, three-mast topsail schooner, armed with twelve-pound carronades and flying the Union Jack - plunged through the waves, elegantly riding the crests, as it sped under full sail, racing briskly before the buoyant lift of a frosty autumn zephyr.

Belowdecks, in the elegant lounge, Farewell was seated at his oak desk, quill in hand and immersed in the task of transcribing and collating the notes he had taken during his extensive talks with the Colonial office and, later, with the Admiralty in the weeks of preparation that had preceded his departure for Africa.

And now, a little over five days out of Plymouth, finally left in the company of his own thoughts, Farewell mentally reviewed the discussions he'd had and was pleased to note that his original observation had been confirmed. An overland approach was indeed impossible. This conviction had been strengthened by the fact that two other men were reported to have attempted the feat after Dr. Cowan, both literally disappearing from the face of the Earth. So this left only the option of an approach by sea, he mused. On the seemingly innavigable shores of the "Wild Coast."

Farewell shifted his gaze from his notes to a detailed map of Southern Africa that he had recently obtained at the Nautical Archives of the British Admiralty. The map, a hydrographical survey of the coasts of British Kaffraria and Natal undertaken in early 1823 by Captain William FitzWilliam Owen, R.N. of the H.M.S. "Leven", delineated Owen's calculations of risk factors inherent in landing on these African shores of the Indian Ocean. According to these calculations (which Farewell found extremely trustworthy), Owen concluded, as further confirmation of Farewell's initial instinct, that the two best spots on the Wild Coast for an attempted landing were indeed either St. Lucia Bay (lying slightly to the South of Portuguese Delagoa) or the mouth of the unexplored Rio de Natal (the Natal River). Owen had gone on to explain (in a brief interview Farewell had been fortunate enough to have with the captain at Plymouth) that were he himself to attempt this extraordinary feat (he used the term "suicidal"), he would "put his money on Rio de Natal".

Rio de Natal! Without hesitating, the lieutenant gripped the quill and drew a fine circle round the spot on the map. Looking up, his smile of satisfaction met his wife's beautiful features.

Elizabeth was nestled in a cosy chair, working on a needlepoint design of a Bavarian landscape - a gift for her mother, a German by birth (from some small town near Munich, the name of which Elizabeth had forgotten) who, at the death of Elizabeth's father had remarried a wealthy merchant, a Johann Lodewyck Peterssen, and was now residing in Cape Town. In fact, it had been in the Cape, Elizabeth reminisced as she threaded her needle through a snowcapped Alp, in the June of 1822, while she had been staying with her mother and step-father, that she had met a young and quite renowned naval officer who was just passing through town on his way to Rio de Janeiro. They had instantly fallen in love - she and the officer - and had been married within a few months, returning to live at Holbrook House where, Francis had insisted with a very British air, all the Farewell women were settled. Smiling at the recollection, she, too, looked up and her eyes became one with those of that renowned naval officer she'd married.

As Farewell gazed at his wife, he sensed that her presence, gave him a waking dream of rest without end, an infinity of happiness suspended without sound and movement, without thought - just joy and an ease of contentment, like a warm summer breeze scented with sweetness; and though the two - husband and wife - were now each engrossed in their own world, both worlds seemed to revolve in harmony round the same central, binding emotion: Love.

Suddenly, in the midst of his joyous reverie, the lieutenant frowned, disturbed by a sensation that was gnawing at his soul, one that was completely unfamiliar to him: a dark sensation of infinite cruelty, of terrible danger, of Death Itself - a brooding violence that weighed heavily on his heart, virtually sucking the breath from his lungs. As he gasped slightly, an eerie sound reached the lieutenant's ears, one that quite resembled the hollow moaning of despairing pain, and, as the sound swelled in his soul, it was abruptly linked to another noise, a distant, innocent noise: - the gentle jingling of ivory tassels.

"What is it, Francis?" Elizabeth was startled by her husband's expression of fear.

"Can you hear that, Elizabeth?" his voice was also hollow, as hollow as the moaning.

"Hear what?" she, too, was frightened now.

"That---." Suddenly the sounds were gone leaving only the splashing of the waves outside the porthole.

"Nothing," Farewell said, forcing a faint smile. "I must have imagined it."

*

Under a full prevailing Westerly wind the "Elizabeth Catherine" made good progress in the next seven weeks of sailing, moving in a southward course over the West European Basin, skirting the outer edge of the AzoresGibraltar ridge, continuing South over the Canary Basin off the shores of La Palma, crossing the Tropic of Cancer and on past the Cape Verde Islands and over the Equator, stopping for a brief stay at St. Helena to replenish the dwindling supplies of fresh water and to restock the hold with food and provisions.

Yet, after pushing off from the beautiful island where Napoleon had met his death, Farewell observed that the ocean had grown strangely calm, its colour undergoing a rapid change, being no longer transparent, but of a milky hue and consistency. Furthermore, the lieutenant noticed that the schooner's sails, though fully displayed, were becoming slack as the wind dwindled, filling the tropical air with an uncanny quietude, - the ship itself moving only under the influence of a strong current that was literally dragging it southwards like the unseen hand of Neptune.

"Remarkable, isn't it?" Wilkins commented as he observed the waning force of the Westerly. "This stillness."

"Aye, Tim!" responded the ship's second mate, Henry Ogle, his powerful framework dwarfing Wilkins as he squinted up at the skies, furrowing the deep crow's-feet round his soft brown, gentle eyes. "'Tis most remarkable, indeed! In the scary sense of the meanin'."

On the bridge next to the two men, Farewell gazed through a spyglass at the horizon directly ahead of the ship's course where the sky and sea blended in varying shades of mauve and lavender: the tell-tale hues of an approaching storm.

"How far would you say it is, Mr. Ogle?" Farewell asked, referring to the storm as he handed the glass to the old, weathered seaman. "Ninety leagues, sir, to be well advised." Ogle replied, peering through the lenses.

"Strike the leelift, Tim," Farewell snapped the orders without hesitation. "And snug her down! No use going into it under full sheet!"

"Aye, aye, sir," Wilkins grinned, savouring the old days when, at a mere 17 years of age, he'd been Farewell's first mate on the good ship "Bacchante" plying the deep-blue waters off the eastern coast of Italy for signs of Napoleon's barques. Feeling his veins recharged with the bubbling vigour of that adventurous period of his early youth, Tim shouted to the "Elizabeth Cather ine's" seamen, his voice ringing with emotion: "Hands by the halyards! In topgallant sails! Stand by to reef!"

In an instant all hands were clambering up the fore and main riggings folding back the stout canvas of the sails with care, as extra lashings were put on the spars, and hatches were looked to in anticipation of the westerly squalls that would soon be upon the vessel.

*

Yet, as the days passed, the ship drew only slightly closer to the storm that stayed well ahead of the schooner, at a constant distance of approximately thirty leagues. It seemed almost as if the lavender clouds had engaged Farewell's ship in a race to see which could reach the Cape first. Indeed, Francis remarked to Wilkins and Ogle, in his usual carefree manner, that he wished he had a way of communicating with those clouds, a way of informing them that the "Elizabeth Catherine" was perfectly willing to let the storm win the race by default if it would promise to maintain a safe distance.

Over the Angola Basin they raced - the ship and the storm - to the Walvis Ridge and the Tropic of Capricorn, and it was here, at the Tropic, that the storm suddenly gave up the contest and called it quits, slowing down to allow the ship to catch up.

The tragedy occurred on Christmas Eve. Elizabeth and Farewell were in the lounge. A small Christmas tree de lightfully decorated with cookies and cutouts, spangles and trinkets, and with a shiny tinsel star perched atop of its spire adorned the room with festivity. The woman was seated at an upright clavicord playing the famous carol "Good King Wenceslas" and singing along, filling the stateroom with the refreshing good will and cheer so proper to the celebration of Christ's birth. Farewell wore an expectant smile as he padded softly up to his wife and stood behind her, gently running his fingers through her long hair and furtively fastening a string of pearls round her neck

"Merry Christmas, Mrs. Farewell," he said, placing a kiss on her brilliant hair.

Feeling the string of pearls on her soft skin, Elizabeth's hand left the clavicord and instinctively moved up to the necklace, her fingertips caressing it. She then rose excitedly and rushed to look at her reflection in a mirror.

"Oh, Francis! They're exquisite!" she exclaimed, throwing her arms around him.

"What were you saying about...males and vanity?" he teased.

"All right, Mr. Farewell. I stand corrected. It is the greatest weakness of both sexes," she conceded, adding quickly, under her breath, "Even though Narcissus was a man."

His laughter laced with the cheerfulness of the moment, Francis returned his wife's embrace. "I love you, Mrs. Farewell!" he told her softly, pressing his lips against her.   A knock at the door broke into their kiss.

"Yes," the lieutenant urged, barely hiding his annoyance.

Wilkins entered the lounge. His expression was grave.

"The monsoon, sir. The break's upon us."

*

The "Elizabeth Catherine's" masts and sails were strained by the intensity of the gusting wind, as the schooner rolled and pitched violently over the turbulent waters of the Atlantic, trembling from trucks to keel, as the force of the tempest blew across her decks in heavy squalls.

Drenched to the bone, the seamen struggled against the howling wind and the slashing rain as they clung precariously to the yardarms high above the decks, engaged in the strenuous tasks of securing the lashings of the mainsail, close-reefing the jibs, fastening the carronades and hauling the anchor inboard.

Squinting against the squalls, soaked by the spray of the water that poured on them from above and below, Farewell and Wilkins stood on the forecastle staring into the wind's eye in an attempt to penetrate its hidden intention and to guess the aim and force of its thrust the thrust of the mighty adversary that had been with them since St. Helena.

The lieutenant took leave of Wilkins, shouting something about wanting to relieve Ogle at the helm - words which Tim only faintly heard above the howling tempest. Making his way up to the quarterdeck, Farewell breathed in gasps, swallowing both fresh and salt water as he ventured to blink hastily against the slashing rain, - with caution, as if suspecting that his eyesight might be destroyed in the immense flurry of the elements.

Suddenly Farewell was apprehensive, disturbed by the familiar uneasiness he had experienced at the outset of the journey - that gnawing of the soul that brought with it the chill of infinite fear and the dark burden of Death Incarnate. Instinctively his eyes moved to the tumultuous sea and he forced himself to open his lids and to squint into the blackness of the storm, and it was then that the gnawing sensation swelled within him until he felt abruptly detached from the sea and from his ship, isolated, as if withdrawn from the very current of his own existence. And in that gripping sensation he was transported to a dimension of complete silence - silence save for the innocent jingling of ivory tassels coupled with the faintest beating of drums, - distant drums that seemed nestled in the most primordial recesses of his being.

Feeling that this mysterious presence was pulling him deeper and deeper into a spiritual abyss of utter darkness and despair, Farewell made a desperate, con scious effort to react to this dimension of silence, and slowly, arduously, he fought it back, gradually feeling himself being freed from the chasm, when the jingling of the tassels and the drumbeat vanished and he almost welcomed the howling wind that returned to torment his ears. Opening his mouth, gasping, the man took a big swallow of water, feeling the salt clawing at his throat, summoning his senses back to full wakefulness.

Steadying himself on the ship's brass railing, Fare well made his way up to the quarterdeck where Ogle was at the helm, his body lashed to the wheel.

"How's she handling, Mr. Ogle," the lieutenant yelled into the second mate's ear.

"Like a Malayan whore with a ballast of rum in her belly," Ogle shouted back, his bellowing voice carrying through the tempest.

Farewell smiled at the remark as Ogle started to undo the lashings in order to let the lieutenant take over the wheel.

"Helm's hard a'weather, sir," Ogle roared to his captain. "She tends to fall off with the wind and go broadside. I've had to spoon'er once or twice."

Farewell nodded, registering the advice. Then, sud denly, as Ogle handed Farewell the tiller lashings, a bolt of lightning struck the boom of the foresail caus ing the spar to break loose and crash down onto the quarterdeck, ripping the mizzen sail. In that same hor rifying instant, one of the mast cables broke, snapping like a whip, its end curling round Ogle's leg, binding it to the mizzen yard. As the mate's scream pierced the thundering skies, the mizzen yard swung out over the high crests hauling Ogle with it, and causing a dis placement of weight that made the "Elizabeth Catherine" lurch violently broadside - at an angle of almost 60 degrees - her masts virtually touching the waves, her starboard out of the water as far as the keel.

As Ogle dangled helplessly over the choppy seas, his life hanging in the balance, Farewell quickly moved to his rescue, inching his way down the yard towards the man's precarious position.

"Cut me loose, sir, or y'll capsize!" Ogle shouted to his captain. "Cut me loose or the sharks'll have us both!"

"Not a chance, Mr. Ogle," Farewell shouted out as he fought his way across the ship and against the elements in an effort to near the man's position. Upon reaching it with great difficulty, Farewell pried Ogle's leg loose from the mast cables. Then, after helping the mate back onto the ship's decks, the lieutenant cut the lines of the splintered mizzen yard, which was instantly claimed by the sea, allowing the schooner to swing safely back onto its natural center of gravity.

Turning, the lieutenant was surprised to see Wilkins and most of the ship's hands standing as if spellbound, gaping at their captain in awe of his heroic deed.

"Get Mr. Ogle belowdecks, Mr. Wilkins!' Farewell snapped at the man, stirring him from his abstraction. "And haul down the yard! I want the foresail replaced before sunset!"

As Farewell watched Wilkins and a few of the seamen lift Ogle's suffered body and carry it safely towards the staterooms, the realisation of his dangerous act suddenly dawned upon him and, though far from being the sort of man who lavishes in glory, the lieutenant's lips wore the shadow of a self-satisfied smile. But that smile was gone as his eyes met Elizabeth's and he recognised, through the flowing curtains of rain, that the woman was far more irritated than impressed by his heroism.

For the entire night and throughout the next day, the "Elizabeth Catherine" was looted by the storm with a senseless, destructive fury, and as the shadows of the night once again mingled with the blazes of lightning, a restless Mrs. Farewell valiantly struggled towards the quarterdeck, the hard determination on her drenched features making her look all the more beautiful.

Upon reaching the deck, Elizabeth wrestled against the tempest to gain the tiller where her husband was lashed, manning the helm, looking exhausted and at the end of his resources, both physical and mental.

"Drink this," she shouted handing him a flask of warm soup. "I'll take over."

"Get back below!" the lieutenant retorted roughly, his eyes verily glazed with fatigue. "This is no time for heroism!" "Exactly!" Elizabeth matched her husband's sternness with her own. "Now drink this!"

Too tired to further react, welcoming the respite she offered, he let go of the wheel (which still remained securely lashed to his body) and gratefully clutched the warm flask in his frost-bitten hands.

"Keep'er broached to," he cried out as she hooked her arms round the wheel.

"Aye, aye, sir," she grinned, planting her feet firmly on the ground; and that grin was obviously contagious, for Farewell returned it.

*

At last, on the morning of the seventh day into the storm, the Eve of the New Year, the "Elizabeth Catherine" sailed out of the darkness and bedlam of the tempest and into a dimension of joyous golden sunshine. On deck, the seamen peered up at the deep blue skies washed in radiance and felt their hearts pervaded by a return to life, a return to hope and to a future.

Grinning at the magnificent skies, Farewell curled an arm round Elizabeth, their faces glowing with new found joy. It was then that, for a moment, the lieutenant considered sharing with his wife the uncanny, recurring sensation that still lingered in his soul with its grappling violence of intention, yet he desisted, not wanting to dampen the joy of the moment, - and also finding it of no use to frighten the woman with an unexplainable occurrence that would soon, he hoped, become a thing of the past.

Ogle limped across the deck with the help of a cane that he had rigged from the remnants of the missen yards and, with a mellow, baritone voice, he intoned "Auld Lang Syne". Eyes moistening with tears, Elizabeth joined in. As did Farewell. And Wilkins, putting a friendly arm round a battered, toothless seaman, his freckles meeting in a broad smile, also added his voice to the song until the entire ship's company was singing in praise of the New Year.

Under white wings the "Elizabeth Catherine" skimmed low over the blue seas like a great tired bird speeding to its nest. Rapid she ran in a straight path towards the Cape until - in that late January of 1824 - its coast stepped out of the horizon into the sunshine to welcome her with the call from the masthead: "Land ho off starboard bow!"

* * *

Cape Town was a leisurely seaport set against the flat-topped grandeur of Table Mountain. Its low, beautifully proportioned houses, with their whitewashed walls and vine-covered pergolas, typified the graceful ease of the early XIX Century. As the only sizeable town in Southern Africa, the Cape had become a metropolis and was often compared to the cities of Europe. Yet, although its broad tree-lined streets, open spaces, and Grand

Parade gave the impression of spacious elegance, the comparison was more romantic than real. In fact, though colourful and lively - crowded with red-turbanned Malays, water-carrying slaves, hawkers, handcarts and ox-wagons - the "city" was, at heart, truly a "town" - with a flavour that was definitely provincial.

*

"A large provincial town," Farewell mused as he stood by the bay window of Lord Charles Somerset's study at the Governor's Mansion. Looking out at the town, his eyes took in St. Mary's Cathedral, the red brick walls and glass panelling of the Botanical Gardens and, beyond it, the bustle of Adderley Street ploughed with carts and carriages running down to waiting ships at Duncan Dock and Table Bay. "As provincial as the heart of its Governor!"

Turning from his perusal of Cape Town, the lieutenant's gaze fell on Somerset's massive frame settled in an overstuffed chair behind his long mahogany desk. A pair of reading glasses were perched on the man's pug nose, their metal supports spanning his voluminous face and disappearing into a tangle of grey whiskers. Sir Charles was intent on reading the letter Sir Henry Bathurst had entrusted to Farewell and Wilkins before their departure for Africa, a missive that was to serve as a reply to the Governor's own letter as well as a formal introduction of the lieutenant as the Colonial Office's "deus ex machina" to the Shakan Affair. Though Farewell had no more than a vague notion of the confidential contents of the missive, he could easily detect that Bathurst's words were having an unsettling influence on the Governor.

Somerset looked up from his reading and gazed vacantly into space, feeling the blood pounding at his temples and the adrenalin of sheer frustration racing through his veins, taxing his already ailing heart with the pulsating vigour of distress.

"How can Bathurst do this to me?" Somerset exclaimed, venting his natural propensity to self-pity on Farewell. "After all I've done for the Cape! The merino industry! The banks! The hospitals! The farming communities! All thriving thanks to my intercession! - And now that I ask for something in return---! A fine thank you from Downing Street! But what do they care? They sit aloof and uncaring in their panelled rooms in the safety of the British Isles with their tea and crumpets, with their Sundays at Ascot, and with their moderate politics and climate, 'Hailing Britannia' while we're left to mind the shop! - And then Bathurst calls me an autocrat because I make decisions on my own. Bloody Hell! Someone's got to make them! Whenever I ask them to hitch their horse to the cart, the bangtail's lame! - And now, this!"

Somerset bitterly crushed the letter in his hand leaving an astonished Farewell to wonder whether the man was about to tear it to shreds. Then he flushed a deep red, making an attempt to recompose himself. Regaining his control with difficulty, Somerset smoothed out the parchment on his desk and, adjusting his reading glasses, he commenced to reread the missive - aloud this time, for the benefit of the lieutenant.

"To Sir Charles Somerset, Governor of the Cape Colony, Colonial Africa," he read. "My Dear Sir Charles, I cannot begin to tell you how alarmed I was upon reading your missive. I assure you that His Majesty and I share your deep concern for the Zulu threat as you so vividly outlined it. Unfortunately, due to economic and military retrenchment policies the Crown has adopted since the end of the Napoleonic Wars, His Majesty's Government is not at this time prepared to sanction the allocation of British troops." Somerset's hands started to tremble as he continued. "However, Sir Charles, after adequate deliberation, the Colonial Office has devised an alternate plan, the architect of which is the bearer of this missive, Lt. Francis George Farewell, R.N. of your acquaintance."

The Governor took a long suffered breath.

"I trust," he read on, "that Your Lordship will conceive that Lt. Farewell's undertaking is entitled to every encouragement and assistance, being one of much hazard, and, if successful, likely to lead to the best possible solution of the problem at hand. - Yours Truly, Sir Henry Bathurst, His Majesty's Secretary for War and the Colonies...."

Somerset lifted his gaze and allowed his eyes to link with Farewell's.

"You?" the Governor found himself saying, his voice burdened with incredulity.

When Farewell nodded in apologetic response, Somerset stared at the lieutenant in silence. Then, surprisingly, a laugh was born somewhere deep within the Governor's cavernous belly and, rising, the laugh surfaced upon his lips in an explosion of terse merriment.

"80,000 ferocious Zulu warriors bent on attacking the Colony," he strained through his merriment. "And what do I have from the Crown and His Majesty to deter them from slaughtering every man, woman, and child in their path? A haughty letter of apology and, nothing personal lieutenant - you?!"

Once again, Farewell nodded grimly as Somerset's laughter returned to its fleshy grotto leaving a sombre expression upon the man's face.

"Pungashe of the Butelezi, Zwide of the Ndwandwes, Pakatwayo of the Qwabes..." the Governor listed the illustrious Nguni kings. "Do those names mean anything to you, Lieutenant?

"No, Sir Charles."

"Justifiably so. That history has yet to be written - with the blood of our settlers, no doubt," Somerset abandoned himself to a feeling of immense fatigue as he rose from his desk and, hands clasped behind his large back, moved to a window to look out at his Town. "They are African cheiftains, Lieutenant. Amongst the most valorous men this continent has produced. Any one of them had the military prowess and and the ingenuity to defeat a Napoleon Bonaparte. Yet they were no match for this Black Napoleon, as they call him - this Shaka Zulu." He spat the name out with a loathsome grimace. "Over two million people, Lieutenant. He has systemati cally exterminated or dispersed over two million peo- ple!" Somerset turned and his eyes met Farewell's. "The population of London! - And you expect to stop him alone?"

By way of an answer, Farewell offered the man an other confident nod coupled with a slight firming of the jawline - as if to reconfirm to Somerset his complete faith in his own abilities.

"Don't you find your behaviour overly sanguine, Lt. Farewell? - Considering the graveness of the situation."

"The spirit requires a touch of levity when faced with the irksome, Sir Charles," Farewell replied, his light-hearted air intact. "Keeps one clear-witted."

A look of utter despondence settled upon Somerset's features as his gaze remained glued to Farewell's and he uttered, under his breath: "What is it that Colonial Jefferson said? 'I tremble for my country when I reflect that God is just'... - I need a drink, Lieutenant. Will you join me?

"I'd be glad to, Sir Charles."

* * *

The spacious emerald-green lawns of the Cape Racket and Country Club were dotted with white tables at which elegantly dressed British subjects, waited upon by Hot tentot servants, whiled away the hours of a leisurely afternoon sipping drinks and chatting casually.

It was to this reserved, stiffly colonial atmosphere that Somerset had brought Farewell, and the two men were now seated in the company of Wilkins, Rev. Josiah Bellow (who had first brought the notion of the Zulu threat to Somerset's attention) and the Xhosa school teacher, Daniel.

"An ivory trading settlement in the heart of Shaka's empire?" Somerset was saying in astonishment. "That's ludicrous, Lieutenant," he added with a sneer. "He'd wipe you out before you had a chance to erect the first lodging!"

Wilkins felt a chill sweep through him at Somerset's words, and a glance at Farewell offered little in the way of reassurance, especially when the lieutenant rejoined, casually sipping his drink: "That's a risk we'll have to take, Sir Charles."

"You're really serious about this, aren't you, Lt. Farewell?" Bellow inquired, his bushy brow furrowed.

"Yes, Reverend. Quite serious. In approximately two month's time, I intend to land a party of handpicked men on the shores of Natal. Ostensibly our presence there will be that of ivory traders but trading will be merely a cover. My ultimate purpose will be to contact Shaka Zulu in order to secure an alliance with His Majesty, King George."

Somerset, Bellow, and Daniel were stunned by the incredible idea, and the sanguine manner in which Farewell had disclosed it. Even Wilkins, who had been the prime mover of the extraordinary scheme, found himself somewhat sceptical upon hearing it presented so offhandedly.

"Alliances, Lieutenant," Somerset remarked rather absently, as if the notion were universally known, "are for civilised people. Not savages!"

At the mention of the word "savage", Wilkins's eyes flitted to Daniel. Reading the apologetic embarrassment in Tim's expression, the Xhosa offered the British youth a thin smile as if to tell him that that sort of racial treatment was very much a part of colonial behaviour - one to which Daniel was quite accustomed. In fact, the teacher's very presence in this exclusive club (upon the condescending invitation of Rev. Bellow) had raised a indignant eyebrow or two. Then, as if to punctuate this note, the Xhosa looked purposefully at the Black waiters that served on the tables, silently making the red-haired young man understand that they were slaves.

"Even if you were successful in obtaining some sort of agreement," Bellow went on in his biased distinction of racial morality, "Shaka would never respect his end of the bargain. The Zulus are Godless heathens. Their values of good and evil, life and death are completely devoid of a moral code. They have no divine prospective in their human relations. They are pagans, Lieutenant; and pagans lack Reason and Ethics!"

"Do they, Rev. Bellow?" Farewell retorted, the venom in him running over, his voice laced with such bitter ness that it's inflection was missed by no one pre sent. "Wasn't Cicero a so-called pagan? And Virgil, Tacitus, Homer, Socrates, Aristotle, Plato....Need I go on?"

"Those men were enlightened, Lieutenant," Bellow noted, his irritation augmented by the faint smile he saw on Daniel's lips. "You can't possible compare them to Shaka! He's a barbarian! An assassin!"

"So was Charlemagne - in his own special way." Fare well's eyes were on fire.

"I fail to see your point, Lieutenant," Somerset spoke in a tone of forced restraint.

"Then let me clarify it, Sir Charles," Francis said, barely controlling his explosive feelings and emotions as he went on, his voice loud enough for a few of the guests at nearby tables to turn in shocked inquiry, "We are hypocrites! We have been since the Crusades and the Inquisition! Since Cortes slaughtered the Aztecs because they failed to embrace our values of ...'good and evil'. - And the only reason our mass-murdering is clothed in righteousness is because Imperialism has a colour: White! The fact that a person of any other race could have the same idea grieves us to no end! Charlemagne was hailed as the 'Divine Sovereign of the Holy Roman Empire' because he was White and Catholic. Had he been Yellow and Pagan, like Kublai Khan, he, too, would have been condemned as a 'savage barbarian'! And yet their methods were quite similar!"

As his captivated audience looked on, awestruck, Francis's intensity grew, as did his conviction.

"Sir Charles, the only chance the Crown has of preserving its positon in Africa, America and Asia is to finally shed its hypocrisy and start treating others as equals. I believe that is the true Christian message, is it not, Rev. Bellow. Or does our moral code justify only our own faults!?" Bellow dropped his gaze in outrage, as Farewell concluded. "As I said, I intend to contact Shaka Zulu in order to negotiate an alliance with His Majesty, King George. - In doing so, I can only hope that King Shaka, though Black and Pagan, will be more 'reason-able' than Pope Alexander Borgia was."

A pregnant hush followed the lieutenant's discourse, as Daniel and a few of the Hottentot servants looked at the eccentric naval officer with deep admiration. Somer set and Bellow exchanged a concerned look, as the Governor forced a superior smile and attempted to dismiss both the lieutenant and his plan with: "I can well appreciate your idealism, Lieutenant. But you obviously have not been made aware of the situation in Africa, and I don't think I shall approve of this absurd mission of yours."

Wilkins bravely broke in, taking up the gauntlet with a challenging: "You've no choice, Sir Charles. Lt. Farewell's mandate comes from Downing Street, and the Colonial Office requests your full cooperation."

Farewell glanced at Wilkins, thankful for his solidarity, as both men rose to take their leave.

"Thank you for the drink, Sir Charles," the lieutenant's tone was surprisingly pleasant as he brushed over Somerset's resentful glare, nodding to Bellow and Daniel. "Now, if you'll excuse us, we didn't brave the high seas for four months to discuss history!"

"Lt. Farewell..." the voice was Daniel's.

"You'll be needing an interpreter and you'll find I'm quite versed in the language of the -- 'heathens'."

As Bellow frowned disapprovingly at his mission employee, Farewell flung his head back and laughed a throaty roar that served as a release of tension and a welcome fresh note in the gossip of the exclusive Country Club.

*

"Did you know my father was a minister, Tim?," Farewell and Wilkins were moving down Adderley Street at a sustained clip.

"Really, sir?"

"Rev. Farewell of Clifton, Bristol." his voice was warm with affection.

"I trust he would've been proud of the stand you took today."

Farewell laughed heartily.

"I seriously doubt that, Tim. In fact, I trust he would have had a good turn in his grave. Like Somerset and Bellow he was a monument to prejudice. For him the Lord created only one species of Man: the White Anglo-Saxon Protestant. The rest of humanity was smuggled in on the Seventh Day, whilst God was sleeping."

Wilkins smiled at the comment, as he and Farewell reached the end of Adderley and strode through the heavy traffic of Table Bay Boulevard heading for the salty wind and spray of Duncan Dock.

"While I'm gone, Tim," Farewell returned with earnest to the business at hand, "I'd like you to do some recruiting for the journey to Natal. We'll need carpenters, mechanics, trappers, blacksmiths, - and a few seamen to compliment the crew of the "Catherine". I suggest you snoop about in a place called "The Gator". You'll find it on the wharf."

"An employment agency, sir?"

"Of sorts," Farewell remarked with a diverted grin as he boarded a small landing craft near the dock and gave the order to push off. "It specializes in the kind of men we'll be needing."

"Where are you off to, sir?" Wilkins asked, as Farewell's craft struck off towards Table Bay.

"Hell," said the lieutenant, the smile gone from his lips.

CHAPTER XXXIII
"ISIHOGO"(HELL)
HENRY FRANCIS FYNN

By the beginning of the XIX Century, the direction of British policy concerning the lamentable question of slavery was to be influenced by the moral implications of the new humanitarian criterion that "all men were indeed created equal" in the eyes of God. The most vehement exponent of this belief was the Earl of Bathurst himself. Speaking in the House of Commons on the 15th of May, 1823, Sir Henry had courageously taken this stand for Equality by resolving "that the state of slavery is repugnant to the principles of the British Constitution and of the Christian religion, and that it ought to be abolished from the British Colonies with as much expedition as possible..."

Unhappily for men like Bathurst, it took over a decade - till the August of 1834 - for that process of Emancipation to be expedited and for all slaves under the British flag to become free.

Unhappily for men like Farewell - who would be buried in the heart of darkness that was Africa long before the Summer of 1834 - the thought of his Brothers' Emancipation remained very remote as ...

...his landing craft bobbed through the dismal night, over the blackened waters of the South Atlantic Ocean off Cape Town's Table Bay. The boat's rowlocks squeaked with a disturbing cadence as the oars were lifted, dripping, out of the tenebrous surface of the sea, swept back and re-emerged, thrusting the shallow vessel closer and closer to the looming shadow of Hell: - the towering monument to misery and despair that was the Portuguese slave ship know as the "Espirito de Guanabara".

Coming up alongside the battered galliot, Farewell took hold of a grimy rope-ladder that swung loosely round the curve of its hull, and, lifting himself out of the landing craft, started to climb up to the ship's bulwarks. Upon reaching them, the lieutenant handed himself over the railing, onto the decks of the "Espirito".

Inspecting his bleak surroundings, the lieutenant made out, here and there, dim yellow lights that hung directly below the flapping blackness of the galliot's sails. Under one of these swaying lanterns, a group of Portuguese sailors was immersed in the beatifying fumes of rum, laughing and talking boisterously as they engaged their leisure playing cards on the splintered surface of an old keg.

"Senhor Fynn, por favor?" Farewell inquired of the men as his figure entered the yellow wash of the lantern.

The sailors looked up, their bloodshot eyes glaring contemptuously at the man's British uniform. After exchanging a smattering of derogatory comments in the Portuguese dialect of Algarve, one of the sailors final ly jerked his thumb downwards, indicating the ship's hold, as he spat out: "Em baixo!"

"Obrigado," the lieutenant nodded wrly by way of thanks as he struck off through the galliot's tenebrosi ty to the open doors of the deckhouse and made his way down the creaky steps leading to the fetid entrails of this dismal vessel of gloom.

Nearing the bottom of the warped stairway, Fare well's senses were sharply stung by the acrid smell of uncleansed, defiled humanity and the pungent fetor of human sweat and faeces along with the sweet cohesive odour of urine. Struggling against a rising wave of nausea, the Englishman reached the last step and, brac ing himself, strode onward, into the dense, suffocating cloud of stench that was the ship's hold, and, as he did so, he froze and caught his breath in a gasp of sheer abhorrence.

Though rather roomy, the hold of the "Espirito de Guanabara" looked quite like the cramped nest of a tightly packed hive of human vermin, with hundreds of black shapes crouching, lying, sitting, standing, writhing, leaning upon and clinging to one another in all the attitudes of pain, abandonment and despair. As Farewell neared this sea of humanity, men and women of all ages, chained to one another and to the lugubrious quagmire that was the hold's pavement the words of Dante's "Inferno" came to mind, the writing inscribed with flames on the Portals of Hades: "Through me is the way into the Woeful City, through me is the Way into Eternal Despair, through me is the way among the Lost People. Leave all Hope, ye who enter!"

"The Lost People", Farewell mused as he moved closer and suddenly felt the oppressive weight of their eyes upon him, -- the proud gazes of saintly vermin that seemed to silently defy him to take pity upon their misery, to regard their suffering with the patronising palliative of commiseration; the proud expressions upon the faces of those who, having lost everything, still retain their noble claim to Dignity.

In the midst of the rippling black sea of torment and agony, Farewell made out the figure of a White man, a shape which looked very much like that of a candid mother-of-pearl butterfly reposing in a field of scorch ed sunflowers. The man, Henry Francis Fynn, knelt in the midst of the sea, his slender stethoscope pressed against the emaciated rib cage of an old man as he listened to the faint beating of the slave's aging, broken heart. If Fynn had sensed Farewell's presence, it was not immediately obvious, as the doctor's attention remained fully concentrated on the dying human being that was hunched on the floor at his knees.

"Mr. Fynn? Henry Francis Fynn? My name's Farewell," the lieutenant finally announced, evoking no response whatsoever from the other White man. "I sent a message round to your lodgings," Farewell added, as if to better clarify his presences in that god-forsaken hold. "With reference to your participation in my up coming expedition to Natal. As my medical adjutant and superintendent of cargo." The lieutenant started to feel slightly uncomfortable, restless as his voice became strained. "I understand that your experience in both areas is quite extensive."

Without lifting his ear from the scrutiny of the stethoscope, Fynn turned his pale features to look at his visitor. His eyes briefly took in Farewell's uniform with laconic indifference before shifting back to his patient in time to hear the weary beating of the old man's generous heart as it shuddered once, than twice - and fell silent, forever. Raising his head, Fynn glanced at the slave's death mask, and, with a saddened sigh, tossed the stethoscope into a sagging, weathered carpetbag and produced from the same a dog-eared, black leather Bible. Simply, as if Baptism were a natural extension of his medical training, as if for the 24 year old Irishman, saving souls were the unaffected corollary to saving lives, Fynn placed his open hand on the slave's forehead and, clutching the Bible to his own chest, recited, mechanically, with a slight brogue: "I baptise you in the Name of the Father, the Son, and the Holy Spirit," and, as his fingers drew the lids closed over glossy, lifeless orbs frozen in an expression of pleading, he added, perfunctorily, "Amen".

"I know," Fynn said to no one in particular, to him self perhaps, to Farewell, or to the trenchant, suffered gazes of the slaves, as he rose and ambled across the hold nodding to the unspoken reproach: "I know. I should baptise them before they die, but I never have time enough. Too busy trying to save the body to think of the soul. - Never time enough!"

The lieutenant eyed Fynn in frank assessment as the Irishman moved to a corner of the hold where his medical instruments were scattered on top of a crate. Resting the Bible and the carpetbag next to the other tools of his noble trade, Fynn poured distillated alcohol onto his hands and arms and lit the inflammable essence, turning his limbs into burning torches before quickly plunging them into a barrel of water that extinquished the peculiar ceremony with a soft hissing.

"They say it prevents infection," Fynn explained, giving the definite impression that he was now address- ing the lieutenant. "Though after four bouts of malaria, I'm starting to doubt its efficacity."

"Is that their main ailment? Malaria" Farewell asked, indicating the slaves.

"That and sundry assortments of many others," Fynn said, listing some as de dried his hands. "Yellow fever. Dysentry. Livergrown. Phthisic. Dengue. -- "

Once again, Fynn looked at the lieutenant, and Fare well was surprised to notice how light the Irishman's eyes were, looking almost transparent in the tenuous light of the hold.

"And ailments of the soul," he added absently, with a tired smile. "Which are harder to diagnose and almost impossible to cure. Only by the grace of God will they reach their destinations alive. Or perhaps it is His will that they do not."

"Are most of them bound for the Americas?" Farewell shifted his gaze back to the writhing sea of lost humanity and found it swirling round him in eddies of attentiveness, taking silent part in the conversation of which they were the center of focus.

"Yes," Fynn retorted as he started replacing his instruments in the discoloured carpetbag. "Havana, Cape Corrientes, Rio de Janeiro, Buenos Aires, Reunion, the Rappahannock Plantation in Virginia. - Their bitterness will spread throughout the world like an infectious plague - one for which there is no cure - and the des cendants of their descendants will rock their babies to sleep with 'nursery rhymes' of a distant birthplace called Africa where the seed of their people was trampl ed by the greed of conquest and by the folly of those who would play God with men who they feel are beneath the comprehension of their culture. And when those children grow into men and finally break the shackles of slavery, it will be too late for Africa, for those nursery rhymes will have been sung not in the dialects of Bantu, but in English, French, Portuguese and Spanish." Shutting his bag, Fynn once again faced the Englishman, and instantly dismissed from his mind the weighty words he had just uttered, changing both his mood and the flow of the conversation with an abruptness that indicated the Irishman's familiarity and cohabita tion with suffering. "Your message. Yes...I remember it. It left me somewhat perplexed, Lieutenant. To what purpose are you venturing into those forsaken regions?"

Farewell was somewhat taken aback by Fynn's sudden swerve of topical direction, and, a slight smile twich ing on his lips, the lieutenant matched the other man's nimbleness of mind by answering without hesitation: "For a man called Shaka. What do you know of him?'

Like a bolt of lightning striking a pool of water and spreading instantly to each and every liquid parti cle, the jolting current of the name

"Shaka" electrified each and every soul in that suffered "Inferno" that was the ship's hold. The very mention of the Zulu emperor provoked a violent excitement in the slaves, as lips moved rapidly and hollow with a vague mutter full of desolation, like the far off murmur of the rising wind.

"Does that answer your question, Lieutenant?" Fynn said, his pensive eyes on the "Espirito's" disconsolate cargo.

* * *

There are often in the affairs of Man - unexpectedly, even irrationally - illuminating moments when an otherwise insignificant sound, some perfectly common place gesture, or perhaps an object or a smell, suffices to suddenly reveal to us, with chilling clarity, what our life has been, what it has become, and the compla cency that has drained motivation from our existence.

Such was the sudden revelation experienced by Anna Schmidt Peterssen as she looked upon the lovely needle point design of the Bavarian Alps that her daughter, Elizabeth Catherine Farewell, had sewn for her on the long trip across the seas. As the older woman's kind, gentle eyes took in the idyllic alpine setting with its snowcapped mountains, its rolling hills dotted with a farmhouse or two, its meadows sprinkled with diasies and wild flowers, Anna felt a knot of tension tightening at the nerves below her heart, momentarily taking her breath away, leaving her on the verge of tears. Being quite reserved by nature, the sort of woman who rarely reveals her innermost emotions, allowing only the more innocuous, the more superficial feelings to transpire even in the relatively safe environment of the family, Anna fought back the desire to cry as she felt the undertow of the Past tugging at the margins of her being, sweeping her into the currents of a "prior identity" - one she had, at some point, chosen to forget.

"You were born in a place very similar to this, Elizabeth. Feldkirchen - in the Bavarian Alps." Anna told her daughter with a soothing German accent as her eyes strayed to the scented apple blossom beyond the Georgian window seat of her Cape Town home. "And I was born near there. And my parents were born near ther. And my parents' parents before them. - Funny how you forget the importance of heritage down here. We're all so busy building, building a future, we often forget we ever had a past." Anna allowed her tone to filter through the blithesome veil of regret. "Our hopes are so projected into what we will become, we lose touch with what we were -- and we reach old age out of breath, never quite knowing for sure what all that run ning was about!" A smile came to her lips as she repeated, somewhat amused by her own near-sightedness. "All that running! Laufen, laufen, immer laufen! - And towards what?"

"Stop talking like that, mother," was Elizabeth's reprimand. "You're not old."

"Yes, yes, of course," she left the compliment unattended. "Not old but old enough to start looking back, to start judging my own life. Weighing it with," she knit her brow, scratching her forehead, " - what would Johann call it, - ah, yes -," she smiled, "a balance sheet! God hands out the balance sheets if you are lucky enough to reach sixty. And he expects you to fill them out before you die, somewhat like those new tax forms they have, where you must print your name, your occupation and how much money you stole."

Elizabeth started laughing at her mother's theatrical diatribe, as Anna went on, her expression an interesting mixture of joviality and deep sadness.

"Except in God's balance sheet, you must fill in - neatly written and legible how much Time you stole from Creation. And as you stop to look back, the Past suddenly loses a lot of its glamour and you say to yourself: 'Why did I always play it so safe! Wouldn't it have been well worth it to risk a bit more for the sake of greater happiness, greater hope, greater love. You see, my dear, -" Anna cupped Elizabeth's hand in her own, gently patting it as she spoke. "When you're as young as you are, its the months and the years that count, but when you're sixty, its the seconds and the minutes you think of, and, when you fill out the 'balance sheet' there is always a special place reserved for "Moments of Happiness" - it doesn't say "Years of Happiness", mind you, - there is no such thing - God is far too conservative for that! Just moments! And it is then that you regret not having risked a bit more for the sake of those moments - not having seen the trees for the forest." The older woman paused, her eyes returning to the apple blossom as her mind reached back to another tree, just like it, in Feldkirchen, and she wondered how tall it had grown. Elizabeth sat in silence, watching her mother's brief reverie, not knowing what to say until Anna sniffed slightly and turned to look back at her with a broad smile.

"But enough of my rambling!" she chided herself, ironing out the needlepoint on her lap, her hand brushing over it repeatedly, as if she were subconsciously attempting to erase its idyllic patterns. "Tell me, what is this work Francis is doing for the Colonial Office? Is it interesting?"

Elizabeth was somewhat reluctant to answer the question, anticipating that Farewell's projected journey to Natal and the hazards it evinced would leave her mother frowning with preoccupation. Indeed, it did just that. And when Anna strove, in a pleading tone, to have her daughter intercede with Francis on behalf of good sense in order to induce him to abandon "this madness" (as she called it), Elizabeth conceded that her own apprehen sions were far greater than those of her mother. The very thought that the man she loved would attempt the impossible in so many varying forms: landing on a "wild coast" where no one had yet landed, venturing into an unexplored wilderness where no White had set foot to bend the mighty will of a brutal, bloodthristy savage king risking his own life so that the ungrateful 'King and Country" can lavish in undeserving glory. - the very thought of it chilled her to the bone. Yet, being a very practical woman, Elizabeth also knew that any emotional interference in the matter would be useless and counter productive.

"I knew what Francis was like when I married him, mother. We all knew what he was like!," she remarked by way of an answer to Anna's reproachful glances and, above all, as a purely personal need for intimate relief from her own anxiety. It seemed, in fact, as Elizabeth spoke, that she was addressing primarily her own courage and bravery in a desire to give herself strength. "I fell in love with my eyes open, mother - wide open! And I loved him because I loved what I saw, because I loved the way he was. The way he is today! And even if I knew how to break through his stubborn streak and change his mind, I'm afraid that by doing so I might inadvertently change him - and myself in the bargain - and that would be disastrous!" Now it was Elizabeth's turn to take her mother's hand in her own and to squeeze it. "It's like those moments of happiness on that 'balance sheet' of your. They have a price, don't they? Those risks you spoke of that one must take in return for greater love. Well, mother, all the worry, all the fears, all the heartache with which Francis unwillingly burdens my soul is the price I must pay for being the happy wife of Francis George Farewell!" Her eyes were mositening, he voice choked with emotion. "And in the end it's well worth it, believe me! When they give me that 'balance sheet', mnother, I want to be able to say I gave Happi ness its best shot!"

Anna Schmidt wore a set, loving smile on her beauti ful features as she handed Elizabeth her handkerchief and watched her dry her tears.

"I never realised I had such a wise young daughter," she grinned.

"It's not wisdom, mother," she replied, sniffing through her smile. "It's just love."

*

"The victims of hatred," Fynn's brogue wound round the phrase, binding it in his own bitterness. "The Masane tribe, the Nxumalos, the

Hlubis, the Cunus, the Ngwanes, Fingoes, and countless others! -- the banished of Southern Africa. That's where those slaves come from! Fleeing from Shaka's spears into the open arms of white slave traders who are only too happy to turn their hope lessness into a profit."

Farewell and Fynn had made the long journey back from 'Hell" and were now strolling through the night, down the Old Beach Road near the shores of Mouille Point and Table Bay. The Irishman's noble pale features were drawn tense with the earnestness of his words.

"In a way, Lieutenant," he went on, "these people are the ultimate victims of recent history. IUf you'll favour my comparison, they are like the 'Wandering Jews' of Africa, escaping from the 'Pharaoh' Shaka into the 'Babylonian Captivity' of the Portuguese, English, Spanish and French slave ships."

"From what I hear, Fynn, the 'pharaoh's' empire is quite vast. Logic dictates that he must give his people something in return for their fidelity of they would all be 'wandering'." Farewell's remark came not in defense of Shaka, but purely as a remark meant to restore a center of balance to Fynn's seemingly one-sided view of the Zulu.

"You've read 'Faust", Lieutenant?" Fynn inquired.

"Marlowe's, Beacon's, Lessing's, or Goethe's?" Fare well rebutted with a sly smile.

"Touche," the Irishman grinned back. "Take any of them. - What was Faust given in return for his 'fidelity'?"

"Are you implying, Fynn," Farewell frowned at his interlocutor, "that Shaka is a Mephistopheles? Offering his people - what? Power? - in return for their souls?" the lieutenant's sarcasm swelled. "I find that preposterous, I'm afraid! He's an emperor, Fynn like many others! With the scruples of a Nero, if you like - but Satan--?!" Farewell laughed out loud. "Don't be ridiculous!"

"There is a legend amongst the native sangomas - the witchdoctors," Fynn started by way of reply as his eyes moved to the moon and they twinkled upon seeing that - rather appropriately, considering the story he was about to reveal - it was a very bright, very full moon. "The legend of a Child. A Prophetic Child. One whose birth was announced almost a thousand years ago - or so they say. One whose lifetime is to initiate an era in which the name of his tribe will signify total war, terror and death. - Or so they say.

There was a certain solemnity in Fynn's speech that struck a disturbing note in Farewell's soul, darkening his mood.

"That tribe is Zulu, Lieutenant," Fynn said thickly, glancing at the other man. "And many look to Shaka as the incarnation of that Prophecy."

"Come now, Fynn!" Farewell forced a laugh. "You look far too intelligent to believe in that hocus-pocus!"

"I've seen that Child, Francis! And so have you!"

The Irishman's extraordinary remark caused the lieutenant to take notice of this frail man of medicine at his side, and he stopped and, furrowing his brow, his face registering his astonishment, his self-confidence somewhat as he probed Fynn's transparent eyes.

* * *

The Gator was one of those renowned seaside drinking establishments where burly men in shirt sleeves with coarse, weather-beaten faces dispensed out of varnished barrels the illusions of strength, of mirth, of happiness and heroism - the fantasy of splendour and the poetry of life.

When Wilkins had first sighted the "agency" in the less respectable quarters of the wharf and set eyes upon its ramshackle wooden construction suspended between the docks and pileworks driven into the muddy shore, he had harboured a lurking suspicion that Farewell had somehow "missed the mark" and sent him to the wrong place. Then, when the freckled representative of His Majesty's Colonial Office had passed under The Gator's warped sign, through its dilapidated doors, and into its tumbledown interior where he had been faced with a sultry, boorish collection of creatures immersed in the boisterous task of heavy drinking, the youth had paled slightly, feeling a light-heartedness stealing upon his frail senses. And when a terrifying hush had fallen upon the pub's crude patrons and all eyes had turned to gaze somewhat menacingly at the clean-cut, well-dressed, wholesome-looking young Englishman, Tim had stuttered a tense "Good afternoon," and at the same moment had fervently wished he could have found a more appropriate way to announce his entrance.

The rest of the encounter had been - as Wilkins had later put it - "down hill all the way!". In fact, to Tim's good fortune, in his stuttered presentation of the expedition to Natal, the word "ivory" had presented itself relatively soon - soon enough to save him any real physical harm. And the brutes, upon hearing this five-letter definition of bliss, had perked their ears and gathered round the young man, offering him drinks and crippling pats on the back in return for full information on this man Farewell and his "Trading Company".

The entire recruiting process took a little under three and a half hours and twenty-seven shots of rum, and at a few minutes after midnight (when Tim had mercifully passed out), eight men had joined forces with Lt. Farewell, -- eight valiant men who Wilkins (upon reawakening the next day to a mere twenty percent of his usual capabilities and upon taking better scrutiny of the motley conscripts) recorded in the following manner in his unofficial Colonial Office Chronicle & Diary:--- John Cane (known as Cane)- a Scot; a mountain of muscle who appears to be slightly under thirty (though with a face that could match any age); a seraphic disposition with elementary needs and instincts; devoted; a loner; shy, and hard to befriend - yet, once his affection has been won, it is probably undying; a carpenter by trade (and blacksmith), a worthy colleague of the good St. Joseph; Popham - a half-breed: Venda Tribe cum Dutch; speaks most local Bantu dialects fluently; good substitute translator should Daniel fail us; suffering from what could be more properly diagnosed as the Half-Caste's Spirit: the spirit in which are trapped both White and Native - the one ardently hating the other (an odd microcosm of racism); expansive in manner with a heart in which lurk a hive of suspect designs; an explosive character on which one should keep an eye at all times; Richard & Thomas Holstead - both hailing from Liverpool; father and son; the one having inherited the violent nature of the other; greedy, both of them, but, as the Lieutenant had cause to point out, this sort of greed is to be expected in adventure-seekers and they are, quite undoubtably, specimens of courage; both builders and seamen by trade if their word can be trusted; Dan Hockley (known at Hockly) - Welsh; crude soul in his twenties (or so he says; though I would put his age not above 16); illiterate and naturally without schooling (save for the tutelage afforded by over five years of seafaring); a wild but kind disposition; learned to probably lie, steal, and kill(?) for survival's sake, no doubt; classified as an excellent seaman; appears to take orders well if they are instilled with a good dose of fear; George Biggar (known as 'Heron', due to his long legs) - East Side of London; an older version of Hockley; has travelled round the world in a lifetime of seafaring; thrives on adventure; seems to have been through "it" all and a better man for it; I would feel quite safe to turn my back on him (for a moment or two, but not before checking his pockets); seems to be a genius in the repair of all articles of a mechanical nature; Alex Thompson - says he hails from North America (Canada); a proper trader who has actually hunted the elephant for its tusks; seemed to be rather well off from the way he spoke at out interview (strange that he should want to join another man's expedition - unless, of course, his finances have taken a sharp turn for the worse); good man to have aboard (unless his motives radically diverge from the camaraderie he demonstrated during our chat);   Michele Disantamaria - Italian (in the full sense of the meaning); yet, as we had occasion to see with Napoleon, they make good sailors; superstitious (the pendants round his neck are reminiscent of an Ottoman shrine); says to be a practicing religious man, though there is quite a bit of idolatry indigenous to his breeding (one such idol which is continuously on his lips is a certain "San Gennaro, or Ginnaro" - perhaps the influence of the beverage, Gin); has a great love of Life and living (though its definition seems somewhat removed from our own); speaks rather good English (said he learned it during the war though only God knows which one!); to be trusted as long as there is no financial consideration attached;--

*

"Natal, the Portuguese word meaning Christmas," Farewell was presiding over an instructional briefing of the official landing party. "The Day of Birth. Yet its coasts have brought only death since Vasco Da Gama discovered them almost three centuries ago."

The lieutenant stopped to review the faces of the men united in his presence: Wilkins, Fynn, Daniel, the "Elizabeth Catherine's" second mate Henry Ogle, John Cane, Richard and Thomas Holstead, George Biggar ('Heron'), Hockly, Michele Disantamaria (becoming known as Ginnaro), Alex Thompson, and Popham. "So diversified," he thought to himself. "Each with a different past, yet all now sharing the same, extraordinary future!", and, as he looked at them he wondered how many would still be alive in a year's time. Indeed, would he still be alive?

"1552, the 'Sao Joao', wrecked. 1683, the 'Wains worth', wrecked," the lieutenant nonchalantly continued to list the casualties of the "Wild Coast" as the men looked on, the litany of the word "wrecked" causing their expressions to droop. "1689, the 'North', wrecked. 1699, the 'Fidelity', wrecked. 1705, the 'Postlooper', wrecked. 1718, the 'Hope', 1782, the 'Grosvenor', 1796, the 'Hercules' --- all wrecked!"

"Doesn't sound terribly encouraging, sir," Wilkins admitted, eyeing his recruits and wondering whether - after this day's meeting - he might have to start his conscription work anew.

"On the contrary, Tim," Farewell smiled with his usual confidence. "I find this list most encouraging." Upon seeing the youth's nose wrinkled in perplexity, the lieutenant added: "Are you still up on your nautical history, Tim?"

"I believe so. - Yes, sir."

"Then tell me," the lieutenant pensively paced the floor of his schooner's lounge - in which the meeting was being held. "What did all those ships I mentioned have in common?"

"They were all large vessels, sir," Tim replied in a wink. "Galliots, barquentines, men-of-war...the sort of merchant ships one would find suitable for long voyages."

"Exactly," Farewell was quite pleased with the youth's ready erudition. "Large and heavy! Weighed down by gun decks, bulkheads, turrets, and oversized galleries! Ships like that displace thousands of tons and have draughts of well over twelve feet! No wonder they sank! They were no match for the sandbars and storms that make landing on that coast virtually impossible! - And that's one mistake we'll try to avoid!"

The men seemed somehow heartened - more by the casual tone of Farewell's voice than by the words he actually spoke.

"We'll use a more appropriate craft - a sloop would be perfect: large enough to brave the winds, yet small enough to sail in shallow waters without running aground." Moving to Captain Owen's hydrographical survey map of the coasts of Natal (hanging prominently from the lounge's beamed ceiling), the lieutenant referred to it as he described the proposed trek. "We'll sail up the coast on the sloop, hugging the shore for safety, until we reach the mouth of the Rio de Natal - the Natal River. Then we'll anchor offshore, wait for the tide and - ride it in!" The lieutenant motioned with his hand as if it were the sloop braving the tide into the waters of the river, as the men looked on - all retaining expressions that bordered on scepticism. Sensing the doubt that plagued their spirits, Farewell added, with disarming mettle: "And you, Mr. Ogle, will skipper the 'Elizabeth Catherine', following our sloop from a position out at sea -- ready to come to our assistance if," he smiled, "my confidence is ill-conceived. - Are there any questions?"

There were none, as a few smiles tentatively flourished on lips previously drawn in tense assessment.

"Then---," the lieutenant raised a bottle of West Indian Rum and pried the hefty cork loose. "To Natal, gentlemen!"

As the neck of the bottle was freed to release its scented nectar, the men cheered and laughed in forced merriment, as Farewell passed the bottle around. Yet, in their hearts, there still lurked the shadow of fear. Even if they should make it over the waves and into the river's mouth ---

--- what of Shaka?

Shaka Zulu - the native emperor's name blazed in Elizabeth's heart as she stood at the lounge's thres hold, her expression grave as she beheld the joviality that enshrouded the man whom she loved; and as the anguish clutched at her throat, her soul could not help but wonder whether she would ever see him again.

CHAPTER XXXIV
"UKUMA NJALO NGOKUNGAFI"
(IMMORTALITY)

"We're at full cable, sir!!" Wilkins yelled desperately over the howling of the wind. "She's dragging anchor!"

It was the morning of the fifth day into the long awaited sea journey to the Kingdom of the "Black Napoleon". As Farewell had planned, the expedition's sloop (a fine specimen of 20 to 30 tons and bearing the name "Julia") was at the mouth of the Rio de Natal, anchored offshore with the intention of waiting for the tide in order to "ride it in" -- or thus the lieutenant had sanguinely outlined the proposed approach in his briefing.

Yet, unlike the illustration used in the briefing, the "Julia" was unexpectedly submerged and overwhelmed by the elements, violently embroiled in a maelstrom of slashing rain and roaring surf; and the passengers of the ship (Farewell himself, Wilkins, Fynn, Daniel, and the eight of the expedition) were fighting for dear life to save themselves and their precious living cargo of horses, goats, and pigs, as well as the crates and barrels that made up the expedition's stores and supplies.

At Wilkins's call that the anchor was dragging, Farewell squinted against the rain and the spray of the saltwater, his eyes narrowing to focus on the entrance to the Rio de Natal and the jagged, razor-sharp cliffs to which the "Julia" was being inexorably pulled by the relentless currents. Spinning round, the lieutenant peered over the sloop's helm and made out the hazy outline of the "Elizabeth Catherine" which, as integral part of the plan, was two miles out at sea, fully reefed against the storm and riding the waves - "ready to come to Farewell's assistance (or so he had told his men) in case his confidence had been ill-conceived". Fully trusting in the support function of his schooner and the courage of his mate Henry Ogle (who was at its helm), the lieutenant braced himself and called out to Wilkins, his voice roaring over the storm: "Cut the cable!"

And, as all hands held their breaths, many quite expecting this breath to be their last, and as Michele clawed at the golden trinkets round his neck and uttered a silent prayer to "San Gennaro", - Wilkins obeyed and freed the drenched anchor line with a slash of his knife, causing the "Julia" to shoot towards the river's mouth like a bullet fired from a gun!

Over the flashing turmoil and the uproar of the surf, the ship ran blindly, dishevelled and headlong, as if fleeing for her life. Her bow sliced onto a sandbar, causing the craft to shudder from stem to stern, then, when it seemed that the keel had been caught in the rift of sand and gravel, the "Julia" miraculously shuddered again and broke free. Clearing the bar, she came up buoyant and soared over the crested waves. Then, barely sweeping past the cliffs that flanked the river's mouth, the sloop skimmed on into a vast body of calmer waters where she spun round on her poop and gradually slowed to a standstill, bobbing innocently on the tranquil surface of her new habitat.

Though the danger of being listed as one of the many wrecks of the "Wild Coast" seemed behind them now, the men remained perfectly still, unable, unwilling to move for fear they might break the spell that held them prisoners in its illusion of safety. Eyes flitted back and forth in attempts to penetrate the storm that still raged round them and take stock of their new surround ings. Although the mantle of rain and fog stubbornly clung to the "Julia", making visibility almost nil, Farewell and his companions gradually realised that their safety was real. When that revelation struck their spirits, wide grins appeared on their haggard faces. Then, their confidence mounting, the men broke their silence, all trying to speak at once in a babble that grew within a short time to loud, joyous cheering and an explosion of wild hooting that was soon accompanied by the stamping of feet and the clapping of hands. As eyes shone large and wild with deliverance, the men started singing and dancing on the decks of the sloop, involving the horses, the goats, and the pigs in their merriment. Some of the men spilled over the "Julia's" sides into the shallow waters of their new home, crying excitedly, splashing, dashing aimlessly here and there with the foam swirling at their waists.

In the midst of this gaiety, Farewell did not have a moment's worry for the "Elizabeth Catherine" which he felt confident was still out at sea where she would wait for the storm to lift so that it's temporary captain, the astute and masterly seamen Henry Ogle, could - according to Farewell's plan - ascertain the safe landing of the "Julia" before sailing back to Cape Town. The lieutenant had no reason to worry about his schooner. The sloop had been the one in danger, not the larger ship, and now that the "Julia" had cleared the perilous sandbars, for Farewell, to all intents and purposes, the first part of the expedition had been successfully concluded.

Yet, what Francis Farewell did not know was that the devastating storm raging round his schooner was too much for the heavy vessel to bear. The foremast cracked be neath the strain of the wind and lumbered down, swaying against the riggings, tearing them, before it came crashing onto the quarterdeck. Farewell did not know that the "Elizabeth Catherine" was listing leeward as the waves snapped her bowsprit and jackstays and as the ocean flowed in great swells onto her decks and through the gaping rift left by the foremast, filling her holds and belowdecks with foaming surf. Farewell had also no way of knowing that a desperate Ogle fought the fury of the elements till he realised, with tears of strained anger diluted to despair by the saltwater that streamed down his face, that the fight was over and that the sea had won. It was then that Ogle limped across the schooner's decks shouting the words which cause the greatest grief for men of the sea: -- "All hands to boats! Abandon ship!"

*

When the storm had subsided, and visibility returned to normal, the men of the "Julia" were able to take stock of their landing site. It was then that they rea lised, to their great surprise, that it was not the mouth of a river, but rather an enchanting bay -- that the "Rio de Natal" was, in fact, "Natal Lagoon", "Natal Bay", or, more properly, "Port Natal" (as it would sub sequently be called). As the men gaped in awe of their beautiful surroundings, they saw that on three sides the bay was encompassed by gently rising bush country, fringed by a tangle of tropical vegetation to the North and West, and, to the South, a narrow, thickly wooded headland that shielded the bay from the pounding surf.

There was also an almost uncanny silence about the place. Indeed, apart from the distant roar of the sea, the only sounds to be heard were the chattering of monkeys, the squawk of waterfoul, and the rustling of hippos wallowing in the reeds at the water's edge.

In was in this peaceful port that the landing party spent their very first and quite rousing night. Wilkins described it in his Colonial Office Chronicle and Diary as:---

"We selected a hollow under rising ground to protect us from the winds, and began cooking our dinner.

"Very tired after our journey up the coast and the harrowing passage over the sandbars, we soon went to sleep. We had, however, not been long in that condition when, about midnight, a storm broke over us. Not only we, but our bedding, became thoroughly drenched, and a stream of water which rushed through the hollow forced us to move to higher ground. Having done so, we employed ourselves in making a blazing fire and wrapping ourselves in our wet blankets when we were suddenly surprised by the howling of troops of wolves. We increased our fire as far as the rain would permit us, in hopes that the wolves would be kept at a distance, but, in defiance of the fire and our yells, they approached and stood menacingly before us. Since our firearms were wet from the rain, we had no better mode of defence from these creatures than by standing back-to-back with firebrands in our fists. Several came so close as to snap at us, yet we were able to strike them back with our firebrands....which had the life-saving effect of scaring the wolves away."

Thus the first truly Colonial night of the freckled Colonial Officer. At the next awakening, he wrote:---

"On the following morning the mechanics, Richard and Thomas Holstead with Hockly, Cane and Biggar set to work to cut timber and build a twelve foot square house of wattle and daub, while I and Fynn walked round the head of the bay in search of inhabitants. We came across none, though we found several footprints..."

Wilkins spent the rest of his first day examining the area - which (besides the "footprints" that gave it a Robinson Crusoe flavour) appeared to be quite desert ed. It was in the course of this exploration that he noted in his Diary:---

"The Port of Natal abounds with Hippopotamus and fish of various sorts and the soil in its vicinity, in my opinion, is particularly productive being blessed with Indian corn which is large and in great abundance. The plains near the bay are very extensive and, should a proper colonial settlement be established here, I'm sure the homesteaders would find the pastures for their cattle rich. There is also an abundance of timber for shipbuilding (that quite closely resembles the cedar) and at the head of the harbour are fine tall spars fit for masts. Overall, I am convinced that we have found the ideal spot for the development of this area, the port being a natural haven, sheltered and lush enough to provide the most immediate needs..."

In his imperialistic zeal - so proper to those of his Downing Street Office - Tim seemed to have been carried away by his plans for development of the area, completely forgetting (or so this entry in his Diary would suggest) the powerful Lord of this "natural haven", the Zulu king on whose land they were now tres passing. A forgetfulness that would quite soon be rectified.

In fact, the members of one of Shaka's scouting parties (who had been routinely patrolling the coastal regions near the umNgeni River) had been quite shaken to see a strange "creature with white wings" floating on the waters of a calm lagoon. The warriors had been even more shaken to see "peculiar animals that looked some what like themselves - only without colour" walking about the woodlands in the course of a protracted inves tigation of their surroundings. Hurrying back to the capital of their Empire

(Shaka's Citadel, "Bulawayo"), the scouts had soon informed the Zulu Prime Minister, Ngomane, of what they had seen.

The next morning, at Shaka's request, a Zulu regiment - the iziCwe with its commander Mgobozi, along with Generals Joko and Nqoboka (as observers) had been dispatched to the coasts of the Great Ocean to look into the matter and to report back to Shaka himself. Moving at a constant trot, the regiment reached the vicinity of "Port Natal" on the afternoon of the second day. The iziCwe's arrival at the site of the "Julia's" landing was recorded by Wilkins in the following manner:---

"As Fynn, I and the Lieutenant sat on the idyllic beach listening to the sounds of the bush, watching the tumbling surf and discussing the best method with which contact could be made with the Zulu King, I happened to feel upon the ground beneath me a peculiar quaking, as if a herd of sea-cows were prancing about in the vicinity. And, at the same time, a sound reached my ears similar to that of male voices intoned in heroic chanting (I was instantly reminded of the recountals I'd heard of Bonaparte's marching troops). My curiosity aroused, I chanced to look up and suddenly became aware of an extraordinary sight. A huge army of natives, like some great black sea, was moving down the coast towards us. So dense was this mass of running men that it was impossible to make out where it ended. Fynn, the Lieutenant and I were instantly on our feet and in the company of our silent, gaping comrades Daniel, Cane, the Holsteads, Biggar, Popham, Hockly and the others, who came in time to witness this army drawing nearer at an unbelievable pace, and, indeed, the closer it came, the more terrifying it appeared. Armed with shields and assegais, these warriors were quite obviously a very different breed from the Cape Africans, being tall, powerfully built men, with bodies developed to the extreme and an unmistakable arrogance that left no doubt as to their superiority..."

As Wilkins pointed out, the closer the iziCwe trotted, the more threatening was its aspect, the more deafening its chanting. But what Tim could not know was that, at the head of the approaching regiment, Mgobozi, Joko, and Nqoboka shared the Swallows' stunned apprehension, their eyes taking in these amazing creatures "from the sea" with a feeling of mounting, spellbinding trepidation that belied there "unmistakable arrogance".

When the "great black army" had come close enough, Mgobozi raised his arm in silent command and, in perfect unison; the warriors broke their measured trot and came to a standstill. Their chanting stopped and silence reigned supreme as both fronts - the Swallows and the Zulus - inspected each other with intense interest, with a shade of bewilderment and with great inquisitiveness - neither side really knowing what to do, neither willing to make the first move.

On the one front Wilkins, Fynn, Farewell and the rest of his party remained immobile, vigilant, as Cane tightened his grip on the musket in his hands, as Richard Holstead steathily extracted the pistol from his belt, and as Thomas Holstead's hand hovered over the sheath of his large hunting knife. On the other front, the soldiers of the iziCwe stood like so many statues, clutching their ixwas in iron grips, as Joko knitted his brow, his inspecting gaze lingering on the incredible redness of Tim's hair, as Nqoboka took in the half-built house of wattle and daub, and as Mgobozi's eyes shifted to the "Julia" tied near the lagoon's shoreline, gently riding the surf that unfurled onto the sandy beaches.

Fascinated by the legendary "animal with the great white wings", the commander of the iziCwe walked across the sand drifts, strode into the bay and waded out to the sloop, stopping waist-deep in the water next to the ship's bow. With childish wonder, Mgobozi gaped at the sloop's mast, at its reefed sails (the white wings "tucked back"?), at its riggings, its yards, at its pointed bowsprit jutting out like a spear. Collecting his courage, readying his ixwa (just in case this really was "an animal"!), Mgobozi reached out and touched the ship, tentatively at first, then with rising confidence as a cherubic smile came to grace his lips. Curling his hand round the sloop's bowsprit, the general tugged on it and let go, his smile turning to a diverted chuckle as he watched the "Julia" bob up and down on the surface of the bay.

Sharing in their friend's legitimate fascination, Nqoboka and Joko laughed along with Mgobozi, as did Farewell, Wilkins and Cane, - the human factor in the general's joyous exploration of the unknown coming as a temporary equalising element, one of levity, in this otherwise high-strung interracial encounter.

Yet, when the general reached up and grabbed hold of the leechlines of the staysails and started tugging on them, Farewell's smile vanished as he anticipated the shock that was forthcoming. In fact, the leechlines sud denly came loose, causing the staysail to unfurl and plop down, flapping in the wind. The sudden movement in the sail scared a seagull that was perched on the sloop's mainyard, and the bird, screeching loudly in protest, fluttered away. Startled by the unfurled canvas and the bird's shrill cry, Mgobozi shrank back, his ixwa poised as he glared wide-eyed at the ship, wondering what he'd done to make it "come to life".

Hearing Joko's laughter swelling merrily at his expense, Mgobozi snatched a glimpse of the fleeting seagull and, upon realising what had happened, the general of the iziCwe blushed slightly with a touch of embarrassment. A good-natured smile tugging on his lips, he turned to eye his warriors who stood silently at attention, secretly wondering whether they had noticed that, for a fleeting instant, the "Whip of Qokli Hill" (as he had been named after the immortal conflict with the Ndwandwes) had been frightened by a small fledgling.

His laughter dwindled by renewed curiosity, Joko strolled by the horses (which he viewed with only pass ing engagement) and attached his puzzled scrutiny to the long blond hair of Thomas Holstead. Beguiled by the "human straw", Joko swatted Thomas's braided pigtail and watched it sway back and forth like a pendulum, before he flicked up the blade of his ixwa and cut it off, grinning at the plaited blond treasure in his hand.

"You cheeky son of a bitch!" Thomas said, feeling the back of his head where his long hair had once been, his passionate phrase to be prominently featured in Tim's Diary as the "first true articulated communication between His Majesty's Government and the Zulu Empire" ("Not terribly promising", Wilkins added to the Chroni- cle as a postscript). Quick to strike back (like all men who've been raised on the docks of Liverpool), Thomas yanked out his hunting knife and, finding no long hair, sliced off one of the feathers on Joko's headdress.

Instantly, as one man, the warriors of the iziCwe lowered their spears and stomped their feet on the ground, ready to vindicate this insult to the pride of one of their commanders. This thunderous show of instant support had a chilling effect on the Whites, who paled (becoming even more the colour of sorghum), their hearts pounding the adrenalin through their bodies. Joko and Thomas eyed each other menacingly, both men looking quite prepared to precipitate the Anglo-Zulu Encounter into a bloodbath.

But just as Farewell prepared to intervene, the disarming laughter of the general of the iziCwe came as a welcomed break in the tension. Indeed, it was now Mgobozi's turn to find diversion at the expense of his friend, and circling Joko, the stout general cast an amused eye on the amputated feather, his merriment soon being shared by Nqoboka and with great relief - by Wilkins, Cane, Hockly, Biggar and the others (who had already seen the ominous spectre of death looming over them). Only Fynn remained curiously unmoved by the events at hand as he watched them unveil with conscious detachment.

"Tell them we come in friendship," Farewell said to Daniel, taking advantage of this lighter mood to strike up a true avenue of communication. "From the King of the Whites, tell them. And that we wish to meet with Shaka."

As seemed to be the norm in this part of Africa, the mere mention of the Zulu's name had a sobering affect. Mgobozi's laughter suddenly faded to a scowl, as his stern gaze whipped to Farewell.

"Ukhuluma-ni?!" Mgobozi demanded of Daniel, angrily inquiring of the other Black man what the Swallow had said.

"Febana ka Mjoji..." Daniel told Mgobozi. "He comes with friendship from King George." And went on to explain that George, "Joji" (in its phonetic equivalent), was the Whites' king, and that his representative, "Febana" ("the one who brings friendship" as Farewell would be called in Zulu) wanted to meet with Shaka.

With a suspicious glare, Mgobozi studied the faces of Farewell, Wilkins, and Fynn. By way of an answer to Farewell's offer of friendship, the Shakan general lashed out, grabbing a trembling Daniel by the arm and hauling him away into the midst of his warriors. Seconds later, upon their commander's sharp order, the regiment turned and trotted away, causing the earth to quake under the men's stomping feet -- leaving an anxious void on the shores of "Port Natal".

"What do you suggest we do now, sir?" Wilkins found himself asking - in a manner that was most rhetorical.

"There's only one thing we can do, Tim," was Farewell's response. "Wait. We've made the first move by coming here. Now it is his turn."

* * *

"How many are they?" Shaka asked, his massive frame reclining by the fire of his immense new Royal Hut in the Citadel of "Bulawayo" (meaning -- "The Place of The Kill").

"Twelve, Sigidi," Mgobozi answered, his eyes flick ering from his king to his statuesque image perfectly reflected on the hut's polished black floor.

"Where?"

"On the coast, Baba," the voice was Joko's. "South of the umNgeni."

The Zulu Emperor remained silent, his body unmoving, his feline eyes fixed on the crackling flames.

"Where there any other landing parties in sight?" he finally asked, his voice not much above a whisper as his pensive gaze shifted to Thomas's pigtail resting on the palm of his large hand.

"No, Sigidi. They were alone."

Again Shaka remained silent, his eyes alive, his brain seething with considerations, plans of action. Then: - "Post lookouts near their camp. I want a full report on their every move."

Bowing with a respectful "Bayete, Nkosi", the generals moved to leave.

"Mgobozi," Shaka asked, looking up and meeting his friend's eyes for the first time.

"Baba...?" the general replied, stopping at the hut's entrance.

"Are they..." The Zulu's voice had a restive quality that was most uncharacteristic, one that betrayed that same peculiar apprehension he'd suffered after his en counter with the White Elephant - that peculiar emotion akin to fear. "Are they..." he repeated, "---like us?"

Sensing his friend's brooding disquietude, the gene ral pulled a smile and answered, in an attempt to bring a touch of levity to his monarch's burdened heart. "No, Sigidi. - That would be impossible!"

"Yes," Shaka said with a weary voice, returning the smile. "Impossible."

When the generals had left, Shaka's eyes returned to the pigtail in his hand and he remained in silence, only the crackling of the fire breaking the stillness that enveloped him.

"What do you think, Ngomane?" he asked after a long pause.

"A scouting party, Nkosi," came the Prime Minister's reply from the shadows of the mammoth hut.

"Hmmmm," Shaka nodded, musingly. "They've probably been sent to assess our military strength. Which means their people are afraid. That's why they speak of -- 'friendship'. - Friendship," he repeated with a wry smile, "a word that veils many subtle meanings."

"Who can tell, Baba," was Ngomane's salubrious re ply. "They might mean it. If Dingiswayo had been in your position, he would've jumped at the chance of a possible alliance."

At the mention of his mentor, Shaka's features softened with an affectionate smile. "I think even an idealist like Dingiswayo would've found this particular alliance somewhat hard to visual ise." Twirling the pigtail in his hand, Shaka casually toyed with a possible name for the fictitious alliance. "The Nguni-White Confederacy? The Bantu-White Paramountcy? The Zulu-Swallow Nation? It all sounds very short lived, doesn't it?"

In a deliberate gesture of finality, Shaka tossed the pigtail into the fire and watched the "straw" burn, quickly curling within itself and fizzling with tiny explosions of blue and yellow. The Zulu's gaze shone brilliantly as he witnessed the striking ease with which the lapping flame overpowered this "effigy" of the Swallows, seeing in the braid's incineration a sign of his own upcoming supremacy over the emissaries of "Joji". When Shaka's sonorous voice returned to flood the hut, the tone was considerably more purposeful as he barked out to an Ufasimba guard: "Bring him in!"

The guard relayed the order to the outside and, seconds later, Daniel had been dragged into the hut and was put in the presence of the great African Lord. Cocking his eye in the teacher's direction, Shaka's gaze strayed critically over the Xhosa's dishevelled three piece European suit, over his soiled white shirt, his cravat, and the faded bowler hat perched on his head. Though Shaka remained divested of expression, Ngomane stifled a smile upon beholding this extraordinary apparition - the fantastic incarnation of (so the Prime Minister told himself) the Nguni-White Confederacy that Shaka had previously attempted to visualise. "Yes," Ngomane nodded silently as his eyes perused Daniel, "the concept does look quite short-lived."

Sensing the immense power wielded by this imposing Zulu Emperor, the infamous protagonist of the "Mfecane" - the expansionistic "crushing" of hundreds of innocent tribes, and in awe of Shaka's overwhelming charisma, Daniel unwittily faltered as he neared the giant imperial figure near the fire and, though his heart was a torrent of hatred for this ferocious Oppressor of the tragic Fingoes, the Black man found himself instinctive ly removing his bowler hat in sign of respect. In that same instant, the stone-faced Ufasimba guards thrust the teacher onto his knees and pressed him flat against the floor causing the hat to slip from his hands and roll across the polished black pavement, coming to a stop at Shaka's side. The king snatched up the strange "head dress" and eyed it as he initiated his inquiry of the odd social specimen who lay prone before him.

"What is your tribe?"

"Xhosa," Daniel replied in the Zulu language, his voice betraying his loathing for what this mighty king stood for.

"Where were you taken prisoner? In the South?" Shaka asked, sensing the Xhosa's aggression and feeding on it as he casually studied the bowler's silk headband.

"I am not a prisoner, Nkosi," Daniel replied, sur prised by the Zulu's question, causing Shaka's own surprise to become evident as the king looked up, his brow raised in wonder.

"You mean to say," the emperor sought clarification, "you joined the Whites -- willingly?"

"Yes, Nkosi," was the level rejoinder.

"Why?"

"They gave me a dignity I lacked," Daniel strained to meet Shaka's searching eyes. "A chance to break with the past."

Ngomane was intrigued by the answer, as Shaka paused to allow his experienced gaze to probe deeper into the man's heart.

"The raven has also been known to 'willingly' build his nest near monkeys," the Zulu considered out loud. "But he is never their equal and he would be a fool to think he could be. That is why when he sleeps at night, he always keeps one eye open. - Are you," the king's lips wore a humourless smile, "their equal?"

In the rigid immobility of his hatred for Shaka, Daniel preserved an austere silence, his eyes remaining locked with the king's.

"In my Nation," the Zulu boasted, as if to deliberately provoke the Xhosa, "any man, irrespective of his origin and the wealth and status of his family, can become a chieftain and commander through merit alone. Do the Swallows offer you the same - 'possibility of dignity'?" When Daniel's silence stubbornly persisted, Shaka's smile broadened and a twinkle came to his eye, as he concluded, in a mocking whisper: "Then you are chasing the moon's reflection in a stream."

When Shaka paused again in pensive silence, Ngomane studied his king and found himself considering that a man like Shaka, who is entrusted with so much arbitrary power, must continuously, unrelentingly believe in himself - even to the point of self-induced megalomania. Or else how could he go on bearing the oppressive burden of his ever-increasing responsibilities. That is why many manifestations of superiority, that could easily be taken as gratuitous - like the burning of the plaited hair and this needless boasting - were of great importance to the delicate balance of such a powerful man's heart. "Of vital importance," Ngomane pondered. And the Prime Minister saw traces of the same vainglorious behaviour when Shaka spoke again.

"What do you do for the Whites? Are you a spy?"

"I am a teacher, Nkosi."

Perceiving the deep-rooted pride in the Xhosa's response, Shaka cast him a sidelong gaze. "There is solidity about his character," the king told himself, "and that cannot exist without courage."

"Do the Swallows want to learn our ways," the king said out loud.

"I teach my people - their ways."

Shaka's feline eyes shot sternly back to his interlocutor. "Is that not betrayal?" he demanded of the Xhosa.

"No, Nkosi," Daniel was unwavering. "All a man can betray is his own conscience. And this sort of learning is a matter of the mind, not the soul."

Shaka's gaze remained rivetted on Daniel, not really knowing how to accept his reply. "What do you teach?" he finally asked.

"To read and write."

Seeing the monarch's features clouding over with perplexity, Daniel intuitively adjoined: "May I show you, Nkosi?"

Ever vigilant, the king hesitated before finally nodding to the Ufasimba. When the guards had relinquish ed their hold on Daniel, the Xhosa got up rubbing the stiffness out of the back of his neck. As Shaka looked on - his distrust momentarily tempered by curiosity - Daniel neared the fire and, taking a piece of charcoal in his hand, wrote on a straw mat, in bold letters, the word S H A K A.

"'Shaka'," the teacher said, indicating the name. "A 'written' word that is 'read' -- Shaka."

The king peered down his nose at the odd drawing and uttered, tentatively, barely concealing his mounting fascination as he poised his long forefinger in indica tion of the lettering and asked: "That is I?"

"Yes. It is the visual representation of your name," the Xhosa told his rather unique pupil. "And this is my name - 'Daniel'," he explained as he wrote his own name on the mat next to the dreaded five-letter word whose mere mention could cause most of Southeastern Africa to take pause.

"What is this used for - this pattern?" the king queried with an annoyed grimace. "Witchcraft? Casting spells?"

No, Nkosi. It is a way of transmitting ideas - feel ings over vast distances."

"I have messengers for that!" Shaka's tone was curt.

"Yes, I can imagine you have," Daniel fought back his exasperation, mentally reproaching himself for having initiated this ludicrous demonstration. "But this assures you that what you speak here will be heard there in exactly the same words."

"I'm already assured of that," the Zulu glanced at Ngomane with a lopsided, impudent grin. "If my messen gers should dare to misrepresent me, they are impaled."

Now it was Daniel's turn to probe the other man's features using his own scholastic mind to dig deep for a key to a potential weak point. As the teacher's mind raced, his thoughts turned over the reality of this man, Shaka, as Daniel knew him to be. The Xhosa inwardly reflected that one who resigns himself to kill (as the Zulu undoubtably had), need not go far for the resigna tion to die. In fact, Daniel guessed quite astutely and accurately, the Zulu monarch's relationship with Death must be rather intimate. And consequently, Daniel deduced, so must his relationship with the Supernatural. With this in mind, the teacher resumed his instruction with a renewed sense of direction.

"Writing can also be used to 'store' what you speak today so that it can be 'heard' generations from now," he told the emperor, adjoining with deliberate emphasis: "It is a form of - 'immortality', Nkosi."

Having built his empire with no clear preconceived goals save for the grandiose visions of his own inex haustible ambition implanted by the hatred and quest for revenge of his mother, Nandi, the Great Female Elephant, - and having created a "fantastic" realm with nothing to go by but his own creative fantasies, it was always obvious to Ngomane that beneath Shaka's outer shell of iron determination there should lurk the sensitiveness of a dreamer (the outer shell being as strong as the inner core is vulnerable). That is why the Prime Minister was not amazed to notice how the very mention of the world 'immortality' had an instant captivating effect on the king, causing intense interest to flash in his eyes. Though this flaring note of engagement was also not lost upon Daniel, Shaka quickly attempted to veil his interest under feigned indifference.

"The Swallows have blinded you," he told Daniel. "The only way to store ideas or feelings is in the mind and in the heart." Shaka tapped his head and chest. "And the future generations will always hear the voice of the Wind bringing them messages from long ago -- " his voice fell to barely a whisper as he added: "-- of Shaka."

"Yes," the Xhosa replied, bitterly, unnerved by the king's arrogance. "And that voice will speak of tyranny!"

"Is that what your Whites think of me? A tyrant?" Shaka shot back, apparently unmoved by what Daniel had intended as an insult (indeed, for Shaka being called a tyrant was rather flattering).

"That is the opinion brought to them - 'by the wind'."

Shaka returned the defiant smile that had appeared on the Xhosa's features and retorted: "You say they have given you a chance to break with the past and better yourself. Doesn't that really mean that they have deprived you of your past and," he dropped his gaze to Daniel's three-piece suit, "...forced you to be like them? Isn't that also tyranny?" "I am still a Xhosa!" he replied calmly, having rewon his composure.

"Are you, 'Danl'?" he said, mocking the man's ac quired name. "Or have you retained only the colour of your skin?"

Daniel was momentarily chilled by Shaka's insight and, noticing this, the emperor ran swiftly to his point.

"Their king? He is called Joji, I am told. Is that correct?" Shaka asked matter-of-factly.

Not trusting himself to reply, Daniel remained silent and nodded stiffly.

"I think Joji and I have a great deal in common," Shaka taunted the other man. "We both know the meaning of the word -- 'persuasion'." Suddenly Shaka's voice was sharp and cutting. "And in force of my own persuasion, since you seem to have mislaid your identity, 'Danl', I will give you one of which you can be proud. From now on you are Zulu and you shall act as my interpreter. If you do well, I shall reward you handsomely. If you fail me, I shall kill you and each and every member of your party!"

With those terrifying words, the Zulu turned away from the Xhosa, dismissing him with a wave of the hand, hissing to the guards as they hauled him away: - "And have him take off those ridiculous garments!"

The Zulu's eyes were then gravitated back to the writing on the mat - the name S H A K A. Without shifting his gaze from the 'immortal' name, the monarch ordered: "Alert all my regimental homesteads, Ngomane. I want my armies assembled at Bulawayo by the end of the month."

"A new campaign, Baba?" Ngomane was confused by the request.

"You might say so," a smiled of eerie diversion twitching on Shaka's lips. "Though I would call it more of a 'show'. For the Swallows."

"Ten regiments for a handful of men, Baba? Who come - in friendship?" The Prime Minister could barely con tain his astonishment. "Don't you find that precaution somewhat overreaching?"

"Are you my friend, Ngomane?"

"Yes, Nkosi," he replied, his devoted gaze meeting his king's. "I am."

"In spite of the fact that I can take your life at a moment's notice?"

"In a way, that is the basis of our friendship, Baba. We have a life in common," Ngomane found himself smiling. "My own."

"And so it will be with the Swallows," Shaka replied with mischievously. "When they've seen my military power, my capability to destroy their people at a moment's notice, then Joji and I will discuss 'friend ship'. My friendship! Unlike Dingiswayo, mutual fear is the only sort of alliance I believe in. - I will give them a reception that will truly be 'heard' generations from now - with or without...this scribbling!"

On that note, Shaka picked up the mat, holding it aloft on his fingertips, and blew forcefully on the word S H A K A, smiling confidently as he saw the charcoal dust flutter away. Yet that smile vanished when he

noticed that a faint black tracing of his name still clung stubbornly to the straw and that no amount of blowing could make it vanish. Indeed, upon closer scru tiny, the outlined impression of the written word seemed to be there to stay --
    ---forever.

CHAPTER XXXV
"FEBANA KA MJOJI"
("HE WHO BRINGS FRIENDSHIP FROM KING GEORGE")

"Our pirates and buccaneers," writes - in the Year of Our Lord 1683 - an esteemed and celebrated public figure of the North American Continent, "have already, by their money, their gallant manners, their sense of public reputability and esteem, and their freedom of intercourse with the people, so ingratiated themselves into the public favour that it is no easy matter to bring them to trial and almost an impossibility to give them the punishment they might deserve. Indeed, so great is the public's love and admiration for these licentious robbers that, when brought to trial, the courts of law become scenes of altercation, discord, and confusion."

In the following year - 1684 - as a reaction perhaps to this growing "love and admiration" that the public nurtured for these gallant bandits of the High Seas, who (as XVII Century Robin Hoods) stole from the rich and shared with the poor, a law was passed by the Government of His Britannic Majesty Charles II and subsequently underwritten by the governments of France, Holland and Spain, forbidding piracy "on the seas, tenures, and possessions" appertaining to these four powers.

The reaction was that - out of spite, it seemed - piracy increased with astounding rapidity. New laws were passed by these nations in 1686, 1688, 1689, 1691, 1693, 1694, and 1697, yet these laws merely helped to give the corsairs more prominence and publicity, heightening their popularity in the eyes of the masses, turning the "licentious robbers" into out-and-out heroes.

In 1698, the Earl of Bellamont was instructed by His Majesty William III to "put an end to piracy". Complying with the king's command, a vessel of war was fitted out and placed in command of one William Kidd, who was re presented to Bellamont as "a man of honour and integrity and well acquainted with the persons and haunts of the buccaneers". Kidd received a commission as a privateer with directions to proceed against the pirates (all over the world and especially in their habitual waters of North America), and hold himself responsible to Lord Bellamont himself.

Yet, "men of office" like the Earl of Bellamont and all those who believed that a man's dignity and honour rest in his obedience to "King and Country", failed de plorably in their understanding of that subtle timepiece called the human heart. These men, whose own hearts were so endured by bureaucracy to have lost all resilience, often ignored that ultimately one's dignity and honour rest in his obedience to an inner voice which is far louder than the roar of Parliament.

Thus, instead of attacking the pirates, William Kidd (known as Captain Kidd) formed a new contract with his crew, turned pirate himself and became the most infamous and successful of them all -- depredating the North Atlantic for over three years until he was seized in Boston and punished capitally in May, 1701.

Yet the pirates raged on.

New laws were passed against these freebooters, and new ships were outfitted to give them chase. But, for the pirates, the "chase" was definitely most of the fun and, by 1717 over fifteen hundred pirates were active on the coasts of the Americas alone - with principle head quarters in the Bahamas and the Carolinas.

Finally, in 1718, an organized effort was made by a strong united front of five countries and these pirates were caught and hanged by the score. And, in 1718, the death of a chap named Robert Theach - also known as Blackbeard - gave the man the distinction of being "The Last of the Pirates".

Or almost! - In seems, in fact, upon scrupulous inspection of Blackbeard's last notations that three days before his hanging, he was visited in his prison cell by a long lost love, a beautiful young Creole named Theresa Maria.

The next year, in the spring of 1719, this Creole bore a son whom she appropriately called Roberto Ticia (the name obviously deriving from her pronunciation of Robert Theach). Roberto - who would be known as El Louco (The Mad One) - soon took to the Seas (blood rarely lies) and joined a band of corsairs who, irrespective of the universal proclamation made by the British king that "piracy in the West Indies was dead", continued to pillage the West Indies, moving their successful enterprise to the Barbary Coasts where, in 1763, El Louco met and fell in love with Maria la Doida de Bahia. In the Spring of 1764 a baby boy was born to them in a squalid barraca on Isla Isabela of the Galapagos. They named him Roberto de Louco e Doida de Bahia Filho Barbanegra de Ticia - known (for obscure reasons) as "Parmananda".

In the Spring of 1792, Parmananda "secured" his first ship (a Portuguese galleon bearing the name of the Blessed Virgin "Santa Maria de Portimao") and, in an attempt to make an honest living (as he had promised his mother on her deathbed), he applied the ship to the le gitimate task of transporting prisoners from Batavia and Malaysia to the dungeons of Lisboa and Faro. Yet, by 1820, when fast ships began to appear on the oceans of the world, Parmananda found that his aging, heavy-bowed, broad-beamed galleon, was no match for the sleeker and more rapid schooners, cutters, wherries and clippers that plied the routes of the South Seas. Business started to slack and, by the middle of 1824, the "Santa Maria de Portimao" had become (with all due respect to the Mother of Christ) an old wenching bird with lame wings that fluttered from port to port at the mercy of Charity and the baser instincts of Man.

Of course Parmananda could have taken to piracy. There was plenty of work to be had in the China Seas. And (in those lean years after 1820) he had often been tempted to do so, his blood (spiked with the passionate erythrocytes of Robert Theach) virtually boiling at the thought of buccaneering. Yet there is something about a Latin and his mother that defies both Logic and Hunger, and, in his moments of weakness, Parmananda was reminded of that fateful promise he had made at the deathbed of Maria la Doida. So he remained relatively honest (though not without "recursos proprios" - "his own resources") and relatively kind, though definitely a pirate at heart.

A pirate at heart -- as Elizabeth Farewell would soon have reason to experience.

*

The sea was slate grey and whitecapped in that April of 1824, and the wind had plenty of the coming Winter in it. The wench known as the "Santa Maria de Portimao" laboured across the face of the Indian Ocean off Natal, its lumbering frame set against the backdrop of the rising sun, its patchwork sails unfurled and swollen with a crisp morning breeze, its tattered hull defying the pounding waves.

The galleon's first mate, Socrates Marinho, dressed in colourful pantaloons and a tightfitting shirt drawn over a sinewy chest, stood on the ship's groaning quarterdeck, his spyglass pointed at the horizon.

"Capitao!" Marinho yelled over his shoulder, causing Captain Parmananda to look up from his crate of Batavian oil and direct his swarthy, ruddy features in purview of his first officer. "O que tem?!" the captain grunted in his deep, throaty voice, a grimace of annoyance running parallel to the transverse scar that marred his face a magnificent scar, starting at the bridge of the left eye, snaking across the aquiline nose and finally furrowing its way into the man's matted, tangled "black" beard.

"Olhe!" Marinho replied, pointing to the horizon.

Grunting again, Parmananda trudged to Marinho's side, his flowing vestments flapping in the wind and looking very much like the remnants of a rummage sale in the Grand Bazaar of Constantinople (with odd splashings of silks and satins in indiscriminate combinations of orange, yellow, blue, red, etc., etc.).Upon reaching the quarterdeck, Parmananda snatched the glass from his mate and narrowed an eye at the horizon. A smile gradually dawned on his face as he noted flotsam from a wreck bobbing on the waves: - bits and pieces of a schooner's bowsprit, parts of a splintered hull, and a Union Jack.

"Um Navio Ingles," Parmananda said in a religious whisper, as if he were savouring his favourite meal. "'Union Jack' - Almirantado." Lowering the spyglass, the captain grinned through gold teeth repeating: "Almirantado. O Governator Somerset tera muito prazer em nossa - cooperacao. Eh, Marinho?," he chuckled, "muito prazer!"

*

"Captain Parmananda," Somerset chided, "What a pleasure to see you!"

Roberto de Louco e Doida de Bahia Filho Barbanegra de Ticia, known as Parmananda crossed the large study belonging to the Governor of the Cape Province and was pleased that he had not prepared any definite plan of action. Being, like his boat, a bit of a wench himself, the extraordinary captain of the "Santa Maria de Porti mao" had decided that he would keep his options open. He would go to the Governor, he had deliberated, and "take it a step at a time", keeping both his ears and eyes on the alert, ready to take advantage of any possible way of making money that might present itself ("Com legali dade! - legally!", he had reminded Marinho, adding with a cherubic smile: - "Im memoria de maezinha cara."). It was this sentimental manner of "freely coasting" into opportunity that gave Parmananda the reputation for be ing, in the realm of "legal buccaneering' far sleeker and slicker than any schooner, cutter, wherry or clip per.

"O prazer e meu, Eminencia!" the captain replied, bowing low, feigning servility and meekness with an adroitness that brought a smile to Marinho's lips.

"You're looking prosperous," Somerset noted with biting sarcasm, irritated by the mock mendacity of this Portuguese shark. "Has the 'begging' been going well?"

"I cannot complain, Eminencia," replied the captain as if the governor's question had been a legitimate inquiry between two businessmen. "Se um homem trabalha, ganha dinheiro. Se nao, nao ganha nada! We were born to work and toil, praza a Deus!"

"All right, enough of the theatrics," Somerset's irritation was mounting. "What brings a pirate like you to my office?"

"Ah, ah, ah, Eminencia," Parmananda shook a repri manding finger at the governor. "There are no more pirates! Your king has said so and your king is no liar! - Come se diz?, 'Hail, Bretanha, Bretanha rule the Seas!'" The captain opened his palms by way of intimate confession, "Ainda que tenho saudades...even though I miss the occupation of my family, I tell myself, there are no pirates and Bretanha is your friend. Temos uma alianca fraternal, you and I, Eminencia. And I come to you with..." cupping his hands, "O coracao nao maos! - with my heart in hand!"

"Get to the point, you piece of driftwood," was the governor's crude reply to the other man's touching dis play of friendship.

Parmananda's face remained frozen in a gold-toothed grin, as he slipped the Union Jack out of his silk robes and spread it out on the floor like a carpet.

"Where did you find this?!" The sight of the Admi ralty banner so abruptly presented to him had a chilling effect on Somerset.

Parmananda spun round to face Marinho who answered, on cue: "Trinta e dois graus longitude este. Vinte e sete graus latitude sul."

"Was a good-size ship," Parmananda added, nodding with severity. "Schooner. - Perhaps you have heard of it, Eminencia...?" The captain produced a tattered logbook from his flowing vestments and read the gilt lettering on its black cover. "'Elizabeth Caterina'. You know it?"

"Where there survivors?" Somerset asked eagerly.

"In those waters, Eminencia...? Imposivel!"

An odd look of relief crossed the governor's fea tures and Parmananda, being an experienced "reader of men's expressions", caught that look with interest and scrutiny and his hawk eyes remained glued to the gover nor as Somerset spoke again.

"That hardheaded fool," Somerset spat out as he snatched the logbook from Parmananda. "I told him it was suicidal!"

"Suicida, Eminencia?" Parmananda queried in his art ful guise. "What was suicidal? Was this schooner per haps...trying to land on coast?"
Somerset became instantly suspicious of the leading question and, eyes narrowed on the "driftwood", he kept his own counsel as Parmananda went on.

"Do not look at me like that, Eminencia," the cap tain smiled at the other's suspicious air as he paced the floor, systematically trampling over the Union Jack. "I did not sink it, I only pick up the pieces and ask myself - 'Porque, Parmananda? Why do these men risk to land on that 'wild' coast?'"

"I didn't say they were trying to land," Somerset shot back.

"Seguro de no!" the captain was quick to agree. "Es Parmananda que lo diz. He ask: 'Porque?' - Why? - Is it the ivory?" he started, as if thinking out loud. "Is the king of Bretanha not rich enough? Does he now want to get to the ivory of Natal before the Portuguese Colony of Delagoa? To -- come se diz...'beat Portugal to it?' Or is it something else the Admiralty wants?"

"I hate to dash your hopes, Parmananda," Somerset said, the venom in him running over. "But there is no money in this for you. No matter how many 'porques' you ask yourself."

"Maybe yes - maybe no, the ways of the Lord are infinite! Talvez - maybe we find a way. Maybe she can help us?"

"Who," the governor's frown was suspicious - yet in trigued.

"'Elizabeth Catherine'," Parmananda said, tapping the name on the logbook triumphantly.

* * *

"The place selected by Lt. Farewell for his resi dence is of a singular appearance being on slightly sloping terrain with a commanding view of the bay. His house is not unlike an ordinary barn made of wattle, plastered with clay and with a thatched roof, without windows naturally, and with only one door composed of reeds. A far cry, I dare say, from the considerably airier domiciles on which he has cut his teeth and the mere fact that this intrepid man should have bent him self to enhancing such quarters with his presence is a tribute to his dedication..."

Thus wrote Wilkins in the Colonial Office Diary at the end of the first week at Port Natal. Continuing:---

"My own quarters are contiguous to those of Lt. Farewell, and about twenty yards from them, while those of Cane and the Holsteads are closer to the bay and have the appearance of the roof of a house placed designedly on the ground, the gable end of which, being left open, serves as a door. The abodes of Hockly, Biggar, Thompson and Gin-aro are quite similar to those of the Holsteads and Cane, while Popham insisted upon having a proper house and set out to build one at the expense of much toil and resulting with a low construction that quite resembles a log cabin. Fynn is far less pretentious and seems quite quiescent and comfortable in a small round ed hut similar to those of the Hottentots. A makeshift abode was also prepared for Daniel, should the poor soul be returned to us.

"Lt. Farewell has also instructed the men to commence building a fortress, which he proposed calling Fort Farewell (as a token tribute to all those of the expedition, no doubt). This fort is to cover a surface of about two hundred square yards, and is to be con- structed in the form of a triangle. As we go about this task (which I am sure the Lieutenant devised as a means for soothing the tension that has gripped the men since Daniel's abduction), I am often reminded, at varying intervals throughout the long day, of Lt. Farewell's words: "We must wait now, Tim. We have made the first move by coming here. Now it is Shaka's turn.", and I wonder how long it will be before the Emperor makes another appearance through his troops or by way of messenger, or..."

The day after this entry in the Chronicle & Diary, the answer to Wilkins's question came by way of Mgobozi and a small detachment of about 200 men who arrived at the Port to announce that the king was now prepared to receive Farewell ("Febana kaMjoji") and the members of his party who bear the "friendship of King George". The men of the "Julia" were stunned by Mgobozi's arrival - a reaction caused not so much by the return of the dread ed Zulu warriors, nor by the news that they would soon be in the presence of the Mighty Mountain of Africa, as by the huge quantity of ivory they brought with them - enough of it to tease the appetite of even the holiest of men (let alone the eight recruited at The Gator).

"He's trying to impress us," Farewell noted upon inspecting the gleaming tower of tusks that loomed on the beach before him.

"And doin' one 'elluva job, I'd say," Cane replied, his pupils dilated on the elephant teeth.

"Don't get your hopes up, Cane," the lieutenant said in an attempt to keep the other's man feet firmly on the ground. "I have a feeling that whatever ivory we obtain in this kingdom will have to be hard won."

As if understanding Farewell's words, Mgobozi pried his attention away from the odd constructions with which the Whites had "cluttered" the bay area, and addressing Popham in Zulu, urged the Black man to relay the mes sage to the leader of the Swallows' party.

"He say the Great Elephant, the Son of Zulu, wishes us to accept these gifts with his greetings," Popham turned to tell Farewell. "He says Shaka is now ready to meet with our leaders as soon as it is convenient."

"Awfully decent of him, sir," Wilkins responded to this act of generosity on the part of the Zulu King. "Do you suppose we've misjudged the chap?"

"Yes," Fynn answered the question with an ominous taint to his voice. "He's far shrewder than I'd anti cipated."

"Tell him we'll leave immediately," Farewell told Popham, and, as the Black man obeyed, the lieutenant turned to the men: "Wilkins, Fynn,

Thomas, Cane, and Popham will accompany me. The others will remain here to look after the ship and settlement, and to finish the construction of the fort. And, gentlemen," he added gravely, "You had better keep a good watch on the 'Julia'. - That sloop is our only link with the outside world."

*

It was a colourful procession that made its way up the coast ("following a sea-cow path", as Wilkins later wrote) on the first stage of the 200-mile journey to Shaka. Mgobozi and his warriors led the way at a steady trot, their feet drumming the sand, whilst, in their tow the party of Whites followed on horseback, wearing the best of their fineries and decked in the formal attire considered suitable for an audience with a king.

In his gala naval uniform, complete with cocked hat and epaulettes, Farewell himself was the most splendid looking of the European group; contrasting sharply with Fynn who was far less formal in his wrinkled linen pants and shirt, and in his soiled straw hat that was pulled low over his pale features, shading his quick translucent eyes - eyes that continuously scanned the scenery, registering and storing impressions on all levels of consciousness. Riding next to Farewell, Wilkins seemed guilelessly invigorated by the trek, bubbling with "colonial enthusiasm", as, behind him, Cane and Thomas were more cautiously reserved, both men being fully armed with pistols, muskets, and hunting knives. Last of the cavalcade, Popham brought up the rear, laconically leading a packhorse laden with gifts for the Zulu monarch.

As the day wore on and Farewell's party followed the lead of the trotting Zulus ("who seemed quite inexhaustible and remarkably fit", as Tim later noted in his understatement), the journey proved fascinating for the Whites. Fording the umNgeni River, they were delighted by the hippos wallowing in the shallow waters, by the bushbuck, impala and giraffe lining the river's banks. And, as this new world was revealed to them, the men gazed at the unfamiliar animals in wonder.

Responding to the Whites' fascination in discovery, the impalas, too, seemed to cock their heads at the procession of strange, exotic creatures, casting astounded looks at the horses and the bipeds on their backs (who, indeed, appeared to be natural extensions of the horses themselves).

At the beginning of the second day, as the sun rose over the Indian Ocean, the cavalcade forded the Amatikulu River and veered inland for the first time, leaving the sandy shores behind it. Instinctively, Wilkins hitched up on his saddle and looked over his shoulder at the already distant sea, silently bidding it a fond and apprehensive adieu. Noticing the melancholic expression on Tim's face, Farewell offered the freckled member of the Colonial Office a warm understanding smile.

"Are you wondering whether you'll ever see it again, Tim?" the lieutenant asked, matter-of-factly, as if reading the man's mind.

"I'm not usually given to that sort of reverie, sir," Tim replied somewhat defensively. "But, yes - the thought had crossed my mind."

"You're in Bathurst's Office, Tim. In that capacity, you must've realised that if our explorers were given to looking over their shoulders - well, there would be no Colonies! - Look ahead, Tim," the lieutenant exhorted with bold-heartedness. "You're about to enter a region that no white man has ever seen. The moment is historic and your name will be emblazoned in the annals of history!"

Invigorated by the thought of being personified in History, Wilkins straightened up in his saddle and looked forward, a gratified smile dawning on his lips, - when, as an afterthought, Farewell added dryly: -"I just hope it's our history and not theirs."

*

As, on the third day, the expedition made its way across a vast savannah dotted with acacia trees, the first inland homesteads (both regimental and private) started to come into view and the Europeans' first impression of these villages was expressed by Wilkins:---

"We were instantly struck with amazement at the order and discipline maintained in the 'savage' country through which we travelled. Especially the regimental homesteads showed that cleanliness was a prevailing custom, for there were considerable spaces were neither dirt nor ashes were to be seen..."

Yet what was to be seen, by the gawking Zulus, were the Whites themselves (the first such specimens any of these Africans had ever seen)! And, as the members of the homesteads (including some of the more valiant warriors) gathered at the gates of their villages to look upon these "creatures", their attitudes ranged from open-eyed curiosity to suspicious defensiveness, for fearful uncertainty to superstitious dread. Strangely enough, of Farewell's party only Popham felt awkward under these gazes of scrutiny; being a half-black coming from a settlement of Whites, he now suddenly felt half- white in the Africa of the Africans.

In his Diary Wilkins noted the curious response of the Zulus in the following manner:---

"While we rode through the unexplored hinterland, I was much taken aback by the extraordinary congregation of natives who had been induced to assemble from all quarters for the purpose of seeing 'white men' for the first time. Their expressions of amazement (which our appearance excited) were so outlandish that, at times, I could not abstain from smiling at them. Most were afraid to approach, but some came close to us and gathered round, inspecting our horses, our gear, our skins and hair (there was quite an interest aroused by my own, I should note reservedly). All the natives were friendly without being offensive, and innocently curious without being troublesome. The youthful seemed delighted and the aged pleased; some danced, others sang; all manifesting their gratification, it seemed (or was it another motive besides gratification which I failed to grasp?) at our being in their kingdom. This first contact with the natives I found quite refreshing inasmuch as the res ponse to our presence was of an entirely humane nature. Only one thing caused me some perplexity, - the peculi arity in the age groups. It appeared, at first sight, that none of the natives were younger than twelve or thirteen. An odd observation which I immediately dismissed from mind in the conviction that this first impression must be erroneous and the fruit of the novelty of it all..."

Wilkins had not erred. And Mgobozi knew it and, as the general of the iziCwe cast furtive glances at the Whites, he wondered how long it would take them to notice the tragic truth of Shaka's domain - the truth of the empire without progeny.

*

"On the Fourth Day out, we arrived at a pleasant pass at the base of a steep mountain, which we ascended, and from the summit of it took a view of the surrounding country. The whole extensive surface was grand and imposing, and I viewed the landscape with sensations of admiration and wonder. Indeed, the interior exhibited a happy variety of hill and dale in pleasing undulations, and vast plains and meadows alive with varied species of figs, palms, thorny trees most of which were complete ly new to us in both configuration and colours, along with wild shrubbery teeming with insects of a tropical nature. These plains and dales were intersected with many beautiful streams, affording a refreshing coolness to the weary traveller. At a distance, mountains of unusual magnitude raised their stupendous heads, and occupied a large proportion of the landscape...

"As we journeyed over vast, amber plains and the greenest and most fertile of hills, we passed many herds of extremely beautiful antelope which seemed to take no alarm at our approach and we saw some deer of a small species unknown to us (apparently like the koodoo, though remarkably light and timid) who ran off at our approach, bounding over the surface with surprising agility, and we viewed swarming birds of the most diversified kinds, together with guinea-fowls and wild turkeys, springbok, a peculiar breed of genet cats, giraffes, monkeys of all sorts, and falcons (to the Lieutenant's delight). It is also of vital importance to note here that, as we had much cause to verify at the expense of our 'urban' nerves, exotic wild animals of every description infest this part of the world, making it dangerous in the extreme, and compelling the traveller to be ever on the 'qui vive' lest he should stumble on the leopard in his lair, or the buffalo hidden in the fastnesses of the surrounding woodlands. Venomous reptiles and insects of various denominations are also to be found; and the serpent, "moving its slow length along," may be seen frequently in line of the traveller's progress. Indeed, this land is a veritable Cornucopia of God's Creation... "

But, although Nature was present in abundance, it was a very specific species of animal that caused Thomas's eyes to open wide.

"Good Lord Almighty!" he said, more as an exclamation of pure greed than as a praise of God, as his eyes took in an immense herd of elephants gathered peacefully round a lake - their wet tusks and hides shimmering in the radiant sunshine.

"There's a fortune there for the taking," Cane commented as he eyed the ivory in a rather cold, calculating manner, apparently untouched by the objective beauty of the scene.

Recognising the all too familiar glitter of human avarice, Mgobozi decided it was time to make the Swallows conversant with the law of the land - the Law called the Will of Shaka. His eyes fixed on Thomas, the iziCwe commander snapped a few short phrases to Popham which were relayed as: "He says that the Great Sigidi is a generous king and that the Swallows have already seen that in his gift of ivory. Yet he warns the Swallows not to take advantage of his generosity."

"What the hell's that supposed to mean?" Thomas demanded, a violent twinkle flaring in his greedy eyes.

"That if we touch one of those pachyderms without his permission," Cane retorted gravely, "our lives won't be worth an hour's purchase!"

"I thought we came here to hunt ivory, Farewell," Thomas snorted contemptuously to the lieutenant, eliciting Mgobozi's pensive glance. Throughout their journey, the general had been studying the Whites, making mental notes of their behaviour, of their strengths, their weaknesses and their attitudes to their new environment (in case Shaka should need relevant information before his meeting with the Strangers). And, in the last four days, the man had noticed that one factor was paramount in the White's behaviour: they all had the seed of individualism, - each man's own fate being far more important to him than the fate of the collective group, each man's action being marred by a desire for independence within the group that was total ly lacking in its respect for collective cooperation. Each of the Swallows, Mgobozi had decided, was like a lone cloud on an otherwise clear blue sky, floating harmlessly across the firmament, too divorced from those of his own kind to create the danger of a storm. Yet there was danger all the same, Mgobozi sensed in his soul, for in their intrinsic lack of solidarity, in their need to be "free", the hearts of the Whites spun wild, covetous and deceptive, like the hearts of scavenger wolves who have lost their pack and roam aimlessly, minaciously in search of food. The Swallows are born rebels, the general told himself as his looked upon Thomas's cruel blue eyes, with their drooping cynical lids, as he looked upon his fierce aggressive nose (so greedy in its lengthy pointedness, so unlike the rounded generosity of the African nose), and upon the threaten ing deep-lined brow of the predator. And though Mgobozi did not understand what Thomas had told Farewell, he could well distinguish the insubordination in the tone of his voice (the rebel warrior defying his commander) and, being a disciplined soldier, the Shakan officer could not help but be disgusted -- and on the alert.

"You'll get your ivory," was Farewell's curt rebut tal to Thomas's intransigence. "We all will," he added, turning to Cane. "Just as soon as we have the King's permission to hunt."

"What if he doesn't give it to us?" Holstead's tone remained defiant, rebellious.

"That will mean that our mission has failed, Thomas," the lieutenant snapped back, his tone razor sharp, gelid. "And, in that case, we'll find that our lives are a far greater treasure than ivory."

*

"We rose early on the dawning of the Fifth Day, and pursued our journey as soon as the heavy dew would permit, crossing the rivers Mafote and Nondote - the later being greatly infested with alligators (we were told that recently two of the local natives had been carried off by the beasts in the act of crossing one of the river's fords; a piece of intelligence which I re ceived with due trepidation and preceded to cross the river with great haste leaving some of my stores behind me). We travelled about fifteen miles further on this day (relentlessly closing the gap that seperated us from Shaka's Citadel), moving through a clear and rich country of pasturage in which we saw several homesteads and many herds of fat cattle. The sun beamed on us warmly, and we found it advisable to halt occasionally under the shade of the surrounding foliage..."

It was on one of these "occasional halts" that Thomas wandered off alone on horseback ("for a spell of fresh air," as he'd grumbled angrily to Cane), his mind apparently still on the ivory. And, in the lone gallop across the savannah, Holstead inadvertently trampled over a nest of ostrich eggs. What followed was as comical for the men, who chanced to glimpse it from a distance, as it was tragic. In fact, in retaliation for this attack on her home, the female ostrich came crashing out of the bush in blind angry pursuit of the transgressor. Yet when the bird and Thomas's horse spotted each other, both creatures froze in terror. The horrified ostrich then emitted a loud shrill and scampered off, whilst the horse, frightened out of its wits by the peculiar creature, whinnied panicstricken, and rearing, landed Thomas on the ground. The man picked himself up and, cursing in fury, began chasing across the dusty plains after the huge, fearful bird.

At the sight of the enraged man racing after the prancing bird, the Zulus were gripped by a fit of infectious laughter which quickly spread to the Whites - infuriating Thomas all the more. Finally, realising that he could not catch the fleetfooted creature, Holstead stopped and aimed his musket in vengeful fury.

"Thomas!" Farewell shouted in alarm, but too late. The man had already pulled the trigger and the first shot in the history of the Zulu Empire rang out over the African veld, sending all God's marvels of wildlife fleeing in panic.

The fatally wounded ostrich tumbled forward, somersaulted, and slumped to the ground, blood spurting from the bullet hole in its back, tinging the dust of the savannah a deep red. Anticipating their reaction, Farewell's head whipped around to look at the alarmed eyes of the Zulus rivetted on the musket, the shot still ringing in their ears. But Farewell and his men were far more alarmed than Mgobozi's troops as they awaited, petrified, for the Zulus to respond to the "stick that spits fire".

Mgobozi eyed his soldiers and noticing their terror (a terror which he himself shared), the commander had the presence of mind to realise that he had to do something promptly to regain the confidence of his men and control of the situation. Walking over to the lifeless, prostrate figure of the bird, the iziCwe commander inspected the bullet wound in its back before turning his furrowed brow to the musket in Thomas's hand, the barrel still smoking with the scent of death. Lifting his gaze to Holstead, Mgobozi addressed him with scorn - a tirade of harsh, guttural words.

"What the hell did he say?!" Thomas roared to Popham.

"That what you did is the way of a coward," Popham translated with a touch of trepidation, instantly causing Holstead's lips to compress in anger. "He said - though your weapon is good, your heart lacks dignity."

As if to underline his statement, Mgobozi nodded to Thomas and spun round, walking away. Embarrassed and inflamed to reprisal, Holstead yelled after the general: "You black bastard!" and trained the barrel of his musket on the Zulu's back.

Sensing the White man's move, Mgobozi froze and tightened his grip on the ixwa and turned ever so slowly to face Holstead. "Give me that musket, Thomas," Farewell's strict command rose sharply, overbearing in its fervour.

"Whose side're you on, Farewell?" Holstead sneered. "Mine or that bleedin' kaffir's?"

"I said give me that gun," the lieutenant repeated through clenched teeth, his ferret-like words causing his entire party to freeze.

"Not bloody likely!" was the barbed reply.

With quick, keen precision of intent and movement, Mgobozi half turned and his eyes darted from Thomas's musket to Farewell and back. Perceiving the gist of the men's exchange, the general decided to take matters into his own hands and administer a taste of Shakan discipline.

So -- in a split second (one that Thomas would remember for the remainder of his days), the Zulu had closed with the white man, made contact, hooked his shield round the tip of the musket's barrel, pulled the weapon back and away (swatting it out of Thomas's hand), and aimed for the Swallow's heart - the blade of the ixwa breaking the skin, drawing blood, stopping a hair's-breadth from the kill.

As the son of Richard Holstead urinated down the inside of his trouser leg, Farewell and his men were spellbound. The speed and execution of the "Method" was unlike anything they had ever seen.

"So much for the superiority of our firearms," Wilkins constated to no one in particular. "You'd best be a crack shot, 'cause you'll never have a chance to reload."

Relinquishing his prey (who was still in a state of shock), Mgobozi picked up the musket and, striding to Farewell, handed the lieutenant the weapon his subordinate had refused to relinquish. The two men's eyes locked in a brief spiritual exchange and, though they spoke quite different languages, there was no misunderstanding: Mgobozi had control, Farewell did not.

Appalled by the violent exchange between their commander and the Swallows, the Zulus, though perfectly disciplined, hesitated slightly before responding to Mgobozi's call to move on. They then fell into perfect formation and trotted off to continue the journey to Bulawayo, leaving the Whites to face their trembling companion.

"That was uncommon clever what y'done, Thomas," Cane told Holstead, his manner remaining casual. "Hope you brought a change of underwear."

"You stupid fool," Farewell hissed into Thomas's face. "You've shown them the worst side of our nature. If you ever disobey me again, I won't be as merciful as he was. - I'll kill you!"

*

"The morning of the Sixth Day opened very fine" Tim wrote in the Chronicle & Diary, "and looked most auspi cious for travelling. Whilst each of us went about the task of breaking camp and preparing our packs for the next stage of the journey, I chanced to snatch an infor mative glance or two in the direction of our native guide (a stout black named Mmgoboosi). My inquisitive ness was in virtue of the brief but exceedingly violent clash that had occurred the previous day between the Zulu and our Thomas (a most lamentable episode, I might add - one which will bring little good for us no doubt). In my discreet inspection of the man, I noticed that he tended to his morning chores of washing and the like with an air as cheerful as was his habit. If he still harboured any ill will for Thomas, it was not apparent in the least, and I found myself inwardly praising him for his commendable spiritual resourcefulness. Indeed, at one point, as Thomas was saddling his horse, he happened to cross Mmgoboosi's path and, though the Zulu looked directly at our man, his face registered no emotion whatsoever. It appeared that he was looking through him, as if Thomas's physical presence were no longer visible for him...

"Our morning's course brought us through a rich country, beautifully intersected with streams of pure limpid water, and we made rapid progress, so that by noon we had travelled over fifteen miles and found ourselves in the midst of another knotting of villages. As expected, natives appeared at the gates of the homesteads to gawk at us in wonder and, once again, I had occasion to note that these family groups were completely lacking in the very young - those under the age of twelve, or so. This disturbing impression was driven home to me as I chanced to ride alongside the Lieutenant and Fynn and overheard the comments:--- The Lieutenant: "Have you noticed it, Fynn?"; Fynn: "Yes. I have. I wonder where they are hiding their children?".

"This exchange, coupled with my own observation, left me pensive for the remainder of the day, causing my mood to take a turn for the worse. As did the general aspect of the weather.

"In fact, towards evening, as the sun disappeared, the whole horizon was overspread by one dark and dismal cloud. The wind, which had been increasing as we advanced, now began to blow from the westward with some force, and everything indicated an approaching storm. With the help of Mmgoboosi, we prepared for the worst by erecting a temporary shelter of branches and some foliage cut for the purpose. We also kindled fires round us to keep off the wild animals, the whole of this part of the country being infested (or so we were told) with leopards, panthers, and hyenas. We had no sooner secured the horses and seated ourselves in this newly constructed refuge, than the pitiless storm gave vent to its fiercest rage. The thunder crashing in awful peals, and the lightning incessantly spreading over the skies before us, made our momentary situation far from enviable. Yet the condition of the Zulus was even more desperate, the men squatting in the midst of the downpour, their faces turned upwards to the storming skies with a look of complete enchantment. Looking at them and at their beatific expressions, one would have thought that they quite enjoyed this violent demonstration of heavenly might. I was later informed by Popham that there exists a superstition amongst the natives that the name itself, 'Zulu' or 'Zooloo', is somehow related to the heavens and that the Zulus think themselves to be 'Children of the Heavens' (I quote). An interesting piece of folklore reminiscent of the Celtic gods ("paganism", as Rev. Bellows would have called it) as well as our own Christian concept of 'A Father in Heaven whose children we are". In a greater sense, I suppose this similarity of thought in such disparate cultures is to be expected. If Christ's revelation is real, it must, by right, be universal...."

And, whilst Wilkins was engrossed in these "imperialistic" musings (which would later be transcribed to his Diary), the rain was indeed coming down in torrents and, in the tempest, Fynn and Farewell found themselves by the fire in the company of Mgobozi.

"Tell him," Farewell started, urging Popham to interpret his words for the iziCwe general, "that we find his country is splendid! A veritable paradise!"

Popham glanced at the downpour, before lackadaisically shrugging his shoulders and conveying the compliment to Mgobozi who nodded in agreement and grinned with proud affection, directing, in turn, a question at to lieutenant.

"He asks if your country is as beautiful?" Popham told Farewell.

"Oh, yes, tell him," Farewell was quick to reply. "Though very different in its beauty. Perhaps one day he can see for himself."

Popham faltered slightly before passing on the lieu tenant's remark, wondering whether that same invitation to England would ever be directed at him, a half-caste, a man without a country by birth and definition.

Mgobozi gazed at Farewell in long assessment when he heard Popham's translation. This valiant, courageous soldier (who, as a soldier, was capable of a bloodthirsty violence that literally took away the breath of the beholder), was, in his roots, quite benevolent at heart and quite vulnerable in matters of sentimentality. Consequently, though he looked upon the Swallows with guardedness, Mgobozi was moved by the invitation to visit the other man's home, and offered Farewell a grateful smile - a smile that vanished instantly as soon as he had heard the translation of Fynn's next comment.

"But tell him," the Irishman remarked over the loud patter of the rain, "that we find it odd that we have seen so few young families. And babies. Young children."

When Popham was through, Mgobozi dropped his graze, his fists tightening with restrained emotion, his mind racing in an effort to offer an honest rebuttal to Fynn's legitimate observation, a rebuttal which would need to accurately represent what the concept of being a "Shakan" Zulu had become for an entire generation of Africans. As Mgobozi thought of this, his mind now reached back to that other fateful rainy day when he had asked Shaka for the right to marry his sister, Nomcoba (for whom he secretly nurtured love and admiration). The Zulu King had laughed at the thought of marriage, chid ing with a scowl: "For soldiers marriage is a folly. Their first and only duty is to protect the nation from its enemies. Later, Mgobozi," he had told his friend, "when the nation is secure, we will consider duties and allegiances of another nature - like a wife, families..."

Though the commander of the iziCwe did not, could not know it, his present train of thought evoked by the Irishman's remark was quite similar in content to what Fynn had told Farewell in Cape Town: - in a way Shaka had offered his people power, pride, "a purpose" in return, not for their souls as such, but for their pri vate and personal Future. As Ngomane had put it, he and Shaka had a life in common: the Prime Minister's. So it was with his people. Shaka and the Zulu Nation had a future in common: Shaka's. His people had given him "all they could have been" in return for "an identity today" of which they could be proud.

And, being profoundly trustworthy and honest, Shaka Zulu had kept (and was keeping) his part of the bargain rather magnificently. Strange as it may seem (consider ing the bloodshed), Shaka was as sublime a moral teacher as he was a martial genius. The Zulu had, in fact, built his empire on the most noble and respected disciplines of life: - submission to authority, obedience to the law, discipline of mind and body, freedom from the heart's palliatives (superstition and the like), respect for superiors, order and self-restraint, fearlessness and sacrifice, civic duty, etc. Shaka had caused these "excellencies of Life" to be so rigorously enforced that they had become truly second nature for his people. To the point where the Zulus could indeed have called themselves (in the Greek sense) "citizens of excellence", if - and only if they could have lived in excellence without war! Indeed, the only "weak point" (so to say) in Shaka's overall method was that, though valid in es sence, it was founded on Hatred, not Love (and Shaka himself would soon see this - when Fynn would tell him about another King of Kings, Christ, the True and Only Lord of the Heavens).

But now, as the heavens poured their rains over Mgobozi, the general considered that the price he and his generation had paid for this "purpose", this "excellence" was a future without children (which is a future without a future). Shaka had never planned it as such, it had just happened, as a side effect of his policy of Total War and Total Dedication to the Paramount King. Since it was ludicrous to think that a soldier could have a wife and family (indeed, the responsibilities and sentimental ties of a family would inevitably weaken the man), no one in the Shakan Armies was permitted to marry "until the wars were over and peace was secured". Since 1811 (when the campaigns began in earnest), the entire youth of the nation was held in a state of enforced celibacy, the men in their military homesteads or on the front, the maidens either home alone or in the corresponding "female guilds" (which Shaka had recently founded under the command of his sister Nomcoba, and under the supervision of Nandi). And, on those rare occasions when the Youth was allowed to have sex (i.e. a day spent in ukuHlobonga), it was unlawful for the female to fall pregnant (to form a "family", in other words). Indeed, willingly or unwillingly, it mattered little to Mgobozi right now, through the celibacy of his Armies and through the Mfecane and the Fingoes, Shaka had infected all of Southeastern Africa with his own disease: - the spiritual illness of the "outcast without a family living in a constant state of hatred and war". It seemed that the Empire of Shaka Zulu was the flesh and blood of Shaka Zulu ---

--- and his people were slowly forgetting they had ever been anything else.

And the years had passed, and that day "when the nation was secure" had never come and was nowhere in sight (especially now that the Swallows had made their first advance). And he, Mgobozi, was almost forty, as was Joko, Dlaba, Nqoboka, and Shaka himself, -- almost forty -- a ripe old age for starting a family; "too late", many would say.

And there were no children. No fresh blood since 1811 - when Shaka had become commander of all five Mtetwa regiments.

"What will it be like ten years from now?" Mgobozi asked himself. "Or in twenty years' time?" Yet he had a more pressing consideration as he turned to look back at Fynn. He had to answer the question in a manner that would be true to his own people. Finally, he did, in a voice that could not hide his sorrow.

"He says," Popham translated, "a soldier cannot divide his life between his home and his country. He says the time will come for founding families and raising children once the nation is secure."

As if reading Mgobozi's mind, Farewell urged the half-caste to inquire: "Ask him, does Shaka forbid the young to marry and have families?"

Upon hearing the question, the general stiffened and his reply remained curt. Then, rising, he strode into the rain to join his troops.

"What did he say?" Fynn asked Popham.

"Our young wish to serve the Nation -- he said."

With a deep sorrowful sigh, Fynn commented: "Sparta."

"'Trained for war, Lacedaeminia'," Farewell recited, quoting Aristotle's remarks on the warrior city of Sparta. "'And all her institutions taught her to fight. - Savage and egoistical, she satisfied the pride of her subjects and won the praise of those who admire power and success, but what did she do for the world? - A war machine perfectly fitted to destroy but incapable of production!'"

"'Sparta'," the lieutenant looked up at the lightning that was brilliant in the heavens and quoted the great Greek historian Thucydides. "'A monolith of war, - dead in every part of its towering figure'."

"Life to Life, Death onto Death," the flashing Heavens seemed to say, in answer to the Swallow. "Such is the Way of the Sword." Then the Thunder of Africa roared as if to ask Farewell: "What is your way, Febana? What is the Way of King George's Friendship? Do you bring Life? Or the Plague of your own Hypocrisy?"

But Farewell could not hear the Heavens, for his thoughts were on Shaka, and in his mind he was now wondering how to best exploit this weak point in the Zulu Nation, how to use it to make his mission successful.

"Is the Way of King George's Friendship the Plague of your own Hypocrisy?" the Thunder of Africa asked once again.

But there was no reply from the Locust.

The Plague had begun.

CHAPTER XXXVI
"UKUZWA"(LIFE)

"The dawn brought more favourable weather," Wilkins wrote in his Chronicle & Diary for the Colonial Office, in an attempt to accurately represent the Seventh Day of his African trek to Shaka Zulu. "The wind had sunk, and the rain had ceased; we therefore rekindled our fires, dried our clothes, and prepared to go on...

"We travelled about six miles to the banks of the Emvuzane, and found the river greatly swollen by the previous night's torrents and quite impassable - or so it seemed. Yet, Mmgoboosi exchanged some words with the Lieutenant (via Popham) and we were told to take places on the banks and wait for a remedy that would soon be forthcoming.

"At about 11 P.M., just as the sun was shedding its influence on our wearied hearts, Mmgoboosi returned with oddly dressed beings called 'inyangers' or 'water doctors', who had apparently come to somehow spirit us to the other side of the river. And, as I turned to look upon the doctors, I was appalled to notice that the point which they had chosen for our crossing was a contracted neck through which the stream was forced with a fearful velocity, and where large stones, slippery and dangerous to tread upon, were strewn in every direction, looking (to a layman such as myself) almost impossible to step upon without being carried off by the currents. However, with all these formidable obstructions, the water doctors insisted on selecting this place for there were few alligators to be found. We were asked to strip and place our clothes in a bundle that in the course of the passage over we were to carry above our heads.

"As we set out to do so, a great many natives soon congregated on both sides of the Emvuzane with eager curiosity and for the sake (or so I was made to suppose) of seeing a white man without his habiliments...

"Having thus successfully crossed the River Emvuzane, with a loud clapping, laughing and cheering of the locals, we proceeded over a rich and luxuriant plain for about two miles. Nothing could exceed the verdure which spread round the hamlets scattered within its space, and the foliage of the mimosa tree rivalled in attraction the beauty of the savannas (where this tree grows in great abundance).

"After journeying for about four miles, the landscape drastically changed its aspect; instead of a rich loamy soil of great depth, we arrived where we found gravelly soil, without much vegetation. And, in the distance, we made out the contours of a small mountain or hillock, conical in shape which our guide, Mmgoboosi, told us conceals a large hollow (like the spent crater of a volcano, or so I understood it to be). The name of the Hillock has a sharp clicking sound to it (a loud smacking of the tongue against the palate). A sound that greatly resembles the word 'Choklee' or 'Qoklee'...

"As our cavalcade neared the Hillock, we were stunned to see an immense congregation of vultures and buzzards that virtually blocked the rays of the sun like a vast, deathly cloud. Approaching closer, we were able to take stock of the horror that lay beneath this circling black cloud. Spread before us, covering the soft earth like an immense carpet, were the gruesome skeletal remains of hundreds, nay!, thousands of dead! As I looked upon this disconcerting sight, I was reminded of the 24,000 dead at the Battle of Austerlitz, - yet those here seemed many, many more - and, alas, unburied!

"Whilst we gaped in abhorrence at the terrain unfolding at our feet and rolling clear up the slopes of the Hillock, for acres and acres, white and blinding to the eye with sun-bleached bones and skulls, Mmgoboosi spoke with pride of a great battle. The greatest battle of the Great Sigidi! The Battle that sealed the Empire for the Son of Zulu! The Battle where One Man and his Mind destroyed the thousands! (or so Popham relayed to us)...

"Mmgoboosi went on to speak with pride of this sea of bones as we looked on in awe and shocked silence. Our guide had many words to tells us, but we were able to grasp only the essential, for at length Popham slouched over in his saddle and started retching convulsively and in a manner which made my own stomach turn queasily. And I distinctly recollect Fynn's soothing voice suspended over the hideous battlefield with his recital of: "The Lord is my shepherd, I shall not wander. He maketh me to lie down in green pastures; He leadeth me beside the still waters; He guideth me by paths of virtue for His name's sake. Yea, though I walk through the Valley of the Shadow of Death, I will fear no evil, for Thou art with me, Lord; thy rod and thy staff they comfort me..."

* * *

"'It chills me to witness the watery grave close over us'," Elizabeth was reading the last entry in the logbook belonging to the schooner that once bore her name. "'But to a Christian, death anywhere is but a portal through which he passes to Glory...'."

"Commovente, no?" Parmananda asked Marinho with a crooked smile of derision, as the woman paused to clear the emotion from her throat.

"'I only pray'," she continued, "'that through our sacrifice, the Lord will spare the 'Julia'...'." Closing the tattered book, the women rested it on her lap and looked up, her strangely composed gaze meeting Somerset's.

"This is not my husband's writing, Governor. It was written by Mr. Ogle, I believe. He was captaining the 'Elizabeth Catherine' at the time of the sorrowful ...'incident'."

Parmananda leaned back in his chair, his brawny arms crossing above his prominent belly, his brow corrugated with a bewilderment that the Governor voiced.

"I don't understand, Madam," Sir Charles made his pressing inquiry. "Do you mean to say your husband was not on that mission?"

"There were two ships, Sir Charles," Elizabeth's voice was firm yet colourless, as Parmananda's fiery eyes shot to take intense scrutiny of the woman. "My husband was on the second vessel, the sloop referred to in that last entry in the logbook. The 'Julia'." Shifting to look at Parmananda, she asked, a slight tremor in her voice: "Was there any trace of her, Captain?"

Parmananda's quick eyes flickered from Elizabeth to Somerset as his mind raced to plot his answer. Finally he opened his arms and exhaled a breath of confidingness.

"At sea, Senhora," his voice bore the weight of his experience, "one piece of wood is much like another. It is often hard to distinguish between what one finds. -- Especialmente with the winter storms that..." he spun his hands round each other in sign of turbulence, "make a - mistura - a mixture of small and big together. But I can say with good conscience that it is difficult, Senhora, almost impossible for a sloop to survive where a schooner sinks. It would be strange."

Elizabeth caught her breath and stiffly queried: "What are you saying, Captain? That my husband might be dead?"

"Por amor de Deus, Senhora!" Parmananda exclaimed rising from his seat and taking a step in Elizabeth's direction. "Only God can say who is dead. And we mortals...ah, we can only hope and pray and do all that is humanly possible to help our loved ones. -- Yes, we must never give up hope. For their sake. No matter what the expense..." his eyes seemed to assume a pleading quality as he said once again, with deliberate emphasis: "No matter what the expense."

Somerset's brows were drawn in inspection of the 'driftwood' as he marvelled at how surprisingly proficient Parmananda's English could be if he wanted to be understood.

And Elizabeth understood.

"The expense," she silently echoed to herself as she held Parmananda's gaze. "I wonder how much that hope would cost me?"

* * *

"Having left the horrendous spectre of Choklee Hill behind us, we continued to advance reaching valleys of great beauty," Wilkins continued in his Diary, "overspread with vegetation of all kinds growing in splendid luxuriance. We here met with trees indigenous to this quarter of the globe, the timber of which appeared of a very solid and close texture (and admirably adaptable for ship building, I might add). Our track was pleasant, but sometimes irregular...

"As evening began to spread its dark mantle over the horizon, and the buffaloes started making their appearance, emerging from the thickets of the forest to indulge in the grateful herbage it afforded, we sought to find an asylum for the night, but apprehending danger from these animals, we were obliged to make a circuitous movement to avoid them. This detour brought us in the vicinity of a homestead from whence we had occasion to hear the miserable wailing of a dirge..."

The Swallows' curiosity aroused, the group inched closer to the homestead and, from a vantage point, was able to see a large funeral cortege making its way through the long shadows of the approaching night. The procession consisted of the deceased's close family and relatives, as well as a sizable following of wailing old women. Next to the corpse of the departed, that of a young girl, her body bound in hides and drawn up in the sitting position (as was the custom), was the hovering predacious figure of the local "inyanga" (the medicine man, described by Wilkins as: "of tall build with the head and neck longer than the body and greatly disfigured by disease, his shoulders and limbs betrimmed with a medley of the most fantastic trappings, with circlets of lion-claws round his neck, and other adornments, grisly and revolting, that enhanced the flash of deep cunning in his eye").

"A funeral?" Wilkins asked Popham, the British youth's eyes alight with engagement.

"Yes," Popham nodded, adding that obviously a member of the homestead had died and the family was taking the body out to the veld to be buried.

"Do you suppose we could look closer?" Tim wanted to know, his curiosity becoming evermore audacious.

Popham relayed the question to Mgobozi who, upon hearing the Swallow's somewhat macabre request, turned to Wilkins and inspecting his pale skin and freckles replied with a smile.

"He says," Popham was also smiling as he translated, "Men who have skins the colour of spirits should be welcome at a funeral."

Chuckling at the remark, Wilkins dismounted and found that Fynn, Farewell, Thomas and Cane shared in his desire to have a closer look.

"But do not interfere with the ceremony, he says," Popham went on, "or the 'inyanga', the medicine man, may accuse you of being 'umTakati'...a 'wizard' -- and that co uld mean death."

Cane and Thomas suddenly had second thoughts and returned to their mounts, leaving an intrepid Farewell, Fynn, and Wilkins to venture out to the burial site in the company of Popham and Mgobozi.

The procession had reached the shallow grave and the sitting figure of the deceased young woman was in the process of being interred, when the hideous features of the inyanga screwed up in astonished rage as his bilious eyes widened on the approaching White men. The medicine man emitted a shrieking cry, like that of a wounded vulture, and hysterically flapped his arms at his side, retreating to cower in a corner of the grave where he gawked with trepidation on the "inhuman" faces of Farewell, Fynn, and Wilkins. As the women also caught sight of the Swallows, the wailing abruptly ceased and the cortege's tearful grief temporarily gave way to gaping amazement and fear. The doleful mourners shrank back in terrified scrutiny of the newcomers - believing, indeed, that they were confronted with the visiting spirits of the departed.

Fynn's clinical gaze wandered from the astonished semblances of the Zulu homesteaders to the body in the grave, and, in his assessment of this native mode of burial, he made a mental note of the way the cowhides were wrapped round the corpse's legs and torso and tied in place with long cords of braided roots. The Irishman's scientific inspection moved on to the flaps of hide that concealed the cadaver's face, leaving only the lips exposed for---

Suddenly Fynn's blood ran cold in his veins. The lips. Ever so slightly -- they were moving. Quivering. As if the cadaver were trying to speak.

"She's alive!" the man of medicine said under his breath, the words chilling him as he uttered them.

"What?" snapped back Farewell, his eyes darting to Fynn in shock.

"They're burying her alive!" the Irishman cried out in horror, dashing towards the gravesite.

"Fynn!! For God's sake, what are you doing! Come back here!" yelled Farewell in apprehension, as he chased after him.

But it was too late. Fynn was beyond listening to anyone or anything but his own medical pledge to saving lives. Under the contemptuous glare of the snorting inyanga, and to the complete stupefaction of the Zulu family, the White man had leapt into the grave and was tugging on the cords that bound the woman's neck and face in an effort to facilitate her breathing.

Mgobozi, having already reached his conclusions regarding the Swallows' rebellious, independent natures, now wondered whether this rebellion was also directed against "immovables" such as Death. In light of this new inquiry, the general quickly scanned the situation and decided to wait and see what this White man was up to, - without intervening (despite the look on the face of the homestead's lord who would seem to be urging the Shakan commander to act on his family's behalf).

Momentarily stunned, Popham, Farewell, and Wilkins glared at their comrade's apparent insanity, as Fynn frantically tore open the kaross, exposing the 'deceas- ed's' face. When he had done so, they all caught their breaths upon viewing its captivating loveliness the congealed cataleptic features of a 'sleeping beauty'.

"She's burning with fever," Fynn cried out as he pressed a hand over her forehead. "Help me carry her back to the village," he exhorted, looking up at the lieutenant.

Uncharacteristically, the young hero of the Napoleo nic Wars hesitated in the face of this life-and-death emergency, his eyes flitting from Fynn to Mgobozi and back as indecision seared through his brain. He had no doubt that the woman was alive; Fynn was far too good at his work to make such a mistake. "Yet, should she be sacrificed?" the lieutenant wondered. "For the sake of show. So as not to get their backs up. Wouldn't it be better to let them bury her and be rid of the affair, then perhaps to jeopardise the mission by intervening and ---"

"Francis!" Fynn's voice broke in to the other man's abstraction. "If we don't act soon, she will be dead!"

So, as Mgobozi pondered over "Febana the Leader of the Swallows" being so emphatically directed by one of his own subordinates, Farewell dismissed his "utilitarian considerations" and leapt to Fynn's assistance and to that of the 'sleeping beauty'. Yet, even as he did so, another utilitarian pursuit had lodged in his mind - one which he thought sure would prove rewarding.

*

The entire night Fynn fought against the devouring and dehydrating fever to save the young woman (whose name came to be known as Tsani), using all the concoctions and medications at the disposal of his weathered carpetbag. While the family and the irate inyanga looked on, the Irishman laboured over the girl's lovely features in a bid to snatch them from the snarling jaws of Death that had already sunk its fangs into the tender flesh of her soul.

By daybreak, Fynn's efforts were rewarded. Tsani opened her eyes and focused them on her saviour. And, as she did so, her seraphic gaze took on the lineaments of disbelief as she cocked her head, gaping at the unfamiliar smiling White face and wondering whether she was in the hallowed presence of some extraordinary Ancestor. Only when she turned her attention to the beaming smiles of her mother and father did the 'awakening beauty' realise that she was still alive. An awareness that made Fynn's presence all the harder to explain.

"Wayengummangalisi," Tsani's father told his daughter, nodding to Fynn by way of introduction. "The Miracle Worker," he explained to his 'resurrected child'.

"Wayengummangalisi," Tsani repeated, taking Fynn's hand in her own soft touch and pressing it against her pale lips.

"I suppose I'll be executed as a wizard now," Fynn said fatalistically as he washed his hands by the currents of a nearby stream.

"On the contrary, Fynn," Farewell grinned. "They think you've resurrected her."

"That's blasphemous!" Fynn shot back, his face suddenly a mask of outrage. "And preposterous!"

"And most useful," Farewell put in, slyly.

"Useful?" the Irishman echoed in surprise as he splashed water on his face, feeling the tingling freshness reviving his tired senses.

"Can you imagine, Fynn," the lieutenant started by way of explanation, "how Alexander the Great would have reacted to the medical innovations of Leeuwenhoek, William Harvey, and Lavoisier? Or how Caesar would have looked upon the stethoscope in an age when the heart was merely a poetic symbol for courage..?"

"What the deuce are you rambling on about, Francis?" Fynn demanded rising from the riverbed and vigorously shaking the water off his body.

"What did they call you back there...?" Farewell's eyes were twinkling. "Ah, yes - 'Um-mangalisi'. 'The Miracle Worker'."

The two men stopped to stare at each other in silence. As realisation gradually crept over Fynn's features, his initial outrage grew to the stinging malaise of righteous anger.

"Medicine is a noble science, Francis!" he said sharply to his companion. "A mission of devoted men - not charlatans! - I know what you're thinking and I'll have no part of your devious scheme!"

As Fynn angrily scooped up his carpetbag and strode off, Farewell cried out after him: "Too late, Fynn! - You are already part of the scheme!"

Fynn froze in his tracks and half-turned to peer back at the other man.

"You have been since you chose that very special profession of yours! You said it yourself - on that slave ship. 'Only by the Grace of God will they be able to reach their destinations alive.' Do you for one minute doubt that for many of those poor souls you enacted that divine miracle, that you were 'um-mangalisi'? And you've repeated it now. To all intents and purposes you have resurrected her. - Don't you see, we'd be foolish not to use that to our advantage!"

"Yes, Farewell, I do see!" Fynn spat out with scorn, the tension of his weariness being translated to bitter indignation. "I see how a man without scruples could easily become a god in this country! But you overlook the fact that I, Henry Fynn," his brogue grew thicker, "believe in God and the integrity of my profession, and I will never use my profession to play god! So don't expect me to!"

"Very well, Fynn," Farewell said casually, unruffled by the other's outbreak. "I won't. But I have a feeling that Shaka will when he's learned about this 'miracle' of yours. And I submit that you'll be in no position to refuse him as you have me. Besides," an amused smile tugged at the corners of his mouth revealing how exhilarated he was by this paradoxical turn of events. "This all fits in to your Faustian notion of the Zulu King. Who better than God is suited to deal with Mephistopheles?"

* * *

"Are you sure that she was dead, old man?" Shaka's voice was lowered in a harsh whisper, and a moody darkness fell on his face as his eyes, trained on Tsani's father, grew still and gelid. "Before you answer, remember that your own life is at stake!"

"Yebo, Baba Nkosi," answered Tsani's father, his trembling body flat against the floor of Bulawayo's royal hut, his eyes cowering from his emperor's piercing gaze. "Yebo, Baba Nkosi!" the old man repeated in the throes of despair and pleading anxiety. "I was told, assured by the inyanga! - Yebo, Baba Nkosi!," he repeated again, his words spasms of sheer fright. "Would I go to bury my own daughter alive?"

Shaka regarded the man's quivering figure pressed fearfully against the ground like a terror-stricken lizard and was satisfied that he told the truth.

"You may go," he said, dismissing Tsani's father. "I will award you twenty of my best oxen for your fidelity."

Looking up, the old man's fear was suddenly replaced by a twisted grimace of deliverance. "UShaka ngiyesabu ukuthi nguShaka, UShaka kuyinkosi yasemaShobeni," he muttered subserviently, praising his lord and the Heavens above for the two miracles of the day: the resurrection of his daughter and twenty cattle as sign of gratitude from the Great Mountain!

"Baba Nkosi," Njani's father bowed repeatedly, backing out of the hut.

When his slithering frame was gone, Shaka's eyes fell on the mat with the outline of the name S H A K A which he had fastened to one of the upright posts of the Royal Hut - to hang as a symbol of the Swallows' "immortality".

"What do you think?" his voice at length returned to address his mother who had been sitting in silence, in the shadows, throughout the tense interrogation. "If what the old man said is true, their sangoma has powers that we ignore."

Nandi's clear eyes shown brilliant in the tenebrous, inclement light of the hut's interior. Remaining silent, the woman strode forward, nearing the flickering light of the hearth that rose to lap her ever-beautiful features with its warmth, ironing away the telltale lines of age that were beginning to steal across her otherwise soft, moist skin. Upon reaching the robust upright post, the woman stopped to gaze vacantly at the mat on which her son's name was inscribed in black - the colour of death.

"We have no need for their immortality, my son," she said after a long pause. "A mountain cannot die. Nor can the lifeblood of a stream stop flowing to its purpose in the Sea. You are the Mountain of Africa. And the Lifeblood you have given this land will flow forever in the veins of our people. Do not search for more."

"But there can be no harm, mother," Shaka said with childish insistence, "in having their Magic at our service."

"Those who wish to be served by Magic are destined to become its servants, Shaka," was her hushed reply. "If what the old man says is true, it means they base their lives on illusion, while you have taught your people to live in Reality! Even if the Swallows had a hundred lives each, those lives would not be worth the life of one Shaka, because you, my son, are Lord of the Heavens!"

"The leopard is also a lord, mother," Shaka's eyes met hers. "A sovereign among Masters. You told me that. Each proud day of his life is worth hundreds of days in the life of a raven. Yet, if the leopard were offered wings to fly, he would be foolish to refuse them."

"No, Shaka," Nandi replied with the same gentle, loving insistence with which she had guided her son from the most tender of ages, offering the maternal spark that ignited the Blaze of Africa. "He would be foolish to accept. The leopard's kingdom is the Earth. On the earth he is a Master. In the skies he becomes a victim! If the Swallows offer you wings to fly, it is because they wish to make you their victim."

    Nandi's voice grew still and she turned to gaze into the dense blackness that clung to the recesses of the Royal Hut. It was then that she fancied that she could hear, over the crackling fire, the howling of the wind high atop the Pinnacle of Kings and the eerie voice of Sitayi as the sangoma whispered to the Great Female Elephant, the Mother of the Language, the Mother of Africa - an eerie voice that came almost as a threatening reminder: "Nandi, daughter of Bhebhe. From your womb has come the Language of the Heavens emblazed in the Heart of He who has been made great. His Fame and that of His House has radiated into the sun. And that Mighty Nation of Red Spears and Thundering Shields of Light has been born. His Shadow and the Glory and Fear of the AmaZulu has spread throughout the Earth - as far as the eye can see. All things obey Him; All kneel at His feet for he is enthroned as the Sacred Sovereign of whom the Ancestors spoke when they sang to the Wind. - Be true to your Heritage," Sitayi's whisper became harsher, menacing. "Or, as the Heavens gave you greatness, so shall they destroy your seed with the Blood of Its Blood. - Such is the Way of Loyalty."

CHAPTER XXXVII
"DINGANE KaSENZANGAKONA ZULU" (THE NEEDY ONE)

Shaka Zulu, "Odlung'emanxulumeni" - "He who raged amongst the Nations", "Ilangfa eliphahl'elinye ngemisebe" - "The Sun that eclipsed all the Universe with its rays", the Great Mountain of Africa, UShaka, had fourteen half-brothers and five half-sisters, and one full sister.

The full sister, the only one Shaka loved like a sister, was Nomcoba of course, daughter of Senzangakona and Nandi, who, in 1824, at the arrival of the Swallows was 32 years of age, a spinstress and commander of the four Shakan "Maiden's Regiments" (which, though never actually engaging in war, were forced to live the disciplined, celibate life of the military homesteads).

The five half-sisters, ignored by their illustrious brother and treated with indifference, were: Nomzitlanga (daughter of Mkabi & Senzangakona), Sikaka (daughter of Magulana & Senzangakona), Nomqoto (daughter of Bibi & Senzangakona), Nozicuba (daughter of Songiya & Senzangakona), and Ntikili (daughter of Songiya & Senzangakona). All five were either in regimental homesteads or at esiKlebeni or Bulawayo at the time of the White's arrival.

The fourteen half brothers, all younger of course, were Ngwadi (son of Nandi & Gendeyana), the only one to share Shaka's affection, who was (at the arrival of the "Julia" in Port Natal) 21 years of age and in his uFogisa Regimental Homestead...

...and the other sons born to Senzangakona and his sixteen wives: Dingane (son of Mpikase & Senzangakona), Mhlangana (son of Mzindswase & Senzangakona), Bakuza (son of Sondaba & Senzangakona), Sigiyana (son of Bibi & Senzangakona), Mpande (son of Songiya & Senzangakona), Magwaza (son of Ncaka & Senzangakona), Nzibe (son of Songiya & Senzangakona), Kolekile (son of Ncaka & Senzangakona), Gowujana and Sigwebana (sons of Mehlana & Senzangakona), Gqugqu (son of Mntuli & Senzangakona), Mfihlo (son of Kishwase & Senzangakona) and Nxojana (son of Mangcengeza & Senzangakona) -- all of whom were barely tolerated by Shaka's uncaring disposition towards all Senzangakona's offspring.

Of these thirteen half-brothers, sons of Senzangakona, seven were dead by 1824: -- Bakuza, Gowunjana and Gqugqu had fallen in action in the Mtetwa-Butelezi War; Sigiyana (his father's official heir to the throne) had been eliminated by Shaka in 1816 when the Zulu had entered esiKlebeni to take his rightful place as the Language of his People; Sigwebana and Mfihlo had fallen at Qokli Hill; Nxojana had died of dysentery during the march to Dlovunga.

Of the remaining six half brothers: Kolekile, Nzibe, Magwaza, and Mpande were in the Ama-Wombe and U-Nomdayana Regimental Homesteads at the time Wilkins started writing his Diary, and Dingane and Mhlangana were in the iziZimazane Regimental Homestead.

Of these six, only three were to ever entertain the thought of actually regaining the Zulu throne from their "usurper" brother, Shaka. They were: Dingane, Mhlangana, and Mpande.

Of these three, two would become kings.

Of these two - only Dingane would rule in Shaka's place.

Dingane kaSenzangakona Zulu. The second-born grandson of Jama kaNdaba.

Born in 1793, six years after Shaka's birth, Dingane was still in his mother's belly when his intrepid halfbrother had escaped death by fleeing in the night from esiKlebeni, the royal residence of Senzangakona, in the company of his sister Nomcoba, and his mother Nandi. Dingane had been a mere toddler when Shaka and his 'family' had struggled against the ill will, the hatred and the resentment of Nandi's people to survive and make a life for themselves in the Langeni village. He had been a small boy of eight when Nzobo had set fire to Mfunda's homestead and when Shaka, Nandi, Nomcoba and his grandmother had been banished and forced to "wander" during the calamitous, and now legendary Famine of Madlatule of 1802. The second-born son of Senzangakona had been barely eleven when Shaka had first officially taken his stand against his father's people in the courageous speech given in Kondlo's Qwabe Homestead.

And, at the age of eleven, for the first time Dingane had started to feel how desperately difficult it was to be the second-born in his House, the younger brother of the Child who was destined to be the "Great Elephant, the Language of His People". Indeed, though Dingane had been tall for a boy his age (as tall as many of the men at esiKlebeni), with broad shoulders and strong, sturdy arms and, though he had been clever, quick-witted and a remarkable hunter, it had been virtually impossible for him (or any youth, for that matter) to stand comparison with the exceptional physique, the beauty, and the strength of body, mind, and character which distinguished the unique human being that was his brother, Shaka.

And the weight of that comparison had burdened Dingane's soul day after day, year after year, taxing his youth and adolescence. It had seemed to him that the brother he had never met, the brother who was always in distant lands making a grand name for himself, was not distant at all -but ever-present to haunt and torment his life at esiKlebeni.

A life he had lived in the shadow of Shaka. One that had caused the robust son of Mpikase to grow up with little or no affection, with little or no praise, with little or no pride in himself and what he could become. He had always been looked upon by his drunken father (whom Dingane knew had an obsessed, maniacal love for both Shaka and his mother, Nandi), by his uncaring mother, and by the other "whores" Senzangakona had married looked upon by everyone, it seemed as the "other son", "the second-born, the second best", "the Needy One". Even the king's sister, his aunt Mkabayi, whom he had sincerely loved, had shunned his affection, limiting their relationship to a one-sided recounting of the heroic tales of his brother's exploits as one of Dingiswayo's soldiers, the head of the Brigade known as "Shaka's Fifty" and to Mkabayi's grandiloquent boasts of how Shaka would make the Zulus great.

As was to be expected, Dingane had responded to the impossible comparison by exerting his own quite definite personality, one which he had honed to become the exact opposite of his brother's, to the point where Dingane's very existence was not one of "action", but one of reaction to Shaka's - one in which his consuming envy drove him to want to be all that his brother was not.

Where Shaka was ever-inquisitive, ever-curious about Life and its many manifestations, Dingane became phlegmatic and reticent, looking upon Life as a river that flowed aimlessly at his feet. Where Shaka was generous and giving of his mind and body, Dingane became lazy and greedy.

War and dominion were the ruling passions of Shaka; while women, luxury, and ease absorbed the whole mind of Dingane. Shaka was bold and daring, his name striking panic in the hearts of his enemies; Dingane became too inert to be feared and too compliant to be obeyed by anyone. Shaka was born and nurtured in combat, Dingane preferred and cultivated the languid superficial profer rings of peace. One was dedicated and a born warrior, the other had a soul, capricious and vacillating, that seemed devoted to only comfort and pleasure.

Even when his father had been dying, Dingane had never aspired to the kingship of the Zulu clan; it would have been contrary to his spiritless disposition to allow so ambitious a thought to cross his mind. And when Shaka came and took the throne in 1816, after murdering his brother Sigiyana, Dingane was quick to fall to his knees and cry out "Bayete, Nkosi! Bayete!"

Yet where Shaka was sincere, Dingane had become insipid and deceitful. And, though he formally and publically declared his approval of Shaka's usurpation of the throne and solemnly promised to honour, to defend and to serve the new King of the Zulus, in his heart Dingane was waiting; - waiting for the moment when he would destroy the hated brother who had broken his youth and robbed it of all affection and praise; waiting for the moment when he could take Shaka's place as the First Son of Zulu.

The moment finally came in 1824 when two specific events were to stir Dingane out of the dull routine of the iziZimazane Regimental Homestead (where his life was made a torture by the unending training, the exhausting manoeuvres, and the strict codes of discipline - a forced existence so divorced from the leisure and ease he relished, one which could only inflame his loathing of Shaka).

The first event was a chance meeting with Pakatwayo kaKondlo of the Qwabes. An encounter in which Dingane was made vividly aware of the hatred the son of Kondlo nurtured for the man who had taken away his throne. And in the course of further meetings both men vowed to kill Shaka as soon as the opportunity presented itself; they were soon joined in their conspiratorial quest by Zwide of the Ndwandwes and General Soshangane - both men having returned from their protracted stay in the North country to vindicate the bloodbath of Qokli Hill and the Destruction of Dlovunga.

The second event was the opportunity itself: - the landing of the "Julia".

Pakatwayo, Dingane and his brother Mhlangana (whom Dingane had had no trouble recruiting to the "cause") met in the Plains of eNtsangoana the same day Mgobozi, Farewell and his party were crossing the open graveyard known as Qokli Hill.

"When?" asked Dingane kaSenzangakona Zulu, male child of sixth wife Mpikase, the "ever-second" son of his father's house, the half brother of the Mighty Sigidi.

"When the Swallows have reached kwaBulawayo," was the reply of Pakatwayo kaKondlo, dethroned king of the Qwabes. "That is the time to strike. No one must doubt that his death was caused by the arrival of the White men. They are the answer for which we've been waiting. - Finally."

"And what of Shaka's network of bodyguards?" asked the treachery of Mhlangana kaSenzangakona, male child of wife Mzondwase, third son of his father's House. "They are virtually impenetrable and incorruptible.

"Nothing is impenetrable," Pakatwayo observed, the moon's reflection glowing harshly on his keen eyes - eyes that betrayed a soul full of loathing, vengeance and murder. "No one is incorruptible. Just prepare the way to your brother's side, and my men will tend to the rest."

* * *

"Those hypocrites have given him up for dead!" Elizabeth paced the elegantly furnished drawingroom of her mother's home at Cape Town.

"One would think it Sir Charles's duty to send a ship out to sift that coast," Anna Schmidt Peterssen remarked, looking up from her tea. "After all, Francis was serving the Colony!"

"Is," corrected her husband, Johann Peterssen, with a touch of reprimand as he gazed at his wife over the top of his Dutch newspaper. "Is serving the Colony."

"Oh, mother," Elizabeth exclaimed, too beside herself with worry and exasperation to catch her stepfather's subtle distinction. "Sir Charles never thought Francis would succeed! From the very start, he looked upon the whole mission as an act of betrayal on the part of His Majesty's Colonial Office! He wanted full regiments, not a lone adventurer! And I suppose the Governor's only too happy to see that he was right! I think that in his heart of hearts he wants to believe Francis has failed! It would justify his own failure if the Colony fell to the Zulus!"

"And where does that leave us? The settlers?!" Anna frowned apprehensively, suddenly losing all interest in her home cooked 'Marillen" cake.

"It leaves us where we have been since Britain took over," Johann looked up again from his paper, his Dutch accent swelling with acrimony as he was reminded of that fateful summer in 1803 when the British Government first took the Cape away from the Dutch East India Company, changing the rule of Cape Town in both institutions and language (the second factor being far harder to cope with). "It leaves us in Limbo, dats where! Gott verdam! Praying for a White Paradise in a Black Hell!"

"Johann!" was Anna's reproachful rejoinder. "Must you always be so frightfully Dutch?" "Ja!" Johann nodded with vehemence, causing his reading glasses to ride up and down his prominent nose using his fleshy cheeks as pivot points. "Ja! As long as the Cape is so frightvooolly British, I remain as frightvoolly Dutch as you remain frightvoolly German! - Have another 'Kuchen'!" he huffed, nodding to the cake.

Elizabeth grinned at her benevolent stepfather. Yet Anna remained serious, asking her daughter: "Are you saying that Sir Charles doesn't care whether we go under or not?"

"Yes, mother! That's the whole point!' Elizabeth exclaimed. "He does not care. Not really! Somerset has done his 'duty'. He's sent his son and Major Cloete to guard the northern frontiers of British Kaffraria with their 2,000 troops..."

Johann looked at his stepdaughter, musefully following her train of though. He knew she was referring to the autocratic decision the Governor had made shortly after his heated meeting with Farewell. In that decision, Somerset, feeling that the "Shakan Emergency" could not wait for the outcome of the "insane remedy offered by Bathurst's Office", had exercised his "authority as Governor in times of crises" and, bypassing the Colonial Office, he had instructed his son, Lt. Colonel Henry Somerset, "to make such military arrangements as circumstances may require". Accordingly, Col. Somerset - with Col. Josias Cloete and Capt. Scott Aitchison of the 25th Regiment of Foot - had left Fort Frederick at the Cape and proceeded with his troops and some English and Dutch volunteers (2,074 in all between enlisted men and recruits) to the outer limits of British Kaffraria (those limits that bordered with the Shakan threat). There Col. Somerset had set up base at Rev. Bellow's mission station in order to keep a vigilant watch on the situation and be ready to intervene when necessary (as if these 2,074 men could do anything even remotely resembling an "intervention" against a Zulu military tidal wave). "Madness", Johann told himself as he listened to his step-daughter's telling remarks.

"Cloete reckons that if Shaka attacks, the 25th Regiment of Foot can hold the Cape for a week or so," her tone was caustic. "Long enough for Somerset to book passage back to Plymouth with his sad tales of how futile it is to keep Africa from the Africans!"

"Aren't you being a bit churlish, my dear," Anna noted, suggesting, somewhat naively: "Why don't you write to His Majesty. He has both the ways and the means to help. I'm sure he'll listen to you. After all, this whole idea was partially his own!"

"King George would never even read my letter, mother," Elizabeth scoffed. "He has more pressing matters to tend to. Such as what wallpaper to use in Buckingham and whether the columns at Windsor should be Doric or Corinthian!"

Johann looked up, his eyes laughing behind his thick spectacles, as Anna pursed her lips.

"I never realised how much Francis's rebellious spirit has influenced you!"

"He's just opened my eyes, mother. To a lot of things!"

"I will need time," Johann declared, removing his glasses and neatly and religiously folding his newspaper in his usual ritualistic manner. "A week perhaps. Or two. But I think I shall be able to raise the money to purchase another ship to go out and search for your..." his rosy cheeks dimpled with a smile, "- rebellious spirit."

"Thank you, Papa," Elizabeth returned the man's beaming affection with sincere gratitude. "But like all our other battles, Francis and I must fight this one alone."

Johann and Anna exchanged a deliberate glance in which the one acknowledged deep respect for the offspring of the other.

"Besides," Elizabeth went on, looking out at the beauty of Table Bay, "I don't need a ship. What I need is a captain and a crew! And that's what's going to be difficult to secure! Cape Town's a small place and word gets round! After the wreck of the 'Catherine', the name Farewell may have become taboo for any self-respecting seamen! They're all so terribly superstitious!" Suddenly Elizabeth froze and, echoed, musefully: "Self-respecting - but of course! -- Perhaps he is the answer after all."

"Who?" Anna asked.

"Captain Parmananda," Elizabeth exclaimed.

"You can't be serious, Elizabeth!" Anna retorted. "That man is a..."

"A mercenary,-- " Johann broke in grinning. "A cutthroat. A pirate! A buccaneer! - As bad or worse than they say he is!"

"Yet, he's the sort of man Francis would choose were he in my place," Elizabeth went on completing her own and her stepfather's line of reasoning. "Just the sort he would choose!"

"Have you considered the fact that all this might be..." Anna found it difficult to add: "Useless?"

"No, mother!" Elizabeth was adamant. "He's alive! I can feel it!"

CHAPTER XXXVIII
"BULAWAYO"(THE PLACE OF THE KILL)

"On the tenth day, after having travelled about 200 miles through a most picturesque country, and crossed several rivers," Wilkins recorded in his Colonial Office Chronicle & Diary, "we arrived at the summit of the Ongoyee Mountain from which the view was particularly grand and imposing. Looking out at the valley below us, my eyes caught a sight which nearly took my breath away, one that I trust I shall remember for the remainder of my earthly days and perhaps beyond that...

"On the gentle sloping hills of the opposite side of the valley, at a distance of a mile or so away, lay Shaka's great homestead. It was unlike anything we could possibly have imagined. Indeed, on the journey upcountry we had ocassion to see many native homesteads (some belonging to minor chiefs), yet impressive and extensive as some of these were, they bore little resemblance to what I now saw Shaka's royal residence to be...

"It might have been likened to a gigantic platter or disc (some four to five miles in circumference) resting on the incline of this immense valley and surrounded by an encircling outer palisade. Centered on the homestead's enormous circular cattle-pen and parade grounds, a mass of over 1700 huts (or so we were later informed) radiated over an area of five to six square miles, giving the impression of a closely packed town. The upper segment of the 'platter' was further hedged around to form the private quarters sacred to the king (the 'isiGodlo', Popham told us it was called). The vastness of the establishment was emphasised by the dense mass of people gathered within it. Even from a distance there was no mistaking the size and animation of the crowd. The muffled sounds of chanting voices and stamping feet drifted across the valley to our enchanted ears, adding a savage resonance to the bellowing of Shaka's huge herd of cattle. Furthermore, in the midst of the Citadel, carpeting the parade grounds, was also collected the amassed strength of Shaka's armies. The soldiers (80,000 we were told) presented a magnificent sight in their full wardress and with their sea of rippling shields of all colours and waving ostrich plumes giving an ominous display of sinister military beauty and efficiency...

"I feel I can safely say that no other white man has witnessed such a scene; it was awesome!"

"Bulawayo," Mgobozi said, making a sweeping gesture in the direction of the mammoth residence, his even white teeth shining bright between lips parted in a beaming smile of pride. Having thus "introduced" the Citadel to the Swallows, the general directed his searching gaze upon the Whites, pleased to see their stunned appreciation.

"Oh my God!" was Farewell's only remarked upon viewing the Zulu Citadel.

"Is that an exclamation or a prayer, Francis?" Fynn asked, the Irishman remaining far less impressed by the magnificence of the Shakan Homestead.

"Both, Fynn," the lieutenant sighed, shifting his attention to Wilkins. "Well, you have your first 'Shakan Affair' report for the Colonial Office, Tim. Five words: 'We don't stand a chance!'"

Mgobozi neared Popham, barking out an order in Zulu before trotting off towards Bulawayo.

"He says we are to wait here until we are called for," Popham diligently translated.

"Who's moving," Cane put in, casting a timorous look at the immense sea of warriors packed within the homestead's perimeters.

"Why is it, gentlemen, that we British are so suicidally inquisitive?" Farewell inquired as his gaze reached out for the gigantic residence and lingered on its seething humanity, the topic of his impromtu discourse catching the Swallows somewhat by surprise. "I mean, what are we doing here?"

"Why, trying to avert a catastrophe, I would think, sir," Tim ventured, blinking back his amazement at the time and place chosen by the lieutenant to make such an odd inquiry.

"Yes, Tim. That's our purpose now. But what was our purpose three centuries ago?" Farewell's words caused both Cane and Thomas to gaze back down at the gargartuan "native" setting. "I speak not only of the British, but of the Dutch, the Portuguese, the Spanish, Italians, Frenchmen, Greeks, Norsemen, the Prussians...Why is it that we Europeans always have to go to the world?! Why doesn't the world ever come to us?!"

"Perhaps the world's shy, Francis," Fynn suggested with a diverted twinkle of his transparent eyes.

"Montezuma shy?!" the lieutenant rebutted. "Hardly, Fynn!"

"Greed?" Cane proffered as a possible motive for the European colonies.

"Every man's greedy, Cane," Farewell shot back. "Be he an Inca or a Bushman."

"Our superior technology, then." Tim submitted, his involvement in the discussion temporarily dulling Bulawayo's spell. "Or our advanced Science."

"Not enough, Tim," was the lieutenant's response. "History proves that when people need to migrate, they always manage to develope the technological know-how to do so. - We migrate for no apparent reason at all. We're looking for trouble, it seems. And we usually find it."

Cane nervously cleared his throat as his attention was gravitated back to the thousands of Shakan warriors.

"It's the thorn in the side of our personality, I'm afraid," Farewell observed. "Christopher Columbus lived in a world of bliss, before he decided it was round. And Magellan was a perfectly carefree sailor, languishing on the beaches of Tras os Montes, before he started asking himself if a ship could reach the East by going West. I think the answer is that we suffer from an infectious disease back home, one you won't find in your medical books, Fynn: - our curiosity is stronger than our fear."

"Infectious, sir?" Tim queried. "Do you think Shaka might catch it?"

"Oh, he already has, Tim. Or we wouldn't be here."

"...with whole skins," Cane added, laconically.

*

"Shoulders back, Fynn. Chin up!" Farewell exhorted. "Pretend we rule the world!"

Three hours after Mgobozi's departure, a messenger was sent up to the Swallows announcing that the Great Shaka was prepared to meet with Febana and his sangoma (which was interpreted to mean the medical man, Fynn). And now the two White men were riding towards the fantastic Citadel flanked on either side by cordons of magnificently attired Zulu warriors of the amaWombe Regiment whose stately figures traced a path down the slopes leading to the gates of Bulawayo. As the lieutenant had urged, his own shoulders were now thrust back, causing the epaulettes on his naval tunic to jut up at the sides.

"A bit late for masquerading, isn't it, Francis?" Fynn noted as he cast a suffered glance at his companion's military air.

"On the contrary, Fynn. The show's just begun, the curtain's rising, and we are alone on the stage. I suggest we give the public..." he nodded to the gaping of Bulawayo, "...it's money's worth."

"I was never very good at improvising."

"There'll be very little of that, Fynn. The minute we reach those gates, I'm sure we'll be presented with a carefull planned scenario."

"'Macbeth'?"

"More like 'Hamlet'. The plot will be based on indecision - keep your protagonist guessing. And the underlying theme will be insanity."

"If anything happens to them," Tim said through clenched teeth as he watched the two men moving towards their Fate. "His Majesty shall hear from me!"

"Do you intend becoming the Ghost of Windsor, Tim?" Cane had a wry smile. "Haunting George at midnight with the rattling of chains."

"I'm afraid I don't follow, Cane," Tim said stiffly.

"If Farewell and Fynn die, m'lad," the tall, goodhearted carpenter told the red-head. "We're next." His eyes moved to Holstead as he underlined: "Every man Jack of us."

While "Febana and his Sangoma" rode closer and closer to the immense brooding black throng packed in the six square miles of the Royal Homestead, the Zulus thrilled by the novelty of the "special attraction" - gawked wide-eyed and enraptured at the peculiar representatives of the Swallows' King Joji who had travelled on the Bird of White Wings to see the Great Mountain. And the Zulus were impressed. Not by the Swallows themselves, but by the fact that "the world had come to them!" (to paraphrase Farewell's previous remark); and the Heart of the Heavens was swollen with pride at the thought that these white creatures should have found it necessary to travel from afar "bringing the Friendship" of the monarch of the Other World; - an act of subservience (or so it was seen) which only helped to heighten Shaka's greatness in the eyes of his own people.

On top of the Royal Dias (the nine-foot high clay mound overlooking the parade grounds) sat Shaka's Royal Entourage: Ngomane, Mbiya, Lutuli, Ngwadi, Kuta, Mzilikazi, Mgobozi, Nqoboka, Joko, and Dlaba, - next to the females, Pampata, Nomcoba, Mkabi and Mkabayi (both the first wife and the sister of Senzangakona having been integrated as part of the "family" upon Nandi's request, out of her feelings of guilt and gratitude: - indeed, in their own quite special ways, the two women had saved the Child's life: Mkabi, by unwittily allowing him to be the first-born through the stillbirth of her own child (Nandi's guilt); and Mkabayi, by planning young Shaka's escape and making way for his greatness (the gratitude).

And, in his greatness, Shaka was under the vigilant eye of the omnipresent Ufasimba and concealed within the high palisades of the isiGodlo, the Emperor's Private Quarters, the fenced-off "Holy of Holies" of the Mighty Shrine of the Heavens called Bulawayo, "The Place of The Kill" - the Kill: that primal, elemental process of survival, pure, artless, often cruel, unreasoning, but never senseless, that, along with Death, had been

Shaka's companion since early childhood. As the Emperor stood peering furtively through the thatching of the isiGodlo at the approaching Whites, a few select uDibi Boys, their bodies dwarfed by Shaka's massive build, were smearing the king's torso and arms with sheep-fat and native butter thus creating a shimmering gloss on his light-brown skin, and dressing him with his brown and black kilt of furry tails, with his armlets of burnished copper and his leglets of ivory tassels, with his leopardskin and his head-dress bearing the quivering crane feather. Shaka found it unbearable to stand throughout this process of dress and adornment, as the blood buzzed through his veins with a tingling sensation procured by his overwhelming expectation and curiosity...

And a good measure of fear. Though he was reluctant to admit it even in the privacy of his own heart, the Emperor was to some degree in apprehension of the meeting with the Strangers. The chilling, inscrutable feeling that had entered the Zulu's soul during the course of his struggle with the iNto eMosayo, the White Elephant, had left him deeply troubled. For the first time in his life, he felt that his spirit was living symbiotically with an emotion foreign to his otherwise healthy psychic constitution, - one over which he had little or no control; an emotion that, like a parasite, was growing and thriving at the expense of carefully honed attributes such as self-assuredness, equanimity, caution, restraint, perceptiveness and sharp insight. He felt that some malignant cancer had inadvertently, unaccountably entered his soul and was spreading, inexorable, to infect all levels of his being. He lived in apprehension that this devouring darkness would catch him unawares, - in the absurd, irrational dread that he would finally fall victim to his own Weapon of Supremacy: the Unknown.

Accordingly, Shaka's brain was on fire with blazing animation and obsession, as his eyes remained wide and glued to the distant gates of his Citadel where the tiny figures of Fynn and Farewell inched closer, gaining the entrance to his magnificent residence.

Upon reaching the end of the human cordon of Zulu warriors, Fynn and Farewell passed through the gates of Bulawayo and pulled up on their reins, stopping on the wide, oval track (nearly two miles in circumference) that encircled the inner fencing of the huge cattlefold. As the enthralled masses pressed closer to the Whites, the two men reacted to the claustrophobic proximity of tens of thousands of people in their own, quite disparate ways: - Francis George Farewell, ecstatic, wearing a broad smile as he viewed Shaka's subjects, his features aglow with the light of his adventurous spirit; Henry Francis Fynn, horrified, feeling irredeemably afloat in the Black Sea of Shaka's power, his delicate soul reminded of all the ships on which he had fought to save lives, ships like the "Espirito de Guanabara", and his tender heart recognised that, like those chained slaves, the thousands now present in Bulawayo were also slaves - the ones who had stayed behind to serve their original master.

"Good afternoon, gentlemen," came Daniel's voice out of the crowd. "Welcome to Dante's 'Inferno'. I hope your journey was pleasant. My name is Virgil and I am to be your guide."

Upon seeing Daniel's smiling features striding towards them through the hive of Zulus, the man of medicine and the naval lieutenant had mixed reactions. They were delighted at first to constate that he was still alive and somewhat amused to see the Xhosa doning the attire of a Zulu induna (crowned, rather incongruously, with his dusty bowler hat).

"Daniel...?" the lieutenant asked, just to make sure it was really their man.

"Don't tell me you're surprised to see me dressed as an African, Lieutenant," the Xhosa joked good-humouredly. "My years of Christianisation couldn't cope with that."

"No, I think you look rather smashing, in fact," Farewell remarked, causing a smile to lighten Fynn's grave features. "That is what the Colonies are all about after all, isn't it, Daniel? - Zulu induna's in bowler hats quoting Italian poets. I'm merely surprised to see you at all, I suppose. - What have you done to win Shaka's confidence?"

"If my instinct is correct, I would say that he thinks he needs us, Lieutenant," Daniel replied, raising his voice over the milling throngs of Zulus that jammed round him. "He thinks we have 'Aladdin's Lamp'."

"And what does he want from the Genie?" the question was Fynn's.

"A foolproof remedy."

"For what?" Farewell inquired.

"Dying," was Daniel's reply.

*

"UShaka ngiyesab'ukuthi nguShaka! Shaka, I fear to say he is Shaka!" Joko chanted in a sonorous voice, his ixwa raised, its blade stabbing the skies ovehead. "UNomakhwelo ingonyama! Ugaqa libomvu nasekuphatheni! - He who is like the lion. He whose spear is red even at the handle!"

"Oth'esadl'ezinye wadl'ezinye, wath'esadl'ezinye wasdl'ezinye, - He who while devouring some, devoured others, and he who devoured others as he devoured some more!" roared the four thousand heroic voices of Joko's uYengonglovu Regiment as a reponsory to their general's invocation, all ixwas raised, their gleaming blades shintillating in the sun.

"UShaka ngiyesab'ukuthi nguShaka!" entoned Mgobozi. "UNomakhwelo ingonyama! Ugaqa libomvu nasekuphatheni!"

"Oth'esadl'ezinye wadl'ezinye, wath'esadl'ezinye wasdl'ezinye," came the thunderous cry of his iziCwe, which, singing as one man, offered the refrain of the "Song of Shaka" (as it was called - both the music and the lyrics a creation of Shaka himself):

"UShaka ngiyesab'ukuthi nguShaka!" sang Nqoboka in a melodious crescendo. "UNomakhwelo ingonyama! Ugaqa libomvu nasekuphatheni!"

"Oth'esadl'ezinye wadl'ezinye, wath'esadl'ezinye wasdl'ezinye," was the deafening response of the four thousand of Nqoboka's iziPikili Regiment.

"UShaka ngiyesab'ukuthi nguShaka! UNomakhwelo ingon- yama! Ugaqa libomvu nasekuphatheni! -- Oth'esadl'ezinye wadl'ezinye, wath'esadl'ezinye wasdl'ezinye!" The verse and the refrain of Shaka's Song rippled through the 80,000 troops, regiment by regiment in turn: by Dlaba and his iNyelezi Regiment, by Kuta and the four thousand of the u-Kangela Regiment, by Mzilikazi and the AmaPen- jana Regiment, by Ngwadi and the uNomdayana Regiment; followed by the generals and men of the uNomdayana Regiment, the amaKwenkwe, the iziKwembu, the iziZimanzana (with the voices of Dingane and Mhlangana loudest of all in the praises of their hated brother), then the Jubingqwanga, the uDlambedlu, the iziPezi, the uMbonambi, the uNteke, the uGibabanye, the uFojisa, the imFoplosi, and the inDabankulu; completed by the chanting of Nomcoba and the Maidens's Regiments: the two thousand of the umVutwanini, the two thousand of the inTlabati, the imBabazane and the uluSiba.

The voice of the regiments swelled as the entire population joined the warriors and maidens in their song, flooding the earth "as far as the eye can see" with the praises of the Zulu Emperor. Then the quaking litany was fluidly transmuted to the booming roar of the Zulu National Anthem (another of Shaka's creative efforts) which exploded from the gates of Bulawayo and ununundated the countryside, deluging all of Creation in its triumphant, heroic notes.

Floundering in this boundless ocean of extolment and exaltation, a prey to its strong emotional currents, to its crested grandiloquent waves that broke bombastic onto the rocky cliffs of militant glory, swirling in the powerful eddies of Shaka's might, Farewell and Fynn were petrified and gaped in a dazzled trance at the chanting multitude, jolted by the intensity of the Zulus' collective pride.

From his post of attentive stalking within the secreted confines of the isiGodlo, Shaka lapped up the prasies and the glory of his Anthem. As his flaming eyes took scrutiny of the effect his power was having on the awestruck Whites, the Zulu's tigerish lips curled away from gleaming white teeth in a smile that was an orgasm of pure paroxysmal ecstasy. When his teeth parted, Shaka growled out a short, staccato order that sent on of the Ufasimba guards shooting out of the isiGodlo and racing round the perimeter of the stockade and through the densely packed crowd that quickly parted to make way for the imperial messenger. Reaching the Whites' position at the foot of thew cattlefold, the Ufasimba guard relayed the Emperor's demands to Daniel who turned to gaze up at Farewell with a mischievous glint in his eye.

"Your horses intrigue the Emperor, he says," Daniel interpreted. "The Great Mountain wishes to learn more about them."

"Could you be more specific, Daniel?" the lieutenant responded with a furrowed brow.

"I believe," said Daniel, "if my interpretation is correct, that he wants to see the animals...in motion. At a trot, perhaps, or at a gallop. So as to ascertain their speed and capability."

"I see," Farewell said, his voice devoid of emotional texture. Looking around at the crowded mass of humanity he added, "And where are we to carry out this," he hesitated searching for the word, "-- 'experiment' without trampling anyone?

Daniel turned to converse briefly with the Ufasimba guard. Well understanding the predicament and in an effort to clear a path for the horses, the Shakan warrior raised his hand and barked out a sharp, urgent order which was relayed from guard to guard across the entire diameter of the residence. As a further sign of Shaka's impeccable organisation, the guards caused the masses to instantly part, thus forming an open track (of approximately ten meters in width) round the entire twomile circumference of the inner stockade - a track of soft soil which, in size and condition, could very well have rivalled the racing institution of Ascot or that of the lesser yet more adjacent Cape Town Turf Club.

With a sporting air of good-hearted improvisation, Farewell motioned Fynn to follow and the two set their horses at a brisk gallop round the huge oval concourse. They Zulus seemed captivated by the exceptional manoeuvre of the two Swallows who expertly and effortlessly piloted their mounts over the swerving terrain, speeding past the electrified excitement of those closest to the circular band of turf. And, in the midst of the gaping throng, the emotional states of the two Whites were again disparate, - with

Farewell enjoying himself tremendously whilst Fynn wore a sour look and sulked in the indignity of this 'circus' in which he had been enlisted as unwilling protagonist.

Shaka's feline eyes remained rivetted on the galloping animals, his keen reasoning power discerning the mares' superb command of both speed and elegance - qualities that the Emperor held in the highest esteem. Without extricating his entranced gaze from the animals' progress round the circular track, Shaka barked out yet another order to the Ufasimba and, in an instant, three superb specimens of athletic fitness had saluted their king with an emphatic "SI-GI-DI!" and were moving in the the direction of the track at a steady trot.

To Fynn's and Farewell's utter amazement, the three Ufasimba warriors veered onto the track and flanked the horses, their own pounding feet falling into step with the animals' trundling hooves.

"They've been sent to outrun us," Farewell remarked upon realising that the three warriors were attempting to match the animals' speed with their own.

"Do you think it possible?" Fynn queried. "A man outrunning a horse."

"Ordinarily, the very thought of it would be preposterous," the lieutenant noted. "But the way these men are trained..." leaving the thought suspended, Farewell spurred his horse and, rising in his stirrups, his body well forward in the saddle, he propelled his mount into a headlong gallop, bolting away from his companion with: "Faster, Fynn. We must play Shaka at his own game!"

Swept away by Farewell's decisiveness and the challenge of the sport, Fynn spurred his own mount and shot off in hot pursuit; whilst the three Ufasimba guards, true to their strict military training, tapped their seemingly inexhaustible reserves of speed and endurance and, defying the humanly possible, gave chase, catching up to the beasts, matching the horses' formidable gait with their own elegant powerful strides. In the heat of the contest, Farewell felt greatly invigorated, his full lips drawn back in a reckless smile that he directed at the Ufasimba runner racing at his side. Sensing the Swallow's regarding glance, the warrior looked up, and when his eyes met Farewell's, for an instant the shadow of a smile crossed his otherwise Spartan features. And that smile serving as a gauntlet, the race began in earnest.

Round the track they competed - the warriors and the steeds, neck and neck; - the rippling, sinewy thighs of the horses pitted against the elongated, muscular flesh of the warriors' churning legs, the foaming sweat on the saddles and the steaming hides matching lungs distended beyond the resilience natural to human tissue and faces taut with blinding exertion. Round the track the warriors raced, bending the norm of human endurance to a Will that is suicidal in its commitment to please their Lord. Mile after mile the horses galloped at breakneck speed, spurred onward by the Swallows' need to excel in a land where excellence was the order of the day. Round and round the track, under the fascinated gazes of the Zulu multitude and before the blazing eyes of their Emperor - eyes alight with a maddened glint.

All those who watched shared in the gripping passion and in the thrill of the race - Wilkins, Cane, Thomas, and Popham. - Mgobozi, Nqoboka, Kuta, Ngomane, Pampata, Nomcoba. All who watched - save for Mkabayi. She, alone, saw the race for what it was: a dangerous farce. Indeed, Mkabayi knew that one must never encourage a contest when one is already clearly, unequivocally superior. By doing so, one makes the mistake of risking defeat unnecessarily.

And that uncalled-for defeat was soon rather vividly brought to the fore when one of the Ufasimba warriors emitted a gurling, tortured sound as his mouth sprang open and the blood pulsated forth, flowing down his chin and onto his chest. Yet the disciplined warrior kept running, until his lungs burst and he toppled to the ground in a lifeless heap that was soon trampled under galloping hooves.

Within the isiGodlo, Shaka's eyes were wide with outrage as, within seconds, the other two warriors also collapsed, one dying on the spot, the other clawing at the soft turf, gasping in a pitiable attempt to relieve his rended lungs.

Having 'won' the race, Farewell and Fynn pulled up on their reins, bringing their sweaty, toilworn mounts to a walk. As the lieutenant leaned forward, stroking his horse's drenched, frothing hide, the man's attention was arrested by the brutal look of accusation that now marred the faces of the dense populace. Having been victorious over the Ufasimba runners, the Swallows had also indirectly struck a victory over the Great Mountain himself, and it was obvious that this did not sit well with the multitude. Unaccustomed to defeat, the Zulus looked upon this subjugation of the three Ufasimba runners as a suspicious act of treachery on the part of Shaka's visitors. An act that was ungracious to say the least.

"I think we've made a mistake, Fynn," Francis voiced his concern, as the accusing looks of the populace remained framed in his vision. "Look at those faces."

"Mistake, Francis?" There was irony in Fynn's tone as his attention was directed on the Zulus. "What should we have done? Lose on purpose?"

"That would have been more diplomatic, I trust. We are guests here. No use going out of our way to antagonize the lord of the household."

"The 'circus' was Shaka's idea, Francis," the man's brogue was thick with bitterness. "The most diplomatic thing we could have done was to show him that we're not clowns!"

Fynn's words had barely been breathed when suddenly and in perfect unison and coordination, the tens of thousands of people that crowded the royal homestead sank to the earth, their faces and bodies flat against the ground. Caught unawares by this unexpected show of complete submission, Fynn and Farewell gazed in wonder at the immense, immovable mass of humanity that now carpeted the vast citadel. Searching for the cause of this unique demonstration of obsequiousness, Fynn's eyes wandered to the summit of the Citadel's sloping incline and suddenly a chill ran down his spine as his eyes widened in awe.

The tall, massive figure of Shaka Zulu, the Nkosi yama Kosi, the King of Kings of Africa, had appeared at the gates of the isiGodlo. The imposing Emperor's majestic silhouette was perfectly centered in the towering posts of the isiGodlo's threshold and cast against the crimson, luminescent brilliance of the setting sun - making the Great Mountain look very much, indeed, like a supernatural apparition. Feeling the overmastering charisma and sovereignty wielded by that "apparition", Lt. Farewell instinctively eased out of his saddle, swung his leg free and dismounted. Fynn did likewise, his eyes never budging from the remarkable vision cast against the flaming sky of dusk.

Then unexpectedly for the Swallows who looked on spellbound a second glimmering silhouette appeared next to Shaka's and was set against the incandescent sun, partially eclipsing its radiance: - the figure of Nandi, daughter of Bhebhe, the Nkosikasi Indlovukazi, the Great Female Elephant, the Queen of Queens of Africa, Mother of the Child, Sister of the Heavens. The Zulu Queen's attire had the gentle amber glow of golden grain interwoven with the silvery shimmer of moonshine, the soft fabric of a warm Summer breeze embroidered with the chilling boldness of Winter's lightning. Her body was slender, shapely, sculpted by the artistic hand of the Master Supreme. Her features had a wild beauty, voluptuous and untamed, a splendour of lineaments that defied age and reason.

And Farewell and Fynn looked upon the silhouette of the Mother next to the silhouette of the Son of Zulu and both men stood frozen in their immobility, as if the blood in their veins had been transmuted to ice; and they knew, with absolute certainty, that these being were no mortal creatures in the sense of common man, they knew that they were in the presence of something that broke away from the norm in obedience to the Supernatural's deference to Mankind. And for both men (especially Fynn), the meaning of the legend named Shaka was driven forcibly home. There was no doubt in their minds why this man, why this women wielded power. Shaka and Nandi were Power in its most unquenchable form!

In the complete stillness and silence that had gripped Bulawayo, a gentle breath of wind touched the ivory tassels on Shaka's legs causing them to jingle - ever so slighty. When that jingling floated across the Citadel and reached Farewell's ears, the lieutenant who had braved the Napoleonic Wars, the hero of the Battles of Lissa, Ragusa, Cattaro, and Manfedora, "the valiant Farewell of the 'HMS Bacchante' known to Admiral Nelson himself, - Francis George Farewell was chilled to the bone by unreasoning terror as, in his soul, the familiar sound of the tassels was linked to the sensation he had experienced twice on the foresaken "Elizabeth Catherine" - the dark sensation of brooding cruelty, of terrible danger, of Death Itself. And in that instant, at the sound of those tassels that rang with the titillating notes of ivory, and at the sight of those silhouettes, Francis George Farewell knew - in a manner that defies any notions of logic - that he was face to face with his own death.

Unreasoning, illogical yet certain!

Yet, being resilient by nature (as are most eccentrics), Farewell reacted to the chill of the moment with the warming influence of inquisitiveness and, instead of running away from the terror that gripped him, he raced into the embracing arms of Adventure and smiled. Little realising that that embrace was his own grave.

The Zulu sovereign stole a deliberate glance at his mother before striding away from the isiGodlo's threshold. And silence continued to hold Bulawayo in its vicelike grip, as Shaka advanced whilst the prostrate, cowering bodies of his faithful subjects shrank from his path like the Red Sea parting before Moses. From their vantage point high atop of the oNgoye Mountain, Wilkins, Cane, Thomas and Popham witnessed this extraordinary show of submission, their minds boggled by such sheer veneration.

Reaching the center of the cattlefold, Shaka stopped near Mgobozi and with a sweep of his long articulate fingers, motioned to the general to rise. Mgobozi obeyed and, with him, in perfect, practiced synchronization; the other generals did likewise, Nqoboka, Kuta, Joko, Dlaba, Ngwadi - all of them. Then, with astounding precision, the entire iziCwe Regiment (shields red and white, plumes on headdress blue) rose as one man and stood at attention. A heartbeat later, the isiPikili Regiment (shields white, plumes red) rose and stood at attention. Dlaba's iNyelezi Regiment (shields white with black patches, plumes white) rose and stood at attention. Ngwadi's uFogisa Regiment (black shields, red plumes) was next. Then the warriors of the uYengonglovu (white shields with one black spot, red plumes) did the same. Followed by the amaWombe, the amaPela, the imFolozi - one after the other, all the regiments rose and stood at attention - ixwas thrust brilliantly against the face of the sun - until the 80,000 male troops plus the 8,000 of the Maidens' Guilds were on their feet and displayed across the length and width of the parade grounds in exact geometrical formations -- one hundred and sixty rows of five hundred warriors each, all rows perpendicular with the sun and staggered at regular intervals of ten paces.

As Shaka reviewed his armies, pleased by the perfection with which the 'show' had been executed, Farewell voiced in hushed admiration: "Amazing! Utterly amazing! These troops make the Changing of the Guard at Buckingham look clumsy!"

Consistent with the day's impressive display of perfect discipline and subjugation, the Emperor's flickering eyes turned to the track where the impromptu race had been held and grew still and expressionless with anger as they fell upon the kneeling body of the only surviving 'defeated' Ufasimba runner. Looking up, the warrior's and Shaka's eyes locked. Well knowing the punishment for having disappointed his Emperor, the warrior raised his arm in salute of Shaka and shouted a loyal "SI-GI-DI!" before bowing his head in stoic anticipation. The Zulu Sovereign's features darkened with resolve, and, glancing at a detachment of Ufasimba guards, Shaka nodded, giving the order. Without the shadow of hesitation, the guards neared the kneeling figure of the runner and, grabbing hold of his head, twisted it round, swiftly extinguishing life with a dull snap of the spinal chord.

An execution that was fast, clean, and 'merciful' (within the context of a "total war morality"), yet, seen objectively (as by the Swallows), a blatant act of butchery that left the two Whites staring in disbelief and horror at the cold-blooded proficiency of Shaka's death machine; a macabre excellence in murder that was made all the more disconcerting by the absurd loyalty with which Zulu warriors - such as the hapless 'martyr' who had just been dispatched to the Heavens - willingly faced death to please their king, - willingly faced the Ultimate Unknown to escape the punishment of Shaka's Own Unknown. Indeed, as the Song of Shaka stated so plainly: "UShaka ngiyesab'ukuthi nguShaka!" - "Shaka, I fear to say the name Shaka!"

And the Composer and Master of Shaka's Song, having witnessed the execution of the runner with complete, gelid detachedness, casually shifted the center of his attention to the curious four-legged creatures that had so facilely routed his warriors. Totally disregarding the Whites (for which he appeared to entertain no immediate interest), Shaka strode past Farewell and Fynn (without so much as looking at them) and neared the horses.

The Zulu Lord's inquisitive eye betrayed that he was impressed by these animals that possessed so much speed and endurance - even when burdened with the weight of a man. Reaching out, Shaka stroked one of the horses, feeling the heat of the animal's hide, smelling the familiar pungent odour of the sticky, frothing sweat that moistened his hand. The Emperor then shifted his scrutiny to the horse's powerful quadriceps and sinewy leg tendons, patting the steed's broad shoulders and brawny chest, running his inspecting fingers over the strong muscular neck and the forceful elongated jawline. Then, as a thin smile twitched on his lips, the Zulu took hold of the horse's mane and - under the astonished eyes of his subjects - jumped onto its back, sitting awkwardly in the saddle with his long legs swinging free, straddling the animal's belly, his feet nearly touching the turf.

Fynn shot a worried glance in the direction of his British companion, both men anticipating full well what was about to happen. In fact, sensing the unskilfulness of his rider, the horse whinnied and reared, bucking his legs and hurling the King of Kings of Africa to the ground.

As Nandi stiffened, paling with solicitude for the well-being of her son's body and pride...

...one single gasp burst forth from Bulawayo's terror-stricken multitude,- a single exclamation that rang loud and anguished like the suffered blast of a cannon. And in that same instant, over a million hearts stood still -- as the Language of the Heavens spat out a mouthful of dirt and slowly got to his feet. His face a mask of rage, the Zulu returned to the animal's side and, closing his large hand around the horse's snout, he held it in an iron clutch as he bent the steed's gaze to meet his own ferret-like stare. And their eyes communed, that of the man and that of the beast, as did their hearts, and the horse felt Shaka's wild, ferocious, domineering spirit. Incapable of understanding the abysmal depths of naked, brutal human passion, the animal felt only the incoherent, unsettling impetuousness of untold aggression. And pierced to the very core of his being by the glacial sting of Shaka's overbearing authority, the animal emitted an anguished neigh. Chopping excitedly at the turf with his hooves, the steed stirred in the man's grip in an attempt to break loose. But Shaka tightened his hold and, tearing his truculent glance from the horse's glassy orbs, the Emperor cast a commandeering look in the direction of the man who had succeeded where he had failed, in the direction of the horse's rider, Francis George Farewell.

As further proof of the unreliability and fickleness of men's souls, far from being fearful, the lieutenant detected himself somewhat thrilled by this unusual encounter with this unique potentate and, strangely mollified by the intrinsic danger of the situation, the naval officer smiled disarmingly and slapped the inside of his thigh - as if to communicate to Shaka that, when riding a horse, one must clutch the animal's belly with his legs.

Frowning inquisitively, Shaka repeated the gesture, slapping the inside of his own mighty thigh. Farewell's smile broadening, the man nodded approvingly to the Great Mountain, causing Shaka's anger to be diluted into a smile of tacit understanding; - and causing Fynn to regard both men with flitting incredulity.

With renewed decisiveness, and whilst Bulawayo held its breath, Shaka leapt back into the saddle, his formidable legs squeezing the animal's belly like steel pincers. Once again the steed attempted to throw its obstinate rider, but Shaka had learned his lesson. Gripping the mane, the Emperor gave the beast a stinging slap on the rump and bolted off at a sustained gallop round the track, steering the horse with painful jerks on the dense, black hair at the animal's neck. Gradually, as the Swallows and Zulus looked on in bated fascination, the Zulu sovereign exercised his taming influence on the horse until his own equestrian dexterity looked almost as smooth and effortless as that of the more experienced Whites.

"Learns fast, doesn't he?" Farewell was grinning as he followed the Zulu's progress round the course.

"Yes," Fynn admitted in a studiously calm tone. "And he's learned quite a bit today. About us especially." His eyes met with Farewell's. "Now he knows we're his equals, Francis, and that puts us at a great disadvantage!"

Oddly enough, as Mkabayi and Nandi held each other's eyes, they shared the same thought. By proving that he could be the Swallows' equal, Shaka had put himself at a definite disadvantage! Indeed, most of the charisma of a Great Mountain lies in the fact that it cannot be scaled.

And, as Dingane kaSenzangakona Zulu, the "secondborn", saw his hated brother and Emperor galloping round the track roaring with exhilarated laughter, he, too, smiled.

"Yes," Dingane told himself with a knowing nod. "Pakatwayo was right. The arrival of the Swallows was a most advantageous event in their bid to rid themselves of the usurper.

CHAPTER XXXIX
"PAMPATA"(THE ONE WHO FLATTERS)

"On the morning following the magnificent display of Zulu might and opulence which Shaka had staged for our benefit (or such was the opinion of Lieutenant Farewell; one with which I and Fynn whole-heartedly agreed), I was roused at a good hour by the gentle scratching of a Vivira civet cat which had found it opportune to burrow the exit to its underground chambers at an inch or two from the position in which I was fastly slumbering..." or so wrote Tim Wilkins in the Colonial Office journal.

"Finding it impossible to regain the threshold of sleep (indeed the pomp and festivities of the previous day came abruptly to the fore in such vivid detail that my disorientation returned in all its reeling impetuosity), I left my companions still quietly immersed in their repose, and made my way down the lovely slopes of the Ongoyee Mountain by Bulawayo (where we had been instructed to pitch camp for the night). Moving through the prickling early-morning mist that clung to the verdure, I chanced to glance down at the Shakan Citadel where the immense sea of humanity that carpeted its concourse was starting to stir with the first gentle ripples of wakefulness. As if with a will of their own, my eyes found themselves gravitated to the immense isiGodlo - the Emperor's secreted Palace - and my mind found itself wondering: 'Does he still sleep or is he awake?', 'What is he doing? - What planning, plotting, designing, scheming?', and 'How will it effect our lives? The lives of the Cape settlers? The life of Tim Wilkins, Colonial Office?'. I am pleased to say that a feeling of youthful adventure accompanied these thoughts and that, though apprehension remained well imbedded in my overall disposition, being manifested through a kind of a perpetual tingling about the belly and loins, I was now starting to entertain with growing conviction the likelihood that our mission might be rewarded with success...

"The Lieutenant had said it: Curiosity is stronger than fear! And so it may well be! -- And is Curiosity not part of the process of Learning, and is Learning not the Mother of Knowledge? And (if I may be permitted to stretch the dialectics), is not Knowledge (in its vanquishment of Ignorance) the ultimate Pacifier? Indeed, could we reach Peace by the circuitous way of Curiosity?

"Lost in these optimistic contemplations, I found myself near a cataract of much grandeur and of a picturesque character; its water falling over a rugged surface of rocks which divided it into a variety of courses and gave it an appearance of singular beauty. Finding that the cataract fell into a spacious basin, I undressed and, casting all care to the wind, plunged into it, giving myself up to the joy provoked by the refreshing sparkling sensation I felt on my skin...

"A little while later, whilst I sat in the vicinity of our camp transferring to paper my memory of the previous day's events, and while Farewell, Fynn, Cane, Holstead and Popham joined me in wakefulness, special messengers appeared from Bulawayo bearing a request from the King to mount our horses, all of us, and proceed to his quarters for our first formal meeting...

"And so, in short order, we had traversed the Citadel (my God!, that oppressive, asphyxiating throng!) and gained the entrance to Shaka's isiGodlo where a domestic instructed us to proceed further. Upon entering therein, we found His Majesty in the shade of an euphorbia surrounded by his court (or so I took it to be). Present was the Queen-mother herself, a woman of singular beauty (whom I was informed bore the soothing name: Nan-dee), the Emperor's paternal aunt (Machabayee, sister of the King's deceased father, Issenzangakoona), Ngoomanee (the Zulu Sovereign's chief confidant and counsellor, or so Popham informed us) and Mmgoboosi in the company of other Zulu generals (as I surmised by their colourful shields, their short swordlike weapons, and the undulating plumage borne on their heads).

"In the center of the dignified group was Shaka himself. To our great surprise, the monarch was completely nude and in the process of having his morning bath and toilet -in the true Pompeian sense: 'al fresco' and in public. Three comely young maidens came with water, carrying it over their heads with their arms extended, which I perceived was the usual way they bore everything to their king. One girl held a broad black dish before him, while another poured in water for His Majesty to wash, and a third stood by ready with a further supply in case of need, holding it in the position before described, without daring to put it down (though I could easily espy that the burden was quite onerous for such a young lad)...

"Whilst bathing from head to foot (using a paste of bruised fat as 'soap'), Shaka idly conversed with his court (remaining, I might add, stoically aloof to the proximity of these lovely women to his naked figure), leaving us to wait, unseen (or so it appeared) and unattended, till he was ready (in his own good time!) to include us in the purview of his attention. While we thus stood 'in reception', as it were, I had the opportunity of taking a rather minute surveillance of the Zulu Potentate and, complimented by subsequent impressions and overviews (obtained during the course of the day, as well as in my chats with Daniel concerning the King), I was able to reach the following portraiture which I humbly set forth at this time as follows:---

"Shaka Zulu is about thirty-eight years of age, upwards of six feet four in height, with a commanding appearance and admirably proportioned. He is well featured (extremely resembling his mother) and of great muscular power; of a light brown complexion, approaching to a bronze colour and, unlike many other males we had ocassion to see, bearing no sign of circumcision. Nothing can exceed his piercing and penetrating eye, which he rolls in moments of anger with surprising rapidity, and in the midst of festivities with inconceivable brilliancy. His whole frame seems as if it were knit for war, and every manly exercise; it is flexible, active, and firm. He is reserved, even to the extreme, and seems to weigh every word before he utters it in a need to be distinct and to be understood. He, however, speaks often parabolically, and with more circumlocution than is desirable, until his searching eye has discovered the motives of the individual to whom he may address himself. He appears neither so credulous nor so superstitious as many of his people, and seems exceedingly anxious to acquire information of all kinds. -- As the Lieutenant had guessed, he is, indeed, most curious!

"And genial! - Shaka rules his people by perpetually keeping them in a state of terror, and this command and ascendancy over them is greatly facilitated by his continually impressing them with the power of Things Unknown and the Supernatural - devices which he (and his mother, it must be said) practices with incredible effect, keeping his poor, abject, deluded subjects in a state of constant oppression. In his pretense of the mystical, Shaka goes to such extent as to excite a belief in his populace's minds that he has the power of knowing all their thoughts, and of seeing all their most secret actions, and it is said that he inherited this power from the spirit of his forefathers, who have deputed it to him. In this sublimely staged act, the Zulu Lord has succeeded in establishing a sort of "Zulu-cratical" form of government (the term is Daniel's and I leave it as such for I can find no better way of describing a system that has no comparison in neither ancient nor modern history). A form of ruling that can neither be totally comprehended nor digested, and such a one as gives protection to no living creature; that puts the subject at the mercy of a despotic king whose nod may consign them to death, innocent or guilty; a mode of governing that puts the subjects in a suspended state of existence not unlike that which intervenes between the first and last shocks of an earthquake, when all are in consternation, fearing that the next moment they may well be swallowed during a devastating convulsion. A unique and extravagant way of government, and Shaka himself being a ruler of great cleverness and enterprise, like few this world will ever have cause to know.

"And a cruel sanguinary King!, as shall become clear in what is set forth in further commentaries of this our first meeting in the Royal Citadel Bulawayo...

"After his wash, the gentle breeze having functioned as a towel, the three maidens (under Shaka's complete indifference to their alluring presence) proceeded to dress their Emperor in his kilt of ox-tails, in his tassels and furs, and in his customary headdress with the long crane feather. And when he had seated himself on his chair of state - consisting of a huge roll of rush matting - and when his body had been bedecked with a large cape of red lowry plumes and his demeanour had assumed a stateliness proper to the power he wielded, the Zulu monarch finally deigned our party with a flashing gaze, his first in our direction...

"'Joji! Your king. Is he the only king of the Swallows?' he finally demanded of us through the official interpreter Daniel. To which Farewell replied that, 'No, he was not.' 'Is he the most powerful, then?' Shaka further demanded to know. 'Yes, you could say that,' the Lieutenant deemed it advisable to acquiesce (so as to strengthen our own negotiating position, no doubt). The King remained momentarily pensive, his entrancing gaze pausing on each of our faces in turn - Popham's, Cane's, Holstead's, Fynn's (upon whose semblance he lingered at length with deep scrutiny), and myself before coming round to Farewell again. He observed us with great interest, as if attracted by that illusive something - a line, a fold, perhaps the form of an eyelid, the curve of a cheek, that trifling trait which makes no two faces on earth alike; he observed us as if each of our faces was the very foundation of what we were, as if, all the rest being hereditary, mystery, or accident, that illusive something for which he searched was the only real factor that had been shaped consciously by the soul within. Then at length, he smiled a strange smile that evinced little humour, one that seemed more a grimace of suspicion. 'Is Joji as handsome as I?' he inquired through Daniel. An unaffected grin of amusement crossed Lieutenant Farewell's lips (he was visualising, I would presume, the somewhat opulent, gouty semblance of our Britannic Majesty), and he found he could favour the Zulu whilst retaining the honour of honesty, and said "No, he is not."

"Evincing a compelling interest in his Hanoverian counterpart and an obvious conviction of his own superior moral and physical charms, Shaka was emboldened to point to his large, beehive-shaped palace of thatching and, transferring his attention away from Farewell, to demand of Fynn whether King George 'could boast so good a one?' To which Fynn, being a tyro at diplomacy, responded, 'Yes, and much larger'. 'Ay, perhaps as large,' said Shaka, 'but not so good!' 'Oh, yes. Just as good,' Fynn answered in stubborn truthfulness (eliciting all our dismay). 'You have not looked well enough at mine,'

Yet - fortunately for the five Swallows present in this historic African encounter - the man to open the large Continental coffer bearing the offerings for the Son of Zulu, the man to give way to the "presentation of the gifts" was Francis George Farewell - handsome, lean, athletic, and not the Son of Hanover - gross, bloated and by no means palaestral.

The coffer, expertly prepared and packed by Farewell (with the assistance of Elizabeth, it should be mentioned), contained every description of beads at that time procurable in Cape Town, a great variety of woollen blankets, a large quantity of turned and lacquered brass bars, sheets of copper, brass bangles, and a full-dress military coat of the Royal Navy with epaulettes covered with gold lace.

Being above all a military man, the Zulu's attention was instantly gravitated towards the coat which Daniel explained was part of the uniform worn by the Swallow Regiments that manned the 'birds with the white wings', the "umkhumbi ohamba ngoseyili" or "sailing ships". Lifting the coat out of the trunk on the tips of his long, expressive fingers, Shaka held it out at an arm's length, studying it diligently before attempting to don it (in the fashion in which he saw Farewell was donning his own naval tunic). Yet try as he may, the Zulu Emperor could not force his mighty arm into one of the sleeves without tearing the seams to shreds, and his comical endeavours to do so evoked a ripple of amiable chuckling from Ngomane, Mgobozi, Nqoboka, Joko, Mzilikazi and the others Shakan generals (even Nandi and Mkabayi stifled smiles), as well as some good-hearted quipping from the lieutenant's companions. Indeed, since the tunic was Farewell's, the Zulu's inability to wear it came as a vivid disclosure of the supremacy of Shaka's physical might over that of his British guest, and, while those present smiled, Fynn was caused to ponder over how many other Foreign "gifts" would be "tight-fitting" for the prodigious frame and figure of Shaka and, similarly, for the greatness of spirit of the continent in the shape of a heart: Africa.

Finally abandoning all attempt to take possession of this item of military apparel, Shaka shrugged his massive shoulders with benevolent surrender and passed the coat on to Mgobozi who, being of shorter stature, easily slipped into the uniform and wore it proudly, verily beaming with joy, the gilded epaulettes shining brilliant in the wash of black and white plumes that showered down from the commander's headdress.

Leaning forward, Shaka bent his insatiable scrutiny upon the trinkets and necklaces that cluttered in their splendour an entire compartment of the Continental coffer. Reaching in, the Emperor rummaged through the treasure of baubles and adornments and, finally selecting a magnificent beaded necklace, fished it out of the pool of jewelry. Rising from his throne, the imposing monarch neared his mother and affectionately draped the colourful beads round Nandi's long, slender neck. A thin smile that bore the tracings of coquetry was born to grace the beautiful woman's sensual lips as her hand was instinctly lifted to the necklace, the fingers gently running over its polished surfaces.

Prompted by Nandi's justifiable feminine act of self-admiration, Farewell produced from the interior of the coffer a small silver hand mirror and gave it to Shaka, gesturing that the King should pass it on to his mother. Greatly intrigued by the unfamiliar object the lieutenant proferred, the Emperor snatched it out of the Englishman's hand and, knitting his highly emphatic brow, he turned it round in his grip, studying the mirror from all angles, wondering of what use it might be. Then, as soon as Shaka caught sight of his own reflection, his features were transformed. As Nandi, Mkabayi, Ngomane, and the other members of the Zulu entourage looked on with growing perplexity, marvelling in stunned silence at their lord, the Zulu Sovereign gazed with compelling entrancement at the image in the Swallows' silver object; an image so clear and true, one that so resembled that of a real man, yet -- with no depth, two-dimensional.

Shaka was suspicious at first as he looked at that man in the mirror who seemed to emanate from the Supernatural, and his suspicion grew upon noticing that the face in the polished glass seemed to be purposely, defiantly imitating Shaka's own facial gestures - as if in mocking! The King turned his head to the right and to the left, up and down, to the right and to the left again and caught his breath upon realising that the man in the mirror was doing the same, with perfect mimicking. Then he touched his face and felt the pressure of his own fingers on his skin and saw that the image on the flat silver object was experiencing the same sensation.

And then he knew. And the realisation momentarily chilled him.

The man looking at him from within the mirror was the same as the man without. And Shaka gasped again, catching his breath deep in his lungs, deep in his soul. And gradually, as he realised that the essence of the looking glass was harmless, the chill left him and his heart was warmed by inquiring delight.

With startling objectivity and with the growing gratification of a Narcissus, Shaka began to inspect this man in the mirror, his finely-chiselled features, his soft, agreeable good looks, and the Zulu's stiffened expression also softened. And he smiled, immensely pleased with this own face. Shifting his attention from the overall face to the hair of the reflected image, the Zulu noticed - with a trace of dismay that he voiced in a murmured sigh - that it was beginning to grey: the first telltale signs of age. Reaching up, his eyes still locked on the mirror, he plucked at the sundry strands of hair, as if to dispel their whiteness, and his gaze automatically shifted to his mother's hair that was partially grey with her advancing years.

"Age," Farewell told himself as he witnessed and interpreted Shaka's inner turmoil. "How right Elizabeth had been! - Vanity was indeed the greatest weakness of all males. Be they falcons, Huns, Englishmen or Zulus! - Was Vanity truly the key for which he had been searching," the lieutenant considered as Shaka returned his attention to the mirror in his hand.

And the King literally froze, as his eyes met the eyes of the man in the mirror and he saw the soul of the man he had become. It was as if Shaka the innocent boy of six, the helpless and hopeless outcast who was unwittily thrust into a life of forced wandering, was suddenly face to face with Shaka the man, Shaka the product of that helplessness, of that hopelessness, of that wandering. And as the child looked upon the Child, as the little boy who had been captivated and intrigued by The Kill looked upon Sigidi the Killer, as the bold young lad who had wanted no enemies left behind looked upon the Emperor of the Method and the Mfecane -- Shaka's soul experienced an uncanny leap into the void of Timelessness and of Space and Interlude without Dimension. And the Past took stock of the Present in defiance of the Future.

And all looked on as the mirror began - ever so slightly - to tremble in the Emperor's mighty grasp. Finally tearing his eyes away from his own image, Shaka turned to his mother and extended to her the silver glass. As he did so, his eyes welling with bewilderment, the Zulu monarch seemed to be silently and with childish inquiry requesting of Nandi a multitude of answers. "Look, mother!" his soul reached out for hers as he pressed the mirror into her hand. "Look! Is this what I am? What I have become? What we both have made of me? - How long, mother? How long have you been able to see what I now see for the first time? How long has this image in the glass been the image of your son?" A tempest of queries that sought instant relief from their spiralling squalls.

And sensing Shaka's plea, Nandi took the glass from his trembling hand and looked into it searchingly. And she instantly saw it. Reflected on her own reflection was both Shaka the boy and Shaka the man: the Past and the Present she herself had forged into the "unreachable" Future that had been her dream as a young girl (the quest she had shared with her father Bhebhe). Yet the image she now saw did not evoke the joy and exhilaration that had accompanied that dream of her youth. Though the Power was there, in that image, there was still that young boy's hopelessness; though the power was there now, they were both still outcasts, she and her son, and would remain outcasts as long as the goal of their ambition remained as "unreachable" as the ever-distant horizon.

"What is it I really wished for so fervently when I was young?" Nandi pondered as if in response to her heart's query. "And what does this person I'm looking at wish for?" she asked herself as she continued to glance at the mirror. "Who is she? What is she doing wearing my soul?"

Involuntarily, as if suddenly tired, Nandi dropped her hand to her lap, causing the mirror to tilt slightly in such a way as to trap on its smooth surface two images, side by side - that of Nandi and that of her son. In awe of the new impression that was now framed in the magic silver, mother and son peered at the mirror, at their conjoined semblances that seemed to symbolize their combined and interwoven existences. And, as the two looked at each other, at their reflected selves, Time did, in fact, stand still for all those present in the isiGodlo.

"Remarkable, the oversight," Farewell whispered almost to himself as he gazed at the extraordinary mother and son, the two most powerful people in southeastern Africa. "Centuries of poets and, to my knowledge, no one has ever thought of giving the Fallen Angel a mirror. - It's poignancy is highly dramatic!"

"Oh, but they have, Francis," Fynn caught the lieutenant's hushed remark and softly replied, "All poetry that does not reflect God is the mirror of the Fallen Angel!"

In short order, when the "presentation of gifts" ceremony had sufficiently pleased the Emperor, the entire group moved to the interior of the huge Royal Hut where, upon solicitation, maidens arrived bearing large baskets of boiled beef and several earthen pots of milk which were proffered to the White guests by way of refreshment. Leading this lovely procession of females was the splendid, ever youthful Pampata (who was now approaching 33 years of age), her usual reserved, withdrawn and timid air faithfully evidencing the meaning of her name: "Pampata, - the One who Flatters"...

..."the One who Flatters". And such had been her life for the past eighteen years - ever since that fateful morning when, in her diligence, she had gone down to the river near her grandfather's homestead to fetch water and had discovered the seemingly lifeless figure of her magnificent "Enchanted Prince" slumped on the pebble-strewn banks of the Guluzana.

From that moment of blissful discovery that marked for her the sudden awakening of an overbearing, all-consuming love (the only sort of emotion one could feel for an overbearing, all-consuming man such as Shaka), Pampata's life had no longer existed in its own right, but only as an existence "complimentary" to that of "her prince". Since that first meeting, her purpose in living had been to complete, to fawn, to "flatter" the life of the object of her passion without asking, without expecting anything in return except the right to live by his side. A love that was destined from the start to be unrequited inasmuch as there seemed to be no place for a woman in Shaka's life, save for that very special niche in his heart reserved for his mother. As Nomcoba had told Pampata, "My brother thinks sandals slow him down. Can you imagine what he must think about women?!"

The one-sided love of the "flatterer" which had always, from its outset, worn the emotional cloak of an obsession.

Unrequited.

With exception, of course, of that one instant of abandon nine years ago, - that fleeting instant suspended in Time and beyond Reality, - that luminous flash of emotion that will forever burn in the darkness of her love, like a solitary star in a barren universe. The instant of that second encounter by the stream, the time when he had held her in his arms, in the desire of his embrace, and she had known - with joy, with deliverance, with tears - that he was the master of her life and that she could find sunshine only in his presence. And in that great tumult of passion, as the love and gratitude welled forth from her heart, uncontrollable, uncontrolled, she felt that her hopes, her dreams, her past, all that she had ever been was turned to cold ashes and that her life was starting anew in the expression of boundless felicity that was the Present and in the pledge of a bright and splendid Future.

Yet that pledge had never had the chance to be fulfilled, nor had that future of boundless felicity ever found expression. For the spark of that passion had been extinguished too quickly, and, in confusion, he had fled from her and his impotence, leaving his name on her lips in an anguished cry that evoked untold pain and infinite remorse. Then, in the days and months that followed, Pampata's mind was ever reeling with thoughts of going to him in an attempt to break through the shell he had formed round his heart, a barrier meant to keep her away. Yet, though words upon words seared through her mind, the woman soon realised that she was incapable of saying anything to her love that would accurately reflect the tumult of her heart. So she kept that pain locked within her, with no mode of release. And soon the words she could have said became the words she should have said - and the years fled from her.

Nine years in all.

When Shaka had first realised that he was impotent, after his aborted attempt at making love to Pampata, his first reaction had been to destroy all evidence of this "un-manly" quality - which meant, of course, destroying her, the first and only women with whom he had attempted to have sex, the only woman to have made him aware of this physical blemish on his otherwise impeccable constitution. Yes, - he had thought of eliminating Pampata and, with her, the reminder of his "crippling" handicap.

Yet the deep-rooted sense of justice he had inherited from Nandi had railed against murdering the fragile, lovely creature who had once saved his life,- the gentle girl for whom (he had to admit) he nurtured a gratifying devotion, something akin to tenderness. And in the light of calm reflection, Shaka had stopped to analyze the woman's behaviour, and his cold rational had found it faultless, devoid of treachery and ill-will, - merely the sincere and artless comportment of a woman in love. He therefore had decided that the most convenient and even-handed measure was to sever the relationship and forget her, convinced that Pampata's lips would remain sealed with respect to his "infirmity" (vowing to himself that if she breathed a word of what had happened, that breath would be her last).

And, absorbed by the intense concernment and impetus of his military campaigns (especially Qokli and the Capture of Dlovunga), which overrode all else, completely annihilating any thought of private life, Shaka had forgotten both the woman and the "malady" -- save for rare moments (especially in the first couple of years) when a certain effort of his mighty Will was necessary to dispel his lingering desire and, above all, his brooding anger at being incapable of controlling every single aspect of his physical make-up.

Indeed, in his forceful resolution to banish his impairment from mind, Shaka had become, to all intents and purposes, "asexual", a "High Priest of War" committed to a life of abstinence. And, in this Rule of Abstinence, all that could remind him of his impotence was also proscribed from the life of his Empire. Consequently, for Shaka's Nation, - children, families, and indulging in frequent sex were soon relegated to the distant Past with the pretense and justification that (as Shaka had voiced it to Mgobozi) "for soldiers marriage is a folly; their first and only duty being to protect the nation from its enemies". This corban way of life ushered a Shakan reality and "morality" which - in its "impotence" - was by force destined to be founded on "total war, total obedience to the Paramount King"; -- the

"Perfect State" where the sovereign is a general and his subjects warriors, the "Perfect State" in which Desire is perennially assuaged by Affection's ultimate palliatives: Death and the Kill.

Shaka himself probably never really took stock of how direct, of how deliberate, of how consequential the link was between the impotence of the Man and that of his Nation. Conversely, he objectively believed that his policy of Forced Military Celibacy was vital to the security of his kingdom and in no way saw it as a by-product of his own celibacy (not even in the realm of coincidence). As a result, he never looked upon his Nation's "sacrifice" as the fruit of his own, because, since his earliest childhood, Shaka had never considered a life dedicated to his "companion Death" as anything but totally fulfilling!

And so - in the frivolous nature of Life's Cycles and Courses - Shaka's existence had ultimately come round to resemble that of his father inasmuch as it was a life committed to "forgetting her".

Of course the love, the passion, the tempestuous emotions had been of a quite different nature with Nandi and Senzangakona, and it would be improper to allow the comparison to hold, yet, in Shaka's heart, "pushing Pampata out of his mind" meant forgetting a very significant part of himself, a part that is invariably forged to many other sentiments that are responsible for a person's emotional and physical equilibrium, - sentiments which, if ignored, can, in the long run, lead to a severe derangement of the mind, mental illness, and ul timately -- a form of insanity.

But before the insanity --- comes the weariness and the isolation.

The return of Pampata to her Emperor's side was the fruit of the isolation that had gripped Shaka's soul in the years directly preceding his death, the years in which he built Bulawayo, the Place of the Kill, the colossal Citadel, larger and greater than any "in the world" (larger than Joji's, as he had insisted with Fynn) - the Grand Home where the Outcast could withdraw into his own power, like the mighty Eagle finds refuge on a mountain's dizzying heights. Indeed, in light of Shaka's emotional state, Wilkins had been most exact in his analysis that "seven thousand years of tried and tested double talk" could well cope with the aggression of the "savage king". Towards the end, those last few years, the Great Mountain was looking for just that: "double talk", soothing double talk that could help him in his never-ending process of - forgetting.

Pampata, being the custodian of Shaka's secret (one which he had shared with no one, not even Nandi), was asked to join him "in the shell" of Bulawayo where her presence was somehow comforting for him. He felt relaxed with her because, in her tacit knowledge of his impotence, her feminility was no threat to him and he felt free to tap the warmth of her undying love without being expected to perform in return. With Pampata, the secret of his body's impotence somehow justified the impotence of his heart. And, in his quest for isolation, this factor made Pampata unique, for not even Nandi could perpetually be - "the One who Flatters"...

...As Pampata entered the Royal Hut with the procession of maidens bearing food and drink for the White visitors, no one could have guessed from her sure step, from her erect proud figure, from the composure of her lovely features, that she carried a weighty spiritual load under the visible burden of the bowl of fruits resting on her head. In her supple figure, so graceful and free in its walk, behind those soft eyes that spoke of nothing but of unconscious resignation, there slept all passion and all feeling, all hopes and all fears. As they looked at her, Fynn, Farewell, Wilkins, Holstead, Cane - all they could see was her alluring beauty, her sensuousness, her desirable fragility, her freshness. As they stole admiring glances at this creature, - no one, not even Shaka, could penetrate her disguise and look into a heart that was dead, or rather, a heart that pumped another's blood. More than ever before, Pampata now lived for her Emperor alone, and, as she went about a life that was his life, she bore his secret with the quietly despairing patience and restrained anguish of a woman who harbours in her womb a child she fears will be deformed.

As Pampata rested the bowl on the floor in front of her master's guests, she stole a curious glance at the men whose skins were the colour of sorghum, and the Whites returned her gaze, captivated by her gentle loveliness. Shaka watched the exchange, critically, studying how "his woman's" beauty could influence the Whites and wondering, with a slight pang akin to jealousy, whether Pampata also found these men attractive.

Flushing slightly with a tinge of coyness, Pampata realised - to her own surprise more than Shaka's - that she was somewhat enjoying the effect her loveliness was having on the Swallows. And, as she rose to leave, her eyes met Farewell's and she quickly turned away in something that resembled embarrassment, but was then suddenly assailed by an irresistible longing to look again at those handsome, "pale" features. Stopping in the motion of rising, Pampata allowed her large eyes to flit back to the lieutenant and, in so doing, she found that their looks became momentarily engaged in mutual admiration. A brief exchange. One that was abruptly interrupted as soon as the female sensed her master's displeased glance. Shifting her gaze to meet Shaka's glaring reprimand, Pampata abandoned her bowl of refreshments and scampered to the Emperor's side. She assumed a halfsitting attitude, her head resting against his powerful thigh and her arms joined on her lap in limp indifference, her features wearing the resignation of a wornout mind in a worn-out body, the sort of pose assumed by people who are either desperately ill or phlegmatically sad.

"As you said, Lieutenant," Holstead commented with a caustic smirk as his eyes ran down Pampata's body. "No 'huntin' without his permission. - Though I wouldn't mind takin' this ducky in tow to once."

Upon seeing the White man's crooked smile and easily recognising the facial aspects of intransigence (the defiance Mgobozi had told him was so much a part of the Swallows' character), Shaka lashed out and grabbed Daniel's arm, hissing his question in Zulu, his eyes remaining rivetted on Thomas.

"He wants to know what he said," Daniel related to Farewell, wincing at the painful pressure the Emperor was exerting on his arm.

The lieutenant shot a spiteful look in Holstead's direction before turning back to Shaka with a charming smile. "Tell him, we think she is lovely," Farewell commented, nodding to Pampata. "Tell him, he is a very lucky man to boast of such a woman."

Shaka cocked his ear to Daniel's translation, never removing his gaze from Thomas's features. Hearing the lieutenant's conciliating remark (which Shaka knew to be one of pure mitigation), the Zulu lord tightened his hold on Daniel's appendage and roared, "Ukhulumani?!

"He wants to know what he said, Lieutenant," Daniel repeated, feeling the tips of Shaka's fingers on the verge of crushing his forearm. "What he really said."

"So tell him," was Farewell's only riposte. One that evoked the tense sidelong glances of his companions - especially the man in question, Holstead himself, who was already wondering in what atrocious manner he would be dispatched to the Other World.

With a deep sigh of resignation, Daniel translated, slowly, word for word, Holstead's taunting comment, trying his best to correctly interpret "ducky" and "in tow" so as not to be too offensive. Throughout the nervous rendering of Liverpool English to Zulu, the Emperor held Thomas's apprehensive gaze steadily with his own, and the White man was surprised and delighted to see that when Daniel was finished, the Zulu wore a broad smile.

"Yebo," Shaka told Daniel levelly. "Ngiyamazi naShaka."

"Yes," Daniel translated. "So it is with Shaka," he added. No "hunting" without his permission.

Then, the smile dwindling, Shaka's attention moved to Farewell and he spoke with a deep tonality and with an inflection of reproach, the clicking on the consonants "c", "q", and "x" coming loud and sonorous: "Akusici, mandoda, ukunqivumela ngoba nithenga ameshlo ami. Ngiphikiseni! - Ngizonikhumbuza, Febana, ukuthi isizwe esinevuso sifana nomximba obuthakathaka odinga ukubuyi- selwa ebuzimbeni bawo ngemitshopo ebuhlungu." During the king's somewhat lengthy discourse, those who understood him - Daniel, Mgobozi. Ngomane, Nandi and the others - kept their gazes fixed on Farewell as if they shared the reprimand that transpired in the Emperor's harsh words.

When Shaka had finished, the lieutenant shot a perplexed look in Daniel's direction.

"Now it's my turn to ask what he said," Farewell rejoined, his voice sharp and brazen.

"He says that it does you no good to agree with him, or to be kind to him just to buy favour in his eyes," the Xhosa told the naval officer. "It would be better for you to be always truthful with him. Even to the point of disagreeing."

Farewell narrowed his eyes at Shaka, studiously, feeling a sudden and profound respect for the Zulu. "Of course," the lieutenant reminded himself, "behind such overwhelming power, there must always be a foundation of honesty, of frankness!" The Englishman then directed an averted gaze at Nandi and spied in the depths of her emerald green eyes the source of that honesty, - as well as the root of that power.

"He also said," Daniel was continuing, "that he wishes to remind the leader of the Swallows, Febana, that an army in a state of unrest and intransigence is like a sick body that must be restored to wholesomeness with treatments that are often painful."

"Yebo," Farewell said, smiling at the Emperor. "So it is." And his teeth clenching with rage and indignation at having been thus reprehended, the lieutenant cast a deliberate glance in Thomas's direction and made a mental note to restore the "body of his army to wholesomeness" as soon as the opportunity arose.

Then, dismissing from his mind the entire parenthesis of tension, Shaka took the silver hand mirror from its place in the Continental coffer and graciously proferred it to Pampata, urging her to look at herself on the reflecting surface of the glass, pressing the object into her hand as if he were making the girl a present of her own beauty.

Unlike the Zulu King and his illustrious mother, Pampata had nothing to fear from her own reflection, nothing to glimpse in her own eyes except a resignation born of unfulfilled love which, though unpleasant to observe, is never terrifying. In fact, as she looked at the reflection in the glass, Pampata found herself giggling at the pretty face that giggled back at her.

His eyes on the mirror, Shaka ran a hand through his hair and inquired of Farewell, via Daniel, in a manner that toyed with nonchalance: "What is the age of your king, he asks."

The lieutenant stifled a knowing smile as the word "Vanity!" came forcefully to mind. "Early sixties, tell him," the officer said aloud.

Again Shaka's words were translated as: "And his kingdom, he asks, did Joji build it alone?"

"No, tell him," Wilkins broke in. "He had help. From his father, and his father before him, and the father before that."

Shaka frowned at the translation and inquired through the Xhosa teacher: "His ancestors?, he asks."

"Yes," Farewell replied lifting a brow. "I suppose you could say that."

Once more the Emperor's melodious voice became: "He wishes to know how many wives George has."

Hearing the question both Nandi and Pampata shifted their inquisitive gazes to the Great Mountain, as Wilkins thought of George's poor wife, Queen Caroline who had recently died (of neglect, disuse, and boredom, it was said), and answered: "None, tell him."

Shaka seemed pleased by his counterpart's "celibacy" and offered his reply in approval of George's sagacity.

"He applauds the wisdom of his brother, Joji, in having no wives," Daniel related with an even tone. "That accounts for his advanced age, he says. Joji and Shaka seem to have much in common."

The Emperor cordially laughed at his own joke, encouraging the Whites to politely join in. Farewell's interest, however, was caught by the silent figure of Pampata curled up like a domestic animal at Shaka's feet, her eyes lowered, her lips pursed in suppressed misery, and, as the lieutenant beheld her state, he was unable to conceal a trace of pity. It seemed to him that this frail creature, whose past and present were unknown to him, was the ultimate victim of Shaka's "joke".

The emperor's hawkish gaze caught Farewell's look of commiseration, and in an instant the smile was gone from Shaka's lips and his features were transformed, taking on a ferocious look, angular, severe and scheming, which left the Whites to wonder whether another soul had suddenly entered his body. Looking up, Shaka barked out an order to his ever-present Ufasimba guards and, in a matter of seconds, Tsani, the young girl whose life Fynn had saved, was led into the hut, her thin frame trembling with fear as her eyes widened on the imposing figure of her Lord and Master.

Fynn was stunned by the unexpected presence of his peculiar patient. An undertone of sheer, unreasoning terror gripped him and he felt his blood race through his veins, throbbing at his temples with the adrenalin of premonition. The Irishman's eyes darted from Tsani to Shaka and back, as he uttered a silent prayer and heard the Zulu speak in a cadenced, deliberate tone that bore the resonance of Cruelty.

"He asks," Daniel started, his voice quivering slightly with emotion. "In your country, to whom does Life belong? To the king or to his subjects?"

Caught completely unawares by the question, Farewell faltered, his mind reeling with a myriad of answers that ranged from the ridiculous to the commonplace. Finally he found the coolness and the insight to respond.

"Each man in our country, tell him, is the lord of his own life," the lieutenant said, trying to keep his voice steady. "Only his own life. - The king included,- tell him."

Listening to Farewell's response, Shaka's features took on no appreciable modification, remaining entranced in a steely glitter of resolve. When he spoke again, his voice was devoid of any specific inflection.

"Can your king make you go to war, he asks," the Xhosa's own tone was starting to show signs of strain.

"Yes," the lieutenant answered, confused by the line of questioning.

"And can you die in war he asks," was Daniel's translation after the king's brief query.

"Yes," Farewell replied and suddenly caught his breath upon realising where Shaka's sophistry was leading him.

A shrewd smile now appeared on the Emperor's lips as he supplied the conclusion to the deductive reasoning.

"Then you are wrong, he says," Daniel reluctantly adjoined this phrases to the rest. "It is your King who owns life."

Mzilikazi, Mgobozi and Ngomane locked gazes. They knew that Shaka's argumentation also applied to generals and commanders like themselves who obeyed orders and sent their men to die. In fact, in this line of reasoning, all reality and all values ultimately rest in the king's hands because, through the focalization of standing armies and War, Life itself is at the beck and call of a country's ruler.

And, before either Farewell or Fynn could offer a suitable rebuttal to Shaka's deduction, the Emperor spoke again, his words now carrying the full weight of his authority. When the Zulu had finished, Daniel's lips trembled as his eyes flitted to a terrified Tsani, and he murmured: "He says that, like with Joji, the same principle applies to the Zulu Nation. Here, too, Life belongs to Shaka. - Her life belongs to Shaka," Daniel indicated that he was referring to Tsani. "You had no right to give her life without the Great Elephant's permission."

Then Shaka nodded to the Ufasimba, and Pampata closed her eyes. Those two simple, elementary gestures - nodding and closing the eyes - which, in themselves, are innocent, pure, unaffected bodily expressions, were, in the context at hand, enough to cause the blood to drain from Fynn's features. The Irishman's mouth fell open in a tortured scream that remained paralysed in silence - save for a rasping gurgle that seemed to tear at his throat, as...

...one of the Ufasimba guards sank the blade of his ixwa into Tsani's heart. The woman spat up blood and phlegm and sank to the ground, while the Whites looked on spellbound and petrified. Wilkins was the first to find his breath and fell forwards, retching convulsively, vomiting into the Continental coffer onto the trinkets presented by "Brother Joji".

Fynn - his face a mask of rage - jumped to his feet as if to strike out at Shaka for the senseless, barbaric murder of this innocent girl, but Farewell speedily intervened, stopping the man of medicine before the Ufasimba could drench the afternoon in more blood.

"What the hell do you think you're doing, Fynn?!" Farewell hissed under his breath.

"In the name of God!" Fynn's brogue made his words almost incomprehensible, - as did his tremulous rage. "He must pay for this!"

"We are in no positon to be judge and jury, Fynn!"

"Then what would you have me do?!" Fynn's eyes were blazing. "Pretend it never happened?!"

"Yes, Fynn!" was Farewell's vehement reply. "That's exactly what we must do if we value our own lives."

As Fynn struggled to compose himself, Shaka's voice returned to chill the interior of the Royal Hut. And, when Daniel offered the translation (which rode the edge of the Xhosa's bitterness), Fynn suddenly realised with appalling clarity that just as Shaka had needed to tame Farewell's horse, he now wished to tame them.

"In the future," was Daniel's suffered translation, "the Swallows will use their powers only for the benefit of the Great Elephant himself and those he chooses."

Nandi, who had watched the horrifying scene with the impassivity of a granite expression, leaned towards her son and spoke softly to him, her feline eyes alive with cunning.

The Emperor stiffened at his mother's words and, as the members of the Zulu party became fully aware of what the woman had said, - a tenseness pervaded the hut's stifling air with a bolt of electrifying horror mingled with the tingling excitement of anticipation.

In answer to Farewell's questioning look, Daniel whispered in a voice that seemed disembodied: "The Queen says, if the Swallows truly have these powers, let them prove it. Let them resurrect her again."

A diverted smile danced across Mkabayi's lips as her face took on an expectant cast, her eyes roaming eagerly to the Whites, her soul feasting upon the disconcertion and complete disarray she read on their despairing visages.

It seemed that the Royal Audience, which had started on a rather cordial note, had gradually and relentlessly precipitated into the abysmal depths of a nightmare. Yet, true to his form, once again Farewell the Adventurer found that he responded best in times of great danger and stress. And knowing full well that he could not admit that there were no "White supernatural powers" involved in the "resurrection" of Tsani (indeed the very idea of a "resurrection" had been Farewell's own), an astonishing elasticity of spirit came to the officer's assistance and the young hero of Nelson's Fleet found himself answering: "With all due respect to Her Majesty, we have made the inexcusable mistake of disobeying the Emperor once. I find it is our sovereign duty as His Majesty's guests not to make the same mistake again. As the Great Elephant wishes, from now on our powers will be used only for his own benefit and on his own behalf."

Daniel, who translated this rather "tongue-in-cheek" reply, found himself smiling at the brazenness of Farewell and his British "imperial" stock; -- this stock of men who created the colonies with often little more to go on than pure exercises of the imagination coupled with the futility, with the charm and sometimes with the deep, hidden truthfulness of dreams. "Britannia is hailed", Daniel considered deep in his African soul, "because, quite frankly, only Britannia knew how to 'pull it off!'"

Yet, even with that "imperial elasticity", few if any have the power to "pull off" a resurrection. Knowing this, Farewell was pleased to see that Shaka seemed satisfied with the answer. Yet, as the Emperor turned to instruct the Ufasimba to carry out the body of the poor young girl, Nandi intervened once again, a thin, challenging smile grazing her lips.

"The Queen says," Daniel told Farewell with an expression that seemed to say 'she's called your bluff', "that it is precisely for the benefit of the Great Elephant that the Swallows must prove their powers."

Lieutenant Farewell held Nandi's gaze levelly with his own. Then, retaining his poker face, Farewell shifted his attention to Shaka and noticed - to his astonishment - that the Emperor was faltering with indecision. The

Zulu searched the lieutenant's face as if to ask, "Can you really do it? Do you really have these powers?", before nodding in agreement with his mother's wish.

Being a gambler by nature, Farewell also nodded to himself with a deep sigh and, shrugging, turned to Fynn, urging in a hushed tone: "All right, Fynn. Resurrect her."

"Are you mad?!" the Irishman's eyes shot to his comrade.

"No, damn it," Farewell was angry now. "But you were when you jumped into that blasted grave! Now do something for the love of God!, or you'll be digging all our graves!"

Fynn's eyes remained fixed on Farewell's. Then, realising the dilemma, with no choice but to play out his part in the farce, the Irishman uttered a silent prayer and took up his weathered carpetbag in a bid to perform a miracle. Rising, feeling the full burden of this grotesque travesty, Fynn approached the "sleeping beauty" and taking out his stethoscope, pressed it against her breast, confirming what he had already known to be the case: - Tsani's "slumber" was, indeed, eternal.

Whilst the man of medicine went about this impossible chore, Farewell continued to regard the Son of Zulu in a level, steady gaze. Shaka's fiery eyes were rivetted on Fynn, and the lieutenant noticed that, as it became increasingly more obvious to the Emperor that Febana's "sangoma" may truly be unable to perform the miraculous transition from death back to life, Shaka's desire to believe in the unbelievable became all the more obstinate. Indeed, in the African Sovereign's tempestuous soul, Fact and Folly were travelling at a collision course - drawing closer and closer to impact as Fynn faltered over Tsani's body, his lips moving, quivering, in a dolorous prayer to the God of life Who is also the True Lord of Death.

And Farewell saw, as he took full scrutiny of Shaka, that the Child who had been raised as a Master in the path of his companion Death wanted, desperately wanted and needed to believe that the "immortality" of the Swallows did indeed exist and that resurrection was possible.

Along with the Englishman, Nandi and the Zulu royal entourage were also silent witnesses to their king's obsession. Especially Nandi was saddened by her son's need to possess the "unreachable". Her idea of insisting that Fynn do the impossible was conceived to prove to her son that it was, indeed, impossible! Yet now she saw that his obsession had blinded him and that her experiment, intended to be one of liberation, had only shackled his heart all the more.

Shaka tore his gaze away from Fynn's pathetic figure bowed powerlessness, and his face darkened with suspicion as his eyes strained after the "immortal" lettering on the mat hanging from the hut's central post, the five symbols that were joined to spell S H A K A.

"Isihlahla somgqwabagqwaba esibasasishulwephi," came the voice of the Son of Zulu riding the crest of his torment. "Satshalwaphi safike sahluma!"

And rising, the Emperor shot an accusing glance at his mother - the first such sign of accusation, and stomped out of the hut under the shaken and astounded countenances of Nandi, Pampata, Ngomane, Mgobozi, Mzilikazi and the others.

Farewell's questioning eyes met Daniel's.

"If the immortality of the Swallows is a lie, he says," Daniel translated in a hushed, solemn tone. "Then this girl's blood is on their hands not mine. If their immortality is a lie, he says, then their hearts are like their silver glass, a reflection of people without the dimension of depth."

Dropping her gaze, Pampata looked once again at her own reflection in the mirror and, as she saw the tears streaming down her cheeks, she thought of Illusion. And she saw, in the mirror, the falsehood that lies deep in the necessities of existence, in life's secret fears and burning ambitions, in the deep-rooted mistrust of ourselves, in the love of Hope and the dread of uncertain days. And she sensed, eyeing her own reflection, that Illusion, being the greatest foe of Reality, is the most soothing of all deceptions.

CHAPTER XL
"UKUVUSA"(RESURRECTION)

Towards the end of the Year of Our Lord 1824, Algoa Bay was a small British settlement hugging the irregular shoreline of the Indian Ocean east of Cape Town. The settlement, forming the last link with civilisation for ships venturing out of the Cape Colony in the direction of India, was a desolate spot of lonesome and dreary wilderness, far removed from the mellow environs of Cape Town, - a spot where traces of human industry were few and human residence was confined to an old Portuguese stone fort and a scattering of rough huts set amidst the windswept sandhills.

It was to these forsaken faubourgs of civilty that Elizabeth Farewell ventured on the tracks of the picturesque corsair who seemed to be the only probable link between herself and the man with whom she had shared her life for well over two years, the man who (it was presumed) had fallen victim to the Wild Coast. She arrived on a night in late September. The wheels of her horsedrawn carriage splashed over the muddy road as the vehicle clamoured through the mist and drizzle, skirting the sandhills and moving towards the desolate taverns and public houses that cluttered the margins of the harbour near the old fort. The carriage came to a stop near a line of warped docks.

"The road ends 'ere, m'lady," said the driver with a Cockney twang, addressing his passenger through the open trap on the vehicle's roof.

The door of the carriage swung open and an embroidered lace umbrella was thrust out and unfurled against the rain, followed by Elizabeth's elegant, noble figure. The woman quickly scanned her penumbral surroundings and her eyes fell knowingly on the gaping portals of the public houses that clung to the fort.

"Thank you, Henry," she said squinting up againstthe rain to peer at him. "I shall continue on foot.

Henry, the coachman, - a seasoned cabby who would appear to have furrowed the streets of London before emigrating to the Colonies and finding employment in the merchant trade of Elizabeth's step-father, Johann Peterssen, - shot a glimpse at the menacing environs and, in apprehension for the safety of his aristocratic passenger, commented with due worry: "Would you be wantin' me to wait, m'lady?"

"No, that won't be necessary, Henry," she retorted evenly. "I trust I shall be returning by ship."

With that, Elizabeth walked away, stepping over a puddle and into the darkness, leaving Henry to shrug his shoulders fatalistically and to veer the horses back in the direction from whence they came.

Reaching the fort, her elegance and gentility sharply contrasting with her grim surroundings, Elizabeth moved down the line of taverns and Portuguese baiucas, checking their quaint and singular names before stopping in front of a sign that bore the red painted lettering "Refugio Bahia". With a trace of reticence and apprehension, the woman neared an open door, lit from within, that yawned onto a flight of stairs leading down to a basement tavern. Bracing herself with fortitude and thoughts of the man she loved, she stepped into the harsh wash of light given off by the flickering lanterns and started down the whitewashed steps, towards the loud, drunken singing and the festive Portuguese music that spewed up from the entrails of the "cantina" or "baiuca" (the sort of stormy establishment that thrived in abundance along the seacoasts of the world in the "glorious" centuries in which buccaneers found favour in the ports of Africa, the Americas and the Far East).

The interior of the tavern sought by Mrs. Farewell was living evidence that not much had changed in Algoa Bay since the Age of Portuguese Piracy. Indeed, though the British had taken over the Bay and renamed it Port Elizabeth, the Portuguese community was hard to die and the patrons of the "cantina" were pirates still both rowdy in their mannerisms and suspect in their scruples. In the lapping hues of the tavern's red and yellow candles, long wooden tables, littered with melted wax that clung to the surface in twisted, baroque shapes, were populated by swarthy sailors engaged in boisterous conversations with women of loose decolletes and morals. In a corner of the establishment, a group of musicians (of half-breed extraction) were engrossed in the joyous, hypnotic sounds of the "maxixe" (the proud forerunner of the Colonial "batuque" of the 1870s, later to explode in the Brazilian "samba" of the 1900s).

Elizabeth stopped at the foot of the stairs allowing her eyes to become accustomed to the play of dazzling lights before being able to take in her surroundings. As she did so, a good deal of the apprehension drained from her as the gaity of the music and the atmosphere flooded into her heart and, swept away by it, she found herself smiling. A hush soon descended on the colourful gathering as, one by one, the "pirates" and their "ladies" had cause to notice in their decadent midst the presence of this refined gentlewoman verily exuding dignity and class.

"Miragrosa!" bellowed Roberto de Louco e Doida de Bahia Filho Barbanegra de Ticia, known as Parmananda. "Que coisa miragrosa!" the large man echoed from the bowels of the baiuca, addressing Elizabeth, his interweaving of Portuguese and English filling the tavern with swells of theatrical vehemence. "It is miracle, Senhora! Mi-ra-cle!" Just this night I sit and I say -- 'Marinho!' - You remember Marinho, no, Senhora? Marinho, my first mate! You meet him! Good man, Marinho," Parmananda nodded, causing his first mate, who was seated at the end of the long table, to beam with joy at the boisterous show his captain was staging. "He speak five languages," Parmananda boasted, disengaging his arm from the lower back of a young woman and holding up his five spread fingers. "Cinco! Fluentemente! El fale Portugues, Ingles, Alemao..." The "pirate" let his voice trail off as he frowned, continuing with affected sincerity. "I say, 'Marinho - that poor woman, Senhora Farewell! Alone! Sozinha sem marido! Que pena, que pena, que pena! What a pity! We must do something, Marinho', I say. 'To help such a lady! Such a real lady!'..." Even Elizabeth found herself smiling along as Parmananda slapped his hand on the table and inquired: "But what can we do, Marinho?', I ask -- 'What?!'..."

..."What, Senhora Farewell? What makes you come to Parmananda?"

The foaming surf glistened with the moon's reflection as it broke under the tattered wooden planks of Algoa's docks. The captain's mood had changed considerably from his clowning in the taberna as he now walked at Elizabeth's side, their lone figures skirting the edge of the shoreline.

"What makes you come in search of me?" his voice was hard, his expression resolute. "It is the sloop called the 'Julia'? I am right, no?"

"Your perceptiveness, captain," Elizabeth retorted stiffly, with a touch of bitterness, "is rivalled only by your gift of gab."

The woman suddenly stopped in her tracks and turned to face the man's scarred features. Now it was her turn to be stern and resolute as she asked: "How much do you want to find my husband?" The captain fell pensive, gazing at the splintered boardwalk at his feet. As usual, the "driftwood's" plotting, conniving mind was turning over sums of money and the best mode of their procurement. He had not been surprised by Elizabeth's arrival. He had known she would come. His blood, the blood of Robert Theach known as Blackbeard, the blood of his mother, Maria la Doida and of his Buccaneer father, El Louco, had buzzed in his veins with the promise of riches at that very first meeting with the woman in Somerset's study. It was just a matter of time! And now that she was there, Parmananda knew that her love and devotion to her husband could be translated into wealth for him.

"1000 British Sovereigns," he finally said. "In gold, " he emphasized, looking up at her. "Portugal's alliance with Britain is solid, but not immortal. Gold is both."

"That's an outrageous amount!" Elizabeth could hardly contain her helpless rage.

"I agree, Senhora. It is outrageous!" He lifted his gaze to the starry sky. "Only O Cristo can bring back those who are no more. Go to a priest. He will find your husband for a few shillings - the cost of a votive candle and a prayer at the Altar Maior!"

The chiding in his tone only caused her outrage and helpless anger to augment. How she hated it! Being there in the middle of the night on this foresaken wharf discussing the life and death of the person she loved most with a human shark, negotiating the price of her husband's salvation with a freebooter who mentioned Christ and Gold in the same breath and with the same revering buffoonery! Yet she had no choice. Even after her talk with her mother and stepfather, she had tried the other sea captains at Cape Town, just to be sure. And, as a verification of her initial feeling, she found that Superstition did indeed rule those seamen's hearts. Word had gotten round and Francis Farewell's name and that of the "Elizabeth Catherine" had become taboo. No one, - no "self-respecting" sailor - would ply the Wild Coast in search of a ghost ship and its helmsman! No one except a freebooter.

"Three hundred," she countered.

"Senhora!" the corsair rejoined with reprimand. "It is sacrilege to bargain with the souls of loved ones. - One thousand."

"Five hundred, captain," she retorted steadfastly.

"A good price," Parmananda admitted, grinning politely. "A credit to your generosity. Many men would accept." He shook his shaggy head sadly and added: "But not Parmananda. Boa noite, Senhora," he bowed respectfully before starting off in the direction of the distant sounds of the baiuca.

"Captain Parmananda!" said Elizabeth sharply.

The man stopped and cast her a sidelong glance.

"Why should I trust you, captain?"

"Because," he said simply, "you have no choice, Senhora. You and I are the only ones who believe your husband is still alive." The man's eyebrows went up as if to punctuate: "That is why you have travelled so far to see me."

The woman held the captain's gaze steadily with her own before sighing deeply and agreeing at last: "Very well, captain. You shall have your money."

"Excellent, Senhora," a broad smile creased the sea wolf's weathered features. "Excellent!"

*

The sign on the shop window in Port Elizabeth's small commercial district read, in elaborate gilt lettering: JONAH BIGSBY & SON - JEWELLERS, ENGRAVERS, WATCHMAKERS, LAPIDARIES & GEMOLOGISTS. As Elizabeth stood in front of the shop, she hesitated slightly. One thousand gold sovereigns was indeed a great deal of money!

She had come to Algoa bearing in her purse a bank cheque for 700 sovereigns (sure that that should be more than enough for the "transaction") which she had drawn, fully liquidating a joint account that she shared with her husband at the Cape of Good Hope Merchants' Savings Company of Buxton Street, Cape Town. That meant she still needed 300 hundred in order to comply with Parmananda's act of "piracy". Of course, Francis had much more than that in his own account but, what with Britain's new rulings on conjugal property, there was no way she could draw from her husband's finances without first undergoing the process of inheritance (as the bank director had told her with a severe curling of his moustache). But, of course, that was completely out of the question inasmuch as Francis was still alive - and he was still alive, she had told the bank director, there was no doubt in her mind about that. Asking her mother or her stepfather for the extra amount was also completely out of the question (even though Johann had offered his full support). No, this was a battle she and Francis would need to fight and win alone! And so that left....

...Jonah Bigsby, a dapper man who quite resembled a tallish elf, pushed aside the curtain behind his shop's window-dressing, revealing his pudgy, perennially flushed cheeks. As Elizabeth looked on from the street, peering through the gilt lettering, the jeweller leaned forward, gently resting a diamond bracelet on a velvet cushion. Sensing the woman's inquiring presence, the man's bulging eyes suddenly darted up to look beyond the horizon of his pince-nez where they took in the noble, 'expensive' figure of Mrs. Farewell. When their eyes met, Elizabeth smiled and, returning that smile, Jonah bowed with reverence and dignity, as his myopic orbs greedily reviewed the potential customer. Bowing again, Jonah shut the curtain and reappeared almost instantly behind the brass rod. Then, with another bow and another smile, the man took his leave, his magnified eyes inviting the woman to enter the hallowed recesses of his establishment. Once again Elizabeth hesitated, musefully fingering the contents of her purse before setting her jaw with determination.

A small bell rang over the shop's door, accompanying Mrs. Farewell into the small, stuffy entrails of Bigsby & Son, Jewellers, where Jonah's corpulent frame bent at the waist in greeting.

"Good day, Madam," he cooed in a mezzo-soprano. "Magnificent, isn't it? One of a kind!"

Elizabeth frowned, taken aback by the remark.

"The bracelet you were admiring," Jonah explained. "The one I just placed in the window. All pale-blue stones. Translucent. Faultless. Quite a rarity - even in this part of the world! A bit expensive, I'm afraid," he chuckled good-naturedly. "But for a lady such as yourself, I'm sure we can...meet halfway, as it were. On the price, I mean. You'll find we're most cooperative," he chuckled again, adding, "No use hiding our light under a bushel, so to speak."

"Yes. Quite right," Elizabeth smiled curtly. "But that bracelet's not why I'm here, Mr--."

"Bigsby. Jonah Bigsby. In person and at your service, so to speak."

"I'm interested in a string of pearls, Mr. Bigsby," she said, opening her bag and producing from within it the splendid necklace Francis had given her for Christmas. "Like these," she said, gingerly placing the gleaming necklace on the counter directly facing the shop's proprietor.

Jonah's attention was instantly bent upon the necklace in delicate scrutiny. Fitting a magnifying lense over his pince-nez, he studied the pearls with great care, thinking out loud.

"A delicate play of oriental lustre," he said, with mounting appetite. "Coupled with a perfect droplike shape. Be hard to find such excellence in these parts. These are Indian, I'd say. Batavian perhaps. But not far from there, I'll be bound. The rose colouring's a dead giveaway!" Looking up, he gazed at Elizabeth, his one eye twice the size of the other, "May I ask where you acquired them, Madam?"

"A gift, Mr. Bigsby. From my husband."

"A seaman, no doubt."

"Lieutenant," she answered proudly. "Royal Navy. Napoleonic Wars." She paused a beat before casually asking: "How much would a necklace just like this one cost me, Mr. Bigsby?"

"Hard to say, Madam," the man's prominent forehead corrugated with concentration. "Our dealings with the Orient have always been somewhat strained. The Portuguese, you know."

"Yes," Elizabeth agreed, thinking of her own strained dealings with Parmananda.

"And of late they have become more stressed than usual. If I were to favour you with an estimate, I'd say - quite a bit, I'm afraid."

"How much, Mr. Bigsby?" she restated her query.

"Six hundred sovereigns. Five-fifty, perhaps," his smile reclaimed its paramount positon on his florid face. "But, for a lady such as yourself, I'm sure we could---"   "I'll take it," she broke in.

"Beg your pardon, Madam?" Bigsby blinked behind his pince-nez.

"I said I'll take it, Mr. Bigsby. In gold, if you please. No use hiding our light under a bushel, so to speak."

*

Farewell's Admiralty map of Southeast Africa (the hydrographical survey of British Kaffraria and Natal undertaken in 1823 by Captain Owen, R.N.) was spread open on one of the massive wooden tables of the "Refugio Bahia". Having received his outrageous payment (which Elizabeth had had the "courtesy" of transmuting to gold sovereigns), Parmananda was seated in the company of Marinho and Elizabeth in the inspection of the map that the woman had provided as an indication of her husband's projected landing site. Reaching for a candle, the "pirate" tilted it slightly so that's its quivering glow illuminated the contours of the Wild Coast.

A drop of melted wax fell onto the map, covering the spot Elizabeth had indicated. As the wax dried over Rio de Natal it turned a deep red - the colour of blood.

* * *

"The morning following the senseless and monstrous assassination of the native girl, Shanee, I awakened, as was becoming my custom, at the first greying of dawn only to find that the weather, quite befitting my own mood and that of my companions, was dreary and cloudy, and that the rain was falling heavily, attended with thunder and lightning, and gale winds blowing from the westward in strong blasts..." Such was the entry in Wilkins's diary (drafted without the usual steadiness of hand and quill) directly following the quest for resurrection that had marred with blood the first encounter between the Swallows and the Son of Zulu. Continuing, the journal set out: "Towards midday, the weather having the appearance of being somewhat settled, a messenger arrived at our camp with the news that the King was indisposed and that we were to occupy ourselves as we thought best until such time as further instructions were forthcoming. Having all of us the desire to remain tranquil in order to recover from the deep fatigue and depression procured by the horrendous murder which had been thrust upon us, we received the news with a touch of relief; and, as the Lieutenant, Fynn, Thomas, Cane and Popham engaged in making short excursions in the vicinity of our station, I remained behind to make a further entry in the Diary which was fast becoming a regular solicitude...

"As I settled down with pen in hand to relate the episodes of which I had been witness (the horrendous murder which I have referred to above), I was reminded of my days of journalism and my Editor, Ol' Hardy, who often had had cause to remind me that when a writer treads on new ground, he possesses few advantages and many and great difficulties. The assertion of Solomon, in his time, 'that there was nothing new under the sun,' seemed to justify him in his opinion. Yet if Ol' Hardy could have reason to venture to this part of the world and spend, as I have, a protracted time in the company of Natal's despotic emperor, he, Ol' Hardy, would have found that even the wise Solomon can be wrong. Shaka Zulu and his Nation are, indeed, 'new under the sun'!

"In previously delineating my portraiture of Shaka, I have had special regard for his physical appearance, his disposition and behaviour, his mode of government (which I have taken the liberty of referring to a Zulucratical), and his unique ascendancy over his abject, oppressed subjects. In this portraiture, I have merely hinted at his cruelty without going into greater definition. And, indeed, even now when I am confronted with the task of relating the death of the poor native girl (whom Fynn had had the sad office of doctoring back to health), I realise that by detailing the enormity of this misdeed (truly "new under the sun"!), I may well be setting the passions of my readers in such an array against Shaka that they would no longer be willing to encourage in their minds any favourable aspects of the man. Yet, in light of my task as writer of this journal and my commitment to objectivity (a lesson learned from Ol' Hardy), I find that, for the purpose of allowing my readers to draw their own conclusions, I cannot spare them the pang that my agonising narration may occasion.

"The world has heard of monsters - Rome had had her Nero, the Huns their Attila, and Syracuse her Dionysius; but for sanguinary diablery, Shaka has outstripped them all..."

And so Tim went on and, after the vivid, and quite florid narration of Tsani's death, Wilkins further wrote that towards late afternoon, when the rains had ceased, yet another messenger arrived bearing news that seemed considerably out of context. The Swallows were told that the Great Mountain was much delighted by the presence of the White men in his realm and that there was to be a great celebration held that evening in honour of the guests who had travelled so far in friendship.

Though more than adequately versed in his medical profession, Fynn could not yet have known of terminologies such as schizophrenia. If he had, he might well have used the word to define Shaka's consistently odd behaviour; - an eccentric conduct which the Irishman had noticed during his brief stay in the Royal Residence and which his experienced mind considered and judged as highly anomalous and whimsical - to say the least! "He's mad, you know! Quite mad!" Fynn was to remark to Farewell. "And I'm afraid that at the end, we may well need Aladdin's Lamp to save ourselves!"

The great celebration was initiated towards evening, when the setting sun had caused the towering palisades of Bulawayo to cast long shadows over the immensity of the Citadel. The parade grounds (where the Zulu Royal family and the Shakan armies were gathered in gala attire) had been festively and brightly lit up with burning bundles of dried reeds held high by the immobile, statuesque warriors of the Ufasimba. And when the darkness set in, and the musicians gave way to the dancing and singing, to the clapping, chanting and shrill ululating of the maiden's regiments and the stamping of feet and the martial drum beats of the regular armies, -- and as the tens of thousands who were amassed in Bulawayo were swept up by the regalement and gaity, no one (save for Dingane and Mhlangana) noticed Pakatwayo's two armed men dressed like Ufasimba warriors as they stealthily entered the vast homestead and took their places near the other Shakan bodyguards; no one noticed the two men as they easily blended with the other members of this special regiment and slowly, relentlessly inched their way under the flickering light of the torches, moving closer and closer to the top of the stockade and the majestic figure of the King who sat next to his mother and his White visitors, Farewell, Fynn, and the others.

Only Wilkins was absent (due to an awkward touch of dysentry) and he related the tragic events of that celebration as follows:

"...yet that evening, I was suddenly attacked with a bacillary inflammation which, from its severity, reduced me to such an ebb of debility, as rendered me quite incapable of any exertion. I was thus forced to remain at our campsite, a silent witness to the brilliant lights, to the enchanting, entrancing music and to the gaity which held the Emperor's homestead in their spell...

"Having abstracted myself for a time in reading, along about midnight, I would put it, I was induced by my curiosity to leave the light of my tent and take a peep at the dancing and singing in the Citadel. I had not been many minutes in this contemplation, when I heard a horrendous, excruciating shriek rise up from the parade grounds, followed by a general confused bustle and crying, along with a great wail that seemed to explode from the multitude that packed Bulawayo. Women shrieked despairingly. Men shouted out in anger. Panic-stricken people ran in all directions like ants that have suddenly lost their orientation. Many collided with others. Those who fell to the ground were trampled underfoot in a world that seemed suddenly to have gone berzerk..!

"Having quickly left the campsite in the company of our interpreter Popham, I was able (through excitement, no doubt) to temporarily overcome the disability of my ailment and gain the portals of the Shakan residence. As Popham and I pressed our way through the frenzied throng, we endeavoured to ask anyone who would stand to listen what the occasion was of this extraordinary commotion. At length I found out, to my great astonishment and apprehension, that Shaka, while dancing, had been stabbed (I was later informed that the blade had gone through the arm and penetrated the left breast). I immediately turned away to search for the others, Fynn, the Lieutenant, Cane, Holstead, Daniel, yet, there was such very great noise going on, and the crowd so dense that it was almost impossible to move. Then, to my further chagrin, Popham joined in the general uproar. Following the example of many others, he fell down in a fit so that I could neither ask questions nor come by any information as to where my companions were and if, indeed, they were still alive...

"I attempted alone to gain the top of the stockade, but the people round me pulled me some one way, some another; all were in a state of madness. And the crowds were increasing and the uproar was becoming more dreadful, in consequence of the shrieking and crying, making my situation very awkward and extremely unpleasant..."

And, in the collective hysteria that followed the assassination attempt, only Mgobozi and Joko had the dexterity and quick-wittedness to pursue the two killers who flagrantly bore the illustrious plumes and colours of the Ufasimba. Catching one of the men, Mgobozi threw him to the ground, wrenching his arm behind his back, snapping it at the elbow.

"Kill him!" shouted Dingane suddenly appearing from the shadows, wearing a look of indignation and rage. "Kill him to appease the people!" he urged once again, his crafty eyes wearing the glint of eagerness that suppressed his guilt and his fear of being discovered as one of the instigators of the assassination attempt.

"That verdict is not ours to decide, Dingane," was Mgobozi's answer. "Sigidi will deal with this man as soon as he recovers."

"If he recovers," was the roguish whisper of the second-born of his House. "We must be realistic," he told Mgobozi and Joko with a cagey, conspiratorial drone to his guileful voice. "We must face the possibility that the Great Elephant may die. And, for the good of the Nation, leadership must be quickly restored! As quickly as possible."

"And who is to provide that leadership?" the surprise was quite evident in Mgobozi's scornful tone. "You, Dingane?"

"Yes, general," the "Needy One" suddenly roared, venting a lifetime of frustration and hatred, the lifetime he had spent in his brother's long shadow. "I am Dingane kaSenzangakona Zulu! The direct descendant of Jama, Ndaba, Mageba, Punga and Zulu kaMalandela! - In the name of my Ancestors, general, the Forefathers I share with your king, I order you to kill this man who has dared to raise a hand against my brother." The urgency took hold of his wily voice as he raised it in emphasis. "Kill him now! Or I shall!"

His troubled eyes fixed on Dingane, Mgobozi remained defiantly unmoving, until Shaka's half-brother was verily trembling with rage at the general's "insubordination". Deciding to take matters into his own hands and in a bid to save himself from discovery, Dingane snatched the ixwa out of Joko's grasp and, thrusting down on Pakatwayo's henchman, sank the blade deep into the assassin's chest, extinguishing life in an instant. Then, handing the weapon back to Joko, Dingane spun round on his heels and strode off, into the midst of the crazed populace.

In a matter of seconds, he was faced with Mkabayi's steady, level gaze.

"You've destroyed the evidence," she whispered to her brother's son, referring to Pakatwayo's henchman whose lips Dingane had just sealed with a thrust of the ixwa. "But you've not abolished your guilt." A cunning smile tugged on the corners of Mkabayi's thin lips. "If you had not spared him from being tortured, I wonder what he would have told us about you, Mhlangana, Pakatwayo and...ah, yes -- the Ndwandwes?" Dingane could barely hide the intense shock occasioned him by his aunt's telling remark. His mind raced, seething with verbal parries and rebuttals in an effort to fashion for himself some sort of riposte to Mkabayi's chillingly accurate imputation. Yet, well knowing the astuteness of his father's sister, Dingane soon realised that all confutation was meaningless with a woman of her intellect. So the man allowed a thin smile to twitch at his insidious mouth as he made a mental note that she would have to be dealt with, later - after his securement of the Zulu throne.

"How long have you known?" Dingane said in a voice imbued with resentment.

"Since you were born, Dingane," she replied in a provoking tone. " Since you were born I knew this day would come. Then, when I was told you and Mhlangana were meeting regularly - and secretly - with the Qwabe and the Ndwandwes, it was not hard to deduce the rest. It is a shame I couldn't discover when, or this crime could have been prevented." The venom rising within her, Mkabayi added, with sharp revulsion: "You're a fool, Dingane! Is your lust for power so great that you would betray your own people - the proud destiny of the amaZulu?!"

"Shaka has betrayed our people!" Dingane's shrieked emphatically, losing his self-control and lowering his guard, his voice gaining force as the pitch rose with hatred, like an evil wind hissing over the brooding violence of the sea. "He has betrayed us! By destroying his father's life! By stealing what is rightfully mine as the oldest legitimate heir! - By building a Nation of warriors! By giving us a decade of war in which young girls are left barren to turn into old maids, and young men are castrated by the bondage of fear and the fear bondage! - Endless bondage!" he cried, his trembling voice barely audible over the tumult that raged round him. "Endless wars, endless blood, endless, endless hatred and murder!"

"And victory! And glory!" Mkabayi shouted over the commotion that had gripped Bulawayo, her own frenetic voice mingling with that of the crazed multitude. "And an Empire! The greatest this land will ever know! Do you really believe such power can be achieved without a price!? He has made the dreams of our forefathers become reality, and now you -- you have turned those dreams into a nightmare! What will you tell the Nation, Dingane. What would you have our people believe? That one of his own warriors, his faithful Ufasimba warriors, would turn a spear against their lord?"

"You underestimate me, my father's sister," Dingane replied with artful cunning, snatching glimpses of the mob and smiling with confidence upon realising that he has not been overheard. "My plan is worthy of even my brother's superior strategy. The people will be told that it was Destiny!" Dingane's voice was lowered in a reptilian hiss. "As a man lives - so shall he die. I will tell the amaZulu that his death was decided by the Ancestors."

"For what reason?" Mkabayi spat out.

"Betrayal!" Dingane softly retorted, the word riding the putrid breath of his ambition and loathing. "Of his People. We will tell them that the Ancestors presaged that the Great Mountain was on the verge of succumbing to the magical spell of the Strangers from the sea. We will tell them that the Son of Zulu had to be stopped before he destroyed the Nation with his own hands, with his own..." the man's features screwed up in a derisive smile with the utterance of the word: "...'curiosity'."

Mkabayi stiffened, unable to offer rebuttal as Dingane added with the concentrated malice of a lifetime: "I think they'll believe that, Mkabayi. After all - it's not too far from the truth, is it?"

*

The Son of Zulu, the Great Mountain of Africa lay in his Royal Hut, the crimson glow of the crackling fire bathing his majestic frame in lapping tongues of black and red - the colours of death and dying. As his proud heart faithfully pumped the torrid blood of his fever through his body, searing his mind, his thoughts confusedly reached through a cloud of darkness groping for the glimmer of life. Yet, reach as he may for the lustre of living, Shaka felt the irrefutable nearness of his Companion Death, and he felt Death's sweet, etherial presence sapping the invisible supports of his strength with the promise of Peace. He had a sensation of eternity close at hand, demanding no effort, soothing, gentle, kind and comforting, - offering a solution to the loneliness and to the desolation of a life where no one except his mother could ever be made to understand him. And, as he sensed his Companion's breath on his soul, he felt a glow of quiet contentment at the ease with which the Ultimate Kill could be affected. He need only let go.

Yet he did not. He could not. Not yet, at least. Not like this!

In an effort to find a stationary point in the world that was swirling round him, Shaka concentrated on the sensation of pressure he felt on his arm, - the pressure of someone's soft touch, a caress, the delicate feel of fingertips on his skin. Using this sensation as a lifeline, Shaka gradually drew himself out of the maelstrom of abandon and began to resurface to the reality of consciousness and to the throbbing, excruciating pain on his left flank.

Opening his eyes, the Zulu saw Pampata's lovely features through the luminous veil that cloaked his febrile vision. In her undying devotion, the woman was kneeling at his side, bent over him, hugging his mighty arm in her gracile embrace. Upon realising that her lord had returned to wakefulness, Pampata sniffed back her tears and her full lips parted in joyous anticipation. Yet, with little regard for the lovely young woman, Shaka shifted his gaze beyond Pampata in search of his mother.

When his eyes met Nandi's, when he saw her eternal beauty frozen in grief and despair, he saw in her the eternity of his existence and he realised that death would mean losing her: the womb, the warmth, the guide and the guardian of his life and of his love. He realised that she was and always had been his reason, his main reason for living, and that all that he had created had meaning only if it was a gift acceptable to her. Indeed, "as far as the eye can see" was only as far-reaching as Nandi's desire.

Lifting his arm, breaking free of Pampata's embrace, Shaka extended his long fingers and took hold of his mother's hand. He felt her warmth, the pulsating regularity of the blood rushing through her veins, - he felt her life and suddenly he, too, needed to live, - for her, in her, and with her!

Nandi ever Nandi!

"Febana," the King said in a voice that was the echo of Death.

Farewell's eyes were on Pampata, on her suffering, on her unrequited devotion, on her features lowered in anguish. Upon hearing his name, the man glanced at Shaka in utter astonishment and found himself answering, "Yebo?" Shaka swivelled his head round on the mat and found Farewell's eyes. Then, reaching out with his other hand, beyond the lieutenant and beyond the ageless figure of Majola (who had, once again, been sent by Sitayi to administer Life), the Emperor clutched Fynn's wrist.

"Sondela!" The King's voice reflected this urgency as he addressed the Irishman.

"He says to come closer," Daniel said in a whisper.

Reluctantly, feeling the Zulu's hold on his arm, Fynn inched nearer to the fire and the massive, imposing figure of the Great Mountain. As Shaka spoke, the Irishman held the King's gaze and was amazed to see in the Zulu's piercing eyes a glint of supplication and the semblance of vulnerability.

And as the King spoke, and as Majola heard his words, unnoticed by those present, she rose from the Child's side and left the hut - the watery eyes on her wrinkled visage shining with an eerie mixture of resignation and requital: the Son of Zulu had preferred the illusive "magic" of the Swallows to the immortal gift of his Heritage. The Darkness of his own Betrayal had started. The Betrayal of Africa!

"He asks--," Daniel started, his voice suddenly choked with emotion. "He asks, can you save him? Can you give him back life as you gave life to that girl?"

Looking up, Fynn found that both Nandi and Pampata where looking directly at him, their appealing expressions betraying cautious hope and eager expectation.

"Has everyone gone mad?!" Fynn's strained voice was laced with distress as his eyes shot to Daniel and Farewell. "That girl wasn't dead!" He was starting to feel claustrophobic, caged behind the iron bars of delusion and folly, and the animation of his tone displayed it quite clearly. "She was in a coma! Catatonic! The transitory stages of hypoglycemia! She would have recovered on her own if they hadn't tried to bury her! - Can't you understand that?!"

"Yes, I do understand, Fynn," the calm reply was Daniel's. "But he won't." The Xhosa's eyes met Shaka's intensely inquisitive stare. "All he can relate to is Light and Darkness. He sees the Darkness coming and he thinks you can give him back Light."

"Would you rather wash your hands of the whole thing thing, Fynn," the lieutenant queried, noticing the Irishman's reluctance to lift a finger for Shaka's wellbeing. "Let him bleed to death and die! Let God condemn him as you have?!"

'And why not?" Fynn's brogue was raised in righteous indignation. "Men like him deserve to die!"

"Do we?" Farewell snapped back, trying to conceal his mounting anger from the wondering gazes of Pampata and Nandi. "Do we deserve to die, Fynn? Do you hear that mob out there?" The man's arm lashed out to point a shaky finger at the turmoil that raged outside the hut. "You're a cultured man, Fynn. Think of Caesar and the interregnum of anarchy led by 'honourable' men like Brutus and Cassius! - The same may happen here! Shaka's armies without Shaka may be a greater threat than we ever thought possible! And I fear we will be the first victims of that anarchy!" At the mention of his name, Shaka's attention darted to the naval officer and the King listened, looking at Farewell attentively, as if understanding his every word. "We have a chance to win Shaka's favour, don't you see that? We cannot allow that chance to slip through our fingers!" The lieutenant took a deep breath and added with vehemence: "If we control his soul, we control the future of Southern Africa! Don't you see that?!"

Daniel peered at the lieutenant, spellbound.

"Control his soul?!" Fynn exclaimed, his voice vibrating with suppressed emotion. "How? By proving that we have powers over life and death?" His tone was suddenly sarcastic. "That is the game we're playing - isn't it, Francis?!"

"Life and death?" the hushed amazement was Daniel's. "Do you realise what you're doing, Lieutenant?"

"Yes, I do, Daniel," Farewell seemed suddenly dwarfed by the magnitude of his own daring. "And may God forgive me."

"I trust he will," Fynn's thin smile had the twisted contours of a scowl. "If for no other reason, God cannot fault your imagination. But there's something you've forgotten, Francis. We do not have those powers, and with my 'normal' medical abilities, I'm not sure I can save him. The spear's penetrated his side, and he's spitting up blood and phlegm that would indicate a puncture of the lung! If that is the case, then he is as doomed as that girl he murdered!"

"Than you must pray, Fynn," Farewell curtly adjoined.

"Pray?" the brogue swelled in outrage. "For him?" The Irishman's glaring eyes whipped to the huge frame of the dying sovereign.

"No. For us," was Farewell's level reply.

Daniel's gaze remained fixed on Farewell and his mind re-evoked the words once spoken by that eccentric, idealistic Englishman. "We are hypocrites," he had said. "We have been since Cortes slaughtered the Aztecs because they failed to embrace our values of good and evil."

"What are those values? What is Good and Evil for these men with skins of sorghum who play at God and can win the trust of a man such as Shaka?" Daniel pondered as he watched Fynn open his carpetbag in search of another miracle.

Yes, Daniel decided, he would pray. "For us."   But above all he would pray for Africa.

"Nkosi sikelela Africa," he whispered. "God bless Africa" and preserve it from those "whose reflection lacks the dimension of depth".

CHAPTER XLI
"INKOLO"(RELIGION)

"Communique forwarded by My Lords Commissioners of the Admiralty to His Majesty's Secretary of State for War and the Colonies, Downing Street..."

Lord Henry Bathurst, the 3rd Earl of Bathurst, who had, for a little over a decade, held the dignified post referred to in the communique, braced himself mentally and, directing his gaze to the text of the Lord Commissioners' missive regarding the Shakan Affair, read aloud: "Subsequent to the notification referred to Their Lordships by Sir Charles Somerset, Governor of the Cape Colony, Colonial Africa, we herewith advise that Lieutenant Francis George Farewell, R.N. is to be deemed missing in action..."

Slipping off his spectacles, Bathurst detached his gaze from the communique and added gravely: "...presumed dead."

"How?" inquired David Worthing with a pang of helpless rage. "That Zulu savage?"

"It wouldn't seem so, David," Bathurst remarked, resting the communique on his massive oak desk and sinking back in his worn leather chair, his voice becoming weak and colourless. "From Somerset's notification it would appear that Farewell never succeeded in making contact with Shaka. Indeed," his tone grew severe, "it is doubtful that his party ever set foot on the shores of Natal." In response to Worthing's questioning gaze, Bathurst elucidated: "I'm told they were shipwrecked, David. During their first landing attempt.

Worthing compressed his lips in disheartenment and crossed the large study, stopping in front of the high windows that framed Downing Street. The Assistant UnderSecretary looked out, yet instead of the forest of towering red-brick chimneys and smokestacks that were cast against a dreary London day, he saw the rambunctious, freckled face of his junior colleague Wilkins, the youth's brazen smile alight with the fire of his red hair.

"Poor Tim," Worthing said to Downing Street. "I shudder to think that I was the one to approve of his going down there." He pursed his lips again in a show of restrained vexation. "We should've known better than to trust that man Farewell! He was too cocksure of himself!"

"Is that what you would have us tell the Crown, David?" Bathurst inquired of his subordinate, causing Worthing to turn and meet the Earl's level gaze. "That we made an error in judgment and put the future of Britain's holdings in Southern Africa in the hands of a foolhardy adventurer?

- Adjoining, perhaps, the extenuation that we had no choice, as all other channels of action seemed closed to us?"

"No, Henry," Worthing sighed in admission. "In fact, I'm afraid we'll be rather hard put to explain any of this to His Majesty."

"I can just imagine what George will say," Bathurst remarked, imitating the monarch's gruff voice: "'Why do I have the lurking suspicion, Bathurst, that your Office has muffed it?'" Worthing found himself smiling at his colleague and friend, as the Earl considered somewhat disparagingly: "We've one last hope: - Major Cloete's troops in British Kaffraria. A mere two thousand men to defend the Cape from the massive tidal wave of Shaka's Empire. Not terribly encouraging, is it?"

Bathurst's attention was gravitated to the Cross that hung over his study's door. As if the question was directly and logically related to the problem at hand, the Colonial Secretary asked his colleague after a slight pause: "Are you a religious man, David?"

"Religious---?" Worthing echoed, his eyes also moving to the Cross. "I suppose so. Or so I would wish to think having been brought up in a stark Anglican regime. From the time I was old enough to reach up and touch the candleholders on the family organ, the 'Rock of Ages' has been 'cleft for me' every Sunday. I can still remember my mother's dainty fingers poised emphatically over the keyboard whilst her gracious feet pumped air into the 23rd Psalm - whoosh-whoosh, whoosh- whoosh - and my father standing behind her, urging me to sing along. And all those graces recited before meals, thanking God for 'These Thy Gifts' and steamed carrots - steamed carrots, Henry! Can you imagine a ten-year-old thanking God for steamed carrots?!" The Earl matched Worthing's tender smile of remembrance as the Colonial UnderSecretary added: "I have to be religious, Henry. I wouldn't want to think that my parents went to all that trouble for nothing. - But if you mean, do I believe in miracles, well...even if I didn't, Henry, this Shakan Affair would be a good time to start." Worthing strode towards the door and opened it to leave. "In fact, I'm beginning to think only a miracle can help us."

"Quite..." Bathurst agreed, drifting into a pensive abstraction. "Quite," he repeated under his breath as Worthing left the study to compile his report for His Majesty concerning the "tragic" Shakan Affair.

"Unless, of course, the Will of God is divorced from the Crown's and those miracles work against us..." the Earl of Bathurst mused aloud to the empty room, as he lifted his head to look wonderingly at the books and atlases that occupied an entire wall of his study. His glance ran over the Mercator Projection map of the World, featuring, in a predominantly centralised position, the stout, bulky contours of the earth's second largest continent: Africa. And with a mounting burden of remorse and dejection, his eyes took in the territories of this huge "colony" for which he was directly responsible,-- territories that extended from the balmy islands of The Canaries, longitudinally across The Barbary to the fertile fields of Alexandria and Goshem on the Nile's Delta, and to the Holy Land of Pathros and Mizraim, to the Red Sea and, beyond it, the rocky plains of Sinai: the Cradle of Man, the Site of God's Garden in Eden; -- and, latitudinally, from the Northern Sahara of the Tuaregs, down the Soudan and Ethopia, past the vast "Regions Unexplored" of the African interior, to the British Colony of Good Hope and its Cape.

"From the Cradle of Man to Good Hope," Bathurst silently told himself as his purview raced over Africa, from top to bottom. "From the Cradle of Man", The Beginning, the Remotest Past, the Focal Point of Creation -- to "Good Hope", Europe's antipode, the name itself indicating the prospect of a Glad Future.

"But for whom?" - As Bathurst said aloud those three words, he felt a pang of repressed emotion clutching at his throat; and, for the first time since he had held the massive responsibility of his burdensome post, an impetuous, implacable sea of thoughts and considerations burst through the restraining bulwarks of his usually guarded English soul, giving way to a tortuous stream of consciousness.

"Africa!" the name echoed with a resonance of greatness in the Earl's heart, a greatness that existed in its own right, independent of the European countries that would subjugate this land.

Africa - the word cudgelled his brain - "the Mother and Father of the Universe", Man's first home, the Birthplace of Culture, of Civilisation; the continent where (in Ethopia, Kenya, Tanzania, and the Lower Nile) Man had walked "erect" whilst anthropoids in Europe still scampered about on the limbs of trees; the land where Man was "Sapiens" almost a million years before the European "Homo Habilis" could make Fire without the direct intercession of God's Lightning.

Africa - Bathurst felt the name of "his colony" take possession of his being - the home where Noah's proud sons, Sem, Ham, and Japeth planted the Seed of the Generations of Man after the Flood when (as Genesis, Chapter 11 recounts) "the whole of the Earth was of one language and of one speech, and the Lord said, 'Behold The People is one ...and nothing will be restrained from them which they have imagined to do'!"

"The People is One!" Bathurst repeated the divine expression - the expression that in the language of The People translates as "Bantu"!

"Africa," the name welled in the Earl's soul eliciting its grandeur, and Sir Henry considered God's Will in the Shakan Affair and how the Colonists could best defend themselves from the Zulu Empire. Yet, as His Majesty's Secretary for the Colonies perpended the White Cape's defense from the threat of Black Africa, Bathurst was reluctantly, yet inevitably led to consider that if God is Just, He might very well be inclined to favour Shaka's imperialism over Europe's, to have a preference for the Zulu's spontaneously 'savage' methods over the calculating cold-blooded methodology of the Dominion by Force stubbornly advocated by Parliament. If God is Just, the Englishman considered, why should He side with us and not Shaka when faced with the African reality called slavery: millions of God's People being forced to live a life of estrangement in their own country as well as in the "exile" of the Americas (the "Babylonian Captivity" - as Fynn had called it).

Slavery. At home and abroad! An existence where fear and the urge to survive make deception a way of life. A merchant trade in human flesh that was transforming Africans into the most humiliated peoples in history. Shuddering, Bathurst thought of the cages, the irons balls, the whips, the chains - torture, rape, forced labour, starvation, murder - all part of the totality of the Black experience since the first White man landed on this continent's shores at the turn of the XVI Century.

Slavery at home and abroad! - The Earl's stream of consciousness eddied and swirled round this human tragedy to which his office was so closely related!

"And whilst this trade in 'niggers' continues to flourish," Bathurst's muted abstraction went on with rising sadness and the venom of injustice as he looked at the map of the world centered round this heart-shaped continent, "and whilst this systematic destruction of the African civilisation is allowed to go on unabated, bringing about the annihilation of the human dignity of the Black man, causing the genocide of the Sons of Noah, and the deportation of millions upon millions of Africans to the New World with a 'madness of method' that will permanently and irreversibly change the racial map of this planet, -- whilst this treachery goes on, do the British have any right to ask God for a miracle against Shaka's might? - Do David Worthing's Anglicans or Sir Henry Bathurst's Evangelicals have any right to pray for Africa when their prayers are directed only for the benefit of their own people? Bathurst knew that the answer could be but one: - No.

"And in a greater sense," Sir Henry considered, feeling his own religious devotion stirring within him, "what is the Church doing against this domestic and foreign slavery of the African people?" - Again the answer came instantly to mind. One word: Nothing! - On the contrary, the Church was doing all it could to advance the cause of this 'White Colonisation' of the world and to aid the Europeans in their bid to become lords of the rest of the planet using the verses of Matthew, 28:19 as a justification for brainwashing, pillaging, bondage and murder - "Go ye therefore and teach all nations, baptising them in the Name of the Father, and of the Son and of the Holy Ghost", - the divine mission that European Greed had transformed into a means not of Salvation, but of Domination in the name of the "father" that is Caesar, not God!

And, as Bathurst's consciousness was cast off in thoughts of the "Miracle" of Colonising Christianity, he was reminded of the appeal that had reached his office in the form of a letter written by a White traveller who had found passage on a slave ship plying the Atlantic from the Gulf of Guinea and the Congo to the American plantations of Virginia; a White traveller who had found St. Paul's Charity: "I love the religion of our Blessed Saviour," he had written on that vessel of doom, "I love that religion which comes from above, in the wisdom of God which is first pure, then peaceable, then gentle, without partiality and without hypocrisy. I love that religion that makes it the duty of its disciples to serve the poor and the socially oppressed, to serve those who suffer in the name of Justice. I love that religion which makes its followers do onto others as they themselves would be done by. It is because I love that religion that I hate the slave-holding, the woman-whipping, the mind-darkening, the soul-destroying religion that is imperialism's distortion of the meaning of Christ's Word. Loving the one I must hate the other; holding to the one I must reject the other."

"Loving the one, I must hate the other; holding to the one, I must reject the other". Those words reflected Bathurst's own need to be consistent with his Faith, and his thoughts were steered towards his own personal struggle in favour of the abolition of slavery and he was reminded of the declaration recently made by the Bishop of London (words which caused the Earl's soul to recoil in recollection): "The right of holding slaves is clearly established in the Holy Scriptures," the Bishop had said high atop his pulpit, "it is established both by precept and example, and neither the letter nor the Spirit of Scripture demands the abolition of slavery. Conversely, these Blacks are so uncivilised that the moment they are free, or on their own, they are totally uncontrollable. But if one punishes them regularly, one may expect a conditioning of their minds towards God."

"In light of this 'justice'," Sir Henry silently mused, his eyes permeated with the moisture of compassion, his mind struggling against the strong currents of his conscience in an attempt to return to his official duty and the Communique of My Lords Commissioners of the Admiralty. Yet, still rebellious, his heart cried out: "How on earth, how in Heaven can we pray for God's help in a land where our Christianity, our mission of salvation is - as Wilkins had put it - tried and tested double talk!"

How on earth, indeed?! - Sir Henry brooded once more.

And, as Mercator's Map of the world loomed over the bowed, seated figure of His Majesty's Secretary for War and the Colonies, its continents, its seas, its oceans and islands, its rivers and mountains seemed to whisper to the Earl, forcing themselves on his mind, quoting from the "Book of Injustice", the "Gospel According to Africa": -- "When the missionaries came," went the first quote, that of Jomo Kenyatta, "the Africans had the land and the Christians had the Bible. They taught us to pray with our eyes closed. When we opened them, they had the land and we had the Bible."

"The difference in colour," was the text of the second quote taken from the sermons of Dr. Malan, first National Party Prime Minister of South Africa and proud reverend of the Dutch Reformed Church, "is merely the physical manifestation of two irreconcilable ways of life, between barbarism and civilisation, between heathenism and Christianity..."

In Genesis 11, God willed that his Creation should be of one speech, of one language, - One! Yet Man was blind to God's will and Man said, "Let us build us a Tower, whose top may reach unto Heaven..." Man was blind to God's will and said, Let us be as gods!. And Man built the Tower and called it "Babel" meaning "confusion" of languages.

The enslavement of the African Continent was Man's second attempt "to ge as gods", Man's Second Tower of Babel. Yet this dealt not with the "confusion of languages", but with the Language of Confusion: our Civilisation's tried and tested double-talk.

* * *

"'If I had all the eloquence of men and of angels, but speak without Love, I am simply a gong booming or a cymbal clashing'..."

The clashing voice of Reverend Josiah Bellow, Anglican clergyman, esteemed pioneer of the B.B.C.A.M. (the British Board of Commissioners for African Missions) was vehemently intoned in the immortal verses of St. Paul's Letter to the Corinthians. Perched high atop of the thatched pulpit of the mission station's makeshift church, the man of God was addressing a mixed gathering that packed the interior of the preaching establishment in three very distinct, very "separate" subdivisions of pews: the first sector (closest to Bellow, to the pulpit and to the Cross of Christ) was filled with the White members of Bellow's small community: his wife and children, his white assistants and (as Somerset's special precautionary measure against the Zulu threat to the Colony) Colonel Josias Cloete (the commander of the over 2000 British troops and volunteers), Captain Scott Aitchison and some of the more religious officers and men of the His Majesty's 25th Regiment of Foot; the second sector was occupied by the mission station's Xhosa and Tembu school teachers and "converted native pupils"; and the third section of the church (that closest to the door) was flooded with the gaping, awesome semblances of the impoverished, foresaken Fingoes.

"'And though I have the gift of prophecy, and understand all mystery, and all knowledge; and though I have all faith so that I could move mountains, and have not Love, I am nothing...'!"

Mrs. Rebecca Bellow compressed her lips and nodded in silent agreement with St. Paul's words so masterfully expressed by her husband. Knitting her brow, the woman's attentive glance flitted to the rear of the church where the Black sea of Fingoes seemed entranced by the expansive gestures and rhetorical flourishes that emanated from the heights of the pulpit. And, as the pungent, acrid smell of this displaced humanity reached Rebecca's gracile nose, and as the drops of perspiration formed and fell from her armpits, staining her white silk dress, the reverend's wife listened to her husband's powerful voice and thought, with resignation, of her great sacrifice called Africa. "Christ will save them," she told herself as she smiled at the Fingoes, her heart swelling with righteousness. "Christ will whisper in their ears that the worst that the world can do is a small thing to those who believe, and that however harsh the ways of Providence may seem, God has a very special place for these Blacks in His heart". Her smile broadening at the refreshing thought, she returned her attention to the White section of the Church, and her eyes fell on Col. Cleote. She found herself thinking how handsome he looked with his greying whiskers, his deep blue eyes and in his spiffy uniform with gilded waistcoat and tight white breeches.

"'Love does not behave itself unseemingly and thinketh no evil'," Bellow recited from memory. "Love always beareth all things, believeth all things, hopeth all things, endureth all things. And Love never faileth; but whether there be prophecies, they shall fail; whether there be tongues, they shall cease; whether there be knowledge, it shall vanish away...'"

And the Fingoes looked on, barefooted and dirty; they looked on as Bellow spoke, not understanding, but feeling, sensing deep in their souls that they were about to be redeemed from sins they had never committed, that they were being given answers to questions they had never asked.

"'When I was a child'," the reverend continued with St. Paul, "'I spake as a child, I understood as a child, I thought as a child; but now I am a man and all childish things are put behind me'."

Captain Aitchison straightened up, arching his back in a proud military countenance.

"'For now we see through a glass, darkly; but then we shall see as we are seen. Now we know in part, but then shall I know even also as I am known'." Bellow paused and, leaving the verses of St. Paul, his mind swerved to the iron tracks of his prepared sermon and, smiling, he leaned forward.

"Dearly Beloved," he started, directing his words to the Whites and to the school teachers. "Our mission here is divine. We have been chosen to bring God's Love to the Children of Africa, to teach the ignorant His ways, to lead the simple of Heart to the great complexity of divine providence. We must reach them..." Bellow lifted his gaze to the Fingoes, "and teach them that nothing happens without the Will of God, that this God is a God of order and that just as they," he nodded in the direction of the Black sea, "are called upon to serve their earthly masters, so must we serve God. Just as they are punished by their masters when disobedient, so are we punished by God if we disobey Him. We must make it clear to them that if we had never come to their land, they would never have heard of the Saving Grace of Our Lord and, for them, He would have died in vain! But fortunately," the reverend smiled at the Fingoes, "we are here, and they have the opportunity to gain eternal happiness through our Lord and Saviour Jesus Christ. It is with that comforting thought that---"

"Colonel Cleote!" the call came from the rear of the Church, interrupting Bellow's harmonious voice. "Colonel," the soldier called out again, pressing his way through a sticky throng of Fingo children.

"What is it, Corporal?" Cleote's eyes flickered uneasily from Bellow's lips pursed in restrained anger to the approaching youth.

"Sir!" the Corporal snapped to attention and announced: "News from the North, sir. - About Shaka!"

A despairing moan was issued from the back of the church and Cloete felt his heartbeat quickening, as Reverend Bellow and his entire congregation gaped at the Corporal in watchful anticipation.

"Has he mobilised his troops?" the Colonel asked.

"Hardly, sir," was the Corporal's response, as he adjoined with a thin smile: "That is, of course, unless the Zooloos are given to being commanded by spirits!" "Speak plainly, Corporal," Cloete was beginning to lose his patience.

"Well, sir. From what I've been able to sift from the reports...we have every reason to believe, sir, that--well, sir...the bloke's been murdered!"

A shocked gasp jolted the first sector of the church as, spellbound, the Whites gaped at the Corporal.

"Shaka Zulu - Dead?!" Cloete said incredulously. "Are you sure?"

"Yes, sir," the Corporal nodded. "I've taken the liberty of checking my native sources. And they're most reliable, I'd say. There seems to be quite a commotion up North. He was stabbed through the heart, they say. Nighly a week ago."

"The Lord be praised!" Bellow cried with obvious relief.

"Amen, Reverend," Cloete grinned, rising from his seat and turning to his officer. "Captain Aitchison."

"Sir?" Aitchison also rose and saluted his superior.

"Assemble all patrol units and volunteers. We return to the Cape at sunrise!"

"Isn't that a bit hasty, sir," Aitchison retorted. "The Zulus may regroup under new leadership."

"Highly unlikely," answered Cloete with confidence. "Shaka was a fluke! A one-time occurrence for Africa. Without him those natives will revert to their natural state of snivelling old women! - No, we have nothing more to fear, and may the Lord be praised."

"Amen!" exclaimed Bellow, and swatted an African fly that had gone for his jugular.

CHAPTER XLII
"UBUSHA"(YOUTH)

Excerpt from the Colonial Office Chronicle & Diary as composed and updated by Tim Wilkins, Assistant to His Majesty's Assistant UnderSecretary for War and the Colonies, African Division: -- "'Nec audiendi qui solent dicere, Vox Popoli, vox Dei, quum tumultuositas vulgi semper insaniae proxima sit. - And we must not listen to those who keep saying that the Voice of the People is the Voice of God, since the riotousness of the crowd is always very close to madness.' Thus wrote the renowned poet Alcuin to the Emperor Charlemagne in the Year 800 A.D. As I consider this dictum written over a thousand years ago by the scribe of one of history's most powerful monarchs, I distinctly (and humbly) perceive the similarity between Alcuin's state of mind (at the time of the writing of his Latin Epistle) and my own inner turmoil as I now put pen to paper in the midst of 'tumultuositas vulgi' ('the madding crowd'). Like Alcuin who wrote of the singular exploits of the XIX Century Emperor of the Holy Roman Empire, I, too, - as selfordained 'raconteur' of the extraordinary circumstances of our expedition's dealings with Africa's Charlemagne, Shaka Zulu - am burdened by the fact that many of the occurrences related by me are so outrageous in import and so exorbitant in scope as to easily overtax the credibility of my readers (which I daresay are accustomed to a norm of existence that is greatly divorced from our native experience). I therefore hasten to adjoin that the incidents recorded here (which occurred directly after the attempted assassination of Shaka) are 'the truth, and nothing but the truth'!

"'Tumultuositas vulgi semper insaniae proxima sit,' Alcuin had written, and how appropriately! Indeed, far from being the Voice of God, the riotousness of the crowd at Bulawayo was as "close to madness" as can be achieved...

"As I had cause to note earlier, directly following the stabbing of the Zulu King, a collective state of pure bedlam and pandemonium had exploded forth from the multitude that packed the Citadel. Then, as the news of the murderous event spread throughout the land like fire through an arid field of wheat, the entire Zulu population found in Bulawayo its Mecca, and swarmed to the Royal Residence in varying states of delirium, fear and frenzy...

"Throughout the first night, the crowd increased so much that the noise of their shrieks became unbearable and, what with the heat and the pressing, asphyxiating mob, I felt as if I had been precipitated into the most abysmal reconditeness of Hell! Morning showed the horrid sight in a clear light. I am satisfied I cannot describe the terrifying scene in any words that would be of force to convey an impression to any reader sufficiently distinct of that hideous scene. Immense crowds of people were constantly arriving, and began their shouts when they came in sight of the Residence, running and exerting their utmost powers of voice as they entered it. They joined those already there, pulling at one another, throwing themselves down, without heeding how they fell, men and women indiscriminately. Many fainted from over-exertion and excessive heat. Several died trampled or suffocated. Others took their own lives, finding their situation too distressing to bear...

"As I strained through this crazed throng, greatly fearing for my own life and for that of my companions, I was suddenly faced with the most sickening part of this tragical episode. As part of the deranged, lunatic reaction to the eventuality of their beloved King's death, whole detachments of the Oofasimba Corps (the 'King's Own' guards) sifted through the crowds, dealing death with a blunt strike of the knobkerrie or a thrusting stab of their short spears. Some were put to death because they did not cry for their sovereign; others because they did not cry enough; and still others for putting spittle into their eyes (to simulate tears). And some were cruelly dispatched for sitting down to cry out of pure exhaustion...

"And so it went on, day after day for nearly a week: wailing, screaming, moaning, despair, thirst, starvation and death - until the turf of Bulawayo's colossal stockade was carpeted with human carrions, and the sky above was speckled and darkened with the horrendous swooping and hovering of buzzards and vultures..."

On the morning of the eighth day, Dingane kaSenzangakona Zulu strode through the chaos and carnage of the Shakan Citadel with a manner and bearing that were a reflection of the man's growing and markedly treacherous conviction that his plan with the Qwabe Pakatwayo had had the desired effect, and that he would soon be the Overlord of the Nation his half-brother had conceived and built.

Gaining with difficulty the top of the sloping cattlefold, Dingane stopped at the gates of the isiGodlo which were vigilantly guarded from the seething, rampageous throng by Mgobozi, Nqoboka, Mzilikazi, Joko and a contingency of the Ufasimba. In response to Mgobozi's restraining hand, the son of Senzangakona met the general's hostile gaze with a confident, placid air.

"Would you deny me access to my dying brother's side, general?" Dingane asked with disturbing calmness, his deceitful features sharpening to sternness upon adding: "Would you deny the legitimate heir to the House of Zulu the privilege of entering the isiGodlo?"

In response to these questions uttered with guileful rhetoric, Mgobozi's gaze shot to Ngomane who, as Prime Minister of the Shakan Nation, had tacitly been accepted as the focal point of authority whilst Shaka lay "indisposed". The older man nodded his approval, prompting Mgobozi to laggardly relinquish his hold of the crafty second-born grandson of Jama. Regarding the iziCwe commander with a superior smirk and a smile of comfortable diversion, Dingane swept past Mgobozi and into Bulawayo's Holy of Holies.

Moving towards the Royal Hut where Shaka had been concealed for over a week, Dingane's petulance flitted perusingly over the anxious faces of Cane, Holstead and Popham - who sat hunched together in the protective custody of the Ufasimba (the Swallows' presence in Bulawayo having become quite precarious since the Great Elephant had fallen prey to the assassin's blade). The two Whites and the half-breed followed Dingane's progress across the dusty turf with solicitous deference, well knowing that their fates might soon hang on the whims of this man's flippant personality.

Approaching the mammoth Royal Hut, Dingane matched a tense look with Nandi and Pampata - who sat in the shade of the euphorbia, unmoving - inaccessible -, their marmoreal features betraying a heart grown cold and shorn of hope. At the entrance to the King's hut, Shaka's half-brother found Wilkins, Farewell and Daniel squatting by the abode's threshold next to an immobile, spartan Ufasimba brigade. As the Swallows ran a restless eye over Dingane's surreptitious features, the Zulu spat out an interrogative that Daniel translated as: "He wishes to speak to our 'sangoma'."

Before any rebuttal was forthcoming from Farewell or Wilkins, Fynn emerged from Shaka's hut and blinked into the light of the sun in an effort to reacquaint his fatigued, bloodshot eyes to the brilliance of the heavenly globe.

"Sinjani isimo seNkopsi na?" Dingane asked stiffly of the man of medicine.

"He inquires after the king's health," said Daniel.

"Tell him that the King's condition is stationary," Fynn replied, scratching the skin under the matted, tangled strands of beard that had invested his cheeks and jawline and were descending in twisted wisps over his pale lips. "Tell him, the minute there is any change - any improvement - he and the people will be informed."

After Daniel's translation, Dingane's expression remained harsh and accusing. "Uma beqamba amange," he responded tartly and with a resounding click on the "q". "Bazongcwatshwa nayo iNkosi."

Fynn bent his attention to Daniel: "He says he hopes the Swallow's sangoma is not lying. He says if the King is dead and you are keeping the truth from the Zulus, your carcasses will provide the cushions for Shaka's grave."

Fynn's weariness had obviously honed his usual mildness of manner into listless impassivity, for, instead of reacting with apprehension, the Irishman was amused by Dingane's rejoinder and, with a crooked smile, commented under his breath, "If I ever needed a good reason to lie about his death - now I have one." Out loud, he told Daniel, motioning to the hut: "Tell him that if he doesn't believe me, he can go in and check for himself! I'm just trying to save the man, not hide him!"

"Ungangena uzibonele," Daniel told Dingane, and the Needy One glanced at the gaping entrance to the hut and the brooding darkness that dwelt beyond it with a nervous impatience and a slight quiver of the lips that greatly resembled fear. When those lips moved to speak, Shaka's half-brother had returned his attention to the Swallows, and his features were set in perfidy. "Ngizobuya ngokushona kwelange!" he scowled and strode off, out of the isiGodlo.

"He says," the Xhosa teacher interpreted, "he will be back at sunset to be further informed."

"The successor to the throne, no doubt," Wilkins remarked, following Dingane's departure with lingering inquiry.

"Yes," Daniel told him with wry mocking. "Patience was never a virtue in royal families."

"How is he, Fynn? - Really." Farewell's eyes were locked on the Royal Hut.

"He's dying, Francis," the Irishman advised the lieutenant, his voice vibrating with regretful irritation. "And there doesn't seem to be a damn thing I can do about it! If his fever doesn't break by sunset, he won't survive another night."

The news evoked a hot flash of fear to rush through Wilkins and Daniel as both men had the rather curious sensation that, however cruel and despotic, Shaka was easier to cope with then the dangerously volatile and unreasoning populace that moaned, wailed and dealt death beyond the relative safety of the isiGodlo's high palisades. As if reading the Swallows' minds, Ngomane cast a deliberate glance in the direction of the violent mob and, nearing them, addressed Daniel with a look of museful preoccupation.

"Sezizinde izinsuku," the Prime Minister spoke with a dignified cadence laced with urgency. "Sekunesidingo sukuthi isiswe simbone uShaka, manje."

"It has been many days, he says," the Xhosa told the Whites. "Too many days. The people must see Shaka. Now. Before the Unity of the Nation is threatened by civil war and anarchy."

"He's right, you know," Farewell agreed.

"That's impossible, Francis," was Fynn's exasperated brogue. "He's not well enough to stand, let alone walk to those gates!"

Farewell followed Fynn's raised hand to the portals of Bulawayo's secreted inner residence.

"Then we must help him," the lieutenant replied, simply and with an adventurous twinkle to his eye.

Within the darkened recesses of the Royal Hut, near the glowing hearth that disgorged billowing medicinal fumes into the abode's suffocating interior, Joko and Farewell lifted the prodigious, muscular frame of the Zulu sovereign from his bed of mats. The Emperor's body fell limp in their grasp, his arms dangling at his sides, his eyes closed and his head thrown back in an attitude of lifeless abandon, the veins standing out like whipcord in his long, sinewy neck.

Struggling under his massive weight - made all the more unwieldy and cumbrous by its state of passive vacuity - the two men, with the help of Mgobozi and Mzilikazi, raised the Great Mountain to a standing position. Then, as Wilkins helped to support the torso and shoulders, Fynn and Pampata dressed the king in his most sumptuous and dazzling attire, completing the regal wardrobe with the crane feather and the ivory tassels, which Farewell himself fitted to the monarch's huge arms and legs (in defiance, perhaps, of that familiar "jingling" sound which had more than once elicited in the lieutenant's soul that inexplicable sensation of dark cruelty and imminent death).

Then, as they steered the towering sovereign towards the hut's door, Farewell caught sight of a small porcelain jar protruding from Fynn's carpetbag. The jar was labelled "ROWLAD'S MACASSAR OIL", and the Englishman knew that the substance was used not only as a dressing for wounds and as a disinfecting tincture, but also (in the more extravagant circles of London) as a blackening hair dye.

"A hair dye!" the lieutenant exclaimed in his heart, as his attention darted to Shaka's greying temples and he was reminded of how the King had dejectedly taken notice of this disturbing sign of advancing years when he had viewed himself in the silver mirror.

And it was then that Farewell's Folly took another dauntless step in the direction of Africa's defilement. Indeed, whilst Mgobozi, Mzilikazi, and Pampata looked on with suspicious mystification, and whilst Wilkins and Fynn frowned in bewilderment, the naval officer smeared the Macassar Oil onto Shaka's head, working it into the hair, staining the grey with a "rejuvenating" measure of youth.

"An added touched, Fynn," Farewell grinned upon meeting the Irishman's questioning gaze. "For the sake of show."

Shaka's imposing body dwarfed both Farewell and Mgobozi as they supported the King's weight, guiding his leaden footfalls that moved, as if self-propelled, in the direction of the isiGodlo's tall portals.

Immobile in the shade of the euphorbia, Nandi looked on, spellbound by the figure of her son who looked so extraordinarily vulnerable in the buttressing grasps of the two human crutches. Then, when she lifted her gaze and saw the youthful shine of his hair, she froze in marvel and amazement. "Immortality," the word surfaced uncontrollably in her mind. "Could it be true that---?" she strangled the thought before it took possession of her soul.

Cane, Holstead and Popham stood wide-eyed and gaping upon spotting the remarkable procession as it stopped a few feet from the isiGodlo's gates.

"Tell him he must continue alone," Farewell ordered Daniel. "Alone - tell him!"

"Bathi bacela, iNkosi," Daniel spoke to Shaka. "Iqhubeke yodwa."

Yet Daniel's words, deprived of urgency and force, passed through the King's febrile mind unnoticed, like the breath of the wind, like the flight of a cloud; and Shaka remained unmoving, his body gradually slouching in the men's grip as unconsciousness regained a hold on his being. Sensing the emergency at hand, Farewell put his lips to the Emperor's ear and hissed: "Iqhubeke yodwa!" - repeating the command with fervour and authority.

The mighty Son of Zulu - his eyes remaining closed, his face retaining the dusty pallor of death, his features drenched with cold sweat and taut with exhaustion - heard Farewell's words spoken in the tongue of his birth and was jolted from his stupor into reeling awareness.

"Bathi bacela, iNkosi! Iqhubeke yodwa!" Farewell repeated once again, deliberately and sharply emphasising each word, perfectly echoing Daniel's pronunciation, - hoping, praying that the King understood.

Then, after a seemingly interminable pause, Shaka's body quivered and stiffened, and - almost imperceptible - the King nodded in agreement.

When the men disengaged their hold on the Great Mountain and left Shaka's side, the Zulu fought to keep his balance; then, calling upon his superhuman reserves of endurance and will power -- he took a step, alone, forward, in the direction of the maddened multitude.

Oddly enough, Dingane was the first to hear it; over the wailing, the moaning, the shrieking, the shouting, and the tumult, he heard it: - a soothing sound that gently penetrated the cacophony of the chaos like the whisper of a Fallen Angel in Hell. The sound of -- jingling ivory tassels.

The blood rushed from Dingane's features, blanching his lips and causing them to tremble as if touched by a icy wind. And the Needy One, the perennial "second-born, second-best", whipped his head round and caught his breath, gasping, gawking at the majestic figure of his half-brother standing - alone - at the gates of his private palace. Simultaneously with Dingane's own silent scream of insurmountable wonder and astoundment, the entire Zulu populace stood still as one man, and the wailing, and shouting, and weeping was, in a throttled instant, congealed to complete and utter silence.

The jingling returned - bloodcurdling in the deafened immensity of the Citadel. And, in that same breath of Time, Shaka's eyes sprang open and devastated the multitude with the intensity of their glare, - a look of infinite rage and immeasurable power. Overwhelmed by the ravaging deluge of Shaka's glare, the Zulus fell to the ground in one grand, whimpering sea of praise.

"Bayete!! Bayete, Nkosi!!" muttered Dingane fearfully, and in false praise.

"Bayete! Wena We-Silo!" cried Mhlangana, his face pressed against the worm-ridden corpse of a slaughtered matron.

"Bayete!! Bayete!" came the thunderous roar from the tremulous populace. Their Lord, the Great Mountain of Africa was alive and, for many, for most, immortal! Then, as one by one they noticed his blackened shiny hair, the tide of reverence swelled with the realisation that their Emperor had risen from the ashes of death with renewed youth!

Hearing that avalanche of praise, Shaka's tigerish lips pulled back in a smile that burst forth in maniacal laughter. Then the Emperor's body straightened with a flood of newfound vitality, and his eyes sparkled with a queer, malicious gleam and with the fire of life that momentarily curbed the suppressing onrush of Death's tide.

"He needed a dose of power, that's all," Farewell nonchalantly told Daniel. "That's usually the best medicine for a man like him!"

Hearing these words, as if understanding them, ever so slightly Shaka's eyes rolled to meet Farewell's smiling features. The Zulu returned that smile and in his feline countenance was the reflection of qualities completely foreign to his nature: pregnable trust, credulousness, susceptibility, and the hint of something that resembled gratitude.

And Nandi saw that smile and sensed something was wrong - alarmingly wrong! But she knew not what it was. Her attention returned to Shaka's "rejuvenated" hair, and, cocking her ear - ever so slightly - she shuddered deep in her soul as if she could hear the Hush of the Wind and its Voice...

*

...From the Summit of the Pinnacle, Sitayi read from the Book of Injustice, from the Gospel According to Africa, and her eerie sibilation penetrated the Firmament, whispering: "Life, Youth, Immortality. - What other shiny trinkets will they offer you in return for your Land, for your Birthright, for Your Freedom...for your Heart. What other shiny, resplendent trinkets will they offer you, My Child?"

"With what will they buy your innocent soul, Africa?"

*

"When do you expect full recovery?" Farewell asked of his thin, frail medical adjutant as they strolled alone in the vicinity of Bulawayo, their senses invoking the therapeutic beauty and magnificence of the African flora and fauna in order to momentarily relieve themselves from the tension and disquietude procured over the past few days.

"Even a creature as exceptionally robust as Shaka needs time to reclaim the thresholds of life." Fynn answered as his eyes roamed to the waters of the Mhlatuze that flowed placidly at their side. "Give him a couple of days at least." He turned to look at Farewell with a wry smile. "Before you engage him in further discussions on that 'alliance' with 'brother Joji'."

"Do I perceive irony in your tone, Fynn?" Farewell grinned at the Irishman good-heartedly. "Do you still feel that killing your Mephistopheles is the best way to save our Colony?"

Fynn hesitated musefully before answering, his gaze becoming instantly lost in the swirling currents of the African river. "Kill him?" he thought. Never! - On the contrary! There was something terrifyingly grotesque in the state of Shaka's soul which greatly excited Fynn's religious and scientific imagination and which made the Irishman long to know more about this extraordinary creature. Indeed, Shaka, Nandi, their relationship and the power they wielded was as unique and as fascinating as only something inhuman or "superhuman" can be, and Fynn craved to better explore the mind of "his Mephistopheles"; to learn, perhaps, or - to teach, to listen or to share. He wasn't exactly sure. Yet one thing he did know: he was glad Shaka was still alive. For many reasons. Most of them quite personal. And as far as the Colony was concerned, well - call it selfish, if you will, but there were few things further from his mind.

"Though intriguing from a purely literary point of view, Francis," Fynn finally spoke in reply. "The concept of curing someone to then murder him is, in practice, ludicrous - especially for a medical man such as myself. Besides," he smiled, "after the assassination attempt, I'm starting to think that Shaka's hut is the safest place for us in Natal."

The lieutenant laughed out loud, adding: "Especially after that 'miracle' of yours."

"Francis," Fynn's expression became suddenly grave as he stopped and took hold of the lieutenant's arm. "We've saved the man's life. I trust his gratitude will be tangible enough. Do you think we could dispense with other 'miracles for the sake of show'? You know: -- Aladdin's Lamp, resurrection, Macassar Oil...How does that old adage go? 'Fools rush in where Angels fear to tread.' Well, since we've been here, I fear we've done a great deal of rushing and very little treading. I daresay the Angels won't let us get away with very much more."

"Oh, I don't know, Fynn," the lieutenant still wore his disarming grin. "The Angels have always struck me as a rather understanding lot. - But I do agree. We'll wave the supernatural ploy. - If Shaka will let us." In response to the Irishman's brow knitted in puzzlement, Farewell explained: "Like most great men, Fynn...Shaka is a 'believer'. The Empire he has built was firmly installed in his imagination long before it actually became a reality. As you say, you've saved his life - yet now I fear you must still deal with that imagination."

"Are you saying he wants us to play God?" Fynn was astounded by the notion.

"Not exactly, Fynn," Farewell retorted in search of clarity. "But when you've reached the top of the mountain, as Shaka has life can become...well, very lonely and solitude plays odd games with one's mind. Think of Alexander the Great. When he realised there was nothing left that needed conquering, he begged Aristotle to supply him with a Supreme Being who could fill the sudden emptiness he felt in his heart. - I think God exists because we need Him..." frowning, shaking his head in indecision, the lieutenant considered: "Or is it the other way around? - At any rate, Fynn, you must brace yourself. You may soon have to account for that Bible you're carrying."

* * *

"Was he a member of the Ufasimba?" Shaka lay on his bed of mats, his voice laboured and his ponderous chest heaving with the lingering onus of fever and pain. At his side was Pampata, and, beyond the crackling hearth, were Ngomane, Dingane, Mgobozi, Joko, and Mzilikazi.

"No, Baba," Mgobozi replied. "He was an imposter."

The relief was visible on the Emperor's face, as his eyes remained lost in the interweaving play of the lapping flames and he asked, softly: "Did he confess to anything before dying?" "No, Baba," Joko shot Dingane a deliberate gaze. "We were deprived of the opportunity of questioning him."

Dingane felt the tension tightening at his neck and shoulders. He compressed his lips and lowered his gaze in a bid to conceal any expression that might devulge his true state of mind and his fear of being discovered. When his eyes were once again raised, he was chilled to find Shaka's galvanising stare fixed on his own.

"A shame" Shaka mused aloud with a long, telling sigh that caused a suspicious uneasiness to steal over Dingane's features.

"May I speak, Baba," came Mkabayi's voice from the threshold of the Royal Hut.

"Come forward, woman," the Emperor said in low, sonorous tone, shifting his gaze to take scrutiny of the unexpected visitor.

As the sister of Senzangakona strode into the hut, Dingane turned to stone, his uneasiness rising inexorably to a pitch of sheer dread and terror. Then, when his paternal aunt stopped at his side and shot him a deliberate oblique glance, the Needy One heard her say: "I know who was responsible for the attempt on your life, Baba," - and the breath caught in his throat and his heart beat frenetically with a rush of adrenalin. Dingane returned the woman's sidelong glance, and his wide, horrified eyes shone with chastened pleading and with a craven supplicant appeal.

The brief exchange was not lost upon Shaka's keen purview. "Well..?" he said, urging Mkabayi to speak.

"The assassins were sent by Pakatwayo," she confessed, and Dingane's vision blurred slightly and he felt the hut's pavement reeling at his feet.

"The Qwabe?" Shaka queried intrigued. "How can you be sure?"

"Perhaps my brother's son can tell you, Nkosi," she replied and passed the task of elucidation onto her dastardly nephew. Yet Dingane remained silent, not trusting himself to speak.

"Well..?" Shaka urged once more, his eyes locked on his half-brother.

"It is so, Baba," the Needy One was groping for traction in his bid to save himself.

"How do you know?" Shaka's voice was now forceful and sharp.

"After you were wounded, Baba," Dingane started, his perfidious mind racing to fashion a shell of lies round a core of truth. "I sent spies north of the Pongola. They tell me that Pakatwayo has been meeting secretly with Zwide and Soshangane..."

Shaka's face hardened at the mention of the Ndwandwe king and his commander whom he knew had escaped the Battle of Qokli Hill and the Destruction of Dluvunga. Mzilikazi was also suddenly strident with anger at the memory of Ntombazi, the hideous witch who had beheaded his father.

"They have built a new and powerful army trained in the ixwa and the methods of Shaka," Dingane went on, his tone gaining in confidence as he related the objective truth, omitting only his own direct involvement. "The spies tell me that an attack on kwaBulawayo was planned as soon as Pakatwayo and Zwide received confirmation that the Great Elephant had fallen."

"You surprise me, Dingane," Shaka said after a short pause, a thin smile punctuating his loathing for the man who shared his lineage. "I had no idea you cared about the security of the Nation, as long as that Nation is still mine." The eyes of the two half-brothers met and locked. "Mgobozi and Joko tell me that after my - accident - you were quite vehement in reminding them that we share the same Forefather's. Was it your intention to suggest that - should anything happen to me - you would rule in my place?"

Dingane quickly lowered his eyes, fleeing from Shaka's probing gaze. The Emperor's question hung heavy in the hut's suffocating air, its tortuous implications - those of treason and murder - suffusing the blue-black fumes emitted by the burning medicinal herbs.

"I cannot know how my words were interpreted, Baba, nor can I control the effect they have had on others," Dingane finally replied, his shifty eyes remaining lowered so as to conceal their glint of falsehood and deceit, so as to avoid the contention of Mgobozi's and Joko's ferret-like accusation. "I can only say that my words were born of fear." Dingane looked up now, confident that he could deliver the rest of the reply without revealing his faithless plotting. "Fear that the Nation you have built could be torn ashunder through lack of guidance. But I've no need to feel that any longer for you are alive and well."

"Yes, Dingane," Shaka said in an uncanny whisper which caused the blood to turn to ice in the other man's veins. "I am alive and well." When those feline eyes closed, dismissing his half-brother, the Emperor ordered: "Mgobozi, alert all the regimental homesteads. We march on Zwide and Pakatwayo after the harvest. For the second and last time"

"Yebo, Baba," Mgobozi bowed in obedience.

"And choose fifty of the Ufasimba and have them impaled. In the center of the cattlefold - where all can see."

A charge of amazed terror shot through all present.

"But, Baba---" Mgobozi started.

"Even if the men were imposters," Shaka broke in. "My regiment should have realised it before the blow was dealt!"

"Yebo, Baba," the commander of the iziCwe bowed in submission.

"Leave me now," Shaka's voice became suddenly weary, as if his tense conflict with Dingane had drained him of all energy. "I must rest."

When the others had left, and Ngomane was alone with his sovereign, the King asked, his lids still drawn in darkness: "Have they found the second assassin?"

"Yes, Nkosi."

"And has he...talked?" The Emperor's tone had become impersonal, like that of a man in a trance.

"Yes," Ngomane nodded and adjoined, with a touch of regret: "After much...coaxing. In essence, he confirmed Dingane's relation of the facts."

"In essence," Shaka echoed with a faint smile. "Only in essence. My father's treacherous son forgot the most important point:- the fact that he, too, was a part of the assassination plot."

"You truly believe that, Nkosi," Ngomane was shocked by the news.

"This morning I believed it, Ngomane. Now, after our meeting, I am sure. His treachery was there for all to see. It was in his own eyes, as well as in those of my father's sister."

"And yet you let him live?"

"I need him alive, Ngomane. He will attract the dissenters like cow-dung flies. And when they are ready to strike again, I will be prepared!"

*

"Thank you for your silence." Dingane fell into step with his aunt, the springiness in his stride betraying his great relief and elation. "May I ask to what I owe your unexpected allegiance?" "Family," Mkabayi said curtly, without turning to acknowledge the other's presence. The woman had never liked Dingane and his attempt to kill Shaka certainly did nothing to improve the man's image in her eyes. "I will not condemn the son of my brother to certain death."

"Could it also be due to the fact that you are known to be a 'cautious' woman?"

Mkabayi stopped to face Dingane and her hatred for him grew as she read his eyes and saw the execrable decay of a soul infested with the purulence of falsehood.

"We all know that you have always supported Shaka thoughout his troubled life," Dingane told her with a cunning smile. "You have often gone as far as risking your own reputation to defend that man and the 'dream' of the empire he was to build. And now that that dream has become reality, I wonder..." His features took on the ugly taint of malice. "If you ever had to choose between Shaka and the Nation, with which would you side?"

"They are one and the same!" she snapped back feeling the bitter taste of bile rising in her troat.

"Of course! Of course! One and the same!" Dingane was quick to agree - too quick. "But what if they were not," he resumed his train of thought, spinning his web. "What if the day came when you felt Shaka was - unintentionally, perhaps, and through weakness - destroying his own dream--" Dingane's brow arched with emphasis, "Your own dream. What if that day came? With which would you side. -- The Man or his Empire?"

Mkabayi held Dingane's gaze steadily with her own. Though she was loath to openly admit it, the Needy One's words struck a familiar note in her heart, and she knew that his insinuations, though culled from guile and hypocrisy, somehow reflected thoughts she herself had secretly entertained. Disturbing thoughts! And, under Dingane's subtle, vile inducement, she was inevitably drawn to consider Shaka's peculiar behaviour in the recent past: the grand - ludicrously grand! - reception he had staged for the Swallows; his attempt to "be like them" which had been exemplified in Shaka's stubborn need to tame Farewell's quadruped; the absurdity of having to make a point of his privileged position by killing that young girl, Tsani, who the Swallows had saved; and then, the entire canvas of the "immortality affair", absurd in concept, yet of great danger "for the Nation" if it were truly to become Shaka's obsession.

Yes, Mkabayi could not help but admit to herself that the danger was there -- personified by the presence of the Swallows! In fact, now that she thought of it, even when Shaka had been stabbed, he had appealed to Fynn's "magic", dismissing Majola, dismissing the salva'tion offered by his own people in a bid to possess the "powers" (if powers they truly be!) of the Strangers from the Bird with White Wings!

Yes, the danger was there, she told herself and an'swered out loud: "If I had to choose between the Man and his Nation, and I was certain that one could and must exist without the other, I would choose the less vulner'able. As you say, Dingane..." Mkabayi smiled as an odd and rather morbid intimacy suddenly sprang up between them. "Your father's sister is known to be a cautious woman."

*

That same afternoon, in compliance with the Zulu Emperor's wish, fifty members of the Ufasimba were marched to two perfectly symmetrical, parallel lines up upright stakes planted in the central clearing of the stockade. And, whilst the Zulu population looked on in dread and horror, the fifty men were lifted onto the stakes and impaled.

* * *

"Ego sum Via, et Veritas, et Vita..." intoned the Portuguese priest aboard the old wench of a galleon that bore the name "Santa Maria de Portimao". I am the Way, the Truth, and the Life. "...Nemo venit ad Patrem nisi per me."

Parmananda, Marinho, and the picturesque crew of the "pirate" ship knelt piously upon the tattered, warped planks that stretched across the vessel's maindecks, - all heads lowered in prayer, parched hands joined in supplication.

"Te benedico..." the priest solemnly uttered in blessing, a manicured hand appearing from under his heavy gilded chasuble and snaking its way to the silver container of Holy Water proferred by an altar boy. "In nomine Patris," a splash of blessed water rained upon the captain and crew of the galleon, a holy droplet tracing a divine path down Parmananda's scar. "Et Filii, et Spiritu Sancti."

"Amen," grunted the old galleon's captain, rising heavily to his feet. Then, plucking a gold sovereign from the folds of his arabesque attire, the illegitimate grandson of Blackbeard ambled to the representative of God and pressed the coin into the priest's spongy white grasp with his own dark calloused hand.

"Deo gratias, Capitao," the Catholic cleric nodded, pocketing the shiny sovereign, and thus consummating on Earth what the Lord had blessed in Heaven.

"Espero que sim, Padre," Parmananda grumbled with a menacing tone that had all the makings of a threat, as he brushed past the prelate and made his ponderous way across the gangway and onto the docks of Cape Town.

"Adeus, Senhora," the "driftwood" smiled, taking Elizabeth's hand in his own in the guise of a departing salutation.

"When should I expect to hear from you," the woman inquired, her gaze instinctively wandering to the recently sanctified ship that was a thousand sovereigns heavier - her thousand sovereigns.

"Six days, six weeks, six months..." Parmananda replied with disturbing carelessness. "Only God can tell how and when we find your husband. And, as you see..." The captain raised an arched finger in indication of the priest and altar boy. "We are in His hands now."

"Why do I have the feeling that I'm making a terri'ble mistake, captain?" Elizabeth asked, her blue eyes roaming over the sloping ridges of Parmananda's devious face.

"Eu creo, Senhora, that it is racial," the "pirate" considered, scratching his beard and screwing up his swarthy features in feigned concentration. "The Ingles are brought up to hate the Portugues 'to distrust them! It is part of history! But we will prove that history is wrong! Eh, Senhora...?" the man grinned, displaying a remarkably polished gold tooth. "We will show history! I, a Portugues, have your money - and you, an *Ingles*, have my word! Eh, Senhora! We will see which is worth more!" Treating Elizabeth to a short chuckle, the man kissed her hand and bowed: "Adeus, Senhora Farewell. Parmananda will find your husband! He will show history his word is worth your gold!"

Elizabeth's searching glance lingered on the "driftwood" as he turned and sauntered back to his ship, shouting out the orders to cast off.

"Yes," she whispered to herself with little convinc' tion and with mounting anxiety. "We will show history."

"Mrs. Farewell?" A young male voice intruded upon her muted reverie. "Thomas Pringle, Editor, 'South African Commercial Advertiser'," the thin man touched his hat by way of personal introduction, when the woman had turned to regard him with an inquisitive glance. "If you will permit, madam, I have an inquiry or to to make."

"In reference to what, Mr. Pringle?" was Elizabeth's curt, defensive rejoinder. She knew that the "Commercial Advertiser" was, together with the "South African Chro'nicle", one of Cape Town's leading "public opinion" newspapers. She had recently read an article it had published regarding her husband and Shaka, one that had left her outraged!

"Your husband," Pringle answered with a mellow, win'ning voice. "And Shaka Zulu."

"That's old news, isn't it?" Elizabeth remarked caustically as she spun round and started off down the wharf.

"Is it?" Pringle shot back, falling into step at her side.

"As your newspaper has so dauntlessly reported, Mr. Pringle, they're both dead!" Her voice tingled with bit'ter irony as she quoted from the article: "'Francis Grorge FArewell, His Majesty's valiant knight pitted against the Zulu Dragon - inflicting death even as the warmth of life drained from his own veins'! - I have rarely read such trash, Mr. Pringle, even in the shoddi'est of drawingroom plays! It nettles me to no end to have my husband's name tainted by your waggish tabloid!" She quickened her step, adjoining a blunt: "Good day, Mr. Pringle!"

"I agree, Mrs. Farewell," the journalist would not be put off and clung to her side. "It was trash! But poerhaps we can make up for it by printing the truth. With your help, that is."

Elizabeth stopped and started stiffly out at Table Bay, her arms clutched defensively in front of her.

"And what is the truth, Mr. Pringle?" she asked at length.

"'His Majesty's valiant knight pitted against the blindness and racial bigotry of the Cape's Governor'."

She spun round and their eyes met.

"Somerset firmly believes," Pringle told her, "that the only way to deal with these 'kaffirs' is to blow their heads off. From what I hear, your husband's outlook was more humane. His eulogy could be quite a lesson for the future administrators of Colonial Africa."

Elizabeth dropped a suffered gaze at the mention of the word "eulogy". Pringle caught that look and suggest'ed: "But then there's no need to write a eulogy, is there? He's alive, isn't he."

"And on what do you base that assumption, Mr. Prin'gle?" Elizabeth inquired with a tense, humourless smile.

"On your woman's intuition and on the thousand gold sovereigns you've paid that pirate Parmananda to sift the Rio de Natal in search of a 'ghost' whose name you bear."

Their gazes remained locked in mutual scrutiny, her desire to trust the man weighing her growing distrust of all men.

"I admire your resorcefulness, Mr. Pringle," she said, remaining impenetrable to coaxing. "But I suggest you concentrate your efforts on more current topics. As I said, my husband's old news!" Disengaging her atten'tion from the man, Elizabeth strode off.

"If you should reconsider, ma'am," Pringle shouted after her, "I think that you'll find that our 'waggish tabloid' may prove to be your best ally. And, perhaps your only one." Elizabeth slowed to a stop. When she turned to look back at Pringle, the journalist's eyes were on the "Santa Maria de Portimao", it's patchwork sails swollen against the wind as the vessel crossed Table Bay towards the open sea -- in search of a ghost named Farewell

CHAPTER XLIII
"NKOSI JAMA KOSI"(KING OF KINGS)

In the life of individuals as well as nations, there comes a moment when, for no definite or easily definable reason, a whole course of events is suddenly and unpre'dictably changed and a Hidden Hand is caused to come to the rescue of Creation. Though capricious and often mer'curial, this mysterious "divine meddling" in the Affairs of Man is ever-present in the History of our worn-out Earth, and the books that relate Humanity's gradual and systematic defloration of the virginal planet Mankind was given are teeming with examples of battles won and lost for reasons that defy human understanding. Indeed, even devote men of science like Charles Darwin - who consumed their lives searching for the Moves of the Hidden Hand - often (in moments of deep contemplation) had reason to entertain the fantastic notion that the Missing Link in Man's evolution might be Divine. In other words, as Thomas A Kempis stated simply in his XV Century writings on "The Imitation of Christ": "God is amongst us...and only He can fully know the Course of all People and Things."

Even People as complex and inimitable as Shaka Zulu and Things as outlandish and Kafkaesque as his soul. In light of this, if one were to explore the Last Act in the existence of one of the world's most magnificent and most tragic Emperors without accounting for the workings of this capricious Hidden Hand, one might, like Darwin, make the mistake of leaving Life's dramatic evolution with a Missing Link.

The fire in the Royal Hut had dwindled to ashes when Shaka reopened his eyes. Gradually and with a formidable effort of the will, the king overcame the debilitating languor of his enduring fever and glared at the hearth's red embers, allowing their throbbing glow to quicken his pulse towards full wakefulness.

When the King's mind was revived, with sensation came the remembrance of what was probably the most significant journey in his recent existence: - those few short steps that had brought him from the stupor of death to the gates of the isiGodlo. And he remembered Febana at his side, and the urgent command the Swallow had uttered in Zulu: "Bathi bacela! Iqhubeke yodwa! - Alone! You must continue alone!"

"Alone". That seemed to be the one word that best defined the Zulu's life, and Febana's reminder that he should "continue alone" had a much greater meaning for Shaka than the few steps he was obliged to take unaid'ed. For him, in his feverish state, it signified that he should not surrender to the soothing solution to Loneli'ness offered by his companion

Death; it signified, for Shaka, that he should cling to life and "continue" down his solitary rode.

"Continue alone!"

And he had. He had reached the high portals of his palace and, once again, his Citadel, his world had been alive with his praises. Yet the lingering joy of his recent return to glory was suddenly and forcibly erased by the sharp pain that ripped across his flank. And it was then that he was reminded of Dingane's treachery, the treachery of his own House - one which would lead to another great war with the Ndwandwes.

And he felt tired. Ever so tired.

How long had it been since the stabbing? A day? Two days? A month? - How long had it been since he'd last rested? A year? Two years? A lifetime?

Alone.

As his eyes remained entranced by the hearth's flickering red glow, and as the events following the stabbing were summoned to the fore of his pulsing, febrile consciousness, an arresting thought occurred to him: the Swallows, Febana's sangoma, had been respon'sible for his "resurrection"! If they had never come, or if they had somehow delayed their arrival on the shores of his Kingdom, he, Shaka, - would be dead!

The deduction was simple: he owed the Swallows his life!

And then there came another thought. Disquieting! The Swallows, Febana, had literally carried him to the portals of his thatched palace so that his people would have proof that he had survived. If the Whites had not had the foresight to do so, or if Febana had delayed this important verification, - might Dingane have swayed the masses against their King? It was possible, Shaka knew. No monarch, not even the Great Elephant, is ever completely sure of his own power; especially when that power is founded on an emotion as volatile as Fear. Yet fortunately, Febana had had the keen-wittedness to readily thwart the threat of Dingane's treachery.

The next deduction: through Febana's intercession, he owed the Swallows his continued hold on Power!

Life and Power. Two immensely important commodities for a man whose State is founded on Total War, Total obedience to the Paramount King, Total Control through Fear of the Unknown.

Then the momentous implications of his train of thought struck him with a blow as debilitating as the assassin's blade. If he really owed these Strangers with Skins of Sorghum something as crucial as his own Life, as the retention of his Power - how could he ever again have total control of his empire?

"In my Kingdom," he had told the Whites, "Life be'longs to Shaka?" Yet, after this "resurrection", was that still the truth? To whom did life belong - now? To whom did Shaka's Life belong - now?

Sheer panic suddenly gripped the Zulu and an unfami'liar feeling of trepidation entered his heart. Scanning the interior of his hut, realising he was alone, the Emperor had the urgent, immediate need to see Nandi, to take her hand, to feel her warmth, the reassurance of her touch, - to hear the soothing voice that had made bearable a lifetime of suffering.

Grimacing against the sharp pain of his wound, Shaka drew a breath and hitched himself up to a sitting posi'tion with the intent of crying out to his guards to fetch his mother. But as he was poised to do so, the King's eyes fell on Fynn's carpetbag that the Irishman had left in the close vicinity of his patient's mat. His monumental curiosity aroused, Shaka reached out, and his large hand hovered warily over the "magic" medical kit before his confidence grew to the point of snatching it up by the handle. Placing the bag on the floor before him, the King eyed it with a mixture of watchful awe and suspicion. Then, with a good dose of circumspection, his palms perspiring slightly with the tension of suspense, Shaka reached for the metal clasp that secured the bag's spine and carefully lifted it (in the manner in which he had seen Fynn do it). Finally, after yet another wary pause, drying his sweaty hands on his massive thighs, swallowing back the nervousness, Shaka opened the medi'cal kit, gingerly, with deliberate regard for its myste'rious contents, - for the "Unknown".

Rocking forward on his haunches, Shaka peered into the Swallows' carpetbag and smiled with childish antici'pation at the thrilling new world that was contained within it. A world of bottles, and glass, and metals that shined resplendent. A world of instruments and gadgets made of bronze, copper, and brass. A world of measuring and weighing with dials, meters, and knobs. The world of the Whites' technology and of their desire "to be as gods". And seeing this world, Shaka sucked in his breath and placed a hand over his mouth, which he had opened in marvel.

Then, grinning with excitement, he reached in and, with a light touch of his long mighty fingers, caressed the myriad of mysteries that were nestled in the medical kit.

His hand closed round Fynn's stethoscope. Lifting it, he pressed it to his ear and, mimicking the Swal'lows' "sangoma", he feigned an expression of intent lis'tening, as if a heartbeat were trapped within the instrument itself. Then, grasping a small binocular microscope, he looked it up and down, running a fascina'ted eye over its lenses and knobs. At length, his peru'sal moved on to study a surgeon's cranium brace, a pair of artery forceps and scissors, catheters, tourniquets, blood-letting scarificators, cupping glasses, apothecary jars, skull saws and ligature silk...

A fascinating new realm of the Playthings of Healing.

He brushed his finger along the polished edge of a metal scalpel, and, finding the instrument razor-sharp, he experimented with the tool on the surface of his arm until a trinkle of blood rose to stain his skin.

Grinning all the more, fascinated by the tiny "wea'pon", Shaka held the scalpel like a miniature ixwa, locking with an imaginary shield to thrust its blade into the heart of an invisible foe. Then, tilting the blade to examine the unique and refined method with which the Swallows had ground the metal to a highly sharpened edge, Shaka's attention was abruptly caught by his own reflection on the surface of the gleaming iron. He looked at his own mouth, the lips curled in amuse'ment; at his chin and cheeks, the skin blotched with prickly patches of beard and stubble; he gazed at his eyes and saw the lingering glossiness of fever; he looked at his hair and...

He froze, as his heart leapt with an electrifying jolt that verily took his breath away. The grey was gone and the deep, uniform blackness was the same as it had been in the Zulu's youth.

Youth!

Life! Power! Youth! - Immortality! Was it really true, then? Did they really have such Magic?!

And his mother's words returned to him: "You have no need for their Magic! You are the Mountain of Africa and the Lifeblood you have given this land will forever flow in the veins of Our People. Do not search for more! - If the Swallows offer you wings to fly, it is because they wish to make you their victim."

"No, mother!" Shaka said aloud, his voice echoing in the empty Royal Hut. "I will become their victim only if I do not make their knowledge, mine!"

"It is illusion!" Nandi's voice resounded in his heart.

"Is it illusion that I now live, mother?" he asked the hut's darkness. "Is this illusion?!" he hissed, plucking with a quivering hand the strands of "rejuvena'ted" hair.

And the panic returned to pound through his veins with a rush of frenzy. And the perspiration of excite'ment intensified to drench his body with the tangy odour of pulsating anxiety. All reticence gone now, Shaka turned over the carpetbag, ripping it, shredding it, dumping its contents onto the hard floor of the hut with a crashing of metal and a shattering of porcelain and glass. His chest heaving with the burden of unreasoning apprehension, the Zulu Emperor frantically rummaged through the instruments, and tools, and shards of glass and porcelain in a blind, pathetic and absurd search for the secret to the White's power.

All of a sudden, the King's attention was gravitated to Fynn's black Bible protruding from the midst of the bag's bestrewed contents, and he fell into complete stillness, his eyes narrowed on the odd "instrument" with renewed curiosity. Picking up the book - the first he had ever set eyes on - Shaka gazed at the gilded Cross on its cover and wondered of what use this con'traption might be. Was it too a bringer of Life, of Youth, of Power?

Awkwardly, the King bent back the pages and frowned in bewilderment at the printed words that snaked across the thin white paper in perfect parallel formations of twos, threes, fours and more; -- the lettering being displayed in a "military" fashion, just like his regi'ments on the parade grounds.

"Shaka," Daniel's voice came to his mind. "A written word that is read...Shaka."

The King whipped his gaze round to glare at the mat fastened to the hut's central post and his flaming eyes ran over the lettering -- S H A K A.

"Shaka," he breathed his own name as if "reading" it, and repeated it once again, with hesitancy, as if the five-letter word belonged to another man, to another dimension.

"Writing," the Xhosa's voice was re-evoked, "is used to store what you speak today so it can be heard genera'tions from now. It is a form of immortality."

His brow furrowed with increasing fascination, mixed with a fierce, stark, elementary craving to assimilate and possess knowledge - and, through it, the Unknown. The King's eyes rolled back to glare at the Bible that was flopped open in the cradle of his fingertips. With a clumsy sweep of the hand, he flipped back the pages to a goldleaf etching depicting the Sermon on the Mount. And seeing that tall, broad-shouldered, handsome man with the long dark hair and beard standing august and impos'ing high atop of a rocky hillock, His arms spread as He addressed the multitudes that gaped at Him entranced, -- seeing the Image of Christ, Shaka was instantly captiva'ted, and the Zulu could see that, like himself, this charismatic Man must represent Ascendancy and Power!

With ever-mounting inquisitiveness, the King's hand swept to another etching: Christ on the Jordan, standing in a fishing boat, preaching to the huge, enraptured throng of men, women, and children who clung to the lake's banks. As Shaka's mind took in the figure of the Man addressing the enthralled masses, the Zulu was auto'matically reminded of himself, and of the huge populace that was at his own beck and call. And he sensed an affinity with this Man, a common purpose in - Power!

Feeling the overbearing allure and attraction of the Book's protagonist, the Emperor eagerly sought out another etching and found the engraving of Christ's triumphant return to Jerusalem on the Palm Sunday before His death. Here, too, Shaka read the overriding presence of Power! It was in the stately manner in which the Man rode on the back of the quadruped. It was on the faces of the immense crowd of the Holy Land that pressed to get closer to Him.

Shaka grinned, his eyes beaming in resonance with the majesty of the Man in the Book. He then turned to another etching, and the Zulu's eyes sprang wide in startled consternation and terror, as a murmur of grief escaped his lips with an undertone of painful regret.

The picture which had thus evoked the wonder and sorrow of the Great Mountain was that of the Crucifixion. Incredulously, Shaka gawked at the body of Christ hanging from the Cross, at the iron stakes driven into his hands and feet, at the Crown of Thorns, at the human skulls scattered on Golgotha, at Mary the Mother of Christ and at the weeping figure of Magdalene, and at the hostile Roman guards who held weapons that were disturbingly similar to the ixwa.

Deeply distressed, his proud soul railing against what he saw, Shaka swivelled the Book to the left and to the right, and lifted it closer to his eyes, narrowing his lids in closer inspection of the chilling portrayal of the Passion. His attention was snagged by the deep gash on Christ's side made by the soldier's spear, and Shaka looked at his own chest and at the spear wound on his left flank.

And he sat mystified, his mind reeling in the maelstrom of implications that his fervid belief in the Supernatural elicited, - a swirling vortex of fantastic explanations for this extraordinary and telling coincidence. "Could this similarity of wounds indicate that this Man had also been betrayed by one of his own House?" Shaka mused. "Had there been a Dingane in His life as well?"

The remarkable affinity which he had previously sensed with the Man of the Book, grew to disconcerting proportions in Shaka's soul and, his eyes fixed incredulously on the etching, he wondered how such Power could end in humiliation, solitude, betrayal, and the most infamous of deaths!?!

And, in his feverish mind, Shaka resolved to know more about this "Master turned Victim", and to avoid the mistakes He made.

*

"Ngubani lo?!" Shaka asked imperviously, his raging eyes clouded with impatience, the Bible (open to the etching of the Crucifixion) clutched tightly in his outstretched hand.

"Who is He? He asks." translated Daniel, and Fynn felt his heart sink in his chest.

The Irishman had sensed something was wrong when the messenger had come, bringing urgent word from the Great Elephant that he wished to see the Whites' "sangoma" immediately. He had known there was something diabolical afoot upon noticing (with deep anguish and revulsion) the writhing bodies of the impaled Ufasimba guards. And he had been sure that the Emperor's ferocity had been revived (along with his good health) when he had spotted his torn carpetbag and the tools of his trade scattered on the floor of the Royal Hut. Yet, he had never entertained the notion that he would have to "introduce" the Son of God to the Son of Zulu.

"The ways of the Lord are infinite," Fynn told himself as the shadow of a smile toyed with his lips. Infinite and highly unpredictable. There had been many times in Fynn's adventurous life when he had been called upon to abide by his Faith, to stand firm in God's name, to administer the teachings of Christ, to baptise and pray, - to be a good Christian in other words. But he had never been called upon to explain Christ and who He was, who He is. And, quite frankly, the Irishman wasn't sure he could explain Christ conclusively - not even to himself, let alone to a potentate like Shaka who did not appear to be terribly amenable to long theological and scholastical dissertations on the works of St. Thomas's "Summa Theologica", or the varying definitions of the Greek "dichaion", or the "articulus stantis aut cadentis ecclesiae", Luther's "justicium coram Deo", or the "Corpus Mysticum" and the Transubstantiation of the Body and Blood of Our Saviour.

No, Fynn sighed as he gazed at the Crucified Christ on Calvary - no Latin and Aramaic, here, - no Councils of Trent and Constantinople, no interpretations of the Church's interpretations of Scholasticism's interpretation of the Middle Ages' interpretation of Paul's interpretations of the Imitation of a Man called Jesus who is God.

No, Fynn reflected. Shaka wanted nothing more than what all simple Christians want: Christ "in a nutshell". Yet how can you fit into a nutshell the Alpha and Omega, the Beginning and the End of the Universe?

With Faith, the Irishman motivated himself. And a touch of Hope and Charity.

And, of course, a great deal of simplicity.

"He was a king, tell him," Fynn answered at length, his eyes moving from the Bible's etching to the concentration etched on Shaka's face as his flaming, impatient eyes darted to Daniel.

"Yinkosi," the Xhosa translated in one word.

"Joji...?" the Emperor inquired, amazed.

"No, not George," Fynn replied, waving the translation with a wry smile. "He was the King of Kings. Christ."

"Akusiyena uJoji," Daniel interpreted, smiling inwardly at the idea of "teaching" the Christ he had learned at Bellow's Mission Station to a creature as extraordinary as the Zulu King. "Yinkosi yama Kosi. - uCristo."

"uCristo?" the Zulu inquired with a loud click.

"uCristo," the Xhosa nodded. "Inkosi yama Kosi."

Suspicious, Shaka leaned back and crossed his mighty arms in front of him, the Bible still clutched firmly in his fist. His probing gaze rolled from Daniel back to Fynn, and he held the Irishman's steady look as he paused to allow the possibility of another "King of Kings" besides himself to be digested by both his pride and his intellect. Standing near the hearth, immobile, Nandi watched her son, and her emerald-green eyes were devoid of expression save for a watchful vigilance, - a guarded, sharp-eyed defense of the Child from the illusions of the Swallows' "magic".

"uCristo," Shaka's sonorous voice returned to fill the hut with its biting inquiry. "Wayemkhulu Jojo na?"

"Was Christ greater than George? he asks."

"Yes," Fynn could not help smiling again at the colossal understatement. "Greater than George. Greater than--," the man of medicine hesitated slightly. "Greater than Shaka, tell him."

Daniel's astounded gaze shot to Fynn, and he tensely and fearfully queried of the White man: "Are you sure you want me to say that?"

"Only if you believe it, Daniel," was Fynn's level reply.

After a brief pause, in which the Xhosa's soul weighed his Christian belief against the probability of imminent martyrdom, Daniel courageously returned his attention to the Zulu King and translated: "Yebo, Nkosi. Wayengaphezula ka Joji. Engaphezula ka -- Shaka."

As further proof of the Zulu's extraordinary nature, instead of assuming rage or resentment, Shaka grinned, his eyes gleaming, charged with excitement by the rivalry suggested between himself and "uCristo".

"Ukufa ngalendlela," Shaka remarked, glancing down at the etching in the Bible with a depreciatory air. "Akuyifanele inkosi."

"This death, he says," Daniel told Fynn. "Hanging from a tree near weeping old women. - It is not worthy of a king.

"No, it is not," Fynn admitted with an air of sadness.

"Cha, akuyifanele," the Xhosa told Shaka, his voice translating both the words and the sadness of the other man.

Having expected to elicit a reaction of anger, Shaka was greatly disturbed by the dispassionate tone of the rebuttal, and, considering it suspect, he observed the two men with a long questioning gaze before breaking his own silence with: "KwaKwenzenjani na?"

"How did he come to die? he asks."

"He was betrayed, tell him," Fynn sighed, his chest heaving with the burden of Judas's treachery. "By those he loved most."

"Wanikelwa yibona," came Daniel's Zulu. "Labo owayebathande kahule."

"Yebo," Shaka nodded, Fynn's reply confirming the Zulu's suspicion that a true affinity existed between himself and the Man of the Book. "Yebo," he repeated, starting to see what the other "King of Kings" had done "wrong". "Kwakuliphuta, inKosi kakufanele ibenothando."

"Yes, he said," came Daniel's voice. "It is a mistake to love. Especially for a king."

Fynn sensed, more than heard a short, muffled gasp of deep affliction, and he shifted his gaze to Nandi. When his eyes met hers, their souls touched one another, fleetingly, before the Great Female Elephant withdrew from the Irishman's searching glance to peer musingly into the shadows. Yet in that fleeting moment, Fynn perceived Nandi's deep melancholy, her most private distress, her solitude, and he was prompted to consider the most saddening aspect of Power: the tears of Christ at Gethsemane.

"Lamabutho," Shaka was saying, his attention narrowed on the etching of the Passion. "Kwakungamabutho akhe na?"

"He asks:- the warriors near the tree, with the spears - were they part of his regiments?"

"He had no regiments, tell him," Fynn wore a set smile, the pride of being Christ's representative welling in his soul. "Only twelve men. Unarmed."

"He won't understand that sort of self-sacrifice," Daniel mused aloud. "Why don't we just tell him that---"

"Daniel," Fynn broke in, catching the Xhosa's eyes. "Do you understand that sort of self-sacrifice? Really understand it?"

"No, I suppose not," the Xhosa admitted at length.

"Nor do I," Fynn confessed. "And no matter how many books they write on the topic, it will remain a mystery. So...why don't we just relate the facts and give Faith a chance."

"Very well, Doctor," Daniel answered with an affectionate smile that betrayed his growing respect for the other man. Turning to Shaka, who had observed their brief exchange with a wondering glance, the Black teacher explained: "Wayenganawo amabutho, Nkosi."

"Yize kunjalo," Shaka hissed with scornful incredulity. "Wena umbiza ngekosi yamaKosi?! Wayengaphezula ka Shaka?!"

"And you call him the King of Kings?! he asks.- Greater than Shaka?"

"Yebo, Nkosi." Fynn's reply needed no further elucidation.

"Yini?" Shaka's voice was raised in exasperation.

"Why? he asks."

"You see his lips, Nkosi. They are moving..." Fynn started calmly, by way of an answer.

"Uyabona, Nkosi, ukuthi uyakhuluma," Daniel told the Emperor, and Shaka instantly furrowed his brow in a close inspection of the etching.

"He is speaking," Fynn went on. "He is saying: 'Forgive them, Baba, for they know not what they do."

"Uthi, bathethelele ngoba abazi ukuthi benzani," was the translation uttered with a tonal quality of a prayer.

"Yekela?" Shaka's voice rose to a sharp emphatic roar, as his indignant gaze shot from the Bible to Febana's sangoma. "Ungabusa kanjani ngokuthethelela?"

"Forgive?!, he says. How could anyone expect to rule with such a foolish strategy?"

"Many are of the same opinion," the Irishman softly agreed.

After Daniel's short translation, the King leaned forward on his throne, his face coming but inches from Fynn's, his eyes trained on the "sangoma" in silent indagation of the Irishman's meekness of reply. From the moment Fynn had remarked that "uCristo" was greater than Shaka, the Zulu had felt invigorated by the anticipation of some sort of verbal conflict in which their wits -- his own and that of the man who had "miraculously" saved his life -- would be pitted against one another in a healthy contest (that Shaka had all the intentions of winning). Yet, instead of an enlivening row, Shaka had been faced only with absurdities clothed in dispassionate humility and resignation. How, the Zulu now wondered as he peered inquisitively at Fynn, could men who possess the keys that open the coveted portals of Life and Youth be so naive as to believe in a King of Kings whose whole reign seemed to have been founded on Faith and Folly.

"Umfowabo, nJoji," Shaka finally asked. "Uthini yena na?"

"And what does George think of this King? he asks."

"George, most of his country, most of his people," Fynn's words were modulated with a level, objective quality, "and people all over the world, worship this King as the Messiah - the divine sovereign announced by the Ancestors."

"uJoji nawo onke amaKhosi," the Xhosa said, disturbingly aware of the intensity with which Shaka received and weighed each spoken word, "omhlaba akhonze kuyo lenkosi yamakosi."

When Daniel had finished, Shaka sat motionless and stupefied, staring blankly ahead in dumb amazement. This coincidental affinity with the Man in the Book was, for the Zulu, becoming most disquieting. Indeed, the Swallow's definition of uCristo's mission seemed to echo Shaka's own Covenant with his Land, his place as "the divine sovereign of whom the Ancestors spoke when they sang to the Wind". Could there have been two Covenants, two Prophecies? - Shaka reflected in his muted abstraction. One for the Zulus and one for the Swallows? Were there two "Nkosi yama Kosi" - one for the Whites and one for Africa? And, if so, which was stronger? Which would ultimately prevail? Which would be the Language of the "People as One - Bantu"?

With these pressing uncertainties searing through his brain, the Emperor shot his mother a fierce look of supplication through which transpired the confounded state of his mind. Yet Nandi could do little to appease her son, for she too was greatly shocked by Fynn's reply, and, outraged by the existence of this usurper "King of Kings" who would challenge her son's prophetic supremacy, her feline eyes glared defiantly at the Irishman.

Unable to entirely perceive the true motivations behind Shaka's appealing anguish and the accusatory harshness of Nandi's gaze, Fynn inadvertently proceeded to make matters worse by announcing, with praiseworthy religious fervour: "Christ is Lord of the Swallows, Lord of the Zulus, Lord of all men. - He is the Son of God, Lord of the Heavens."

When Daniel had painstakingly finished rendering Fynn's words into Zulu, Shaka asked, with a sinister, eerie scowl: "Amandla akho uwathatha kuyena?"

"Do you derive your powers from him? he asks."

"He is Power, tell him!" the Irishman's voice was raised in a manner, emphatic and bold, which left Daniel wondering whether martyrdom was not imminent after all. "With Christ in your heart, tell him, you are stronger than all the regiments on earth."

"Uma unoCristo," the Xhosa referred, trying to clear his voice of his apprehension, "ungaphezula kwawo onke amabutho omhlaba."

"Kuleli amaZulu, yinye inKosi yama Kosi," Nandi spoke unexpectedly, her voice riding the strident sibilance of a threatened snake protecting her nest. "Lowo nguShaka!"

"The Heavens belong to Zulu, she said, and Shaka is their son," Daniel related as he watched the magnificent figure of Nandi striding to the King's side. "If the Swallows wish to be his friends, she says, they must remember that in this land there is only one King of Kings - Shaka!"

Fynn's chest heaved with submission. "He had been a fool," he told himself with a feeling of awful desolation, "- a fool to think the idea of Christ could ever find respondence in this abysmal Hell; to think that God could ever reward him with such a bizarre and singular conversion."

"Yebo, Baba," Fynn bowed and neared the throne. But when he reached out to retrieve his Bible from the Zulu monarch, he found that, surprisingly, Shaka hesitated, as if he were reluctant to part with the Book.

Fynn smiled, reminding himself that the Ways of the Lord of Heaven are indeed infinite, and said: "Tell him the Book is a gift - from the Swallows."

"Izinkonjane, Nkosi," came the Xhosa's translation. "Ziyakupha lelibhuku." Shaka's sinister expression altered slightly upon hearing of Fynn's present. The Emperor merely nodded his acceptance and tightened his hold on the Bible. Yet, as Fynn and Daniel offered their salutations and turned to leave the Royal Hut, Shaka spoke again and, as he did so, the Xhosa froze in his steps and a doleful moan was wrenched from his soul.

"What did he say?" Fynn was anxious to hear.

"He wants to know," Daniel could barely formulate the words. "He wants to know if...if Christ also resurrected."

"Holy Merciful Mother...!" Fynn prayed in a hushed, suffered brogue and added: "Forgive us! -- Francis was right." He whispered to himself, the tears of despair welling in his eyes. "He does want us to play God!"

Then, slowly turning back to face Shaka, the man of medicine nodded, answering: "Yebo, Nkosi."

Instinctively both Nandi and Shaka bent their attention on the etching of the Passion, and, for them, that limp figure of Christ was suddenly and miraculously bestowed with the breath of Life. And, for both Nandi and the Child, that handsome, bearded Man in whom the Swallows believed was no longer just a drawing. In light of His Resurrection, Christ had assumed for them an objective existence. So real and so tangible that Shaka was caused to look up at Fynn and ask: "Ikhaya lakhe likuphi?"

"Where does he live? he asks," Daniel said with a deep sigh.

"I was expecting that question," Fynn admitted, and ran a dejected hand over his angular features. What had started out as an attempt to wedge the "Corpus Mysticum" into a nutshell, had unwarily evolved to the threshold of the Ascension. "No," Fynn mouthed the word with a bitter taste of anguish. I cannot be expected to explain the Ascension to the Emperor of the Zulus! God must understand that, and He must allow me a concession or two ...'for the sake of show'.

"Tell him--" Fynn said, avoiding Daniel's eyes. "That He's in England. With George."

"What?!" the Xhosa retorted in a strained hiss.

"Well He is in England, isn't He?" the brogue was laced with exasperation. "Figuratively speaking."

"Shaka isn't figuratively speaking!" the Xhosa rebutted.

"All right, Daniel," Fynn's tension was about to explode to a surface of anger. "You play missionary. You explain the Ascension to him! And don't leave out the part about the glowing clouds and the chorus of Angles."

"You sound like you don't believe in it," the Xhosa was shocked.

"Of course I believe in it!" the Irishman hissed under his breath. "That's the whole problem! I don't need to understand it! I believe in it! 'Credo ut intelligam', if you know what I mean!"

"You European Christians are a very strange breed," Daniel retorted with pursed lips.

"Just tell him what I said and stop discriminating, will you, Daniel." Fynn was angry now.

"Ikheya lami lisekwaJoji," Daniel translated, not daring to meet Shaka's penetrating eyes.

Shaka regarded the two Swallows with suspicious intrigue, while his long fingers lazily traced the contours of his deep black hair.

*

"The Macassar Oil, Francis! Did you really think he wouldn't notice it?! He thinks we've rejuvenated him. Physiologically as well as aesthetically! - And now he wants us to to the same for his mother!"

"Simmer down," was the lieutenant's soothing reply as his gaze wandered pensively to a distant herd of elephants languishing in the muddy waters of a shallow pool where the two men were accustomed to come in search of peace and concentration. "In principle I think the entire matter is definitely veering to our favour. And I think you've done marvellous work. By the way," there was a hint of derision in his tone, "where did you tell him the Holy Saviour was staying - at Buckingham or Windsor?"

Deeply grieved by Farewell's flippant air, Fynn compressed his lips in sign of annoyance. The Irishman was already sorry that he had dared to toy with the unmovables of his life. Indeed, for this devout Catholic, the Resurrection and the Ascension were not only matters of Faith, but of deep respect as well, and Fynn now felt that his hasty reply (born of cowardice, as he saw it) was a lack of respect on his part - respect for God.

"I'm sorry, Fynn," Farewell was truly penitent. "That remark wasn't called for. But I do feel - whether you find it dastardly or not - that what you did has greatly furthered our cause. - You've used Christ to link Shaka to Britain, you see. And now we must comply with the Zulu's wishes and make that bond more secure by rejuvenating his mother."

"By what...?!"

"In a manner of speaking," Farewell was quick to adjoin.

Yet as Fynn gazed at the lieutenant, he glimpsed a sparkle in the other's eye that greatly troubled him: -- the glint of idle boastfulness that accompanies vainglory.

The glint of what the Latins called "Superbia".

The Sin of the Fallen Angel.

*

Dressed in her most fastuous attire, verily glistening in the resplendent morning sunshine, Nandi sat aweinspiring and majestic on top of the nine-foot-high Royal Dias at the summit of Bulawayo's parade grounds. At her side were Shaka, Farewell, Wilkins and the Swallows, and Pampata, Mkabayi, Nandi's daughter Nomcoba and son Ngwadi, Mbiya, Ngomane, and the Zulu generals.

A devotional stillness held captive the intrigued and enchanted populace of the Zulu Nation that was pressed into the five-mile circumference of the Shakan Citadel. Henry Francis Fynn strode to the top of the dias wearing his old straw hat and a look of despondence, feeling very much like a reluctant harlequin in some grotesque slapstick pantomime plucked from the pages of John Rich or Laurence Sterne.

Gently opening the porcelain jar labelled "ROWLAND'S MACASSAR OIL", the dejected Irishman proceeded to debase the two most cherished things in his life: - his profession and his faith. Pouring a splash of the dark liquid onto Nandi's head, Fynn worked the oil into the Queen's hair, rubbing it deep into the roots, spreading it with a uniform renascence of youth's colour.

When all the grey was gone, and the hair was once again completely black, when all were gaping in silent marvel and veneration, Pampata neared her Queen and proferred the silver mirror that Shaka had given her during the first tragic audience with the Swallows. Before directing her gaze at her own reflection, Nandi faltered, casting her son a look of deep uncertainty. Shaka smiled at his "youthful" mother and, pleased, nodded, urging her to take scrutiny of her renewed freshness, of her beauty now once more intact.

Nandi gasped with a surge of elation at the sight of the reflection that seemed a reflection of what had been. Biting her lip to withhold the tears and to conceal her commotion from her subjects, the Queen of Queens of Africa, the Nkosikasi indlovukazi, the Great Female Elephant rose to her feet and stood tall for all to see. An instant later, the entire populace had sunk to the ground and lay pressed against the turf, virtually trembling with superstitious devotion for the rejuvenated mother of their immortal lord.

Nandi shifted her attention back to her son who was now beaming with joy and pride, and she smiled. The appeasement of the great vanity inherent in all beautiful women seemed to have momentarily won a place for the Swallows in her favour. And when the tears of gratitude could no longer be restrained, she wept and thought of the Mighty Leopard who had been given wings to fly, considering that perhaps her son had been right after all to seek out the Power of the Strangers. True Masters, she resolved, have nothing to fear from "Magic", for their entire existence is a thing of illusion.

Farewell was also beaming with pleasure. His "alliance" was going well, he thought and, turning to look at Fynn, was surprised to see that, like Nandi, the Irishman was also crying.

"...and forgive us our trespasses," Fynn was lost in silent prayer, "as we forgive those who trespass against us. Lead us not into temptation, but deliver us from..."

The words stuck in Fynn's mind, and he found it impossible to finish the prayer, for his heart kept changing the words. Instead of "deliver us from evil", his soul resounded with "deliver Africa from us".

*

Directly after the "Rejuvenation Ceremony" (as Wilkins was sanguine enough to call it in his Diary & Chronicle), Shaka officially pronounced his deep gratitude to the Swallows, uJoji, and uCristo for the Life and Youth that had been awarded to the Son of the Heavens and His Mother. Addressing Febana through Daniel, the Emperor urged the leader of the Whites to relieve the Great Mountain of his burden of debt and to suggest a manner in which Shaka could make his gratefulness more tangible.

Without hesitating, Farewell gave thought to his ivory "Trading Company" and resolved that a conferral of land might well be a suitable gift for all concerned. Indeed, Shaka had so much of it, a few square miles more or less made little difference. "Besides," the lieutenant remarked to Wilkins with a cunning smile, "perhaps the best way to keep Shaka from going to the Colonies, is to bring the Colonies to Shaka."

And so the land grant was drawn up by Febana, and the conferral sealed in front of the entire Zulu Nation in a ceremony that would be a landmark in the Rape of Innocence. In the grant - to all intents and purposes - Francis George Farewell, R.N., His Britannic Majesty's Representative in the Shakan Affair, was buying Land with a coinage that sparkled far more than silver or gold: - the currency of Life Renewed.

The document was officially read aloud by Wilkins (as the man of the Colonial Office) and simultaneously translated by Daniel. It read:

"I, Inguousi Shaka, King of the Zulus and of the country of Natal, as well as the whole of the land from Natal to Delagoa Bay, do hereby, on the Seventh of November, in the Year of Our Lord eighteen hundred and twenty four, and in the presence of my Prime Minister and General Staff and of my own free will, grant, make over and sell onto Francis George Farewell & The Farewell Trading Company the entire and full possession in perpetuity to themselves, heirs and executors, the Port or Harbour of Natal together with the islands therein and the surrounding country, together with all the country inland extending about one hundred miles backward from the sea shore, with all rights to the ivory, rivers, minerals, and articles of all denominations contained therein. The said land to be from this date for the sole use of Farewell & Company, their heirs and executors, and to be by them disposed of in any manner they think best calculated for their interests, free from any molestation or hindrance from myself or my subjects.

"In witness whereof, I have placed my hand being fully aware that in so doing I bind myself to all the articles and conditions that I, of my own free will and consent, have agreed upon before the said F. G. Farewell whom I hereby acknowledge as the SOLE CHIEF of the said country with full power and authority. I do this as a reward for the Whites' kind attention to me in my illness from a wound and for their exceptional regard for the Queen Mother."

Signed,
SHAKA, his X mark, King of the Zulus,

Native witnesses: Ngoomanee, his X mark
Mmgoboosi, his X mark
Daniel (Zulu Interpreter), his name

It should be noted that, though Shaka himself showed little or no reluctance in undersigning this document and carefully and fastidiously scratching his "X" on the place indicated, both Ngomane and Mgobozi were greatly disturbed by this concession that made the Swallows Shaka's official neighbours, and the Prime Minister and the general of the iziCWe hesitated before giving witness, and finally did so only under the forceful urgings of their Emperor.

It should also be noted that Mkabayi sat through the land grant with ever-increasing apprehension for the emotional state of the Son of Zulu (that she saw as a form of ingenuousness) and for the wellbeing of the Empire he had created. Being a highly rational and practical woman (devoid of weaknesses like vanity), Senzangakona's sister gave no real importance to concerns as frivolous (or so she saw it) as "rejuvenation", and it mattered little to her whether or not the Stranger's blackening oil truly had the "magical" properties Shaka seemed to believe it had. No, Mkabayi had no need or desire to be "forever young". Indeed, in her dedication and unselfishness, all she cared about - all she had ever cared about - was the "long life" and health of the Nation, and she was now troubled to see that its King had given away a chunk of the Zulus' sovereign land in return for a self-indulgent, purely personal gain for himself and Nandi. Consequently, when Mkabayi's eyes met those of Dingane, when she saw the Needy One's knowing smile, she could barely conceal from him her deep preoccupation for the future of Shaka and his relationship with Those with Skins of Sorghum.

After the concession had been signed and witnessed, Shaka rose and thus addressed the Zulus: "Ngithi ziqapheleni izimanga," his voice roared to all corners of his Citadel, "zabamhlophe. Isizwe sonke masibahlonipke ngendela..."

Daniel's instantaneous translation went: "He desires his people to look at the Swallows and to see their bond with the Heavens, and to consider Shaka's own greatness and courage in having broken with Fear and dared to share his land and wealth with Joji's and uCristo's friend's from the sea. He expects his Nation to pay the Whites the respect due to Kings and to..."

"The History of Weaponry distilled into a sticky, dark liquid," Wilkins whispered to Farewell under Shaka's portentous oratory. "Macassar Oil! And to think the Colonial Office thought it was whiskey!"

"I never thought hair dye could become a political asset," Fynn grumbled under his breath.

"That's because you're not a practical man, Fynn," smiled the lieutenant smugly.

"All right," Fynn retorted. "I'll be practical! The jar of dye's almost empty. What happens when it runs out and those hairs start sprouting back on their royal skulls."

"Ingenuity, Fynn," "Chief Febana" whispered out of the corner of his mouth as his set smile remained trained on the Zulus ("his" Zulus now). "Ingenuity's the 'dye' we'll use when the bottle runs out. And I'm confident that we've quite enough of that - a supply as lasting as our own daring."

*

The next morning it was decided (between Shaka and his new chief Febana) that the Swallows should travel back to Port Natal in order to check on the other members of the expedition (indeed, Biggar, Gin-naro, Richard Holstead, Hockly and Thompson must, by now, be worried to no end about their absent companions) and to officially settle in to the newly-acquired "colony" of the Farewell Trading Company. It was further decided (to Holstead's and Cane's great joy) that an elephant hunt would be organised to celebrate the land grant and the new bond of "friendship".

In less than seven days, the Whites' cavalcade was in sight of the Indian Ocean and the smattering of huts and makeshift abodes that comprised the residential area of Port Natal. The reunion that followed was characterised by boisterous merriment and muted incredulity as the men who had stayed behind (and who had given up hope of ever seeing their comrades again) were told of the trials and tragedies, and of the unexpected and overwhelming final success of the first mission to the Zulu Emperor.

The next few weeks were occupied in the completion of Fort Farewell - which Wilkins was to describe as: "...situated on the flat near the entrance to the Bay and covering an area of about two hundred square yards with foundations that, under the Lieutenant's instructions, were built in the shape of a triangle."

Finally, after over a month of hard work, on the Eve of Christmas, 1824, the Union Jack was run up on the fortress's pole and the "Julia's" cannon (which had become an integral part of the Fort) was bravely fired, and - with the high-handedness of XIX Century imperialism - the Port of Natal and its surrounding hinterland were declared British territory.

*

The Great Elephant Hunt (as Wilkins was to call it in his Journal) took place from the third to the tenth of January, 1825. The troupe engaging in the "sport" was mixed, with both Zulus and Whites taking part. Mixed was also the manner of execution - ranging from the Shakan hamstring method to the more merciful practice of firing muskets. In these eight days, 31 bulls and 42 cows met their death in a hunt that was deemed most "successful". The tusks were cut and loaded onto the "Julia" in preparation for the first return voyage with cargo of the Farewell Trading Company. Being that all the men (save for Farewell, Fynn, and Wilkins) were most anxious to revisit the environs of their habitual existences, and inasmuch as the "Julia" (with its weighty cargo) had the possibility of carrying only a limited human charge, straws were drawn, and four men were selected to return with the ship.

On the 16th of January, 1825, the sloop "Julia" left Port Natal with sixteen tons of ivory and a crew consisting of Richard Holstead, Hockly, Biggar, and Alex Thompson (who bore a missive written by Farewell for his wife Elizabeth; and another for Lord Charles Somerset informing the Governor that "to date, I do not feel that Shaka is a threat to our White Settlers; on the contrary, he has shown his benevolence by recently appointing me one of his chieftains"). The sloop was to journey to the Cape, dispose of its cargo in a reliable wharfside warehouse (belonging to Elizabeth's stepfather, Johann Peterssen) and return to Port Natal in time to transport another load of ivory before the end of Summer. It was also deemed necessary that, on her voyage back to Natal, the sloop should carry a crate of porcelain jars with a "black, sticky liquid" known as "Rowland's Macassar Oil" (the "long lasting brand" - it was noted - the sort that didn't easily wash off).

When the "Julia" left on January 16th, it was stressed by Farewell that, all other orders being equal, she (or another vessel in her place) must return no matter what! Indeed, the lieutenant vehemently pointed out, without a ship the expedition was marooned and at the mercy of a man whose hair would keep growing - even after the porcelain jar was empty.

But, after sailing from Natal's Bay, the "Julia", her cargo, and her crew were never seen or heard from again.

And no one ever really knew what Fate she had met on that foresaken Wild Coast.

No one. - When asked years later, even Elizabeth Farewell's explanation was merely a conjecture. Yet - call it woman's intuition - till the day she died she seemed sure that the loss of the "Julia" was directly linked to the disappearance of her thousand gold sovereigns and of a man known as Parmananda (who, due to hard time, may have found it condonable to break the word given to his dying mother).

"We will show History, Senhora, which is worth more. Your money or my word!" the buccaneer had said.

And, like Parmananda, Farewell's Folly would also show History that was worth more: - the land of the Africans or the word of Strangers.

CHAPTER XLIV
'UCRISTO"(CHRIST)

"The New Year of 1825 began quite auspiciously," was the entry in Wilkins's Colonial Office Diary, "with the success of the Great Elephant Hunt that proved to be good sport all around and an additional cohesive element in the congenial relationship that seemed to be budding between ourselves and Shaka. Indeed, the Zulu King further evinced his friendship towards our party by personally participating in the hunt and, I might add, promptly showing himself to be the best man on the field, bagging over ten of the one-and-thirty bulls that went to plenish our impressive and successful catch.

"Towards midmonth, the Lieutenant, Fynn, Holstead, Cane, Popham, Gin-naro, and I witnessed the launching of the "Julia" with her sparse crew of four (Biggar, Hockly, Richard Holstead and Thompson) and her large cargo of ivory. For myself, I admit that upon watching the sloop's bows glide gently into the sea, I felt somewhat elated by the prospect of the riches embodied in the gleaming white elephant tusks that, at our mission's end, were to be apportioned to each of us in equal shares through the Farewell Trading Company. Yet, at the same time, I was quite unnerved by the thought that we'd now become castaways (in a manner of speaking) and was greatly concerned for our welfare, knowing that the brooding restlessness I now experienced at our ship's departure would stay with me until her sails appeared once again on the horizon...

"To our good fortune, our small community of seven (Daniel was still obliged to reside at Bulawayo) was soon augmented by a sizable contingency of locals, both woman and men (most still able-bodied and labour-worthy) who readily attached themselves to Port Natal and, building their beehive huts in the sloping bush country at our shoulders, were most desirous and keen to be of service to us in any way possible...

"Under the Lieutenant's orders, we soon had the cooperative natives engaged in planting a field of corn for our Colony, which they completed much to our satisfaction and, in the turn of a couple of months, the harvest-bird (which the Zulus hailed with joyful acclamations) had made its appearance...At the direction of Cane, Holstead, and Gin-naro (who avows to have been a farmer's son in his native Naples), the locals soon began to cut and to garner the corn with every demonstration of delight at the favourable season. Their labour (united with that of our own men) was a pleasing sight to contemplate, and, thinking of my post at the Colonial Office, I felt enlivened to see these ignorant, wild, untaught, and unsocial creatures industriously labouring in harmony with the Whites in the highly valued occupation of reaping the fruits of the soil, which their own efforts had sown.

"This communal harvest revived in me many pleasing anticipations, and, in those pleasant, peaceful days, I was convinced that if the natives could be brought to congregate in bodies, settle near us, and live in social order under our protection, in time we might present a little Colony which would become flourishing, and realise much benefits and happiness to the whole of its inhabitants; a Colony that, by example and the enforcement of consistent rules and regulations, might, in time so improve the moral condition of our Zulus as to remove them altogether from the darkness in which they had been born and nurtured...

"It was in this serene and reposeful period - from Christmas, 1824 to the April of 1825 - that we bent our efforts upon the learning of the Zulu language so as to facilitate communion with the locals and in order to impress Shaka (on our next visit to his Citadel) with tangible proof of our desire to be a united fellowship in Natal. The time required to learn the language so as to be understood by the natives depends on the facility one has for the acquisition of foreign tongues. I am proud to relate that the Lieutenant, Fynn and I were in possession of the language in less then three months, whereas Cane and Holstead took considerably longer. And Gin-naro (for lack of interest, perhaps) acquired only a smattering of words, relying heavily upon hand gestures to make himself understood (which, incidentally, was also the manner in which he spoke English)...

"Towards the termination of that first Harvest at the Port, Fynn returned from his monthly visit to Bulawayo -- visits which he was required to make for the purpose of administering (in a solemn ceremony in the presence of the entire Zulu populace) Rowland's Macassar Oil to the 'royal crowns' of both King and Queen Mother (before the sprouting greyness became dangerously manifest). As I looked upon Fynn's approaching figure - pale and gauntly - riding on the back of his weary mount, I was reminded of Don Quixote returning from one of his valiant battles with the windmills of Spain. And in truth, judging from Fynn's appearance and the melancholy expression that had become his 'African mask', Miguel Cervantes might well have used the Irishman for a model in the creation of his tragicomical hero, - 'the mad Knight of the Rueful Countenance' (as Quixote was called). Indeed, dispensing the 'elixir of life' in an empire founded on blood and death is as absurd as being a knight-errant in an era when Chivalry was long past; keeping Shaka 'young' was very much a 'tilting of windmills'.

"And this overall 'quixotic' impression of our beloved doctor was enhanced by his singular appearance -- which I shall now attempt to set forth. Mr. Fynn is in stature somewhat tall, with a prepossessing countenance. From necessity his face was disfigured with hair, not having had an opportunity of shaving himself for a considerable time. His head was partly covered with a crownless straw hat; a tattered blanket, fastened round his neck by means of strips of hide, served to cover his body, while his hands performed the office of keeping it round his 'nether man'; his boots he had discarded for some weeks, whilst every other habiliment had imperceptibly worn away, so that there was nothing of a piece about him. And, if the reader finds occasion to smile at this description, I hasten to remind him that the rest of us looked very much the same -- bearded, long-haired, and garbed in the worn and shredded remnants of our European attire, and greatly supplemented by skins, hides, and decorative plumes. In the spirit of this forced masquerade, the Lieutenant had gone as far as donning a headdress of sorts that was meant to distinguish him as the official leader of our group, - as Chief Febana. And though Mr. Farewell insisted that he wore this distinction solely for the benefit of our natives, some of us (especially Fynn) had cause to wonder whether the Lieutenant wasn't indeed truly enjoying the role of a Zulu Chieftain...

"On the morning of the day directly following Fynn's return - a morning in April, it was - we were a little surprised at receiving an early and unexpected visit from Maloori, one of the most illustrious elder tribesmen of our Colony, a man of consequence and one who apparently shares the favour of the Zulu Royal Court (being related by blood to the King's Councillor Lutuli). This man, Maloori, alleged charges against two of our party. Charges which gravely threatened our relationship with Shaka, as well as our position of respect and predominance in the mixed community of Port Natal. According to the allegations, it seemed that Holstead and Popham, whilst out hunting one day, had met Maloori's young wife and offered her some beads to induce her to comply with their impure lustful wishes. When the faithful and indignant female had boldly refused their proferred presents, it was alleged that, whilst Popham held a musket to the poor woman's head, Holstead accomplished by force what he could not obtain by persuasion or bribe, and violated the unwilling girl.

"Shocked by Maloori's accusation, the Lieutenant ordered that Holstead and Popham be immediately presented to him. At first, the two men denied the charges, but, after a violent outburst on the part of Lt. Farewell (who had reason to suspect Holstead of lying), Popham confessed to the ignoble crime, forcing his accomplice to follow suit.

"We were all quite aghast and outraged by this dishonourable conduct on the part of our men, which so defeated our general good intention of elevating the moral condition of our Colony's natives. Our spokesman, the Lieutenant, found he could say nothing of any effect to our illustrious visitor - especially since the whole affair had already been communicated to the King himself. Consequently, Mr. Farewell, Fynn and I resolved to set out at once to Bulawayo in the hopes of saving the situation...

"On the eve of the sixth day, we arrived at the entrance of the Citadel's private quarters and were soon admitted. A domestic informed us that the King was holding an 'en-daba' (a council) with his warriors for the purpose of discussing an upcoming military campaign: a major war against a King Zweedy (I gathered the name to be) and his tribe of Nawandees. When we were finally brought to the King's presence, Shaka received us very coolly and showed no apparent impression (favourable or otherwise) relative to our acquired knowledge of his language...and, to our surprise, instead of immediately mentioning the violation of Maloori's young wife, the Emperor acquainted us with the war he was planning against those who had made an attempt on his life and spoke of the necessity of our accompanying him. We were, quite understandably, taken aback by the proposal and attempted to explain to him the nature of the laws of Joji's country and the duties they imposed on its subjects - especially in regard to attacks on other nations. Hearing this refusal, the King's voice took on a good deal of wrath and he reminded us of how dependent we were on him - especially after the departure of our vessel.

"When the Lieutenant would not be swayed by the threat and renewed our refusal to fight at his side, Shaka finally referred to the disgraceful behaviour of our two men, Holstead and Popham. He told Lt. Farewell that the incident had not come as a complete surprise to him, for when the Whites had first arrived at Bulawayo, his general Mmgoboosi had already informed him of the regrettable lack of discipline that existed in our ranks (it was here that Shaka made direct reference to the episode of the killing of the ostrich, and to Holstead's repeated contempt for the Lieutenant's orders). The King also saw fit to remind us of Holstead's behaviour at our first meeting in Bulawayo, at the shameful way he had leered at Pampata -- highly disrespectful for a guest in a foreign land. It was predictable, Shaka noted, that a man like that, without proper correction, would inevitably jeopardise the wellbeing of all. And, in an effort to resolve the matter of Holstead once and for all, the King remarked, matter-of-factly: 'He will have to die! To appease Maloori, Lutuli and his family. A death as disgraceful as the violent crime committed.' - 'Impale ment,' he suggested, in a manner that caused us to recoil, like from a serpent's hiss or a lion's growl.

"In an effort to save our undeserving companion from a fate truly 'worse than death', we readily acknowledged that he and Popham had done wrong and deserved severe punishment, but endeavoured to persuade the Emperor that impalement was not 'the custom amongst the subjects of Joji (and uCristo, Fynn quickly added)' and that perhaps we could devise another, more 'traditional', penalty.

"Oddly enough, Shaka's tone became abruptly milder, more familiar, and he observed, running a hand through his blackened hair, that 'he was still our friend' and would do 'his utmost to respect the custom of Joji's and uCristo's subjects'. Yet, he confessed, he must appease his Elders who were quite impassioned by the regretful incident. 'Accompanying him to battle might be a way of gratifying them,' he remarked, coming round full circle to his original request. 'After all,' he adjoined, 'Febana was his chief, and it was the custom, when the King proceeded in person to war, for all generals and chiefs to follow'...

"And so it came to pass that we -- all of us: Fynn, the Lieutenant, Cane, Daniel, Gin-naro and I, and a terrified Popham and Holstead -- found ourselves 'marching to war' with our courage, our muskets and the "Julia's" cannon. For myself, I must admit that, at the outset of the campaign, I felt no ordinary sensations of anxiety and apprehension. I was young and inexperienced, had not yet been in a military engagement, and knew not what awaited me. - Had I known, I daresay I would have had forebodings of no pleasing description...

"On the 17th of April, 1825, we crossed the Encootoo Hills and were on the banks of the Eencome River ..."

On the dawning of the day following the annotation in Tim's Diary (to wit: April 18, 1825), the two massive armies met on the opposing slopes of the iNcome Valley to engage in what would go down in History as the most extraordinary and fantastic battle ever fought on the African Continent.

On the one slope, closest to the river, were the Zulu forces (68,000 men divided into seventeen regiments) combined with Chief Febana's seven valiant "Swallow Recruits"; - on the countering slope were marshalled the combined forces of King Zwide, General Soshangane, and King Pakatwayo kaKondlo Qwabe (40,000 men divided into ten regiments that went by the tribal designation of "Ndwandwe", though all the original populace of the kingdom which once bore that name had been annihilated by Shaka in 1821, at the Destruction of Dlovunga).

As both fields waited in silence for the commencement of hostilities, each front expecting the other to make the first move, Shaka sat on a rocky precipice, surveying the serried enemy ranks with an appearance of marked deliberation. The Emperor knew (from the thorough investigations undertaken by his spies) that, under the command of Soshangane, Zwide's forces had trained extensively in both close combat and Shaka's famous "Method". He was also aware of the fact that the "new Ndwandwe" troops not only possessed weapons similar to the ixwa, and were highly and most efficiently drilled in endurance and speed, but had discarded the use of sandals, and were familiar with Shakan tactics such as the "cattlehorn formation". - Indeed, Shaka mused as he scanned the enemy lines, to all intents and purposes, Zwide's troops were "Shakan" in all but name and inspiration.

Something new was needed, Shaka told himself. A tactic, unexpected and outlandish, that would astonish and confuse. As his mind ruminated these thoughts, his eyes fell on the handful of Whites who, despite their Zulu regimental gear (which they wore over their shredded European garments), stood out in the midst of his regular troops like a foamy crested wave on a sea of amber. The King narrowed his eyes on Febana, taking scrutiny of the exceptional appearance of the Swallows' commander, with his white ostrich feathers mounted on his cocked hat and with his ornate cape of fur tails tied to his shredded epaulettes. "He and his men are already unexpected and outlandish," Shaka considered with a smile. "More than enough to astonish and confuse". He had already sensed they could be of great use; that was one reason why he had insisted that they join him in battle.

But of what use - specifically? - the King asked himself as his attention wandered back to the Ndwandwe forces. How can seven men make a difference with an enemy 40,000 strong?

Then the idea struck him. And, as it took shape in his mind, the Zulu murmured in a note of whispered excitement: "uCristo". Rising, moving down towards his waiting regiments, Shaka felt suddenly elated. For him the Battle of iNcome River had just taken on a new and different texture. It was to be not only a struggle between his own armies and Zwide's, but an outright challenge of his "rival King of Kings", and a significant gage of Fynn's allegation that "Christ is Power!"

"You and your men will march against the enemy alone," Shaka calmly announced to Febana, leaving the Englishman congealed in a pose of astounded consternation. "My armies will cover you if and when you need assistance."

Mgobozi, Nqoboka, Mzilikazi, Joko and the other Shakan generals knit their brows in stark disbelief at their King's seemingly preposterous command; while the Swallows stood dumbfounded, too spellbound to react, their wide, horrified gazes flitting inexorably to the opposing hillock that was swarming with enemy troops.

Regaining mobility in his legs, the lieutenant neared the Emperor and cast a long, searching look that dwelt on the Zulu's inscrutable gaze. Glimpsing an impenetrable earnestness in those fiery feline orbs, Farewell sought to cast some edifying light on the darkness of this absurd request. With a hushed tone that suppressed an inclination to scream, he inquired: "You want us - the eight of us - to fight them, all forty thousand... alone?"

By way of an answer, Shaka smiled.

"It can't be done," the lieutenant concluded somewhat off-handedly, his mind racing to fathom the tragic complexion of the King's thoughts whilst his heart sincerely hoped that the entire incident would prove to be a regrettable jest. "It just cannot be done," he repeated. "But, then, you know that of course. Don't you?"

The Emperor remained silent and smiling, his eyes locked on Farewell. It was a moment before the Zulu spoke, asking: "Do you not have Christ in your heart?"

The lieutenant's head cocked slightly down and to the side, like that of a man poised to listen to a faint, distant sound. Of all the questions, all the possible questions that could have been proferred in this specific context, this was the last, the very last Farewell had expected to hear, and he was suddenly aware of a rushing sound in his ears, as if all his blood had taken on the consistency of a mountain stream after heavy rains.

"W-what?" the English adventurer asked, barely controlling a dry, uneasy laugh.

"Your sangoma has told me," Shaka's eyes were dancing to the notes of his sinister imagination, "that a man with Christ in his heart is stronger than all the regiments on earth."

A short, suffered gasp was torn from Fynn's throat.

"Is that not true..?" the Emperor inquired, his brows arched in feigned innocence.

Biting deep into his upper lip, Farewell cast Fynn a look of alarmed inquiry.

"Did you -- did you say that, Fynn?" the lieutenant queried, prompting a shower of inquisitive glances to rain upon the tense figure of the penitent Irishman.

"Yes," Fynn answered, not daring to meet his companion's gaze but glancing, instead, at a flock of weaver birds swooping overhead.

"I see..." Farewell retorted thickly, glancing at the birds as if they, too, were responsible for Fynn's misdeed. "Yebo, Baba," the lieutenant returned his attention to Shaka. "It is true. - But the meaning of the statement must be taken...differently."

"Differently?" Shaka inquired, quizzically, as all eyes now shifted to Farewell.

"He did not mean real regiments, Baba," the Englishman was starting to perspire. "He meant--. He meant--. Tell him, Fynn," he urged, turning to Fynn, "Tell him what you meant."

"I--." And that is as far as the Irishman got before a rattling peal of nervous laughter shook his frail figure.

"You will march against them. Alone," Shaka repeated his request with a note of impatience. "We will see who is the true King of Kings! Who is -Power!" he spat out the word. "If your Christ truly wishes to be the Lord of the Zulus, he must deserve it -- as I have!"

Dismissing further dispute, cutting off all avenues of rebuttal, Shaka spun on his heels and struck off to join his generals in silent observation of the Whites' next move.

After a brief exchange of flitting, terror-stricken glances that served to confirm the collective stupor of Febana's men, - one by one, their hearts on fire with flashing visions of imminent and savage destruction, the Swallows shouldered their muskets and gripped their kegs of powder and bags of shot. Then, facing the rocky plain of their "Armageddon", the eight men bunched together, shoulder to shoulder, elbow to elbow, and inched pitiably forwards in the direction of their Ndwandwe foe, tugging behind them the wooden two-wheel carriage that bore the weight of the "Julia's" cannon.

"Who taught you catechism?" Farewell asked Fynn, the hot breath of his anger grazing the Irishman's cheek.

"Fr. Patrick Mulligan," the man of medicine replied, the pride in his voice sounding somewhat incongruous. "Holy Trinity Church. Dublin."

"Blast the Irish!" Holstead muttered.

"You're a fine one to talk," Wilkins shot back, addressing Thomas. "If we're here at all, it's because of you and Popham!"

"D'you reckon he really meant it, lieutenant?" Cane wondered. "Us fightin' them alone, I mean."

"That would appear to be the case, Cane," Farewell replied glancing over his shoulder at the Zulu ranks that remained stubbornly unmoving.

"Where's his sense of 'ppreciation," Holstead scowled. "We saved his bloody hide!"

"Ask, Fynn," Daniel rumbled. "He's the theologian."

"I think the answer's quite obvious," the Irishman replied defensively. "Shaka's testing us, that's all. He wants to see if our actions speak as loud as our words! It's a question of faith?"

"Well next time 'Nero' asks you to prove your faith," Farewell's irony was biting. "Would you please refrain from mentioning the Colosseum!"

"Couldn't we surrender, sir?" the timid inquiry was Wilkins's. "It's been done before you know. Honourably, I mean."

"Yes, Tim. I suppose we could," Farewell rested his glance on the Ndwandwe forces that loomed down on them from the countering slopes. "Yet I have the lurking suspicion that those gentlemen do not take prisoners."

"Hardly seems worth it - all this!" Cane remarked sorrowfully.

"Worth it?" Gin-naro echoed. "Not worth it at all -- dying in someone else's war, on someone else's land, in someone else's uniform. But then, come to think of it, dying in your own war, on your own land, in your own uniform isn't hardly worth it either. In fact," Gin-naro knit his brow thoughtfully, "you know what's not worth it at all?"

"What?" the question was Popham's.

"Dying," the Italian said and sighed deep in his chest.

"What absurd strategy is this?" Pakatwayo's expression was clouded with bewilderment and annoyance as he cocked his blazing eye at the closely packed handful of Whites who were crossing the saffron "arena of battle" like so many martyrs nigh to a tryst with the lions of Rome.

"Idiotic!" Zwide scoffed, his headdress of long blacks plumes quivering with his rebuke.

"That's what your son said at Qokli, Zwide" Soshangane's rejoinder was cautious. "If he hadn't chaffed Shaka's tactics then, he and Dlovunga might have been spared. - I've faced the Zulu before and I've learned what it means to underestimate him." "Then tell me, Soshangane," Pakatwayo was ironic. "Why has he sent out those monkeys? - To amuse us?"

The Ndwandwe general allowed his wondering gaze to linger on the minute contingency of Whites. In the years after his escape from Shaka's armies, Soshangane had rambled and roved to the North of the Pongola River, in the territories bordering on the Greater Zulu Empire. In those lands he had lived with the Tembe and Swazi tribes near Delagoa Bay, and had heard tales of the White men who inhabited the Portuguese Colonies of the Indian Ocean. And though he had never met these Strangers, he had been told that, like Shaka, these creatures should also not be underestimated for they are indeed capable of every wickedness.

"No, Pakatwayo," Soshangane was still pensive. "They are not there to amuse us. Though often incomprehensible to all but he, there is always a reason behind Shaka's moves, no matter how 'idiotic' they may appear.- Sikhunyane!" the general shouted to one of his officers. "Send down a handful of warriors. Lets see if their blood is the same colour as ours!"

Upon spotting the detachment of Ndwandwes trotting towards them, Farewell's intrepid blood was raised in temperature, and his military training came to the fore, immediately vesting him with the duty of commanding the defensive martial operation.

"Prepare to fire!" he barked out to his men, bringing the semblance of order to the chaotic state of their hearts. Reacting on instinct alone, the Whites got down on one knee and levelled their muskets at the wild, truculent assault of the approaching enemy.

"For all our exaggerated notions at the outset of this mission," Wilkins wryly commented peering down the barrel of his rifle, his eye shut in sighting, his mind reviving the idealistic words uttered in Cape Town with Reverend Bellows and the Governor - words that evinced a desire to find peace with the Africans through brother- hood. . "Well - perhaps Somerset was right after all." Sensing the lieutenant's questioning gaze, the Colonial Officer added: "It's all boiling down to blowing their heads off, isn't it, sir?"

Farewell found it difficult to ignore the telling remark and faltered slightly before regaining his usual stouthearted resolve. "It's do or die, Tim" he told his freckled English coadjutor, "the colour of the enemy has little to do with it". Then, positioning his finger on the trigger to spark the flintlock, he shouted to all: "Aim! --- Fire!

When the gunshots echoed throughout the valley, four of the approaching Ndwandwe warriors were hit by the barrage of leaden pellets and tumbled to the ground, collapsing over their shields that toppled like so many playing cards. Stunned by the unfamiliar weaponry, the rest of the small detachment stopped in their tracks, struck dumb by the mystifying accuracy of the sticks that spat fire and killed from afar.

"Reload!" ordered Farewell, pouring a fine stream of gunpowder into his muzzle-loader, and ramming another two-ounce pellet down its long slender barrel. Enheartened to some degree by the comparative success of their first defensive measure, the other Whites readily obeyed, preparing their weapons for another round.

The survivors of Soshangane's armed detail were too slow in snapping out of their startled daze and, when they had finally worked up their courage with bloodcurdling screams and had resumed their headlong charge, the Whites, following Farewell's lead, were poised and ready for the next volley.

"Fire!" the lieutenant repeated the command, his voice resounding with authority on the valley's opposing slopes, its echo mingling with the gunshots that ripped through the advancing enemy, ushering death to the survivors of the first Ndwandwe detachment.

"Functional at a distance, like the traditional spear," Soshangane considered the effectiveness of the "fire-sticks" with abstracted musing. "Yet, like the Shakan assegai, the weapon is not thrown away. -- Most impressive! And efficient against limited odds. But what if---" the general's thought trailed off as he turned to Sikhunyane and snapped: "Send down a full regiment. And let no one return until those eight men are dead!"

As the Ndwandwe officer trotted off to obey the directive, Pakatwayo knit his brow in astonishment: "Four thousand against eight? I'll admit, their weapons are quite capable, but...well, don't you find those odds a bit embarrassing for our pride?"

"The pride of war is at the service of victory, Pakatwayo," Soshangane retorted dryly, his gaze reaching out to the opposing slopes where Shaka and his troops were immobile in their spartan ranks. "And when faced with a formidable foe like the Zulu, one can never be too careful...no matter how 'embarrassing' the odds. -- That's another lesson I learned at Qokli. One that cost us almost 25,000 men."

"Should we prepare to attack, Baba?" Mgobozi asked as he took notice of the huge Ndwandwe regiment rumbling down the slope and spilling out onto the valley in the direction of the tiny White army.

"Not yet, Mgobozi," Shaka answered distractedly, his gaze locked on the Swallows with the glint of consuming interest and a myriad of contrasting intents.

With due objectivity, Shaka knew that the handful that made up Febana's minute "regiment" had no chance whatsoever of offering even a modicum of opposition to the thunderous advance of the trotting thousands that made up the enemy ranks. Their firearms were far too slow in reloading, Shaka reflected, and after a volley (two at the most), the surging sea of Ndwandwe troops would overwhelm the Whites like the ocean's tide unfolding on a lowly splinter of driftwood. Yet Shaka hesitated to move to their rescue, his mind shunted to indecision by a tumult of confused and diverging thoughts that combined to cloud his judgment for the first time.

Mgobozi was deeply distressed by Sigidi's surprising and peculiar reluctance to act, one which evinced an unheard-of lack of resolve and purpose, one which was fast turning strategy into improvisation; and, in apprehension for Shaka's wellbeing, the iziCwe general addressed his friend and sovereign, his words probing the secrets of the Zulu's heart and, inadvertently, bringing his King's dizzying whirl of conjectures into focus.

"They will be massacred, Sigidi," Mgobozi commented dispassionately, feeling no real concern for the Swallows' fate. "Is that what you want, Baba? - Or do you seriously believe they will be saved by their...magic?"

His lips wearing an eerie smile, Shaka cocked his eye at his oldest friend. "I'm beginning to believe, Mgobozi, that the greatest of Man's illusions is his desire to have none. - You were with that girl, weren't you. The one who was...dead. You saw them bury her. And yet she lived. - And you saw the gash on my chest. It was fatal - and yet I live." Shaka's smile broadened as his eyes returned to the handful of Swallows and the advancing storm of Ndwandwes. "And yet I live," he said again with the inflection of a prayer. "Do you feel that I am wrong, my friend, in wanting to 'investigate' further?"   "I am a soldier, Baba. My role in life is to kill. The role you yourself taught me. If I were to entertain the notion that my victims could come back to life, my personal victories would become farces. - Yet, I cannot say that you are wrong in anything you do, for your life is well beyond my reproach." Mgobozi's attention also moved to review the ludicrously disparate armies on the field of battle. "Yet I say - very well! Let them die! Let us finally put an end to this 'investigation' of yours. -- While there is still time."

On the battlefield, time was rapidly running out for Febana and his men. The entire Ndwandwe regiment had reached the valley and had fanned out in formation, with twenty charging rows of two hundred men each. As if the overbearing superiority of this human avalanche were not sufficiently marked, the men - all 4000 of them - started chanting in unison, their quaking voices raised over the martial rhythm of their pounding footfalls, which advanced on their humble quarry of eight in the prospect of literally trampling them to death.

Like Shaka, Farewell had also taken ready note of the futility of attempting to face this massive attack with the muskets alone. Though viable against lesser odds, the firearms were far too slow in reloading to take on a full regiment. Two, perhaps three volleys - the lieutenant had calculated - and that would be the end of them. - No, he was aware that something else was urgently needed to stop, or at least slow, this crushing onslaught.

Predictably, Farewell's attention came to rest on the hefty cannon of the "Julia". His mind racing, the lieutenant quickly computed possible trajectories of fire that would do the most damage in the enemy lines, and arrived at the disquieting conclusion that their present position was wrong - both trigonometrically and militarily. They needed to be lower and more protected.

Scanning the adjoining landscape, Farewell's eyes snagged on a deep gully less than 150 meters away: the perfect place to lodge the "Julia's" gun. Looking up, the lieutenant's gaze met Cane's.

"D'you think we can make it in time?" the large man asked, reading Farewell's mind.

"We'll have to, won't we," was the lieutenant's fatalistic rebuttal, his attention darting, with growing alarm, from the Ndwandwes - who thundered ever-nearer - to the bulky cannon. It was then that man was reminded of the large gun's considerable weight.

"Do you think you can lift it?" he inquired of Cane.

"I'll 'have to, won't I," he grinned and curled his mighty arms round the cannon, grunting with exertion as he hoisted it up onto his broad shoulders and started off, lumbering towards the gully at a steady, sustained pace. With an appreciative smile, Farewell easily lifted the wooden gun carriage and fell into step with his muscular companion, urging the others to follow, carrying what they could.

Thus, what had started out as preposterous was now tainted with burlesque, as the small group of valiant Whites scurried, helter-skelter, towards the relative safety of the nearby gully:-- with Cane in the lead (swaying precariously under the onerous gun), with Farewell at his side (half-submerged by the upturned carriage, its wheels spinning free in the wind), with Wilkins, Fynn, Daniel, Holstead, and Popham at their heels, hefting bags of shot, cannonballs, and a keg of powder, with Gin-naro bringing up the rear -- and with 4000 warriors literally breathing down their necks at a distance of less than two hundred meters.

In point of fact, visualising the peculiarity of this scenario - so reminiscent of the farsical "Commedia dell'Arte" - it should not come as a total surprise that Gin-naro, the only Italian of the group, was the one to panic. Indeed, feeling the earth virtually quaking behind him, the Neapolitan lost his nerve and, turning, stopped, losing contact with the others as he blindly fired his musket at the swarming enemy throng.

One could hardly have missed, yet Gin-naro did (as a further sign of his emotional disarray). And, as he made a desperate and pitiful bid to reload his weapon, the surging sea was upon him. With a soul-rending scream that touched the Heavens, the Italian was overwhelmed by the human stampede and trodden underfoot until his body was a hashed and macerated pulp of flesh and bone.

It would be nice to think that his demise was quick and merciful, - yet it was not. -- Michele "Gin-naro" Disantamaria died the most excruciating of deaths, having ample time, in the midst of the ghastly ordeal, to wonder what he had done to wrong his patron San Gennaro. Ample time to hear the voice of his poet compatriot Dante Alighieri whispering: "Tu proverai si come sa di sale Lo pane altrui, e com'e' duro calle, Lo scendere e salir per l'altrui scale -- O Patria! Perche' ho abbandonato le tue spaggie dolci per La chimera?!" - "And, wandering, you shall discover how salty is the taste of another man's bread, and how hard is the way up and down another man's stairs - O Land of my birth! Why did I leave your sweet shores in search of idle fancy?!"

The Whites could barely react to Gin-naro's tragic slaying for they were deep in the midst of a tragedy of their own. In effect, in their frantic bid to reach the gully before the Ndwandwes overpowered them, the Swallows were incapable of reacting to anything but the mad rush of adrenalin that endowed their legs with uncommon speed and their minds with instinctual reflex.

John Cane was the first to arrive at the natural intrenchment, and he indecorously slide down into the ravine on the seat of pants, balancing the large gun on his arched back. Farewell was close behind, and, in a matter of seconds, he had the carriage set up on the gulch's inclined hollow.

Whilst the others gained the margin of the gully and frantically leapt, dove, rolled and slide into its basin, the lieutenant helped Cane mount the gun on its wooden trolley and tilt its muzzle at the desired angle of detonation.

"Fire at will!" Farewell shouted to the men; and, as he and Cane hurriedly loaded the cannon's muzzle with gunpowder, Wilkins, Fynn, Holstead, Popham and Daniel aligned the sights of their muskets with the human tidal wave that was now a mere hundred meters away.

Fire, reload, fire again. - Two volleys were unloaded into the serried ranks of the approaching regiment, felling a few of the warriors but in no way slowing the enemy's inexorable attack.

Reload and fire once more. The third volley. And the enemy was but twenty meters away, when Farewell rammed the powder in place with a rod and loaded one of the iron projectiles into the cannon's muzzle.

Before the next volley, Cane had touched a lit taper to the mighty gun's fuse. It burned and fizzled, and, as the Whites looked on fearfully, the fuse declined to give the expected result - leaving a vacuum devoid of movement and breath...

Then, abruptly - a resounding boom, deafening and hollow, tore the sky asunder, and a billowing cloud of white and grey phosphide was forcibly expelled from the cannon's muzzle, propelling the ball on a collision course with the enemy. The blast hit the Ndwandwe line at point-blank range, cleaving out a wide channel for itself through the solid human wall. Dozens upon dozens of warriors were literally blown apart in an horrendous burst of blood, and shredded flesh, - the fragments and pulpy chunks of their dismembered bodies showering onto the ranks that followed.

Petrified by the resonating blast and the carnage it caused, the regiment stopped short in its tracks, and stood gaping at the Swallows with superstitious terror; - the same terror with which Soshangane, Zwide, and Pakatwayo gawked at the modest assemblage of seven men who had stopped the advance of thousands with an unearthly device: a weapon in which were harnassed the explosive energy of thunder and the battering force of a hurricane.

Like Shaka, Mgobozi, Mzilikazi, Joko and, indeed, the entire Zulu army were positively boggled by the devastating efficiency of this bewitching weapon. All eyes were expectantly directed at the gully in suspended animation, as Cane touched his taper to the cannon's fuse, and a second blast breached a trail through Ndwandwe flesh, hacking the large detachment in half with its searing thrust.

Overcoming the numbness of their terror, panic suddenly took hold of the regiment. The surviving warriors shed all semblance of military instruction and became like a maddened swarm of ants, running wildly in all directions, hysterically trampling one another in a bid to flee before the next pestilential barrage.

"All regiments attack!" roared Soshangane, regaining the faculty of speech.

"Attack!" Zwide echoed the order, his voice throaty and hoarse, like that of man jarred to wakefulness from a nightmare.

"Attack! Attack!" the order was repeated by Sikhuyane and rippled down the line of Ndwandwe generals.

Obediently, the remaining 36,000 troops assembled in formation, yet the men's expressions reflected their dire reluctance to descend onto the field of a battle in which the enemy was tainted with the superhuman.

Shaka's gaze whipped to the countering slopes and his attention seized the very shades of the Ndwandwes' movements. Yet, even though he observed that Zwide's entire army was now grouping to charge the Whites, the Zulu Emperor still dangerously wavered on the brink of indecision. Events, necessities, things, -- Shaka had lost his grip on them all it seemed, and he felt as if the surges of the heaviest sea were running through his mind and soul. Aware of the accelerated beating of his heart, he sensed that the hitherto inexpugnable supremacy of his authority and influence was being insidiously menaced by this extraordinary font of marvel and untold capability that he himself had willingly, blindly and - obstinately tapped. Yet, despite this realisation, Shaka remained momentarily paralysed in immobility. He would not, - he could not draw back from his challenge to the Whites and their uCristo, for the gears of the machine he had set in motion had acquired a momentum of their own and, too late, he now knew that he was becoming the victim of a betrayal he had perpetrated upon himself! Indeed, the Swallows had "called his bluff" (if in truth it had been a bluff) and were now, to all intents and purposes, anigh to a victory that was Power Itself.

Cane's expression disclosed far less conviction of the Whites' capabilities as he eyed the immense Ndwandwe army that was sweeping down towards their position.

"We've powder enough for three more blasts," the "gentle giant" told Farewell with a trace of even-tempered resignation. "At intervals of thirty seconds each, that gives us 'bout a minute'n a 'alf to live."

"Not if we load her with the supernatural, Cane," was Farewell's brazen reply. And, as Cane and the others snatched wide-eyed glimpses at the approaching sea of warriors, the lieutenant quickly slipped off his cape of fur tails and started tying it round a cannonball. When it was securely in place, he drenched the singular projectile with the kerosine from a lantern and stuffed it into the cannon's muzzle, ramming it in place with the rod. He then checked the surrounding landscape with an eye to determine an appropriate line of fire.

"Tilt it up sixty degrees, Cane. And light the fuse, will you," the lieutenant coolly remarked.

"Why'd you do that, lieutenant?" the large man asked, slanting the muzzle to the requested inclination and bending the flame of his taper to the fuse.

"An added touch," Fynn laggardly replied, glancing at the enlivened smile on Farewell's face and grimly guessing what he had done. "'For the sake of show', no doubt."

When the cannon's roar returned to deafen and torment the iNcome Valley, its cast-iron tube spat a blazing projectile through the air that looked remarkably like a comet "Febana's Comet". And even though, unlike the other blasts, the flaming bolide soared harmlessly above the enemy's position, it did far more damage - from a spiritual and emotional point of view. In fact, both fronts (the Ndwandwe as well as the Zulu) were jolted to a staggered, open-mouthed inertness that left them goggling at the "astral body" hissing across the sky, its flickering reddish glow dancing on their gaping entrancement. Then, to complete the "supernatural" spectacle Farewell had so efficiently staged, with astounding precision the fireball crossed in front of the face of the sun - momentarily eclipsing its heavenly light -, and collided with the rocky summit of a hillock.

Its forward thrust deadened, the fiery globe bounced back and changed direction, spitting flames as it rolled down the slopes and into the the midst of Zwide's marching troops. Terrified, the Ndwandwes scrambled out of the "comet's" way, falling over one another in an effort to avoid the meteor as it whistled past them, singeing their skin. The bolide's "metaphysical flight" finally climaxed when it bounded into the iNcome River and was spent in a hissing cloud of steaming white smoke.

Silence gripped the valley, and, awe-struck, the Ndwandwes stood frozen in place, their gazes locked on the billowing cloud that rose from the surface of the river. Stirring from his own stunned abstraction, Shaka realised that he had hesitated too long, and that the Swallows' overwhelming triumph spelled impending victory - a victory that might well be his own defeat.

"Phase One!" The Zulu Emperor exclaimed, inciting his armies to charge. Yet the men wavered, unsure of what course to take.

"It is too late, Baba," Mgobozi told his King, reflecting the men's unsettling hesitancy. "The Swallows have already made the Kill. We march in only as scavengers!"

"Phase One!" Shaka's roar was laced with fury as he repeated the command.

"Yebo, Baba," Mgobozi sadly yielded to his Emperor's wish and, saluting, trotted off to face his regiment. When in position, the general of the iziCwe thrust his ixwa into the air and bellowed - for what he sensed would be the last time: "SI-GI-DI!" -

"SI-GI-DI!" echoed the iziCwe.

"SI-GI-DI!" shouted Joko and his uYengonglovu.

"SI-GI-DI!" cried out Nqoboka and his men of the iziPikili.   "SI-GI-DI!" the praise was resounded by Dlaba and his iNyelezi, Ngwadi and his uFojisa, Mzilikazi and his amaPenjana -- by all the regiments, as the men loyally stomped their foot on the ground in a thundering quake and trotted off to engage the enemy in a battle that had all the undertones of a farce.

Before following his men, Mgobozi cast one last look of parting in Shaka's direction. When their eyes met - for a fleeting instant - it seemed to the Zulu Emperor that the eyes of the faithful, loving companion of his youth wore the saddened forbearance of a farewell.

"Better late than never," Holstead grumbled with obvious relief upon noticing the Zulus entering the field of war.

"Amazing, isn't it?" Wilkins's commented, giving vent to his imperialistic scrutiny. "How these natives react to elementary technology."

"Yes, quite amazing," Fynn scowled, revolted by the afternoon's "metaphysical massacre", his eyes glued to Farewell as he added: "As I once had occasion to note, a man without scruples could easily become a god in this land."

"What did you expect me to do, Fynn," Farewell rebutted, sensing the accusation in the Irishman's pale blue eyes, "sit back and watch us get killed?"

"No, Francis," the medical man admitted. "In fact, I applaud your ingenuity. What disturbs me is the fact that you were enjoying it! And if there's anything worse than playing god, it's playing Gulliver!"

Though the battle motions were the same -- Contact! Lock shields! Pull back and away! Aim for the heart! -- and the courage faultless, for the Zulus something was missing at the Battle of iNcome River. Particularly in the hearts of the old-time Shakan generals like Mgobozi, Nqoboka, Dlaba, Joko and Mzilikazi. A precious commodity called - Purpose!

Somehow the men felt as though they were fighting in someone else's war. The exhilaration of the old days, the days of the "Fifty", the days of eNtuzuma Hill, the days of Qokli were gone, replaced by the realisation that their King had allowed the Whites to "steal the show" and the pride of the amaZulu. Even the glorious "Method" was reduced to the men hacking their way through the enemy lines with a reckless vehemence that hinged on the suicidal.

For the first time in his life, Shaka himself did not take part in the fighting. Indeed, had he not from the battle's outset chosen the role of the spectator?

Nqoboka was the first to fall. Then Ngwadi, Shaka's beloved brother. And finally - Mgobozi-ovela-entabeni.

When the conflict was over and the dead were counted, it was difficult to determine at first sight who had won - even though the Zulu losses were far fewer than the Ndwandwe. Indeed, if one were obliged to decide the outcome of the Battle of iNcome River, one would not greatly err in saying that, in a way, both Zulus and Ndwandwes had lost, - and that only Febana had won.

When the conflict was over -- Shaka strolled listlessly through the funereal stillness that hovered over the valley. His glance fell on his bother Ngwadi, his mutilated frame contorted in death. And, once again, Shaka heard the voice of that small child who was the blood of his blood asking from the recesses of long ago: "Is it dead yet?"

"Yes, Ngwadi," Nandi's voice surfaced from the Past. "It's dead."

"How can you tell?" came the spectral whisper of Ngwadi the child.

"It's in the eyes," Shaka heard himself saying out loud, echoing the answer he had given his brother almost twenty years ago. "Look closely. Can you notice something's gone?"

Shaka looked down at his brother's open eyes. Yes, something was gone, he knew. From that barren gaze, and from Shaka's own heart.

Forever.

"But where has it gone?" the voice of Ngwadi the child haunted the battlefield.

"It is in the air," the Zulu King said aloud, answering the voice of his brother's ghost, the voice that he alone heard. "It is all around us," he sighed looking at the death that was all around him.

Death. The Lord of Grief. The Lord of Pain. The Lord of the Kill. One is either its Master or its Victim, there is no middle way.

And today, at iNcome River, for the first time in his life, Shaka fervently wished that there were a "middle way".

Moving past the detachment of Ufasimba who were holding captive both Zwide and Pakatwayo (purportedly Soshangane had fled once again), moving past the remains of Nqoboka, the King's eyes finally fell on the everboyish features of Mgobozi. The breath of Life still clung to the brave warrior and, when Shaka neared him and knelt at his side, the man reached out and clutched his Emperor's arm with urgency, his blood-flecked lips forming the words: "There is nothing more dangerous than a soldier who has no idea what he's doing on the battlefield. He can cause his own death as well as that of his comrades."

Shaka's eyes met those of his friend.

"My words," the King admitted. "Your words." he smiled and, when the smile faded: "What were we doing today, Nkosi?"

Shaka dropped his gaze, and there was stillness as the wounded warrior allowed his rended lungs to fill with air. Then:---

"Baba...the Swallows will never serve you. Their purpose is to have you serve them. And today, they have shown that it is possible." As the words chilled Shaka's heart, Mgobozi swallowed and continued: "The weapons, the 'magic' they used against Zwide will one day be turned against you and all those whose skins are not the colour of sorghum."

"They came to me in friendship, Mgobozi," the King rebutted, stubbornly adhering to his obsessed faith in the Strangers. "They fought at my side, and we won!"

"No. They won!" Mgobozi's voice was weaker, his words spoken with the clarity of Light that comes with Ultimate Darkness. "The battle is theirs, and they share victory with no one. Such is the way of their loyalty. They are like the Snake who slyly enters the hut bringing silent death. And, with the subtlety of the Snake, they have replaced your friends, your isangoma, and, today -they replaced you, Baba."

Shaka stiffened, his mind railing against the words spoken by his friend, his soul finding it easier to suffer for his mistake than to own to it.

"Today they were Sigidi - one against a thousand. When the hills and valleys of this land sing of the Battle of iNcome River, they will not sing of the amaZulu. There will be no praises for Mgobozi-ovela-entabeni. There will be no praises for Shaka."

"You cannot see clearly, my friend," Shaka's voice was unusually weak and colourless. "I will call the Swallows' sangoma. He will drive back the darkness."

"No, Baba," Mgobozi shook his head with a wane of resignation upon realising that his words were lost on his Emperor and friend. "I would rather die than live to see the death of your people. My people." His eyes moistened with tears that, falling, traced a path through the blood on his face. "Shaka...You have given them our gardens in which to plant their seeds, if you let them steal our sunshine, the harvest will be theirs."

"One of us is wrong, Mgobozi," Shaka held firm in his desire to believe. "Soon you will know who it is. Guide your spirit back to me and let it whisper in my ear."

"It already has, Shaka," was the simple reply. "In Death the Past, the Present, and the Future blend in the words I speak - but you do not wish to hear. -- Sala kahle, Mngane," he said with a faint smile, dying. "Bayete, Nkosi, wena wa silo. Bayete, Nkosi yama Kosi, wa-hlula amakosi!"

"Hamba kahle, Mgobozi," Shaka replied, feeling the gelidness taking possessing of his friend's hand. "Bayete - uya kuhlasela-pi na! Go well, my brother. My heart goes with you."

Placing Mgobozi's hand in the gentle grasp of his Companion Death, Shaka rose heavily to his feet and turned to face the Swallows and their bewitching cannon. His expression hardening with resolve, the Zulu King neared the Whites with measured strides, his eyes remaining rivetted on the mighty gun. Then, stopping, the Son of Zulu rested his hand on the iron muzzle and swivelled it round so that it was perfectly aligned with Zwide and his ignoble accomplice Pakatwayo. Realising what was about to happen, the two ex-kings started whimpering in dispirited appeals as the Ufasimba moved well away from their position, leaving them alone to face the gun.

"Give it fire!" Shaka commanded, his flaming eyes resting on Farewell.

"We will not be your executioners!" Fynn interjected, facing Shaka's anger with stouthearted resolve.

"And those dead?!" the King hissed motioning to the bloodied field which was partially bestrewed with the gun's dismembered victims. "In whose name did they fall? Were you my executioners or your own? Which king guided the massacre - I or your..." his tone became harsh as his tigerish lips formed the words: "---'Forgiving' Christ?!"

Fynn's eyes locked with Shaka's in a silent battle of wills and wits. Finally the Irishman had a deep sigh and, snatching the taper out of Cane's hand, he lit it and touched it to the fuse.

Seconds later, Zwide's and Pakatwayo's horrified cries were forever silenced by a resounding blast.

* * *

The Great Mountain decreed that the General of the iziCwe, Mgobozi-ovela-entabeni, should be buried in a manner befitting a king. Accordingly, a colossal pit (seven meters by seven, and seven deep) was dug in the center of the concave crater situated on the summit of Qokli Hill. At the northern end of the pit, the side closest to the river, a large niche (three meters by three) was carved into one wall of the grave. The niche was squared and panelled with polished ivory and adorned with shells from the Sea, and bedecked with the sparkling trinkets, baubles and pearls contained in Febana's Continental coffer.

The remains of Mgobozi were caused to assume a sitting position and wrapped in leopardskins (the symbol of Zulu Supremacy and Power), in the hide of the cheetah (the symbol of Speed), in the braided skins of Elephant (the beast of Endurance), and in the coloured plumes and feathers of the Bateleur Eagle (Strategy).

The Burial Ceremony was held on the Third Moon of uNtlaba (April 22, 1825). The entire iziCwe was present, as were Joko and his uYengonglovu, Dlaba and his iNyelezi, Kuta and his u-Kangela, Mzilikazi and his amaPenjana; and the Regiments of the uFojisa, of the uNomdayana, of the amaKwenkwe, of the iziKwembu; and the iziZimanzana, the Jubingqwanga, the uDlambedlu, the iziPezi, the uMbonambi, the uNteke, the uGibabanye, the uNomdayana, the imFongosi, and the inDabankulu; completed by the Maidens' Regiments: the two thousand of the umVutwanini, the two thousand of the inTlabati, the imBabazane and the uluSiba.

The body of the deceased general was carried down to the niche by Joko and Dlaba and "seated" on a throne made from the foot of the "iNto eMosayo" - the giant White Bull Elephant.

Interred with Mgobozi was the cannon of the "Julia" - which was placed in front of the niche, its muzzle pointing away from the general and tilted upwards, sixty degrees (the trajectory of "Febana's Comet").

A stone slab was placed at the site of the grave with the lettering "MGOBOZI-OVELA-ENTABENI" (which Shaka had ordered Daniel to inscribe in his best and clearest writing - the writing that would be most "immortal")

Also present at the ceremony were the Swallows with their Chief Febana. For the occasion, Farewell had shed his naval tunic for a flowing robe of genet tails and lion fur, and his cocked hat for a magnificent headdress shaped from a strip of leopardskin and crowned with ostrich feathers. Fynn stood beside the lieutenant and, as he snatched glimpses at the Englishman's self-satisfied expression (that of a true "African Chieftain", the proud victor of the Battle of iNcome River), the man of medicine realised that, like Icarus, Francis George Farewell had now taken flight on the wings of Febana ka MaJoji - the tragic flight that leads to destruction. And, looking at the lieutenant, Fynn realised that, aside from the ivory, the Farewell Trading Company dealt in the barter of dreams.

Nandi and Nomcoba did not take part in the ceremony. Both women were in mourning for the death of Ngwadi and had retired to a lonely vigil by the tangled thorn tree where they had buried the son of Gendeyana next to the gravesite of his maternal grandmother Mfunda.

Shaka was also absent from the funeral.

Responding to a need to be alone, to be far from people and their words, to be rid of the earth itself and the harrowing dimension that was the Present, the Emperor had wandered from his Citadel.

And wandered.

And - in obedience to an inward voice, to an impulse beating in his blood, to a vision of things sublime, of things past - in obedience to the warmth of Love that had created him, the Son of Zulu had descended the slopes of emTonjaneni and found himself on the banks of the Mkumbane.

And the stream was exactly as it had been a lifetime ago - when Nandi had first met Senzangakona, when their tempestuous love had taken shape and been mirrored on the surface of its turgid waters.

The same. Exactly the same. Almost as if it had been waiting for the Child it had conceived to return to the site of Love's anguish to complete the Cycle of the Language.

And as Shaka crouched, motionless, lost in the Mkumbane's gurgling, swirling currents, his mind was borne afloat in the trance-like stupor of wakeful dreaming in which Fantasy and Reality are blended to bring balance to the soul's image of itself. In this state, Shaka fancied that he saw the image of his mother on the surface of the stream's rippling waters - an image from long ago, when Nandi had been young. And, on the reflecting surface of the water, the youthful Nandi neared her son and, overcoming her hesitancy, took hold of his powerful arm and embraced it, resting her soft cheek on the curve of his shoulder.

And it began to rain.

Stirring from his abstracted reverie, Shaka gaped at the reflection and was chilled by the realisation that the touch was real, that, miraculously, the vision from the Past was present. And, as the youthful Nandi grazed his skin with her lips in a gentle kiss, Shaka felt her warmth igniting his passion, and slowly he abandoned himself to that caressing, restoring touch.

Turning, Shaka took hold of the woman in his arms and pressed her body against his own, loosening the bonds of his pent-up sensuality. Then, gently resting her on a bed of leaves, the Child took his Mother -- and, though he saw it was Pampata, though he knew it was Pampata, though he heard her words of love whispered in his ear, Shaka closed his eyes and made love to the only Love of his life.

Nandi ever Nandi.

A flash of lightning pierced the unfathomable and pellucid depths of the Heavens bathing the top of a distant hill where two figures stood in the rippling tapestries of wind and rain, their grisly silhouettes set against the lavender clouds. Another bolt of harsh light washed the silhouettes in a steely glitter which made their ghostly features look all the more horrid.

The two figures - that of Sitayi and, at her feet, the immobile shape of a hyena - seemed to be waiting, watching, probing.

At length, Sitayi looked up, her blind, vacant orbs of pastel-blue reaching into the Infinite as she searched for the Cycle of Genesis.

And, when the sangoma knew all was well and that the Second Child of the Prophet's Song had been conceived, she and the hyena turned away from the Mkumbane and, shambling off down the hill, -- the rippling shroud of rain claiming then back onto the still, silent shores of Mystery.

CHAPTER XLV
"SINDA"(ESCAPE)

"...and Jesus said onto her, 'Thy brother shall rise again'. And Martha saith onto Him, 'I know that he shall rise again at the Resurrection on the Last Day.' And Jesus said," Fynn related from memory, "'I am the Resurrection, and the Life; he that believeth in me, though he were dead, yet shall he live. And whoever liveth and believeth in me shall never die."

The Union Jack over Fort Natal flew at half mast, and the small settlement of makeshift huts was veiled in a light drizzle and an air of solemnity, as the remaining Swallows: Farewell, Fynn, Wilkins, Cane, Holstead, Daniel, and Popham were gathered round the site where they had buried the mangled remains of their Italian companion. The Cross (formed out of elephant tusks) that jutted out of the soft African turf at the head of the grave read:

HERE LIES MICHELE 'GIN-NARO" DISANTAMARIA
BORN ? - DIED, APRIL 18, 1825
AT THE SERVICE OF HIS MAJESTY'S COLONIES
R.I.P.

Clearing his throat, Fynn intoned, off-key: "Rock of Ages cleft for meee, let me hide myself in Theeeee..."

One by one, awkwardly, the others Swallows joined in the singing as best they could, considering that most of them could remember neither tune nor lyrics to the popular hymn. Fynn and Farewell barely succeeded in sustaining the absurd choir until they, too, reached a point where the words failed to come to mind. Mercifully (for Gin-naro, perhaps) the hymn slowly dwindled and naturally evaporated into an uneasy silence.

"May he rest in peace," the Irishman addressed the grave, sprinkling a handful of damp earth over the rounded mound of freshly dug soil.

"'Cause we sure as 'ell won't," grunted Holstead, eliciting the stunned and indignant glances of his companions. "No sacrilege intended, mind'ya," Thomas was quick to add, "it's just that -- well, it's been four months, mates. I think it's time we faced the fact that the Julia's either lost or not comin' back. Which means we're land-locked. - Now that makes a sailor like meself feel sort of all-overish. 'specially after two funerals in one week."

The sting of Holstead's remark was obvious on the other men's faces. And no one, not even Farewell, could honestly say there was no truth in his words. Yet the lieutenant was quick to offer his optimistic rebuttal.

"We may be land-locked, Holstead, but the land is ours! With a proper concession - signed and sealed!"

"By a man who almost got us all killed!" Thomas shot back, peremptorily dispelling the pretense of solemnity that had somewhat honoured Gin-naro's funeral. "The way I see it, lieutenant, the only concession we've got is to a graveyard - our own. Sign and sealed! And as for the ivory," Holstead cast an annoyed glance at the elephant tusk made into a Cross. "You can't get much wear out of a tombstone. 'specially if you're under it!"

"How do the rest of you feel?" Farewell asked his men.

"Fact is, sir," Cane was the first to reply, "we're in bad need of a ship. Somethin' to sail us out of 'ere quick, in case Shaka should go gettin' more notions of how to test our faith, if you know what I mean."

"I think we'd all like nothing better, Cane," Fynn saw that the lieutenant was trying to remain calm and condescending as he went on: "But ships don't grow on trees, do they?"

"In a matter of speakin' Lieutenant," Holstead retorted, "they do. There are plenty of trees here to turn into a ship -- of sorts."

"Quite right, Thomas," Farewell concurred in a patronising tone, his eyes carelessly scanning the timbered bush country that bordered on the sandy shores of Port Natal with its "fine tall spars fit for masts" (as Wilkins had written in his Diary). "And we shall have our ship, as soon as Shaka feels there is a need for one."

"That just may be our problem," Popham muttered almost under his breath. "Being so dependent on that mad King's needs and whims."

Farewell's face ironed out upon noticing that the others were in muted agreement with Popham's disquieting remark.

"You surprise me, gentlemen," Farewell assumed an air of healthy reprimand. "Do you really think that the six of us...alone, could build anything worth navigating without the assistance of Shaka's warriors? It would take us a year or two! And even then our work couldn't possibly go unnoticed. Not in an Empire whose King has eyes and ears everywhere! - No!" he shook his head vigorously, "it's out of the question! Not without Shaka's approval."

"I wasn't thinking of anything fancy," Holstead would not be dismissed. "A few logs and a sail would do. And if we shove off at night - well, Shaka'll be none the wiser."

Sensing he might be losing his hold on the men's fidelity, Farewell raised his voice and strengthened his argument: "There are over four hundred miles of coastline between here and the nearest harbour, Port

Elizabeth! With 30-foot waves and razor-sharp reefs! - You say you're a sailor, Holstead, do you really think we could make it on a raft! "I just say it's worth a try," Holstead was adamant. "Better'n sitting around waitin' for that madman to make his next move! We survived one battle by the skin of our teeth! I reckon we won't be that lucky next time! "

"Need I remind you, Holstead," the lieutenant was becoming angry, "that it was your misdeed that occasioned our problem in the first place!"

"And need I remind you, Lieutenant," Thomas's riposte was biting, "that the idea of fightin' them alone was Fynn's! Or Christ's, should I say. Which only goes to prove that no matter what we do, that tyrant can turn it against us if he wants to. - Why he even impales his own bodyguards by the dozens, doesn't he?! Nobody's bleedin' safe around 'ere!"

"But what of the threat to the Colony. And our mission?!" Wilkins interjected with a somewhat exaggerated dose of naive patriotism and with a hint of indignation. "We can't shove off when we're making such good progress!"

"Eight men against 40,000 screamin' warriors," Cane could not screen the sarcasm from his voice, " and he calls it 'progress'!"

The few chuckles of wry amusement that ensued were instantly quelled by the lieutenant's vehemence.

"Yes, Cane, it was progress! - Any good card player knows that the least likely time to fold is when he has called his opponent's bluff. - Shaka dared us to do the impossible and, to all intents and purposes, by surviving we proved that we can perform the 'miraculous'. It would be a shame to give it all up merely because a few of us," his disapproving ferret-like glance flitted past Holstead, "have gotten cold feet. We owe ourselves and the Colonies much more!" The man's tone sharpened to sternness as his face flushed with wrath. "As head of this expedition, I and I alone will establish the manner and the time of our departure! Meanwhile, there'll be no more talk of doing anything behind Shaka's back! - Understood!?"

And with that, the lieutenant spun on his heel and trudged off.

Two hours later, Fynn found him in a remote corner of the bay, perched on a rock and staring musefully at the waves unfurling onto the long, shallow sandbars. Nearing the lieutenant, the Irishman flopped down on the beach beside him.

"The Lt. Farewell I once knew," the Irishman said softly, "would have been on that raft within the week - just to see if it was possible. -- But not Febana."

Farewell dropped his gaze and stiffened.

"Have you forgotten why we're here, Fynn," Farewell's voice was throaty.

"Have you?" came the answer. "You don't really want to leave, do you, Francis?"

The lieutenant turned and rested his glance on the Irishman; yet he had no reply.

"I though you were enjoying it," the man of medicine pressed on, his brogue moderate and mitigating. "But I never thought it would become your obsession. Yet, I should have guessed as much. You are the product of a military upbringing. Taught to thrive on power and reckless bravery. And - in a place like this," the man's pale eyes encompassed the beauty of the coast's wilderness, "divorced from the hindrances of Western cynicism and protocol, a man like you can find far more room for advancement. Febana ka MaJoji may have a far greater future that Lt. Francis George Farewell, R.N. ever dreamed possible!"

"You're being ludicrous," Farewell retorted in a dull voice that lacked the colour of true conviction.

"That's quite likely," Fynn considered. "But then so much of what's happening here is ludicrous. You've called not only Shaka's bluff, but the bluff of the past ten millenia of what we cherish as - civilisation. Life, Death, Youth, Resurrection, Friendship and Power - you name it! Why we've even turned the sanctity of a Christ in whom we both believe into a political device!" A bitter laugh escaped the Irishman's lips. "Shaka may be becoming the victim of our sophistry, but, what's worse - so are we! Especially you, Francis! - Though we are dressed to play the part," Fynn's attention fell on Febana's leopardskin attire, "we could never be Zulu, and that has little or nothing to do with the colour of our skin! - Francis! You need that ship more than the the men do. They may be losing their nerve, but you're losing something far more precious and irreplaceable: -- yourself!"

Farewell detached his gaze from his companion's intense eyes and found the glimmering reflection of the setting sun on the surface of the ocean. And though his mind longingly caressed thoughts of Elizabeth, his home, his country, his people -- he felt an all-consuming fever raging deep in his soul, a fever called Africa.

And Farewell thought of the Colonies and had the distressing suspicion that that fever was born of unrequited love, of an unrequited desire to possess. "It's true, what Fynn says," the lieutenant silently mused. "No matter what we do, Africa will never be ours! This Grand Lady who is impersonated in the greatness and in the beauty of women like Nandi - will never be ours! Even if we rape and defile Her, our violence can only enhance her arcane and impenetrable dignity."

And Farewell felt suddenly jealous of Africa! Of the land he could never possess, the land he could never be truly a part of. He felt an insensate, poignant, tormenting, and unreasoning jealousy! An emotion that rode on the sweat smell of sorghum and the acrid, tangy odour of the lion. And he knew he must escape. Escape. - Now!

If he was still in time, - and, in time, start anew a life far away from the inscrutable majesty of this magnificent Lady.

"It wouldn't be a bad idea to go back and see the Governor," Farewell finally said, drifting back to himself as if awakened from a trance. "Make a full report for His Majesty. See Elizabeth. - It wouldn't be a bad idea..." he repeated, still pensive.

"Not a bad idea at all," Fynn was beaming with delight. "By now they're surely all wondering what happened to us."

"Hmmm," was Farewell's bemused reply. "But Shaka mustn't think that we're escaping. That would ruin everything. The building of the ship must be justified.

"Granted." the Irishman fell pensive. "Then you shall have to give him a reason, a good reason. One he will believe. And I would remind you that he's far too cunning to buy anything but the truth. - You came here to form an alliance with King George, didn't you? That was the unblemished truth of your mission at its outset. - Well, tell Shaka that the time is now ripe for the two sovereigns to seal that pact." Intrigued, the lieutenant shifted round to look directly at Fynn. "We will escort Shaka's emissaries to Cape Town where a proper peace treaty can be drawn up between His Majesty's government and the Zulu Empire." Fynn smiled in conclusion: "Therein lies our need for a ship."

"You're making it sound easy."

"It can be," was the level rejoinder. "If you remember which king you truly represent."

* * *

"...and what makes you think I am so willing to send my emissaries to your kingdom?" asked the Son of Zulu, the gleam in his sparkling eyes evidencing defiance more than inquisitiveness.

"It reflects, I believe," Farewell suggested in a deliberately amiable tone, "your own personal desire, Nkosi."

A silent spectator to the verbal duel between King and "Chieftain" that was being enacted in the privacy of the Royal Hut, Fynn took note of the Emperor's powerful neck muscles tightening with the suggestion of annoyance.

"Does it..?" the King brusquely petitioned his interlocutor. "How?" he demanded, crowning a piercing sidelong glance with an impervious brow.

The lieutenant briefly withheld his rejoinder and sat cocooned in his own thoughts, allowing the patterns of his argument to take shape. Disturbed by his companion's hesitancy to reply, Fynn fervently hoped that Farewell's quick-wittedness and cunning had in no way been damaged by their "honest talk" on the beach. Securing another ship was most important - for many reasons, Fynn mused, calling to mind the bottle of "magic" Macassar Oil in which were left only a precious handful of applications.

"For almost a year now, we have lived in the sphere of your kind hospitality," Farewell at length riposted. "We have been generous in sharing with you the gifts of our culture..."

Fynn stifled a wry smile, as he listened attentively to the lieutenant. "No," the man of medicine considered. "There's been no damage to the lieutenant's cunning." If anything, the realisation of "which king he truly represents" had served to sharpen the man's artful craft.

"Just as you have been generous in sharing with us the fruits of your conquests by acknowledging our right to live on the harbour and environs of Port Natal," the Englishman continued, unravelling the fabric of his inveigling appeal. "We have striven to build a life together under the auspices of peace and friendship - and, even in war, we have fought side by side and we have won."

Shaka suddenly perceived Mgobozi's dying words reverberating in his heart, and he was somewhat appeased to hear the lieutenant use the pronoun "we" - "we have won".

"Indeed," Farewell was saying, "most aspects of our permanence here have gone to prove that it is possible for Whites and Zulus to live in harmony. And I feel that Joji should be made aware of the good will we have established. I feel that the time is ripe for us to take the next step towards a formal alliance that will provide more lasting unity."

Shaka regarded the Englishman with lingering circumspection and felt a suspicious uneasiness pass through his mind. Though his heart held strong in its desire to preserve his relationship with the Swallows, and though Febana's words sounded right in essence, there was something in the Swallow's tone that made Shaka wary.

"Unity," the Emperor repeated, weighing the word objectively. "An interesting concept, Febana, especially when referred to kingdoms like our own, populated by men who are so obviously," he extended his open hand as if to indicate its colouring, "-- different. Can day and night find...unity? Or is their 'alliance' merely a cycle in which one replaces the other?"

Farewell grinned, finding in the high intellectual stamina of his illustrious host a source of constant inspiration.

"If it is a cycle, Nkosi, there can be no true replacement," the lieutenant considered aloud, evolving the King's analogy. "We go to sleep at night trusting that, though it is dark, the Day will return, and, in the course of the Day we are never so foolish as to think that the Night has abandoned us forever. In fact," Farewell eyed Shaka candidly, concluding his parry in their verbal battle of wits, "they need each other - Night and Day - to complete the Cycle of the Heavens. And, in the reality of that Need, lies their intrinsic Unity."

Catching the ball on the bounce, Shaka pulled back his full lips in a challenging grin. "And you think I need you?!" he asked and instantly poised his ear for the reply.

"Yes, Nkosi," the lieutenant's tone was flat and dispassionate, a statement of facts. "If you did not need us, you would have killed us. -- Long ago."

A brief interlude ensued in which Shaka's gaze remained locked with Febana's. Then the King tilted his head back in a burst of uproarious laughter that swelled to assail the huge royal hut. Both Fynn and Farewell were contaminated by the jovial effusion, and chuckled along, though their eyes disclosed no real amusement. At length Shaka was still again, and when he spoke, his question took the Whites unawares.

"And why do you need me, Febana?" the King queried with striking sincerity.

Fynn directed his pale eyes at the lieutenant and thought of all the banal answers one could provide for such a seemingly rhetorical question. Answers that were all based on the "Fear of Shaka".

"You are the Future of this land, Baba," Farewell remarked, his response most pleasing to Shaka as well as to Fynn (who found it a curious mixture of truth and flattery). "Anyone who wishes to make his home here, needs you."

"Yes," the Emperor's mighty head bobbed up and down in agreement. "I am the Future. Joji and uCristo must be told that."

At the mention of Christ, Fynn wondered how much longer he could keep the Holy Lord "physical, earthly, and a resident of Buckingham" before he was forced to take up the matter of Jesus Returning to His Father.

"Very well. You will leave at dawn," Shaka deliberated, jolting Fynn from his thoughts of the Ascension, and Farewell into state of attentive alarm. "With two regiments which will serve as a..." he was searching for the term, "...'royal escort' - to your king's Citadel and back."

"It is very far, Baba," the lieutenant heard himself say, visualising the trek overland to Cape Town - or, in more fantastic terms, the journey on foot across Africa to England.

"We have time," the Zulu rebutted, crossing his arms as if he had already begun to wait.

"Yes," the lieutenant concurred, regaining his verbal footing. "But there is no need to waste it, when it can be better employed in more constructive purposes. Besides, such a journey would be most hazardous. - We felt that," he quickly inserted, "it would be more practical to go by sea."

An appreciable fraction of a second elapsed before the real import of Farewell's words reached Shaka's intuition, causing the King to freeze, his head inclined slightly to the side as he peered at Febana enigmatically. Though the lieutenant had coloured his plan well, the underlying shades of Reality shone through, and Shaka sensed that this planned departure might be without return, and in his ever-suspicious mind the words "by sea" were inexorably linked to the notion: "escape".

And when the king conjured up an image of his world deprived of the Swallows', he was suddenly gripped by a disconcerting emptiness. It was then that he had the insight to realise that Mgobozi had been right: - like the Snake, the Whites had insidiously entered his hut, his heart, his Heavens; and he now truly "needed them". He needed the assurance of their "magical influence"; he needed the wealth of their knowledge and the tools of their Power; he needed the thrill of impenetrable mystery inherent in the fabulous and illusory Protagonist of the Swallows' Book: the Master made Victim, the Absurd "Rival" King of Contradictions Who rules the Realm of the Preposterous with the Sceptre of Love.

Yet, on a purely human level, Shaka realised that he had become accustomed to the inimitable companionship of these outrageous Strangers from the Sea, and that, if they were to leave, he would miss the stimulating disputes and refreshing intellectual "battles" (with their own Speed, Endurance, and Strategy) that he waged with Febana and his sangoma -- so unlike the fleshless, onesided relationship based on Fear that he had established with his own people.

No, they would not leave him forever, Shaka resolved. He would prevent it.

"By sea...?" the King replicated at last. "I was not told that your vessel, - the craft with the white wings had returned."

"It hasn't, Baba. - But we shall construct another, with your help," the lieutenant's attention happened to fall on the mat with Daniel's "immortal" lettering and he added, "a much finer ship. - One that will impress Joji. - We shall call it...the 'Shaka'."

"The 'Shaka'?" Shaka echoed, barely concealing his childish joy and the immense gratification of knowing that there would be a ship carrying to distant shores the "immortal letters" imprinted on "Daniel's mat".

"It shall be the finest of ships," Farewell smiled.

"And who would accompany you on this...Embassy to Joji?"

"My men of course," the lieutenant said, casually, avoiding all emphasis, "and those who have the right to speak in your name, Baba. Your Prime Minister and two or three of your chief indunas. - To make the embassy credible."

"I see," the Emperor said, his tone suddenly eerie, sinister. Fynn and Farewell echanged an uneasy glance as they heard him comment, "You have spun your web well, Febana. Yet you failed to consider that the Great Elephant is not a fool. Do you really think I would just let you all leave as you came -- returning home with my Prime Minister and chief indunas as 'trophies' to prove that your 'hunt' was successful?"

Stunned to immobility, Farewell stared at the King in dumb amazement until the sound of his own voice stirred him.

"I don't understand, Nkosi," the Englishman's words were hollow with incredulity as he felt all hope of leaving suddenly dashed. "That was never my intention."

"Nor is it mine, Febana," said the King, withdrawing into the shell of his boundless authority. "Yet, the idea is in principle valid, and we will do as you suggest," he appended, to the Swallows' further surprise. "With one minor change. You, Febana, and umFekethile will go alone. While you," the Zulu turned to glare at Fynn, "and the others will stay behind. As an indication of your good will and 'friendship'."

Farewell was crushed by the news. It meant that only he and Wilkins ("umFekethile" signifying "the Freckled One"), would be allowed to take advantage of the ship whilst Holstead, Popham, Cane, Daniel and Fynn would be left behind. It meant, absurdly enough, that the two who originally wanted to stay would sail, and that those who had insisted on sailing would remain "land-locked".

Feeling totally defeated in his intent, Farewell attempted to offer a rebuttal, yet Shaka complemented his embittering decision by dismissing the two Whites with: -- "My 'need' for you and your people will be endured till after the next harvest. If you are not back by then, your companions will die."

"One year," Farewell told Fynn as they strode across Bulawayo. "One year to build a ship, seal an alliance with the British Empire and return.- It can't be done!"

"Where have I heard that before?" Fynn remarked, amazed to find that he could still smile.

* * *

"...and so, with our determination and bold-spirits in hand," Wilkins set down in his Diary on the dates successive to the tense summit with Shaka, "we set out to accomplish this mammoth task; namely: to build a vessel with the native material and timbers as we might be enabled to procure suitable for the purpose. Although the undertaking appeared quite laborious, if not nearly impracticable (particularly in the short time given us), the realisation that something was being done for the purpose of effecting a link with the outside world greatly helped to palliate the discontentment of our comrades - which was of no ordinary magnitude..."

Further excerpts from the Chronicle & Diary (selected and abridged from entries written throughout the rest of the Year 1825) reveal, as quoted here:--

"Yet, even before our labours on the ship could commence, the collective inquietude and vexation (felt especially by Holstead, who, I might add, had been a cause of dismay from the mission's onset), was greatly augmented by the news that only the Lieutenant and I would embark on the journey. As could be expected, Holstead and Popham made this a point of great contention, going as far as suggesting that there might have been foul play on the part of our mission's valiant leader. Fortunately Fynn (who had been present at the meeting with Shaka, and was unquestionably respected by each of us) quickly put an end to this defamatory intimation by forcibly asserting that Lt. Farewell had done his very utmost to secure passage for all, and his failure to succeed in this effort was due only to the King's innate distrustfulness. Furthermore, Fynn went on to appeal: 'We've months of building ahead of us,' he put the matter to Holstead in most laudable terms. 'A great deal can happen in that period, Thomas. Perhaps the King will change his mind. I personally will have regular court visits in my 'elixir sessions' (as he called them in jeering). I shall bring up the matter with as much tact as is given me, and, if God so wills it, I shall endeavour to represent the collective cause'. Indeed, in his great self-sacrifice, Fynn went as far as to suggest that he alone remain behind as 'hostage', whilst the others be allowed to return home. This act of magnanimity served to ingratiate the men and to instil hope in their dissident hearts, especially when he told them, as indication of his good sense: 'Little can be accomplished by dissension. So let us set out in our work and pray that the wheel of fortune will spin to our favour.'..."

"The entire first half of June," continues the abridged quote from Wilkins's Diary, "was employed in the studying of various ship designs and plans with an eye to selecting the most feasible blueprint for our purposes. We were most elated to find that Cane - besides being an expert builder and woodworker - was also a practical shipwright, and had been brought up to the trade...The design finally chosen was that of a standard two-masted ketch-rigged trading coaster with standing bowsprits and jib-boom, and an arrangement of head sails and gear that closely resembled the tabernacle format of the schooner. And, though this sort of detail is foreign to the purpose of this Chronicle, I herewith note its dimensions to be: Length: 87.5 ft, Breadth: 22.0 ft, Depth: 9.5 ft, Tonnage: a calculated 95 tons gross..."

"Towards the first part of July, Lt. Farewell, Cane, and I crossed the environs of the Bay to view the country, and to select a fit place on the coast for the location of the dockyards where the vessel would be built and fitted for sailing. The spot conceived to be most convenient was situated on the declivity of the hill on the western side of the Harbour, parallel with the isthmus of Fort Farewell and adjacent to a great wooded area providing lumber for ship building..."

Leaving a direct quote of Wilkins, it must be related that the Colonial Office Chronicle & Diary goes on to cover - in relative detail - the actual building of the vessel which was started in July, 1825 (when "trees were felled, stripped of bark and squared, and the keel was laid down on the sandy declivity") and brought to an end on Christmas Eve of the same year. The Diary entries in this period show a quite smooth and tranquil progression in the construction of the vessel. The annotations disclose how the Whites ("assisted by a large portion of the eeseeSway Regiment") cut and trimmed the timber, shaping it into the rise of the keel and the arching bow, the hull and the gunwales; it reveals how Zulu women pounded cowhide and skins into a paper-thin consistency and sewed the leathery material into sails ("...of the square and stailsail variety, with slanting leeches and reinforced clews endowed with lined peaks for added security..."); the Journal describes how the masts, the yards, the spars, the jibs and sprits were trimmed from branches and sapling, how the fitted hull was smeared with animal fat, and how the finished decks and booms were lacquered with a substance of thick red ochre (similar to the "isiBuda" paste).

As set out in Tim's Diary, the entire "laborious undertaking" lasted approximately six months; - a period of time, which, under the extraordinary circumstances, may truly be rated as an astonishing feat (especially by those who are familiar with the hazards of ship-building).

No exceptional event was reported by Wilkins in this period, save for a "tragic interlude" in the month of November "which almost caused all our hopes of a departure from Natal to vanish forever".

It seems (according to the Chronicle & Diary) that, at one point in the course of the ship's construction ("...early in the span of August"), Holstead had arranged a nocturnal encounter with Popham. In the secrecy and seclusion of the dense bush country near the Port, the two men seemed to have reconfirmed their unshakeable fear that the Zulu King would remain inflexible in his decision that all but Farewell and Wilkins be detained in Natal (virtually in a state of "house arrest"). In consequence, the two men determined "to take matters into their own hands, and squirrel away as much building material as would go unnoticed by the others...for the ultimate purpose of manufacturing a raft with which to escape on their own".

Having done so, Holstead and Popham completed their clandestine vessel, and "choosing the moonless night of November 13th, they undertook to launch it in the covert shadows of the rocky cape known as Point Fynn". Yet the two dastardly men forgot to take into consideration what Farewell had once noted: to wit, that they were in "an Empire whose King has eyes and ears everywhere".

On the morning of November 14th (the Diary further relates), the inhabitants of Port Natal awoke to a "lovely summer day, not excessively hot, nor exceedingly humid". Yet, whatever might have been "lovely" about this mild summer day, was instantly overshadowed by the sight of Popham - impaled on a post jutting out of the promontory's jagged rocks, his expression of absolute anguish and excruciating pain frozen in the chilling jaws of rigor mortis.

Sheer terror and abhorrence seized the handful of Whites inhabiting the Port (or so Tim noted in this specific entry). And when Farewell searched the vicinity for the perpetrator of this hideous crime, he found Shaka in the company of a trembling Holstead who was being fixedly held at bay by a detachment of Ufasimba.

"...only in the face of such incidents as Popham's impalement," is the direct quote that follows this ghastly event (dated November 5, 1825) "is the reader reminded that, though Shaka had many facets to his character that were agreeable and even pleasant, courteous, and generous, - nothing could restrain his ferocity and the joyous impulse he felt as seeing the blood of innocent creatures flowing at his feet...."

On the Eve of Christmas, 1825, Tim wrote: -- "We had now our ketch ready for launching - everything having been completed for that purpose, - and after naming her the 'Shaka' and inscribing the nominative on her bows (in a gala Yuletide ceremony which greatly delighted our Host), she glided gently down the slipway into the sea. Then, floating on the bosom of the ocean, she brought her bows up to the billows, as if evincing the desire to take a longing farewell of the spot that had given her birth - a Birth which had coincided with that of 'uCristo'. Though she looked odd (even comical, some would say) with her rough bows and splintered decks painted in red ochre, her heavy cowhide sails of patchwork flapping in the wind, - she looked proud and as seaworthy as any polished Admiralty frigate We called her 'Farewell's Ark' without feeling that we had wronged Noah..."

"Soon after, Lt. Farewell and I embarked and hoisted the Union Jack on the mainmast next to a rudimentary 'Zulu Flag' of Daniel's design - a soft leopardskin hide bearing the emblem of the blue crane feather and the ivory tassels...."

"When the 'Shaka' had been laden with its cargo of cattle, foodstuffs, ivory and other 'gifts for Joji', the Shakan Emissaries joined us on board - with a great deal of uneasiness and sharp reluctance as well as apprehension, I might add (indeed, they had never set foot on a "creature with white wings"). They were: Ngomanee and the indunas Lutuli and Kuta...

"In the late afternoon, after taking due leave of our comrades in a very emotional goodbye filled with the promises of a successful journey and a speedy return before the Harvest (or, at least before April - which was deadline set by Shaka), our noble vessel glided out of the bay. Fynn, Holstead, Cane, and Daniel looked after us - barely hiding their sorrow. The idea was then inexorably brought to the fore of my silent reverie: 'Will we ever see them again,' I inquired aloud of the Lieutenant. 'That, my dear Tim,' he answered, 'depends a great deal on how this nautical abortion endures the journey, and on how the Governor and the Cape Authorities react to our unique venture. We can only hope that God is truly with us, and that Somerset's curiosity is stronger than his prejudice. -- What is it they say on Christmas Eve, Tim? - 'Peace on earth to men of good will'? Well then, Peace to us all is my wish, and may the political institutions of Pilate that look upon peace as an undesirable commodity spare us from another Crucifixion'...

"Such were the Lieutenant's words," Wilkins remarked at the end of the annotation, "and now that he is no longer with us, those words cause my heart to pain in their telling recollection of the past."

CHAPTER XLVI
"BABA"(FATHER)

At the end of the second month following their encounter on the banks of the Mkumbane, Pampata knew she was with Shaka's child, and the unexpected and astonishing realisation evoked in her a feeling of great intimacy, of cherished possession, and a deep sense of fulfilment.

An immense wave of pride, gratitude and love welled forth out of her heart towards the Prince of her life, and she felt closer to him than she had ever thought possible. A part of him. Inexorably and joyously linked to his grandeur by and through the seed that dwelt and grew in here womb.

And with a sudden and elating singleness of conviction, she perceived this to be her true Destiny - the Order and Purpose that the Ancestors had ordained from the first moment she had met her Lord in the domains of the Eminent Dingiswayo. She now clearly understood that her principal role in life had never been to be loved by Shaka, to be his wife and cherished companion, nor yet had she been fated to share his hopes, his fears, his dreams, his innermost thoughts. No, her Destiny, the destiny of "The One Who Flatters" was greater, far greater (or so she considered it): she had been chosen to maintain his excellence through the propagation of his seed; to bear his child, the offspring of the Great Mountain.

It mattered little - she rationalized - that the first attempt at conception so many years ago had been ineffective. That could have been only due to the fact that conditions were not yet ripe. The Nation, Shaka's Nation, his Empire had still been a dream then. There would have been no place, no need to have a child -- then. It had been too soon. Far too soon. He, himself, had not been ready.

Yet now, so much was different - Pampata reflected cupping her hands protectively over her belly with a fanciful smile of pure bliss. The Nation was there now for the whole world to see and praise, and its august Sovereign appeared to be approaching a less self-seeking and a less "heroic" stage of life. More prepared, possibly, to be the Father not only of an Empire, but of a child.

Or so Pampata speculated, basing her assumption on the fact that the Zulu King had visibly changed in the past year. Ever since the Strangers had arrived. He had become more contemplative and introspective, more accessible; - yes, he had become more "human", she decided.

Yet...

"Yet how would he react to this unexpected news? - Would he go against his own ruling on forced celibacy and accept the child?" she wondered, remembering that, in keeping with Shaka's own law, it was forbidden "to have a family", forbidden for a female to fall pregnant without the express consent of the Emperor. In her case, naturally, there had been no such formal consent, and - through neglect born of enrapture, so to say - she had received him without due precaution.

That meant - according to the imperial decision - that she would be forced to ingest the foul-tasting "iHlunguhlungu" root that medicinally induced the interruption of pregnancy - and with it (in Pampata's own case), the termination of a life's dream.

"But would Shaka require her to abort his own flesh and blood just to set an example for his troops?!" - she asked herself, her heartbeat quickening at the very prospect of such a ghastly occurrence. "That would be preposterous, mad! He was King, after all, and could do anything he wished! And it was every King's legitimate right to have an heir to the throne!" And she secretly hoped it was his wish as well.

"No," Pampata vehemently resolved, "he would never ask her to abort!"

Never!

Then she faltered, recalling that the word "never" was just not a part of this unpredictable man's vocabulary. Indeed, with Shaka, Life was a guessing game. That was part of his charm and the foundation of his Power.

And yet? Would he, could he order the death of---

Clutching her belly, Pampata fancied that she felt the child stirring and caught her breath, strangling the very thought of any harm befalling this tiny promise of life that her body was feeding. But the doubt kept whirling in her mind in a dizzying frenzy of mounting anxiety that left her confused.

There was only one person who would know what to do.

Nandi.

*

"Does he know?" was the first question Nandi put to Pampata upon learning of the pregnancy.

"No, Ndlovukazi. - I thought it best if I first sought your advice."

"You have done well..." the Queen of Queens retorted, leaning back away from the purling glow of the hearth, and receding into the protective darkness of the shadows that clung to the curved thatching of the hut's walls. For Nandi, the news of Pampata's state had been unexpected, and the Royal Mother now sat unmoving, her mind needing time to cope with the implications at hand. She weighed the courses of action open to her, and deliberated on how to best deal with this event that might virtually change Shaka's life, her own, and their life together as the inseparable mother and son. Nandi's first consideration was, of course, Pampata herself, and she realised, with a trace of self-reproof, that she had never really given the woman adequate importance. There had never been cause to - or so Nandi had thought. Obviously, she had been wrong. Pampata's place at her son's side was apparently more than just decorative.

And this bothered the Queen.

Tilting her head slightly, Nandi rested her investigating glance on the younger woman, and, as if seeing her for the first time, her feline eyes exposed Pampata's body and soul to a deliberate and attentive scrutiny. And she was suddenly conscious of spawning jealousy opposing her effort to remain objective.

The effusive glow of the fire threw into conspicuous relief the smooth, unwrinkled contours of Pampata's features, causing her brilliant black eyes to take on a lustrous, passionate sheen - the throbbing femininity that invariably accompanies gestation. "She is beautiful, of course," Nandi conceded unwillingly. "Of no arresting beauty," she quickly retaliated, "nor striking in appearance (as she herself had been at that stage of her life). - Just pretty. Very pretty. And at an age when a woman is in love with love, and with desire itself! A dangerous age," the Queen Mother mused in recollection of her own overbearing affair with Senzangakona, "an age when one is most likely to seek the... 'unreachable'."

And for Pampata, Nandi reflected with a feeling of possessive pride, the Son of Zulu definitely was and must remain..."unreachable".

She would see to that! No one would contest her rightful and undisputed place at her son's side.

No one!

Yet she was carrying his child. The child of her own child! And that could not - that must not be changed, the Queen decided, realising, with compelling insight, that she already felt a great wave of affection and warmth for the tiny creature in the other woman's belly whom she longed to cradle in her arms.

In juxtaposition, Nandi could not help but think of her own first pregnancy - the one specific factor that had changed and revolutionized her life!

"Nandi, daughter of Bhebhe is with child," she remembered the joyous tidings confided to the Langeni messenger over forty years ago, and she remembered the answer, the cold-hearted, merciless answer that had been the beginning of the end of her Love: "Senzangakona kaJama Zulu knows no one by the name of Nandi, daughter of Bhebhe."

Repudiation!

"How would Shaka react to the same tidings?" - his mother wondered. Would the "Beetle" ever risk having a "Beetle" of his own who might one day contend his father's place on the throne. "Never leave an enemy behind," Shaka had told his troops. Would he now allow such a potentially great "blood" enemy to be born?

"Most certainly not," Nandi feared, and it was then that she knew, with crystal clarity and with a fierce rapacity, that she wanted that child, the "illegitimate" offspring of the "Bastard Outcast" who had blazed a path across Africa. She felt that she wanted that "royal" child, the true blood of her blood, almost as much as she had wanted Shaka.

"And no one must stand in her way!" - she brooded fervidly.

The Queen's gaze returned to linger on Pampata's eyes, - eyes so alive with the contrasting passions that accompany motherhood. Passions veiled under the gloss of profound vulnerability.

"You have done well to come and seek my advice," she finally said aloud, the sound of her voice carrying the undertones of conspiracy and satisfaction. "You have done well, my child..."

*

And thus it came to pass that in the first Moon of the Month of uNtlangulana (June, 1825), Pampata was sent far away to the Hills of eTaleni near the emHlatuze River, to live in hiding in one of the personal homesteads of the Queen of Queens: a place called emKindini.

The irrefutable wish of the Great Female Elephant was that the young woman should remain in this concealed outpost until the child was born and until such time as she herself saw fit to inform the Emperor of the momentous event.

Since Nandi daughter of Bhebhe had always been a withdrawn and "private person", confiding in no one except, eventually, in her son (which was in this case impossible), it was never clear - even after the Queen's untimely death - exactly how she had intended proceeding with Pampata, with the child (once it was born), with the fact of the birth itself and its secret circumstances and implications which drew in their wake a plethora of plots and schemes. The fact is, there were rumours at emKindini that the sangoma Majola had twice visited Pampata (in the month of August, and again in October), and a shepherd from iBabanango swore that in November he had seen the Wise Sitayi herself at that very homestead.

It was even murmured amongst the Queen's handmaidens that the Nkosikazi was plotting something. Indeed, considering Nandi's undying ambition and her very special attachment to her son, it can never be completely excluded that the idea of killing Pampata after the birth of the child had not crossed the Queen's mind.

It had.

But - as it happened - Death came in another form.

*

Seven months after Pampata's meeting with Nandi, on the seventh day of the seventh moon of uNyaka, in the Year 1825 (the date corresponding to the launching of the ship "Shaka"), on a placid night that heralded the mild Zephyrs of Promise, under the starry vault of the Heavens where the moon shone peaceful and true - a child was born in emKindini.

And before her lips shed the tingle of her joyous smile, in obedience to the mandate of Those Who Inhabit the Mountains, Pampata gave the child, a boy, the name Ukuma kaShaka Zulu.

Ukuma kaShaka - the "Immortality of Shaka".

The First Born of his Nation.

The Child who was the Language of the New Africa, the One Destined to deal with the Plague.

uBaba ya MaBantu - the Father of the People As One...

*

...and from the Pulpit high atop the Pinnacle of Kings, Sitayi read the night, and her heart conceived that all was good and well. Yet, as she swept up the Wind, wielding the Force of the Heavens, the sangoma felt the Darkness rolling back on to the Birth of the Heir Apparent.

Leaving the Gates open to the Plague that would rage for ten-and-two before the Advent of the Appeaser.

*

Though all the Emperor's spies had had express orders to find her, Joko was the one who finally approached his King with the information that she was hidden in Nandi's homestead at EmKindini.

He also told Shaka of the child.

His child.

Near the fumes and reddish glow of the fire, Pampata sat curled on a mat nursing her son, the child she shared with the Great Mountain; and as she looked down at the babe, with tender and pensive eyes, it seemed to the woman that in all the range of human sentiment there was no joy that could be elevated and spiritualized more than the gift of life born of love.

Beyond the hearth, far from its warming glow, Nandi sat in silent appraisal of the other woman's enchanted rapture, and she felt pity for Pampata, for herself, and for the artless guile of the human condition. Yet she realised - with a pang of compassion - that the young woman's love must be very genuine to have sustained her through emotional privation and disillusionment. And, appreciating that devotion, Nandi decided to wait, to let Pampata enjoy the child - just a little while longer. After all, the Queen mused, she had deserved it. It was a fine boy! Beautiful and with eyes like his father - the eyes of Nandi.

Pampata was the first to sense his bodeful presence, and she froze, wide-eyed, terror-stricken. Then Nandi heard his restrained breathing and, detecting the danger etched on the other woman's face, her eyes leapt to life, taking in the semblance of her son standing at the hut's entrance, his powerful legs framing its threshold.

Slowly, with leaden footfalls, Shaka advanced upon the hunched figure of the mother of his child, and, well recognising the glint of savage fury in his eye, Pampata shrank back in dread, clutching the babe protectively to her breasts.

"Shaka..." the young woman hazarded addressing the man to break the disquieting spell of his wild gaze. Yet Shaka disregarded Pampata, as he moved to the mat and knelt by his own flesh, glowering at the child with the consternation of incredulity, dazzled, crazed by the presence of this living externalisation of himself.

Feeling suddenly weakened, - as if his son were already sapping his blood, contesting his father's right to live, - Shaka could not contain a desire to reach out with a trembling hand and lightly graze the boys face. And Pampata smiled when his hand touched her son, their son, and, seeing this act on the part of Shaka as a sign of hope, she gently rested the baby in the cradle of his grasp.

The child instinctively clasped Shaka round the neck, pressing close to him with the sweet smell of milk and of Life. Aghast, the Emperor stiffened in repulsion, in horror, in the mysterious revolt of his heart; whilst his son clung to him - holding fast as if this Titan of Cruelty were a refuge from harm, from fear, from sorrow, from the Unknown.

And while the babe clung to his neck, and while Pampata dared to hope, Shaka sensed that the weakness was taking hold of his heart, sapping, sapping, sapping; and the King said nothing - felt nothing, save for the unavailing regret that it was too late, that it had always been too late. For him. For the Son of Zulu.

The passion of wrath returned sweeping away all distraction, and Shaka felt the choking fumes of bitterness rising to his lips. Hooking a long finger round his son's chubby arm, the King disengaged the child's embrace and, continuing to ignore Pampata, he returned the infant to his mother and shifted his spectral gaze to Nandi's petrified countenance.

"So you have deceived me," he began in a hoarse, provoking tone. "Just as you deceived my father! With the curse of an unwanted child!"

Pampata gasped, her eyes flitting from Nandi to Shaka with the sting of hurt and incomprehension.

"Shaka--," Nandi tried to retort in supplication, as her son neared her.

"I have made you Queen of Queens," his accusation with rising to a fever pitch, "the most powerful woman in the world? But that wasn't enough for you, was it mother? You wanted more!" His flashing eyes were cast on the infant. "You wanted me! To possess me through him!"

"I love you, Shaka..." Nandi could barely withhold her tears.

"Love?" the Emperor sneered his contempt. "We are incapable of that emotion, mother. All we feel, all we have ever really felt is vengeance and hate.- Hate has been our reason for living! It is the one emotion that has inflamed our ambition!" The man's tone was suddenly overwhelmed by a commanding sadness. "Love never had a chance...with us. If my father hadn't loved you, he would have been a man. If he hadn't loved me, he would have been a king. Instead he lived the life of a dog, whilst we fed on his affection like scavengers!"

As she looked on, stunned beyond feeling, Pampata realised that she had inadvertently become the silent, neglected spectator not of a tragedy, but rather of some grotesque comedy of errors where Nandi was irreversible cast as protagonist. Indeed, even though the son in Pampata's arms was her own, for Shaka there can be but one woman, one mother...

Nandi ever Nandi.

"No!" Nandi yelled over her tears. "I loved him! I loved your father."

Jolted by the astonishing revelation, Shaka stood perfectly still, his head slightly cocked to the side, his bewildered gaze rivetted on his mother. He had never heard her voice such a confession. Indeed, since his early childhood, Nandi had always told him quite the opposite. And he was now hurt, hurt and startled.

"I loved him, Shaka! " the Daughter of Bhebhe wept aloud. "I loved him more than all else! More than---"

"Me?!" the Son of Zulu broke in. "More than me, mother?" his brows arched in an insidious twinkle.

"Different," Nandi's head was spinning and her words came confused. "It was different. I was..." Sighing, she fell silent.

"You see, mother?" Shaka's smile was uncanny, macabre. "It's all too confusing for us. Hating was easier," the King turned to look back down at his son. "Much easier," he repeated in a hollow voice.

"He is the future, Shaka," Nandi pleaded. "Through him we---

Spinning round, his eyes on fire, Shaka lashed out and struck Nandi across the face, a deafening blow that hurled the woman to the floor of the hut, bringing blood to her lips and nose.

"No mother!" the King's chest was heaving with his fury. "Not we! No longer we! - It is time for the 'Beetle' to go on alone! He is the Future! - He alone."

When Shaka left the hut, his maddened, anguished eyes met Joko's and the King nodded, giving the order, and strode away, into the night. His pace quickened when he reached the gates of emKindini, and moved out onto the moonlit contours of the veld. He walked faster, and faster, leaving the homestead behind him. And moments later, he had almost reached the horizon; yet the night was still and, though he was far, Pampata's hysterical screams reached his ears nonetheless.

As did the wailing of an infant. The shrill, despairing wail of the promise of life that was claimed by Death, the Companion.

And though Shaka knew what had happened, he felt nothing but the sudden void that had gripped his heart.

So she had loved him.

Suddenly nothing made sense anymore.

CHAPTER XLVII
"ILIKAPA"(CAPE TOWN)

Bright and early on the morning of January 21, 1826, Old Man Samuel (as he was respectfully called by the Cape Town Port Authorities) shuffled up the spiral staircase of the newly-constructed Mouille Point Lighthouse. Reaching the lantern-dome high atop the tower, Samuel threw open the windows (as was his daily habit), and sucked the salty air deep into his lungs. Then, run- ning an admiring gaze over the azure expanse of Table Bay shintillating in the silver rays of the morning sun, the old man suddenly gasped, forcefully expelling the breath of salt air, and stood gaping, astonished to the point of wide-eyed disbelief.

"What the---!" murmured Old Man Samuel, the excla- mation dying on his lips as he hurriedly pressed the lense of his bifocals to the eyepiece of his brass fourdraw telescope and trained its sights on a distant object floating off Hout Bay. When he had the "object" clearly framed in the spyglass's magnifying field, his disbelief grew all the more upon realising that he was looking at a craft, of sorts -- though his extensive nautical experience could barely conceive of a more specific definition for the vessel. Its design, the shape of the hull, the decks s (painted red!) and the elongated bow, would tend to put the "ship" in the category of a trawler, - the old man assessed - though its squat keel resembled that of a barge and its double-masts were spaced like those of a Bermuda ketch. "And those sails!" Samuel thought in marvel, "what the hell are they made of?!"

But what most astounded (and amused) the elderly lighthouse keeper were the passengers of the fantastic vessel. Adjusting the focus on his telescope, Samuel could distinctly make out three black men at the forwards decks of the ship (next to a glistening pile of ivory!), dressed in fabulous attire with leopardskins and plumes galore! And, aft, at the helm (near the cattle), two whites ("Or were they Arabs?" - the old man wondered) with flowing beards, long hair pulled back in pigtails and donning colourful hides and feathers. In all his years of naval service, he'd never seen anything quite like it!

"Daniel!" Samuel cried out, his voice rumbling down the hollow interior of the lighthouse. "Daniel! Get up here? Hurry!" the old man ordered, evoking the cadenced sound of footfalls running up the metal steps.

"What it is, Sam?" Daniel was out of breath and wiping the shaving foam from his face when he reached the observatory deck.

"Feast your eyes on this beauty, m'lad," the old man grinned to his young assistant relinquishing his place at the telescope. "Must've been built to escape from bedlam!" "My God!" was Daniel's first reaction as he concentrated his gaze on the disheveled, bizarre ship. "Look! There's a name on it!" "Daring batch, whoever they be," the old man chuckled. "What is it?"

"S-H-A-...K-A, I think. It's hard to make out," the young man muttered. "And flying a Union Jack."

"Shaka..." Samuel repeated under his breath, padding to a large nautical ledger and running his arthritic finger down a list of registered ships. "Shaka. Nope! Nothin' here! Run off and inform Burgess. You'll find him by Graving Dock this time o'day, I'd reckon. Ask'im if and where she's to tie up. Then come up and fetch me, hear!" the old man chuckled again. "I wouldn't miss seein' this lunatic whore of a boat for nothin'!"

On the "lunatic whore" in question, Wilkins and Farewell were at the gunwales peering at Cape Town for the first time in almost two years. Their reactions were mixed. In the one case, Wilkins, the freckled member of the Colonial Office felt unmistakably enthused by this return to "civilisation" which he saw as triumphant, - being that the architects of the promised alliance with the Zulus were virtually "at hand".

The feelings of the lieutenant, however, were somewhat more complex as he gazed out at the familiar shapes and patterns of his culture. The naval officer sensed an odd detachment from those vine-covered pergolas, from those constructions build of "mud and wattle", and from the paved sidewalks where pedestrians wearing cotton and lace strolled with thoughts of shopping, tea & scones, banking hours and the poetical works of Moore. He felt somehow divorced from it all, as if he no longer belonged, as if he had somehow "outgrown" his culture's certitudes and values.

And Farewell's heart could not help but disclaim that world -- just as the butterfly, in its natural development, is made to shed the confinement of its grub. And though he wished to take flight, the man still knew not in whose sky he belonged. So he faltered, his wings still ensnared in the comfortable larva of the commonplace.

"I wonder what's going on in their minds...?" Wilkins's voice served to rouse the man from his reverie.

Turning, the lieutenant followed the young man's gaze to Ngomane, Lutuli, and Kuta who stood stoically facing the Swallows' citadel with eyes, impenetrable and gelid that evinced no emotion whatsoever. It was as if the three Zulus had lost all feeling.

"They've been like that since the Cape came into view," Tim noted. "Do you suppose they're afraid?" "No, Tim," was Farewell's level rejoinder. "Just cautious. They're in our territory now and, like the Leopard, they've withdrawn into a guarded shell of watchful diffidence. And our alliance will depend a great deal on what they see..."

A short while transpired before the first "Cape Swallows" made contact with the extraordinary craft. Here, too, there was watchful diffidence (on both sides) as a longboat jounced over the waves and pulled up alongside the "Shaka". Flying the banners of the Cape Harbour Authorities, the boat was manned by Hottentote oarsmen and commanded by a young British subject wearing the uniform of a Chief Petty Officer. Old Man Samuel and Daniel were perched in the back of the longboat, their eyes wide and attentive in their inspection of the curious vessel. "Who commands this...this," the Petty Officer, Burgess by name, found it hard to say, "this 'ship'?"

"I do, Officer," Farewell announced, realising that he had instinctively assumed a stature, erect and proud, that was military in bearing. "And who might you be?" Burgess inquired of the bearded man, his eyes flitting from the ivory, past the cattle, to Farewell's headdress of ostrich feathers.

Suddenly reminded of how "peculiar" he must look to his own people (indeed, to his own Navy), the lieutenant faltered somewhat before saluting the other Officer and identifying himself as: "Lt. Francis George Farewell, R.N. - Here on official business with Sir Charles Somerset, Governor of the Cape."

In spite of the light sea breeze, Samuel's chuckling reached Farewell's and Ngomane's ears, causing both men to stiffen. Casting an eye in the Zulu's direction, the lieutenant was aware of the Prime Minister's probing gaze, and he felt angry with his own people for making him look the fool in front of his "guests".

"I see," replied the Petty Officer to Farewell's formal introduction and his lips were tainted with an ironic smile upon noting, "We fail to find your ship in our registers..." he paused slightly before adding, with little conviction: "... 'Lieutenant'."

"I should imagine not," came Farewell's biting riposte. "One need not be an accomplished sleuth to deduce that this barque is obviously unregistered! Just one look at it would suffice for that purpose!" "Quite!" Burgess stiffened slightly, his lips pursing with the bureaucratic obstinacy of a die-hard conservative. "And what is your port of departure?"

"Natal," Farewell was starting to fume.

"Have the Port Authorities there provided you with a Lloyd's Certificate of Navigability?"

Finding his obduracy astounding, Farewell stared at Burgess long and hard before starting: "Mr..."

"Chief Petty Officer Burgess," Burgess quickly supplied the name and rank. "Mr. Burgess," the lieutenant tried to remain calm, "Lloyd's of London do not have offices in that part of the world. Indeed, there are no offices of any type whatsoever -- in that part of the world. Do you understand?"

"Are you implying you have no Certificate of Navigability?" came Burgess's even rejoinder.

"Precisely!" Farewell barked, losing control. Then, struggling to regain his composure, the man took a deep breath and pulled a humourless smile. "Mr. Burgess, I realise that you are merely doing your job and I appreciate your position, and ask that you allow me to make my own positon clear." Another deep breath, then: "I am in the company of the representatives of the largest empire in this part of Africa..." Farewell brought Burgess's attention to Ngomane, Lutuli, and Kuta. "Perhaps one of the largest in the world. A militant empire, Mr. Burgess." Farewell's features hardened. "And your present obstinacy may not only cost you your stripes, you may well be held responsible for a catastrophic diplomatic blunder!" The last three words being spewed in a vocal crescendo of outrage.

"If it is the largest empire in Africa," the Petty Officer remained unflinching in resolve and insensitive to Farewell's angry threats, "why can't it afford a proper ship and..." his eyes brushed past the hides and feathers, "...uniforms?"

"Because it is not seafaring!" "Do you have any documentation to prove this -- 'diplomatic status' of yours?" Sensing that Farewell might well be on the verge of homicide, Wilkins stepped in and nodded to the Port Official with a pleasant smile: "Mr. Burgess, my name is Wilkins," he said, sweeping the feathers away from his face. "I'm with the Colonial Office, Downing Street. And, in that capacity, I am quite able to corroborate both Lt. Farewell's statement and his status as a representative of His Majesty's Government. If you will allow us to moor, I'm sure the Governor will supply you with whatever else you might need for your records."

Chief Petty Officer Burgess was straightfaced as his eyes shifted back and forth, from Tim to Farewell, to Tim. The thought might have crossed the man's mind that he was at grips with lunacy, though it was not obvious, in his deadpan reiteration of: -- "This ship is illegal. It has no right to be, let alone be here! Therefore, you are herewith denied permission to moor, and liberty to enter the harbour. – So either sail away...'Lieutenant', or sit here and rot!"

"Sit down, Lieutenant," Sir Charles smiled, though his eyes were bitter. "May I offer you some rum! Or have you forgotten what that is?"

"Rum..?" Farewell echoed wryly, crossing Somerset's study and taking a seat in front of his massive mahogany desk. "The Colonists' greatest weapon, isn't it? Next to Bible-hawkers and guns." He was conscious of a great lassitude under his effort to be sarcastic as he went on: "All part of the Crown's unofficial policy when extending its boundaries amongst the so-called natives." The man's tone became mordant and acrimonious. "First it sends in the Bible-hawkers to delude their simple hearts. Then the rum-seller to capture their stomachs. And finally the armies to 'take rightful' possession." Farewell accepted the glass of rum the Governor proferred and swallowed a sip, feeling the warming nectar burn its way down to his stomach. "Yes, Sir Charles, I remember what rum is."

Somerset slumped into his chair and fell silent, his eyes locked on Farewell as he ran the edge of his glass over his lips, sniffing the rum's sweet scent in absorbed musing.

For over a year now, the Governor had secretly looked upon the lieutenant's "disappearance" as a blessing. It had given this autocratic politician the rare and timely chance of proving Downing Street wrong and thus reconfirming his own precious autonomy as Governor of this distant British Colony.

Indeed, though Somerset had had the foresight to look upon Bathurst's and His Majesty's proposed solution to the Shakan Affair as both ludicrous and fool-hardy, the ill-advised and impetuous lieutenant had pushed off all the same, leaving Reverend Bellow and the Governor himself insulted and outraged in the wake of Farewell's arrogance. The man's swift demise (or so the wreck of the "Elizabeth Catherine" and the vanishing of the "Julia" would vividly indicate) had come merely as the expected corollary to Sir Charles's prophecy born of long colonial experience. Farewell's presumed death had served to strengthen Somerset's position as the "de facto" Regent of the Cape Colony. It had demonstrated to the Colonists that Sir Charles knew better than Downing Street what was good for this beautiful African outpost; it had demonstrated that though George was officially King here, he, Sir Charles, was in charge.

Yes, it had been a rare and timely opportunity, Somerset knew. Indeed, even if Shaka did attack, History would remember Charles Somerset as the Cape's last and most valiant lord.   But now - Farewell was back, alive and well, outrageously dressed as a Zulu and commanding a ship that was an insult to the "waves that Britannia ruled".

Somerset knew he must be rid of him - swiftly and with as little ado as possible.

"I once considered you merely an idealist, Lieutenant," the Governor said at length, in response to Farewell's sarcastic observation regarding the weapon called rum. "One of the many harmless visionaries that pollute this century. Yet now I see that you are far more dangerous. Though you are critical of your own people, I fear that you are as much of a hypocrite as you suggest we are."

"I have done my job, Sir Charles, and I have done it well!" Farewell's voice trembled slightly with incense. "They're not worth it!" he told himself. "These petty bureaucrats who would drag the whole world down to the level of their own complacency!" Why had he ever asked Burgess to take him to shore? He should have known better than to try reasoning with such narrow-mindedness! Then aloud, he went on: "The Cape has had two years of grace and we are now standing on the threshold of a lasting peace with the Zulus. - But if you treat those proud men on my ship like animals," he was tingling with rage from head to foot, "by refusing us permission to moor, by refusing to meet with them - there may be nothing but your biased folly standing between this Colony and 80,000 dedicated warriors! - And, Sir Charles, I have seen them in action. If Shaka sets his hearts on the Cape - it's his!"

"That has the distinct flavour of a threat, Lieutenant," the Governor retorted stiffly. "And since you are making it in the name of some one who is officially dead - I must assume that you do not represent some selfstyled savage chief - but that you yourself are that chief." "What are you saying?" was Farewell's astonished reply, as, for the second time that day, he was made aware of his peculiar attire.

"Our reports indicate that Shaka died last year," was Somerset's curt remark.

"I am also 'officially dead', Sir Charles," the lieutenant tried to smile, but couldn't. "Yet as you can plainly see, that is a fallacy! And Shaka is also alive! Very much alive, I might add!"

"We have only your word for that, Lieutenant," the Governor's accusation was far from veiled.

"Tim Wilkins's can..."

"...corroborate your statement?" Somerset's irony broke in. "Yes, Lieutenant. So we've been told."

"Are you insinuating," Farewell was taken aback, "that I have made myself," a spurt of laughter accompanied the designation: "...King of the Zulus?!"

"It wouldn't be the first time," Sir Charles was smug, as if speaking with great wisdom and varied experience. "Those natives think we Whites are born leaders! And the road from inference to fact is often very short - especially when there is untold power at the end of the journey!"

Gaping at the Governor, Farewell slowly rose to his feet and ambled to the study's window. Looking out at the distant shape of the "Shaka" anchored at the entrance to the harbour, Farewell suddenly became aware of a sharp sense of disorientation that was so profound it bordered on vertigo. Reaching out, the man rested his hand on the windowsill and, as his balance returned, he found himself grinning.

Said simply: - he liked it; he liked being considered "King of the Zulus", and he could barely hide it from his own heart! The joy of it verily shone on his face (forcing him to look away from the Swallows' Governor).

When he finally did turn around, he had shed the restraint a man keeps up for his own sake, and he was glowing with an inner strength that greatly disturbed his interlocutor.

"In point of fact, Sir Charles, it was Febana speaking now and not the Lieutenant, and even the tone of his voice had changed, "it makes no difference, no great difference at all whether you are dealing with Shaka Zulu or...Febana ka MaJoji. - The Zulus' request remains the same: - permission to moor and an audience with His Majesty's representative. Or there shall be war!" Crossing the study, he nodded: "Good day, Governor. I await your decision."

"Dammit, Farewell!" the Governor was furious. "Whose bleedin' side of the fence are you on?!"

"I'll leave that for you to determine, Sir Charles", Febana retorted, delegating to the other man the responsibility of allocating his own identity.
"Do you truly expect me, the Governor of the Cape, to lend an ear to a bunch of savages bobbing about on a piece of flotsam?!"

"Yes, Sir Charles, I do," the tone was amazingly peaceful and stolid. "Because that is your job! You are the Governor...of...the...Colonies. If you find it hard to speak to 'savages', I suggest you resign. In the Early XIX Century, the distinguished British and Dutch burghers of Cape Town were quite accustomed to the quaint and curious semblances of "savages". Daily, they were confronted with Hottentotes, Malays, Bushmen, Xhosa, Fingoes, and other Bantu of disparate and variegated tribal origin, and little or nothing could leave these Colonists agape.

Yet - be that as it may - all the noble citizens who happened to find themselves in the vicinity of Strand Street and Adderley in the late afternoon of January 21, 1826, stopped and regarded with gawking awe a very extraordinary "savage" named Febana ka MaJoji as he stormed out of the Governor's Mansion, his ostrich feathers in the wind, striding angrily in the direction of Kaiser Geracht Street and the home of Mr. and Mrs. Johann Lodewyk Peterssen.

The local papers who "covered" the incident (i.e. "The South African Chronicle" and the "Commercial Advertiser" with the pen of Thomas Pringle) went on to report that the bizarre creature ("...a latter-day Robinson Crusoe," Pringle wrote, "who was subsequently identified as one of our most valiant naval officers, the missing Francis George Farewell") indulged in a brief chat with Mrs. Anna Peterssen ("...who appeared to be quite beside herself with amazement and delight at seeing him") and then hurried off ("followed by a vibrant mob of curiosity seekers and fans of the freakish"), down New Market, to the luxurious Heerengracht Hotel.

As had become her custom in the past months of solitary, dejected vigil (after having given up the faith she had too generously entrusted in humanity and in men such as Parmananda), Elizabeth Farewell was dining alone in the Heerengracht's open veranda when she chanced to espy an excited murmur rippling from table to table as the diningroom's elegant patrons caught sight of a person more than a little unusual. The reactions - ranging from shock to outrage to amusement - finally culminated in suppressed amusement.

Looking up, Elizabeth's attention was gravitated to the source of the patron's sport and diversion, and she was quite astonished to see a most singularly dressed bearded individual. The woman's wonderment was heightened upon realising that the man had approached her table and was eyeing her with the glint of deep affection, his gaze lingering on her features with fond attachment.

When startled recognition slowly crept into her heart, causing it to flutter madly like a moth near a strong light, Elizabeth breathed in hushed reticence: "Francis?"

"I believe so," came the "creature's" ambiguous rejoinder.

*

That night - in the Hotel's "Imperial Suite" - Mr. and Mrs. Farewell made love for the first time in a little under two years. Francis showed himself to have in no way lost the expertise and manly craft that had so often ignited Elizabeth's passion; and his touch, gentle yet assertive, swept her away into the torpor of sensual bliss.

Yet, on one level of consciousness, in some remote side-alley of her mind, Elizabeth felt as though she were making love to a complete stranger. At first she attributed this sensation to the long period that had elapsed since their last sexual encounter. It was to be expected - she rationalized - that after such a great stretch of abstinence, even her own husband's desire should appear somehow unfamiliar and foreign. But when he entered her, and their bodies were one, she read his mind and his heart and knew that a part of his soul was elsewhere. Far, far away. On a dimension of feeling that evinced a man, - another man - who was confused, vulnerable, lost...and in search of comfort.

*

Elizabeth reposed in her low bed-place under a snowy white sheet and light coverlet, her head sunk on a lace pillow, her expression distant and musing as she gazed out the Heerengracht's window at the throbbing globe of the rising sun. The faint scent of lavender reached her senses and she turned to look up at her husband who had reappeared from the bathroom, his beard shaven and revealing, once again, the sharp, smooth mould of his handsome visage.

The two exchanged a smile that bore the undertones of uneasiness. They were both aware that, - though they still loved each other, needed each other very, very much - something was missing, gone, perhaps irreclaimably! And now both suffered, and both were reluctant to voice their concern for fear that they might give body to their apprehensions.

Turning away from Elizabeth, Farewell faced his own reflection in a full-length mirror as he undertook (after another sort of long abstinence) to don a brand-new ornate uniform of a lieutenant in His Majesty's Navy. Dressing, his attention moved up and down the length of his reflected image on the two-dimensional surface of the mirror, and he was aware that his own semblance seemed strange to him, like a photograph of the person he had been two years ago. - Before Shaka, before Port Natal, before the Battle of iNcome River, before Febana ka MaJoji, -- before it all!

Whilst Elizabeth looked at the man who was her love and had been her life's companion, she wondered (with the lingering feeling she'd had during their love-making) whether that life together was still possible, and her mind sifted the words they had exchanged in the course of a sleepless night. She had inquired about his journey and, of course, the conversation soon swerved in the direction of Shaka Zulu, and Francis spoke freely about the King with a boyish exhilaration that tended to ascribe extraordinary potency to people and agents in themselves powerless.

"In our very first month in Natal, and once in the company of this incredible Emperor," he had told her, among other things, with a gleam of recollection, "I immediately perceived that my imagination had hitherto been running in conventional channels and that, by comparison, even my dreams had always been drab stuff! - Shaka is as exceptional a being as anyone has ever had cause to encounter, with tastes that lean naturally towards the marvellous and the monstrous. And a genius!" Farewell had told his wife, "Indeed, my stay in Natal brings back to mind that unforgettable night of my youth when I boarded the ship 'Bellerophon' on its journey to Saint Helena. Our illustrious cargo: -- a defeated general named Napoleon Bonaparte. When asked what was the greatest attribute of any good soldier, Bonaparte told us: 'Le Courage de l'improviste' - 'spontaneous courage'. And on that principle is based the chess game in which Shaka and I find ourselves contenders," the lieutenant had confessed to Elizabeth. "And if I cannot emulate the Zulu King's brilliance, at least I must try to match his endurance. That is how we will save the Colony..."

Yet in her heart, she felt that the Colony and its safety were now "drab stuff" for her husband. And she fervently hoped, as she looked at him slipping into his blue naval tunic, that she, too, had not been relegated to the "conventional channels" of Farewell's past imagination.

Buttoning the top of his white shirt, the lieutenant hooked it closed at the collar, fumbling somewhat with the clips, and then started to tie the elaborate knot of his military cravat. And he struggled with that knot, his fingers finding it awkward as he tied the silk band, untied it, and tied it again, his frustration growing to rail against his incompetence. It seemed as though Febana ka MaJoji had forgotten how to dress Lt. Farewell.

"Would you mind terribly, darling?" he smiled apologetically at length, giving up, and delegating the tying of the cravat to his wife. "I'm afraid I've lost my touch."

As the woman's nimble fingers swiftly and expertly interwove the blue silk into a large knot, she allowed her gaze to take closer scrutiny of her husband in the light of day and to probe those blue eyes that seemed somehow spent with care. Farewell stiffened under that look, and when the cravat was tied, he thanked her awkwardly, and quickly returned to take refuge in his reflected self, buttoning his waistcoat and straightening the tunic. When he was through, he stepped back and critically observed his own image, his eyes taking in the smartly dressed officer standing before him.

"There were so many times over the past couple of years," he admitted to Elizabeth's reflection. "When I thought I would never again see myself like this."

"And do you see yourself now, Francis?" she inquired, examining the man in the looking-glass. "What an odd remark, darling," he forced a smile, pretending to not understand.

"If I think of all the hours, the days, the months I've spent hoping and praying for your return," she neared the mirror, addressing Farewell's "other" self. "Yet now that you're here, finally here -- I feel more lonely than ever because I realise that you may never really return."

Francis remained speechless, as his wife inched closer and, reaching out, touched the mirror's cold, hard surface.

"You have become like this image on the glass. Every detail of Lieutenant Farewell is there except life." Their eyes met in the mirror and locked. "Who owns that life, Francis? - Is it Shaka's?"

Farewell crossed the room and gazed out the window, his contemplative eyes resting on the Cape's innumerable houses with their quiet, conventional lives gathered round their firesides. Thinking of those lives, real yet artificial in their desire to preserve the fantasy of peace, the lieutenant was saddened by the clarity with which he suddenly saw what he had been before Shaka - what he could never be again.

"Francis," his wife was beside him, her hand on his shoulder, "What's happened to us? What's happened to you?" Farewell turned to face her, and, for the first time since his return, he looked at Elizabeth, taking her features in as he had a thousand times before. And he saw her beauty, her strength and bravery, her steady loyal eyes, and her long hair which hung wavy and soft. He saw his wife, the woman he loved and had married "in sickness and in health, till death did them part". He saw her for what she was and knew that she belonged to Farewell Mansion, to England, to Holbrook House, and to those conventional lives gathered round firesides. He knew that she deserved to belong to that life and that he should not, could not take her away. And he was deeply sorry that he had mislaid the keys to that world.

Yet he said nothing, and she continued at length.

"I've watched you plunge headlong into ventures that would give cold feet even to the most brazen of men," she was saying, "yet you've always survived because you had the capability of mastering situations and their effect on you! You were always above the event with your freewheeling style, avoiding any real personal involvement, and you were invulnerable because elusive. It was that tongue-in-cheek spirit that justified your apparent recklessness, - that made you a winner!" She took his hands and pressed them to her breasts pleadingly. "But it's different this time, isn't it, Francis? You've cut loose all your emotional anchors and your involvement is complete."

Francis felt the emotion clutching at his throat, stripping his response of all pretenses.

"Through no fault of my own, Elizabeth. I assure you," he confessed, throwing open the chasm of his wife's despair. "No matter how well you play, you cannot always control the game in its entirety. Especially when your opponent is as formidable as Shaka. You just find yourself putting more and more chips on the table until its too late to quit." "It's never too late, Francis," she squeezed his hands with a strength born of helplessness. "You still have me."

"Then I ask you to wait, darling," he took her in his arms. "It's selfish, I know. Yet I see no other way. We must both wait until I am ready to really return."

A loud rap at the door roused them from the intimacy of their embrace.

"Come in," the lieutenant said, letting go of his wife and crossing to the door where he was faced with the brusque countenance of Petty Officer Burgess.

"Sir," Burgess saluted, somewhat stunned to now see a real lieutenant - clean-shaven and spiffy - wearing Farewell's voice. "Ma'm," he nodded to Elizabeth.

"What news do you bring me, Mr. Burgess?"

"The Port Authorities and the Governor's Commission have deliberated and reached their verdict," he announced, stone-faced, as Francis and his wife froze in anticipation. "Inasmuch as the 'Shaka' has no papers," the Petty Officer continued, "and inasmuch as the Port Authorities do not wish to create an embarrassing precedent, - your ship has been denied permission to enter the harbour and moor."

Farewell's face ironed out with rage, and Elizabeth closed her eyes in despair; - by forcing her husband's hand, the Governor may well have cast him out of her reach forever.

"Furthermore," Burgess continued, "whereas the Zulu Empire has no recognised diplomatic status with the Crown, an audience with Sir Charles Somerset has been deemed inadvisable."

"This is madness!" exclaimed Farewell, feeling the bitter taste of rejection - made all the more bitter by the fact that it was coming from those he considered his own people. Begging your pardon, sir," the Petty

Officer interjected, "so was your idea of thinking they would ever treat those primitives on an equal basis."

Farewell's eyes darted to Burgess with the intensity of his mounting outrage, and he ordered stiffly: "If that's all, Mr. Burgess, I--"

"That's not all, sir," the other man interrupted, somehow relishing the moment. "You and Mr. Wilkins are requested to board a ship for Plymouth at your earliest convenience in order to offer the Crown and the Admiralty a clarification regarding your involvement in the... Shakan Affair."

"A Court Martial, Mr. Burgess?" Francis was indignant.

"A clarification, sir," Burgess restated with formal rigidity. "As to where your true allegiance lies, I believe."

"The Governor's just made that very clear for me, Mr. Burgess," was the even, vibrant riposte. "Very clear," Farewell added, clawing open his cravat. "Tell Sir Charles and his Commission that I..." the words caught momentarily in his throat as he cast a fleeting gaze at his wife with an expression that was at once rueful and supplicant; Febana now had to make a decision that would change Farewell's life. "Tell him that I am -- Zulu!" And with that he strode out of the suite with an air that portended deliberate finality.

"Most unfortunate, Madam," Burgess considered looking after Francis. "From what I hear," he affected a tone of well-bred politeness, "your husband had such a brilliant record! A promising career! - To toss all that away for some ungrateful savages..."

"I couldn't agree with you more, Mr. Burgess!" Elizabeth snapped, aggrieved and bitter. "Men like Sir Charles aren't worth it!" Upon reaching the harbour and Duncan Dock, Farewell pushed his way through the crowd of curiosity seekers which had gathered to gawk at the "freak ship". Having become somewhat of a sideshow celebrity himself, the lieutenant's progress through the dense mob was accompanied by a flurry of heated comments and spurts of jeering and laughter.

Boarding the longboat, the lieutenant sharply ordered the Hottentot oarsmen to transport him back to his ship. As the vessel pushed off towards Table Bay, Febana ka MaJoji furiously ripped off Lt. Farewell's military cravat and tunic and hurled them into the crowd -- where the ornate jacket was quickly and boisterously dismantled by the throng of human predators and souvenir hunters.

An hour later, the longboat had left the territorial waters of Cape Town Harbour and was pulling up alongside the "Shaka".

"Do we push off, sir?" suggested Wilkins, registering the lieutenant's despondent look.

"No, Tim," came the venomous answer. "We stay put! Until we rot, if need be!" Tim's worried eyes shifted to Ngomane and he saw that the Prime Minister, upon Farewell's return and upon diagnosing the outcome of his mission on shore, had assumed an austere expression, his features shrouded in dignity and pride. Slowly, the Zulu turned away from the Swallows and moved to the gunwales, gazing out at the crowds collecting on the wharf - the crowds that had come to witness the fate of the "freaks". And, as he looked at the milling throng of curious "monkeys" on the wharf, the Prime Minister of the Zulu Nation was reminded of the revealing words spoken with his Emperor before his departure for "the Unknown":---

"You have given them land, Baba," he had told his King, "wealth, and the status of chieftains. And now you send me to speak of peace without conquest. That is not you, Nkosi, That is not Shaka! - Your People are wondering, -- they are asking, how can the Conqueror of Nations have been bewitched by a handful of jackals?"

"My people have become very daring in thought," the Emperor had told his most illustrious induna. "Could it be that it is your own question that echoes in their hearts?"

"My question, Baba," Ngomane had humbly replied, "is what is the Great Elephant receiving in return for his generosity?"

"The power of their knowledge," Shaka had said in earnest.

"Then I can only hope, Baba," had been Ngomane's unusually bold rejoinder, "that their knowledge is not the fabrication of lies, or all that you have built will become theirs."

And as he remembered this talk and looked upon the jeering faces of those who would give the Great Elephant knowledge, Ngomane kaMqombolo Zulu suddenly felt like a fool

CHAPTER XLVIII
"INDALULO"(BETRAYAL)

In Mark's Gospel there is a verse that is wondrous in its simplicity, its wisdom, and its insight into the human condition. And, quite befitting the narrative of the Great Mountain, this Biblical passage is so indicative of Shaka's moral and mental state after the "execution" of his son, that when Fynn first read it to the Emperor, the Zulu was so intensely affected by its words that he spent the rest of the day in silent and solitary contemplation.

The passage (which Fynn dubbed "Shaka's Verse") reads: - "For what shall it profit a man if he shall gain the world and lose his own soul?"

This was his verse, Shaka's, and he thought of it often towards the end... Towards the end, when he and his Companion Death had become so close that the time was fast approaching for their encounter in the Dimension of Eternity, - when he had became aware of the illusion of Human Fellowship on earth vanishing before the naked truth of Man's insatiable greed, his colossal hypocrisy, his disconcerting ineptitude to rise to his place in Creation, -- towards the end of his short life, Shaka the Great Elephant of Africa, Shaka "Udlungwana - The Ferocious One", Shaka the King of Kings whose hands were stained with the Blood of his Blood, Shaka the Inscrutable - would sit near the banks of the Mkumbane, at the site of his conception, immersed in the deepest of reflections, wrung by the faltering of his convictions and commitments, probing the imponderable in an attempt to justify the obscure desires that had moved his conduct throughout his life.

And in this reflection, his thoughts would wander back to the impulses, to the passions, to the prejudices, to the follies, to the arrogance, and to the hidden fears that had conditioned him since childhood, and he would think of Nandi, and how he had cast her off, out of his life. And the guilt would overwhelm him, infesting his soul with the notion that though he had "gained the world", he was irremediably losing himself.

He would sit on the banks of the river and stare at his open hand, the hand that had dealt the blow that had caused Nandi's lips to bleed. He would look at it, that hand, for hours on end, suspended in the timelessness of infinite remorse, and his eyes would grow wide and moist with despair; and he would think of the crucified hands of uCristo ("the true victor of iNcome River" - as he now saw Him), stained with the blood of Man's guilt (or so Fynn had told him). His guilt (or so Fynn said).

And feeling the weariness, a profound numbness of spirit devoid of even the most elementary desires, Shaka sensed that uCristo, too, must have been weary when he forgave those who had hung Him from a tree, and he found consolation in the other King of Kings Who, through His Passion, had become for Shaka as much a Companion as Death Itself.

He would sit, towards the end, this Mountain of Africa, - with Fynn, listening to the words in the Swallows' Book, searching through the Life, the Death, and the Resurrection of his "Illustrious Rival" in an attempt to find himself and the soul he had lost.

And in uCristo, Shaka found not only a rival, but his first and only peer.

"'...and Jesus went about all Galilee, teaching in their Houses of Prayer, preaching the Gospel of the Kingdom that was to come and healing all manner of sickness and all manner of disease among the people, bringing sight to the blind and resurrecting the dead...'" Fynn was perched on a rock near the stream's gurgling waters, the Bible cradled in his hands, reciting slowly whilst he effected, as best he could, a most provocative translation of the English to Zulu.

"And His fame went throughout all the land, and they brought onto Him all sick people that were taken with divers diseases and torments, and those which were possessed with evil spirits, and those which were mad, and he healed them...'"

Shaka crouched by the water's edge, his feet immersed in the currents that swirled and eddied round his ankles, his unblinking gaze fixed on the stream's rushing flux as he listened, reflected and absorbed.

"'...And seeing the multitudes, uCristo went up to the top of a high mountain and addressed the people, saying, Blessed are the poor in spirit: for theirs is the Kingdom of the Heavens; Blessed are they that mourn: for they shall be comforted; Blessed are the meek: for they shall inherit the earth; Blessed are the merciful: for they shall...'"

And Shaka stood unmoving, a statue of attentiveness, listening, his piercing stare poised on the stream as if his mind were scouring a channel through the water, through the earth, to the Hell that was secreted in its core.

"'...Blessed are the peacemakers,'" Fynn continued, "'for they shall be called the Children of the Heavens. Blessed are you, when men shall revile you, and persecute you, and shall say all manner of evil against you falsely for my sake; rejoice and be exceedingly glad for great is your reward in Heaven...'"

"He said that...?" the King's voice came from an alien place borne on the shoulder of disbelief.

"He said that, Baba," Fynn confirmed.

"And Joji and your people - you believe in this...his Litany of Victims?"

"Yebo, Nkosi. We do."

The Emperor pondered the point, and Fynn saw in the magnitude of his inner turmoil that he, too, wanted to believe the words of this "Litany of Victims". In fact, though he was a born Master, in his present weariness Shaka wanted - desperately - to benefit from the Truce of Victims that was the Truce of God: a cessation of the hostilities that had commanded his existence. And this Sermon on the Mount was the perfect balsam for his wounded heart. Yet - though the desire to believe was there - Fynn knew that this Biblical passage was just too absurd for one such a Shaka to accept prima facie. It would take time, the Irishman knew, - all the time in the world.

And as the King pondered the point, and in his need to understand the workings of uCristo's mind, the mind of a man who was obviously so important for the Swallows, Shaka was suddenly inspired by a refreshing thought that left him smiling.

"So His reign is also founded on Man's fear of the Unknown." The comment caused Fynn to frown. "Though I must admit His Laws are far more elaborate than mine. I am content to have my people's loyalty onto death. His influence seems to go beyond that."

"Of course, Baba," came the Irishman's zealous reply. "He is God."
"The Creator of Heaven and Earth?" Shaka's smile broadened.

Fynn remained silent. - They had discussed God and come to some sort of formal stalemate inasmuch as the concept of the God of the Swallows was nothing new to Shaka. Indeed, the Zulu belief was that The Creator, The First Cause, "Unkulunkulu" (the old, old one) had made all things. He had made man and woman, wild animals, cattle and game, snakes and birds, water and mountains, and the sun and the moon. And He was a God very similar to the Whites' God, because He was the same God by another name. And Shaka, though quite grateful for this gift of Creation, had no intention of discussing at length (let alone worshipping) something as remote as "the First Cause". Only uCristo interested the King, and when Fynn told him that God and Christ were one and the same (the Father and Son), Shaka merely smiled and changed the subject.

As he did now. With the elegance of essential philosophy.

"There is little logic to be expected on this earth, my friend," Shaka remarked with calm judgment, "not only in the matter of thought, but also of sentiment. That is why gods and tyrants are so necessary. - And He was far more of a tyrant than a god," the King remarked, indicating the Bible.

Fynn's outrage brought laughter to Shaka's lips, and the Zulu quickly adjoined.

"What is it He says..?" the King knit his brow in the strain of recollection, "'he who is not with me, is against me'. -- I couldn't have put it better myself."

In his genuine desire to reach Shaka's heart, Fynn's tone in the defense of uCristo was firm yet not aggressive: "His is the Message of Love, Baba. Yours is a corollary to..." the White man strangled the half-born thought and the word remained unspoken until Shaka supplied it, cocking his eye at the other man.

"Hatred? - Yes," the King readily agreed. "But they are so surprisingly alike - Love and Hatred, and in many ways totally indistinguishable because Fear is at the core of both. - Fear," he was scowling now with heavy, despondent eyebrows. "Fear of living, fear of losing, fear of loneliness. And the more you love another," Shaka paused, his thoughts embracing Nandi and the unrequited passions of Pampata, "the closer you are to hating yourself. - Fear of freedom, fear of feeling, fear of fear! And at the end there is Death - the only lasting cure to the disease called living!"

Perceiving the sudden tired resignation in Shaka's voice, Fynn was deeply touched by the sad state of his heart, and he held the Emperor's gaze, unaware of the tenderness and compassion his own eyes betrayed -- till the King himself brought it to the Irishman's attention.

"You look at me oddly, my friend," came the mellow voice lowered in a hush. "Do my words bother you? They should not. All those blesseds, blesseds, blesseds - are they not at the service of Fear and Death?"

"He brought us Life, Baba," there was a flash in Fynn's eyes as his devotion communed with the other's darkness. "A reason for living, a reason for loving. Without fear."

"And you believe this, -- Joji and your people?"

"Yes, we do?"   "Then why did you hang him from a tree?"

The messenger arrived towards sunset and fell to the ground at his King's feet. So engrossed was Fynn in this unique Biblical session, he failed to hear the news the warrior brought. And when the White man looked up, he noted with shock the King's crestfallen expression.   Rising heavily to his feet, Shaka hurried off bidding Fynn to follow him.

"What is it, Nkosi?" the Irishman was at his heels.

"The Great Female Elephant," was the anguished reply. "She needs the One Who is Power." He ran all night, with Fynn's horse trotting at his side. And by daybreak, as the two men had reached emKindini, they could hear the disconsolate sounds of the wailing women who had gathered in the Royal Residence to mourn the ailing Queen of Queens.   When the Emperor entered the homestead, the wailing instantly ceased, and the milling crowd that packed the enclosure of the palisades fell to the ground and parted before their sovereign and the Swallows' sangoma, forming a path that wound up the sloping incline towards the threshold of Nandi's dwelling. - And Shaka moved up the path, with Fynn at his side.

The King's eyes were rivetted on his mother's hut and, as he strode closer and closer, his terror fed on his apprehension and grew in his heart, threatening to burst it open. Yet, for fear of betraying his inner upheaval to the watchful glances of his prostrate subjects, the Emperor remained expressionless as he accosted the small door and, bracing himself, ducked in to the dwelling - with Fynn close behind.

The interior of Nandi's private abode was infested with surging clouds of fetid fumes and asphyxiating billows of medicinal toxins that the hearth disgorged in great ebbing waves of blue and white. Shaka and Fynn were stung by the oppressive stench, and narrowing their eyes against the suffocating smoke, they could barely make out the human shapes that were crouched and huddled within.

Through the swirling stew and vapours, they saw Pampata and Nomcoba who cowered, horrified and unmoving, near the hideous features of Majola and the deformed semblances of the witchdoctor Sopane of the Mountain and his insidious subordinates, Mgidi and Mqalane.

A muted, ghoulish chanting accompanied Sopane's animated fingers as they mixed, stirred and sprinkled the ingredients of his magic into a steaming bowl. Lifting the bowl from the crackling flames, Majola rested it at the side of the noble, magnificent figure that lay beautiful and unstirring in the midst of the gruesome and diabolical assemblage.

When Shaka's eyes became accustomed to the fumes, he shifted his attention from the gazes of Pampata and Nomcoba, impenetrable in their grief, to the squatting "birds of prey" who hovered over the body of their illustrious patient. Then, when her marmoreal features suddenly came into view, Shaka gasped at his mother's death mask, and a choked groan was wrenched from his soul - a squalling lament that tore through the hut's interior, causing all to turn and face their Emperor with eyes betraying a range of feeling that spanned from servility to accusation.

Fynn's attention was also arrested by the Queen's noble figure. Noticing that her stillness was not total indeed, the breath of life still rose in her chest - the Irishman's medical instinct came to the fore and he shouted to the oppressive gathering.

"Ya phandle!" Fynn exhorted, "Everyone out! She can't breath! She needs air!" - When all hesitated to comply, Shaka repeated Fynn's command, giving way to an excited flurry of movement.

When the "supernatural entourage" had scurried out, and Pampata and Nomcoba had slipped tensely past the King, avoiding his probing, crazed eyes - Fynn moved to Nandi's side and felt the raging heat of her fever.

"She's very ill, Nkosi," the Swallow confessed. "I fear that---"

"Shaka!" came the sharp, sibilating whisper, cutting Fynn short. -- "Shaka!" Nandi repeated, her eyes springing open with the flaming intensity of her body and soul.

The Great Mountain shrank from that uncanny whisper, and, wearing the timorous look of the scolded child, he sidled to his mother's mat and beheld her piercing stare - a look that was now well beyond the reach of Affection.

"Come closer," she hissed, and Shaka arched forward, his face nearing hers.

"Closer!" she hissed again, like a serpent before striking.

Cocking his head to the side, the Son of Zulu bent his ear to his mother's lips and felt the searing fire of her breath.

"You..." she spoke with difficulty. "You...have... killed...me!"

The King caught his breath in startled grief, accusing the mighty blow of her words. His eyes widening with insurmountable pain, Shaka gaped at his mother in trembling appeal and moaned: "No! No, mother! I love you! I have always loved you! We---"

"Too late!" she silenced him with an eerie smile. "Too late," she said again. "No more we! You are alone!" she said and closed her eyes in dismissal, leaving Shaka with the immense weight of his guilt. "Alone" - without the solace of the one who had been the only island in the sea of his solitude.

Slinking away from his mother's side, like an animal beaten by its mistress, the Master of Outcasts skulked into the shadows, crouching in their darkness. And though Fynn could not see the King's suffering -- which he sensed must be boundless - he heard Shaka's soft whimpering, the bewailing of a soul's perdition, the snivelling complaint of Hell Itself.

And then there was silence, and Shaka reappeared, his eyes glowing with the gleam of maniacal intention.

"Save her," he growled at Fynn. "Or my guilt will become your own."

"It will take a miracle, Baba." Then find one!" he said pointing to the Bible in Fynn's hand. "There are plenty in there to choose from."

The entire Nation responded to the news of its Queen's illness, and by evening immense crowds had gathered round emKindini, converging on the emaTeku and emBuzane streams to the North and West, amassing as far as emPongo Hill to the East.

And they stood in stillness - the tens of thousands that carpeted the valley and hills round her homestead, -- they stood in fear, eyes fixed on Nandi's hut, hearts beating in resonance with the laboured breathing of the Son of Zulu who sat outside the dwelling, his head bowed in suspended emotion.

At length Fynn was beside the Emperor, and when their eyes met, the Irishman merely shook his head in sign of defeat.

"There is nothing I can do, Baba," he told the Zulu. "The Nkosikazi is beyond my medicine."

Yet he clung to hope, and moments later the Emperor was once again at his mother's side. With trembling fingers, he reached out and touched her lips, and though they were still, and though they were cold, - he felt the timid breath of life graze his fingertips.

The breath that could return to utter words, - words to dispel the guilt.

Furiously rummaging through Fynn's carpetbag, the King found the Rowland's Macassar Oil, and snapping off the bottle's neck, he frantically smeared the dark "elixir of life" on Nandi's hair, on her face, on her shoulders, on her breasts, on her arms. And all the while he spoke to her in moaning appeal and in pining entreaty.

He spoke to his mother's limp frame, addressing it with sobbing recollections of things past, with the pitiable laughter of vain hopes, with the voice of a child and that of a man. And he smeared the oil onto her death mask and begged her to believe in this "Restorer of Life" - to believe, as he himself did.

"They would have another child," the Child told Nandi daughter of Bhebhe. "And this time he would be allowed to live - to live and grow to be a man. The greatest of men! The Son of the Mountain!" - he told her through his tears.- "And again they would be a family!"

"And Nomcoba would marry Mgobozi," the Zulu told his mother who was already dead. "And they would have children and the family would grow. And Ngwadi he, too, would marry and bear sons and daughters to sons and daughters! And they would talk of Love, he and his mother," - the King told her corpse. And -- "Nandi..." he sighed.   And he fell silent.

The tears came in waves of convulsive despair, he lifted her, gently pressing her lifeless frame to his massive chest, tinging his tears with the dark liquid that was the Swallows' Promise of Life.

"Bring her back to life! Bring my mother back to life!" Shaka roared as he strode through the multitude of Zulus and approached the Irishman. "Resurrect her!"

Upon spotting the stains of Macassar Oil on the Emperor's face and body, Fynn's heart quickened. "If the bottle was now broken," the Swallow silently mused, "so was the spell, -- he and his companions had nothing more to lose by telling the truth". - And suddenly he was aware of a deep feeling of relief. Farewell's Folly had finally reached its moment of truth, and now even death seemed more acceptable than the lingering torment of falsehood. "I cannot, Baba," came the reply. Simply. Evenly. "He came back to life!" the King of Kings pointed to the Book of his Rival. Fynn was silent. "And I did!" The King of Kings pointed to himself.

Fynn remained silent.

"You will not resurrect her?!" Shaka's eyes narrowed menacingly.

"I told you, Baba," his chest heaved with a deep sigh, "I cannot. I never could."

"You will not." Shaka decided, deaf to Fynn's confession, his brows joining in anger.

"May I speak, my brother's son?" Mkabayi moved out of the throng and stood facing Shaka. The King nodded with a glint of diffidence, and the woman went on: "I think it is time for the Great Elephant to acknowledge that the Creatures from the Sea have no powers that exceed our own. They are merely more cunning in their lies."

With a crafty smile, Dingane shifted his eyes from Mkabayi to Shaka, and stood poised for the reply.

"What have you to say?" the Emperor curtly inquired of Fynn. "Is there truth in Mkabayi's words?"

"The truth, Nkosi, is that your mother is dead," the Irishman was deeply afflicted. "And though I wish I could restore her to life, I cannot! No one can."

Shaka looked at Fynn with a long, questioning gaze. Though the truth was now staring him in the face and, with it, its myriad of disconcerting implications, the Emperor hesitated before a falsehood that was too immense for his heart to conceive. "Could it really have all been a lie?" he wondered and asked aloud, his voice vibrating with repressed emotion: "You cannot heal death?"

"No." "You never could?"

As further confirmation of the delicateness of the human heart, Fynn found he could say nothing on his own behalf, nor on behalf of uCristo Who had, once again, fallen victim to Man's impudence. So Fynn cried. For himself, for Christ, but above all for Shaka.

"And -- and this?" the Zulu inquired, gaping at the Macassar Oil on his hands.

"A dye, Baba," Fynn's short, joyless laugh came through his tears. "Just a dye. Makes grey turn black again. - An illusion."

The atrocity perpetrated against him and his Nation was colossal, and an outrage of equal proportions was to be expected. Yet, while all looked on awaiting Shaka's mammoth wrath, the King remained perfectly still, staring at the Swallow, his features etched not with wrath, nor with outrage, but evincing amazement and grief - profound, bitter, - the immense and blank desolation of a small child robbed of a toy. The wondrous toy of Prometheus, which even Christ had refused!

And whilst the Nation looked on, stunned by the Emperor's apparent weakness, Shaka stood powerless, his arms limp at his side. Paralysed. The void left in his soul by Nandi's death, - a void already immeasurable - had now become infinite.

Speech, action, anger, reprisal, - all appeared useless and vain, not worth the effort of will or pride that was needed to give them effect. And Dingane, Mkabayi, and the Nation looked on and snatching glimpses of his subjects, Shaka read on those faces that his deception had become their own. Yet he stood stock still, feeling something like a heavy chain that held him there; his stupor as immense as the Folly of which he had been prey.

"Folly!" Shaka told himself, and the spark of this realisation was fanned to raging flames when Ngomane's words returned to haunt him: "You have given them land, wealth, and the status of chieftains, -- your people are wondering how the Conqueror of Nations could have been so bewitched by a handful of jackals. Your people are wondering what the Great Elephant is receiving in return for his faith?"

And, rolling his wide eyes to look at his people, the Son of Zulu heard himself reply: - "The Power of their Knowledge."

The Power of their Knowledge!

And Shaka laughed, and his laughter seemed to be torn out of him against his will, brought violently to the surface from under his misery, his self-contempt, from under his despairing wonder at his own ingenuity!

Then, as Joko, Mzilikazi, Dlaba, and the people looked on, spellbound, Shaka hid his face and wept.

And when he looked up again, his tears of disconcertion had given way to a wild, maddened distress. Lashing out, he plucked the Bible from Fynn's hands, and clenching his teeth, he wrenched it apart, tearing at the pages, shredding the words of uCristo that spoke of immortality, of life, of forgiveness, and of glory through rebirth.

Finally, feeling that his solitude was complete and unbearable, the Great Mountain sank to his knees and emitted a bloodcurdling howl that rended the Heavens with its anguish.

The Wail of Africa betrayed.

Three days after the death of Nandi, Daughter of Bhebhe, a grave was dug for the Queen under the lone thorn tree that marked the final resting place of her mother Mfunda and her son Ngwadi. According to the instructions of the Great Elephant, the pit was of gigantic proportions - large enough to contain all that which were the Promise of Life and the Promise of Youth. - Yet, though poetic, the meaning behind the Emperor's decree was far from figurative, and the funeral of the Queen of Queens - held on the Full Moon of uNdasa (February, 1826) - can be recorded as the one most horrendous incident in the entire tragic story of Zulu's most illustrious Son.

In fact, all men and women under the age of sixteen, and all women (illegally) found with child -- over a hundred and fifty thousand people in all -- were buried with the Queen.

Alive.

And it is said - by Those Who Inhabit the Mountains - that, to this day, on the Eve of the Full Moon of uNdasa, the anguished cries of their spirits can still be heard throughout Africa. But only by those with Skins of Sorghum who would pollute this Proud and Believing Continent with their lies and who would lay waste the Promise of Africa's Youth and the Promise of its Life with their Parliaments and with their House of White Hypocrisy.

The Emperor's second decree came seven days after the funeral and messengers were sent to every part of the empire to make it known to all. According to the extraordinary mandate it was ruled that:---

"When the Great Female Elephant, the Over-ruling spirit of Life and Vegetation had died, it was deemed probable that the Heavens and Earth would unite in bewailing her death, and thus the sacrifice for man should be great. Therefore: - no cultivation would be allowed for the following year but only as much as necessary to feed the armies; no milk would be used but, as drawn from the cow, it should be all poured upon the earth; no sexual intercourse of any nature was to take place for a period of a year; and women found with child would, together with their husband and other children, be put to death."

This inhuman edict, virtually condemning the entire population to starvation and unnatural abstinence was, through abject fear, received with acclamation, and regiments of soldiers were dispersed throughout the realm to massacre all those who failed to obey.

The third decree came three days later. In consequence, Daniel was led to Bulawayo and crucified in the center of the stockade (with a hammer and nails that Cane was forced to supply).

The other Swallows, Fynn, Cane, and Holstead were confined to a heavily guarded permanence at Port Natal until the Great Elephant would decide how best to deal with the treachery of the Creatures from the Sea.

Then, notwithstanding any promises made to Febana (which now seemed truly ludicrous), as the final and most decisive move arising from his mother's death, Shaka called upon all his generals and officers to meet in a huge "indaba" summit that was held at Mgobozi's grave on Qokli Hill.

In this summit, the Emperor outlined the details of a new ambitious military campaign that would be initiated by the next moon.

A campaign that was hailed by all the regiments as Shaka's greatest, grandest, most ambitious - and most justified (considering recent revelations): the Campaign against the Locusts residing in iliKapa.

The Campaign against Joji's Swallows at the Cape

CHAPTER XLIX
"AMAFUTHA E-MACASSAR"(MACASSAR OIL)

The same Full Moon of uNdasa that dispassionately witnessed the wails and plaints of the mass execution that was Nandi's requiem, shone bright and phosphorescent over the entrance to the harbour of Cape Town, enveloping the fearless ship named the "Shaka" in a breathless silence.

All were sleeping on the ship. All except a disconcerted and somewhat forlorn Zulu chieftain named Febana ka MaJoji. He sat slouched on the rough bark planking of the maindeck, his head propped against the hardwood mast, gazing up at the blue-white brilliance of the heavenly globe and listening to the flapping of the furled cowhide sails and the uneven, affected breathing of his slumbering companions Wilkins, Ngomane, Lutuli and Kuta.

It had been over a month now, - he considered. A month of "sitting and rotting" in hopes that Sir Charles and the Authorities of the Cape would change their minds about officially "meeting with a bunch of savages bobbing about on a piece of flotsam" (or so Somerset had vividly described the requested peace talks).

Yet as the days passed, the lieutenant knew that the likelihood of such a meeting actually taking place diminished appreciably. In fact, thanks to the local newspapers and to the extensive word of mouth coverage amongst the Colonists, the "Siege of the 'Shaka'" (as Thomas Pringle had cynically called it in the "Commercial Advertiser") had become a topic of heated public debate (in taverns, homes, and even churches) and consequently the proposed "Anglo-Zulu Summit" (again, Pringle's terminology) had become a matter of principal for both Farewell and Sir Charles.

Yet Sir Charles was obviously the more powerful of the two, - Farewell reminded himself. Especially in these parts of the world, and the Governor had a great deal more to lose by "giving in" than Francis did. In fact, for Somerset, agreeing to the meeting would mean bowing to the will of a British Naval Officer who had shunned the orders of the Cape's highest official and gone as far as withdrawing his own allegiance to Britain by designating himself as "a Zulu".

Outrageous!

No, the lieutenant mused with a pang of regret - the likelihood of his alliance being sealed was far off, and the fault rested not in the "barbarians", but in the inflexible prejudice of the "enlightened" Europeans. Indeed, in the Shakan Affair, Colonial bureaucracy and British pride were proving to be far more cruel than the Zulu despot.

Zulu. He had said he was Zulu.

Farewell's attention shifted from the moon to the sleeping shapes of Ngomane, Lutuli, and Kuta wrapped in hides and snuggled under the protective cover of the open foredeck. And as he looked at the black men, their polished ebony skins radiant in the moonlight, Febana was caused to reflect upon Fynn's revealing remark: "We could never be Zulu," the Irishman had told him before his departure, "and that has little or nothing to do with the colour of our skin!"

It was true, Farewell knew. No matter how much he felt with them and for them, he was not and could never be one of them. And that was a fact of Nature more than Politics. Even an idealist has to be practical at times, he admitted in his heart. And it's all very well to say, "there's but one race: the 'Human'", and its fine and true to believe that Man's only colour is the colour of Blood - but what happens when all the lofty words have taken flight and one is left with only his ideals to cure his dysentry. Being true to God and one's nature is a strenuous task - very strenuous! And all the euphemisms in the world won't make you belong where you don't.

That is the Curse of Babel.

The Curse of Colonization.

Not Zulu. No longer British. -- What then?

"Who am I, Moon?" he whispered to the moon. "Where do I belong?"

And the Moon, which had remained dispassionate in the wails and plaints of Nandi's burial, responded to his query, twinkling slightly in sympathy, and it seemed to Farewell that it answered: "Be true to your heritage, or your death will be the death of your people".

At daybreak, the "freak show" caused by the permanence of the "Shaka" was, as usual, brought vividly to the fore, with the milling throng of "monkeys" on Duncan Dock growing to outrageous proportions. Enterprising young boys and men set up their refreshment stands and others sold souvenirs and ribbons with the word SHAKA printed on them, whilst fishing boats picked up a regular flow of money by taking tourists to the mouth of the harbour where they could take a closer gawk at the bizarre craft that was stubbornly anchored at the Cape's entrance.

On the craft in question, the five "freaks" gazed back at the crowds with deep disillusionment etched on their haggard countenances. Even Ngomane - who had never really believed that their mission would be fruitful - was profoundly saddened by these "sadistic" masses since he now saw, with discomfiting clarity, that the future of Africa would have many such "freak shows" and that ultimately, in the face of this White abuse, the cruelty of Africans like Shaka would be exculpated and glorified.

"Look at them," Farewell told Wilkins, regarding his own people with scorn, "a cross-section of our 'superior culture' - cold-blooded, uncaring, ruthless! - They're like parasites! Feeding on our resolve. Waiting, hoping we'll push off so they can go back to their complacency with renewed purpose!" His voice grew bitter and harsh. "If I think of all the young men who gave their lives at Lizza, Waterloo, Trafalgar...so that these vultures could live in peace and - freedom! My God! It hardly seems worth it!"

"Aren't we doing the same thing now, sir? Risking our lives, our dignity so that they can live in peace and freedom?" Tim's voice had grown weary during the past month and less disposed to the elation of excitement. The youth had come a long way since Downing Street and, like Farewell, he too felt that he'd somehow out-grown his roots. Yet, unlike the lieutenant, he knew where he belonged: - back in Britain, in the Colonial Office! There was a great deal of work that needed to be done to save the Colonies and he was itching to roll up his sleeves! But for now, his first loyalty was to Farewell and he would remain at his side for as long as the lieutenant needed him. With that in mind he added: "If it's not worth it, sir, why are we here?! 'Rotting' on this ship? What are we trying to prove?!"

The question was valid, of course, and as Farewell reflected upon it, he realised that he wasn't completely sure what it was he was doing, stubbornly anchored to threshold of his civilisation. Perhaps, in a figurative sense, Febana ka MaJoji was laying siege to Francis George Farewell in a bid to "take full possession" of his body and soul. Or maybe it was Febana acting alone, trying to justify his name: - "the one who brings the friendship of George" - willy-nilly!

Whatever the reason, their permanence on the "bobbing flotsam" could not be protracted much longer. It was February, and if they weren't back in Natal by April, Fynn and the others would die! There was no doubt in the lieutenant's mind that Shaka would be true to his intimation.
It now seemed that Farewell's Folly needed another miracle, - Febana prayed. And quickly.

Elizabeth Farewell had been assiduous, going out to the dock every morning and staying till late afternoon. In the restless languor of her helplessness, she felt that she should at least be there, as close to Francis as possible - just in case.

Though in the first week or two, she'd been far more active. There'd been meetings with the Governor, with the Cape Council, with the Merchant's Guild (of which her step-father was an esteemed member), with the Clergy (the Anglicans of Rev. Robert Jones and the Methodist Chapel at St. George's), and with the Ladies' Fund at Groote Kerk. All to no avail!

The situation was just too novel, and, as is common with the "Unknown", no one wanted to take the responsibility of setting a precedent that might prove embarrassing. Especially after news got round of what Farewell had told Burgess about his being Zulu! The churches just couldn't cope with that. Why the religious community was there to convert the heathens to European ways (Rev. Jones had told Elizabeth) - not vice versa, as seemed to be the case in Francis's own "conversion".

So Elizabeth was left alone with her despair. Now that her husband was back, within sight and reach, no longer "lost at sea", she felt she had lost him more than ever to the fathomless depths of an ideal. And as she stood on the wharf gazing longingly at the "Shaka", she, too, fervently prayed for a miracle. Only a miracle would change his mind, or perhaps---

Suddenly Elizabeth froze and saw the answer staring her right in the face. It was a copy of the "South African Commercial Advertiser".

"How blind of me!" she exclaimed out loud, spinning on her heels and starting off through the crowd.

*

In the offices of the "Advertiser", Thomas Pringle was pleased to see Elizabeth again.

"Of course I remember you, Mrs. Farewell. - What brings you to the hallowed halls of our 'waggish tabloid'?" he asked, barely concealing the jest. "Do you want us to run a Lost & Found on Parmananda?"

Elizabeth smiled in spite of her departed gold sovereigns.

"You once suggested that you and your paper might be my allies, Mr. Pringle. Is that still the case?"

"More than ever," the man was grinning with delight. "What's the story? The 'Confessions of a Hero's Wife'?"

"Too seedy," the woman replied, finding her spirits heightening in Pringle's company. "I suggest we appeal to a sentiment nobler than pity,--" her expression hardened. "Anger!"

The next morning, when Sir Charles Somerset opened his newspaper, he was shocked. Elizabeth's Farewell's photograph stared at him in silent reproach with, next to it, the headline: "GOVERNOR OBSTINATE - PEACE AT STAKE". And as he silently read the first few lines, the blood drained from his face and he spilled his coffee onto his newly-pressed polo trousers.

"What is it, Sir Charles?" Colonel Josiah Cloete of the 25th Regiment of Foot was alarmed by the other man's sudden pallor.

"Listen to this, Colonel," the Governor moaned in a hollow voice, and started reading: - "'The Good Ship Shaka has been languishing outside our harbour for over a month now, its passengers virtually prisoners..'" the paleness on the Governor's face flushed to a deep red as he continued: "'To unjustly treat any ship and its crew in this manner is wanton, but when that ship is carrying the emissaries of Shaka Zulu, the commander of Africa's largest standing army, the act also becomes one of profound and flagrant recklessness. We would be excused,'" Sir Charles read on: "'for thinking that some heinous crime or some dastardly act had been committed by this crew, or that the 'Shaka' has been used in the perpetration of piracy, murder, or an act of war against the Colony. But that is not so. The 'Shaka', under the gallant command of the famed Lt. Francis George Farewell, has come to offer lasting peace between the Cape and the mighty and dangerous Zulu Empire. A peace we so desperately need for ourselves and our children! This reporter begs to know why Sir Charles Somerset is being so obstinate.'" The Governor grunted angrily and ploughed ahead with the article. "'Could it be that Lord Somerset has built a circumstantial case in which the hideous spectre of racial bigotry plays a large and unsubtle role? That would seem to be the case, and this journalist and Mrs. Francis Farewell, the gallant lieutenant's wife, wish to remind our Colonial Governor that, prejudice aside, we at the Cape are in no position to snob 80,000 armed Zulus...'"

"Racial bigotry, indeed!" Somerset snarled, letting the paper fall to his lap. "Freedom of the press! Blast it!"

"What do you intend doing, Sir Charles?" Cleote inquired.

"I don't know! This article's no longer part of a public debate! They're getting personal, and no politician can afford to be so transparent. Sooner or later Whitehall may start begging for the same answers Pringle finds are 'so vital for our children'!" The venom rose to add its bitterness to his tone. "I'm afraid I've let this drag on for too long, Colonel. It's starting to effect my image here and at home. - I want it solved! I want Farewell and that ship out of my life! - Once and for all!"

"Then I'm afraid we must meet with them, Sir Charles."

"Very well! - They want an alliance?!" he roared with mounting wrath. "They'll get their alliance. But on my terms!"

*

"Would it bother you very much, Sir Charles," Wilkins asked tactfully, "if we sat on the floor?" In the vast Audience Room of the Governor's Mansion, Somerset and Col. Cloete sat behind a large mahogany desk facing the Zulu delegation. And though velvety chairs had been set up for Ngomane, Lutuli, and Kuta, the three Zulus found this peculiar method of sitting "at right angles" somewhat foreign, thus prompting Wilkins's question and the Governor's response:---.

"I suppose that would be acceptable, Mr. Wilkins," Somerset replied, casting a smug, diverted look in the direction of Cloete and the handful of journalists which he had summoned for the meeting ("to set the Press's record straight with regards to bigotry"). "Quite acceptable," he smiled with affected politeness, "Under the circumstances."

Farewell - whose naval uniform was once again punctuated by his headdress of ostrich feathers - set the example for his small diplomatic corps by sinking down onto the soft pile of an exquisite Aubusson carpet and facing Somerset in an erect and dignified half-squat.

Addressing the journalists as well as Farewell, the Governor started: - "Now, Lt. Farewell, would you please state precisely and concisely your position in the Shakan Affair and what it is that you expect from me, as Governor of the Cape."

Farewell's attention fell on Pringle, and the lieutenant was surprised to see the journalist (whose acquaintance he had never made) grin and wink at him as if to say, "Go ahead! You can do it!" His gaze lingering quizzically on Pringle, Farewell (in his quality as Febana) gave way to his presentation, as Wilkins provided a simultaneous translation for Ngomane.

"As you know, Sir Charles, I and my men have been serving His Majesty in Natal," the man paused briefly, weighing his words upon sensing how enthusiastically the journalists' pens had met paper. "In the course of the two years in which we have been amongst the Zulu People," the lieutenant went on, "I have endeavoured to concile Zulu interests with those of the British government. There have, of course, been many problems. Most of them related to questions of customs - such as you have just witnessed with regards to the seating arrangements. Basic misunderstandings that affect communication. But recently I have had the good fortune to win King Shaka's confidence and trust."

Hearing the translation of this last part, Ngomane shot Farewell a deliberate glance. After the hostile reception afforded the lieutenant at Cape Town, the Zulu Prime Minister was brought to think that the Swallow may well share the "confidence and trust" of Shaka more than that of his own people.

"The result of which," Farewell was saying, "is the Zulu King's desire to show his good will by proposing an alliance with Britain. To that purpose, Shaka has sent his Prime Minister, Ngomane kaMqobolo to represent him."

A few of the journalists stifled a smile when the lieutenant automatically clicked the "q" in the Prime Minister's name. Quickly taking advantage of this air of subtle mocking, Lord Somerset leaned back in his chair, crossed his arms over his belly and assumed a commanding tone.

"You spoke of questions related to customs, Lieutenant. In point of fact, how did Shaka communicate to you the word 'alliance'?"

"I'm afraid I don't follow, Sir Charles."

"Well, you spoke in Zulu did you not?" the Governor had inadvertently taken the reigns of the discourse and was using them to suit his purpose. "And did Shaka - in Zulu - instruct you to go to the Governor of the Cape and seek an 'alliance' between the Zulu tribe and the British Empire. Were those his exact words, Lieutenant?"

Farewell was caught slightly off guard by this illfavoured line of questioning, and he offered no rebuttal as the Governor set his verbal sails to the wind.

"He did say 'alliance', Lieutenant," Sir Charles pressed on, "not 'concurrence', or 'cooperation'? Does Shaka wish to join the British Empire or does he, instead, wish to maintain his sovereignty, in which case, does he wish to establish diplomatic ties, with embassies, or does he..." Somerset smiled, "merely want to meet King George and enjoy some kaffir beer?"

The Governor's apparently good-humoured sarcastic wit met with general laughter from the journalists; the notable exception being Thomas Pringle. And, as Wilkins smiled wryly registering the detrimental effect of those famous "7000 years of tried and tested double-talk", he came to notice Ngomane's eyes still rivetted on the lieutenant. And Tim saw the induna's attention move from Febana's headdress of ostrich feathers to Farewell's naval tunic and back. It seemed to the freckled youth from Downing Street that he saw compassion in the Zulu's eyes - as one might have compassion for the stray antelope that has lost its herd, or the sparrow that is shunned by its flock and must fly alone. "Surely it is not a question of semantics, Sir Charles," was Farewell's adamant reply. "What difference does it make if the word translates as---"

"Excuse me, Lieutenant," Captain Aitchison entered the Audience Room and addressed his superior. "May I have a word with you, Colonel Cloete?" "Of course, Captain. What is it?"

Stealing a peculiar glance in the direction of the Zulus, Aitchison crossed to the Colonel's chair and whispered into his ear. As astonishment slowly crept over Cloete's features, his eyes flitted to Farewell's delegation, and leaning towards Somerset, the Colonel relayed the message in a tense murmur.

"Are you sure of this, Captain?" Sir Charles inquired with a sullen frown, eliciting the intrigue of the journalists and the mounting perplexity and unease of Farewell and Wilkins.

"Quite sure, Sir Charles. This is no conjecture. The declaration was all too formal."

"I see," Somerset grumbled and returned his attention to Farewell. "You were saying, Lieutenant?"

"I was merely suggesting..." the man's gaze ran over the hardened expressions of Cloete and Aitchison as he struggled against perplexity to regain the pattern of his thoughts. "...that it makes no difference if the word is alliance or agreement, Sir Charles. The sentiment is one. The Zulu people are reaching out for the hand of friendship."

"Friendship...?" the Governor echoed with scorn and shifted his attention to Tim. "Mr. Wilkins, would you please convey to the -," he cleared his throat, "'Prime Minister' that we have just received word that his King Shaka has declared war on this Colony and is preparing to march on the Cape with his entire military force."

Crestfallen by the news, Farewell softly murmured, "That's - that's impossible!"

Yet no one heard his remark, for in their dire need to relate this momentous news to their respective tabloids, the journalists had burst clamourously towards the door with a heated flurry of comments. Indeed, the sudden noise was such that Tim had to raise his voice somewhat as he related - in a tone of suppressed emotion - the incredible turn of events to Ngomane, Lutuli and Kuta.

And when Ngomane had grasped what Wilkins was telling him, the blood drained from his face, leaving wrath and indignation welling up within him to rail against his hitherto undying fidelity to Shaka. The Zulu Emperor had made him twice the fool: first by sending him on this absurd mission, and again by making the mission all the more absurd by turning his "quest for an alliance" into a farce! The proud induna of Dingiswayo was not to be treated like a monkey!

"Lt. Farewell," Somerset had risen from his chair and his voice was rigidly official. "Your native friends have twenty-four hours to board their ship and leave the Cape - failing which I shall be obliged to consider their presence here an act of war. - That will be all, gentlemen."

While all left the Audience Room in varying stages of stupefaction and resentment, Somerset felt it necessary to add a corollary to his dispute with the "eccentric".

"Lieutenant," he beckoned, causing Farewell to stop and regard the man with a glance devoid of all sentiment. "A word of warning. Off the record. - Men like you invariably find themselves caught between two fires and rejected by both sides. - You cannot trust these people, because - quite frankly - they will never really trust us! I think today's news proved that. Forget all this nonsense about being Zulu and let them go! Save yourself, man! You've too much at stake!"

"Exactly, Sir Charles," the fog of defeat and weariness had enveloped the man and he spoke from a bygone place that was the graveyard of his enduring hope. "I've too much at stake. I've sacrificed much more than two years of my life. My very soul is in Natal, and I must go back for it."

"Do you really mean to see him again?!"

"I must, Sir Charles," his voice wavered slightly as if it were precariously balanced between resignation and the lingering need to survive. "You see, the war he's declared is not on the Cape - it's on me, Governor. - I am his guide through Paradise Lost and I must now show him the way home."

CHAPTER THE LAST L
INKAWU" (MONKEY)

The Zulus have a Folk Tale about the Hyena and the Moon. As the story goes: -- Once upon a time, in the Present of the Past, a Hyena carrying a savoury bone in its mouth came to a river. Seeing the beautiful reflection of the Moon on the clear water and thinking it a nice fat piece of meat, the Hyena dropped its bone and greedily snapped its fangs at the Moon in an attempt to bite into what it thought was an appetising morsel. Again and again the avaricious animal tried to sink its teeth into the Moon in the water, but to no avail. Finally, exhausted, it gave up and turned its attention from the water only to find that another animal had come along and taken its bone leaving it hungry and frustrated. Therefore, it is said, the Hyena is much laughed at in the Animal Kingdom for its foolishness in throwing away what was good for the sake of a useless, deceiving reflection.

Most certainly this Folk Tale applies not only to Hyenas and Bones, but also to Men and their Cultures. And in that sense, it is a tale from which both Shaka kaSenzangakona Zulu and Febana kaMaJoji Farewell might have found - before their premature deaths - much, much food for thought.

A man - whether he be an adventurer or a warrior, an officer or a king, an Englishman or a Zulu - must never toss away what he is for the deceiving reflection of what he could be, or, like the poor Hyena, he just might end up with the "hunger pains" of disenchantment.

As Francis Bacon put it: "Be so true to thyself as thou be not false to thy condition as Man", or, as Sitayi announced it: "Do not betray your Heritage or your death will be the death of your people".

Both Shaka and Febana snapped at the Moon and, towards the end of their lives, their search for the "unreachable" became a "long day's journey into night".

*

Leaving behind the security of what he was, Francis George Farewell left the Anglo-Zulu Summit and boarded his ship. Destination: Shaka and Febana's "Paradise Lost".

He left behind Elizabeth, his love --- with a kiss and the promise that he would return as soon as he was ready to "really return". He left behind Wilkins, his friend and companion in Hell --- with a pat on the back and the prompting goodbye that rang with finality: "Thanks all the same, m'lad, but I must push off alone. You can be of little help now. Go back to Plymouth and deal with your king, just as I must deal with mine!"

On April 3, 1826 the "Shaka" landed at Port Natal with its four Zulu passengers: Ngomane, Lutuli, Kuta, and Febana.

Fynn and Cane were there to meet their friend.

But Holstead was dead: impaled. After Nandi's death he had tried to escape with another raft.

"Is it true?" were Febana's first words.

"Yes, Francis," was Fynn's dispirited reply. "Nandi's dead, and our lies were buried with her."

The indication that Ngomane was able to secure from Mbiya and Mkabayi at Bulawayo was that Shaka and the regiments had left on the full moon (i.e. March 27) and that they were marching due South with the strategic objective of reaching the Cape in a month's time. That meant (according to Farewell's arithmetic) that Shaka's troops were covering about thirty miles a day. Thirty times five: they were about one hundred and fifty miles away from the Zulu Citadel.

Due South. It would be close, Febana thought. But on horseback, travelling day and night at a steady gallop (with only the briefest necessary stop to rest and feed the animal) he just might be able to catch up with Shaka before he reached the Colony.   He just might be able to.

No! - He had to.

He did.

On April 9, 1826, Febana crossed the umZimkulu River and entered the iNgwangwane Plains northwest of the Cape Colony (about a hundred miles from British Kaffraria).

At sunset, he caught up with Shaka's troops in the vast forest of iMpendle where they had bivouacked for the night.

Tying his horse to a tree matted with fungi and crowded with tall ferns, Febana groped his way through the gloomy forest treading gingerly on laminations of rotting plants and tight clusters of truffles and toadstools that felt pulpy and alive under his step.

The air was still and inexpressibly oppressive. Storm clouds overhead were thickening into a low vault of uniform blackness, and rumbling with the threat of an approaching tempest. And it was dark, frightfully dark.

Suddenly a hooked dart of fire tore the obscurity of the distant horizon, briefly lighting up the gloom of the earth with a dazzling, ghastly flame. The flash cast a harsh light on the tenebrous forest, and suddenly Febana saw warriors everywhere, standing stock-still in silent groups, their eyes fixed on the approaching Swallow like the malevolent sentries of a dark power gone mad.

His back stiff, his jaw level, Febana moved past the warriors feeling an all-consuming violence emanating from their hearts -- a violence that sapped his strength.

Advancing, the lieutenant's eyes fell on the mouth of a cave, lit from within by the tenuous glow of a campfire. Moving towards the grisly cavern, he felt overcome by a sense of foreboding, and, with chilling clarity, he realised that the man he was seeking lay within it entrails. Steadying himself, he approached the cave's threshold, pushed past a hanging kaross, and entered.

The interior was veiled in shades of tenebrosity pierced only by a circle of embers that glowed flatly on the ground as if marking a hole cut in the crust of the Underworld. Febana took a few steps forward, waiting for his eyes to adjust to the darkness. Then, as his senses began to acclimatize, the lieutenant could hear a heavy, irregular breathing and feel the ominous presence of Shaka Zulu.   "Baba, it is I."

Silence ensued. Febana moved closer and could suddenly make out the King's body outlined by the rippling hues of the embers. The massive figure was wrapped in skins and furs, making him look like a huge animal lying wounded in his lair. When Shaka finally spoke, his voice was distant, ghostly.

"Tell me, Febana...How do you trap a monkey?"

The lieutenant was taken aback by the question and the eerie way in which it was delivered.

"Nkosi...?" he asked quizzically.

Again, there was no answer, save for the laboured breathing that was bathed in impatience. With uncertainty, Febana groped for an adequate response, drawing from his knowledge of Zulu hunting methods.

"A gourd is used. With a narrow neck. And bait is dropped into the gourd: - a piece of fruit or something shiny. The monkey---" Febana's voice trailed off as he suddenly realised down which malicious road the Emperor was leading him. Yet Shaka's breathing became demanding and the lieutenant braced himself, continuing: "The monkey slips his hand down the narrow neck of the gourd and grabs the bait. Then...then he is trapped because he cannot get his fist out."

"Once he realises he is trapped," Shaka asked, "Why doesn't the monkey let go of the bait?"

"Because his greed has made him blind." "And for what is he greedy, Febana?" "I suppose -- for what he thinks he cannot have." The silence grew ominous, then:---

"And what new bait have you brought from your kingdom, Febana. Bring it here for this monkey to see! Something shiny...like the freshness of youth, of life, of the past. Bait your gourd again, Febana. My heart yearns for something shiny! My arm yearns to reach out for a thing of Promise or of Hope!"

"And it was that yearning that made the illusion complete, Baba," Febana addressed the shades of Shaka's being. "Without the desire to believe, there can be no magic, because magic is always in the eye of the beholder. Mine were just words. You made them come true for yourself by believing." Febana's voice was calm, free of emotion. He had nothing to lose that he had not already lost. Including life. "The fault is yours, Baba, as much as it is mine."

In the dim light of the glowing embers, Shaka's eyes suddenly gleamed and seemed to take on a lustre of their own.

"Punishing my people is not the solution," Febana went on. "We must search for another. Together."

Rising slowly, the Zulu neared Febana, his imposing frame towering over the lieutenant like a huge bear.

"Together?" he hissed, his soul now impenetrable to persuasion, coaxing, or abuse; to soft words or shrill rivalling; to desperate beseechings or the allure of dreams. "No, Febana! You have proven that you were never with me! So you are against me!" he remarked, paraphrasing uCristo "his rival".

Suddenly Shaka's Ixwa shone in the brilliance of the embers, and the King drew back the deadly Blade as if poised to thrust it through Febana's heart. Yet the Swallow was too deadened to react, and, without flinching, the lieutenant held Shaka's maniacal gaze, watching the weapon flash through the dark. It twirled in the air, its shaft landing softly on the lieutenant's shoulder, the Blade now pointing, magically, at Shaka's own chest.

Their eyes locked - framing forever the brief meeting of two souls touching in despair.

"Kill me, Febana, my foolish friend!" came the raucous voice. "If it is not in your heart to serve me, then serve your own kingdom." Grasping the Ixwa, Febana held Shaka's eyes, reading in them a veiled plea for deliverance. Tightening his hold on the shaft, the lieutenant squared his shoulders to inflict the blow. But - as the Emperor waited for Death, his

Companion, his maddened eyes wearing a silent appeal - Febana stood unmoving.

And the moments passed, and passed, and the silence in the cave became asphyxiating. Then, when it was clear that the Swallow would not, or could not strike, the King's full lips curled back in a sardonic smile. "You are right," Shaka's breath seared Febana's face. "Magic is in the eye of the beholder. The illusion is now complete. You are a man with no mystery. You are a shadow. - Go, Febana! I have no need for you anymore!"

"Where shall I go, Baba?" the question was genuine and born of daunting grief.

"Where I have been."

The next morning, at the heralding of dawn, Febana ka MaJoji looked on powerlessly as the human tidal wave of Shaka's regiments trotted off, in perfect formation, towards the Cape Colony. And as he stood unmoving in the clash of voices and cries that burst forth from the marching troops, his heart sank despairingly - not only for the personal and intense engagement of the past two years of his life and the work of those years which had apparently come to naught, nor yet for the Colonists themselves who would soon fall to the overpowering surge of Zulu might, - no, indeed, Francis was disheartened by his own utter failure to reclaim the heart of Shaka, the heart of Africa - and his own heart. He now felt utterly lost, the victim (as Shaka had said) of an illusion that was complete.

By the Eve of April 11, 1826, the Zulu army had crossed the vast umZimvubu River and entered Griqualand, on the outskirts of British Kaffraria - approximately thirty miles due North of Reverend Bellow's Mission Station. Shaka gave Joko, Dlaba, Mzilikazi, and his other generals the order to camp for the night. At dawn - or so he had planned - when the scouts had returned from their reconnaissance, they would initiate a forced march through Tambook, into the unexplored regions south of the Bashee River and, hugging the coast, enter the Swallows' Domains through to the Gates of Gaika.

That night, after the troops had retired to a sleep populated with dreams of untold conquest, the Son of Zulu remained awake in an effort to nerve himself for the next day's campaign and the untold implications of its success. In fact, he had no doubt that he could win the war. The very fact that Febana had returned to "plead the Swallows' cause" (or so Shaka now saw it in the light of cold reflection) indicated that the White armies were severely deficient in number.

No, victory would be his, he knew, and in his mind he weighed anxiously and attentively his apprehensions and desires against the grand

and ambitious accomplishment of being able to unite under one King of Kings two great peoples - the Swallows and the Zulus; - the accomplishment of incorporating the Swallows in a Zulu Nation in which he, Shaka, would reign supreme over Joji and his People; and over uCristo.

uCristo.

Shaka sighed, deeply, and bent his gaze on his open hand, thinking of the hand of the crucified Christ.

And he thought of Fynn. And of Resurrection. According to the Book, uCristo had died, hung from a tree with "nails" (like the ones Cane was forced to supply for Daniel's death). Yet, on the third day (or so the Book related), His mother and friends had returned to the tomb where He was buried and found it empty. Then, some time later, uCristo had reappeared to his indunas alive again! One of them had even touched Him! He had resurrected!

Was the Book also a lie? - Shaka wondered. And what of his own resurrection? Fynn had said he had never had the power to heal death, yet he, Shaka, had been "healed".

Or had he? Was this too false? Was it all a lie?

Shaka felt his head spin. It was all so devastating for the mind, so confusing, and he truly felt like a monkey with his hand caught in the gourd. His undying desire and need to believe found it frustrating and hard to grasp the fleeting breath of Mystery that is Faith. But one thing was certain and limpidly clear: - in his present confusion he was not prepared to properly rule over Joji and His People - even with all the armies in the world!

He needed to know more. Yet it was too late to ask Febana and his sangoma. He had lost their faith and loyalty by dismissing their trust. It was too late and tomorrow - tomorrow he would march into the "Unknown".
He needed to know more.

In a half daze, Shaka found himself leaving the camp and striding away, alone, through the night -- in the direction of the Swallows' Domain. With no clear directives - save for the intent to scout for knowledge, hunting not the leopard this time (as he had done so often, so many years ago with Mgobozi and Nqoboka), but stalking the vague lineaments of uCristo's shadow in his own soul.

At the greying of dawn, he was high atop of a hill overlooking the first signs of White "civilisation": - the cluster of homes gathered round the church that was Reverend Bellow's Mission Station. Shaka stood in petrified silence, his feline eyes trained in vigilant scrutiny of that outpost. And he saw houses made of wattle and mud, with windows of glass and walls coloured in the nitid hues of the butterfly, - he saw trimmed lawns and flowerbeds, and the careful symmetry of gardens girded in white fencing, - he saw a pole with a flapping cloth with red and white stripes and blue triangles, - he saw the Swallows' horses tied to wagons and buggies with people moving over paths and roads winding and intersecting before houses and stockades.

And Shaka saw men - many men - who looked like soldiers holding sticks that spat fire, - he saw large hollow trunks of iron which resembled Febana's cannon at iNcome River, - and he saw other men and women with their hair tucked under head coverings and dressed in fineries and colourful garments of cloth going into a tall building with a steeple situated in the center of the homestead.

And Shaka was startled to hear a piercing, reverberating sound, cadenced and throbbing - the unfamiliar ringing of a bell. Searching for the source of that rhythmic, resonant sound, the Zulu's attention was gravitated towards the steeple where he saw a large rounded cone swaying back and forth in tune with the metal clanging.

Above the bell, Shaka saw the Cross and he remembered the gilded symbol on the leather cover of the Book. And stirring, he strode down the hill.

In his avid religious fervour, Reverend Josiah Bellow had his fingers firmly curled round the parapet of his lectern whilst he led his mixed congregation in an impassioned rendition of the "warrior" hymn: - "Onward Christian Soldiers". The clergyman's tenor voice rose vibrant over the pulsing drone of the organ and he felt his faith strengthening with the Hymn, fortifying his soul against the heathen threat of the diabolical Zulu Empire, - the bloodthirsty Kingdom of Beelzebub (or so Bellow saw it) that would soon pounce upon the poor sheep of his faithful congregation with its murderous intents and with the brooding treachery of its cruel monarch, the monstrous King Shaka!

Louder and more ardently the Reverend sang, forcing the organ to compete with his melodious zeal as he bent forward over the rim of his lofty pulpit, his head and chest projected over the assemblage of singing faithful like a gargoyle from the battlements of a medieval shrine.   And the faithful sang along, tremulously and with the Fear of God (and Shaka) buzzing in their veins, the horror of imminent and terrible death fanning the flame of their devotion. They all sang along, - with Colonel Cloete, Captain Aitchison, and the officers of the 25th Regiment of Foot occupying the front pews (next to Mrs. Bellow and the White European members of the community), with the native teachers and assistants tucked into the middle rows, and with the "common natives" and the Fingoes wedged in the pews behind them and crowded throughout the back of the church and near the open door.

And when the hymn was finished and Reverend Bellow had bellowed the last note, there was silence as the congregation stopped to catch its breath. - Complete silence save for a bit of shuffling, some coughing and...

...the jingling of ivory tassels.

Hearing the unfamiliar jingling, Bellow, his wife, Col. Cloete, and a few of the Xhosa teachers turned to glance at the back of the church.

They spotted his shadow first - a long, slender shadow running down the church's central aisle. Then, looking up with mounting curiosity, they saw a tall, handsome, muscular black man framed in the open threshold of the House of God, his majestic frame cast against the early light of day that clung to him like a halo.

"A magnificent specimen of native beauty," Mrs. Bellow thought in spite of herself, and blushed as her eyes took in the stranger's regal body (which was completely nude save for his leopardskin loincloth and the tassels tied round his arms and legs). Yet the tall man looked somehow forlorn, the Reverend's wife noticed, as if he had stumbled into the church by mistake, or - as if he had no place else to go. "Surely an outcast," Mrs. Bellow quickly made up her mind. "A beautiful, beggarly outcast! I wonder if I should convince Josiah to take him on as a gardener. He's such graceful strength," she mused, looking at his hands resting easily at the sides of his lean hips.

With a set smile, Reverend Bellow nodded a curt greeting to the newcomer, and made an ample wave of the hand, motioning to the black man to take a place near the "other Fingoes". The tall stranger understood and obeyed, striding into the midst of the dense black throng (that instinctively parted before his advance).

And Bellow plowed into his sermon that was designed to prepare his faithful for the flagellum of the Zulu Advent. The clergyman quoted St. Paul, beseeching the assembly to "be strong in the Lord, and in the power of his might, and to put on the whole armour of God, that ye may be able to stand courageously against the wiles of the 'Shakan' devil".

And he quoted Genesis 17:8, reminding his White Christians that this land, Africa, was theirs by right and by divine behest and that no one could chase them away - not even Shaka. "In fact, it is written:" Bellow told them, "'and I will give onto thee, and to thy seed after thee, the land wherein thou art a stranger, all the land of Canaan - which is the land of the Blacks -, for an everlasting possession'..."

Whilst the Reverend enheartened his assemblage for the bloody onslaught of the savage Zulu, Shaka --- Shaka Zulu stood amongst the Fingoes, towering over their heads, and inspected the interior of the Royal Hut that belonged to his Rival King of Kings.

The Emperor saw the Cross with the crucified figure of uCristo. And he took note that each of those present (including his own people) were holding copies of the Book with the gilded symbol of their Nkosi yama Kosi. And he saw the hands joined in prayer - both Black and White hands. And Shaka realised that these people - both Joji's and his own - were already united under one King of Kings.

Looking up at the Cross and at Christ's lean, muscular body hanging from the nails, Shaka contemplated his Companion and Rival. And he thought of their kingdoms - the one based on Fear of the Unknown which breeds hatred, and the other based on Love of the Unknown which breeds Devotion.

Then - as he looked around and at the Cross, and as he felt the devotion - the realisation was born in his heart that, though they had committed the sins of vainglory and hypocrisy which are the curse of Adam's Children, nothing that Febana and Fynn had said had been a lie. The Magic was right there for him to see and feel.

The Magic of uCristo - His Power, his Immortality, His Resurrection, - all of it, - all of the "Gourd's Shiny Bait" was there and it was as ancient as Africa and as universal as the Heavens. - The Magic of the Beginning.

"In the Beginning was the Word and the Word was with God and the Word was God".

It was not White, nor Black, not Joji, nor Shaka. Nor was it conquerable by him and by his troops, nor by White troops, nor by all the armies of the Heavens and of the Earth.

It was the Word of the People as One. Bantu.

And suddenly, for Shaka, his military campaigns, his life of War seemed ludicrous and he faltered, surrendering his heart.

And when Reverend Bellow looked up, searching for the intriguing black stranger, he was gone.

*

The following day, on April 12, 1826, as the sun reached its zenith, it shone on the retreat of Shaka's armies which were marching back from the boundaries of British Kaffraria in remarkably loose, undisciplined ranks, the expressions on the faces of the warriors reflecting their dismay and sheer discouragement.

Farewell raced through the troops, frantically calling out to individual soldiers, pleading, demanding to know what had occurred. Finally Febana met Joko.

"What is it? What happened?" the Swallow shouted over the chaotic din of the regiments.

"Your lies have defeated the Great Mountain, Febana," was Joko's bitter response. "At daybreak, our armies were ready to crush your world. But when we shouted 'SIGIDI', there was no answer. Shaka was gone!"
"Where?"
"Does it matter? Now?"

*

As the sun shone forth dwarfing the earth, the Son of Zulu reached the foot of the towering spiral of ice that rose straight up from the Summit of the Mountain like a finger pointed at God, its tip vanishing in the dizzying heights.

Steps, steep and perfectly levigated, miraculously appeared on the natural curve of the spiral forming a staircase that wound upwards like the swirl of an immense shell. And Shaka started up the glimmering steps, towards the top of the stairway and the "Isiqongo kwaNkosi", the Pinnacle of Kings.

Hours later, when the sun was already weary from its long trek across the Heavens, the Emperor reached the Platform of the Pinnacle and, as he had done over twenty years before, he padded out to the polished railing of ice that circumvented its margins. Longingly, he allowed his gaze to drift out to the immeasurably vast stretch of landscape that sprang into view: a great expanse of woodlands, sombre and green, undulating as far as a violet and purple range of mountains, - and the canvas of the veld, saffron and amber, rolling like a sea, with glints of winding rivers that flowed into the opaque blueness of the Indian Ocean. The immensity "as far as the eye can see" of the empire that was his!

And, in spite of the vastness of the realm, he knew he had lost all that mattered. All that had ever mattered: - Nandi. - And himself.

"You are either born to die or to kill - there is no middle way".

And The Kill was no longer in his heart.

He must start again. Start it all again. Anew. - As a Master, anew.

Then, sensing a presence at his shoulders, the Son of Zulu turned to meet the vacant orbs of the sangoma Sitayi. And nearing him, the ageless woman spoke of the Immortality that transcends Life - the Immortality that is in the innermost life of his people.

They had congregated in Bulawayo - the hundreds of thousands that were the living, throbbing plasma of the Zulu Nation. Yet that blood was now infested with the purulence of riot and anarchy as word buzzed from ear to ear that the lustrous and venerable Emperor of Zulu had disappeared; - some even whispered that he had shied from the task of conquest - "bewitched by the Strangers from the Sea".

For over a month now he had been gone, and the seed of conspiracy and doubt planted by Dingane was starting to take root in the Hearts of the People. All feared that the Creator of the Realm of Masters had, in the end, chosen the Way of Victims.

But the Heart of Zulu's Son was too honest for that sort of Betrayal, and he appeared to them, finally -- on the Fourth Sun of the Moon of ukwEngula.

When they saw him, an eerie stillness gripped the hundreds of thousands that packed the Citadel, - with all thought, all emotion, all movement, all speech suspended -- as all eyes were cast in the direction of the rising sun which framed the imposing figure of the Great Mountain of Africa - devoid of all regal distinction, save for the Ixwa held limply in his hand.

The Zulus gaped, spellbound, as Shaka strode solemnly down the slopes of Ongoye with a deliberate, harmonious gait, like that of an angel walking on a cloud. His eyes were feverish and his mind burned with the searing images of an ephemeral life based on the quest for Power, as his stately frame drew nearer and nearer to the colossal homestead he had built as a tribute to Glory, - the Immense Glory of Zulu which was expressed in the very rhythm of his walk.

Set against the lavender clouds, his towering might seemed all the more threatening as he moved through the Gates of Bulawayo. His back straight, his head high, his expression imperious, Shaka looked more majestic than ever, somehow untouchable and the crowds shrank away from his charismatic, ominous advance, forming a human path up the inclined turf of the cattlefold to the Royal Dias.

Stopping near the coiled rushes that were his throne, the Language of the Heavens turned and directed his feline eyes at the contours of the distant horizon, veiling in the mystique of unfeeling abstraction the strong currents that tore at his soul and the crazed tempest that was his heart. Then a thin smile appeared on the Sovereign's lips, as if he were suddenly amused by some incidental concern beyond the confines of Life, on a dimension relegated to the stars.

And in the hush that gripped his Citadel, a voice was heard vested in the disembodied solemnity of Death and its Spirits.

"Dingane," the voice pronounced the name as if reading it on the heavenly vault. "It is time."

With wonder, Shaka recognised the compelling voice to be his own.

Thus beckoned, the Needy One stiffened, panicstricken, and in his utter perplexity his eyes shot to Mkabayi. The sister of Senzangakona kaJama Zulu, looked deeply saddened by the deed she knew must be performed: - the Final Act. And, almost imperceptibly, she nodded to her brother's second born.

Dingane took a step forward, out of the crowd, towards the Dias and the throne. Then another step, and another. Suddenly Ngomane was at his side, and an ixwa was pressed into his sweaty grasp. The "second-born" gaped at the weapon in his hand and at the Prime Minister who locked his eyes on those of Dingane in a mute echo of Mkabayi's directive, Shaka's own command.

Dingane's confidence grew. And suddenly his brother Mhlangana was flanking him, his spear poised for The Kill.

"You, too, my brother?" Shaka said to Mhlangana, an uncanny glint giving lustre to his saddened look of resignation. "I would never have thought you capable of such...decisiveness."

The comment caused the man's face to tighten with open hatred and, outpacing Dingane, Mhlangana moved on towards the Man Who was the Language. But Shaka remained immobile, a smile frozen on his lips. Then, turning his back to his brothers, the Son of Zulu strode away, towards the isiGodlo. And the Nation held its breath as Mhlangana lunged forward, silent spectators to the Fate of Gods. And a tortured moan was wrenched from the Zulu multitude, as Mhlangana raised a trembling hand, sinking the ixwa into Shaka's back. And the Heavens were shot through with flashes of crimson and gold, as Dingane struck as well, again and again - stabbing, stabbing, stabbing.

And Shaka stopped as if waiting, his thin smile flecked with blood. And when they were through, Shaka strode on, over the Dias, to the Gates of his isiGodlo.

Then he turned, his serene smile bringing tears to the eyes of Mkabayi and Nomcoba.

Some screamed. Others cried. Some fainted.

And Shaka cocked his ear as if listening, as if measuring his strength against that of his Ultimate Adversary.

Once again, Dingane and Mhlangana neared him, inflicting blow after blow, drenching their ixwas in the fluid of the Heaven's life. Yet the Mountain did not fall.

And the Nation gasped. Was the Son of Nandi truly immortal?

Then, suddenly, lifting his eyes, peering through the shroud of Life, the Great Elephant looked upon the Heavens for the last time, and sank to his knees, embracing his life-long Companion Death with deliverance.

*

Blinded by Shaka's death, the Nation fled -- it fled in panic, in pandemonium, in despair. And though it was day, the skies took on the semblance of night, with great storm clouds forming to the East and running swiftly from horizon to horizon until all of Creation was immersed in the Shadows of Grief.

And the rains came in torrents, violent and hissing. And through the tempest Pampata ran from emKindini. She ran frantically over the muddied landscape in response to the news that the Great Elephant had fallen. She tripped, fell, scrambled to her feet and went on, - she ran, uncaring, unfeeling, her skin scratched and bloodied, her eyes swollen with tears of unbearable anguish, her chest heaving with the gasping, choking breath of unconsolable grief. When she finally reached Bulawayo - on the dawning of the new day - the tempest still raged without respite, as if punishing Man and his Earth for the Death borne by the Heavens. Entering the immense Citadel, she found it to be empty, and gaping round through the gloomy shadows, the woman haltingly moved up the sloping incline, towards the Emperor's throne.

A stab of lightning tore the skies, and a crashing reverberation shook the earth with the pounding might of Zulu. Yet Pampata was insensitive to this violence of the elements brandishing around her, for her entire mind and heart were bent upon finding him - finding the love of her life, the Lord of her World.

"He must be alive!" - her heart screamed out.

Again the lightning gathered violence, and flash after flash seared through the darkness, vividly illuminating the abandoned Citadel, and....

...suddenly, near the Royal Dias, she saw the body.

The heavenly flashing drenched the Emperor's massive figure in a harsh glow that made his corpse look all the more terrifying. And the thunder came to drown her despairing wail, bearing it on the crest of the tempest to the vastness of the Ongoye Valley.

Pampata ran to his side and sank onto the beloved figure of her Lord. Sobbing, she caressed him - his face, his lips, his body, feeling for signs of Life, clinging despairingly to the Hope that Life's sweet breath had not abandoned him.

Another flaming bolt reflected its phosphorescence on the Son of Zulu, evidencing his glazed eyes, congealed in death. And as the inescapable truth was forced upon her, a piercing cry of inhuman torment shook the Citadel.

Then there was stillness.

After a timeless instant, Pampata stirred. Reaching out, her hand closed over Shaka's, and she forced it back, turning his wrist so that the Ixwa was pointing at her own heart.

Then Pampata bent forward, kissed his cold lips, and fell on the Blade. Composed, she felt the searing pain of her soul leaving her, to be replaced by the infinite joy of being united with her Prince.

The rains fell harder, branding the earth with the vengeance of the Heavens. And the blood of Pampata was washed to the ground, streaming over the mud in rivulets, mixing, mingling with Shaka's own blood. And finally the combined Life Fluids of the Mountain and the Flatterer collected in a puddle, together, as one, near the gleaming Blade that had torn Life from the Blood of their Bloods, the child of the Child.

Slowly, ominously, out of the rippling shrouds of darkness and rain, Sitayi's regiment of hyenas moved towards the two bodies, - two serried rows of twenty, in perfect formation. And, as they had once protected the Promise of Life that had been in Nandi's womb, the beasts now silently, protectively, surrounded the Lovers who had been gloriously and ceremoniously united in wedlock by the Ultimate Minister of Man's Faith in himself and in Humanity: Death Our Companion

***

* EPILOGUE *

After an interregnum of two months, Dingane kaSenzangakona Zulu was enshrined as King of the People of the Heavens. His reign, lasting approximately twelve years, marked the beginning of the end of Zulu Glory. The Glory that is still presently defiled and repressed by the Wail of Africa Betrayed known as Apartheid.

Ngomane kaMqombolo Zulu became the Chief Induna of King Dingane kaSenzangakona Zulu, and remained at his service until his death in 1834.

Mkabayi kaSenzangakona Zulu served as the personal Advisor of King Dingane kaSenzangakona Zulu, and was reported to have filled that post of authority until her death on or about the Summer of 1842.

Of the Swallows, John Cane remained at Port Natal (under the protection and auspices of King Dingane kaSenzangakona Zulu). He married a native woman named Rachel in the Winter of 1829 and lived to be old and prosperous. He never left Africa.

Francis George Farewell, known as Febana ka MaJoji, disappeared into the Heart of Africa. Never to be seen again. In was rumoured that a White man fitting his description was haunting the interior of southeast Africa in search of a diviner named Sitayi and a crystal staircase that led to a place called the "Pinnacle".

Elizabeth Farewell waited in vain for her husband's return. After two years, she visited Port Natal and undertook a formal search for him. As the search proved fruitless, she returned to the Cape. Five years later, she remarried and had three children. She named them Francis, Fynn, and Timothy.

Elizabeth Farewell Aspeling never returned to England. It was said that till the day she died of old age in 1871, she would inquire amongst the settlers of Natal after a man named Febana.

Henry Francis Fynn became the personal doctor and religious tutor of King Dingane kaSenzangakona Zulu. The Irishman spent the rest of his life in Natal and was buried there.

Timothy Wilkins returned to Downing Street and stayed on in the Colonial Office until 1827 (when Sir Henry Bathurst resigned as Secretary for War and the Colonies). Tim then returned to journalism, and the publishing of his "African Diary" brought him a considerable degree of fame in Whitehall circles.

In an attempt to return to his "Moment of Africa" (as he called it), he died in a shipwreck off the Wild Coast of Natal in 1829. The last entry salvaged from his new book (which was to be entitled "Farewell's Folly") read:-- "The Imitation of Christ is an escape from the commonplace. And that escape, whether it be down the Road of Sanctity or the Path of Perdition, leads inexorable to the Tears of Gethsemane and the Passion of Golgotha...

"The Imitation of Christ is the Heart of Africa. I find comfort in knowing that in that Grand and Glorious Heart both Shaka and Febana will meet again, converse again, and find friendship again in a dimension that is free from those '7000 years of tried and tested double talk'. - And as for me, well, I pray only that these two great men may find time in their Eternity to take into their confidence umFekethile, The Freckled One. - Nkosi sikelela Africa!...

"We awoke this morning under the strong influence of the Westerlies, and Mr. Hardy, our first mate, remarked that the Southern Cross had not appeared, signifying the likelihood of a storm. I can only pray we make the Wild Coast before it is upon us..."

Nkosi sikelela Africa. - God Bless Africa.

Mother and Father of the Universe. The Word of the People as One - Bantu.

THE END

Printed in Great Britain
by Amazon